1945]

The Economic Organisation of a P.O.W. Camp

By R. A. Radford

Introduction

After allowance has been made for abnormal circumstances, the social institutions, ideas and habits of groups in the outside world are to be found reflected in a Prisoner of War Camp. It is an unusual but a vital society. Camp organisation and politics are matters of real concern to the inmates, as affecting their present and perhaps their future existences. Nor does this indicate any loss of proportion. No one pretends that camp matters are of any but local importance or of more than transient interest, but their importance there is great. They bulk large in a world of narrow horizons and it is suggested that any distortion of values lies rather in the minimisation than in the exaggeration of their importance. Human affairs are essentially practical matters and the measure of immediate effect on the lives of those directly concerned in them is to a large extent the criterion of their importance at that time and place. A prisoner can hold strong views on such subjects as whether or not all tinned meats shall be issued to individuals cold or be centrally cooked, without losing sight of the significance of the Atlantic Charter.

One aspect of social organisation is to be found in economic activity, and this, along with other manifestations of a group existence, is to be found in any P.O.W. camp. True, a prisoner is not dependent on his exertions for the provision of the necessaries, or even the luxuries of life, but through his economic activity, the exchange of goods and services, his standard of material comfort is considerably enhanced. And this is a serious matter to the prisoner: he is not "playing at shops" even though the small scale of the transactions and the simple expression of comfort and wants in terms of cigarettes and jam, razor blades and writing paper, make the urgency of those needs difficult to appreciate, even by an ex-prisoner of some three months' standing.

Nevertheless, it cannot be too strongly emphasised that economic activities do not bulk so large in prison society as they do in the larger world. There can be little production; as has been said the prisoner is independent of his exertions for the provision of the necessities and luxuries of life; the emphasis lies in exchange and the media of exchange. A prison camp is not to be compared with the seething crowd of higglers in a street market, any more than it is to be compared with the economic inertia of a family dinner table.

Naturally then, entertainment, academic and literary interests, games and discussions of the "other world" bulk larger in everyday life than they do in the life of more normal societies. But it would be wrong to underestimate the importance of economic activity. Everyone receives a roughly equal share of essentials; it is by trade that individual preferences are given expression and comfort increased. All at some time, and most people regularly, make exchanges of one sort or another.

Although a P.O.W. camp provides a living example of a simple economy which might be used as an alternative to the Robinson Crusoe economy beloved by the text-books, and its simplicity renders the demonstration of certain economic hypotheses both amusing and instructive, it is suggested that the principal significance is sociological. True, there is interest in observing the growth of economic institutions and customs in a brand new society, small and simple enough to prevent detail from obscuring the basic pattern and disequilibrium from obscuring the working of the system. But the essential interest lies in the universality and the spontaneity of this economic life; it came into existence not by conscious imitation but as a response to the immediate needs and circumstances. Any similarity between prison organisation and outside organisation arises from similar stimuli evoking similar responses.

The following is as brief an account of the essential data as may render the narrative intelligible. The camps of which the writer had experience were Oflags and consequently the economy was not complicated by payments for work by the detaining power. They consisted normally of between 1,200 and 2,500 people, housed in a number of separate but intercommunicating bungalows, one company of 200 or so to a building. Each company formed a group within the main organisation and inside the company the room and the messing syndicate, a voluntary and spontaneous group who fed together, formed the constituent units.

Between individuals there was active trading in all consumer goods and in some services. Most trading was for food against cigarettes or other foodstuffs, but cigarettes rose from the status of a normal commodity to that of currency. RMk.s existed but had no circulation save for gambling debts, as few articles could be purchased with them from the canteen.

Our supplies consisted of rations provided by the detaining power and (principally) the contents of Red Cross food parcels—tinned milk, jam, butter, biscuits, bully, chocolate, sugar, etc., and cigarettes. So far the supplies to each person were equal and regular. Private parcels of clothing, toilet requisites and cigarettes were also received, and here equality ceased owing to the different numbers despatched and the vagaries of the post. All these articles were the subject of trade and exchange.

The Development and Organisation of the Market

Very soon after capture people realised that it was both undesirable and unnecessary, in view of the limited size and the equality of supplies, to give away or to accept gifts of cigarettes or food. "Goodwill" developed into trading as a more equitable means of maximising individual satisfaction.

We reached a transit camp in Italy about a fortnight after capture and received ¼ of a Red Cross food parcel each a week later. At once exchanges, already established, multiplied in volume. Starting with simple direct barter, such as a non-smoker giving a smoker friend his cigarette issue in exchange for a chocolate ration, more complex exchanges soon became an accepted custom. Stories circulated of a padre who started off round the camp with a tin of cheese and five cigarettes and returned to his bed with a complete parcel in addition to his original cheese and cigarettes; the market was not yet perfect. Within a week or two, as the volume of trade grew, rough scales of exchange values came into existence. Sikhs, who had at first exchanged tinned beef for practically any other foodstuff, began to insist on jam and margarine. It was realised that a tin of jam was worth ½ lb. of margarine plus something else; that a cigarette issue was worth several chocolate issues, and a tin of diced carrots was worth practically nothing.

In this camp we did not visit other bungalows very much and prices varied from place to place; hence the germ of truth in the story of the itinerant priest. By the end of a month, when we reached our permanent camp, there was a lively trade in all commodities and their relative values were well known, and expressed not in terms of one another—one didn't quote bully in terms of sugar—but in terms of cigarettes. The cigarette became the standard of value. In the permanent camp people started by wandering through the bungalows calling their offers—"cheese for seven" (cigarettes)—and the hours after parcel issue were Bedlam. The inconveniences of this system soon led to its replacement by an Exchange and Mart notice board in every bungalow, where under the headings "name", "room number", "wanted" and "offered" sales and wants were advertised. When a deal went through, it was crossed off the board. The public and semi-permanent records of transactions led to cigarette prices being well known and thus tending to equality throughout the camp, although there were always opportunities for an astute trader to make a profit from arbitrage. With this development everyone, including non-smokers, was willing to sell for cigarettes, using them to buy at another time and place. Cigarettes became the normal currency, though, of course, barter was never extinguished.

The unity of the market and the prevalence of a single price varied directly with the general level of organisation and comfort in the camp. A transit camp was always chaotic and uncomfortable: people were overcrowded, no one knew where anyone else was living, and few took the trouble to find out. Organisation was too slender to include an Exchange and Mart board, and private advertisements were the most that appeared. Consequently a transit camp was not one market but many. The price of a tin of salmon is known to have varied by two cigarettes in 20 between one end of a hut and the other. Despite a high level of organisation in Italy, the market was morcellated in this manner at the first transit camp we reached after our removal to Germany in the autumn of 1943. In this camp—Stalag VIIA at Moosburg in Bavaria—there were up to 50,000 prisoners of all nationalities. French, Russians, Italians and Jugo-Slavs were free to move about within the camp: British and Americans were confined to their compounds, although a few cigarettes given to a sentry would always procure permission for one or two men to visit other compounds. The people who first visited the highly organised French trading centre, with its stalls and known prices, found coffee extract—relatively cheap among the tea-drinking English—commanding a fancy price in biscuits or cigarettes, and some enterprising people made small fortunes that way. (Incidentally we found out later that much of the coffee went "over the wire" and sold for phenomenal prices at black market cafés in Munich: some of the French prisoners were said to have made substantial sums in RMk.s. This was one of the few occasions on which our normally closed economy came into contact with other economic worlds.)

Eventually public opinion grew hostile to these monopoly profits—not everyone could make contact with the French—and trading with them was put on a regulated basis. Each group of beds was given a quota of articles to offer and the transaction was carried out by accredited representatives from the British compound, with monopoly rights. The same method was used for trading with sentries elsewhere, as in this trade secrecy and reasonable prices had a peculiar importance, but as is ever the case with regulated companies, the interloper proved too strong.

The permanent camps in Germany saw the highest level of commercial organisation. In addition to the Exchange and Mart notice boards, a shop was organised as a public utility, controlled by representatives of the Senior British Officer, on a no profit basis. People left their surplus clothing, toilet requisites and food there until they were sold at a fixed price in cigarettes. Only sales in cigarettes were accepted—there was no barter— and there was no higgling. For food at least there were standard prices: clothing is less homogeneous and the price was decided around a norm by the seller and the shop manager in agreement; shirts would average say 80, ranging from 60 to 120 according to quality and age. Of food, the shop carried small stocks for convenience; the capital was provided by a loan from the bulk store of Red Cross cigarettes and repaid by a small commission taken on the first transactions. Thus the cigarette attained its fullest currency status, and the market was almost completely unified.

It is thus to be seen that a market came into existence without labour or production. The B.R.C.S. may be considered as "Nature" of the text-book, and the articles of trade—food, clothing and cigarettes—as free gifts—land or manna. Despite this, and despite a roughly equal distribution of resources, a market came into spontaneous operation, and prices were fixed by the operation of supply and demand. It is difficult to reconcile this fact with the labour theory of value.

Actually there was an embryo labour market. Even when cigarettes were not scarce, there was usually some unlucky person willing to perform services for them. Laundrymen advertised at two cigarettes a garment. Battle-dress was scrubbed and pressed and a pair of trousers lent for the interim period for twelve. A good pastel portrait cost thirty or a tin of " Kam ". Odd tailoring and other jobs similarly had their prices.

There were also entrepreneurial services. There was a coffee stall owner who sold tea, coffee or cocoa at two cigarettes a cup, buying his raw materials at market prices and hiring labour to gather fuel and to stoke; he actually enjoyed the services of a chartered accountant at one stage. After a period of great prosperity he overreached himself and failed disastrously for several hundred cigarettes. Such large-scale private enterprise was rare but several middlemen or professional traders existed. The padre in Italy, or the men at Moosburg who opened trading relations with the French, are examples: the more subdivided the market, the less perfect the advertisement of prices, and the less stable the prices, the greater was the scope for these operators. One man capitalised his knowledge of Urdu by buying meat from the Sikhs and selling butter and jam in return: as his operations became better known more and more people entered this trade, prices in the Indian Wing approximated more nearly to those elsewhere, though to the end a " contact " among the Indians was valuable, as linguistic difficulties prevented the trade from being quite free. Some were specialists in the Indian trade, the food, clothing or even the watch trade. Middlemen traded on their own account or on commission. Price rings and agreements were suspected and the traders certainly co-operated. Nor did they welcome newcomers. Unfortunately the writer knows little of the workings of these people: public opinion was hostile and the professionals were usually of a retiring disposition.

One trader in food and cigarettes, operating in a period of dearth, enjoyed a high reputation. His capital, carefully saved, was originally about 50 cigarettes, with which he bought rations on issue days and held them until the price rose just before the next issue. He also picked up a little by arbitrage; several times a day he visited every Exchange or Mart notice board and took advantage of every discrepancy between prices of goods offered and wanted. His knowledge of prices, markets and names of those who had received cigarette parcels was phenomenal. By these means he kept himself smoking steadily—his profits—while his capital remained intact.

Sugar was issued on Saturday. about Tuesday two of us used to visit Sam and make a deal; as old customers he would advance as much of the price as he could spare then, and entered the transaction in a book. On Saturday morning he left cocoa tins on our beds for the ration, and picked them up on Saturday afternoon. We were hoping for a calendar at Christmas, but Sam failed too. He was left holding a big black treacle issue when the price fell, and in this weakened state was unable to withstand an unexpected arrival of parcels and the consequent price fluctuations. He paid in full, but from his capital. The next Tuesday, when I paid my usual visit he was out of business.

Credit entered into many, perhaps into most, transactions, in one form or another. Sam paid in advance as a rule for his purchases of future deliveries of sugar, but many buyers asked for credit, whether the commodity was sold spot or future. Naturally prices varied according to the terms of sale. A treacle ration might be advertised for four cigarettes now or five next week. And in the future market "bread now" was a vastly different thing from "bread Thursday". Bread was issued on Thursday and Monday, four and three days' rations respectively, and by Wednesday and Sunday night it had risen at least one cigarette per ration, from seven to eight, by supper time. One man always saved a ration to sell then at the peak price: his offer of "bread now" stood out on the board among a number of "bread Monday's" fetching one or two less, or not selling at all—and he always smoked on Sunday night.

The Cigarette Currency

Although cigarettes as currency exhibited certain peculiarities, they performed all the functions of a metallic currency as a unit of account, as a measure of value and as a store of value, and shared most of its characteristics. They were homogeneous, reasonably durable, and of convenient size for the smallest or, in packets, for the largest transactions. Incidentally, they could be clipped or sweated by rolling them between the fingers so that tobacco fell out.

Cigarettes were also subject to the working of Gresham's Law. Certain brands were more popular than others as smokes, but for currency purposes a cigarette was a cigarette. Consequently buyers used the poorer qualities and the Shop rarely saw the more popular brands: cigarettes such as Churchman's No. 1 were rarely used for trading. At one time cigarettes hand-rolled from pipe tobacco began to circulate. Pipe tobacco was issued in lieu of cigarettes by the Red Cross at a rate of 25 cigarettes to the ounce and this rate was standard in exchanges, but an ounce would produce 30 home-made cigarettes. Naturally, people with machine-made cigarettes broke them down and re-rolled the tobacco, and the real cigarette virtually disappeared from the market. Hand-rolled cigarettes were not homogeneous and prices could no longer be quoted in them with safety: each cigarette was examined before it was accepted and thin ones were rejected, or extra demanded as a make-weight. For a time we suffered all the inconveniences of a debased currency.

Machine-made cigarettes were always universally acceptable, both for what they would buy and for themselves. It was this intrinsic value which gave rise to their principal disadvantage as currency, a disadvantage which exists, but to a far smaller extent, in the case of metallic currency;—that is, a strong demand for non-monetary purposes. Consequently our economy was repeatedly subject to deflation and to periods of monetary stringency. While the Red Cross issue of 50 or 25 cigarettes per man per week came in regularly, and while there were fair stocks held, the cigarette currency suited its purpose admirably. But when the issue was interrupted, stocks soon ran out, prices fell, trading declined in volume and became increasingly a matter of barter. This deflationary tendency was periodically offset by the sudden injection of new currency. Private cigarette parcels arrived in a trickle throughout the year, but the big numbers came in quarterly when the Red Cross received its allocation of transport. Several hundred thousand cigarettes might arrive in the space of a fortnight. Prices soared, and then began to fall, slowly at first but with increasing rapidity as stocks ran out, until the next big delivery. Most of our economic troubles could be attributed to this fundamental instability.

Price Movements

Many factors affected prices, the strongest and most noticeable being the periodical currency inflation and deflation described in the last paragraphs. The periodicity of this price cycle depended on cigarette and, to a far lesser extent, on food deliveries. At one time in the early days, before any private parcels had arrived and when there were no individual stocks, the weekly issue of cigarettes and food parcels occurred on a Monday. The non-monetary demand for cigarettes was great, and less elastic than the demand for food: consequently prices fluctuated weekly, falling towards Sunday night and rising sharply on Monday morning. Later, when many people held reserves, the weekly issue had no such effect, being too small a proportion of the total available. Credit allowed people with no reserves to meet their non-monetary demand over the week-end.

The general price level was affected by other factors. An influx of new prisoners, proverbially hungry, raised it. Heavy air raids in the vicinity of the camp probably increased the non-monetary demand for cigarettes and accentuated deflation. Good and bad war news certainly had its effect, and the general waves of optimism and pessimism which swept the camp were reflected in prices. Before breakfast one morning in March of this year, a rumour of the arrival of parcels and cigarettes was circulated. Within ten minutes I sold a treacle ration, for four cigarettes (hitherto offered in vain for three), and many similar deals went through. By 10 o'clock the rumour was denied, and treacle that day found no more buyers even at two cigarettes.

More interesting than changes in the general price level were changes in the price structure. Changes in the supply of a commodity, in the German ration scale or in the make-up of Red Cross parcels, would raise the price of one commodity relative to others. Tins of oatmeal, once a rare and much sought after luxury in the parcels, became a commonplace in 1943, and the price fell. In hot weather the demand for cocoa fell, and that for soap rose. A new recipe would be reflected in the price level: the discovery that raisins and sugar could be turned into an alcoholic liquor of remarkable potency reacted permanently on the dried fruit market. The invention of electric immersion heaters run off the power points made tea, a drug on the market in Italy, a certain seller in Germany.

In August, 1944, the supplies of parcels and cigarettes were both halved. Since both sides of the equation were changed in the same degree, changes in prices were not anticipated. But this was not the case: the non-monetary demand for cigarettes was less elastic than the demand for food, and food prices fell a little. More important however were the changes in the price structure. German margarine and jam, hitherto valueless owing to adequate supplies of Canadian butter and marmalade, acquired a new value. Chocolate, popular and a certain seller, and sugar, fell. Bread rose; several standing contracts of bread for cigarettes were broken, especially when the bread ration was reduced a few weeks later.

In February, 1945, the German soldier who drove the ration waggon was found to be willing to exchange loaves of bread at the rate of one loaf for a bar of chocolate. Those in the know began selling bread and buying chocolate, by then almost unsaleable in a period of serious deflation. Bread, at about 40, fell slightly; chocolate rose from 15; the supply of bread was not enough for the two commodities to reach parity, but the tendency was unmistakable.

The substitution of German margarine for Canadian butter when parcels were halved naturally affected their relative values, margarine appreciating at the expense of butter. Similarly, two brands of dried milk, hitherto differing in quality and therefore in price by five cigarettes a tin, came together in price as the wider substitution of the cheaper raised its relative value.

Enough has been cited to show that any change in conditions affected both the general price level and the price structure. It was this latter phenomenon which wrecked our planned economy.

Paper Currency—Bully Marks

Around D-Day, food and cigarettes were plentiful, business was brisk and the camp in an optimistic mood. Consequently the Entertainments Committee felt the moment opportune to launch a restaurant, where food and hot drinks were sold while a band and variety turns performed. Earlier experiments, both public and private, had pointed the way, and the scheme was a great success. Food was bought at market prices to provide the meals and the small profits were devoted to a reserve fund and used to bribe Germans to provide grease-paints and other necessities for the camp theatre. Originally meals were sold for cigarettes but this meant that the whole scheme was vulnerable to the periodic deflationary waves, and furthermore heavy smokers were unlikely to attend much. The whole success of the scheme depended on an adequate amount of food being offered for sale in the normal manner.

To increase and facilitate trade, and to stimulate supplies and customers therefore, and secondarily to avoid the worst effects of deflation when it should come, a paper currency was organised by the Restaurant and the Shop. The Shop bought food on behalf of the Restaurant with paper notes and the paper was accepted equally with the cigarettes in the Restaurant or Shop, and passed back to the Shop to purchase more food. The Shop acted as a bank of issue. The paper money was backed 100 per cent. by food; hence its name, the Bully Mark. The BMk. was backed 100 per cent. by food: there could be no over-issues, as is permissible with a normal bank of issue, since the eventual dispersal of the camp and consequent redemption of all BMk.s was anticipated in the near future.

Originally one BMk. was worth one cigarette and for a short time both circulated freely inside and outside the Restaurant. Prices were quoted in BMk.s and cigarettes with equal freedom—and for a short time the BMk. showed signs of replacing the cigarette as currency. The BMk. was tied to food, but not to cigarettes: as it was issued against food, say 45 for a tin of milk and so on, any reduction in the BMk. prices of food would have meant that there were unbacked BMk.s in circulation. But the price of both food and BMk.s could and did fluctuate with the supply of cigarettes.

While the Restaurant flourished, the scheme was a success: the Restaurant bought heavily, all foods were saleable and prices were stable.

In August parcels and cigarettes were halved and the Camp was bombed. The Restaurant closed for a short while and sales of food became difficult. Even when the Restaurant reopened, the food and cigarette shortage became increasingly acute and people were unwilling to convert such valuable goods into paper and to hold them for luxuries like snacks and tea. Less of the right kinds of food for the Restaurant were sold, and the Shop became glutted with dried fruit, chocolate, sugar, etc., which the Restaurant could not buy. The price level and the price structure changed. The BMk. fell to four-fifths of a cigarette and eventually farther still, and it became unacceptable save in the Restaurant. There was a flight from the BMk., no longer convertible into cigarettes or popular foods. The cigarette re-established itself.

But the BMk. was sound! The Restaurant closed in the New Year with a progressive food shortage and the long evenings without lights due to intensified Allied air raids, and BMk.s could only be spent in the Coffee Bar—relict of the Restaurant—or on the few unpopular foods in the Shop, the owners of which were prepared to accept them. In the end all holders of BMk.s were paid in full, in cups of coffee or in prunes. People who had bought BMk.s for cigarettes or valuable jam or biscuits in their heyday were aggrieved that they should have stood the loss involved by their restricted choice, but they suffered no actual loss of market value.

Price Fixing

Along with this scheme came a determined attempt at a planned economy, at price fixing. The Medical Officer had long been anxious to control food sales, for fear of some people selling too much, to the detriment of their health. The deflationary waves and their effects on prices were inconvenient to all and would be dangerous to the Restaurant which had to carry stocks. Furthermore, unless the BMk. was convertible into cigarettes at about par it had little chance of gaining confidence and of succeeding as a currency. As has been explained, the BMk. was tied to food but could not be tied to cigarettes, which fluctuated in value. Hence, while BMk. prices of food were fixed for all time, cigarette prices of food and BMk.s varied.

The Shop, backed by the Senior British Officer, was now in a position to enforce price control both inside and outside its walls. Hitherto a standard price had been fixed for food left for sale in the shop, and prices outside were roughly in conformity with this scale, which was recommended as a " guide " to sellers, but fluctuated a good deal around it. Sales in the Shop at recommended prices were apt to be slow though a good price might be obtained : sales outside could be made more quickly at lower prices. (If sales outside were to be at higher prices, goods were withdrawn from the Shop until the recommended price rose : but the recommended price was sluggish and could not follow the market closely by reason of its very purpose, which was stability.) The Exchange and Mart notice boards came under the control of the Shop : advertisements which exceeded a 5 per cent. departure from the recommended scale were liable to be crossed out by authority : unauthorised sales were discouraged by authority and also by public opinion, strongly in favour of a just and stable price. (Recommended prices were fixed partly from market data, partly on the advice of the M.O.)

At first the recommended scale was a success : the Restaurant, a big buyer, kept prices stable around this level : opinion and the 5 per cent. tolerance helped. But when the price level fell with the August cuts and the price structure changed, the recommended scale was too rigid. Unchanged at first, as no deflation was expected, the scale was tardily lowered, but the prices of goods on the new scale remained in the same relation to one another, owing to the BMk., while on the market the price structure had changed. And the modifying influence of the Restaurant had gone. The scale was moved up and down several times, slowly following the inflationary and deflationary waves, but it was rarely adjusted to changes in the price structure. More and more advertisements were crossed off the board, and black market sales at unauthorised prices increased : eventually public opinion turned against the recommended scale and authority gave up the struggle. In the last few weeks, with unparalleled deflation, prices fell with alarming rapidity, no scales existed, and supply and demand, alone and unmellowed, determined prices.

Public Opinion

Public opinion on the subject of trading was vocal if confused and changeable, and generalisations as to its direction are difficult and dangerous. A tiny minority held that all trading was undesirable as it engendered an unsavoury atmosphere ; occasional frauds and sharp practices were cited as proof. Certain forms of trading were more generally condemned ; trade with the Germans was criticised by many. Red Cross toilet articles, which were in short supply and only issued in cases of actual need, were excluded from trade by law and opinion working in unshakable harmony. At one time, when there had been several cases of malnutrition reported among the more devoted smokers, no trade in German rations was permitted, as the victims became an additional burden on the depleted food reserves of the Hospital. But while certain activities were condemned as anti-social, trade itself was practised, and its utility appreciated, by almost everyone in the camp.

More interesting was opinion on middlemen and prices. Taken as a whole, opinion was hostile to the middleman. His function, and his hard work in bringing buyer and seller together, were ignored ; profits were not regarded as a reward for labour, but as the result of sharp practices. Despite the fact that his very existence was proof to the contrary, the middleman was held to be redundant in view of the existence of an official Shop and the Exchange and Mart. Appreciation only came his way when he was willing to advance the price of a sugar ration, or to buy goods spot and carry them against a future sale. In these cases the element of risk was obvious to all, and the convenience of the service was felt to merit some reward. Particularly unpopular was the middleman with an element of monopoly, the man who contacted the ration wagon driver, or the man who utilised his knowledge of Urdu. And middlemen as a group were blamed for reducing prices. Opinion notwithstanding, most people dealt with a middleman, whether consciously or unconsciously, at some time or another.

There was a strong feeling that everything had its " just price " in cigarettes. While the assessment of the just price, which incidentally varied between camps, was impossible of explanation, this price was nevertheless pretty closely known. It can best be defined as the price usually fetched by an article in good times when cigarettes were plentiful. The "just price" changed slowly; it was unaffected by short-term variations in supply, and while opinion might be resigned to departures from the "just price", a strong feeling of resentment persisted. A more satisfactory definition of the "just price" is impossible. Everyone knew what it was, though no one could explain why it should be so.

As soon as prices began to fall with a cigarette shortage, a clamour arose, particularly against those who held reserves and who bought at reduced prices. Sellers at cut prices were criticised and their activities referred to as the black market. In every period of dearth the explosive question of "should non-smokers receive a cigarette ration?" was discussed to profitless length. Unfortunately, it was the non-smoker, or the light smoker with his reserves, along with the hated middleman, who weathered the storm most easily.

The popularity of the price-fixing scheme, and such success as it enjoyed, were undoubtedly the result of this body of opinion. On several occasions the fall of prices was delayed by the general support given to the recommended scale. The onset of deflation was marked by a period of sluggish trade; prices stayed up but no one bought. Then prices fell on the black market, and the volume of trade revived in that quarter. Even when the recommended scale was revised, the volume of trade in the Shop would remain low. Opinion was always overruled by the hard facts of the market.

Curious arguments were advanced to justify price fixing. The recommended prices were in some way related to the calorific values of the foods offered: hence some were overvalued and never sold at these prices. One argument ran as follows:—not everyone has private cigarette parcels: thus, when prices were high and trade good in the summer of 1944, only the lucky rich could buy. This was unfair to the man with few cigarettes. When prices fell in the following winter, prices should be pegged high so that the rich, who had enjoyed life in the summer, should put many cigarettes into circulation. The fact that those who sold to the rich in the summer had also enjoyed life then, and the fact that in the winter there was always someone willing to sell at low prices were ignored. Such arguments were hotly debated each night after the approach of Allied aircraft extinguished all lights at 8 p.m. But prices moved with the supply of cigarettes, and refused to stay fixed in accordance with a theory of ethics.

Conclusion

The economic organisation described was both elaborate and smooth-working in the summer of 1944. Then came the August cuts and deflation. Prices fell, rallied with deliveries of cigarette parcels in September and December, and fell again. In January, 1945, supplies of Red Cross cigarettes ran out: and prices slumped still further: in February the supplies of food parcels were exhausted and the depression became a blizzard. Food, itself scarce, was almost given away in order to meet the non-monetary demand for cigarettes. Laundries ceased to operate, or worked for £s or RMk.s: food and cigarettes sold for fancy prices in £s, hitherto unheard of. The Restaurant was a memory and the BMk. a joke. The Shop was empty and the Exchange and Mart notices were full of unaccepted offers for cigarettes. Barter increased in volume, becoming a larger proportion of a smaller volume of trade. This, the first serious and prolonged food shortage in the writer's experience, caused the price structure to change again, partly because German rations were not easily divisible. A margarine ration gradually sank in value until it exchanged directly for a treacle ration. Sugar slumped sadly. Only bread retained its value. Several thousand cigarettes, the capital of the Shop, were distributed without any noticeable effect. A few fractional parcel and cigarette issues, such as one-sixth of a parcel and twelve cigarettes each, led to momentary price recoveries and feverish trade, especially when they coincided with good news from the Western Front, but the general position remained unaltered.

By April, 1945, chaos had replaced order in the economic sphere: sales were difficult, prices lacked stability. Economics has been defined as the science of distributing limited means among unlimited and competing ends. On 12th April, with the arrival of elements of the 30th U.S. Infantry Division, the ushering in of an age of plenty demonstrated the hypothesis that with infinite means economic organisation and activity would be redundant, as every want could be satisfied without effort.

[2]

INGREDIENTS OF FAMINE ANALYSIS: AVAILABILITY AND ENTITLEMENTS*

AMARTYA SEN

Famines often take place in situations of moderate to good food availability, without any significant decline of food supply per head. The paper presents an alternative approach to famines, which does not concentrate on availability, but on people's ability to command food through legal means available in the society (including the use of production possibilities, trade opportunities, entitlements vis-à-vis the state, etc.). The approach is explained, focusing on exchange entitlement mappings, fluctuations in which can lead to big shifts in the intergroup distribution of food command. The approach is then applied to the Bengal famine of 1943, the Ethiopian famine in Wollo in 1973, and the Bangladesh famine in 1974, and some general conclusions are drawn about the nature and classes of famines.

The main purpose of the paper is to develop an approach to famine analysis and to examine its implications. The entitlement approach, which contrasts with the more usual food availability approach, concentrates on the ability of people to command food through the legal means available in that society (including the use of production possibilities, trade opportunities, entitlements vis-à-vis the state, etc.). The main line of analysis is presented in Section II, relating endowment vectors to sets of alternative commodity entitlements through an exchange entitlement mapping. Application to famine analysis is discussed in general terms in Section III, including limitations of the approach, while entitlement failures are broadly categorized in Section IV. Then the approach is applied to studying three actual famines: the Bengal famine of 1943 (Section V), the Ethiopian famine of 1973 in Wollo (Section VI), and the Bangladesh famine of 1974 (Section VII). While data scarcity constrains some of the analysis, some firm conclusions do emerge. The limitations of the food availability approach—its cluelessness—come out sharply. Some general remarks on famine analysis are made in the concluding section.

I. THE AVAILABILITY APPROACH

Famines have received a good deal of attention recently, partly because they have continued to occur despite mid-twentieth century

* This paper was completed during the author's visit to Cornell University in September–October 1979. For helpful comments, I am most grateful to M. Alamgir, John Flemming, Keith Griffin, Judith Heyer, Jay Kynch, Mukul Majumdar, Felix Paukert, Debraj Ray, Jaroslav Vanek, Henry Wan, Jr., and to the referees of this *Journal.* The papers draws heavily on my forthcoming book, Sen [1981].

The Quarterly Journal of Economics, August 1981 CCC 0033-5533/81/030433-32$03.20

prosperity,[1] but also because much fear seems to be entertained currently about a coming "world food crisis."[2] It has even been suggested that "the biggest famine in history has just begun" [Dumont, 1975, p. 29].

The traditional approach to famines looks for a decline in food availability: "a sudden, sharp reduction in the food supply in any particular geographic locale has usually resulted in widespread hunger and famine" [Brown and Eckholm, 1974, p. 25]. This approach of food availability decline (FAD approach for short) has some superficial plausibility, since it seems natural to sense a shortage of food when people die as a result of not having food. The FAD approach also fits in well with Malthusian long-run analysis of increased mortality as food supply falls relative to the size of the population.[3]

However, starvation is a matter of some people not *having* enough food to eat, and not a matter of there *being* not enough food to eat.[4] While the latter can be a cause of the former, it is clearly one of many possible influences. The next section is devoted to developing a different approach to starvation and famines based on the notion of entitlement.

II. The Entitlement Approach

Ownership of food is one of the most primitive property rights, and in each society there are rules governing this right. The entitlement approach concentrates on each person's entitlements to commodity bundles including food, and views starvation as resulting from a failure to be entitled to any bundle with enough food.[5]

In a fully directed economy, each person i may simply get a particular commodity bundle that is assigned to him. To a limited

1. Important examples of recent famines include the Great Bengal Famine of 1943, the Biafra famine in Nigeria of 1968, the Ethiopian famines of 1973–1974, famine in the Sahel countries in the early seventies, the Bangladesh famine of 1974, and famines in Kampuchea and in East Africa in recent years.

2. See Ehrlich and Ehrlich [1972], Brown and Eckholm [1974], Aziz [1975], among many other contributions. See also Johnson [1975] and Sinha [1976] for general analyses of the available information.

3. Robert Malthus himself provided a closely reasoned short-run analysis of famines in Malthus [1800], following his long-run analysis of population growth in Malthus [1798].

4. The distinction corresponds to that between "goods" and "named goods," which is central to the welfare-based evaluation of national income (see Sen [1976b]). See also Hahn [1971] for a different use of the contrast, which can be related to Hicks's [1946] notion of "dated goods."

5. It may be worth mentioning that the use of "entitlement" here is descriptive rather than normative, and the entitlement approach presented here must not be confused with Nozick's [1974] moral theory of the same name. Some of the normative issues are discussed in Sen [1977a].

extent, this happens in most economies, e.g., to residents of old people's homes or of mental hospitals. Typically, however, there is a menu—possibly wide—to choose from. E_i is the entitlement set of person i in a given society, in a given situation, and it consists of a set of vectors of alternative commodity bundles, any one of which the person can decide to have.[6] In an economy with private ownership and exchange in the form of trade (exchange with others) and production (exchange with nature), E_i can be characterized as depending on two parameters: the endowment vector $\mathbf{x}$ and an exchange entitlement mapping $E_i(.)$, which specifies the set of commodity bundles any one of which person i can choose to have through "exchange" (trade and production).[7]

I have examined elsewhere the formal characterization of entitlement relations and their use (see Sen [1981], Chs. 1, 5, 10, and Appendices A and B). It should be noted here that the exchange entitlement mapping, or E-mapping for short, will, in general, depend on the legal, political, economic and social characteristics of the society in question and the person i's position in it. Perhaps the simplest case in terms of traditional economic theory is one in which the endowment vector can be exchanged in the market at fixed relative prices into any bundle costing no more, and here the *value* of the exchange entitlement mapping will be a traditional "budget set."

Bringing in production ("exchange with nature") will make the E-mapping depend on production opportunities as well as trade possibilities of resources and products. It will also involve legal rights to apportioning the produce, e.g., the capitalist rule of the "entrepreneur" owning the produce. Sometimes the social conventions governing these rights can be very complex indeed, e.g., those governing the rights of migrant members of peasant families to a share of the peasant output [Sen, 1975, 1981].

Social security provisions are also reflected in the E-mapping; e.g., the right to unemployment benefits if one fails to find a job, or the right to income supplementation if one's income would otherwise fall below a certain specified level. And so are employment guarantees when they exist—as they do in some socialist economies—giving one the right to sell one's labor power to the government at a minimum price. E-mappings will also depend on provisions of taxation.

Person i will have to starve if given his endowment $\mathbf{x}_i$ and the

6. E_i can be seen as a subset of the nonnegative orthant X of n-dimensional real space (given n commodities).

7. $E_i(.)$ is a function from X to the power set of X, the set of all subsets of X:

$$E_i: X \rightarrow 2^X, \qquad \text{with } \mathbf{x} \in E_i(\mathbf{x}), \qquad \text{for all } \mathbf{x} \in X. \tag{1}$$

exchange entitlement mapping $E_i(.)$, no element of $E_i(\mathbf{x}_i)$ contains enough food. The "starvation set" S_i of endowment vectors consists of those commodity vectors $\mathbf{z}$ such that he cannot meet his food requirements through exchange, starting from $\mathbf{z}$ (i.e., the exchange entitlement set $E_i(\mathbf{z})$ contains no vectors satisfying his minimum food requirements).[8]

In standard models of general equilibrium for capitalist economies,[9] it is assumed *in effect* that everyone's endowment vector lies outside the starvation set, and in this way the problem of survival is eliminated. As Koopmans [1957] puts it: "they assume that each consumer can, if necessary, survive on the basis of the resources he holds and the direct use of his own labor, without engaging in exchange, and still have something to spare of some type of labor which is sure to meet with a positive price in any equilibrium" [p. 59]. The advantages of such an assumption for general equilibrium models are clear enough, but it is not the case that, say, barbers, or shoemakers, or goldsmiths, or general laborers, or even doctors or lawyers, can survive without trading. The problem that is thus eliminated by assumption in these general equilibrium models is precisely the one that is central to a theory of starvation and famines.

The "survival problem" for general equilibrium models calls for a solution not in terms of a clever assumption that eliminates it irrespective of realism, but for a reflection of the real guarantees that actually prevent starvation deaths in advanced capitalist economies. This involves bringing in social security provisions, which precisely play this role, and there need be no great difficulty in incorporating such transfers in the formulation of a general equilibrium model with the state providing minimum entitlement transfers.

The real problem is not one of convenience of analysis but of *actual* existence of such entitlement guarantees, and starvation and famines can flourish in different parts of the world precisely because of the absence of such guarantees.

III. Famines as Entitlement Failures

Person i can be plunged into starvation *either* through a fall in

8. The set of commodity vectors, each of which satisfies person i's minimum food requirement, is denoted $F_i \subseteq X$. Person i will be forced to starve because of unfavorable entitlement relations if and only if he is not entitled to any member of F_i, given his endowment vector and his exchange entitlement mapping:

$$E_i(\mathbf{x}_i) \cap F_i = \phi; \tag{2}$$

$$S_i = \{\mathbf{z} \mid \mathbf{z} \in X \quad \text{and} \quad E_i(\mathbf{z}) \cap F_i = \phi\}. \tag{3}$$

9. See Debreu [1959] and Arrow and Hahn [1971].

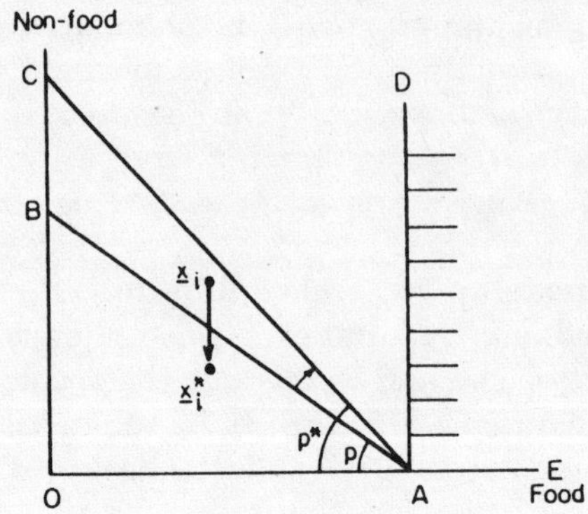

FIGURE I

the endowment vector $\mathbf{x}_i$, *or* through an unfavorable shift in the exchange entitlement mapping $E_i(.)$.[10] The distinction is illustrated in Figure I in terms of the simple case of pure trade involving only two commodities, namely, food and nonfood. The exchange entitlement mapping is taken to assume the simple linear form of constant price exchange. With a price ratio p, and a minimum food requirement $0A$, the starvation set S_i is given by the region $0AB$. If the endowment vector is $\mathbf{x}_i$, the person is in a position to avoid starvation. This ability can fail either (i) through a lower endowment vector, e.g., $\mathbf{x}_i^*$, *or* (ii) through a less favorable exchange entitlement mapping, e.g., that given by p^*, which would make the starvation set $0AC$.

It is easy to see that starvation can develop for a certain group of people as its endowment vector collapses, and there are indeed many accounts of such endowment declines on the part of sections of the poor rural population in many developing countries through alienation of land, sale of livestock, etc., and of consequent hardship.[11] Shifts in exchange entitlement mappings are rather less palpable, and more difficult to trace, but starvation can also develop with unchanged asset ownership through movements of exchange entitlement *mapping*. This will be impossible only if the endowment vector was itself an element of F_i, e.g., in Figure I, if it belonged to the region DAE.

Before proceeding to the use of the entitlement approach, a few of the limitations may be briefly noted. First, there can be ambiguities in the specification of entitlements. Even in capitalist market economies, entitlements may not be well defined in the absence of a unique

10. Note that this account, if taken as a real shift over time, involves a more short-run view of exchange possibilities than in the classic Arrow-Debreu formulation with present contracting of all future transactions.

11. See, for example, Griffin and Khan [1976] and Griffin [1978].

and reachable Walrasian market-clearing equilibrium,[12] and in pre-capitalist formations, there can be a good deal of vagueness on property rights and related matters.[13] In many cases the appropriate characterization of entitlements may pose problems, and in some cases it may well be best characterized in the form of "fuzzy" sets and related structures—taking precise note of the vagueness involved.[14] In empirical studies of actual famines the question of precision is compromised by data problems as well, and the focus here will not be on characterizing entitlements with pretended exactitude, but on studying shifts in some of the main *ingredients* of entitlements. Big shifts in such ingredients can be decisive in outlining entitlement failures, even when there is some "fuzziness" in the entitlement relations.

Second, while entitlement relations concentrate on rights within the given legal structure in that society, some transfers involve violation of these rights, e.g., looting or brigandry. When such extra-entitlement transfers are important, the entitlement approach to famines will be defective. On the other hand, many, though not all, recent famines seem to have taken place in rather orderly societies without anything "illegal" about the process leading to starvation. In fact, in guarding ownership rights against the demands of the hungry, the legal forces uphold entitlements, e.g., in the Bengal famine of 1943 the people who died in front of well-stocked food shops protected by the state[15] were denied food because of lack of legal entitlement and not because of their entitlements being violated.

Third, people's actual food consumption may fall below their entitlements for a variety of other reasons, e.g., ignorance, fixed food habits, or apathy.[16] In concentrating on entitlements, something of the total reality is obviously neglected in our approach, and the question is how important these ignored elements happen to be and how much of a difference is made by this neglect.

12. See Hicks [1946] and Arrow and Hahn [1971].

13. There is also the critique by Dworkin [1977] of "legal positivism" disputing the view of law as a set of "rules," and emphasizing the role of "principles, policies, and other sorts of standards" (p. 27), which are, of course, inherently more ambiguous. See also Summers [1978].

14. A similar problem arises from the ambiguity of values in economic planning, requiring "range"—rather than "point"—specification of shadow prices, leading to *partial* orders (see Sen [1975]).

15. See Ghosh [1944] and also Government of India [1945].

16. Also people sometimes *choose* to starve rather than to sell their productive assets (see Jodha [1975] for some evidence of this in Indian famines), and this issue can be accommodated in the entitlement approach only in a relatively long-run formulation (taking note of future entitlements). There is also some tendency for asset markets to collapse in famine situations, making the reward from asset sales rather puny.

Finally, the entitlement approach focuses on starvation, which has to be distinguished from famine mortality, since many of the famine deaths—in some cases *most* of them—are caused by epidemics, which have patterns of their own.[17] The epidemics are, of course, induced partly by starvation, but also by other famine characteristics, such as population movement and breakdown of sanitary facilities, adding to the force of contagion.

IV. Direct and Trade Entitlement Failures

Consider occupation group j, characterized as having commodity j to sell or directly consume. Let q_j be the amount of commodity j each member of group j can sell or consume, and let the price of commodity j be p_j. The price of food per unit is p_f. Let F_j be the maximum food entitlement of group j. Clearly, $F_j = q_j p_j / p_f = q_j e_j$, when e_j is occupation j's food exchange rate (p_j/p_f).

Commodity j may or may not be a *produced* commodity. The commodity that a laborer has to sell is labor power, and it is his means of survival just as commodities in the shape of baskets and jute are the means of survival of the basket-maker and the jute-grower, respectively. In general, it may be necessary to associate several different commodities, rather than one, with the same occupation, but there is not much difficulty in redefining q_j and p_j as vectors (with $q_j p_j$ as an inner product and e_j a weighted ratio).

A special case arises when the occupation consists of being a producer of food, say, rice, which is also what members of that occupation live on. In this case $p_j = p_f$, and $e_f = 1$, with $F_f = q_f$. Given the selective nature of calamities such as floods and droughts, affecting one food-producing group but not another, it will sometimes be convenient to take the group f to be a *specific part* of that occupation category.

It is worth emphasizing that this drastically simple modeling of reality makes sense only in helping us to focus on some important parameters of famine analysis; it does not compete with the more general structure sketched in Sections II and III. Furthermore, these simplifications will be grossly misleading in some contexts, e.g., in analyzing entitlements in an industrialized economy, because of the importance of raw materials, intermediate products, asset holdings, etc. Even in applying this type of structure to analyze *rural* famines

17. See Sen [1980] for a study of the pattern of mortality in the Great Bengal Famine.

in developing countries, care is needed to insure that the distortions are not too great.

For any group j to start starving *because of* an entitlement failure, F_j must decline, since it represents the *maximum* food entitlement. F_j can fall either because one has produced less food for own consumption, or because one can obtain less food through trade exchanging one's commodity for food. The former will be called a "direct entitlement failure," and the latter a "trade entitlement failure." The former will arise when q_f falls for some food-producing subgroup, while the latter can occur either because of a fall in e_j, or because of a fall in q_j, for a group that sells its commodity to buy food. Such a fall in q_j can occur either due to an autonomous production decline (e.g., a cash crop being destroyed by a drought), or due to insufficiency of demand (e.g., a laborer being involuntarily unemployed, or a basket-maker cutting down the output as the demand for baskets slackens).

It is, in fact, possible for a group to suffer *both* direct entitlement failure as well as trade entitlement failure, since the group may produce a commodity that is both directly consumed as well as exchanged for some other food. For example, the Ethiopian or Sahelian pastoral nomad both eats the animal products directly and also sells animals to buy food grains (thereby making a net gain in calories), on which he is habitually dependent.[18] Similarly, the Bengali fisherman does consume some fish, though for his survival he is dependent on grain-calories, which he obtains at a favorable rate by selling fish—a luxury food for most Bengalis.

In the next three sections of following famines are briefly examined in the light of the framework presented in the preceding sections: the Bengal Famine of 1943; the Ethiopian famine in Wollo province in 1973; and the Bangladesh famine of 1974. They draw on fuller studies,[19] but the intention here is to put them in a comparative perspective, using the ingredients of famine analysis presented here. There will be attempts to answer the following questions in each case:

(1) Was there a substantial food availability decline compared with normal supply?
(2) To which occupation groups did the famine victims chiefly belong?

18. See Chs. 7 and 8 in Sen [1981].
19. See Sen [1980a], which also examines other cases of famines, e.g., those in Sahel countries in the seventies and the starvation of nomads in the Ogaden region of Ethiopia in 1974.

(3) Did these groups suffer from substantial entitlement declines, and if so, what were the characteristics of these entitlement failures (e.g., endowment loss *versus* unfavorable shifts in exchange entitlement mappings, direct entitlement failures versus trade entitlement failures)?

V. THE GREAT BENGAL FAMINE OF 1943

The Bengal famine of 1943 was characterized by an acute period of starvation during May to October of 1943. The death rate stayed up for several years because of epidemics that the famine unleashed. The contemporary official estimate of excess death due to the famine was 1.5 million in a population of around sixty million (see Government of India [1945, pp. 119–20]). However, use of later data, including reverse-survival estimates based on the 1951 census, indicates that 3 million was closer to the mark (see Sen [1980]). The famine was mostly a rural phenomenon, affecting every district in rural Bengal,[20] but Calcutta saw the famine mainly in the form of masses of rural destitutes trekking into the city and dying on the streets (see Das [1949]).

Was there a substantial food availability decline compared with normal supply? The official Famine Inquiry Commission, which produced an admirably detailed report, thought so, and diagnosed that the primary cause of the famine was "a serious shortage in the total supply of rice available for consumption in Bengal."[21] This FAD explanation would have seemed plausible, since there were several factors working negatively on the supply of rice, which is the staple food of the Bengali, and on the supply of foodgrains in general. To wit: (i) a cyclone in October 1942 had affected, in some areas, the main crop (*aman*) of rice to be harvested in December 1942; (ii) import of rice from Burma into India had been disrupted by the Japanese occupation of Burma; (iii) London persistently turned down requests from New Delhi of shipping allocation for importing grains into India; (iv) interprovince movements of grain were largely prohibited except through intergovernmental agreements that did not get organized until after the famine; and (v) a cunning British policy of "rice denial" to the oncoming Japanese led to removal of rice stocks from three coastal districts in Bengal in 1942 (without causing much anxiety to the Japanese, since they failed, for other reasons, to show up).

20. See the *Census of Pakistan 1951* and the *Census of India 1951*.
21. Government of India [1945, p. 77].

TABLE I

FOOD AVAILABILITY IN BENGAL: 1940–1943
Base: 1941 value = 100

Year	Index of rice output	Index of rice supply	Index of foodgrains availability	Index of foodgrains availability per capita
1940	125	124	122	123
1941	100	100	100	100
1942	141	135	131	130
1943	113	112	111	109

Source. Sen [1977b, Table 2].

Nevertheless, a careful tally of food availability in Bengal does not fit in with FAD explanation of the famine. Table I presents the results of food supply calculation, taking into account local production and trade, choosing—wherever the data permit—an assumption as unfavorable to 1943 as possible. Current availability of food grains was at least 11 percent higher in 1943 than in 1941, when there was nothing remotely like a famine. Even in per capita terms the current availability was 9 percent higher in 1943.[22]

I turn now to the second question: who were the famine victims? There is overwhelming evidence that the famine victims came almost exclusively from the rural population.[23] Hardly any came from Calcutta, even if Sir Manilal Nanavati might have exaggerated the contrast in his claim that "in the end not a single man died of starvation from the population of Greater Calcutta, while millions in rural areas starved and suffered" [Government of India, 1945, p. 102]. Within the rural areas, a picture of relative destitution can be constructed from the sample survey carried out in the famine stricken areas of Bengal by Mahalanobis, Mukherjea, and Ghosh [1946]. Using these data, inter-occupation transition matrices can be constructed reflecting changes over the famine period (see Tables 9 and 10 in Sen [1977b]).

22. For the details of the estimation procedure, see Sen [1977b]. Since figures on carryover of stocks do not exist, two-year and three-year moving averages were also considered. The three-year moving average ending in 1943 is just marginally lower than that ending in 1941, while the two-year moving average ending in 1943 is higher than any since 1939–1940 (see Table 2 in Sen [1977b]). Splitting up the availability during 1943 to take note of trade flow variations during the year does not alter the picture substantially either (see Sen [1977b, pp. 40–41]). See also Alamgir [1980] and Sen [1981, Ch. 6].

23. See Government of India [1945], Ghosh [1944], Mahalanobis, Mukherjea, and Ghosh [1946], Das [19], and Mukerji [1965].

TABLE II

DESTITUTION INDICES FOR RURAL OCCUPATION GROUPS DURING THE BENGAL FAMINE

Occupation groups	Index A	Index B
Fishermen	9.6	10.5
Transport	6.0	6.9
Agricultural labor	4.6	6.1
Other productive occupations	4.6	4.6
Nonagricultural labors	3.7	4.5
Craft	3.8	4.3
Trade	2.2	2.6
Professions and services	2.1	2.5
Noncultivating owners	1.6	2.4
Part peasant, part labor	1.4	2.0
Peasants and sharecroppers	1.3	1.4

Source. Sen [1977b, Tables 9 and 10]. Index A is the "transition" percentage to "living on charity"; it represents the percentage of January-1943-population of each occupation group responding in 1944 that they were "living on charity." Index B is the sum of destitution Index A and the "transition" percentage to "husking paddy"—a classic destitution occupation.

They include, inter alia, relative frequencies of destitution of different rural occupation groups, using two indicators: (A) transition percentage to "living on charity," and (B) transition percentage to "living on charity" or "husking paddy"—a typical destitution occupation with easy entry. The destitution indicators are presented in Table II.

The *most* affected groups in this list of rural occupations were fishermen, transporters, and agricultural laborers in that order, followed by "other productive occupations," nonagricultural labor, and crafts. In absolute number by far the largest groups of destitutes came from the class of agricultural laborers (see Mahalanobis, Mukherjea, and Ghosh [1946]). The surveys of the destitutes who trekked into Calcutta also confirm this (see Das [1949]), and so do other rural surveys dealing with destitution as well as occupation-specific mortality (see especially Mukerji [1965]).

The *least* affected group among the rural occupations was that of peasants and sharecroppers, as can be seen from Table II. Other studies again broadly confirm this.[24]

Information about entitlements is very limited. However, Table III presents indices of rice exchange rate e_j for some of the occupations

24. For example, in the villages surveyed by Mukerji [1965], peasant and sharecroppers were the least affected with the exception of landlords and office employees. See also Bhatia [1967].

TABLE III

INDICES OF RICE-EXCHANGE RATE e_j OF RURAL OCCUPATIONS DURING THE BENGAL FAMINE: BIRBHUM DISTRICT AROUND BOLPUR
Base: (a) December 1942 values
(b) Same month 1942 values

Month	Agricultural laborers		Fishermen		Barbers		Bamboo craftsmen		Rice-cultivating peasants and sharecroppers	
	(a)	(b)	(a)	(b)	(a)	(b)	(a)	(b)	(a)	(b)
1941										
December	152	152	119	119	179	179	118	118	100	100
1942										
December	100	100	100	100	100	100	100	100	100	100
1943										
January	106	n.a.	77	68	93	48	100	75	100	100
February	114	n.a.	85	75	100	52	115	77	100	100
March	67	n.a.	55	48	66	34	81	45	100	100
April	55	n.a.	40	39	48	31	71	41	100	100
May	36	n.a.	32	36	32	24	51	32	100	100
June	39	n.a.	46	30	34	22	56	30	100	100
July	41	n.a.	45	31	34	23	55	31	100	100
August	47	n.a.	44	34	34	26	52	34	100	100
September	58	43	67	43	50	32	78	46	100	100
October	58	68	60	60	45	45	67	62	100	100
November	73	126	95	118	57	71	86	106	100	100
December	120	120	126	126	75	75	106	106	100	100

Source. Sen [1977b, Tables 4 and 5]. Rice price is that of grade no. 2 rice. Agricultural wages are those of unskilled, male, agricultural laborers (daily rate). Other occupations are represented by the following commodities respectively: *pona* fish (fishermen); haircut (barbers); bamboo umbrellas (bamboo craftsmen); grade no. 2 rice (rice-cultivating peasants and sharecroppers). Not available is denoted n.a.

from data contemporarily collected in the Birbhum district near Bolpur. The occupation classification in these statistics is rather different from the categorization used by Mahalanobis and his colleagues, except for agricultural labor and fishermen. But the rice exchange rates of barbers and bamboo craftsmen are also relevant, and those of peasants and sharecroppers growing rice can, of course, be put as unity on analytical grounds (as discussed in Section IV). Table III presents these rice exchange rates, defined as the amount of common grade rice that could be bought with one unit of the occupational commodity. They are indexed (a) with the December-1942-value as 100 (to indicate absolute changes), and (b) with the same-month-1942-value as 100 (to filter out seasonal patterns).

The contrast between the obvious stationarity of e_j for rice-cultivating peasants and sharecroppers and the devastatingly steep decline of e_j for agricultural laborers, fishermen, and other groups is striking.[25] This was mainly the result of rice price rise, with prices of other commodities and rural wages falling behind.

There was little information about quantities q_j, except the unquantified, but reported to be large, decline in the amounts of fish caught and river transportation because the government's "boat denial" policy was carried out in 1942.[26] That policy, like the "rice denial" policy, was also aimed at the elusive Japanese, and took the form of destroying or removing boats capable of carrying ten passengers or more in a vast area of river-based Bengal; it did not touch the Japanese, but played havoc with river-transport (widespread in river-based Bengal), and fishing. These quantity losses were reflections of endowment loss, compounding, at least in the case of fishermen, the decline in exchange entitlement mapping resulting from a fall in the rice exchange rate.

What happened to entitlements of the Calcutta population, which escaped the famine raging all around it? While there was a little decline of real wages (see Palekar [1962]), the Calcutta population was effectively insulated from the steep rise in foodgrains prices by subsidized rice being made available through a system of rationing covering more than a million employees and their dependents, and also through a network of "controlled" shops for regular residents of Calcutta. Virtually the whole of the Calcutta population was kept

25. A qualification is worth mentioning here. There is evidence that some peasants and sharecroppers had sold off their stock shortly after the harvest (often to repay loans), and had to buy back grains for consumption later in the year, and would have suffered from the high retail price of foodgrains.

26. See Government of India [1945, pp. 26–27]; also Ghosh [1944].

supplied with foodgrains at prices far below those ruling elsewhere (and indeed also below those existing in Calcutta for purchase outside rationing and control). There is little doubt that the government was successful in its policy of keeping the Calcutta population well fed, based on the belief that "the maintenance of essential food supplies to the industrial area of Calcutta must be ranked on a very high priority among the government's wartime obligation" [Government of India, 1945, p 30]. And indeed, war efforts were not disrupted in Calcutta.

It is not part of my program here to investigate the causation of the change of food prices and declines in rice exchange rates of rural occupation groups. I have tried to go into this question elsewhere [Sen, 1977b, pp. 49–55]), even though the explanations are speculative, and data limitations make any kind of proper testing virtually impossible. The main factors to emerge are as follows: (i) the importance of demand expansion connected with war-related military, industrial, and construction activities along with a massive increase in effective demand and money supply through 1942 and 1943; (ii) speculative withdrawal of rice in 1943 caused partly by panic after early reports of starvation, but also by the extreme profitability of holding rice even under the assumption of stationary expectation (rice prices nearly doubled in 1943, the year preceding the famine) and a relatively low money rate of interest (well below 10 percent); (iii) uneven distribution of the demand for labor reflecting the uneven impact of war-related activities, leaving most rural labor out of the activity boom; (iv) institutional sluggishness of the rural wage mechanism used to largely stationary rice prices in the quarter of a century preceding 1942; and (v) "derived destitution" through collapse of demand for commodities other than foodgrains (such as craft products, rural services, fish and other luxury food, etc.) as the purchases of these commodities fell into destitution.[27]

The pattern of destitution suggests that the failure of entitlements, which was widespread and massive, was mainly *trade* entitlement failure rather than *direct* entitlement failure. Evidence of *endowment* loss was found for fishermen and rural transporters, but evidence of collapse of *exchange entitlement mapping* is much more widespread.

The rise in rice prices, which played a crucial part in this, does *not* seem to have been the result of an availability failure. There is, in fact, very little evidence for availability failure in the famine year. Indeed, rice prices had also nearly doubled in the year *preceding* the

27. See also Sen [1981], Ch. 6 and Appendix B.

famine, i.e., in 1942, a year in which food availability per capita reached a record level (30 percent higher than in the preceding year).[28] The clue lies on the demand side, and the entitlement failures associated with the Bengal famine seem to relate to the powerful, but uneven, expansionary forces working on the economy of Bengal. The Bengal famine was indeed a boom famine.

VI. The Wollo Famine of 1973

The 1973–1974 famines in Ethiopia were associated with droughts. The main—*kremt*—rains in mid-1972 failed in parts of Ethiopia particularly in the northeast, and this was followed by a failure of the spring—*belg*—rains in early 1973. The famine that gripped Ethiopia in 1973 was centered on the province of Wollo. While the *kremt* rains of 1973 were good in the northeast, a new drought situation developed further south. When the famine of 1974 raged over the province of Harerghe, the northeastern famine had substantially ended. So Ethiopia experienced two rather distinct famines during 1973 and 1974, though the former was by far the larger episode, and it is with the former that this section is concerned.[29]

The mortality estimates for the Ethiopian famines vary between 50,000 to 200,000 in a population of about 27 million.[30] Most of the deaths took place in 1973, in Wollo. Starvation reached its peak in Wollo around August of 1973.[31]

Was there a substantial food availability decline in Ethiopia in 1973 compared with normal availability? Data on this are difficult to obtain, and furthermore, the heterogeneity of types of food consumed makes overall indicators difficult to define (unlike in Bengal). The Food and Agricultural Organization of the United Nations does, however, present estimates of food availability per head in terms of calories consumed in the *FAO Production Yearbooks*. The 1973 availability figure, while just a bit lower than that of the preceding year, is hardly lower than for the 1961–1965 period, and a good deal higher than the figures for 1964–1969 and 1970.[32] On this basis there

28. The entitlement decline of many of the occupation groups had already started in 1942, especially of agricultural labor (see Sen [1977b], Tables 4 and 5).

29. For an analysis of the Harerghe famine and a more detailed account of the Wollo famine, see Sen [1981], Ch. 7.

30. See Rivers, Holt, Seaman, and Bowden [1976] and Gebre-Medhin and Vahlquist [1977].

31. See Holt and Seaman [1976, p. 4] and Seaman and Holt [1975].

32. For a more detailed analysis (and examination of data consistency), see Sen [1981, Ch. 7]). The calorie estimates were interrupted in the Yearbooks for 1972 to 1975, but the 1976 Yearbook presents the figures for 1972 and 1973. 1971 is the only missing year, covered neither in the 1971 Yearbook, nor in the 1976 Yearbook.

is no reason to read a food availability decline for Ethiopia as a whole in the famine year 1973. (For a more detailed account see Sen [1981, Ch. 7].)

Should the FAD analysis relate to the Ethiopian food availability or to that in Wollo? It is, of course, always possible to make a FAD explanation work by choosing units sufficiently small, since some people dying of famine must mean that food was not "available" to *them*! However, Wollo is a big province, and given reported transport difficulties, may *deserve* to be considered on its own. I shall later take up the complex issue involved in the choice of focus for FAD, but will turn first to the food production and supply situation in Wollo.

Food production did fall quite drastically in the province of Wollo. As far as the main crop is concerned, dependent on the *kremt* rains of 1972, 90 percent of the districts had "below normal" production, with more than half of them "substantially below normal," according to a Ministry of Agriculture survey. No exact production figures have been reliably estimated for Wollo, but a big food production decline in Wollo seems indisputable [Hussein, 1976].

Was there a substantial movement of food into the deficit province of Wollo from the rest of Ethiopia? While there was some movement, no exact figures exist, but it appears that the movement was not very substantial during the famine year. Indeed, there is a record of movement of food *out of* Wollo into Addis Ababa and Asmera through the famine period (see Holt and Seaman [1976]). This would indicate that while food availability did fall in Wollo, something more than food availability had also fallen.

Who were the famine victims? While there is evidence that the pastoral population, especially of the *Afar* community, was among the first to face acute problems [Holt and Seaman, 1976, p. 3], and had a high proportional destitution rate [Hussein, 1976, p. 19],[33] most of the destitutes came from agricultural backgrounds. Indeed, it appears that "relief-centre populations were mainly made up of members of the farming peoples of principally low-land areas which are many times more densely populated than the Afar region."[34] While there were some urban-origin people in the relief camps,[35] the bulk of the

33. The *Afar* pastoralist suffered not only from drought but also from the loss of some of the best grazing ground, just before the drought, due to encroachment from commercial agriculture (see Bondestam [1974], Flood [1976], and Hussein [1976]). A similar conflict with commercial agriculture seems to have played a prominent part in the famine in the Sahel countries (see Comite Information Sahel [1974], Meillassoux [1974], and Copans [1975]). Sen [1981] takes up some of the issues raised.

34. Holt and Seaman [1976, p. 3]. See also Gebre-Medhin *et al.* [1974], and Belete *et al.* [1977].

35. These included daily male laborers and women in various service occupations: domestic service, water-carrying, beer-selling, and prostitution.

destitutes came from a farming background—a majority from the three *awrajas* (subregions) of Raya and Kobo, Yeju, and Ambassel,[36] belonging to the eastern lowlands of Wollo, severely affected by the failure of the *kremt* rains of 1972.

What about entitlements? For food-growing farmers consuming the food grown, the food exchange rate e_j is trivially unity. Thus, the production failure translates *directly* into an entitlement failure. The farming population faced starvation, since their own food output was insufficient and they did not have the ability to *buy* food from others, as food output is also their source of income.

It is the last point that provides a clue to the relative absence of food movement into Wollo from elsewhere in Ethiopia. For the farmers i in the region affected by drought, the collapse of the food entitlement F_f is a *direct* entitlement crisis related to a fall in q_f, without the overall food availability and markets making much difference (see Section IV).[37]

This explanation could be challenged by arguing that food did not get to the famine-affected people in Wollo because of transportation difficulties, and not because of the lack of purchasing power. Indeed, the roads inside Wollo are few and bad, and a large number of complaints were heard about them in discussions on the famine. If bad roads rather than lack of purchasing power prevented food from getting to the famine victims, then one must treat the province of Wollo rather than the country of Ethiopia as the right focus for a FAD analysis, and must then give food availability decline an important role in the famine. Can this hypothesis be rejected?

There is indeed strong evidence against the hypothesis of transport limitation. First, while roads are few and bad in much of Wollo, two highways run through it, and the main north-south Ethiopian highway linking Addis Ababa and Asmera runs right through the area most affected by the famine (see Holt and Seaman [1976] and Belete *et al.* [1976]). Indeed, much of the early information about the famine came from travelers being stopped on this highway to ask for food (see Holt and Seaman [1976]). Nearly all the relief camps that were eventually set up were located near the highway, not merely because of easy access for supplies coming in, but also because of the high intensity of destitution in that region (see Belete *et al.* [1977]). Underdeveloped roads would not explain the starvation in these famine-affected regions.

36. See Belete *et al.* [1977], Tables I and II.

37. A farmer owning land and livestock can, of course, sell these endowments. But many farmers did not possess saleable land; land and livestock prices were severely depressed; and there was also much endowment loss in the form of livestock death.

Second, as mentioned earlier, there was some movement of food *out of* Wollo through the famine period. This was not very large in volume, but it did provide some support for the market entitlement view rather than the transport-limitation view of food shortage in Wollo.

Third, despite the disastrous failure of food output, food prices did not go up very much in Wollo. When in October 1973 Holt and Seaman started collection of food prices in the hardest hit district of Raya and Kobo, which had more than a tenth of its population in relief camps by May–June 1974,[38] they found that food prices were within 15 percent of the pre-drought levels [Holt and Seaman, 1976, p. 5].

Food prices in Dessie, the main grain market in Wollo, also rose relatively little. Taking the average prices of 1970–1972 as the "pre-famine" levels, prices in the famine year 1973 were, on the whole, remarkably close to pre-famine levels: somewhat higher for some (e.g., teff, millett), and somewhat lower for others (e.g., wheat, sorghum, barley, maize).[39] People starved to death without there being a substantial rise in food prices. In terms of entitlement approach, there is, of course, no puzzle in this. Since the farmers' food entitlement is a *direct* entitlement (without going through the market), a collapse of it can operate without a rise in market prices. On the other hand, the transport-limitation view would have suggested a substantial increase in prices because of the excess demand arising from supply limitation.[40]

The transport-limitation view is, therefore, not easy to defend. Insofar as the starving people in Wollo could draw on food from the rest of Ethiopia *if* they had the market power to pull food into Wollo, the appropriate unit for a FAD analysis has to be Ethiopia rather than Wollo. Food did not move into Wollo in sufficient amount (and some moved out), not so much because the roads did not permit such movements, but because the Wollo residents lacked the market command.

Finally, while the entitlement failure of the Wollo farmer was a *direct* entitlement failure, this led to *trade* entitlement failures of

38. See Belete *et al.* [1977], Tables I and II.

39. See Sen [1981, Table 7.4]. These prices, collected by the National Bank of Ethiopia and the Ethiopian Grain Agency, relate to the Ethiopian calendar. So 1973 corresponds to September 1972 to September 1973. While it begins a bit early (and no time breakdown could be obtained), it avoids the period of very late 1973 in which relief supplies started coming into Wollo in some volume. Also, the main crop failure was clear by September 1972, the *kremt* rains having already failed. I am grateful to Julian Holt for giving me these unpublished official data.

40. The Wollo grain prices in 1973 remained in the neighborhood of—typically only a little higher than—those ruling in Addis Ababa despite the starvation in Wollo, according to Ethiopian Grain Agency data.

other groups. Farm servants and dependents were dismissed. The usual food sales to urban markets were reduced, and demands for urban goods and services were cut, leading to "derived destitution" there. The multiplier process would lead to other destitutions as a consequence. The composition of the relief center population confirms such indirect entitlement failures.[41] If the Bengal famine had the character of a *boom* famine, the Wollo famine certainly looks more like a contraction-based *slump* famine.

VII. The Bangladesh Famine of 1974

The Bangladesh famine of 1974 is associated with floods that came during June to September of 1974 on an inflated Brahmaputra river. Reports of famine could be heard not much after the flooding began, though the official declaration of the famine did not come until late September. Some relief centers (*langarkhanas*) providing cooked food came into operation under private initiative in early September, and massively under government auspices in early October. At one stage nearly six thousand langarkhanas were providing relief to 4.35 million people—more than 6 percent of the total population of the country. By November the crisis seemed to be passing, and the langarkhanas were shut down by the end of November.

Mortality estimates vary widely. The official figure of deaths due to the famine is 26,000. Other estimates suggest that in the Rangpur district alone "80 to 100 thousands persons died of starvation and malnutrition in 2–3 months" [Haque, Mehta, Rahman, and Wignaraja, 1976, p. 43]. Another estimate suggests an excess-death figure of around one million during August 1974 and February 1975, and a further half a million in the year following [Alamgir, 1980].

Was there a substantial food availability decline? There were factors contributing to this. The floods did wipe out a part of the standing *aus* crop of rice, which is harvested in July and August, and also washed away rice seedlings being transplanted for the principal *aman* crop, harvested around December. Importing was proving difficult due to dollar shortage (see Islam [1977]), and food aid from the United States was in serious jeopardy because of the U. S. objection to Bangladesh's export of jute to Cuba, until Bangladesh agreed to stop further export (see McHenry and Bird [1977]; also Sobhan [1979]).

41. See Gebre-Medhin *et al.* [1974], Holt and Seaman [1976], and Belete *et al.* [1977]. See also other accounts of destitution, e.g., Hussein [1976] and Wood [1976].

TABLE IV

FOODGRAINS OUTPUT AND AVAILABILITY IN BANGLADESH: 1971–1975
(Base: 1971 value = 100)

Year	Index of per capita rice output (a)	Index of per capita foodgrains availability (b)	Calories per capita (c)
1971	100	100	
1972	90	103	1,900
1973	95	103	1,913
1974	105	107	2,023
1975	99	100	

Source. (a) and (b) calculated from Alamgir [1980]; (c) is obtained from *FAO Production Yearbook 1976*.

But *did* the food availability in Bangladesh decline in the famine year? Table IV provides the indices of rice production as well as of per capita availability of rice and total foodgrains. Far from being a bad availability year, it seems that 1974 was the year of peak availability in the first half of the decade. A similar picture emerges from the estimates of calorie consumption.[42] It is difficult to defend a FAD explanation of the Bangladesh famine of 1974.

Who were the famine victims? The survey of langarkhana destitutes carried out by the Bangladesh Institute of Development Studies permits us to give an answer to the question in terms of rather broad categories. It appears that the destitutes were almost entirely from the rural areas. The breakdown among broad rural occupation groups is given in Table V. The biggest occupation group among the langarkhana destitutes was that of "farmers" (38.7 percent), followed by agricultural laborers (24.1 percent) and other laborers (20.4 percent). Farmers are also the most numerous occupation group in Bangladesh, and if we look at the relative *intensity* of destitution (see Table V), it would appear that rural laborers as a group had a much higher rate of destitution than the farmers—in fact, about three times as high. Incidentally, if we put the rural laborers together rather than splitting them into agricultural and nonagricultural (there is easy movement between the two groups), then they are also the most

42. The rice *output* figure for 1974 in the *FAO Production Yearbook* is low because it *includes* the December 1974 harvest and *excludes* the December 1973 harvest. The production figures given in Table IV here are based on Alamgir's [1980] estimation that rightly identifies the output relevant for 1974 as including the crop harvested in December 1973, and not that harvested in December 1974, which is consumed over the *next* year. The same method was used in estimating output of foodgrains in Bengal during the Bengal famine of 1943 in Section V above, and in Sen [1977b].

TABLE V

OCCUPATIONAL DISTRIBUTION AND INTENSITY OF DESTITUTION IN BANGLADESH 1974

Occupation	Percentage of total langarkhana population (a)		Percentage of Bangladesh rural households by major sources of income (b)	Destitution intensity (a)/(b)
Farmers		38.7	58.6	0.66
Agricultural laborers	24.1			
Other rural laborers	20.4			
Total rural laborers		44.5	23.7	1.88
Others		16.8	17.7	0.95
Total		100.0	100.0	1.00

Source. (a) and (b) obtained from the results of sample surveys by the Bangladesh Institute of Development Studies, reported by Alamgir [1980].

numerous occupational group of destitution in terms of absolute numbers.

The study by the Bangladesh Institute separated out three districts as "famine districts" namely, Rangpur, Mymensingh, and Sylhet, because of incidence of destitution and effects of the flood as revealed by the survey. The langarkhana data support this diagnosis, and these three are certainly among the top four districts (Rangur, Mymensingh, Dinajpur, and Sylhat) in terms of proportions of their respective total population who lived on langarkhanas (respectively, 17 percent, 12 percent, 9 percent, and 8 percent). In the case of the fourth, Dinajpur, it appears that a considerable proportion of the local destitutes really "came from the adjoining district of Rangpur" [Alamgir, 1980].

How did these three "famine districts" fare in terms of food availability change? Estimates relating to this have been presented in Table VI. Rice production in all three districts *went up* substantially. So did food availability per head. Furthermore, in terms of absolute foodgrains availability per head, these three famine districts were among the *best supplied* five districts in a list of nineteen!

What about entitlements, especially of rural labor? Table VII presents the indices of rice-exchange for rural labor for each month

TABLE VI

INTERDISTRICT VARIATIONS OF FOODGRAINS AVAILABILITY AND CHANGE: BANGLADESH 1974

District	Foodgrains availability per head (oz./day)	Percentage change of foodgrains availability between 1973 and 1974	Percentage change of rice production between 1973 and 1974
Dinajpur	25.1	+23.0	+32.1
Mymensingh	22.8	+10.7	+22.3
Sylhet	22.1	+ 3.3	+10.3
Bogra	20.8	+ 7.8	+25.8
Rangpur	20.1	+ 9.8	+17.1
Chittagong	19.7	+ 7.1	+12.6
Noakali	16.7	− 6.2	+ 6.5
Jessore	16.3	+11.6	+24.6
Khulna	16.2	+17.4	+42.2
Barisal	16.0	−14.0	− 9.6
Rajshahi	15.8	+ 1.3	+ 6.4
Patuakhali	15.7	−34.9	−33.0
Tangail	15.3	+ 4.1	+22.0
Comilla	14.9	− 7.5	+ 3.9
Chittagong Hill Tracts	14.4	− 2.7	+38.8
Dacca	13.8	− 4.8	+ 8.0
Kushtia	12.8	+ 6.7	+22.8
Faridpur	12.0	+12.5	+20.1
Pabna	10.8	+ 3.8	+12.4

Source. Alamgir [1980].

in 1974 with two alternative bases: namely, (a) December 1973 as 100; and (b) the same month in 1973 as 100. The decline of the e_j indices in the months just preceding the famine and through the famine months is very sharp indeed. The fall is a bit less if we use the same-month-previous-year base, which does something to eliminate the seasonal drop, but even there the fall is large. At the peak of the famine the fall is 35 to 45 percent compared with the same month in the previous year, for a group of people already close to subsistence.

The sharpest decline comes just after the floods started, and Table VIII presents the fall of the rice-exchange rate of rural labor during June to October. There was no such decline in the preceding year (see Table VII), and data for earlier years also show no substantial seasonal fall over these months.

TABLE VII

INDICES OF RICE-EXCHANGE RATE e_j OF RURAL LABOR DURING THE BANGLADESH FAMINE 1974
Base: (a) December-1973 values
(b) Same-month-1973 values

Month	Rural wage rate		Price of rice		Index value of rice-exchange rate e_j for 1974 month	
	1973	1974	1973	1974	(a)	(b)
January	4.78	6.22	72.37	92.11	86	102
February	4.91	6.36	76.68	98.93	82	100
March	5.14	7.17	83.84	117.33	78	100
April	5.35	8.22	96.49	136.98	77	108
May	5.47	8.72	96.29	135.68	82	113
June	5.83	8.26	91.11	139.04	76	93
July	6.02	8.61	87.06	141.78	78	88
August	5.81	8.82	85.92	171.25	66	76
September	5.72	8.80	89.47	212.80	53	65
October	5.85	8.64	94.11	251.78	44	55
November	6.00	8.39	89.65	213.73	50	59
December	6.32	8.70	80.90	188.98	59	59

Source. Calculations based on data compiled by the Bangladesh Institute of Development Studies, reported in Alamgir *et al.* [1977, Tables 3.3 and 4.3].

TABLE VIII

DECLINE OF RICE-EXCHANGE RATE OF RURAL LABOR IN BANGLADESH BETWEEN JUNE AND OCTOBER 1974

Area	Wage rate in October 1974 with June 1974 value as 100	Rice price in October 1974 with June 1974 value as 100	Percentage decline in e_j for rural labor between June and October 1974
Bangladesh	104.6	181.1	42.2
Mymensingh	69.0	225.9	69.5
Rangpur	80.0	190.3	58.0
Sylhet	100.0	236.0	57.6
Noakhali	100.0	209.8	52.3
Barisal	87.0	177.3	50.9
Chittagong Hill Tract	100.0	201.3	50.3
Tangail	106.3	211.4	49.7
Pabna	100.0	172.3	42.0
Chittagong	100.0	170.5	41.3
Patuakhali	100.0	167.9	40.4
Dacca	118.9	192.6	38.3
Khulna	96.2	153.9	37.5
Bogra	100.0	158.2	36.8
Dinajpur	114.3	179.1	36.2
Comilla	135.7	205.0	33.8
Jessore	108.3	155.0	30.1
Kushtia	112.0	151.4	26.0
Rajshahi	123.1	156.4	21.3
Faridpur	158.3	164.5	3.8

Basis. Calculated from Tables 3.3 and 4.3 of Alamgir *et al.* [1977, pp. 57–58 and 92].

The decline in the rice-exchange rate of rural labor for the districts are also presented in Table VIII. The three most affected districts in terms of precipitate decline of the rice-exchange rate are Mymensingh (70 percent), Rangpur (58 percent) and Sylhet (58 percent)—precisely the three "famine districts."[43]

What led to this severe exchange entitlement decline? The main factor would appear to be the rise in rice prices, but it is worth noting that in two of the three "famine districts," viz., in Rangpur and Mymensingh, even the money wages fell, respectively, by 20 percent and 31 percent (Table VIII). The floods certainly did reduce employment in those areas in which crops or seedlings got washed away cutting

43. For more detailed analyses of the interdistrict pattern of entitlement decline and destitution, see Alamgir [1980] and Sen [1981, Ch. 9].

TABLE IX

COMPARATIVE ANALYSIS OF THREE FAMINES

Which famine?	Was there a *food availability* collapse?	Which occupation group provided the *largest number* of famine victims?	Did that group suffer substantial *endowment* loss?	Did that group suffer *exchange entitlement* shifts?	Did that group suffer *direct* entitlement failure?	Did that group suffer *trade* entitlement failure?	What was the general economic climate?
Bengal famine 1943	No	Rural labor	No	Yes	No	Yes	Boom
Ethiopian famine (Wollo) 1973	No	Farmer	A little, yes	Yes	Yes	No	Slump
Bangladesh famine 1974	No	Rural labor	Earlier, yes	Yes	No	Yes	Mixed

down the scope for fruitful work.[44] While the floods did not reduce the overall *aus* crop in Bangladesh, and could not reduce per capita food availability in any of the "famine districts" (given the relatively large *aman* harvest in the preceding November–January); nevertheless, the labor market during the *aus* harvesting and *aman* transplanting was clearly disrupted, particularly in the "famine districts." The reduced *aman* harvest of November–January 1974–1975 did not, of course, affect food availability in Bangladesh until *after* the famine was over, but its impact was *immediately* felt in the labor market since wage employment was curtailed straightaway.

But the rise in *rice* prices cannot be explained in terms of labor market disruption, and the question arises as to why rice prices rose so fast just after the floods hit. Anticipation of the coming shortage, seeing the effects of the flood, would have been a possible immediate reason, and there was clearly some speculative rise (see Alamgir [1980]). But inflationary forces operating on the rice market had started pushing rice prices up very sharply much before the floods hit. This had been going on throughout the early seventies (see Faaland and Parkinson [1976] and Islam [1977]). But the rise in the early months (January–April) of 1974 was particularly severe, and there was about a 50 percent rise between January and April in 1974.[45] In this inflationary development the floods that came in June and later could hardly have played a role.

Thus, while floods were associated with the Bangladesh famine and played the part of disrupting the labor market as well as leading to some loss of crops by farmers and consequent destitution,[46] the forces that wreaked havoc must be traced in part to *macroeconomic* factors operating on the economy of Bangladesh. The floods seemed to have made it impossible for some deprived groups, especially rural laborers, to keep up with the expansionary forces pushing food prices up in the economy (see Sen [1981], Ch. 9).

While the *explanation* of the entitlement shifts of the victim groups must remain somewhat speculative, the *facts* of the entitle-

44. See Rahman [1974]. Also Alamgir [1978, 1980].

45. There is a seasonal element in this too, but the rise was much sharper in 1974.

46. The langarkhana destitutes came mostly from the class of landless laborers or the little-landowning peasantry. Of the langarkhana destitutes surveyed, 81 percent owned no land or less than ½ acres, compared with 26 percent for the average rural population of Bangladesh. 99 percent of destitutes owned less than 2½ acres if they owned any land at all, compared with 65 percent of the average rural Bangladeshi population. The tendency toward land alienation had been strong in Bangladesh in the preceding years to the famine (see, especially, Rahman [1974], Khan [1977], Abdullah [1976], and Adnan and Rahman [1978]), and this endowment loss over the years would have made a larger population vulnerable to the famine that took place.

ment shifts are clear enough. It is also established that whatever might have caused these shifts, a substantial decline in food availability could not have played this part, for the simple reason that such a decline did not occur. It occurred neither for Bangladesh as a whole, nor for the "famine districts" within Bangladesh.

VIII. Concluding Remarks

This paper has been concerned with presenting the entitlement approach to famine analysis. The theoretical structure was outlined with critical discussion in Sections II–IV, and then the approach was used for analyzing three recent famines in Sections V–VII. The entitlement approach analyzes famines as economic disasters, not as just food crises. The empirical studies bring out several distinct ways in which famines can develop, defying the stereotyped uniformity of food availability decline (FAD). While famine victims share a common predicament, the economic forces leading to that predicament can be very different indeed.

Table IX presents a comparative picture of a few aspects of the four famines studied, though it misses out many other contrasts discussed in detail in Sections V–VII. (Other famines have been similarly scrutinized in Sen [1981].)

That famines can take place without a substantial food availability decline is of interest mainly because of the hold that the food availability approach has on the usual famine analysis.[47] It has also led to disastrous policy failures in the past.[48] The entitlement approach concentrates instead on the ability of different sections of the population to establish command over food using the entitlement relations operating in that society depending on its legal, economic, political, and social characteristics.

I end with five general observations. First, the entitlement approach provides a general framework for analyzing famines rather than one particular hypothesis about their causation. There is, of course, a very *general* hypothesis underlying the approach, which is subject to empirical testing. It will be violated if famine starvation is shown to arise not from entitlement failure but either from choice

47. In addition to explicit use of the FAD approach, very often it is implicitly employed in separating out the total food supply per head as the strategic variable to look at.

48. The failure to *anticipate* the Bengal famine, which killed about three million people (Section V) and indeed the inability even to *recognize* it when it came, can be traced largely to the government's overriding concern with aggregate food availability statistics (see Sen [1977b], section 7).

characteristics (e.g., people refusing to eat unfamiliar food that they are in a position to buy),[49] or from non-entitlement transfers (e.g., looting).[50] But the main interest in the approach does not, I think, lie in checking *whether* most famines are related to entitlement failures, which I believe would be found to be the case, but to characterize the *nature* and *causes* of the entitlement failures where such failures occur. The contrast between different types of entitlement failures is important in understanding the precise causation of famines and in devising famine policies: anticipation, relief, and prevention.

Second, it is perhaps of a certain amount of interest that famines can arise in overall *boom* conditions (as in Bengal 1943) as well as in *slump* conditions (as in Ethiopia 1973). Slump famines may appear to be less contrary to the "common sense" about famines, but it is quite possible for such a slump to involve contraction of outputs *other than* those of food (e.g., of cash crops). Boom famines might seem particularly counterintuitive, but as discussed, famines can take place with increased output in general and of food in particular if the command system (e.g., market pull) shifts against some particular group. In this relative shift the process of the boom itself may play a major part if the boom takes the form of uneven expansion (e.g., favoring the urban population and leaving the rural laborers relatively behind). In the fight for market command over food, one group can suffer precisely from another group's prosperity, with the Devil taking the hindmost.[51]

Third, it is important to distinguish between decline of food availability and that of direct entitlement to food. The former is

49. Cf. "Now, the people of Bengal are traditionally rice eaters and they would not change their eating habits; they literally starved to death in front of shops and mobile units where wheat was available" [Moraes, 1975, p. 40]. There is, however, little evidence in favor of this account of the Bengal famine; see Ghosh [1944], Government of India [1945], and Das [1949] on people's willingness to eat anything during the famine. The explanation of people dying in front of well-stocked shops has to be sought elsewhere.

50. Such non-entitlement transfers have played a part in some famines of the past. As an example, see Walter Mallory's [1926] account of the 1925 famine in Szechwan: "The Kweichow troops invaded southern Szechwan and after some fighting were driven out. When they left they took with them all available beasts of burden, loaded with grain. The Szechwan troops who replaced them brought very little in the way of supplies and forthwith appropriated the remainder of the food reserves of the district—leaving the population, who had no interest in either side, to starve" [pp. 78–79].

51. When the fast progressing groups are themselves poor, the development of the famine may be accompanied by a reduction in the number of people below some general "poverty line," leading to a recorded reduction of poverty as it is conventionally measured, i.e., in terms of head-count ratio. The problem is somewhat less acute with distribution-sensitive measures of poverty, as proposed in Sen [1976a]. See also variants of such measures discussed in Sen [1973, 1979], Anand [1977], Hamada and Takayama [1978], Osmani [1978], Takayama [1979], Thon [1979], Kakwani [1980a, 1980b], Blackorby and Donaldson [1980], Chakravarty [1980], and Pyatt [1980].

concerned with how much total food there is in the economy in question, while the latter deals with each foodgrower's output of food that he is entitled to consume directly. In a peasant economy a crop failure would reduce both food availability as well as direct entitlement to food of the peasants. But insofar as the peasant typically lives on his own-grown food and has little ability to sell and buy additional food from the market anyway, the immediate reason for his starvation would be his direct entitlement failure rather than a decline in food availability in the market. Indeed, if his own crop fails, while those of others do not, the total supply may be large while he starves. Similarly, if his crop is large while those of others go down, he may still be able to do quite well despite the fall in total supply. The analytical contrast is important even though the two phenomena may happen simultaneously in a general crop failure. While such a crop failure may superficially look like just a crisis of food availability, something more than availability is involved. This is important to recognize also from the policy point of view, since just moving food into such an area will not help the affected population, and what is required is the generation of food entitlement.

Fourth, entitlement shifts also explain why the world has seen so many cases of "food countermovement," with food moving *out of* the famine area, rather than into it. The famine-affected region may lose out in market competition with people from other areas, and it may thus lose a part of even the food supply that it has. Some food countermovement was found in the case of the Wollo famine (Section VI). The classic case of food countermovement is, of course, the Irish famine of the 1840s, and as Woodham-Smith puts it: "In the long and troubled history of England and Ireland no issue has provoked so much anger or so embittered relations between two countries as the indisputable fact that huge quantities of food were exported from Ireland to England throughout the period when people of Ireland were dying of starvation" [Woodham-Smith, 1975, p. 70]. This is not the occasion to comment on the shortsightedness of British policy in Ireland, but to note that market forces would tend to encourage precisely such food movements when failure of purchasing ability outweighs availability decline.[52]

Finally, the focus on entitlement has the effect of emphasizing

52. In China, British refusal to agree to a ban of rice exports from famine-affected Hunan was one of the causes of a popular uprising in 1906, and later a similar thing was involved in the famous Changsha rice riot of 1910; see Esherick [1976]. There is also evidence of food movement from Bangladesh to India during the Bangladesh famine, though the magnitude of such movements is a matter of controversy (see Alamgir [1980]), Ambirajan [1978], and Rashid [1980].

legal rights (see Section III). Other relevant factors, e.g., market forces, can be seen as operating through such a system of legal relations (ownership rights, contractual obligations, legal exchanges, etc.). The law stands between food availability and food entitlement, and famine deaths can reflect legality with a vengeance.

ALL SOULS COLLEGE
OXFORD

REFERENCES

Abdullah, A. A., "Land Reforms and Agrarian Change in Bangladesh," *Bangladesh Development Studies*, IV (1976).

Adnan, S., and H. Z. Rahman, "Peasant Classes and Land Mobility: Structural Reproduction and Change in Rural Bangladesh," Working Paper No. 9, Village Study Groups, Dacca, 1978.

Alamgir, M., *Bangladesh: A Case of Below Poverty Level Equilibrium Trap* (Dacca: Bangladesh Institute of Development Studies, 1978).

——, *Famine in South Asia—Political Economy of Mass Starvation in Bangladesh* (Cambridge, MA: Oelgeschlager Gunn and Hain, 1980).

——, *et al.*, *Famine 1974: Political Economy of Mass Starvation in Bangladesh, A Statistical Annex* (Dacca: Bangladesh Institute of Development Studies, 1977).

Ambirajan, N., *Classical Political Economy and British Policy in India* (Cambridge: University Press, 1978).

Anand, S., "Aspects of Poverty in Malaysia," *Review of Income and Wealth*, XXIII (1977).

Arrow, K. J., and F. H. Hahn, *General Competitive Analysis* (Edinburgh: Oliver & Boyd, 1971; distribution taken over by North-Holland, Amsterdam).

Aziz, S., ed., *Hunger: Politics and Markets: The Real Issues in the Food Crisis* (New York: University Press, 1975).

Bardhan, P. K., and T. N. Srinivasan, eds. *Poverty and Income Distribution in India* (Calcutta: Statistical Publishing Society, 1974).

Belete, S., M. Gebre-Medhin, B. Hailemariam, M. Maffi, B. Vahlquist, and Z. Wolde-Gabriel, "Study of the Shelter Population in the Wollo Region," *Environment and Child Health* (Feb. 1977), 15–22; republished from *Courrier*, XXVI (1976).

Bhatia, B. M., *Famines in India 1860–1965*, 2nd ed. (Bombay: Asia, 1967).

Blackorby, C., and D. Donaldson, "Ethical Indices for the Measurement of Poverty," *Econometrica*, XLVIII (1980), 1053–60.

Bondestam, L., "People and Capitalism in the North-East Lowlands of Ethiopia," *Journal of Modern African Studies*, XII (1974), 423–39.

Brown, L. R., and E. P. Eckholm, *By Bread Alone* (Oxford: Pergamon Press, 1974).

Chakravarty, S. R., "New Indices for the Measurement of Poverty," Indian Statistical Institute, Calcutta, mimeo, 1980.

Copans, J., *Secheresses et Famines du Sahel* (Paris: Maspero, 1975).

Comité Information Sahel, *Qui Se Nourrit de la famine en Afrique?* (Paris: Maspero, 1974).

Das, T., *Bengal Famine (1943)* (Calcutta: University of Calcutta, 1949).

Debreu, G., *The Theory of Value* (New York: Wiley, 1959).

Dumont, R., "The Biggest Famine in History Has Just Begun," in Aziz [1975].

Dworkin, R., *Taking Rights Seriously* (London: Duckworth, 1977).

Ehrlich, P. R., and A. H. Ehrlich, *Population, Resources, Environment: Issues in Human Ecology* (San Francisco: Freeman, 1972).

Esherick, J. W., *Reform and Revolution in China* (Berkeley, CA: University of California Press, 1976).

Faaland, J., and J. R. Parkinson, *Bangladesh: The Test Case of Development* (London: Hurst, 1976).

Flood, G., "Nomadism and Its Future: the Afar," in Hussein [1976].
Gebre-Medhin, M., *et al.*, *Profile of Wollo under Famine* (Addis Ababa: Ethiopian Nutrition Institute, 24/74, 1974).
——, and B. Vahlquist, "Famine in Ethiopia—The Period 1973–75," *Nutrition Reviews*, XXXV (1977), 194–202.
Ghosh, K. C., *Famines in Bengal 1770–1943* (Calcutta: Indian Associated Publishing, 1944).
Government of India, *Famine Inquiry Commission: Report on Bengal* (New Delhi: Government of India, 1945).
Griffin, K., *Land Concentration and Rural Poverty* (London: Macmillan, 1976).
——, *International Inequality and National Poverty* (London: Macmillan, 1978).
——, and A. R. Khan, eds., *Poverty and Landlessness in Rural Asia* (Geneva: ILO, 1976).
Hahn, F., "Equilibrium with Transaction Costs," *Econometrica*, XXXIX (1971).
Hamada, K., and N. Takayama, "Censored Income Distribution and the Measurement of Poverty," *Bulletin of the International Statistical Institute*, XLVII (1978).
Haque, W., N. Mehta, A. Rahman, and P. Wignaraja, *Towards a Theory of Rural Development* (Bangkok: U. N. Asian Development Institute, 1975).
Hicks, J. R., *Value and Capital*, 2nd ed. (Oxford: Clarendon Press, 1946).
Holt, J., and J. Seaman, "The Scope of the Drought," in Hussein [1976].
Hussein, A. M., ed., *Rehab: Drought and Famine in Ethiopia* (London: International African Institute, 1976).
Islam, N., *Development Planning in Bangladesh: A Study in Political Economy* (London: Hurst, 1977).
Jodha, N. S., "Famine and Famine Policies: Some Empirical Evidence," *Economic and Political Weekly*, X (Oct. 11, 1975).
Johnson, D. Gale, *World Food Problems and Prospects* (Washington, D. C.: American Enterprise Institute for Policy Research, 1975).
Kakwani, N., *Income Distribution: Methods of Analysis and Applications*, (New York: Oxford University Press, 1980a).
——, "On a Class of Poverty Measures," *Econometrica*, XLVIII (1980b), 437–46.
Khan, A. R., "Poverty, and Inequality in Rural Bangladesh," in Griffin and Khan [1977].
Koopmans, T. C., *Three Essays on the State of the Economic Science* (New York: McGraw-Hill, 1957).
Mahalanobis, P. C., R. Muherjea, and A. Ghosh, "A Sample Survey of After-Effects of the Bengal Famine of 1943," *Sankhya*, VII, part IV (16).
Mallory, W. H., *China: Land of Famine* (New York: American Geographical Society, 1926).
Malthus, T. R., *Essay on the Principle of Population as It Affects the Future Improvement of Society* (1798).
——, *An Investigation of the Cause of the Present High Price of Provisions* (1800).
McHenry, D. F., and K. Bird, "Food Bungle in Bangladesh," *Foreign Policy*, No. 27 (Summer 1977).
Meillassoux, C., *Femme, Greniers, et Capitaux* (Paris: Maspero, 1975).
Miller, D. S., and J. F. J. Holt, "The Ethiopian Famine," *Proc. Nutr. Soc.*, XXXIV (1975), 167–72.
Moraes, D., "The Dimensions of the Problem: Comment," in Aziz [1975].
Mukherji, K., *Agriculture, Famine and Rehabilitation in South Asia* (Santiniketan: Visva-Bharati, 1965).
Nozick, R., *Anarchy, State and Utopia* (Oxford: Blackwell, 1974).
Osmani, S. R., *Economic Inequality and Group Welfare: Theory and Application to Bangladesh*, mimeo, 1978 (to be published by Oxford University Press).
Palekar, S. A., *Real Wages in India 1939–1950* (Bombay: International Book House, 1962).
Pyatt, G., "Poverty and Welfare Measures Based on the Lorenz Curve," Development Research Center, World Bank, Washington, D. C., mimeo, 1980.
Rahman, Anisur, "The Famine," mimeographed, Dacca University, 1974.
Rashid, S., "The Policy of Laissez-faire during Scarcities," *Economic Journal*, XC (1980).
Rivers, J. P. W., J. F. J. Holt, J. A. Seaman, and M. R. Bowden, "Lessons for Epidemiology from the Ethiopian Famines," *Ann. Soc. belge Med. trop.*, LVI (1976), 345–57.

Seaman, J., and J. Holt, "The Ethiopian Famine of 1973–74, 1. Wollo Province," *Proc. Nutr. Soc.*, XXXIV (1975).

Sen, A. K., "Poverty, Inequality and Unemployment: Some Conceptual Issues in Measurement," *Economic and Political Weekly*, VIII (1973); reprinted in Bardhan and Srinivasan [1974].

——, *Employment, Technology and Development* (Oxford: Clarendon Press, 1975).

——, "Poverty: An Ordinal Approach to Measurement," *Econometrica*, XLIV (1976a), 219–32.

——, "Real National Income," *Review of Economic Studies*, XLIII (1976b), 19–39.

——, "On Weights and Measures: Informational Constraints in Social Welfare Analysis," *Econometrica*, XLV (1977a), 1539–1572.

——, "Starvation and Exchange Entitlements: A General Approach and Its Application to the Great Bengal Famine," *Cambridge Journal of Economics*, I (1977b), 33–59.

——, "Issues in the Measurement of Poverty," *Scandinavian Journal of Economics*, LXXXI (1979), 285–307.

——, "Famine Mortality: A Study of the Bengal Famine of 1943," in Hobsbawm *et al.*, *Peasants in History: Essays in Memory of Daniel Thorner* (Calcutta: Oxford University Press, 1980).

——, *Poverty and Famines* (Oxford: Clarendon Press, (1981).

Sinha, R., *Food and Poverty* (London: Croom Helm, 1976).

Sobhan, R., "Politics of Food and Famine in Bangladesh," *Economic and Political Weekly*, XIV (1979).

Summers, R. S., "Two Types of Substantive Reasons: The Core of a Theory of Common-Law Justification," *Cornell Law Review*, LXIII (1978), 707–88.

Takayama, N., "Poverty, Income Inequality and Their Measures," *Econometrica*, XLVII (1979), 747–60.

Thon, D., "On Measuring Poverty," *Review of Income and Wealth*, XXV (1979).

Wood, A. P., "Farmers' Response to Drought in Ethiopia," in Hussein [1976].

Woodham-Smith, C., *The Great Hunger: Ireland 1845–9* (London: New English Library, 1975; earlier edition, Hamish Hamilton, 1962).

[3]

SOME COSTS AND BENEFITS OF MARKETS: AN EMPIRICAL STUDY*

FREDERIC L. PRYOR

I. INTRODUCTION

The purpose of this essay is to isolate some important major costs of operating the market parts of market economies by comparing these economic systems with centrally administered economies where a considerable amount of market activity has been suppressed. I make a series of quantitative comparisons to investigate three questions: (1) Does a market system permit a savings in bureaucratic personnel by transferring a marketing function from the industrial hierarchy to workers in commerce? Conversely, does the suppression of much market activity lead to greater bureaucratization outside the commerce sector? (2) How much more personnel in the commerce sector and in sales does a market economy require in comparison to a centrally administered economy? (3) How much additional shopping and marketing time is required by customers if the market function is, to a certain extent, suppressed?

All three of these questions have been examined by Gur Ofer in a recent book that focuses primarily on the Soviet Union. The following essay uses data unavailable to Ofer, handles the data in a considerably different (and, I hope, more revealing) manner, broadens the geographical coverage of the analysis to include all East European socialist nations, and deepens the analysis of the interrelationships of shopping time to other aspects of the trade sector.[1]

* The research for this essay was financed by a faculty research grant from Swarthmore College, to which I would like to express my appreciation. I would also like to thank Gudmund Iversen, Bernard Saffran, David Schwartzman, and Laura Tyson for their helpful remarks on a previous draft.

1. Gur Ofer, *The Service Sector in Soviet Economic Growth: A Comparative Study* (Cambridge, Mass.: Harvard University Press, 1973). Ofer's book is the standard treatment of the subject. It deals primarily with comparisons between the Soviet Union and the West and surveys the entire service sector; this study includes almost all of the East European nations in the comparisons and focuses exclusively on the trade sector. Ofer is particularly concerned with the trade sector from the labor market standpoint and expends considerable effort in examining questions about the quality of personnel in the sector, the productivity of the factors of production, the relationship of the trade sector to other economic sectors, and the institutional context in which important decisions about the trade sector are made. My concern is much more narrow and focuses particularly on questions concerning the trade-off between shopping time and personnel in the trade and other sectors. Ofer deals with both time-series and cross-section data; I use only the latter kind of information. Our statistical metho-

II. Bureaucratization

There are several reasons for expecting that a nonmarket economy will have more bureaucratic personnel in the various productive sectors outside commerce. First, the marketing function (i.e., the buying and selling of goods; the obtaining of information about available goods and potential customers, etc.) will be carried out by personnel in the individual sectors of production, rather than by specialized sales personnel in the commerce sector. Second, the market provides certain information in an allegedly inexpensive manner that, in a nonmarket economy, can be obtained only through considerable processing of information by bureaucratic personnel. Countering these two arguments is the notion that a firm will manufacture goods, rather than purchase them, if the transaction costs are more than the costs of administering the manufacturing of the good; if the good is manufactured, the need for bureaucratic marketing personnel to search for sources of supply is reduced.

Bureaucratization can be measured as the ratio of bureaucrats to the labor force (which is defined throughout this paper as the economically active). In order to separate the effects of central administration and market systems most precisely, it seems best to define bureaucratization in terms of bureaucrats outside the commerce sector in relation to the labor force excluding the economically active in commerce. Since data for such a ratio are available for only a limited number of nations, I also examine a more crude measure of bureaucratization in terms of the entire economy. Relevant data may be found in Table I.

By "bureaucrat" I refer to the labor force engaged in office work and administrative tasks. Comparable data on the labor force in various pursuits are available from censuses of occupation, which use the *International Standard Classification of Occupations,* a classification that distinguishes four major groups of office workers; professionals (including technical and related workers); administrative (including managers and lower level executive personnel); clerical workers; and sales workers. Since sales workers receive intensive treatment in the next section, they are handled in only a summary

dologies are quite similar in that each of us uses the same type of multiple-regression analysis; we differ, however, in our choices of the independent and dependent variables. In regression experiments for this essay I tried the variables he used (but with more recent data) and found that my own choice of variables was, for my particular purposes, more satisfactory. For each type of empirical analysis I carry out in this essay, I designate the most important similarities and differences between Ofer and me in footnotes.

TABLE I

MEASURES OF WHITE COLLAR WORK FORCE AND PER CAPITA G.N.P.[a]

		As a percentage of labor force excluding commerce			
Country	Year	Bureau-crats out-side commerce sector	Bureau-crats and sales personnel outside commerce sector	All bureau-crats as a percentage of total labor force	Per capita G.N.P. (U. S. price weights)
Market economies					
Australia	1961	n.a.	n.a.	28.40%	$1853
Austria	1961	n.a.	n.a.	18.29	1200
Belgium	1961	22.19%	25.27%	22.81	1531
Canada	1961	27.19	28.73	28.88	1783
Denmark	1960	17.55	19.09	18.48	1471
Finland	1960	13.69	14.26	15.01	909
France	1962	18.92	20.87	19.17	2055
Greece	1961	5.64	7.80	8.15	626
Ireland	1961	15.48	16.39	15.85	963
Italy	1961	n.a.	n.a.	13.37	1119
Japan	1960	17.00	18.16	17.56	885
Netherlands	1960	23.71	24.63	24.63	1379
Norway	1960	16.67	17.01	19.31	1537
Portugal	1960	7.66	8.10	8.61	449
Spain	1960	n.a.	n.a.	10.94	426
Sweden	1960	21.91	23.84	22.14	1856
Switzerland	1960	n.a.	n.a.	23.76	1927
United Kingdom	1961	25.63	27.86	24.43	1672
United States	1960	28.97	30.64	31.49	2340
West Germany	1961	21.36	22.65	22.57	1801
Yugoslavia	1961	n.a.	n.a.	10.55	585
Centrally administered economies					
Bulgaria	1965	n.a.	n.a.	15.90	876
Czechoslovakia	1961	n.a.	n.a.	22.25	1504
East Germany	1964	26.38	26.38	23.71	1647
Hungary	1960	13.96	16.32	15.11	948
Romania	1966	11.80	11.98	12.60	864
Soviet Union	1959	14.14	14.71	14.59	1031

a. The sources and estimation methods for obtaining the data presented in Table I are discussed in the Statistical Notes.

fashion below. As the dividing lines between professional, administrative, and clerical workers are somewhat nebulous and certain problems of comparability arise when examining market and centrally administered economies, all are lumped together as bureaucrats. This is not, by any means, a very satisfactory measure of "bureaucrat"; but it is, unfortunately, the only measure for which data for many countries are readily available.

Although the relationship between bureaucratization and other facets of the economy has not yet received definitive treatment, it seems reasonable to suppose that bureaucratization is related to the degree of economic development and the economic system. A logarithmic regression form is used for three reasons: to minimize the impact of extreme points; to provide for a ratio measure of bureaucratization in market and centrally administered economies (which is the antilog of the calculated regression coefficient) and to have the other calculated coefficients represent elasticities.[2] Since I use almost a complete sample of economically developed and semideveloped economies for many of the regressions, the calculated coefficients reflect the world as it really is for this set of nations and any tests of statistical significance on the systems variable refers to the universe of possible market and centrally administered economies, of which only a small sample are represented in the world today. The calculated regressions are as follows:

Regression (1):

$$\ln B_a = \underset{(0.827)}{-3.448^*} + \underset{(0.115)}{0.880^*} \ln y + \underset{(0.120)}{0.053}\, S \qquad n = 19, \quad R^2 = 0.79$$

Regression (2):

$$\ln (B_a + W_s) = \underset{(0.700)}{-2.984^*} + \underset{(0.097)}{0.827^*} \ln y + \underset{(0.101)}{0.013}\, S \qquad n = 19, \quad R^2 = 0.82$$

Regression (3):

$$\ln B_b = \underset{(0.505)}{-2.092^*} + \underset{(0.071)}{0.702^*} \ln y - \underset{(0.074)}{0.000}\, S \qquad n = 26, \quad R^2 = 0.81,$$

where

B_a = ratio of bureaucrats outside of commerce sector to labor force excluding the commerce sector

2. More specifically, the following functional form was selected: $X = aY^bP^s$, where X is the labor force variable, Y is an explanatory variable such as income per capita, a and b are constants, S is a dummy variable (equal to 0_s or 1) and P is the proportionality factor. When $S = 0$, $P^s = 1$; when $S = 1$, P^s = a positive number. Regressions were calculated using a logarithmic form of this function: $\ln X = [\ln a] + [b] \ln Y + S\,[\ln P]$, where the expressions in the brackets are the calculated regression coefficients.

B_b = ratio of bureaucrats in the entire economy to entire labor force
W_s = ratio of sales workers outside of commerce sector to labor force excluding the commerce sector
y = gross national product per capita (U. S. price weights)
S = economic system (0 = market economy; 1 = centrally planned economy)
n = number of observations
R^2 = coefficient of determination
* = statistical significance at the 0.95 confidence limit (standard errors are placed below the calculated coefficients in parentheses)
ln = natural logarithm.

The regression results show that bureaucratization appears to be significantly related to the level of economic development[3] but that it does not seem related to the economic system, since the calculated regression coefficients of the systems variable and the t ratios are both very low.[4] The larger and more crude sample of twenty-six nations (all nations in Table I excluding Yugoslavia, which is used as a control country throughout this essay) shows the same conclusions as do the more refined data from the smaller sample. The results are not due to any problem in pooling the data from the different economic systems,[5] and several explanations may be offered.

1. Other causal factors underlying bureaucratization have not been included, and this biases the results. To investigate this possibility, I calculated a number of additional regressions (using the more refined data from the smaller sample) that included such "reasonable" explanatory variables as the percentage of the labor force in agricul-

3. It is interesting to note that the cross-section elasticity of bureaucratization is less than unity, even though the time-series elasticity is greater than unity. This suggests that bureaucratization is related more to the state of technology (i.e., the technical knowledge shared by all countries of the world at a given point in time) than to the level of economic development per se. A similar phenomenon is found for the share of education expenditures in the G.N.P. and is probably due to the same cause. (For further discussion, see Frederic L. Pryor, *Public Expenditures in Communist and Capitalist Nations* (Homewood, Ill.: Irwin, 1968), pp. 213–19.)

4. A similar conclusion is reached by Ofer, *op. cit.*, pp. 39–45, for the Soviet Union alone. When the ratio of bureaucrats outside commerce to the total population is used as the dependent variable (and when the participation ratio is included as an explanatory variable), the calculated regression coefficient for the systems variable is somewhat larger and approaches statisti significance. The labor force ratio is, I believe, a much more valid test.

5. For all regressions reported in this essay, tests were performed (described in Potluri Rao and Roger LeRoy Miller, *Applied Econometrics* (Belmont, Calif.: Wadsworth Publishing Co., 1971), pp. 148–52) to determine the legitimacy of pooling the data in the manner shown in the two sets of nations. For all regressions this legitimacy was established.

ture, the participation ratio (the ratio of labor force to population), a variable to measure the deviation of the population age-sex structure from the "average," and population (in order to see whether scale effects might be important), but in none of these regressions did the systems variable appear important.

2. The results are too "messy" because all sectors of the economy have been included. To investigate this possibility, I calculated a number of regressions for the smaller sample using the degree of bureaucratization outside agriculture and also solely in manufacturing and mining sectors as the dependent variables. The systems variable in these regressions also appeared unimportant.

3. The results are due to the fact that the definition of "bureaucrats" is too inclusive. The definition was narrowed to include only administrative and clerical personnel, and other regressions were calculated using the small sample. Still more regressions were calculated using particular subgroups of white collar workers. Again the results were the same: the systems variable appeared unimportant.

We must thus conclude that the degree of bureaucratization (outside commerce) of market economies and centrally planned economies is not significantly different and that the market system does not permit a savings in bureaucratic personnel by transferring a marketing function from workers in the industrial hierarchies to workers in the commerce sector.

III. Personnel Serving the Market Function

That part of the labor force directly serving the market function includes the labor force in the commerce and finance sector and, in addition, labor force occupationally classified as sales workers in other sectors. Standardized data on the former can be found in censuses where workers are classified according to the *International Standard Industrial Classification;* standardized data on the latter can be found where workers are classified according to the *International Standard Classification of Occupations.* Many nations present data on the labor force cross-classified according to both classifications, and from such tabulations we can easily determine the total workers in sales and in commerce, excluding any double accounting between these two categories.

Of the total workers in sales and commerce in market economies, roughly 65 percent can be accounted for in the West by workers in wholesale and retail establishments. Since such establishments exist primarily to channel goods from the producing sectors to the consumers, it seems reasonable to analyze the relative importance of their work force vis à vis the population. Moreover, the most important causal variable should be the relative volume of marketed goods to the consumer, rather than the total production of goods and services, a consideration that affects the numerical value of the calculated coefficient of the economic systems variable, which is also added.[6] For reasons cited above, I use a logarithmic regression form. The relevant data are presented in Table II, and the calculated regressions (for the countries in this table excluding Yugoslavia) are as follows:

Regression (4):

$$\ln R = \underset{(0.825)}{-1.242} + \underset{(0.137)}{0.774^*} \ln g - \underset{(0.118)}{0.634^*}\, S \qquad n = 21, \quad R^2 = 0.85$$

Regression (5):

$$\ln (R + W) = \underset{(0.725)}{-0.122} + \underset{(0.120)}{0.660^*} \ln g - \underset{(0.103)}{0.594^*}\, S \qquad n = 21, \quad R^2 = 0.86,$$

where

R = retail personnel per 1,000 population
W = wholesale personnel per 1,000 population
g = marketed goods per capita (U. S. price weights)
(other symbols are defined above).

The results show that the work force in retail and wholesale establishments in a nation can be to a large extent explained by two variables; the per capita marketed goods and the economic system. Further statistical tests on these results show that the calculated regression coefficients for the marketed goods coefficient are similar for market and centrally administered economies so that it is legitimate to pool the data in the manner above. Addition to the regression of other possible causal variables such as the percentage of the labor force in agriculture, the participation rate of women (to capture possible effects arising from the fact that women in the labor force do less shopping than housewives), and the population (to capture

6. For a given per capita G.N.P., the centrally administered economies have a lower amount of marketed goods per capita for two reasons: they have a higher investment share in the G.N.P.; and they have a somewhat higher percentage of their labor force in agriculture. For the countries in Table II (excluding Yugoslavia) the marketed goods variable can be regressed against the G.N.P. and the economic systems variable, and the following result is obtained:

$$\ln g = \underset{(0.325)}{-0.771^*} + \underset{(0.044)}{0.934^*} \ln y - \underset{(0.038)}{0.165^*}\, S \qquad n = 21, \quad R^2 = 0.97.$$

For a given per capita G.N.P., the centrally administered economies have about 85 percent (the antilog of -0.165) of the marketed goods per capita.

TABLE II

WHOLESALE AND RETAIL PERSONNEL AND PER CAPITA MARKETED GOODS[a]

Country	Year	Total retail and wholesale personnel per 1,000 population	Total retail personnel per 1,000 population	Per capita marketed goods (U. S. price weights)
Market economies				
Austria	1964	34.9	20.9	$353
Belgium	1966	53.0	36.9	515
Canada	1961	51.0	35.3	481
Denmark	1960	55.4	38.9	430
France	1966	47.0	32.8	540
Ireland	1963	48.0	35.6	286
Italy	1963	47.6	28.6	347
Japan	1960	39.0	21.2	236
Netherlands	1960	49.6	25.6	449
Norway	1960	45.8	29.0	441
Portugal	1960	22.8	13.7	159
Sweden	1960	55.7	38.1	529
U.S.A.	1966	71.1	57.8	802
West Germany	1965	55.3	36.5	628
Yugoslavia	1965	12.4	8.2	161
Centrally administered economies				
Bulgaria	1965	18.1	11.4	212
Czechoslovakia	1965	24.5	13.8	373
East Germany	1966	37.3	21.1	460
Hungary	1965	24.3	14.3	301
Poland	1965	20.4	12.5	211
Romania	1966	9.3	5.2	209
U.S.S.R.	1965	19.7	13.7	341

a. The sources and estimation methods for obtaining the data are discussed in the Statistical Notes.

possible effects arising from economies of scale) do not reveal any other statistically significant or interesting relationships.[7]

From the antilog of the calculated regression coefficients for the systems variable, we can see that centrally administered economies have roughly 53 percent of the retail personnel and roughly 55 percent

7. Ofer, *op. cit.*, Table 32, presents similar regressions for the commerce sector for a sample of nations in East Europe and the West; and he also reaches roughly the same conclusions. Because of this overlap in our work, I discuss these findings in an abbreviated manner. Ofer also investigates sales personnel outside the commerce sector for the Soviet Union alone in a quite different manner than I; but our conclusions are also roughly the same.

of the combined retail and wholesale personnel of a market economy with the same population and marketed goods per capita. Thus, the centrally administered economies achieve a definite savings in personnel at this last step of the market process.

Before turning to examine other parts of the total of the work force in sales and commerce, it is useful to use these results to examine the case of Yugoslavia, a nation with public ownership of the means of production (outside agriculture) but with a marKet économy. Given the same marketed goods per capita in 1965, a centrally administered economy would have 7.8 retail personnel and 13.9 retail and wholesale personnel per 1,000, while a market economy would have, respectively, 14.8 and 25.3. In actuality, Yugoslavia had, respectively, 8.2 retail and 12.4 retail and wholesale personnel per 1,000, thus placing this market economy very close to the predictions based on the existence of a centrally administered economy. Three explanations for these strange results may be offered: (1) the low number of retail and wholesale personnel in Yugoslavia is a legacy of their period of central administration, which lasted from the end of World War II to the early 1950's; (2) the low number of retail and wholesale personnel in Eastern Europe is less a matter of economic system and more a cultural matter that was imposed or influenced by the Soviet Union or which lies deeper in the national psyche of these nations; (3) this is a statistical illusion based on the fact that the relationship between marketed goods per capita and retail and wholesale personnel does not have the curvature specified in the regression equations and the prediction for Yugoslavia (having the second lowest per capita marketed goods of any nation in the sample) reflects this bias. This third explanation can be explored by examining the differences between the predicted and the actual retail and wholesale personnel for the various nations arranged according to marketed goods per capita. Since no pattern is found that would suggest bias in the Yugoslav results, this third explanation can be rejected, and we are left to choose between the first two proposed explanations. After exploring other segments of the work force in commerce and in sales to gain additional perspective, I return to this matter again.

As I mentioned above, in market economies roughly 65 percent of total workers in sales and commerce are in retail and wholesale establishments. Roughly 10 percent is accounted for by sales workers outside the commerce sector, and the remaining 25 percent is accounted for by workers in the commerce sector excluding the work force in wholesale and retail establishments, a miscellaneous group that consists primarily of personnel in various financial institutions and in restaurants and cafeterias. I could find no statistically significant relationships to explain the relative importance of each set of these workers after testing a variety of possible explanatory variables; and in no regression were the calculated coefficients for the economic systems variable or the corresponding *t* ratios very large. Since the sample of centrally administered economies for such experiments numbers only three nations, we cannot be very definite about our conclusions. But it does not appear as if the economic systems variable significantly affects this 35 percent of the total work force of commerce and of sales.

The major impact of the economic system on the number of workers serving the market function thus appears to be in the size of the work force in wholesale and retail establishments and not in the number of sales workers outside commerce or in other workers in the commerce sector (excluding workers in wholesale and retail units). This is a strange empirical finding for one would have expected the reverse, since the centrally administered economies have suppressed the market between producing units, but not between producers and consumers. Three explanations for such results can be given: First, as mentioned above, there may be a savings in bureaucratic marketing personnel by having greater vertical integration than in a market economy. Although this explanation may have a certain validity for the Soviet Union, certain evidence suggests that it is not very important for the rest of Eastern Europe.[8] Second, the sales workers outside the commerce sector appear to be a very small fraction of the labor force in any economic system, so there should not be great differences between centrally administered and market economies. Third, the work force in wholesale and retail establishments does not represent whether or not the economy is centrally administered, but whether or not it is in East rather than West Europe. The importance of this difference may stem either from an underlying cultural heritage or from the influence of the Soviet Union and its economic system or from both factors. The last two explanations are consistent not only with the various regression results, but also with the seemingly strange results obtained when comparing predicted and actual personnel in wholesale and retail establishments in Yugoslavia. Particular facets of the East-West European factor receive further attention below.

8. Such evidence is presented in Frederic L. Pryor, *Property and Industrial Organization in Communist and Capitalist Nations* (Bloomington, Indiana: Indiana University Press, 1973), pp. 240–45.

IV. Expenditure of Shopping Time

If one nation has fewer sales personnel than another, one would expect (other things remaining equal) that consumers in the former nation would spend more time shopping. Consumers would spend more time in traveling to the retail establishments, since these would be fewer in number; consumers would spend more time waiting in lines for the retail clerks, and consumers might spend more time in hunting for the goods they want if the fewer personnel in the wholesale and retail sector meant that less attention was given to stocking the shelves with goods that were actually wanted. A cutting back in sales personnel would mean, in other words, that some of the costs in the distribution sector would now be borne by the consumer in the form of additional shopping.

The analytic situation becomes more complicated when we introduce as a causal variable the economic system, for its direction of impact is quite unclear. There is one major argument that consumers in capitalist nations spend less time shopping, and it is derived from elementary economic theory (before the invention of the economics of information): since the centrally administered economies in Eastern Europe during the 1960's were less responsive to consumer desires and since retail prices did not respond quickly to changes in supply or demand forces, consumers in these nations spent more time shopping, especially in searching for desired goods and standing in queues to obtain scarce goods that had been priced too cheaply. There are several major arguments that consumers in centrally administered economies spend less time shopping: (1) Since retail prices were more uniform, people spent less time looking around for the lowest prices; (2) since the variety of goods was less in these nations, decision making was simplified, and consumers spent less time looking at variants of goods; (3) since there was considerable suppressed inflation in some of these nations, consumers many times bought any good they happened to see, even if it was not exactly what they wanted, in order to be able to spend their income; (4) less attention in Eastern Europe was paid to shopper's amenities so that the phenomenon of "shopping for pleasure" was missing. The net impact of the economic system cannot be determined theoretically until we can judge the relative strength of these two sets of opposing forces.

For statistical analysis the economic system does not stand alone, since the centrally administered economies (and Yugoslavia) had a relatively smaller number of sales personnel than did market economies with similar levels of per capita marketed goods. Separating the systems effect from the sales personnel effect raises some statistical problems, and in order to reduce the effect of the multicollinearity I have chosen to explain shopping time with three variables: per capita marketed goods, a dummy variable indicating that the nation is among that set of nations with a much smaller expected number of sales personnel, and a variable indicating the ratio of sales personnel predicted by regression equation (5) in the previous section to the actual number of sales personnel. The calculated regression coefficient is for the marketed goods variable personnel. It is useful to consider briefly what the signs and the sizes of the regression coefficients might be.

The calculated regression coefficient linking the per capita marketed goods and shopping time should be positive, since with a greater volume of goods shopping should take longer. The elasticity, however, should be less than unity for several reasons. First, the quality of goods purchased per transaction increases with the total value of purchased goods, so the physical quantity of goods does not increase as fast as income. Second, as per capita income increases, so that the opportunity cost of shopping increases, consumers may take measures to reduce shopping time by purchasing refrigerators, buying in bulk, and so forth. The calculated regression coefficient for the dummy variable should be positive, since the smaller number of sales personnel should make for longer shopping time. And the regression coefficient for the ratio of predicted to actual sales personnel should be positive for the same reason (i.e., a ratio more than unity means fewer sales personnel than expected, so shopping time should be longer). By a comparison of the calculated regression coefficients for the last two variables, we can separate the economic systems effect from the effect of fewer sales personnel in a manner described below.

The major difficulty in carrying out such an empirical exercise is finding comparable data on shopping times, especially since the data obtained from the various national time budget studies vary considerably according to the survey techniques employed, the study design, and the definitions used. Adjusting the data from these individual national studies would be a wearisome and dubious enterprise. Fortunately, a standardized international time budget study has been carried out by Alexander Szalai and his associates, which has comparable data for twelve nations.[9] The various national studies were

9. Alexander Szalai *et al.*, eds., *The Uses of Time* (The Hague: Mouton, 1972). Ofer, *op. cit.*, p. 115, presents data from a number of surveys for the Soviet Union alone. He uses the time data in a quite different manner than I, and since we ask different questions of these data, our conclusions cannot be easily compared.

standardized in many different ways. Before plunging into the regression analysis, however, several peculiarities of the data deserve brief comment.

For most countries the data are drawn from a sample from a single city with certain specified characteristics, since shopping time appears affected by city size and composition. The cities chosen (which fell in the range from 40,000 to 200,000) had higher shopping times than nationwide samples from the same country, at least for the two countries for which such comparable data are available, which suggests that standardization of city characteristics was a wise decision. However, the explanatory variables used in the regression refer to the nation as a whole, and thus a source of error is introduced into the analysis. (Unfortunately, requisite city data needed for the regressions were not available.) Because I wish to use the most comparable shopping data possible, I have chosen to use the city data in all cases, even though the use of the national data for the two countries for which they are available would improve the fit of the regressions.

Another difficulty with the time-budget data is the handling of "secondary activities," i.e., activities carried out while the primary focus of activity is something quite different. A certain amount of shopping is carried out in this manner (e.g., when returning from work) and must be included, although the use of such data rests on the assumption that Szalai and his associates were able to achieve standardization on this information, which is extremely difficult to gather.

In order to calculate the average national shopping and marketing time that is due to the economic system, it is necessary to standardize the time budget data for the population structure. This is because the amount of shopping time is greatly influenced by marital status and also, for women, by labor force participation. Fortunately, the time budget data are presented for various subgroups, and I have averaged the shopping and marketing time of married employed males (with a weight of 0.5), married employed females (with a weight of 0.3), and married housewives (with a weight of 0.2) so that we can focus our attention exclusively on the systems effect.

Since there are a number of countries in the sample for which I had to estimate the retail personnel (in many countries data on wholesale and retail personnel are given in a combined category, since the functions are often difficult to separate), I have chosen to use the ratio of actual to predicted personnel in both wholesale and retail establishments, rather than in retail establishments alone. This decision, based strictly on practical considerations, may also be theoretically justified, since the number of wholesale personnel can affect shopping time by affecting the quantity and the type of goods in the retail outlets. These data and the other data used in the analysis are presented in Table III.

TABLE III

SHOPPING TIME, PER CAPITA MARKETED GOODS, AND SALES PERSONNEL DATA[a]

Country	Year	Marketed goods per capita (U. S. price weights)	Ratio of expected to actual retail and wholesale personnel	Average shopping and marketing time (minutes per day): Actual	Predicted: Using (6A)	Predicted: Using (6B)
Belgium	1966	$515	1.026	26.22	27.17	25.95
Bulgaria	1965	212	0.923	29.24	33.50	29.04
Czechoslovakia	1965	373	0.992	37.06	37.57	36.81
East Germany	1966	460	0.748	33.82	32.29	30.88
France	1966	540	1.194	29.18	30.06	29.97
Hungary	1965	301	0.868	27.82	33.65	30.73
Poland	1965	211	0.819	41.96	31.06	—
Soviet Union	1965	341	1.162	40.76	41.05	40.97
U.S.A.	1966	802	1.023	27.90	28.63	29.71
West Germany	1965	628	1.121	32.23	29.43	29.77
Yugoslavia						
Slovenia	1965	298	{1.846 1.020	29.84	{36.77 37.23	{36.13 35.19
Serbia	1965	150	{2.120 1.170	40.16	{36.86 37.30	{32.84 31.95

a. For Slovenia and Serbia the data in the upper rows are calculated under the assumption that these Yugoslav Republics should be classified with the capitalist market economies; and the data in the lower rows are calculated under the assumption that these Republics should be classified with the socialist centrally administered economies. For the calculation of the ratio of expected to actual personnel in wholesale and retail establishments, the following estimates were employed: Slovenia, 20.6 workers per 1,000 population; for Serbia, 11.4 workers per 1,000 population.

The sources and estimation methods for obtaining the data are discussed in the statistical notes and in the text. Szalai and his collaborators also presented time data for Peru, but I was unable to obtain comparable data for explanatory variables and had to drop this case from the sample.

The average shopping time among the capitalist market economies was 28.88 minutes; and among the socialist centrally administered economies, 35.11. (In such a grouping of nations, Yugoslavia is omitted; since Yugoslavia had strong administrative and market elements and had both large public and large private sectors, placing it either among the market economies or among the socialist nations raises considerable problems for the purposes for which the data are being analyzed). That is, the average adult in the socialist centrally administered economies spend 28 percent more time shopping, a difference that is statistically significant at the 0.05 level. Since the East European nations in the sample have lower per capita marketed goods and also, for this particular group of nations, lower ratios of expected to actual retail and wholesale personnel, the difference in shopping time between the two groups of nations holding these factors constant should be even greater.

For the regression analysis (which allows us to hold these other factors constant) I have selected a logarithmic form for the reasons given in Section II. Since there is multicollinearity between the independent variables, the following two-stage procedure was adopted. For the two subsets of nations (capitalist market and socialist centrally administered) I calculated regressions relating average shopping time to marketed goods per capita and ratio of expected to actual sales personnel. Statistical tests were made to affirm that the calculated coefficients were obtained from the same universe. I then averaged the coefficients, calculated the amount of shopping time attributable to the marketed goods and ratio of expected to actual sales personnel (using the averaged coefficient) and calculated a regression for the entire sample of nations to determine the impact of economic system. Although standard errors cannot be calculated for the coefficients, we can determine the coefficient of determination. In carrying out this calculation, it became apparent that the data for Poland lay so far off the calculated regression line that it greatly influenced the final results.[10] Therefore, regressions both including and excluding Poland were calculated. The results are as follows:[11]
Regression (6A):

$$\begin{array}{llllll} \ln T = & 2.519^* + & 0.123 \ln g + & 0.628 \ln R + & 0.385^* D & n = 10 \\ & (0.070) & (0.214) & (0.519) & (0.090) & R^2 = 0.570 \end{array}$$

10. There do not appear to be any institutional factors in Polish trade that might account for the extraordinarily high shopping times (at least as reported by J. Hart Walters, Jr., "Retailing in Poland: A First-Hand Report," in Montrose S. Sommers and Jerome B. Kernan, eds., *Comparative MarKeting Systems: A Cultural Approach* (New York: Appleton-Century-Crofts, 1968), pp. 289–301).

11. The standard errors for the g and R coefficients were calculated from the standard errors of the regressions for the individual economic systems. The standard errors of the constant coefficient and the dummy variables were calculated from the regression with the combined data. This way of handling the regression calculations permits the coefficients to be statistically significant, without the coefficient of determination being significant, a circumstance that occurs in regression (6A).

Regression (6B):

$$\ln T = 1.293^{*} + 0.311 \ln g + 0.852^{*} \ln R + 0.479^{*} D$$
$$(0.032) \quad (0.170) \quad (0.367) \quad (0.043)$$

$n = 9$ (Poland excl.)

$R^2 = 0.876$,

where

T = average shopping and marketing time (minutes per day)
D dummy variable indicating if country is socialist, centrally administered (0 = no; 1 = yes)
R = ratio of predicted to actual retail and wholesale personnel
(all other symbols defined above).

The signs of the calculated regression coefficients are in the expected direction (and, for the marketed goods variable, of the expected size). The antilog of the calculated coefficient of the dummy variable indicates that adult shoppers in Eastern Europe spent 47 percent (regression (6A)) or 61 percent (regression (6B)) more time shopping than did shoppers in the West (other things being equal). Although we do not know the standard errors of the individual coefficients, the coefficient of determination (calculated from information about the variance of actual shopping time and predicted shopping time) of regression (6B) is statistically significant at the 0.05 level and of regression (6A) is a shade below statistical significance at this level.

How much of the longer shopping time in Eastern Europe is attributable to the fewer sales personnel, and how much is attributable to economic system? This decomposition can be carried out in a simple manner.

Regression (5) shows that the nations of Eastern Europe had 55.2 percent (the antilog of −0.594) of the retail and wholesale personnel of the comparable nations in the West, which means that the ratio of "expected" to actual sales personnel (without taking the systems variable into account) was 1.811. If we substitute this datum into regressions (6A) and (6B) (and similarly neglect the systems variable), we find that expected shopping time in the East European centrally administered economies should be 45 percent (regression (6A)), or 66 percent (regression (6B)) greater than in the West. Since these results are roughly equal to the impact of the systems variable per se (discussed two paragraphs above), we must conclude that the lower number of sales personnel accounted for all of the differences in average shopping time between the capitalist market and the socialist centrally administered economies.

The most important conclusion to be drawn from this calculation is that the impact of the systems variable, after taking into account differences in the number of sales personnel, appears negligible. That is, the reasons cited above for expecting the systems variable to influence shopping times in either a positive or a negative direction appear to cancel each other out. The presence of a centrally administered economy and relatively fixed retail prices leading to longer shopping times is offset by such factors as less search time for lower prices or different varieties of a product, quicker buying decisions because of the exigencies of suppressed inflation, and lack of shopping for pleasure.

One brief interpretation must be given to the discovery of greater shopping time in Eastern Europe and, thus, of greater "queueing." This does not necessarily mean that East Europeans spent more time in "visible" queues. Part of this extra shopping time represented the added time to reach the fewer retail establishments; part was spent going from store to store to find one which stocked a particular good; and part was spent waiting for clerks while in stores. Although travelers in Eastern Europe reported the presence of queues in only a few of these nations (notably the Soviet Union), the "invisible" queues were probably much more important in terms of time usage.[12]

Before turning to some broader issues, it seems useful to look briefly at shopping times in various parts of Yugoslavia. Since Yugoslavia combines both market and administrative elements, as well as public and private ownership, comparison of actual shopping times with predicted shopping times with Yugoslavia classified with the capitalist market economies or with the socialist centrally administered economies should yield some useful information. However, since the systems effect does not appear important, it is not expected that our predictions for Slovenia are considerably higher than the actual situation, while the predictions for Serbia are considerably lower. Such opposite variations of the two Yugoslav Republics are difficult to explain; part, however, may be due to the uncertainties of the data, particularly for Serbia.[13] For Yugoslavia as a whole, however, shopping times may be on the average what we expect, given the per capita income and the number of wholesale and retail personnel per 1,000.

12. Queueing time is also conserved because certain scarce goods are known to arrive in the stores only on particular days, so queueing is unnecessary on other days. For instance, in Prague, potatoes seemed available only on Saturday during the summer of 1976.

13. One of the American survey collaborators of Szalai, when I questioned him about the comparability of the Serbian data with the rest of the sample, expressed some of his personal doubts on this matter.

V. Some Broader Issues

Is it economically worthwhile for a nation to cut back on its sales personnel and to force its consumers to spend more time shopping? If we take two comparable nations in West and East with marketed goods of $350 per capita, we would expect (assuming that the ratio of expected to actual sales personnel is 1.000) married adults in the East to spend 11.99 minutes per day (from regression (6A)) or 13.84 minutes per day (from regression (6B)) more time shopping. This works out, respectively, to 83.93 minutes or 96.88 minutes more shopping time per week (the data are on a seven-day week basis) in the East, other things being equal. If we further assume a forty-four-hour work week, this additional shopping time amounts, respectively, to 3.18 percent and 3.67 percent of a work week, or the equivalent of, respectively, 31.8 and 36.7 additional workers per 1,000 adult population. Assuming that nonadults amount to 35 percent of the population, this means that the additional shopping time of adults amounts to the equivalent of 20.7 workers (regression (6A)) or 23.9 workers (regression (6B)) per 1,000 total population.

It is noteworthy that this additional time shopping occurred because in the capitalist market nations, personnel in wholesale and retail establishments amount to 42.3 per 1,000 population, while among the socialist, centrally administered nations or East European nations (however this variable is interpreted) such sales personnel amount to 23.3 per 1,000 (both calculations were made from regression (5), assuming a marketed goods production per capita of $350). Thus, reducing sales personnel by nineteen workers per 1,000 population, roughly the equivalent amount of additional shopping time is spent by consumers in these nations. This invariance in the sum of shopping time and work time of personnel in wholesale and retail establishments between nations of East and West Europe (holding other factors constant) may appear quite startling, and it seems proper to examine more closely some of the factors that I have thus far omitted from consideration.

To what extent are my results due to omission of other factors that might explain the alleged difference in sales personnel in East and West? In his detailed and interesting analysis of the Soviet Union, Gur Ofer offers quantitative evidence that part of the difference between the Soviet Union and the West is due to such factors as underreporting of Soviet sales personnel, relative differences in the quality (especially in terms of education) of the work force in commerce and in other sectors in the two sets of nations, less capital intensiveness of sales establishments, and greater economies of scale in Soviet distribution, and so forth.[14] He also demonstrates that the effect of these factors is relatively small so that such factors can, I believe, be omitted from further discussion.

Much more important in evaluating the relative effects of shopping time and economic system are the side effects that accompany each type of distribution system. In the West the higher number of sales personnel is accompanied by a rampant commercialism on which many place a high negative value in their analysis of the "quality of life." In the East the lower number of sales personnel and the centrally administered economy are accompanied by considerable frustrations of not being able to obtain goods which are desired and for which money is available (a taste of this phenomenon was experienced with displeasure in the West during the Great Oil Crisis of the winter of 1973–1974). There is an additional pressing question: the degree to which consumer sovereignty is realized in either a market or a centrally administered economy, an issue which must remain in the ideological realm because of the lack of empirical evidence.

A final question concerns my assumption that time engaged in one activity is substitutable for time in another activity. More specifically, is it appropriate to compare labor hours in the distribution sector with shopping time? From the standpoint of central economic administrators, the opportunity costs of consumer shopping time may be very low, in which case they are able to achieve more production by cutting back on sales personnel and forcing people to shop longer. From the standpoint of the consumer, the problem is much more difficult to analyze because it depends in part on whether the individual is able to work as many hours as he wishes to. If there is a conventional working day and part-time work is unavailable, then an individual may work fewer hours than he really wishes to (in which case the foregone utility of the extra time spent shopping is low) or more hours than he really wishes to (in which case the foregone utility of the extra time spent shopping is high). Only in an equilibrium situation when a person can freely adjust his working hours might an individual be indifferent between working fewer hours but spending a longer time shopping, or working longer hours but spending a shorter time shopping (with changes in his leisure time net of shopping as well).

For greater clarification of many of these issues, it would be useful for pollsters in various countries to ask standardized questions dealing with peoples's desires for more or less work (and corresponding income) and with consumer satisfaction with goods they are able to

14. Ofer, *op. cit.*, esp. Ch. VI.

obtain with their income. In this way we might develop some empirical evidence on labor market equilibrium and consumer sovereignty so as to gain more solid information on the welfare implication of the cutback in wholesale and retail personnel in East Europe.

VI. Summary

In the first part of this essay I show that the partial suppression of markets of Eastern Europe did not lead to greater bureaucratization outside the commerce sector. In the second part I show that the major effect of the suppression of the market function in Eastern Europe was a savings of personnel in the wholesale and retail sector but not in other personnel serving the market function. I further argue that this may be less a matter of economic system per se than a cultural or political matter.

In the third part of the essay I investigate the impact of economic system on the amount of time spent shopping with the aid of a simple model relating shopping time to the amount of available goods, the number of personnel in wholesale and retail establishments, and the economic system. I present evidence that consumers in East Europe spend more time shopping than in West Europe; I also show that, if we hold the amount of available goods constant, this difference in shopping time can be explained primarily by differences in sales personnel per 1,000 population, and not by the economic system.

In the final section I argue that the hours of retail and wholesale personnel that are saved in Eastern Europe are roughly equal to the additional number of hours that consumers spend shopping because the sales personnel are fewer. The significance of these results depends partly on how one values the side effects that accompany both types of systems, as well as more technical issues such as whether or not the labor markets in the two systems are in equilibrium.

Statistical Notes

In these notes I indicate only in broad brush strokes my procedures and sources. A full list of the fifty-nine sources that were used and the estimation methods employed can be obtained from the author.

1. *Time data.* The time data come from Alexander Szalai and his associates.[15] Data on time spent marketing plus that proportion of time spent carrying out errands and shopping (with the proportion

15. Szalai *et al.*, *op. cit.*, pp. 576, 708, 610, and 678–80.

derived from the more detailed data on p. 582) in which the person spent buying goods were added together. Time spent waiting in line and travel for obtaining goods and services were apportioned according to the fraction spent buying goods. A weighted average of time spent for these activities was calculated from data on married working men (weighted 0.5), married working wives (weighted 0.3) and married housewives (weighted 0.2). For time spent in secondary activities concerning shopping and marketing, a similar procedure was followed except that the weighted average took no account of marital status, since only data for employed men, employed women, and housewives were given, and no account was taken for standing in line or traveling (since presumably these are attributable to the primary activity).

2. *G.N.P. data.* For most of the West European countries, the starting point was a set of estimates for 1955, which was calculated by Milton Gilbert and his associates.[16] These were updated using standard procedures. For other western nations the dollar value G.N.P.'s were calculated according to the method described by Pryor.[17] For the East European nations the starting point was the estimates of the dollar value of their G.N.P.'s that were presented by Pryor,[18] which were also updated using standard procedures. It must be noted that all G.N.P. and all marketed goods estimates are based on the estimates by Gilbert *et al.*[19] of a U. S. gross national product of $380 billion in 1955.

3. *Marketed goods.* For most Western nations the starting point was the set of estimates of Gilbert *et al.*,[20] which was then updated. For the other Western nations special estimates had to be made. For the East European nations, estimates were made of the total share of industrial production and agricultural production that reached the consumer by consulting standardized input-output tables and by making certain assumptions about tax incidence.

4. *Labor force in wholesale and retail establishments.* Whenever possible, I started with data on the economically active in wholesale and retail trade in a census year and then adjusted these data for the year of the time budget study with the aid of such correlative series as workers in trade or total employment in trade. The data came either

16. Milton Gilbert *et al.*, *Comparative National Products and Price Levels* (Paris: O.E.E.C., 1958).
17. Pryor, *Public Expenditures in Communist and Capitalist Nations*, p. 401.
18. *Ibid.*
19. Gilbert *et al.*, *op. cit.*
20. *Ibid.*

from Maurice Lengelle[21] or from various national statistical sources, usually censuses and labor force surveys.

5. *Labor force in sales and commerce.* A cross-tabulation of the economically active in various economic sectors and of various occupations compiled by the O.E.C.D.[22] was the basic source of information. For East Germany and Romania I constructed such tables from census data. The East German data contained the peculiarity that sales personnel outside commerce were not designated.

6. *Other labor force and population data.* The basic sources were Andrew Elias and the O.E.C.D.,[23] but these were supplemented by various other sources. When armed forces were omitted from labor force data, estimates were obtained and added in so that the data for the economically active would follow a standard definition.

SWARTHMORE COLLEGE

21. Maurice Lengelle, *The Growing Importance of the Service Sector in Member Countries*, Series: Changes in Employment Structure, No. 1 (Paris: O.E.C.D., 1966).

22. O.E.C.D., *Statistics of the Occupational and Educational Structure of the Labor Force in 54 Countries* (Paris, 1969).

23. Andrew Elias, "Magnitude and Distribution of the Labor Force in Eastern Europe," in United States, Joint Economic Committee, Congress of the United States, *Economic Development in Countries of Eastern Europe* (Washington, D.C.: G.P.O., 1970); and O.E.C.D., *op. cit.*

[4]

THE JOURNAL OF

POLITICAL ECONOMY

Volume LXVI APRIL 1958 Number 2

THE ECONOMICS OF SLAVERY IN THE ANTE BELLUM SOUTH[1]

ALFRED H. CONRAD AND JOHN R. MEYER
Harvard University

I. OBJECTIVES AND METHODS

The outstanding economic characteristics of southern agriculture before the Civil War were a high degree of specialization and virtually exclusive reliance on a slave labor force. The large-scale, commercial dependence upon slave labor was to distinguish the ante bellum South not only from other regions in its own time but from all regions at all other times in American agricultural history. Because of this unique historical status, ante bellum southern agriculture has been a subject for special historical attention. Above all else, attention has been focused upon the proposition that, even without external intervention, slavery would have toppled of its own weight. This allegation has its source in the assertions of slave inefficiency to be found in the writings of men who lived with slavery: American or English liberals like G. M. Weston, H. R. Helper, or J. E. Cairnes and southern slaveowners who, in a religious, self-righteous age, could find every motive for the protection of the slave system except that it was personally profitable. The argument is to be found most strongly stated in the work of later southern historians, especially C. W. Ramsdell and U. B. Phillips, who take the position that the Civil War, far from being an irrepressible conflict, was an unnecessary blood bath. They argue that slavery had reached its natural limits and that it was cumbersome and inefficient and, probably within less than a generation, would have destroyed itself. To the question why emancipation was not resorted to, they reply that slavery was for the southerners an important (and evidently expensive) duty, part of their "unending task of race discipline." On the other side, Lewis Gray and Kenneth Stampp have strongly contested this view, contending that southern plantation agriculture was at least as remunerative an economic activity as most

[1] This paper was presented at a meeting of the Conference on Research in Income and Wealth at Williams College, Williamstown, Massachusetts, September 4–5, 1957, and is published here with the kind permission of the Conference. We wish to thank the Harvard Foundation for Advanced Study and Research for a grant for computational and secretarial assistance. The Foundation does not, of course, share in any way the responsibility for the views or conclusions of the paper.

other business enterprises in the young republic.

The evidence employed in this debate has been provided by the few, usually fragmentary, accounting records that have come down to us from early plantation activities. The opposing parties have arranged and rearranged the data in accordance with various standard and sometimes imaginary accounting conventions. Indeed, the debate over the value of the different constituent pieces of information reconstructs in embryo much of the historical development of American accounting practices. For example, virtually all the accounting valuation problems have been discussed with relation to the slave question, including the role and meaning of depreciation, the nature and accountability of interest charges, and the validity of distinctions between profits and payments of managerial wages. But, despite the fact that the problem is ostensibly one in economic history, no attempt has ever been made to measure the profitability of slavery according to the economic (as opposed to accounting) concept of profitability. This paper is an attempt to fill this void.

Thus this paper is devoted to establishing methodological as well as historical points. Specifically, we shall attempt to measure the profitability of southern slave operations in terms of modern capital theory. In doing so, we shall illustrate the ways in which economic theory might be used in ordering and organizing historical facts. An additional methodological point is also made evident by this exercise, namely, how the very simple statistical concepts of range and central tendency as applied to frequency distributions of data can be employed in interpreting or moderating inferences from historical facts.[2]

In executing these tasks, we must ask first what it is we are talking about and, second, whether we can say anything that can be proved or disproved. For example, we must ask what the slave economy was. Was it cotton culture? Was it cotton and sugar and tobacco? Was it all of ante bellum southern agriculture? In answering, we shall define slavery in terms of two production functions. One function relates inputs of Negro slaves (and the materials required to maintain the slaves) to the production of the southern staple crops, particularly cotton. The second function describes the production of the intermediate good, slave labor—slave-breeding, to use an emotionally charged term which has colored, even determined, most of the conclusions about this problem.

What do we mean by "efficiency"? Essentially, we shall mean a comparison of the return from the use of this form of capital—Negro slaves—with the returns being earned on other capital assets at the time. Thus we mean to consider whether the slave system was being dragged down of its own weight; whether the allocation of resources was impaired by the rigidity of capitalized labor supply; whether southern capital was misused or indeed drawn away to the North; and, finally, whether slavery must inevitably have declined from an inability of the slave force to reproduce itself.

The hypothesis that slavery was an efficient, maintainable form of economic organization is not a new one, of course. Nor are we, by one hundred years, at least, among the first to conclude that Negro slavery was profitable in the ante bellum South. What we do feel to be

[2] A more thorough presentation of these methodological views may be found in our paper, "Economic Theory, Statistical Inference, and Economic History," in *The Tasks of Economic History*, proceedings issue of the *Journal of Economic History*, December, 1957.

novel, however, is our approach. Postulating that American Negro slavery was characterized by two production functions, we argue that an efficient system developed in which those regions best suited to the production of cotton (and the other important staples) specialized in agricultural production, while the less productive land continued to produce slaves, exporting the increase to the staple-crop areas. It is this structure that we are examining.

We propose to test the hypothesis by putting appropriate values on the variables in the production functions and computing the rate of return over cost, the stream of income over the lifetime of the slave. This rate of return, the marginal efficiency of slave capital, must, in turn, be shown to be at least equal to the rate of interest currently available in the American capital markets. It is further necessary to show that appropriate markets existed to make this regional specialization possible and that slavery did not necessarily imply the disappearance or misallocation of capital. Evidence on the ability of the slave force to maintain itself numerically will be had as a corollary result. For these purposes it is necessary to obtain data on slave prices and cotton prices, the average output of male field hands and field wenches, the life-expectancy of Negroes born in slavery, the cost of maintaining slaves during infancy and other nonproductive periods, and, finally, the net reproduction rate and the demographic composition of the slave population in the breeding and using areas.

Looked upon simply as a staple-commodity agriculture, the southern system must appear to have been burdened—possibly even to have been on the verge of collapse—under the weight of areas of inefficient, unprofitable farming. We submit that this view is in error and that the error arises from the failure to recognize that an agricultural system dependent upon slavery can be defined operationally only in terms of the production function for both the final good—in our case, cotton—and the production function for the intermediate good—Negro slaves. Considered operationally in terms of a neoclassical two-region two-commodity trade system, it must be seen that a slave system produces labor as an intermediate good. The profitability of the system cannot be decided without considering the system's ability to produce chattel labor efficiently.

There are also non-historical reasons for taking up once again the economics of ante bellum southern slavery. A detailed re-evaluation of the profits of plantation slavery in the American South might help us evaluate the possibilities first, that the near-slavery existing today in many highly agricultural, underindustrialized lands is an institution that can be expected to disappear automatically or, second, that dislodging it will require substantial governmental pressure or interference. These are, of course, often key policy questions in former colonial countries that are just beginning to develop modern industrial economies.

The possible relevance of the American experience in this connection increases moreover, as the underlying economic motivations of a slave system are analyzed and established. This happens primarily because, once these motives are recognized, it becomes possible better to understand and predict the political structures that will accompany slavery In other words, the interrelationships between certain economic and political goals of slavery can be better understood once the underlying economic factors are understood.

II. THE ECONOMIC RETURNS ON SLAVE-HOLDING

From the standpoint of the entre-preneur making an investment in slaves, the basic problems involved in determining profitability are analytically the same as those met in determining the returns from any other kind of capital investment. The acquisition of a slave represented the tying-up of capital in what has appropriately been called a roundabout method of production. Like the purchase of any capital, a slave purchase was made in the anticipation of gaining higher returns than are available from less time-consuming or capital-using methods. This model is particularly applicable in the present case, because slave investments, like the forests or wine cellars of classic capital theory, produced a natural increase with the passage of time.

TABLE 1

EXPECTATION OF LIFE AT BIRTH IN YEARS FOR WHITE AND COLORED MALES, UNITED STATES, 1850*

State	White	Colored
Massachusetts....	38.3	39.75
Maryland........	41.8	38.47
Louisiana........	....	28.89

* Reported in L. I. Dublin, A. J. Latka, and M. Spiegelman, *Length of Life* (New York: Ronald Press Co., 1949) p. 54, where the source is given as the L. W. Meech table based on the records of the 1850 Census and first published in J. C. G. Kennedy, *The Seventh Census—Report of the Superintendent of the Census, Dec. 1, 1852* (Washington, D.C., 1853), p. 13. The Maryland colored data are for slaves only; the Louisiana, for slaves and free together.

Investment returns are properly computed by using the capital-value formula, $y = x_t/(1 + r)^t$, where y is the cost of the investment, x_t is realized return t years hence, and r is the internal rate of return[3] or what Keynes called the marginal efficiency of capital. When returns are realized over a number of years, the total earnings of the capital can be found by simple summation in this formula. The criterion for a profitable investment is that the marginal efficiency exceeds the interest rate (in the Keynesian terminology). From this statement of the problem, it is obvious that the following information is needed to determine the profitability of slaveholding from the slaveholder's point of view: (*a*) the longevity of slaves; (*b*) the costs of slaves and any necessary accompanying capital investments; (*c*) the interest rate; and (*d*) the annual returns from slave productive activities, defined to include both field labor and procreation. We shall consider each of these in turn and then put the pieces together to determine the approximate profitability of slave investments.

A. THE LONGEVITY OF SLAVES

Slave longevity corresponds, of course, to the period for which a slave investment was made. We shall limit attention here to the purchase of twenty-year-old Negroes in the immediate pre–Civil War era, and we shall deal only with the typical or median life-expectancy for this group. These limits greatly simplify the problem and still include the vast majority of relevant cases.

There is a scarcity of good longevity data for the period, but it is known that in 1850 Negroes lived just about as long as whites in the two states for which acceptable data are available. The available figures are given in Table 1. There is doubt about the quality of these estimates because they show Negroes in New England expecting a longer life than whites. This is not the case today, nor

[3] Computation of rate of return in this way is preferable to the usual recording of net profit rates on total plantation investment in slaves, land, and durable equipment, because of the reproductive character and the limited durability of slave investments. Clearly, the same characteristics do not apply to non-depreciable investments in land. A non-depreciable investment in agricultural land is, however, quite rare.

was it the case in 1900, when the first good data became available. Also, Negroes would appear in this table to have had a longer life-expectancy in 1850 than they had fifty years later. Although surprising, this may be perfectly correct. Negroes could have received better care under slavery, because plantation owners had an economic interest in keeping Negroes alive. Furthermore, the Negro in the period after emancipation generally lacked the means to participate equally in the new medical advances, in contrast to his position of roughly equal medical care in the period before 1860.

Life-expectation at birth does not tell us much, of course, about the expectation of a twenty-year-old man. Actually, there are no data on Negro life-expectancy at different age levels in the prewar period except for some imperfect estimates made by Sydnor for Mississippi slaves.[4] Using the average reported age at death of those over the age of twenty who died in 1850, he estimated a life-expectancy of twenty-two years for a twenty-year-old Mississippi slave. This figure is probably low for two reasons. First, the estimating procedure tells more about life-expectancy in the years preceding 1850 than after, unless we make the dubious assumption that there was no advance in medical and dietary knowledge around the middle of the century. Second, estimates from deaths reported at the end of ten-year intervals and averaged back over the decade would tend to underestimate life-spans at the younger ages. Doubts about the quality of the Sydnor data are borne out by consideration of the Massachusetts life-expectancy of 40.1 years for twenty-year-old males, white and Negro, in 1850.[5] Looking back at the data in Table 1, there is no reason to expect twenty-year-old Massachusetts Negroes to have a lower life-expectancy than Massachusetts whites, though both clearly lived longer than southern Negroes of the period. Taking all these factors into account, an estimate of thirty to thirty-five years of life-expectancy seems most plausible for twenty-year-old Negroes working as prime cotton hands on southern plantations in the period 1830–50, and a thirty-year life-expectancy will generally be used in the succeeding calculations.

B. THE COST OF THE CAPITAL INVESTMENT

The capital investment in plantation operations included investment both in slaves and in the land and equipment on which the slaves worked. The price of slaves fluctuated widely, being subject to the waves of speculation in cotton. Furthermore, the price depended, among other things, upon the age, sex, disposition, degree of training, and condition of the slave. In order to hold these variables roughly constant, we shall confine our present analysis to eighteen–twenty-year-old prime field hands and wenches. Some summary data on slave prices were compiled by U. B. Phillips on the basis of available market quotations, bills of transactions, and reports of sales in most of the important slave markets of Georgia. His estimates of the best averages for

[4] Charles S. Sydnor, "Life Span of Mississippi Slaves," *American Historical Review,* XXXV (April, 1930), 566–74.

[5] L. I. Dublin, A. J. Latka, and M. Spiegelman, *Length of Life* (New York: Ronald Press Co., 1949), p. 51. It is worth noting that there is general agreement that labor on the rice and sugar plantations was sufficiently more arduous to reduce Negro longevity in such locations. Therefore, the Louisiana estimates are probably inordinately pessimistic, and the Maryland figures are better estimates of conditions prevailing on the cotton plantations. This, in turn, means that the thirty- to thirty-five-year estimates used below are, if anything, a little conservative.

several years between 1828 and 1860 are presented in Table 2. On the basis of these data it would appear that both the median and the mean price for prime field hands were in the range of from $900 to $950 in the period 1830–50. Because of the substantial price increases in the last ante bellum decade, these averages would run substantially higher for the entire slave period after 1830; specifically, about $1,100–$1,200. Since the prices of field wenches usually averaged about $100–$150 less than those of hands, they were probably in the range of from $800 to $850 in the years 1830–50 and between $900 and $1,100 for the entire period 1830–60. (Phillips' averages are substantially confirmed by the detailed tabulation of slave transactions shown in Table A of the Appendix. This is a reasonably exhaustive list of such transactions as reported in the standard references on ante bellum southern agriculture.)

TABLE 2

ESTIMATED AVERAGE SLAVE PRICES IN GEORGIA, SELECTED YEARS, 1828–60

Year	Average Price of Prime Field Hands
1828	$ 700
1835	900
1837	1,300
1839	1,000
1840	700
1844	600
1848	900
1851	1,050
1853	1,200
1859	1,650
1860	1,800

Source: U. B. Phillips, "The Economic Cost of Slaveholding in the Cotton Belt," *Political Science Quarterly*, XX, No. 2 (1905), 267.

As for the non-slave capital, by far the most important was the investment in land. Since the land values varied widely, depending on the quality of the soil and the type of agriculture pursued, experimental control on our calculations requires that attention be confined to cotton culture. The range in cotton-land prices in the period 1830–50 is fairly well bracketed by the $6 per acre paid for poor upland pine land in Alabama and the $35–$40 per acre paid for cleared Mississippi alluvium. Such a range even encompasses the costs of new lands in the Southwest. Although such land was obtained for nominal original cost, the usual costs of clearing, draining, and otherwise preparing it, plus the transportation of slaves and supplies, would amount to something in the range of $20–$30 per acre. There was also variation in the number of acres needed per hand. Counting garden land and woodlots, as well as productive fields, the usual number of acres per field hand was between 15 and 35, the exact figure depending primarily on the quality of the land. This meant an original land investment per hand of somewhere between $90 and $1,400, with $180–$600 encompassing the vast majority of instances.

The price per acre was, of course, related to the durability of the land, which immediately introduces a further dimension into the capital cost problem. Cotton lands lasted between ten and forty years, depending upon original quality and fertilization. In the land-rich, labor-scarce economy of the nineteenth-century United States, fertilization was a rare practice. Furthermore, planters clearly had the choice between operating less capital intensively on low-durability land or more capital intensively on high-durability land. For example, poor Alabama pine land might be expected to last ten years and require 30–35 acres per hand; this meant that $180–$210 had to be reinvested every ten years to utilize the slave force properly. Assuming thirty-year slave longevity and an 8 per cent interest rate, the present value of the land investment for one slave's lifetime was \$302–\$350 for an upland-pine operation. On the alluvium, by contrast, the land would typically outlast the slave in usefulness; assuming, though, that both lasted the same number of years and that 16 acres of cleared and 10 of uncleared land (at \$10 per acre) were used per hand, a total land investment of \$660 per hand is indicated. This difference in value of the land investment was presumably a function of different yields. At any rate, the typical case was probably halfway between these two, involving a land investment of about \$450 per hand.

Similar problems arise in estimating the investment in plows, gins, wagons, cabins, and miscellaneous implements. Such investments ran about \$25 per hand in original outlay and had to be renewed every fifteen years. This gives a total present value in such items (again on the assumption of thirty-year slave longevity and 8 per cent interest) of about \$33. A small investment was required in work horses and oxen, but in this case the stock was likely to be self-replenishing, reducing the costs to interest on the investment at most. Putting all these capital costs together indicates that \$1,400–\$1,450 was a fair approximation of the typical or average total investment per male slave in terms of present values. The range ran from \$1,250 to \$1,650.

C. THE INTEREST RATE

Determining the relevant rate of interest—the rate with which the cotton-slave returns must be compared—is perhaps empirically the easiest and conceptually the most difficult of the tasks in computing the economic returns on slave investments. While there is a relative abundance of data on interest rates in this period, none corresponds exactly to the desired rate. In a strict conceptual sense, the relevant rate of interest is that which plantation owners or other investors in southern agriculture could have earned on their money in other pursuits if slavery had gone out of existence. This is difficult to arrive at on the basis of historical evidence, since it assumes circumstances contrary to the facts. The closest substitute would be earnings on other investments that were *least* dependent upon cotton and southern agriculture. Given the importance of cotton in the American economy prior to the Civil War and the general interdependence of economic systems, even in so primitive an economy as that of the United States in the first half of the nineteenth century, it is difficult to find any conceptually correct figures. The figures that follow are offered in complete recognition of their fallibility on this count, yet they are probably as good as are available.

In the contemporary chronicles it is obvious that southerners and northerners alike considered 6–8 per cent a reasonable rate of return and a reasonable asking price for loans. Figures in this range are repeated over and over again and must be given some significance. This is all the more true because these figures are consistent with reported rates charged on prime commercial paper and other debt instruments in the principal money markets before 1860. The prime commerical rates charged in New York and Boston in the period 1830–65, shown in Table 3, illustrate this point.[6] Similarly, the

[6] In confirmation of these figures, Lance E. Davis, who is now completing a study of New England financial intermediaries (the essentials of which can be found in his Ph.D. dissertation on deposit in the Johns Hopkins University Library), reports that these New England firms consistently realized less than 6 per cent on three-signature prime commercial

rates on New York Stock Exchange call loans, New England municipal issues, and rail debentures, shown in Table 4, fall for the most part within, or below, this same 6–8 per cent range. While the average annual rates fluctuated widely in the years between 1830 and 1850 and the distribution of rates is skewed, the central tendency was clearly close to the 6–8 per cent range. Specifically, the New York average was 9.2 per cent, the median was 8.0, and the mode was between 6.0 and 7.0 per cent. Because of the skew, the median rate of 8 per cent is probably the best measure of central tendency for the present analysis.

The interest rates for the Civil War years, although they lie somewhat outside the time period of this investigation, may be conceptually the most pertinent figures in Tables 3 and 4. The Civil War represents as good an approximation as is achievable of a controlled experiment to determine investment returns in the North under complete divorce from the plantation economy. The difficulty is, of course, that too many other structural changes took place concomitantly with the withdrawal of the southern cotton economy: above all else, the Lincoln administration adopted the very essence of Keynesian expansionary fiscal policies. It simultaneously ran a large deficit budget and closed the economy with high tariffs and buy-American clauses in government contracts. On the supply side of the money market, the war meant that the southern withdrawal was consummated without any flow of capital out of slavery and into other ventures. Consequently, returns on northern investments unquestionably remained

TABLE 3

AVERAGE ANNUAL INTEREST RATES ON PRIME COMMERCIAL PAPER FROM 1831 TO 1860

	New York*	Boston†		New York*	Boston†
1831	5.1	6.5	1849	10.0	12.0
1832	5.3	6.5	1850	8.0	7.5
1833	6.9	6.0	1851	9.7	7.0
1834	14.6	14.5	1852	6.6	6.0
1835	7.0	5.0	1853	10.2	10.7
1836	18.4	20.3	1854	10.4	12.0
1837	14.1	6.0	1855	8.9	7.0
1838	9.0	7.0	1856	8.9	10.0
1839	13.2	9.0	1857	12.9	9.0
1840	7.8	6.0	1858	5.0	4.5
1841	6.9	6.0	1859	6.8	7.0
1842	8.1	7.8	1860	7.0	6.0
1843	4.5	3.0	1861	6.5	....
1844	4.9	5.0	1862	5.8	....
1845	6.0	6.0	1863	5.0	....
1846	8.3	8.0	1864	6.0	....
1847	9.6	6.0	1865	7.6	....
1848	15.1	15.0			

Sources: *New York data:* Federal Reserve Bank of New York, *Monthly Review*, March 1, 1921, p. 3. The figures are also reproduced in A. O. Greef, *The Commercial Paper House in the United States* (Cambridge, Mass.: Harvard University Press, 1938), p. 79. *Boston data:* Joseph G. Martin, *One Hundred Years' History of the Boston Stock and Money Markets* (Boston: The Author, 1898), pp. 52-53.

* Two-name sixty–ninety-day paper.

† "First class three to six months, bankable paper." The rate reported is either one sustained for a major portion of the year or an arithmetic average.

paper in the period before 1840; from 1840 to 1860, however, almost all loans were made at 6 per cent, which was the legal maximum under Massachusetts usury laws. He estimates that these intermediaries realized an over-all return of between 6 and 7 per cent in the period 1840–60 on their total investment; 6 per cent on the debt and 7–8 per cent on equity.

higher than they would have if southern cotton had been withdrawn without offsetting government action and with a flow of southern capital into northern money markets. On the other hand, there might have been compensatory government action even without the war, and the loss of southern funds was at least partially offset by the loss of southern opportunities. The 6–7 per cent average returns in the period 1860–65 can be viewed as indicative of at least what could be achieved in the United States in the absence of cotton investment opportunities.

The realization on short-term, high-quality commercial paper might normally be expected to be below the realization on longer-term investments of the type represented by ownership of a cotton plantation. However, in the period 1840–60 banking practices were rather lax and potentially or actually inflationary, as indicated by the recurrent financial panics of the time. Such unstable financial conditions may have given equity a premium that it might otherwise not have enjoyed. Furthermore, the existence of well-established slave and real estate markets made most plantation investments highly negotiable, thereby reducing the time commitment in such investments. There are some reports available on the realizable returns on longer-term investments; for example, Table 4 presents the rates at which some municipal and railroad development bonds were floated in the prewar period. In addition, Davis reports returns of 16.76 per cent on total capital stock in the 1844–48 period and 5.75 per cent in the 1848–53 period for nine of the larger and more prosperous Massachusetts textile firms.[7]

From these many disparate sources it seems safe to estimate that a wholesale withdrawal of capital from slave operations in southern agriculture would not have depressed marginal investment returns in the prewar United States economy much below 4.5–5 per cent. Similarly, it seems safe to conclude that the withdrawn capital could not have expected to earn returns much in excess of 8 per cent. Between these high and low estimates, a return of 6 per cent seems the most probable and, therefore, appropriate for comparison in our model.

TABLE 4

YIELDS ON VARIOUS ECONOMIC ACTIVITIES, 1857–65

Year	New England Municipal Bond Yields (January Index Numbers)	Call Money Rates at the New York Stock Exchange (Arithmetic Average of Months)	Railroad Bond Yields (January Average for All Railroads)
1857	5.2	9.3	8.1
1858	5.3	4.2	8.7
1859	4.8	5.4	7.4
1860	4.8	6.0	7.5
1861	4.9	5.8	7.4
1862	5.2	5.2	7.5
1863	4.4	6.2	5.6
1864	4.7	6.6	6.0
1865	5.2	6.2	6.2

Source: Frederick R. Macaulay, *The Movements of Interest Rates, Bond Yields and Stock Prices in the United States since 1856* (New York: National Bureau of Economic Research, 1938), pp. A172–A173 and A34–A38.

D. ANNUAL RETURNS

The appropriate return figure to enter in the capital equation is the net return on current account, or the difference between gross sales and all out-of-pocket expenses. The expense deduction is limited to out-of-pocket expenses, because all the book charges that complicate the usual accounting procedures are taken into account in the process of constructing the capital cost estimate.

[7] Lance E. Davis, "Sources of Industrial Finance: The American Textile Industry," *Explorations in Entrepreneurial History*, IX (April, 1957), 201. The figures are based on the companies' financial records to be found at the Baker Library of the Harvard Graduate School of Business Administration.

Estimates of plantation expenses have been taken primarily from three excellent, exhaustive records of the available material: J. L. Watkins' *The Cost of Cotton Production*, Lewis C. Gray's *History of Agriculture in the Southern United States to 1860*, and Kenneth Stampp's *The Peculiar Institution*.[8] A reasonably thorough check of these secondary sources against some primary sources and against one another for consistency indicates that these surveys have been reliably and accurately made. A digest of the estimates is presented in Table 5. The total figure of $20–$21 annual out-of-pocket slave maintenance costs will be used in subsequent calculations. These costs are to be subtracted from the annual gross return figures on slave activities.

TABLE 5

TYPICAL ANNUAL OUT-OF-POCKET COSTS OF MAINTAINING AND WORKING PRIME FIELD HANDS ON SOUTHERN PLANTATIONS IN THE PERIOD 1840–60

A. Food and clothing	
(1) Out-of-pocket costs where most food was produced on plantation and most clothing was hand-sewn	$ 2.50–$ 3.46
(2) Cash costs if purchased	$25.00–$40.00
(3) Out-of-pocket costs where some ready-made clothing and meat, fish, and other food "delicacies" were purchased	$ 7.00–$10.00
B. Medical care	$ 1.50–$ 2.00
C. Taxes	$ 0.39–$ 1.20
D. Supervision	$ 5.00–$15.00
Total, based on means of the estimates above and option (3) under A	$20.00–$21.00

Principal sources: J. L. Watkins, *The Cost of Cotton Production* (United States Department of Agriculture, Division of Statistics, Miscellaneous Series, Bull. 16 [Washington, D.C.: Government Printing Office, 1899]); Lewis C. Gray, *History of Agriculture in the Southern United States to 1860* (Washington, D.C.: Carnegie Institution, 1933), pp. 529–67; Kenneth Stampp, *The Peculiar Institution* (New York: A. A. Knopf, Inc., 1956), chaps. vi, vii, and ix.

For a male field hand the returns considered will be limited to the sales of products realized from his field labor; in the case of a female hand, an addition must be made for the returns realized on the labor and sale of her children. Because of these basic differences in the production functions for the two sexes, they will be treated separately.

For the male field hand, limited to the returns on his field labor, the gross proceeds will depend on the price of cotton and the quantity of his annual output. The output, in turn, will be crucially dependent on the quality of the land on which the slave was employed and, to a much lesser degree, upon the quality and amount of capital goods with which he was equipped. The figures in Table 6 illustrate the possible variation in productivity per hand. These estimates agree with frequent statements in con-

[8] These three secondary sources carefully and consistently record the estimates available from three basic types of primary material. Gray's *History of Agriculture in the Southern United States to 1860* (Washington, D.C., 1933), esp. pp. 529–67, covers the cost estimates intermittently reported in the principal agricultural and business journals read by the planters and traders: *DeBow's Review*, *Farmers' Register*, *Farmer and Planter*, *Southern Planter*, *Southern Agriculturist*, and *Hunt's Merchants' Magazine*. Watkins' *The Cost of Cotton Production* (U.S. Department of Agriculture, Miscellaneous Series, Bull. 16 [Washington, D.C., 1899]) includes the estimates recorded in the Patent Office and the Commissioner of Patents' *Annual Reports*, especially for the years 1844, 1849, 1850, 1852, 1854, and 1855. Stampp's *The Peculiar Institution* (New York, 1956), esp. chaps. vi, vii, and ix, reports the estimates available from diaries and individual plantation records still in existence.

temporary journals that in the typical case a prime field hand could be expected to raise from 3.5 to 4 bales per year. The maximum seems to have been 7–8 bales on the best lands, and 2–3 bales was the minimum on the poorest land.

The relevant price of cotton for valuing these yields is the net price realized at the farm (in order that price and cost data be comparable). This means that export prices at the major ports must be adjusted downward by the amount of freight, insurance, storage, drayage, and factor's commission charges that were properly chargeable to the planter. Gray estimates that these costs generally ran between $2.50 and $4 per bale. Somewhat more detailed information is presented by Watkins, whose findings are summarized in Table 7. The Gray and Watkins findings are fully compatible, and a marketing cost of from 0.7 to 0.8 cent per pound appears to be properly deductible from the export price in determining the price f.o.b. farm.

The export price itself fluctuated widely over the period. As can be seen from Table 8, New Orleans cotton prices averaged almost 50 per cent higher in the thirties and fifties than they did in the depressed forties. Even in the forties, however, the export price level was sufficient to insure an average net farm price of not much less than 6.5 cents. Since prices at any given port were usually equal to the Liverpool price minus ocean shipping rates, the New York and Mobile prices were generally somewhat higher. Taking all this into consideration, 7–8 cents seems a realistic and conservative estimate of the average realized farm price for the whole period.

Finally, the price, productivity, and capital cost estimates must be combined in order to compute the actual profitability of investments in male slave labor for cotton production. Capital costs must be included in the computations, since the present value of the capital outlay will depend, as was previously shown, upon the rate of return. In lieu of a single computation, several cases involving different capital outlays, yields per hand,

TABLE 6

REPORTED YIELDS PER PRIME FIELD HAND

Location	Year	Bales per Hand	Source
South Carolina coastal	1849	4⅓	Watkins
Mississippi (De Soto County)	1849	4	Watkins
Unidentified	1844	7	Watkins
Alabama (Cherokee County)	1855	4	Watkins
Mississippi (Vicksburg area)	1855	8	Watkins
New Southwest land	1850's	5	Gray, p. 912
South Carolina upland	1852	3	Gray, p. 912
Texas	1859	10	Stampp, p. 408
Arkansas River	1859	7	Stampp, p. 408

TABLE 7

COTTON MARKETING COSTS PER BALE CHARGEABLE TO PLANTERS IN 1840

	At Mobile	At Charleston
Freight in	$1.50*	$1.25†
Drayage	0.125	0.13
Weighing	0.125	0.06
Storage (1 month)	0.20	0.24
Insurance (1 month)	‡	0.25
Factor's commission (2–2.5 per cent)	0.80	0.60–1.61
Total per bale	$2.75	$3.03§
Total cents per pound‖	0.69	0.76§

Source: Watkins, *op. cit.*, pp. 38, 39.

* By river.

† From Columbia.

‡ Not reported. Note that the higher (Charleston) figures have been used in the profit computations to follow.

§ Assuming $1.10 factor's commission.

‖ Four hundred pounds to a bale.

and realized farm prices have been constructed; the results are given in Table 9.[9] Cases 1, 2, and 3 are the most typical; cases 4, 5, and 6 represent the situation on somewhat better land. These first six cases, with returns ranging between 4½ and 8 per cent, encompass the majority of ante bellum cotton plantation operations. Cases 7, 8, and 9 represent the minimum of profitability or what might be expected on poor upland pine country or the worked-out lands of the eastern seaboard. By contrast, cases 10, 11, and 12 show the upper range of profitability which was realized on the best lands of the new Southwest, the Mississippi alluvium, and the better South Carolina and Alabama plantations.[10]

The calculations in Table 9 represent an estimate of potential returns for the relatively simple production function of prime field hands. With the female hand or prime field wench the situation becomes much more complex: in addition to her productivity, the productivity of her children and the returns realized on their sale must be considered. Similarly, the extra cost of maintaining the children and the maternity and nursery costs associated with their birth must also be counted.

To make the calculations in this rather complex situation manageable, the following assumptions will be made:

1. Each prime field wench produced five to ten marketable children during her lifetime. (The computations for the ten-child or upper-limit case are shown in Table 10, while those for the lower limit of five children are shown in Table 11.)

TABLE 8

WEIGHTED YEARLY AVERAGE PRICES OF SHORT-STAPLE COTTON (USUALLY LOUISIANA OR MISSISSIPPI MIDDLING OR SECOND GRADE) AT NEW ORLEANS FOR THE CROP YEARS 1830–60

Year	Price	Year	Price	Year	Price
1830	8.4	1840	9.1	1850	11.7
1831	9.0	1841	7.8	1851	7.4
1832	10.0	1842	5.7	1852	9.1
1833	11.2	1843	7.5	1853	8.8
1834	15.5	1844	5.5	1854	8.4
1835	15.2	1845	6.8	1855	9.1
1836	13.3	1846	9.9	1856	12.4
1837	9.0	1847	7.0	1857	11.2
1838	12.4	1848	5.8	1858	11.5
1839	7.9	1849	10.8	1859	10.8
				1860	11.1
Decade average price	11.2		7.6		11.2

Source: Gray, *op. cit.*, Table 41, pp. 1027–29.

[9] No allowance has been made in these computations for the expenses of maintaining slaves in their dotage. This would not appear to be a serious omission. Generally speaking, slaves were considered to be virtually fully productive in field labor until their fifty-fifth birthdays—which corresponds to the average life-expectancy on the purchase of a twenty-year-old slave. Furthermore, the direct out-of-pocket costs of simply maintaining a slave were only $10–$15, figures considerably below productive value in field work. Given the possibility of specialized use of older labor in such occupations as garden-tending, nursery operations, and supervision, it seems doubtful if many slaves lived long enough to be economic drains on current account.

[10] A purist might ask how different returns can be realized in what is ostensibly the same type of economic activity in a relatively competitive industry. The question overlooks the fact that it took a much larger initial outlay to attain productive situations like those in cases 10–12. This is all the more true, since the capital outlay in these cases would be concentrated at the start of the undertaking, while in cases 7–9 some of the outlay would be delayed ten or fifteen years until the land wore out.

Furthermore, we assume that successful pregnancies were spaced two years apart. It must be recognized that these figures represent assumptions more about what was achievable than about actual happenings. Slave infant mortality data are too poor to permit inferences about the latter.

2. The prime field wench was one-half to two-thirds as productive as a prime field hand when she was actually at work in the field. This estimate is based on the fact that, when prime field hands and wenches were hired out, the hiring rate on the latter was usually one-half to two-thirds the hiring rate on the former. Thus, it is assumed that the market hiring rate reflects the relative productivity of the two sexes. In addition, adjustments must be made for the time lost by the female during pregnancy and post-natal period. It is assumed here that three months' productive field time was lost for each successful pregnancy; the entire deduction has been made in the year in which the successful birth took place, despite the fact that it would probably be more realistic to assume that one month and a half was lost on each unsuccessful as well as each successful pregnancy. This allowance for "lost time" is probably too generous, since the only births that really cost any important productive field time were those occurring during the peak agriculture seasons, planting and picking times.

3. The wench's children began to be productive in field labor at age six, with the males becoming self-sustaining by age nine (that is, they then earned the adult maintenance charge of $20 per year), while females became self-sustaining by age thirteen. This can be represented by letting the male productivity go up $5 every year between ages six and nine and letting female productivity increase by $2.50 for every year between the ages of six and thirteen. These rates are in keeping with the previously stated principle that females were roughly half as productive in field labor as males. After reaching a self-sustaining status at these ages, it is further assumed that their productivity continued to rise linearly until the children reached their full adult productivity at age eighteen; thus, male productivity is assumed to rise $10 per year between ages nine and eighteen and the female productivity $5 per year between ages thirteen and eighteen.

TABLE 9

REALIZED RETURNS ON PRIME FIELD HANDS UNDER VARIOUS HYPOTHESIZED CONDITIONS

Case	Present Value of Capital Outlay per Hand	Yield per Hand (Bales)	Average Net Farm Price (Cents)	Approximate Return (Per Cent)
1	$1,350–$1,400	3¾	7	4.5
2	$1,350–$1,400	3¾	8	5.2
3	$1,350–$1,400	3¾	9	6.5
4	$1,600	4½	7	5.0
5	$1,600	4½	8	7.0
6	$1,600	4½	9	8.0
7	$1,250–$1,300	3	7	2.2
8	$1,250–$1,300	3	8	3.9
9	$1,250–$1,300	3	9	5.4
10	$1,700	7	7	10.0
11	$1,700	7	8	12.0
12	$1,700	7	9	13.0

4. The typical wench had as many male as female children. For purposes of computation, the productivity, sales price, and other data for the two sexes have been averaged. For example, the final sales price of a typical child is assumed to be $875, halfway between the average price of $825 for prime field wenches and the average price of $925 for prime field hands.

5. Nursery costs were about $50 per successful pregnancy.

Using these assumptions, hypothetical annual returns for a typical prime field wench can be determined; such calculations are shown in Tables 10 and 11. In constructing these tables, it was assumed that the prime field wench and her children worked on land that returned 3.75 bales of cotton per year for every prime male hand employed; that is, the land is of approximately average fertility. Also, a 7.5 cent net farm price for cotton has been used. The first successful pregnancy has been assumed to occur in the second year after the prime field wench

TABLE 10

ANNUAL RETURNS ON A PRIME FIELD WENCH INVESTMENT (WORKING ON LAND WHICH YIELDED 3.75 BALES PER PRIME MALE FIELD HAND, ASSUMING A 7.5-CENT NET FARM PRICE FOR COTTON AND TEN "SALABLE" CHILDREN BORN TO EVERY WENCH)

Year from Purchase Date	Personal Field Returns	Child Field Returns	Child Sale Returns	Personal Upkeep	Child Upkeep	Net Returns
1.	$56	....	....	$20	....	$ 36
2.	40	....	....	20	$ 50	−30
3.	56	....	....	20	10	26
4.	40	....	....	20	60	−40
5.	56	....	....	20	20	16
6.	40	....	....	20	70	−50
7.	56	....	....	20	30	6
8.	40	$ 3.75	....	20	80	−56.25
9.	56	7.50	....	20	45	−1.50
10.	40	15.00	....	20	95	−50.00
11.	56	22.50	....	20	60	−1.50
12.	40	37.50	....	20	110	−52.50
13.	56	52.50	....	20	75	13.50
14.	40	75.00	....	20	130	−35.00
15.	56	97.50	....	20	95	47.50
16.	40	127.50	....	20	150	−2.50
17.	56	157.50	....	20	115	78.50
18.	40	195.00	....	20	165	55.00
19.	56	232.50	....	20	130	134.30
20.	40	195.00	$875	20	170	920.00
21.	56	232.50	....	20	130	138.50
22.	56	195.00	875	20	120	986.00
23.	56	232.50	....	20	120	148.50
24.	56	195.00	875	20	110	996.00
25.	56	232.50	....	20	110	158.00
26.	56	195.00	875	20	100	1,006.00
27.	56	232.50	....	20	100	168.00
28.	56	187.50	875	20	90	1,008.50
29.	56	225.00	....	20	90	171.00
30.	56	180.00	875	20	80	1,011.00
31.	...	210.00	....	...	80	130.00
32.	...	157.50	875	...	60	972.50
33.	...	180.00	....	...	60	120.00
34.	...	120.00	875	...	40	955.00
35.	...	135.00	....	...	40	95.00
36.	...	67.50	875	...	20	922.50
37.	...	75.00	....	...	20	55.00
38.	...	....	875	...	....	875.00

is purchased; further successful pregnancies occur at regular two-year intervals. The children were sold at age eighteen, and the annual maintenance cost per child was assessed at the rate of $10 per year for one–six-year-olds, $15 per year for seven–twelve-year-olds and $20 per year, the full adult maintenance cost, for those age thirteen and over. The maternity costs have been included in the annual charge for the children's upkeep; similarly, the $16 decline every other year for the first few years in the wench's own field returns represents the allowance for time lost because of pregnancy. Rates of return were computed on the streams of net returns shown in the far right-hand columns of the tables on the assumption that the total investment in the prime field wench, land, and equipment amounts to $1,200–$1,300, figures which would appear to be very good averages. A rate of return of 8.1 per cent was thus obtained for the mother bearing ten children and a return of 7.1 per cent for the mother with five children.

TABLE 11

Annual Returns on a Prime Field Wench Investment (Working on Land Which Yielded 3.75 Bales per Prime Male Field Hand, Assuming a 7.5-Cent Net Farm Price for Cotton and Five "Salable" Children Born to Every Wench)

Year from Purchase Date	Personal Field Returns	Child Field Returns	Child Sale Returns	Personal Upkeep	Child Upkeep	Net Returns
1	$56	....	....	$20	...	$ 36
2	40	....	....	20	$50	−30
3	56	....	....	20	10	26
4	40	....	....	20	60	−40
5	56	....	....	20	20	16
6	40	....	....	20	70	−50
7	56	....	....	20	30	6
8	40	$ 3.75	....	20	80	−56.25
9	56	7.50	....	20	45	−1.50
10	40	15.00	..	20	95	−50.00
11	56	22.50	....	20	60	−1.50
12	56	37.50	....	20	60	13.50
13	56	52.50	....	20	65	23.50
14	56	75.00	....	20	65	46.00
15	56	97.50	....	20	75	58.50
16	56	127.50	....	20	75	88.50
17	56	157.50	....	20	85	108.50
18	56	191.25	....	20	85	142.25
19	56	225.00	....	20	90	171.00
20	56	180.00	$875	20	75	1,016.00
21	56	210.00	....	20	75	171.00
22	56	157.50	875	20	60	1,008.50
23	56	180.00	....	20	60	156.00
24	56	120.00	875	20	40	991.00
25	56	135.00	....	20	40	131.00
26	56	67.50	875	20	20	958.50
27	56	75.00	....	20	20	91.00
28	56	....	875	20	...	911.00
29	56	....	....	20	...	36.00
30	56	....	....	20	...	36.00

These figures are, of course, somewhat higher than those calculated for the prime field hands. A proper working of the market mechanism would suggest that the attainable returns on the two sexes should be approximately equal. That is, the price differential between males and females should be such that the rate of return on the two types of investment turns out to be roughly equal in the typical or average case. The question therefore arises why a somewhat higher estimated return is obtained for the female.

Several answers can be made to this question. First, the difference between the estimated returns for the two sexes may arise because it probably took a somewhat higher return on the females to attract capital investment into that type of productive activity. Slave-breeding and slave-trading were not generally considered to be high or noble types of activity for a southern gentleman. Indeed, many plantation owners would stoop to all sorts of subterfuge to disguise the fact that they were engaging in any part of the slave trade or breeding operations. Second, the investment in the female was a longer-term affair; from Tables 10 and 11 it is apparent that the bulk of the returns on a female were realized twenty or more years after the investment was made, when the children had grown to marketable ages. To the extent that more distant developments are more uncertain, investments in female slaves could be expected to demand a higher return. Finally, the over-all average price of prime field wenches quoted from Phillips may be too low for proved "childbearers"; as is evident from Table A of the Appendix and contemporary comments, a female who had proved herself fertile was worth more than a female who had yet to bear her first child.

But these qualifications do not change the principal conclusion that slavery was apparently about as remunerative as alternative employments to which slave capital might have been put. Large or excessive returns were clearly limited to a few fortunate planters, but apparently none suffered excessively either. This general sharing in the prosperity was more or less guaranteed, moreover, if proper market mechanisms existed so that slaves could be bred and reared on the poorest of land and then be sold to those owning the best. Slavery in the immediate ante bellum years was, therefore, an economically viable institution in virtually all areas of the South as long as slaves could be expeditiously and economically transferred from one sector to another.

III. REPRODUCTION, ALLOCATION, AND SLAVE MARKETS

It thus remains to be determined whether an efficient supply mechanism—efficient in both its generative and its allocative functions—existed in the ante bellum South. That the slave force might reproduce itself was not sufficient; there must also have been a capital market capable of getting the labor to the areas where production was expanding if slavery was to be profitable. It will be useful to introduce the secondary propositions by stating several arguments which together form the orthodox opposition to the present hypothesis. The arguments follow, in every case accompanied by a citation as a talisman against any possible charge that we are setting up straw men:[11] (i) slaves are notoriously inefficient and unwilling workers; (ii) slave

[11] (i) J. E. Cairnes, *The Slave Power* (New York: Follett Foster & Co., 1863), pp. 44 50; F. L. Olmsted, *The Cotton Kingdom* (New York: Mason Bros., 1861), pp. 100–110 (1953 ed.; New York: A. A. Knopf); W. A. Lewis, *Theory of Economic Growth* (Homewood, Ill.: Richard D. Irwin, Inc., 1955), pp. 107–8; (ii) U. B. Phillips, *Life and Labor in the Old South* (Boston: Little, Brown & Co., 1935), pp. 174–75; (iii) U. B. Phillips, "The Economic Cost of Slaveholding in the Cotton-Belt," *Political Science Quarterly*, XX (1905), 257–75; (iv) Lewis, *op. cit.*, pp. 111–13; (v) J. S. Duesenberry, "Some Aspects of the Theory of Economic Development," *Explorations in Entrepreneurial History*, III (1950), 9. This is, of course, intended only as a list of examples, chosen in the hope that they are particularly well stated.

property, unlike wage labor, must be supported in the years before and after the slave is economically productive; (iii) slaveholding absorbed plantation earnings; (iv) slave economies are constantly threatened by decline because they cannot in general maintain the number of slaves; and (v) capitalization of the labor force inhibits the efficient allocation of labor.

The first and second of these arguments are implicitly tested in the computation of the rate of return on slave capital. We are not concerned with efficiency per se, however that might be measured, or with the efficiency of slaves as opposed to free white laborers. The more sophisticated version of this efficiency argument—that slave ineptness forced the planters to use a particularly wasteful form of agriculture—is probably untestable because of the difficulties of identification where impetus or motives are being considered. It might be suggested as a partial answer, however, that extensive farming was not peculiarly a characteristic of slave agriculture or even of plantation cotton culture. It was common to all North American colonial agriculture and, as late as the end of the nineteenth century, was reputed to be characteristic of farming in the Northwest wheat lands. It is, generally, a salient feature of agriculture where labor is scarce relative to land.[12] But, insofar as slaves were inefficient, the inefficiency must be reflected in the returns computed in our model. Similarly, the costs of maintaining slaves in infancy and dotage are accounted for in our cost of production.

The third argument—that the South lost from the payment of interest and the constant enhancement of prices (and, therefore, overcapitalization of the labor force)—rests in part upon two misapprehensions, attributable to U. B. Phillips: (1) that capitalization involves a net loss through the payment of interest and (2) that slaves were, somehow, a fictitious form of wealth. We have already shown that slave capital earned returns at least equal to those earned by other contemporary forms of capital. For the overcapitalization part of the argument, it remains to be shown that slave prices did not run away from cotton values.

The last two of the assertions state the negative of our principal secondary hypothesis, which is that an efficient market system existed for the supply of slaves to the rapidly growing cotton industry of the Southwest from the exhausted land of the Old South. It will be shown below that the slave population, in all but the Louisiana sugar area, more than reproduced itself. It will be further shown that the border states were not being depleted to provide for western needs but that only the natural increase was being exported. Finally, avoiding the emotion-wracked testimony of the time, we will attempt to demonstrate the existence of regional specialization and an efficient market by comparing the demographic composition of the cotton and border states and by examining the price behavior in the market for Negro slaves.

A. THE REPRODUCTION OF THE SLAVE LABOR FORCE

The history of slavery is full of examples of slave economies which could not reproduce their population and collapsed because of a failure of supply. Frequently, as in the Roman case, the supply was dependent upon a steady flow of military prisoners. The Augustan peace and the stabilization of the borders of the empire are credited with the de-

[12] M. B. Hammond, *The Cotton Industry* (New York, 1897), p. 82. See also *United States Patent Office Report* (*Agriculture*), *1852* (Washington, D.C., 1853), p. 374.

cline of Roman slavery for this reason. Similarly, the labor supply in the Caribbean sugar islands could be maintained only by importation. It is generally argued that slavery disappeared from Jamaica because of the inability of the slave population to reproduce itself once the slave trade had been closed and not because of abolition in 1834.

By contrast, the ante bellum cotton-slave economy of the southern states managed to maintain and allocate its labor supply by a system of regional specialization which produced slaves on the worn-out land of the Old South and the border states for export to the high-yield cotton land of the Mississippi and Red River valleys. For the whole nation the Negro rate of increase in the six decades before the Civil War was only slightly below the rate for the white population; for most of the period, the slave rate was very much above that for free Negroes. In the South the disparity between Negro and white rates of increase is in favor of the Negro rate; considering the relative rates of immigration of whites and Negroes after the first decade of the nineteenth century, the discrepancy in natural increase is even more striking. The evidence in Table 12 does not admit of any doubt that the slave population was capable of producing a steady supply of labor for the plantation economy.[13]

TABLE 12

PERCENTAGE DECENNIAL INCREASE IN WHITE AND NEGRO POPULATION, 1790–1860

Census Year	Increase during Preceding Ten Years				
			Negro		
	Total	White	Total	Slave	Free
1800....	35.1	35.8	32.3	28.1	82.2
1810....	36.4	36.1	37.5	33.1	71.9
1820....	33.1	34.2	28.6	29.1	25.3
1830....	33.5	33.9	31.4	30.6	36.8
1840....	32.7	34.7	23.4	23.8	20.9
1850....	35.9	37.7	26.6	28.8	12.5
1860....	35.6	37.7	22.1	23.4	12.3

Source: Bureau of the Census, *Negro Population in the United States, 1790–1915* (Washington, D.C., 1918), Tables 2 (chap. ii) and 1 (chap. v) and pp. 25 and 53. The sharp declines in the rate of increase for slaves in the decades ending in 1840 and 1860 probably reflect the generation cycle following the increase in importations, mostly of mature Negroes, in the years just prior to 1808.

B. SLAVE MARKETS AND ALLOCATION

The more important issue, however, is whether or not the slave force could be allocated efficiently. The natural rate of increase was more than sufficient in the Old South to meet the needs of agriculture in the region, but in the West it was less than sufficient to meet the demands for increased cotton production. By direct export and by the migration of planters with their work forces, the eastern areas supplied the needs of the Southwest. In every decade before the Civil War, the increase of slaves in the cotton states was much above and in the Atlantic and border states much below the rate of increase for the whole slave population. Indeed, in the decades ending in 1840 and 1860, the net rate of population increase in the Old South was only slightly above the level sufficient to maintain the population at a constant level, 4.5 per cent and 7.1 per cent (see Table 13). From 1790 to 1850 the increase of slaves in the Atlantic states was just 2 per cent per annum, while in the Gulf states (including Florida), Arkansas, and Tennessee the rate was 18 per cent per annum. A rough but probably conservative estimate of the export from the selling states between 1820 and 1860 is given by W. H. Collins. Taking the difference between the average natural increase and the actual

[13] See Bureau of the Census, *Negro Population in the United States, 1790–1915* (Washington, D.C., 1918); Gray, *op. cit.*, chap. xxviii; Cairnes, *op. cit.*, chap. iv; E. Halle, *Baumwollproduktion und Pflanzungswirtschaft* (Leipzig, 1897), Vol. I, Book III, 5.3.

rate in the selling states, Collins arrived at the following estimates:[14]

1820–30	124,000
1830–40	265,000
1840–50	146,000
1850–60	207,000

Collins estimated that at least three-fifths of the removals from the border states were due to emigration to the Southwest rather than to export. While this has little bearing upon the issue of allocative efficiency, it does have significance for the corollary assertion that the slaveowners of the border states, consciously or unconsciously, were engaged in a specialized breeding operation, producing chattel labor for the growing Southwest. In 1836 the *Virginia Times* estimated that, "of the number of slaves exported [from Virginia], not more than one-third have been sold, the others being carried by their masters, who have removed."[15] Ruffin supposed that the annual sale in 1859 "already exceed in number all the increase in slaves in Virginia by procreation."[16] Bancroft goes beyond these estimates and states that "in the 'fifties, when the extreme prejudice against the interstate traders had abated and their inadequate supplies were eagerly purchased, fully 70 per cent of the slaves removed from the Atlantic and the border slave states to the Southwest were taken after purchase or with a view to sale, that is, were the objects of slave-trading."[17] Whatever the accuracy of these several estimates, which range from two-fifths to four-fifths of total exports of slaves from the border and the Atlantic states, it is clear that sales of slaves provided an important capital gain for the exporting states. There is ample documentary evidence that planters in the Old South were aware of this, that some welcomed it and depended upon it, and that others were fearful of its effect upon the agriculture of the area and upon the tenability of slavery. Some spoke frankly about Virginia as a "breeding state," though the reply to such allegations was generally

TABLE 13

PERCENTAGE RATE OF POPULATION INCREASE, BY RACE, IN THE COTTON AND BORDER STATES, 1790–1860

Decade Ending	Cotton States* White	Cotton States* Negro	Border States† White	Border States† Negro
1800	42.9	47.4	27.9	24.4
1810	37.5	61.3	23.5	23.4
1820	38.8	48.0	19.5	15.5
1830	40.0	46.8	19.0	14.0
1840	31.3	37.6	21.1	4.5
1850	34.1	35.6	34.5	11.0
1860	27.6	29.0	39.2	7.1

Source: Ernst von Halle, *Baumwollproduktion und Pflanzungswirtschaft in den Nordamerikanischen Sudstaaten* (Leipzig, 1897), p. 132. His sources were Tucker, *Progress of the United States* (to 1840), *Census of Population* (1850 and after), and H. Gannett, *Statistics of the Negroes in the United States*.

* North Carolina, South Carolina, Georgia, Florida, Alabama, Mississippi, Louisiana, Texas, Arkansas, and Tennessee.

† Delaware, Maryland, District of Columbia, Virginia, West Virginia, Kentucky, and Missouri.

[14] W. H. Collins, *The Domestic Slave Trade of the Southern States* (New York, 1904), chap. iii. In the first decade the selling states include Virginia, Maryland, Delaware, North Carolina, Kentucky, and the District of Columbia; the buying states are assumed to be South Carolina, Georgia, Alabama, Mississippi, Tennessee, and Missouri. In 1830, Florida, and in 1850, Texas were added to the buying group. Tennessee, Missouri, and North Carolina are very uncertain assignments, since these states were far from homogeneous slave-marketing areas; some parts imported, while other parts exported, during the period (cf. Halle, *op. cit.*, pp. 282 ff., and Frederic Bancroft, *Slave Trading in the Old South* [Baltimore: J. H. Furst, 1931], chap. xviii, for similar estimates, consistent with those given by Collins).

[15] Quoted in *Slavery and the Internal Slave Trade in the United States of North America* (London, 1841) (by the Executive Committee of the American Anti-Slavery Society), p. 13. On the same page the authors assert that four-fifths or more of the slaves brought into the buying states are supplied by the internal slave trade.

[16] Edmund Ruffin, *DeBow's Review*, XXVI (1859), 650.

[17] Bancroft, *op. cit.*, p. 398.

an indignant denial. Whether systematically bred or not, the natural increase of the slave force was an important, probably the most important, product of the more exhausted soil of the Old South.

The existence of such specialization is evident in the demographic composition of the cotton and breeding areas and in the price behavior in the markets for slaves. Table 14 demonstrates that the selling states contained, in 1850 and 1860, a greater proportion of children under fifteen years and a substantially greater proportion of slaves above the age of fifty than did the buying states. While the disproportions are not great enough to characterize the selling states as a great nursery, the age composition is in the direction which our hypothesis would lead one to expect. The relationship between the prices of men and women in the slave market, when compared with the ratio of hiring rates for male and female field hands, gives an even stronger indication that the superior usefulness of females of breeding age was economically recognized. The relative hiring rates for men and women in 1860, shown in Table 15, can be taken as a measure of their relative values in the field.[18]

To compare to these rates, we have purchase prices of male and female slaves, in the same markets, in 1859 and 1860. The purchase prices should reflect the relative usefulness of the sexes for field work. More than this, however, if there is any additional value to slave women—for breeding purposes, presumably—there should be a premium in the form of a narrower price differential than is found in the hiring rates. The prices shown in Table 16 are taken from Table A in the Appendix. Whenever possible, 1860 is used; wherever necessary, 1859. Table 16 includes age designations and, when available, a description of the grade or class represented in the average price.[19] This evidence is a striking con-

TABLE 14

SLAVE POPULATION BY AGE

(Per Cent)

Age (Years)	1860 Total	1860 Selling States*	1860 Buying States†	1850 Total	1850 Selling States*	1850 Buying States†
Under 15	44.8	45.6	43.8	44.9	45.6	44.3
15–19	11.4	11.5	11.4	11.1	11.3	11.0
20–29	17.6	16.5	18.9	18.0	17.0	18.9
30–39	11.7	10.7	11.8	11.3	10.5	12.1
20–49	36.4	34.4	38.1	36.4	34.6	38.1
50 and over	7.5	8.5	6.7	7.5	8.5	6.6

Source: J. C. G. Kennedy, *Population of the United States in 1860* (Washington, D.C., 1864), "Classified Population," Tables No. 1, by state; J. D. B. DeBow, *Statistical View of the United States, . . . Being a Compendium of the Seventh Census* (Washington, D.C., 1854), Part II, Table LXXXII, pp. 89–90.

* Virginia, Maryland, Delaware, South Carolina, Missouri, Kentucky, District of Columbia.

† Georgia, Alabama, Mississippi, Florida, Texas, Louisiana.

NOTE.—The exclusion of Tennessee and North Carolina is explained in n. 14. Missouri was included with the selling group because of its apparent net selling position in this period.

[18] The rates are quoted in Hammond, *op. cit.*, p. 90, from *Report of the Commissioner of Agriculture, 1866* (Washington, D.C., 1867), p. 116. Three Virginia newspaper quotations in G. M. Weston, *Who Are and Who May Be Slaves in the United States* (undated pamphlet), give ratios ranging between 2 and 2.5, supporting Hammond's estimate. There is a possible overestimate in these ratios, if they are to be used to infer relative usefulness in the field, since some allowance was probably made for time lost for delivery by pregnant females. No evidence has been found on this point, however.

[19] With one exception—the South Carolina, 1860, comparison—the pairings are taken from single sales. In addition, the pairings are made, as far as possible, with slaves of apparently comparable

firmation of the validity of the model. In every case but one, the purchase-price differential is narrower than the hiring-rate differential. The price structure clearly reflects the added value of females due to their ability to generate capital gains.

TABLE 15

ANNUAL HIRING RATES FOR MALE AND FEMALE SLAVES (INCLUDING RATIONS AND CLOTHING), BY STATES, 1860

State	Men	Women	Ratio (Men:Women)
Virginia	$105	$ 46	2.28
North Carolina	110	49	2.25
South Carolina	103	55	1.87
Georgia	124	75	1.65
Florida	139	80	1.74
Alabama	138	89	1.55
Mississippi	166	100	1.66
Louisiana	171	120	1.43
Texas	166	109	1.52
Arkansas	170	108	1.57
Tennessee	121	63	1.92

It is especially interesting in this regard to note that the price ratios in Virginia and South Carolina, the two breeding states represented in the list, show practically no differential. This evidence clearly shows that the Old South recognized in the market the value of its function as the slave-breeding area for the cotton-raising West.

TABLE 16

SELECTED PRICES OF MALE AND FEMALE SLAVES, 1859 AND 1860

State (Year)	Age	Condition	Male Price	Female Price	Ratio
Virginia (1859)	17–20	Best	$1,350–$1,425	$1,275–$1,325	1.07
South Carolina	....	Prime	$1,325	....	1.03
	....	Wench	......	$1,283	
South Carolina (1859)	....	Field hand	$1,555	......	.91
	....	Girl	......	$1,705	
Georgia	21	Best field hand	$1,900	......	.88
	17	(9 mo. inf.)	......	[$2,150]	
Georgia (1859)	....	Prime, young	$1,300	......	1.04
	....	Cotton hand, houseservant	......	$1,250	
Alabama (1859)	19	....	$1,635	......	1.37
	18, 18, 8	....	......	$1,193	
Mississippi	....	No. 1 field hand	$1,625	$1,450	1.12
Texas	21, 15	....	$2,015	$1,635	1.23
Texas (1859)	17, 14	....	$1,527	$1,403	1.09

quality. The Virginia and Mississippi quotations are from average-price listings and are probably most useful for present purposes.

C. THE "OVERCAPITALIZATION" OF THE LABOR FORCE

The aspect of slave economics that causes the most confusion and outright error is that which relates to the capitalization, and, in the ante bellum southern case, the presumed overcapitalization, of slave labor. Phillips speaks of an "irresistible tendency to overvalue and overcapitalize" and argues that slaveholding had an unlimited capacity for absorbing the planters' earnings through the continual payment of interest and the enhancement of prices. For the Cotton Belt this was presumably aggregated into a continuous public drain of wealth, first to England and New England and, later, to the upper South.[20] Moreover, a series of writers from Max Weber down to the most recent theorists of economic growth have argued that capitalization tends to rigidify the pattern of employment. "Free labor is necessary to make free transfers of labor possible. A production

[20] Phillips, "The Economic Cost of Slaveholding in the Cotton-Belt," *op. cit.*, pp. 271 ff.

organization cannot be very flexible if it has to engage in the purchase or sale of slaves every time it changes its output."[21] But this is really a question of how good the market is; no one, after all, claims that manufacturing is made suicidally inflexible by the fact that expanding sectors must buy the capitalized future earnings of machinery. There are three issues to be distinguished in this argument: first, the alleged tendency toward overcapitalization; second, the inflexibility of chattel labor and the difficulty of allocating it, geographically and industrially; and, third, the loss of wealth.

First, was the southerner his own victim in an endless speculative inflation of slave prices? The assertion of an irresistible tendency to overvalue and overcapitalize must mean that he was so trapped, if it means anything. Phillips answered the question by comparing the price of cotton with the price of prime field hands, year by year. He found, or believed he found, a permanent movement toward overcapitalization inherent in American slaveholding. But speculative overexpansion is capable of reversal: from the inflation of 1837 to the bottom of the depression in 1845, slave prices fell as sharply as cotton prices. If the rise from that lower turning point is a demonstration of speculative mania, it was a mania solidly based on the increase in the value of the crop per hand, owing to the concentration of production in more fertile areas, the greater efficiency of the American-born slaves, lowered transportation costs, and the development of new high-yield varieties of cotton from the fourth decade of the century on.[22] Finally, the choice of the initial period in Phillips' analysis exaggerates the decline in cotton prices relative to the price of slaves: at the turn of the century the demand for cotton was increasing rapidly, supporting remarkably high prices, while the unrestricted African slave trade kept domestic slave prices well below the level that might be expected in view of the level of profits. Table 17 and Chart 1 demonstrate the relationship among slave prices, cotton prices, and the value of cotton output per slave (of field work age, ten to fifty-four). Several things become clear in this comparison. To begin, the relationship between slave and cotton prices is significant for Phillips' purposes only if there is no increase in productivity. While he is struck by the fact that slave prices rise more rapidly than cotton prices in the long upswing starting in the early 1840's, it is equally striking to observe that (New Orleans) slave prices rose about one and one-half times between the low point in 1843–45 to 1860, while values of cotton production per hand rose more than three times from the low in 1842. This was recognized in the *New Orleans Daily Crescent* in 1860, as follows:

> Nor do we agree with our contemporaries who argue that a speculative demand is the unsubstantial basis of the advance in the price of slaves. . . . It is our impression that the great demand for slaves in the Southwest will keep up the prices as it caused their advance in the first place, and that the rates are not a cent above the real value of the laborer who is to be engaged in tilling the fertile lands of a section of the country which yields the planter nearly double the crop that the fields of the Atlantic States do.[23]

Furthermore, it would appear that slave prices fluctuate less than do cotton prices. This and the less clear-cut lag of the slave

[21] Duesenberry, *loc. cit.*

[22] Gray, *op. cit.*, chap. xxx; *DeBow's Review*, XVIII (1855), 332–34; Hammond, *op. cit.*, pp. 76–77, 113–19; T. P. Kettell, *Southern Wealth and Northern Profits* (New York, 1860), p. 48.

[23] Quoted in Phillips, *Life and Labor in the Old South*, p. 180. Having quoted this, Phillips, without offering any evidence, asserts: "But surely a peak was being shaped, whose farther side must have been a steep descent, whether in time of peace or war."

TABLE 17

VALUE OF COTTON PRODUCTION AND SLAVE POPULATION, 1802–60, NEW ORLEANS PRICES

Year	Crop (Thousands of Pounds)	Average Price (Cents per Pound)	Value (Thousands)	No. of Slaves, Aged 10–54 Years*	Crop Value per Slave	Price of Prime Field Hand	Crop Value per Hand per Dollar Slave Price
1802.......	55,000	0.147	$ 8,085	550,708	$ 14.68	$ 600	.02
1803.......	60,000	.150	9,000	568,932	15.82	600	.03
1804.......	65,000	.196	12,740	587,157	21.70	600	.04
1805.......	70,000	.233	16,310	605,381	26.94	600	.05
1806.......	80,000	.218	17,440	623,606	27.97	600	.05
1807.......	80,000	.164	13,120	641,831	20.44	600	.03
1808.......	75,000	.136	10,200	660,055	15.45	640	.02
1809.......	82,000	.136	11,152	678,280	16.44	780	.02
1810.......	85,000	.147	12,495	696,505	17.94	900	.02
1811.......	80,000	.089	7,120	717,376	9.93	860	.01
1813.......	75,000	.155	11,625	759,118	15.31	600	.03
1814.......	70,000	.169	11,830	779,989	15.17	650	.02
1815.......	100,000	.273	27,300	800,860	34.09	765	.05
1816.......	124,000	.254	31,496	821,731	38.33	880	.04
1817.......	130,000	.298	38,740	842,602	45.98	1,000	.05
1818.......	125,000	.215	26,875	863,473	31.12	1,050	.03
1819.......	167,000	.143	23,881	884,344	27.00	1,100	.03
1820.......	160,000	.152	24,320	905,215	26.88	970	.03
1821.......	180,000	.174	31,320	933,517	33.55	810	.04
1822.......	210,000	.115	24,150	961,818	25.11	700	.04
1823.......	185,000	.145	26,825	990,120	27.04	670	.04
1824.......	215,000	.179	38,485	1,018,421	37.99	700	.05
1825.......	255,000	.119	30,345	1,046,723	28.99	800	.04
1826.......	350,000	.093	32,550	1,075,024	30.28	840	.04
1827.......	316,900	.097	30,739	1,103,326	27.86	770	.04
1828.......	241,399	.098	23,657	1,131,627	20.91	770	.03
1829.......	296,812	.089	26,416	1,159,929	22.77	770	.03
1830.......	331,150	.084	27,817	1,208,034	23.03	810	.03
1831.......	354,247	.090	31,882	1,247,489	25.56	860	.03
1832.......	355,492	.100	35,549	1,275,061	27.88	900	.03
1833.......	374,653	.112	41,961	1,302,633	32.21	960	.03
1834.......	437,558	.155	67,821	1,330,206	50.99	1,000	.05
1835.......	460,338	.152	69,971	1,357,778	51.53	1,150	.05
1836.......	507,550	.133	67,504	1,385,350	46.79	1,250	.04
1837.......	539,669	.090	48,510	1,412,923	34.38	1,300	.03
1838.......	682,767	.124	84,663	1,440,495	58.77	1,220	.05
1839.......	501,708	.079	39,635	1,468,067	27.00	1,240	.02
1840.......	834,111	.091	75,904	1,507,779	50.34	1,020	.05
1841.......	644,172	.078	50,245	1,568,022	32.04	870	.04
1842.......	668,379	.057	38,098	1,611,269	23.65	750	.03
1843.......	972,960	.075	72,972	1,654,516	44.11	700	.06
1844.......	836,529	.055	46,009	1,697,762	27.10	700	.04
1845.......	993,719	.068	67,573	1,741,009	38.81	700	.06
1846.......	863,321	.099	85,469	1,784,256	47.90	750	.06
1847.......	766,599	.070	53,662	1,827,503	29.36	850	.04
1848.......	1,017,391	.058	59,009	1,870,750	31.54	950	.03
1849.......	1,249,985	.108	134,998	1,913,996	70.53	1,030	.07
1850.......	1,001,165	.117	117,136	1,979,059	59.19	1,100	.05
1851.......	1,021,048	.074	75,558	2,034,482	37.14	1,150	.03
1852.......	1,338,061	.091	121,764	2,080,554	58.53	1,200	.05
1853.......	1,496,302	.088	131,675	2,126,626	61.92	1,250	.05
1854.......	1,322,241	.084	111,068	2,172,698	51.12	1,310	.04
1855.......	1,294,463	.091	117,796	2,218,770	53.09	1,350	.04
1856.......	1,535,334	.124	190,381	2,264,843	84.06	1,420	.06
1857.......	1,373,619	.112	153,845	2,310,915	66.57	1,490	.05
1858.......	1,439,744	.115	165,571	2,356,988	70.25	1,580	.04
1859.......	1,796,455	.108	194,017	2,403,060	80.74	1,690	.05
1860.......	2,241,056	0.111	$248,757	2,460,648	$101.09	$1,800	.06

Source: *Crops:* Computed from the data on number of bales and average weight of bales in James L. Watkins, *Production and Price of Cotton for One Hundred Years* (U.S. Department of Agriculture, Miscellaneous Series, Bull. 9 [Washington, D.C., 1895]). *Price:* Gray, *op. cit.*, Table 41: "Weighted Yearly Averages and Monthly Prices in Cents per Pound of Short-Staple Cotton at New Orleans for the Crop Years 1802–1860." *Slaves:* Bureau of the Census, *Negro Population in the United States, 1790–1915*, "Slave and Free Colored Population at Each Census by Sections and Southern Divisions: 1790–1860," p. 55, and "Negro Population in Years Specified, Classified by Sex and Age Periods; 1830–1910," p. 166. *Slave prices:* Estimated visually from the chart "Approximate Prices of Prime Field Hands in Hundreds of Dollars per Head: . . . at New Orleans . . . ," in U. B. Phillips, *Life and Labor in the Old South* (Boston, 1935), p. 177.

* To estimate the slave population in the intercensal years, the increase over each decade was divided into equal parts and assigned to each year in the decade. The proportion of Negroes in the field-work age brackets (between the ages of ten and fifty-four) was .641 in 1860, .635 in 1850, .621 in 1840, and .610 in 1830. The census-year proportions at the beginning and end of each decade were averaged for use in the intervening years. For the years before 1830, an estimate of .60 was used. There is no implication that we have measured the number of field hands, but it should be noted that the range .60–.65 brackets several contemporary estimates of the proportion of the slave population employed in cotton agriculture (see, e.g., P. A. Morse, "Southern Slavery and the Cotton Trade," *De Bow's Review*, XXIII [1857], 475–82).

CHART I

SLAVE POPULATION AND PRICES AND THE VALUE OF COTTON PRODUCTION, 1802-60

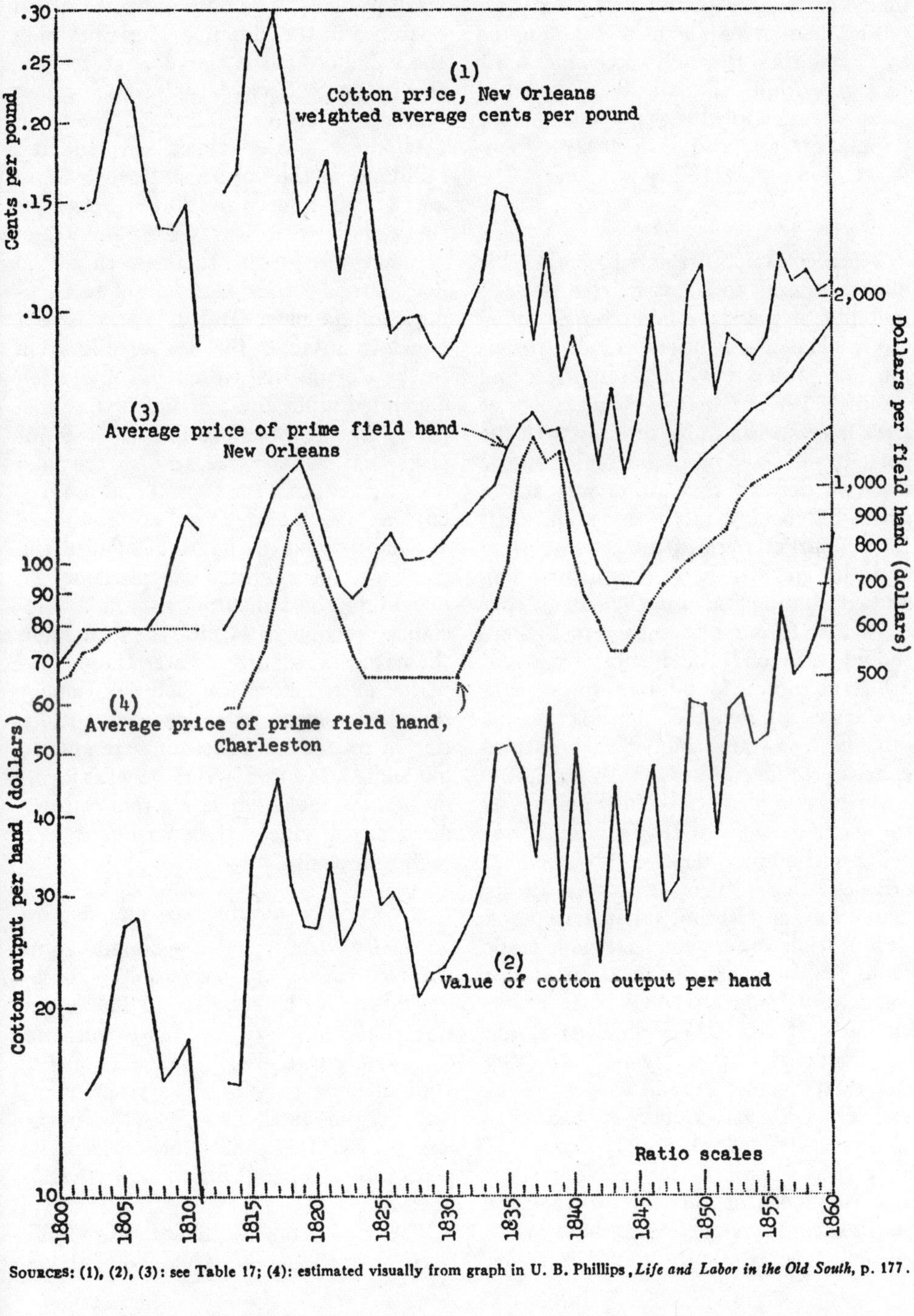

SOURCES: (1), (2), (3): see Table 17; (4): estimated visually from graph in U. B. Phillips, *Life and Labor in the Old South*, p. 177.

prices make it difficult to accept the image of unwary planters helplessly exposing themselves in a market dominated by speculators. It would make more sense to argue simply that the rising trend of slave prices coupled with a growing slave population is in and of itself strong evidence of the profitability of slavery.

D. THE EFFICIENCY OF ALLOCATION

The second point relates to geographic allocation and, to a lesser extent, to the mobility of the slave labor force among crops. The slave prices in all regions move very closely with cotton prices and products per hand. It is clear, too, that the eastern prices move directly with the cotton-area slave prices, although in the last two decades the rate of increase of prices fell behind in the breeding area. If the market were extremely imperfect and the transfer between the breeding and consuming states inefficient, in contradiction to our hypothesis, then there should be much less evidence of regional arbitrage than is found here. In response to the western demand, Virginia and the other eastern states shipped their natural increase to the cotton areas. Indeed, it is frequently argued that the transfer was too efficient and that the Old South was being continuously depressed by the high price of labor occasioned by western demand. Edmund Ruffin, particularly, took this position and argued that slave trade could not bring profits to Virginia but could result only in the paralysis of her industry. If true, this argument would be supported empirically by increasing real estate values on the western lands and decreasing values in the Atlantic and border states. That is, the chain of high cotton profits–high slave prices–increased cost of farming in the Old South should have depressed land prices in that area. Emigration, by reducing demand, should have meant more downward pressure. The only influence which operated in the direction of maintaining the value of land in the older states was the profit to be had from the increase and sale of slaves. Indeed, in 1850 and 1860, the value per acre of farm land and buildings in the border states was $7.18 and $12.33, and, in the Lower South for the same two census years, $4.99 and $8.54. Undoubtedly, the western cotton land earned a considerable rent in farming over the older land. It was this rent which maintained the flow of migration to the Cotton Belt. But that migration depended upon and supported the prosperity of the breeding states. It is not clear that slavery was able to continue only by skinning the topsoil and moving on, leaving exhausted land and low slave and land value in its wake. Quite the contrary, the evidence can plausibly be interpreted as indicating a unified, specialized economy in which the settlers on the naturally superior western lands (superior even before the deterioration of the older regions by single-crop cultivation of tobacco and cotton) were able to bid slave labor away from general farming and to make wholesale removal unnecessary, if indeed there had ever been such a necessity.

E. SLAVERY AND SOUTHERN ECONOMIC GROWTH

Finally, there are two economic arguments about slavery and potential southern growth to be considered. The assertion that slavery per se was inimical to economic growth rests in part upon the alleged inefficiency of slave labor in industrial pursuits and in part upon the loss of capital that might otherwise have gone into industrialization and diversification.

The inefficiency argument is not supported very securely. There were slaves employed in cotton factories throughout the South. Slaves were used in the coal mines and in the North Carolina lumbering operations. In the ironworks at Richmond and on the Cumberland River, slaves comprised a majority of the labor force. Southern railroads were largely built by southern slaves. Crop diversification, or the failure to achieve diversification, appears to have been a problem of entrepreneurship rather than of the difficulties of training slaves. In the face of the demand for cotton and the profits to be had from specializing in this single crop, it is hardly difficult to explain the single-minded concentration of the planter.[24]

In what ways was slavery allegedly responsible for the drain of capital from the South? The lack of diversification, to the extent of a failure even to provide basic supplies, made necessary the import of much food and virtually all manufactured articles from the North. But half of this assertion, the argument that laid the responsibility for the single-crop culture upon slavery, has been found questionable already.

The major avenues by which wealth is said to have been drained from the cotton states were the excessive use of credit (through dependence upon factors' services) and the "absorption" of capital in slaves. The dependence upon advances was, in effect, a dependence upon the New York or London money market and was, therefore, an impediment to the accumulation of capital in the South. Good crop years bring the temptation to expand production; bad years do not bring any release from the factors. But resort to factoring is characteristic of speculative, commercial agriculture, whether or not the labor force is organized in slavery. It is also frequently argued that slavery gave southern planters a taste for extravagant, wasteful display, causing the notorious lack of thrift and the relative lack of economic development, compared to that experienced in the North and West. This is a doubtful inference, at best. Slavery did not make the Cavalier any more than slavery invented speculation in cotton. However, insofar as successful slave management required military posture and discipline, the southerner's expensive image of himself as a *grand seigneur* was encouraged. It is beyond the scope of this paper to offer hypotheses about the reasons for the relative degrees of entrepreneurship in Charleston and Boston; in this context it is sufficient to state that slavery per se does not seem to have been responsible for the excessive reliance upon factoring and external sources of credit.[25]

There remains only the absorption of capital in slaves to set the responsibility for lack of growth in the South upon the peculiar institution. Earnings that might have gone out of the South to bring in investment goods were fixed in the form of chattel labor. For the early years, during the external slave trade, there is some plausibility to this argument, though it is difficult to see how the capitalization of an income stream, excellent by contemporary standards, can

[24] See Robert R. Russel, *Economic Aspects of Southern Sectionalism, 1840–1861* (Urbana, Ill., 1923), esp. pp. 54–64, and "Slavery and Southern Economic Progress," *Journal of Southern History*, IV (February, 1938), 34–54. See also Gray, *op. cit.*, pp. 458–61, 940–42, and Hammond, *op. cit.*, pp. 40–44, 94–96.

[25] Hammond, *op. cit.*, pp. 107–12; Russel, *op. cit.*, pp. 49 ff.; M. B. Hammond, "Agricultural Credit and Crop Mortgages," in *The South in the Building of the Nation* (Richmond, Va., 1909), V, 457–61; Alfred H. Stone, "The Cotton Factorage System of the Southern States," *American Historical Review*, XX (1915), 557–65. For an excellent discussion of the seigneurial impediments to entrepreneurship see W. J. Cash, *The Mind of the South* (New York, 1941), pp. 42–70.

be said to count as a loss of wealth. In the later years there was, except to the extent that northern or English bankers drew off the interest, a redistribution of wealth only within the slave states: from the cotton lands back to the less profitable field agriculture of the older section. And, to the extent that the old planting aristocracy used the profits to maintain the real or fancied magnificence of the preceding century, capital was absorbed. Slavery made this possible, so long as the natural increase could be shipped off. But, as Russel pointed out, slavery also made the profits in the cotton fields and the resultant demand for eastern hands. We are left with the conclusion that, except insofar as it made speculation in cotton possible on a grander scale than would otherwise have been the case and thereby weakened whatever pressure there might have been for diversification, capitalization of the labor force did not of itself operate against southern development.

IV. CONCLUSION

In sum, it seems doubtful that the South was forced by bad statesmanship into an unnecessary war to protect a system which must soon have disappeared because it was economically unsound. This is a romantic hypothesis which will not stand against the facts.

On the basis of the computation of the returns to capital in our model of the ante bellum southern economy and the demonstration of the efficiency of the regional specialization, the following conclusions are offered:

1. Slavery was profitable to the whole South, the continuing demand for labor in the Cotton Belt insuring returns to the breeding operation on the less productive land in the seaboard and border states. The breeding returns were necessary, however, to make the plantation operations on the poorer lands as profitable as alternative contemporary economic activities in the United States. The failure of southern agriculture on these poorer lands in the post bellum period is probably attributable, in the main, to the loss of these capital gains on breeding and not, as is so often suggested, to either the relative inefficiency of the tenant system that replaced the plantations or the soil damage resulting from war operations. These factors were unquestionably contributing elements to the difficulties of post bellum southern agriculture, but they were of relatively small quantitative importance compared with the elimination of slave-breeding returns.

2. There was nothing necessarily self-destructive about the profits of the slave economy. Neither the overcapitalization argument nor the assertion that slavery must have collapsed because the slaves would not reproduce themselves is tenable. Slave prices did not outpace productivity, and the regional slave price structure would imply a workable transfer mechanism rather than the contrary.

3. Continued expansion of slave territory was both possible and, to some extent, necessary. The maintenance of profits in the Old South depended upon the expansion, extensive or intensive, of slave agriculture into the Southwest. This is sufficient to explain the interest of the Old South in secession and does away with the necessity to fall back upon arguments of statesmanship or quixotism to explain the willingness to fight for the peculiar institution.

4. The available productive surplus from slavery might have been used for economic development or, as in totalitarian regimes in this century, for militarism. In spite of this good omen for

development, southern investment and industrialization lagged. It is hard to explain this except on the social ground that entrepreneurship could not take root in the South or on the economic ground that the South did not really own the system but merely operated it. Furthermore, the American experience clearly suggests that slavery is not, from the strict economic standpoint, a deterrent to industrial development and that its elimination may take more than the workings of "inexorable economic forces." Although profitability cannot be offered as a sufficient guaranty of the continuity of southern slavery, the converse argument that slavery must have destroyed itself can no longer rest upon allegations of unprofitability or upon assumptions about the impossibility of maintaining and allocating a slave labor force. To the extent, moreover, that profitability is a necessary condition for the continuation of a private business institution in a free-enterprise society, slavery was not untenable in the ante bellum American South. Indeed, economic forces often may work toward the continuation of a slave system, so that the elimination of slavery may depend upon the adoption of harsh political measures. Certainly that was the American experience.

APPENDIX

TABLE A

Tabulation of Reported Slave Transactions and Valuations

Year	State	Sex	Age	Grade or Condition	No. in Sale	Average Price	Source, Page*
1800	S.C.			Prime field hands		$ 500	P(PSQ)
	Ga.			Prime field hands		450	P(PSQ)
1805	S.C.			Prime field hands		550	P(PSQ)
	Ga.			Prime field hands		550	P(PSQ)
1808	S.C.			Prime field hands		550	P(PSQ)
	Ga.			Prime field hands		650	P(PSQ)
1810	S.C.			Prime field hands		500	P(PSQ)
	Va.			Prime field hands		500	G.665
	La.			Prime field hands (max.)		900	G.665
1813	S.C.			Prime field hands		450	P(PSQ)
	Ga.			Prime field hands		450	P(PSQ)
1818	Ga.			Prime field hands		1,000	P(PSQ)
1819	S.C.			Prime field hands		850	P(PSQ)
	Va.			Prime field hands		700	P(ANS).370
	La.			Prime field hands		1,100	P(ANS).370
	La.			African, "brute Negro"		400– 500	G.664
	La.			Intelligent dom. Negro		1,000	G.664
1820	S.C.			Prime field hand		725	P(PSQ)
1821	Ga.			Prime field hand		700	P(PSQ)
1822	S.C.			Prime field hand		650	P(PSQ)
	Va.	F		Mother of 3	1	300	B.78
		M	4		1	200	B.78
		M	2		1	150	B.78
		F	1		1	75	B.78
1825	S.C.			Prime field hand	1	500	P(PSQ)
	Va.	F		Mother of 3 (see above)	1	200	B.78
		M	7		1	200	B.78
		M	5		1	125	B.78
		F	4		1	90	B.78
1826	S.C.			Prime field hand		475	P(PSQ)
	Ga.			Prime field hand		800	P(PSQ)
1828	S.C.			Prime field hand		450	P(PSQ)
	Ga.			Prime field hand		700	P(PSQ)

* SOURCES

P(PSQ): U. B. Phillips, "The Slave Labor Problem in the Charleston District," *Political Science Quarterly*, XXII, No. 3 (1907), 436.

P(Doc. II): U. B. Phillips, "Plantation and Frontier, 1649–1863," in *A Documentary History of American Industrial Society*, Vol. II (Cleveland, 1910).

P(ANS): U. B. Phillips, *American Negro Slavery* (New York, 1918).

G: Lewis Gray, *History of Agriculture in the United States to 1860* (Washington, D.C., 1933).

B: Frederic Bancroft, *Slave Trading in the Old South* (Baltimore, 1931).

O: Frederick Law Olmsted, *The Cotton Kingdom* (New York, 1953).

GMW: George Melville Weston, *Who Are and Who May Be Slaves in the United States* (pamphlet, undated, unsigned).

TABLE A—*Continued*

Year	State	Sex	Age	Grade or Condition	No. in Sale	Average Price	Source, Page*
1829.......	S.C.	......	....	Prime field hand	....	$ 475	P(PSQ)
	Va., Md.	M	18–24	First	Bid	400– 450	B.30
		F	18–24	First	Bid.	280	B.30
	Ala., La., Miss.	......	18–24	First	Est.	"Nearly twice as much"	B.30
1830.......	S.C.	......	....	Prime field hands	....	450	P(PSQ)
	La.	......	....	Sugar hands, 5:3 ratio, working: children and aged	....	550	G.542
1832.......	S.C.	......	....	Prime field hand	....	500	P(PSQ)
	Miss.	......	....	Price range: $300–$1,000	30	500	B.308
1835.......	S.C.	......	....	Prime field hand	....	750	P(PSQ)
	Ga.	......	....	Prime field hand	....	900	P(PSQ)
	Md.	M	18–25	Likely	Est.	500– 650	B.39
		F	18–25	Likely	Est.	300– 500	B.39
		F	18–25	Best field hand	Est.	300– 400	B.39
		F	7	Servant	Est.	250	B.39
	S.C.	......	....	En route	75	533	B.55
	D.C.	......	1	....	1	100	B.55
		M	7– 8	....	1	400	B.55
		M	18	....	1	750	B.55
		F	....	....	2	650	B.55
		M	....	First field hand	Est.	900	B.55
		M	....	Mechanic	Est.	1,200	B.55
	Ky.	M	....	"Boy"	1	350	B.209
		M	7	....	1	630	B.209
		F	....	"Young"	1	710	B.209
	Miss.	M	23	Coachman	1	950	B.303
		F	....	Seamstress	1	750	B.303
		M	....	Field hand	Est.	800	B.308
		F	....	Field hand	Est.	600	B.308
		......	....	Bodyservant	Est.	1,000	B.308
		M	....	Good mechanic	Est.	900–2,000	B.308
		F	....	Seamstress	Est.	700–1,000	B.308
1836.......	S.C.	......	....	Prime field hand	....	1,100	P(PSQ)
	Tenn.	......	....	(Aver. Tax Value)	....	414	G.666
1837.......	S.C.	......	....	Prime field hand	....	1,200	P(PSQ)
	Ga.	......	....	Prime field hand	....	1,300	P(PSQ)
	Va.	......	....	Prime field hand	....	1,000–1,200	G.666
	Tenn.	F( )	(3 mos.)	....	2	[1,350]	B.207
	La.	F( )	(2)	Young mother	2	[700]	B.336
1844.......	S.C.	......	....	Prime field hand	....	500	P(PSQ)
	Ga.	......	....	Prime field hand	....	600	P(PSQ)

TABLE A—*Continued*

Year	State	Sex	Age	Grade or Condition	No. in Sale	Average Price	Source, Page*
1846.......	S.C.	......	....	Prime field hand	....	$ 650	P(PSQ)
	Ala.	......	....	Mostly boys and women, equal to 10 good hands	13	446	G.542
1851.......	S.C.	......	....	Prime field hand	....	750	P(PSQ)
	Ga.	......	....	Prime field hand	....	1,050	P(PSQ)
1852.......	S.C.	......	....	Prime field hand	....	800	P(PSQ)
				Incl. aged and infirm	42	400	B.167
	Va.	......	....	Not above ordinary	21	553	B.350
					of which:		
		M	....	No trade	1	1,028	B.350
		F( )	(10 mos.)	....	2	[950]	B.350
		F	11	....	1	600	B.350
	Ala.	......	....	Plantation sale	....	700	B.350
1853.......	S.C.	......	....	Prime field hand	....	900	P(PSQ)
	Ga.	......	....	Prime field hand	....	1,200	P(PSQ)
	Va.	M	18–25	Best	....	1,200–1,300	O.595
		M	18–25	Fair	....	950–1,050	O.595
		M	....	Boys, 5′ tall	....	850– 950	O.595
		M	....	Boys, 4′8″ tall	....	700– 800	O.595
		M	....	Boys, 4′5″ tall	....	500– 600	O.595
		M	....	Boys, 4′ tall	....	375– 450	O.595
		F	....	Young women	....	800–1,000	O.595
		F	....	Girls, 5′ tall	....	780– 850	O.595
		F	....	Girls 4′9″ tall	....	700– 750	O.595
		F	....	Girls, 4′ tall	....	350– 450	O.595
		M	45–50	Scarred back	1	460	B.107
		......	....	(Unscarred, est.)	....	(750– 800)	B.107
		F( )	30(2)	....	2	[650]	O.41
1854.......	Ky.	F	....	Very handsome mulatto	1	1,600	B.131
	Ala.	......	Ten under 7	"Highest prices"	18	788	B.350
					of which:		
		M	7	....	1	760	B.350
		M	12	....	1	710	B.350
		M	17	....	1	1,374	B.350
		F( )	37(2–7)	....	7	[5,000]	B.350
1855.......	S.C.	......	....	Prime field hands	....	900	P(PSQ)
1856.......	Va.	M	....	Ordinary field hand	2	1,467	GMW
		M	70	....	1	100	GMW
		M	55	....	1	1,610	GMW
		F	20	Likely, "highest pr."	1	1,700	GMW
		M	12	....	1	1,518	GMW
		F	....	Prime field hand	Est.	1,050	GMW
		M	....	Prime field hand	Est.	1,250–1,500	GMW

TABLE A—*Continued*

Year	State	Sex	Age	Grade or Condition	No. in Sale	Average Price	Source, Page*
1856.......	Tenn.	......	....	Aver. reported tax value	....	$ 689	G.666
	Mo.	M	30–45	Common crop hands	5	1,380	GMW
		F	....	....	....	800–900	GMW
		F	....	Houseservant	1	1,040	GMW
		F	....	Houseservant	1	1,753	GMW
		F	Over middle age	....	2	700	GMW
	Ga.	F	15	....	1	1,280	B.83
		F	14	....	1	1,280	B.83
		F	14	....	1	1,305	B.83
		F	16	....	1	1,525	B.83
		F	18	Pregnant	1	1,500	B.83
		F( )	20	....	2	[1,840]	B.83
		M	18	....	1	1,290	B.83
		M	22	....	1	1,500	B.83
	La.	M	....	"Prices never been equalled"	....	1,500–1,635	GMW
		F	....	....	....	1,200–1,550	GMW
1857.......	Md.	F	14	....	1	900	B.79
		F	....	Small girl	1	880	B.79
		F	....	Small girl	1	350	B.79
	Va.	F	10	....	1	800	B.116
		......	....	....	35	700	B.116
		F	7	....	1	725	B.357
		F	12	....	1	770	B.357
	Mo.	F	9	....	1	805	B.79
		M	5	....	1	487	B.79
		M	2	....	1	325	B.79
	La.	F( )	20(3, 4)	....	2	[2,505]	B.83
		F( )	30(3)	....	2	[1,610]	B.83
		F( )	35(2)	....	2	[1,325]	B.83
	Tex.	M	22	....	3	1,855	B.356
		5M, 5F	11	....	10	716	B.358
1858.......	S.C.	......	....	Prime field hand	....	950	P(PSQ)
	Ga.	M	....	....	2	1,350	B.362
		......	....	....	"Several"	1,100	B.362
		4M, 5F	....	....	9	1,170	B.362
	La.	......	....	....	7	1,538	B.356
					of which:		
		M	36	....	1	1,835	B.356
		M	26	....	1	2,050	B.356
		M	50	....	1	1,225	B.356
		F	20	....	1	1,300	B.356

TABLE A—*Continued*

Year	State	Sex	Age	Grade or Condition	No. in Sale	Average Price	Source, Page*
1859.......	S.C.	......	....	Prime field hand	....	1,100	P(PSQ)
	Ga.	......	....	Prime field hand	....	$ 1,650	P(PSQ)
	Va.	F	10	....	....	1,151	B.79
				Mostly children	39	566	B.79
		M	20–26	Number 1	Est.	1,450–1,500	B.117
		M	17–20	Best plough boys	Est.	1,350–1,425	B.117
		M	15–17	Best class	Est.	1,250–1,375	B.117
		M	12–15	Best class	Est.	1,100–1,200	B.117
		F	17–20	Best grown girls	Est.	1,275–1-325	B.117
		F	15–17	Best class	Est.	1,150–1,250	B.117
		F	12–15	Best class	Est.	1,000–1,100	B.117
		F	14	Tolerably tall	1	1,150	B.349
		M	....	"Enormously high" (price)	1	1,275	B.349
		F	....	"Enormously high" (price)	1	1,300	B.349
		M	15	"Very high" (price)	1	1,188	B.350
		M	18	"Very high" (price)	1	1,395	B.350
		F	10–16	"Very high" (price)	....	792–1,275	B.350
		M	....	Field hand—"should bring more than $2,000 in La. or Texas"	1	1,640	B.351
		M	....	....	1	1,600	B.351
		F	16	....	1	1,400	B.351
	S.C.	F	16	....	1	1,395	B.83
		F( )	....	....	4	[2,700]	B.83
		F( )	....	Excellent houseservant	2	[1,300]	B.84
		F	10	....	1	765	B.79
		M	12	....	1	915	B.79
				Entire Pimlico stock	235	750	B.183
		F	18	Unsound, excellent cook	1	910	B.184
		F	16	Maid, seamstress	1	1,000	B.184
		F	14	Likely	1	970	B.184
		......	....	....	90	1,000	B.341
		F( )	....	....	2	[1,900]	B.352
		F( )	....	....	4	[3,000]	B.352
		F	....	Girl	1	1,705	B.352
		M	....	Field hand	1	1,555	B.352
			12 <8	....	36	1,000	B.352
			3 >40	....	....	....	B.352
		M	....	Common field hand	1	1,630	B.352
		M	40	....	1	1,795	B.352
		M	21	....	1	1,605	B.352
		M	10	....	3	1,150	B.352
		F	10	....	1	1,045	B.352
			13–16	....	2	1,053	B.352
		M	14–38	....	7	1,540	B.352

TABLE A—*Continued*

Year	State	Sex	Age	Grade or Condition	No. in Sale	Average Price	Source, Page*
1859.......	Ga.	......	....	Three of working age	8	$ 1,250	B.83
					436, *of which:*	716	B.232
			126<10	....	....	....	B.232
			182<31	....	....	....	B.232
			88<50	(Several crippled or superannuated)	....	....	B.232
			40>50		....	....	B.232
					of which:		
		M	....	Carpenter, fair	1	1,750	B.232
		F	....	Cotton hand, houseservant	1	1,250	B.232
		M	....	Prime, young	....	1,250–1,350	B.232
		3F, 2M	24, 21, 17, 15, 12	....	5	1,205	B.232
		M, F	....	Plain smith and wife	2	[2,900]	B.232
					126	1,084	B.341
	Ala.	M	....	Very high, 12 mo. credit w/o interest	1	1,859	B.351
		M	....	....	3	1,800	B.351
		M	32	....	1	1,300	B.299
		M	30	....	1	1,290	B.299
		M	22	....	1	1,605	B.299
		M	19	....	1	1,635	B.299
		F	18, 18, 8	....	3	1,193	B.299
		M	12	....	2	1,305	B.299
		F	8	....	1	800	B.299
		M	14	....	1	1,050	B.299
		F	33	....	1	920	B.299
		F, 4M	35, 32, 11, 9, 7	....	5	[5,220]	B.299
		M	13	....	2	1,000	B.299
		F	28, 8, 6, 4	....	4	[2,328]	B.299
		F	15	....	1	1,200	B.299
		F	30–38	....	Several	900–1,500	B.299
		M	....	....	4	1,400	B.299
				Field hands and children	Thigpen estate	1,309	B.356
	Tenn.	.....	15	....	6	1,140	B.357
	La.	M	....	No infants. Sugar estate	55	1,000	B.341
		M	....	Prime field (in above)	....	1,500	B.341
	Tex.	M	....	Blacksmith	1	2,000	B.356
		M	38	....	1	1,308	B.358
		F	14	....	1	1,403	B.358
		M	17	....	1	1,527	B.358
		F	12	....	1	1,255	B.358
		M	12	....	1	1,155	B.358
		M	8	....	1	1,002	B.358

TABLE A—*Continued*

Year	State	Sex	Age	Grade or Condition	No in Sale	Average Price	Source, Page*
1859.......	Tex.	......	28	......	1	$ 1,500	B.358
		......	26	......	1	1,650	B.358
		......	18	......	1	1,800	B.358
		......	9	......	1	1,056	B.358
		......	7	......	1	1,005	B.358
		......	13	......	1	1,005	B.358
1860.......	S.C.	......	......	Prime field hand	......	1,200	P(PSQ)
	Ga.	......	......	Prime field hand	......	1,800	P(PSQ)
	S.C.	F	14	Wench	1	970	B.84
		F( )	30( )	Houseservant, children	4	[2,200]	B.84
		F( )	18( )	With infant	2	[1,160]	B.84
		F( )	25(2, 4)	......	3	[1,470]	B.84
		F	17	Wench	1	1,400	B.84
		F	18	Wench	1	1,165	B.84
		F( )	20( )	......	2	[1,180]	B.84
		......	......	......	30	750	B.185
		......	......	Very prime	72	665	B.185
		......	......	Sea Island cotton hands	34	703	B.188
		......	......	Sea Island cotton hands	20	795	B.188
		M	21	......	1	1,205	B.188
		F	......	Disabled	1	485	B.188
		M	......	Prime	2	1,325	B.188
		F( )	18	Likely	2	[1,160]	B.195
			(7 mos.)	......	1	700	B.195
		F	9	......	68	586	B.205
		4F, 5M	1–40	Prime (5 under 10)	9	450	B.220
		M	......	Carpenter	1	3,500–4,000	B.353
	N.C.	......	8	......	5	600	B.357
	Tenn.	M	12	......	1	800	B.211
		M	7	......	1	400	B.211
		M	4	......	1	300	B.211
	Ga.	M	21	Best field hand	1	1,900	P(Doc. II).73
		F( )	17 (9 mos.)	......	2	[2,150]	P(Doc. II).73
		F( )	18(3)	......	2	[2,500]	P(Doc. II).73
		F( )	30(6)( )	......	4	[4,525]	P(Doc. II).73
				Far from prime	140	625	B.224
					536	1,025	B.354
					of which:		
		F	17	......	1	1,800	B.354
		M	20	......	1	1,800	B.354
		M	30	Field hand	1	2,005	B.354
		M	......	......	Several	2,000	B.354

TABLE A—*Continued*

Year	State	Sex	Age	Grade or Condition	No. in Sale	Average Price	Source, Page*
1860......	Ga.	M, F( )	....	....	3	$ [4,500]	B.354
		25 F and 10 children		Railway builders	108	1,364	B.355
		60 F and children		Ordinary	81	1,100	B.355
		F	11	....	1	1,465	B.355
		F	11	....	1	1,385	B.355
		......	....	....	20	919	B.355
					of which:		
		......	....	(Excluding 5, old and children)	15	1,128	B.355
			3–50	....	Estate sale	1,148	B.355
	Fla.	......	....	Trader's purchase	53	834	B.223
	Miss.	M	....	No. 1 field hands	Est.	1,600–1,650	B.309
		F	....	No. 1 field hands	Est.	1,400–1,500	B.309
		......	....	....	17	1,200	B.357
	Ala.	......	....	High, but for 12 mo. credit	33	1,145	B.84
					of which:		
		M, F	4<6	....	6	[5,200]	B.84
		F( )	....	....	3	[2,600]	B.84
		......	18	....	1	2,045	B.84
	Tex.	M	21	....	1	2,015	B.358
		F	15	....	1	1,635	B.358
		M	10–12	....	1	1,236	B.358
		M, F	6, 3	....	2	500	B.358
		M	35	....	1	2,206	B.358

NOTES

Square brackets indicate total sale price rather than average price and have been used where the age range is extremely wide.

Parentheses have been used to indicate children sold with their mothers.

"Est." is used to indicate estimates of going prices in a market.

Where no entry is given under "No. in Sale," the average has been reported without indication of the size of the market or the number of observations. The Charleston and Middle Georgia averages, taken from U. B. Phillips, "The Slave Labor Problem in the Charleston District," *Political Science Quarterly*, XXII, No. 3 (1907), 436, and given as the first entry in almost all the reported years, are given without indication of number.

The grade or condition or other comment on the sale or valuation has been quoted in the language of the original report whenever possible.

[5]

JOHN P. CASKEY

Pawnbroking in America: The Economics of a Forgotten Credit Market

IN HIS 1930 STUDY of consumer financial institutions, Clark Evans (1930, p. 40), commented regarding pawnshops,

> The actual facts, however, are almost completely unknown. No national statistics of pawnbrokers have ever been compiled, nor, as far as the author has been able to find out, have any been published even for a single city. Neither have any academic studies been made of the business in the United States.

Sixty years later, it is time to remedy this oversight.

Interestingly, monetary economists have produced hundreds of theoretical and empirical studies of banks while completely ignoring pawnshops, popularly known as banks for the little man. This omission is unfortunate because pawnshops are a source of credit to millions of Americans who are excluded from mainstream financial markets. Moreover, pawnbroking has grown in importance over the past decade, probably reflecting an increase in the percentage of the population without access to bank or finance company credit.[1]

[1]Pawnshops in the United States are not only important because of their contemporary role as a key credit source for lower-income Americans, but also for their historical role in the discovery of America. As Samuel Levine (1911, p. 31) points out, Isabella of Castile pawned her jewels to finance Christopher Columbus' first voyage to America. Levine notes this thought led one nineteenth-century writer to comment that if Americans had duly reflected on this incident, they certainly would have placed the three balls in their national flag along with the stars and stripes.

The author gratefully acknowledges the financial support of the Swarthmore College Research Fund. Brian Zikmund collaborated extensively in the background research and expresses his gratitude to the Joel Dean Foundation for a student summer research stipend. Brian and the author are both indebted to the many pawnbrokers in the Philadelphia area and elsewhere who took the time to explain the business to them. J. Huston McCulloch, two anonymous referees, and numerous other economists provided helpful comments on an earlier version of this paper.

This article was completed while the author was a visiting scholar at the Federal Reserve Bank of Kansas City. The views expressed herein are solely those of the author and do not necessarily reflect the views of the Federal Reserve Bank of Kansas City or the Federal Reserve System.

JOHN P. CASKEY *is assistant professor of economics at Swarthmore College.*

Journal of Money, Credit, and Banking, Vol. 23, No. 1 (February 1991)

This paper provides an overview of the economics of pawnbroking in America. Among the questions addressed are: How important is pawnbroking in consumer credit markets? Who uses pawnshops as a source of credit and why? How are pawnshops regulated and what are the characteristics of a typical pawnshop loan? Is the availability of pawnshop credit affected by the business cycle? Why are pawnshops so unevenly distributed across the nation? And, finally, why did pawnbroking die out in Britain but not in the United States, and what explains the 1980s' upturn in the pawnbroking industry?

Before beginning to answer these questions, the degree to which pawnshops have been overlooked by economists should be emphasized. There have been no studies of pawnbroking in North America using data from the past fifty years. Prior to that, the best studies were William Patterson's (1899a and 1899b) comparative study of American and European pawnshops, Samuel Levine's (1913) extensive description of the pawnbroking business, and Rolf Nugent's (1939) estimate of total pawnshop credit. In Britain, pawnbroking has received more attention. Kenneth Hudson (1982) and Melanie Tebbutt (1983) have written fascinating accounts of the historical development of British pawnbroking, and A. L. Minkes (1953) studied the dramatic decline of pawnbroking in Britain between 1910 and 1950. With pawnshops common in much of Latin America and Asia, some attention has been given to their role in developing countries. F. J. A. Bauman and R. Houtman (1988), for example, provide a good description of the functioning of pawnshops in Sri Lanka and Mario Lamberte (1988) studies their role in the financial system of the Philippines.

1. THE IMPORTANCE OF PAWNBROKING IN THE U.S. ECONOMY

There are no official estimates of the importance of pawnshops as a source of credit in the United States. The Board of Governors of the Federal Reserve System does not collect data on pawnbroking and does not include an estimate of pawnshop credit in its statistics on total domestic credit. However, extrapolating from the data provided by a few state regulatory agencies, I estimated total pawnshop credit outstanding at the end of 1988 to have been \$689 million, with pawnshops making about \$1,723 million of loans over the year.[2] For comparison, outstanding con-

[2]From yellow-page listings and reports by a few states' regulatory agencies, I counted 6,853 pawnshops operating in the United States in 1988. To estimate the amount of pawnshop credit outstanding at the end of the year, I assumed the average pawnshop had outstanding pledge loans of \$100,000. Reports by the Indiana, New Jersey, Oregon, and Pennsylvania state regulatory agencies show the eighty-three pawnshops in these four states had average outstanding loans of \$166,916 at the end of 1987. However, pawnshops in the south, encompassing the majority of U.S. pawnshops, operate on a smaller scale. For example, Cash America Investments reports that its 101 pawnshops in Texas, Oklahoma, Louisiana, and Tennessee had an average outstanding loan balance of \$127,653 at the end of 1988, and Cash America shops may be larger than average for this region. Oklahoma, for example, reports that its 369 licensed pawnshops lent an average of \$126,801 per shop over 1988, suggesting an average outstanding loan balance of only about \$50,000. Combining these data, a \$100,000 national average for 1988 seems a reasonable, conservative guess.

Data on the average rate of loan turn-overs is available only for Indiana and Oregon. Over the past five years, pawnshops in these two states lent annually about 2.5 times their end-year outstanding loans. Assuming this average holds nationally, pawnbrokers made about \$1,723 million in loans in 1988.

sumer credit in 1988 totaled $744 billion, of which $371 billion was accounted for by commercial bank loans and $174 billion by finance companies.

By these measures, pawnshops appear to merit academic neglect; they are the source for only about one-tenth of one percent of consumer credit in the United States. By other measures, pawnbroking clearly plays a key role in U.S. credit markets. In 1988, for example, there were approximately 6,900 pawnshops in the United States, more than twice the number of savings and loans or about one pawnshop for every two commercial banks. Moreover, in that year pawnshops made about 35 million loans.[3] Even allowing for multiple loans to a core group of customers, pawnshops must serve several million Americans each year, and perhaps as much as 10 percent of the adult population. However, since the average loan is only about $50, pawnshop lending as a percentage of total consumer credit is much less significant than as a percentage of the population served.[4]

Beyond these aggregate measures, pawnshops are also very important to the millions of Americans, especially the poor and poorly educated, whose risk characteristics exclude them from mainstream credit markets. Because there have been no surveys of pawnshop customers, evidence on who uses pawnshops is limited. However, in interviews with the author, pawnbrokers indicated their loan customers can be classified into two groups. Some turn to pawnshops for credit because they are excluded from bank or finance company loans. Others use pawnshops for their discretion and convenience; cash loans are disbursed in a matter of minutes with very few questions asked. However, throughout the nation, most pawnbrokers say the overwhelming majority of their customers belong to the first group. They characterize these customers as having comparatively low levels of income and education and say many are poor managers of their personal finances.

Available data support the view that low-income individuals turn to pawnshops for credit because they often do not own sufficient collateral to secure a minimum size bank or finance company loan and are judged too risky for unsecured credit. As Alan Andreasen (1975) found in his empirical study of low-income consumers, they are much more likely than the middle class to have unstable incomes and employment patterns. This increases their need for credit but also makes it less likely they will honor debt payment commitments reliably. In addition, many low-income individuals do not maintain bank accounts, almost assuring they will be rejected in a credit check. A recent government study (U.S. General Accounting Office 1988), for example, found that 17 percent of all families in 1985 did not have a checking or savings account. Of these families, 56 percent had family incomes below $10,000 and 24 percent were headed by individuals with eight years or less of education.

Anecdotal evidence also supports the notion that the vast majority of pawnshop customers are drawn from this social segment operating independently of mainstream financial institutions. For example, Cash American Investments, a publicly

[3]In 1987, the mean loan size in Indiana, Oklahoma, and Oregon was $43, $41, and $58, respectively. The simple average of these amounts in 1988 prices is $49. Assuming this was the 1988 national average, pawnshops made about thirty-five million loans to total $1,723 million.

[4]The state of Indiana reports data on the range of pawnshop loan sizes as well as the mean. While the 1987 mean pawnshop loan size in Indiana was $43.11, 80 percent of the loans were for less than $50 and over 90 percent were for less than $100.

traded company owning about a hundred pawnshops located in Texas, Oklahoma, Louisiana, and Tennessee, characterizes its customer base in its 1989 *Annual Report* (p. 4),

> They do not use checking accounts or credit cards, but choose to pay bills and purchase goods and services with cash and money orders . . .
>
> The cash-only individual makes up the backbone of America. He's the hard-working next door neighbor, the guy at the corner service station, or the lady who works as a checker at the local supermarket . . .
>
> Why do these people need a pawnshop? First, there are times when they need extra cash. Maybe a child is ill and the doctor's bill must be paid. Maybe the car needs a new transmission. There are countless reasons why the customer might have an emergency need for cash, but banks and finance companies will not make this customer a loan.

Even more explicitly, Jack Daugherty, the founder and C.E.O. of Cash America, remarked to a journalist (Kleinfield, 1989), "I could take my customers and put them on a bus and drive them down to a bank and the bank would laugh at them. That's why they're my customers."

2. THE BUSINESS OF PAWNBROKING

Many pawnshops operate as one-stop financial centers for their customers. It is not uncommon, for example, for a pawnshop to make loans, cash checks, sell money orders, and handle customers' utility bill payments and income tax forms. In this article, however, I focus only on pawnshops' loan activities.

The Regulatory Environment

While charitable groups and governments in continental Europe and Latin America often operate nonprofit pawnshops as a public service, in the United States pawnshops are almost exclusively privately owned and operated for profit.[5] However, they are regulated by state and, sometimes, local governments. While these regulations vary, there is a general pattern. When someone pawns a good, terms of the loan contract must be specified on a pawn ticket, a copy of which the customer receives. The ticket states the customer's name and address, a description of the pledged good, amount lent, maturity date, and the amount that must be paid to redeem the good. Pawnshops must file daily or weekly police reports listing all

[5]In the late nineteenth-century, charitable organizations in the United States formed nonprofit pawnshops in several major cities to serve the credit needs of the working class. All of these have now closed except the Provident Loan Society in New York City, which still flourishes making loans from a number of branches at an interest rate of 23 percent a year. Its 1894 founders included Solomon Loeb, J. P. Morgan, and Cornelius Vanderbilt.

items pawned and identifying the individuals pawning the goods.[6] Some states regulate the type of items that can be pawned.[7]

Most states regulate pawnshop interest rates and other charges, such as storage or insurance fees. Including these fees, implicit interest rate ceilings range from 1.5 percent a month to 25 percent a month across states. A few states impose no ceilings, and the ceilings are widely ignored in some others.[8] In more than half the states, pawnshops levy implicit interest rates on average size loans of 120 percent APR or more.

Table 1 presents pawnshop usury ceilings and other data for the five states whose regulatory agencies publish pawnshop data. Each of these states imposes a ceiling on pawnshop interest rates and other fees, and pawnshops in these states almost universally charge the ceiling rates. In Oklahoma, as in several other states, the pawnshop usury ceiling depends on the size of the loan, with lower rates for larger loans. For example, in Oklahoma, a pawnshop can levy a 20 percent monthly interest rate on a loan up to $150, a 15 percent monthly interest rate on that amount over $150 but less than $250, and so on. For sake of comparison, the table reports the interest rate on a two-month $51 loan, a typical pawnshop transaction.[9] The reported "implicit" APR interest rate includes storage or insurance fees.

In the case of a loan default, the collateral becomes the property of the pawnshop after the loan is overdue by a specific amount of time, commonly one to three months. Some states require the collateral be sold at public auction. Thirteen states and the District of Columbia require any surplus from the sale of the collateral over the amount owed the pawnbroker, including accumulated interest and any costs related to the sale, revert to the customer. Default rates of 10 to 30 percent are typical in the states for which there are data.[10] As shown in Table 1, default rates as

[6]In response to the popular belief that pawnshops act as fronts for burglars, all brokers adamantly insist that they do not knowingly accept stolen goods as collateral. They point out it is not in their interest because the police can seize the goods and the broker loses the collateral and the loaned money. Given the police report requirement, they also say it would not be in the interest of a thief to pawn a stolen good.

Although many items, especially jewelry, do not have serial numbers and would be difficult to identify from police reports, the data appear to support the brokers' claims. For example, Oklahoma reports that in 1988 the police seized only 0.1 percent of pawned goods for being stolen property.

[7]An interesting example is Delaware, where it is illegal for a pawnbroker to accept a customer's false teeth or artificial limb as collateral.

[8]In states that set no pawnshop interest rate ceilings, such as Alabama, Florida, Iowa, and South Dakota, interest rates on a $50 loan commonly range from 18 percent a month to 28 percent a month.

In some states with low ceiling rates, such as Mississippi, Missouri, and North Carolina, brokers almost universally charge far above the legal maximum. In others, deviations from the law are more limited. For example, I pawned a VCR for $35 at a Philadelphia pawnshop and was issued a ticket showing that in order to redeem it I would need to pay $1.50 in finance charges, the legal fee for a one-month loan of this size. When I went to redeem the item, however, I was informed that I would also need to pay another $1.00 for "insurance," an illegal additional charge.

[9]The table uses $51, rather than $50, because in some states the regulated storage or interest fees may vary at exactly $50.00.

[10]Pawn tickets are legally transferable in almost all states, so it is hard to know the true default rate. In New York City, for example, pawnshops report average default rates well below 10 percent. However, there are also yellow page listings in New York by businesses willing to buy a customer's pledge ticket. The ticket has value if the pledged item is worth more than the principle and interest needed to redeem the item. In no other city have I seen similar public offers to buy pawn tickets, and reported default rates for most states probably only slightly under-represent actual default rates.

TABLE 1

SELECTED PAWNSHOP DATA

	IN	NJ	OK	OR	PA
Year of state report	1987	1988	1988	1988	1988
Average loan size	$42	NA	$48	$61	NA
Default rate, number of loans	20.6%	NA	30.2%	13.9%	NA
Default rate, amount of loans	13.8%	NA	17.0%	9.3%	NA
Max. interest charge on two-month $51 loan	$3.06	$3.06	$20.40	$3.06	$0.51
Max. storage & insurance fees (for item left on pledge two months)	$3.00	none	none	$5.00	$2.55
Implicit APR interest rate on two-month $51 loan (includes storage & other fees)	$71.3%	36.0%	240.0%	94.8%	36.0%

Source: State regulatory agencies

a percentage of the number of loans are higher than default rates as a percentage of the amount of loans, indicating higher default rates on smaller loans.

Characteristics of a Typical Loan

Because pawnbrokers lend only on the basis of collateral left in the broker's possession, brokers do not gather information to determine credit risk but, rather, focus on properly evaluating the collateral. Once this is determined, a cash loan is advanced immediately upon the completion of the pawn ticket. A typical loan requires less than ten minutes.

In most states, pawnbrokers make loans with one- or two-month maturities. However, it is not uncommon for customers to renew these loans by paying the interest on the loan at the end of the month. Brokers report many pledges are redeemed within a week or two.[11] The typical pledge, however, is redeemed in two to three months.

A broker lends a customer a percentage of the value the broker believes the collateral would bring in a sale. The loan to collateral ratio varies over time and across pawnshops, but a loan of about 50 percent of the resale value of the collateral is common. This means the broker almost always makes a one-time gain from a default. However, brokers say they prefer the customer redeem the collateral. A customer who loses his collateral may feel bitterness towards the shop and patronize another, and brokers claim they would prefer to lend repeatedly to a customer rather than profit once from a default. Pawnbrokers report about 70 to 80 percent of their customers are repeat customers.

Commonly pawned items include jewelry, electronic and photographic equipment, musical instruments, and firearms. These items maintain their value over a reasonable period of time and are easy to store, especially jewelry. Examination of police records in Wilmington, Delaware, for example, showed that over a recent eight-day period one pawnshop made 221 loans for a total amount of $10,790. The

[11]In such a case, however, the customer must almost always pay one month's interest charge.

average loan size was $46, and the range of loans fell between $5 and $500. Of the items pledged, 68 percent consisted of watches and jewelry; 21 percent, television, stereo, or video equipment; 4 percent, musical instruments; 2.7 percent, camera equipment; and 2.7 percent, firearms.

Is Pawnbroking Cyclical?

Just as banking is a cyclical activity, one might also expect pawnbrokers to restrict credit in economic downturns. This might occur for two reasons. First, in a recession the same collateral may be worth less than it would be in normal times. Second, if the downturn leads to a decline in pawnshop sales or loan redemptions, the broker may become illiquid and reduce the average loan to collateral ratio. As Cash America Investments explains in its 1988 *Prospectus*,

> The Company is generally able to tighten and loosen credit by adjusting the ratio that the amount loaned must bear to the estimated resale value of the pledged property . . . [S]maller loans in relation to the pledged property's resale value may tend to increase loan redemptions and improve the Company's liquidity. (p. 14)

To check for cyclicality in pawnshop lending, I draw on data from the Indiana and Oregon state regulatory agencies, which have annually reported in aggregated form total pawnshop lending and number of loans over the past thirty years. To represent pawnshop credit conditions, I use the annual average pawnshop loan size (*AVEL*) in constant 1982 dollars. As explanatory variables, I employ the average state per capita income level (*INC*) in constant 1982 dollars and the state unemployment rate (*UNEM*), expecting the loan size to be positively correlated with the per capita income level and negatively correlated with the unemployment rate. A correlation between the per capita income level and loan size may reflect rising average standards of living and cyclical effects. The unemployment variable should represent cyclical effects and, perhaps, structural changes in labor markets.

In the case of Indiana, using annual data from 1957 through 1987, a regression of the average pawnshop loan size on the explanatory variables yields

$$AVEL = 36.7 + \underset{(3.34)}{0.002\, INC} - \underset{(4.04)}{1.62\, UNEM}$$

t-statistics in parentheses $R^2 = 0.44$

For Oregon, the regression results are

$$AVEL = 48.6 + \underset{(0.77)}{0.0002\, INC} - \underset{(0.40)}{0.086\, UNEM}$$

t-statistics in parentheses $R^2 = 0.02$

In both cases, the coefficient signs agree with the hypothesis that pawnshop lending varies with general economic conditions. In the case of Indiana, the estimated coefficients are statistically significant; with Oregon, they are not. Overall, these results suggest pawnshop customers find credit restricted in economic downturns, just as bank customers do.

4. EXPLAINING THE DISTRIBUTION OF PAWNSHOPS

As indicated in Figure 1, even after adjusting for differences in population, pawnshops are highly unevenly distributed across the United States. Texas, with almost 1,300 pawnshops, has the most of any state but Oklahoma and Idaho, with 369 and 110 respectively, have the most pawnshops per capita, a little more than one for every ten thousand inhabitants. New Hampshire, with just one pawnshop, also has the least per capita, one per million inhabitants. The Sunbelt and Central Mountain states tend to have the highest numbers of pawnshops per capita, while the New England and Great Lake states have the least.

Not shown in the figure is another characteristic of pawnshop location. In states with many pawnshops per capita, the majority of towns over ten thousand have at least one pawnshop. In states with few pawnshops per capita, pawnshops are located almost exclusively in major urban areas. What accounts for this skewed distribution of pawnshops?

Before proposing an answer, it is useful to consider two key characteristics of the pawnbroking industry: high customer transportation costs per loan dollar and relatively free entry into the industry. To obtain a loan or redeem collateral, a customer must physically transport the collateral to or from the pawnshop. With an average loan of around $50, transportation costs per dollar of credit are significant, and customers generally patronize the closest shop. Thus, despite probable economies of scale in pawnbroking, strong demand for pawnshop services across a broad geographic area is usually met by numerous, dispersed shops.

Barriers to entry into pawnbroking are small. Pawnshop start-up costs are within reach of most middle-income entrepreneurs (Gregory and Norton 1985). Consequently, new pawnshops quickly enter areas that promise high profits. As they enter, the customer base per pawnshop shrinks because customers switch to patronize the most convenient pawnshop. With the shrinking customer base, profits fall because each pawnshop must cover its fixed costs from a smaller cash flow.

This account suggests an explanation for the skewed national distribution of pawnshops. Because generous usury laws permit small pawnshops to operate profitably and high customer transportation costs mean they will be patronized, one would expect more pawnshops per capita in states with high usury ceilings. One would also expect to find more pawnshops per capita in states that do not require the return to customers of any surplus from a default sale, because this also favorably affects pawnshop profits.

The uneven distribution of pawnshops across the states may also be explained by differences in population densities and the need for pawnshop credit. Some thought suggests population density would have an ambiguous effect on pawnshops per capita. If people are extremely dispersed, pawnshops might draw too few customers

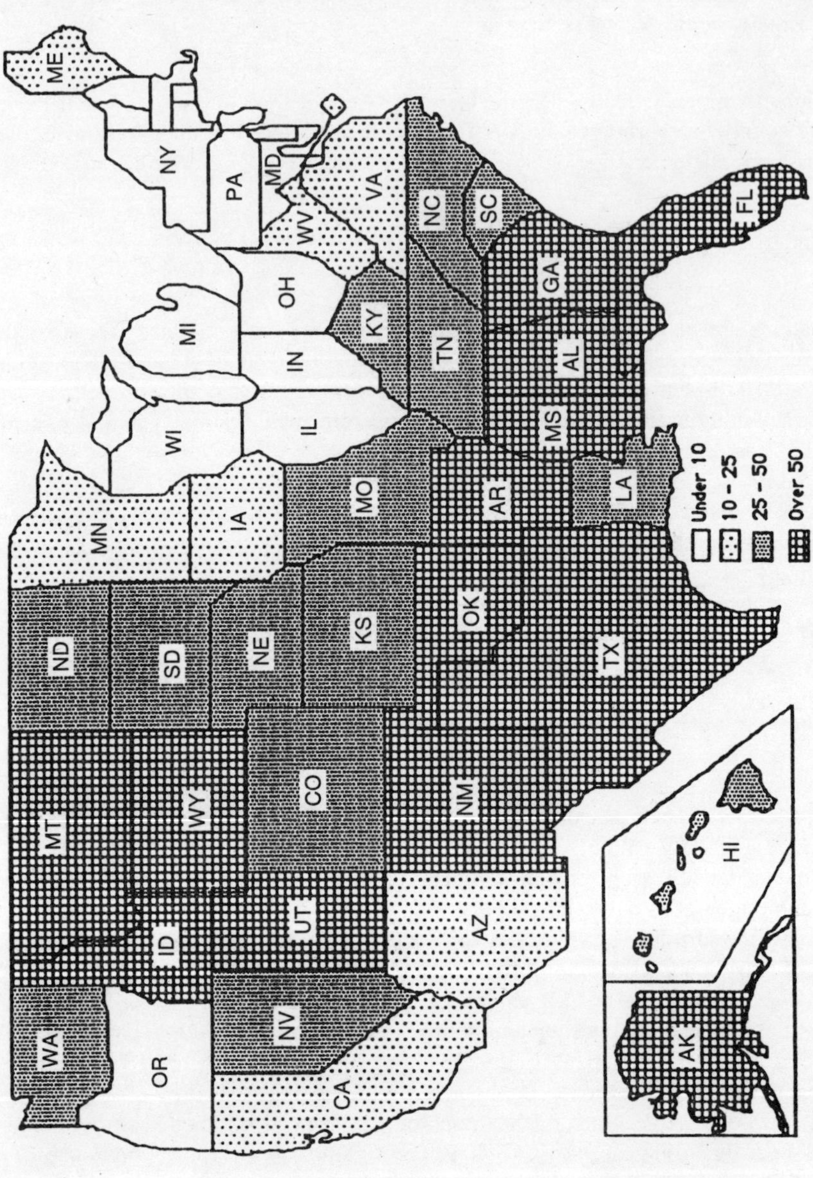

FIG. 1. Pawnshops per Million Inhabitants, by State

to survive. On the other hand, if the population is densely concentrated in a small area, one large pawnshop might serve the whole community. Finally, some states may also have a stronger per capita demand for pawnshop services because a larger percentage of the population is excluded from mainstream credit markets.

To test these hypotheses, the data analysis is expanded beyond the five states in Table 1. For states other than these five, information on the pawnbroking industry is limited to the number of pawnshops in the state, the regulations governing the sale of unredeemed pledges, storage or insurance fees, and the legal interest rate ceiling. A small random telephone survey determined the average interest rate actually charged, including fees, within the states. Because finance charges can vary by loan size and maturity, for comparative purposes recorded monthly interest rates refer to the rate on a $51 loan redeemed after two months. Any one-time storage costs or other fees are included as part of the interest rate.

Using 1987 data and cross-sectional regression analysis, I examined the links between pawnshops per capita, pawnshop regulations, and state demographic characteristics. The number of pawnshops per million capita (PPC) in each state is the dependent variable. Two explanatory variables represent the effect of state regulations on pawnshops per capita: the state monthly interest rate ceiling (*INT*) and a dummy variable (*SUR*) for states with rules requiring any surplus from the sale of the collateral be returned to the pledger. In states without usury limits, the number of pawnshops per capita could affect the interest rate as well as vice versa, so to prevent any simultaneity bias the regression employed only data from the twenty-eight states with clearly binding usury laws.

To control for the effects of population density, the explanatory variables include the population per square mile (*PPM*). Two variables are meant to capture the per capita need for pawnshop services. Based on the earlier discussion of pawnshop customers, measures of state poverty and education levels should serve as rough proxies for the percentage of a state's population excluded from bank or finance company credit. Accordingly, the explanatory variables include the percentage of persons in the state below the national poverty standard (*POV*) and the percentage of people twenty-five years old and over in the state attaining at least four years of high school education (*ED*).[12]

The regression results are

$$\begin{array}{l} PPC = 9.2 + 420\,INT + 253\,POV - 177\,ED + 9.6\,SUR - 0.002\,PPM \\ \qquad\qquad\quad (6.6) \qquad\;\; (2.0) \qquad\;\; (3.1) \qquad\; (1.2) \qquad\; (1.0) \end{array}$$

t-statistics in parentheses $R^2 = 0.80$

The signs on the interest rate, poverty, and education variables agree with the hypotheses and are statistically significant at high levels of confidence.[13] The sign

[12]The source for the demographic data other than the poverty rate is the *1988 Statistical Abstract of the United States*. Robert Plotnick (1988) is the source for the poverty data.

[13]For the twenty-eight states, the average number of pawnshops per million inhabitants was 29.2. The mean of the independent variables was 9.0 percent for the monthly interest rate, 13.4 percent for the poverty rate, 31.0 for the percentage of citizens completing their high school education, and 528 for the population per square mile.

on the surplus rule does not agree with the hypothesis, but the estimated coefficient is not statistically significant. The coefficient on the population variable suggests greater population density is associated with fewer pawnshops per capita, but the coefficient is not statistically significant. Together, the independent variables explain about 80 percent of the variation in pawnshops per capita observed among these twenty-eight states.

Implications for the Regulation of Pawnshops

These results have implications for regulatory decisions. Many states set usury ceilings in consumer financial markets. As Harold Nathan (1980) reports in his survey, economists have generally criticized these regulations as detrimental to low-income consumers because financial institutions under binding interest rate ceilings tend to allocate credit to only the most credit-worthy borrowers, who generally belong to middle- or high-income groups.

This is not the case with pawnshops, however, because all customers provide collateral, eliminating the need to distinguish high-risk from low-risk borrowers. Rather, the major effect of a tight pawnshop usury law is to reduce the number of pawnshops in the state. Thus, in the case of pawnbroking, regulators face a somewhat different trade-off than that faced in mainstream credit markets. A high interest rate ceiling ensures the provision of convenient, very expensive small collateralized credit to all. A low ceiling rate limits convenient access to pawnshops to areas with high concentrations of potential pawnshop customers, that is, largely urban areas, because with low interest rates only pawnshops with high volume lending can cover their overhead.

5. IS PAWNBROKING DYING OUT?

Research on pawnbroking in Britain has shown a sharp decline in the industry since the early part of the century. Minkes (1953), for example, reports that in 1950 there were only 32 percent as many pawnshops in Great Britain as there had been in 1913. At present, 175 pawnshops are said to be operating there, compared to the three thousand functioning in 1900 (Lohr 1987). Minkes, Hudson (1982), and Tebbutt (1983) attribute this contraction in British pawnbroking to the development of new consumer credit sources, rising personal incomes, increased public welfare measures, and growing social stigma attached to use of pawnshops and entry into the profession.

Data on pawnbroking in the United States prior to World War II are limited, but support the conclusion that pawnbroking has not declined in importance in the United States. Rather, the industry has shifted from older major urban areas, primarily in the northeast, to urban and rural areas in the southern and central mountain states. Levine (1913, p. 30) reports that in 1911 there were 1,976 licensed pawnbrokers in the country, or about one for every 47,500 citizens. He also noted that pawnshops were heavily concentrated in the major urban areas of the time. To illustrate his point, he counted 201 pawnshops in greater New York City, 102 in Philadelphia, 77 in Chicago, 72 in Boston, and 47 in San Francisco.

There are now 6,900 pawnshops in the United States, or about one for every 35,700 inhabitants, but they are no longer heavily concentrated in the older major urban areas. A contemporary count for Levine's cities would yield fifteen in New York City, twenty-three in Philadelphia, thirty-one in Chicago, thirteen in Boston, and twenty in San Francisco. On the other hand, there are 893 in Florida, 515 in Georgia, 285 in North Carolina, 369 in Oklahoma, and 1,270 in Texas. Moreover, in these states pawnshops are regularly found in towns of five thousand to ten thousand people as well as in major urban areas.

This raises a puzzle: Why has pawnbroking declined so dramatically in Britain while growing in the United States? At this point any answer must be tentative, but the explanation is probably based on a less comprehensive social support system in the United States and liberal state usury regulations in the United States compared to a strict national usury law in Britain. Less comprehensive social services, such as unemployment compensation and medical care, lead to more unstable incomes and expenditure patterns, increasing the need for short-term credit. In addition, before the mid-1980s, the British pawnshop interest rate ceiling was set nationally, and had remained under 35 percent APR for over a century.[14] States in the United States with enforced interest rate ceilings consistently below 50 percent APR have also experienced a decline in pawnbroking relative to the early part of this century, while states with annual interest rate ceilings of 200 percent or more have seen strong growth.

Contributing to the growth in U.S. pawnbroking and its shift to rural areas has been a significant decline in personal transportation costs. Even with high interest rates, a pawnshop needs a substantial number of customers to operate profitably. In the early part of this century pawnbroking was probably not viable outside of the major urban areas because high transportation costs prevented pawnshops from drawing customers from more than a few miles away. It was for this reason that Patterson (1899a, p. 256) wrote, "The business of the pawnbroker requires not only an urban population, but a dense urban population, such as is found in the great centers of industry . . . [O]utside of the North Atlantic Section there are but few States with even two cities of sufficient size to support the business." With the advent of the automobile and a well-developed highway system, this is no longer true.

Both generous usury laws and falling transportation costs are required to explain the growth of U.S. pawnbroking over this century. One is not sufficient without the other. States in the northeast and Great Lakes region of the United States also experienced falling transportation costs but, because of more restrictive usury laws, pawnshops are rarely found in the small cities and rural areas of these states. Similarly, without the low-cost personal transportation brought by the automobile,

[14]England abolished its pawnshop usury ceiling in the mid-1980s, and the industry has grown strongly in recent years. In 1980, for example, there were 115 pawnshops in England. By 1987, the number had risen to 175 (Lohr 1987).

TABLE 2

OUTSTANDING PAWNSHOP LICENSES

	1980	1982	1984	1986	1987	1988
Indiana	26	25	25	28	28	32
Maine	8	10	8	9	12	13
New Jersey	27	22	16	15	15	16
Oklahoma	NA	279	312	340	351	369
Oregon	11	13	14	13	13	13
Pennsylvania	27	28	29	30	32	37
Texas	787	953	980	1,103	1,195	1,270

Source: State regulatory agencies

pawnshops would probably not exist outside of the urban areas in any region of the country, regardless of the usury laws.

Recent Trends

Table 2 presents recent trends in U.S. pawnbroking for the seven states for which time series data on pawnshop licenses are available. In six of the seven states, the industry expanded over the 1980s, in some cases very rapidly. In Texas and Oklahoma, some of the growth is probably explained by the collapse in oil prices and the resulting economic disruptions, but there is also strong growth in Texas pawnbroking from 1980 to 1982, prior to the fall in oil prices.

To explain the 1980s' growth in pawnbroking, one cannot appeal to changes in transportation costs or usury laws. Rather, the main factor is likely to be an increase in the number of Americans who do not use mainstream financial institutions because of poverty and the effects of bank deregulation. Whether from changes in social support programs or from fundamental changes in labor markets or economic structure, the 1980s were characterized by a substantial increase in the number of low-income Americans. Between 1978 and 1988, for example, the national poverty rate rose from 11.4 percent to 13.1 percent, an increase of 7.5 million people below the poverty line. As discussed earlier, low-income individuals are much less likely to use mainstream financial institutions.

Bank deregulation may be another factor contributing to an increase in the population operating independently of the banking system. Following the Depository Institutions Deregulation and Monetary Control Act of 1980, banks increasingly introduced service charges on small accounts and closed branches in poor neighborhoods (Obermiller 1988). Since people without bank accounts would find it extremely difficult, and most likely impossible, to obtain bank or finance company loans, these trends may indicate an increase in the percentage of the population forced to turn to pawnshops to meet short-term credit needs.[15]

[15]A recent Federal Reserve study (Canner and Maland 1987) showed that 28 percent of families in the lowest quintile for family income did not maintain any depository accounts in 1977. By 1983, 36 percent of families in this group did not maintain either checking or savings accounts.

6. SUMMARY AND CONCLUSION

Because so little is known about pawnbroking in America, much of this study was descriptive. Among the facts presented are the following: Pawnshops provide very small secured loans to millions of low-income individuals. Most states regulate finance charges on these loans, with the majority setting effective ceiling interest rates between 36 and 240 percent APR. With pawnshop finance charges substantially above those found in mainstream credit markets, most customers turn to pawnshops for credit because their incomes or credit histories make them ineligible for bank and finance company loans.

The highly uneven distribution of pawnshops across the nation is largely explained by differences in state usury ceilings. This has a policy implication. Recently, companies have begun to set their sights on building national pawnshop chains, and there is pressure in a number of states to increase pawnshop usury ceilings. In mainstream financial markets, where credit risk is an issue, tight usury ceilings can hurt lower-income individuals' ability to obtain credit. In pawnbroking, such regulations do not have this effect. Rather, tight interest rate ceilings limit access to pawnshop credit to areas with high concentrations of pawnshop customers, that is, mainly urban areas. Regulators considering changes in usury laws should be aware of this trade-off.

This introductory survey also raised a number of issues that deserve further investigation. For example, why have interstate chains of pawnshops begun only recently, and is pawnbroking likely to become dominated by these chains in the future? In addition, in states with few pawnshops, one wonders what credit sources are available to those excluded from mainstream financial institutions. Certainly banks are our most important financial institutions, but economists will have a very incomplete understanding of credit markets if attention is not also given to the financial markets faced by the millions of Americans operating independently of the banking system.

Data for this paper are available from the JMCB *editorial office.*

LITERATURE CITED

Andreason, Alan R. *The Disadvantaged Consumer*. New York: Free Press, 1975.

Bauman, F. J. A., and R. Houtman. "Pawnbroking as an Instrument of Rural Banking in the Third World." *Economic Development and Cultural Change* 37 (October 1988), 69–89.

Canner, Glenn, and Ellen Maland. "Basic Banking." *Federal Reserve Bulletin* (April 1987), 255–69.

Evans, Clark. *Financing the Consumer*. New York: Harper and Brothers, 1930.

Gregory, Charles, and Frank Norton. *Open and Operate Your Own Pawnshop*. Duluth: StarNorth Publications, 1985.

Hudson, Kenneth. *Pawnbroking, An Aspect of British Social History*. London: Bodley Head, 1982.

Kleinfield, N. R. "Running the Little Man's Bank." *The New York Times*, August 13, 1989, 37.

Lamberte, Mario. "An Analysis of the Role of Pawnshops in the Financial System." Philippines Institute for Development Studies Working Paper No. 88-04, 1988.

Levine, Samuel. *A Treatise on the Law of Pawnbroking as Governed by the Principals of Common Law, and as Modified by the Statutes of the Different States of the United States, and the Ordinances of the Municipalities, Regulating Pawnbroking*. New York, 1911.

______. *The Business of Pawnbroking: A Guide and a Defense*. New York: D. Halpern Company, 1913.

Lohr, Steve. "Pawnbrokers in Britain Draw Affluent Clientele." *The New York Times*, September 7, 1987, 25–26.

Minkes, A. L. "The Decline of Pawnbroking." *Economica* 20 (February 1953), 10–23.

Nathan, Harold C. "Economic Analysis of Usury Laws." *Journal of Bank Research* 10 (Winter 1980), 200–11.

Nugent, Rolf. *Consumer Credit and Economic Stability*. New York: Russell Sage Foundation, 1939.

Obermiller, P. J. "Banking at the Brink: The Effects of Banking Deregulation in Low-Income Neighborhoods." *Business and Society* 27 (Spring 1988), 7–14.

Patterson, William R. *The Relation of State and Municipality to Pawnbroking in Europe and the United States*. Ph.D. dissertation, University of Pennsylvania, 1899 (a).

______. "Pawnbroking in Europe and the United States." U.S. Department of Labor *Bulletin* 4, 1899, 173–310 (b).

Plotnick, Robert D. "Poverty and Income Transfer Policy at the State Level." University of Wisconsin-Madison Institute for Research on Poverty, Discussion Paper No. 869-88, November 1988.

Tebbutt, Melanie. *Making Ends Meet: Pawnbroking and Working-Class Credit*. New York: St. Martin's Press, 1983.

United States General Accounting Office. *Government Check Cashing Issues*. Washington, D.C.: GAO, 1988.

[6]

Journal of Economic Perspectives—Volume 3, Number 3—Summer 1989—Pages 23–36

How Auctions Work for Wine and Art

Orley Ashenfelter

At the first wine auction I ever attended, I saw the repeal of the law of one price. The wine being sold was Chateau Palmer, a red Bordeaux, from the glorious 1961 vintage. The results of the auction I watched are contained in Table 1. Each lot (of 12 bottles) of wine for sale was identical, and three lots were sold in a matter of seconds by Sotheby's according to the usual English auction practice. The first lot fetched 920 pounds, the second lot fetched 800 pounds, and the third lot fetched 700 pounds. The first bidder paid 31 percent more for his 1961 Chateau Palmer than did the third bidder!

I was, of course, stunned to see such enormous price variability for identical objects sold at the same time and place. Even more amazing, as I looked around the auction room it seemed obvious that no one else in the room thought anything was amiss. The law of one price was repealed and no one even seemed to notice!

This empirical surprise led me to begin collecting data on wine auctions, to interview auctioneers, and even to buy a little wine.[1] In the meantime I have also had the opportunity (with John Abowd, 1988) to observe and collect data on the auction sale of impressionist and contemporary paintings. This paper reports on some of the empirical regularities that I and others have observed in the actual operation of the auction markets for these items. In view of the rich and diverse array of theoretical literature on auctions it seems high time economists began to spell out precisely what facts it is meant to explain.[2]

[1]Collecting data is an expensive hobby; to support it I began publication of the results of the world's wine auctions in a convenient financial format. See Liquid Assets: The International Guide to Fine Wines, 169 Nassau St., Princeton, NJ 08542.

[2]Recent empirical analyses of oil leases by Hendricks and Porter (1988) and of highway bidding by Thiel (1988) show how rich is the potential for the study of actual auction outcomes.

■ *Orley Ashenfelter is Professor of Economics, Princeton University, Princeton, New Jersey.*

Table 1
Typical Price Sequences for Identical Wines Sold in a Single Auction
(in £ sterling per dozen bottles)

	Chateau Palmer 1961		*Croft (Port) 1927*		*Chateau Margaux 1952*		*Quinta de Noral (Port) 1934*	
Wine Type	*Lot Size*	*Price*	*Lot Size*	*Price*	*Lot Size*	*Price*	*Lot Size*	*Price*
Lot 1	12 bts	920	12 bts	800	12 bts	480	10 bts	400
Lot 2	12 bts	800	12 bts	800	12 bts	480	12 bts	500
Lot 3	12 bts	700	12 bts	750	12 bts	480	12 bts	500
Lot 4			12 bts	650	24 bts	480	12 bts	480
Lot 5			12 bts	650	24 bts	480	12 bts	480
Lot 6			12 bts	650	20 bts	480		
Lot 7			12 bts	650				

Source: Author's tabulation of the results of Sotheby's Auction of Finest and Rarest wines, December 11, 1985.

How "English Auctions" Really Work

Many people think they understand the rules of an English auction because they are so commonly used.[3] Sotheby's, Christie's, Phillips, and the other English auction houses have invented and refined these rules over two centuries, and they are now common in many other parts of the world. It is well known that in an English auction the bidding begins low and edges upward as bidders escalate their bids. When the bidding stops, the item for sale is said to be "knocked down" or "hammered down." The price at which an item is knocked down or hammered down is called the "hammer price."

What is not so well understood is that the items knocked down have not necessarily been sold. Here is the reason. The seller will generally set a "reserve price," and if the bidding does not reach this level the item will go unsold. Auctioneers say that an unsold item has been "bought in." (This terminology is somewhat misleading since unsold items are rarely, if ever, bought by the auction house.) An item that has been bought in may be put up for sale at a later auction, sold elsewhere, or taken off the market. John Abowd and I (1988) found that about one-third of the Impressionist paintings put up for sale in the early 1980s did not find buyers. In wine auctions, on the other hand, the typical "buy in" rate ranges from 5 percent to 10 percent. It is my impression that the typical buy in rates for other auction items—European paintings, silver, furniture, and jewelry—fall between these extremes.

[3]What is called an English auction is, in fact, Roman. The word auction comes from the Latin "auctio," which means to ascend.

Auctioneers are very secretive about whether and at what level a reserve price may have been set, and there is a real auctioneer's art in getting the bidding started on each item without revealing the reserve price. For example, the auctioneer may have to accept and announce fictitious bids "off the wall" or "from the chandelier" to start the "real" bidding. Bids from off the wall are legally being placed on behalf of the seller. At the same time, sellers are forbidden by contract with the auctioneer from bidding in the auction. This is the protection that the auctioneer offers to the prospective buyers to ensure that they are not being artificially "bid up."

If you sit through an auction you will find that every item is hammered down and treated as if it were sold.[4] Only after the auction does the auctioneer reveal whether and at what price an item may have actually been sold. In short, the auctioneers do not reveal the reserve price and they make it as difficult as they can for bidders to infer it.

Although the above description outlines commonly accepted practice in auctions, many economists who write about auctions describe them differently. For example, Milgrom (in this journal) states "the auctioneer begins with the lowest acceptable price—the reserve price—and proceeds to solicit successively higher bids from the customers until no one will increase the bid. Then the item is 'knocked down' (sold) to the highest bidder." As I have noted, real auctioneers do not reveal the reserve price in this way, and many "knocked down" items may be unsold. In another example, Graham and Marshall (1987) state that, "when the bidding stops, the auctioneer will generate a false or phantom higher bid if he feels that the high bidder is 'good for another bump'." However, inventing fictitious bids above the reserve price is certainly unethical and probably illegal, too. Since the auctioneer's rules are known to an entire array of personnel who often move on to become bidders or their agents, it would soon become common knowledge if an auction house systematically engaged in the generation of fictitious bids above the reserve price. No auction house that values its reputation—and the long run profits its reputation secures—would systematically engage in this practice.[5]

Secret reserve prices and high "buy in" rates have some interesting implications for the theoretical study of auctions. In the optimal auctions model of Riley and

[4]There are exceptions to this rule. In New York City the auctioneer is legally required to state whether an item has been sold at the conclusion of the bidding. The New York auctioneers did not reveal this information before this rule was promulgated, and they do not reveal this information in other locations except where required by law.

[5]It should be appreciated that an auctioneer faces a real tradeoff in deciding whether to follow the standard ethical auction practices. If the auctioneer gains a reputation for following these practices he receives the benefit that buyers will be willing to reveal their true valuation of an item, and this will, in the long run, lead to higher prices for the items sold. On the other hand, there are always short term gains to be obtained by abandoning the standard practices. I do not mean to suggest that all auctioneers follow the standard practices considered ethical in the auction trade, although I do believe that the large auction houses with substantial reputations follow them. Many sellers try to give the impression that they follow standard auction practices even when they do not, apparently because they believe that it increases their sale prices to uninformed buyers. Some of the most amusing examples of this practice are depicted by the home shopping clubs broadcast on late night cable television. This kind of cheating seems to be endemic to any kind of economic activity where reputations are valuable.

Samuelson (1981), for example, the reserve price serves to extract a slightly higher price from the bidder with the highest valuation of the item on offer.[6] The reason is that in an English auction the seller only receives an amount equal to the second highest valuation placed on the object among the bidders. By setting a reserve price the seller takes a chance on extracting part of the valuation gap between the two bidders with the highest valuations in exchange for the risk of losing the sale altogether.

However, this optimal auctions model is probably not much help in understanding how reserve prices are set in most auctions. First, since it is a dominant strategy for each bidder in an English auction to bid up to their true valuation of the object, the optimal reserve price is identical no matter whether it is kept secret or not. This model therefore offers no explanation for why the reserve price should be secret. Second, in the optimal auctions model the reserve price is independent of the number of bidders. It follows that the probability that an item will be sold increases with the number of bidders. In fact, however, as I noted above buy in rates are very high for some types of items despite a large number of bidders. Moreover, buy in rates differ systematically across types of items in a manner that is almost certainly not related to the number of bidders in these auctions. It seems very unlikely that actual buy in rates can be explained primarily by the considerations important in the optimal auctions literature.

One likely explanation for the secrecy surrounding reserve prices is that it serves to thwart "rings."[7] There is always random variation in the interest and turnout of bidders; when the turnout is low, some sellers may prefer that their goods be bought in and offered for sale at a later date rather than risk a collusive ring bidding to depress the item's price. The auctioneer may also engage in other practices that weaken rings. For example, the auctioneer typically does not reveal the identity of the purchaser, if there was one, and this creates strong incentives for the ring members to bid privately in opposition to the interests of the ring.

An explanation for the key determinants of the seller's reserve price may be found in models of search (Mortensen, 1970), where the seller may expect to offer the item at auction more than once, or even to sell it privately to a dealer as an alternative. The highest observed price in a particular auction may be thought of as a "job offer" which will be accepted only if it exceeds the reserve price. In these models there is a "natural rate of unemployment" that may well be related to the "normal buy in rate" that characterizes auction markets. Abowd and I (1988) find that time-series movements in the auction market for Impressionist paintings do seem consistent with the dynamics of search models, so perhaps the other characteristics of these markets are consistent with them as well.

[6]The term "reserve price" is an unfortunate choice of words in this context. In reality virtually every seller has some price below which they would not agree to sell an object; the theory of optimal auctions indicates why, for strategic reasons, a seller should set a reserve price that is strictly higher than the minimum price for which they would sell the object.

[7]Webster defines a "ring" as, "An exclusive combination of persons for a selfish, and often corrupt, purpose, as to control the market."

Competition Among Auction Houses

It is sometimes said that the auctioneers at Christie's (still owned by Englishmen) are gentlemen who try to act like businessmen, while the auctioneers at Sotheby's (now owned by Americans!) are businessmen who try to act like gentlemen. There is no doubt an element of truth to this characterization of the style of these two auction houses. The competition among auctioneers is more than a matter of style, however. The auction business is an interesting example of an industry where the cost of building a reputation may act as a significant entry barrier to new competitors. Surprisingly little attention has been paid in the literature about auctions to the role of the auctioneer.

In principle the auctioneer acts on behalf of the seller, but the auction house typically receives compensation from both the buyer and the seller for items that are sold. The *buyer's premium* is a percentage of the sale price paid to the auctioneer by the buyer. In most auction houses the buyer's premium is 10 percent of the sale price, and the amount is generally not negotiable. The *seller's commission* is a percentage of the sale price paid to the auctioneer by the seller. It varies with the type of item being sold, ranging from 15 percent for wine to as little as 5 percent for certain kinds of paintings. (Thus, if a single lot of wine is sold at an auction for a hammer price of $100 the buyer will pay $110 to the auctioneer, and the seller will receive $85 from the auctioneer.)

If an item goes unsold, the auctioneer will receive neither a buyer's premium nor a seller's commission. To make sure the seller bears some of the cost of auctioning but not selling an item, auctioneers usually charge the seller a fee on unsold items. This fee is often a percentage of the reserve price set by the seller, which obviously gives the seller an incentive to keep the reserve price low. In addition, some auction houses will not allow a seller to put up an easily recognized item for resale until some time has passed. Sometimes it is claimed that when an advertised item goes unsold its future value will be affected. Such items are said to have been "burned."

Whether an item can be "burned" has some implications for the set of assumptions used in studying auctions. When bidders have independent private valuations of the items on offer, as in Riley and Samuelson (1981), it should not be possible for any item to be burned. The failure of an item to sell should not influence its future salability either at auction or privately. But in models where bidder valuations are correlated, as in Milgrom and Weber (1982), the failure of an item to sell is informative about the value it might achieve in another sale. If an object can be burned, the assumption of correlated valuations becomes more appropriate. However, it is not clear whether paintings really are burned, or whether this is a fiction invented to encourage sellers to be satisfied with lower reserve prices.

Most auction houses now collect a much larger part of their revenues from the buyer's premium than was true in the past. The most commonly given reason is that auction houses have been increasingly forced to bargain down the size of the seller's commission when they deal with large consignors. Since it is far more difficult for a

Table 2
Wine / Hammer Price Differences Across Auction Houses

	% Difference from Christie's London Prices			
Auction House	*Spring 1986*	*Fall 1986*	*Spring 1987*	*Fall 1987*
Sotheby's London	−12%	0%	+5%	−4%
Christie's Chicago	+14%	+18%	+15%	+4%
Butterfield's San Francisco	+27%	+21%	+10%	0%
Christie's Amsterdam	−16%	−8%	−8%	−8%
Christie's Geneva	+13%	+37%	+25%	+19%
Sotheby's Geneva	+27%	+34%	+27%	+30%

Source: "Liquid Assets," *The International Guide to Fine Wines*, Issue No. 4, Spring 1988.

large number of small buyers to bargain effectively, the buyer's premium has provided a new source of revenue. This suggests that real bargaining costs have changed in recent years, but I am unaware of why this might have happened.

The result of an interesting natural experiment in the variation of the buyer's premiums is contained in Table 2. This table contains a comparison of the hammer prices (that is, not including the buyer's premium) for identical wines sold at six auction houses at four points in time. In the spring of 1986 buyer's premiums were 10 percent in Sotheby's London, Christie's Chicago, Butterfield's San Francisco, and Christie's and Sotheby's Geneva auctions. The buyer's premium was 16 percent in Amsterdam at this time, and there was no buyer's premium in Christie's London auctions.

It is reasonable to consider Sotheby's London, Christie's London, and Christie's Amsterdam auctions to be conducted in the same market. The other auctions take place in markets that are divided by both regulatory and transportation cost barriers. Rational buyers will, of course, discount the price of a wine to the extent that it carries a buyer's premium. Thus, the price differences among Christie's London, Sotheby's London, and Christie's Amsterdam auctions in Spring 1986 are consistent with the assumption that these auctions are taking place in a single market and that buyers have caused buyer's prices to be equalized. Prices in the United States and Geneva, on the other hand, offered opportunities for arbitrage in early 1986.

In the fall of 1986, Christie's instituted a 10 percent buyer's premium in their London auctions. The Christie's auctioneer had earlier condemned Sotheby's for instituting a buyer's premium, and had promised not to follow suit, but some aspect of the commercial realities did not allow Christie's to keep this pledge. Most observers believed that having instituted a buyer's premium which would definitely generate some revenue, Sotheby's had then proceeded to negotiate with the larger trade-oriented sellers over the seller's commission and had threatened to take away some of

Christie's larger and more lucrative clients. Christie's put a halt to this behavior by implementing their own buyer's premium.

As shown in Table 2, the institution of a buyer's premium by Christie's London immediately resulted in a realignment of hammer prices, so that buyer's prices remained the same among Christie's and Sotheby's London auctions and Christie's Amsterdam auctions. In the meantime, buyer's prices have also converged between London and the United States, albeit much more slowly. Perhaps some arbitrage did take place. Geneva prices, on the other hand, remain remarkably high, suggesting the existence of some permanent barriers to trade between Switzerland and both the U.S. and England.

The Price Decline Anomaly

I believe it is common knowledge among auctioneers that, when identical lots of wine are sold in a single auction, prices are more likely to decline than to increase with later lots. This does not mean that price declines always occur, but they are far more common than would be expected by chance alone. Table 1 provides some examples of the pattern of results that you are likely to see in a wine auction.

A more formal analysis is contained in Table 3. I have compared the prices of every pair of identical wines sold in the same lot size in the years 1985 through 1987 in London, Chicago, and San Francisco. Although it is most common for the price to remain constant, prices are at least twice as likely to decline as to increase. This pattern is true for every auction house in London or the United States.

Table 3
The Distribution of Price Patterns for Identical Wines Sold in the Same Auction (August 1985–December 1987)

	Auction House			
	Christie's London	*Sotheby's London*	*Christie's Chicago*	*Butterfield's San Francisco*
Later Price Higher	271	143	90	20
Later Price Lower	628	430	183	41
Later Price Identical	1498	1073	226	39
Mean Ratio (2nd to 1st price)	.9943	.9875	.9884	.9663
Standard Error of the Mean	.00128	.00188	.00335	.0103
Number of Comparisons	2370	1646	499	100

Source: "Liquid Assets", *The International Guide to Fine Wines*, Issue No. 4, Spring 1988.

Table 3 also contains the means (and estimated standard errors) of the ratios of the second to the first prices. If prices followed a random walk these ratios would be unity, but all the ratios are less than unity, and the differences are statistically significant. However, since the cost of buying and then selling these lots of wine will rarely, if ever, be less than 15 percent of their value, these discrepancies will not support a profitable trading strategy. Still, if you attend a wine auction it is worth remembering that it does not pay to be too aggressive in bidding for early lots of a particular wine!

Most auctioneers are aware that later bidders on similar items are more likely to pay lower prices, but they are uncomfortable about revealing this information to uninformed bidders. Apparently most bidders, like economists, expect to see identical items sold at identical prices! When inexperienced bidders see exceptions to this rule they may think something fishy is going on. As a result, auctions are set up to disguise this regularity. For example, the auctioneer will usually offer smaller lots of the same item before larger lots. Since most bidders see nothing anomalous in quantity discounts, declining per unit prices seem more acceptable. Of course, the statistical analysis I reported above deletes cases where different lot sizes are being offered, and this selection bias has probably led me to underestimate the extent of the decline in prices.

Auctioneers have another device for limiting the extent to which bidders are likely to see price declines for identical items. When a series of lots of identical items is offered, the winning bidder on the first lot has the option of immediately taking all the subsequent lots at the same price.[8] This rule has two effects. On one hand, for a bidder who wants some (but not all) of the items on offer, it increases the risk of waiting for the lower prices that may materialize with later lots. Risk averse buyers are thus forced to pay a real price for any attempt to exploit the typical pattern of price declines: they may lose the opportunity to buy any of the lots they want. Thus, this rule increases the seller's revenue so long as there are risk averse buyers. In addition, since the option to purchase several lots is often exercised, bidders will in this case see a uniform price for all items. (This is also another reason to believe that I have underestimated the extent of the anomalous declines in prices that would otherwise have taken place in Table 3.)

These anomalous price declines appear to be characteristic of many other auction markets. For example, Penny Burns (1985) compared the behavior of student subjects and a group of experienced Australian wool traders in a simulated auction environment identical to that used in the wine auctions described here. After a few "weeks" of simulated trading, the students learned to maximize their profits and market prices followed a random walk throughout trading "days." The wool traders operating in

[8]Since the buyer must exercise this option immediately, this rule does not establish an option value for risk neutral traders which could be used to explain the price decline anomaly. Here is the reason. Since the option expires as soon as it is purchased, it is only of value if it is exercised. If it is exercised, however, there will be no price decline. Thus, the existence of an option value is not consistent with the price declines. For those who like empirical tests of such theoretical arguments I might also add that Butterfield's San Francisco auctions have no "buyer's option"—but the price decline anomaly is even more severe there.

the same environment did not learn to maximize their profits and market prices in their simulated trading declined as in the wine auction results above. Burns asked the wool traders whether they had noticed the pattern of declining prices and reports that, "Despite its consistency over 15 consecutive auction sessions, they had not seen the price fall!" This suggests that in the market trading to which they are accustomed, wool traders do not consider a declining price pattern to be a signal of unexploited profits.

These results suggest that risk aversion or quantity constraints play a significant role in real auction markets. Indeed, assuming bidders are risk averse may simply be a convenient analytical device for dealing with the fact that many bidders at auctions are buying to fill orders and are effectively quantity constrained. In fact, the mechanism used in practice by the auctioneers that gives the first buyer the option to purchase subsequent lots at an identical price is clearly related to the optimal auction design suggested by Maskin and Riley (1984) when there are risk averse bidders. Theoretical work on auctions will almost certainly have to remove the assumption of risk neutral bidders if it is to explain the full range of interesting empirical results from real auctions.

The Information in Auction Results: An Externality

A young woman called me with an unusual request just before Christmas: "Professor Ashenfelter, my husband was killed in a car accident last month, and I am going to have to sell his wine cellar. A relative has offered to take the wine for $3,000, but I am suspicious it may be worth more. Would you tell me what it is worth?"

Oh my, what a sad situation. Knowing that younger wine collectors have young (and not very valuable) wines I wasn't quite sure what to say. So, after offering my own condolences I asked, "What sorts of names are on the bottles?"

"I have a list; there are Chateau Lafite, Chateau Latour, Chateau Mouton..."

These are, of course, the names of the finest red Bordeaux wines. Maybe, I thought, this young woman had a little better luck than I had first guessed. So I asked, "What vintages are on the bottles?"

"There are quite a few. The oldest is 1945, but there is 1961, 1959..."

As it turned out, my estimate was that this young woman's wine cellar would fetch about $18,000 if it were put up at auction, about six times what her relative had offered her!

This story illustrates one way that regular auctions confer information benefits that are typically not captured by the profits of the auctioneer. In essence, the presence of an auction system provides a way for an uninformed seller to obtain approximately the market value for the items they own.

The value of a public auction system as protection for uninformed sellers has long been understood in Europe, but it is not widely appreciated in the United States. In both Sweden and Austria, for example, the auction houses are run as state-owned monopolies. The major auction houses in both the U.S. and England are certainly not state-owned, but they are watched with some care by institutions like the Metropolitan Museum of Art, which disposes of its property only through public auctions.

My advice to the young woman whose wine cellar I appraised was, of course, to sell her wine at auction unless she could find a private buyer who would pay her at least (the certainty equivalent of) what I estimated she would receive for the wine if it were sold at auction. The information on prices I used would not exist without a system of public auctions. In other words, the auction system allows traders to make private transactions outside the auction system, but if everyone traded in this way there would be no auctions in the first place. I believe that the inability of auctioneers to capture a significant part of the benefits of the information they produce leads to less use of the auction system than is optimal for society.

Of course, some people oppose the use of the auction system as a matter of principle. For example, many wine merchants argue that the auctioneers pose "unfair competition" because they do not have to maintain an expensive inventory and therefore the prices realized at auction will be lower than the merchant's. To an economist, such special interest pleading is hard to take seriously, but state legislators are not so immune. The result is that wine auctions are illegal except in Illinois and California.

The Information in Auction Results: Taking Advantage of It

In 1987, not long after public wine auctions had begun in California, I asked Dennis Foley of the San Francisco auction house of Butterfield and Butterfield how I could find the "real bargains" in his wine auctions. He said, "Buy the wines Robert Parker doesn't like. Parker's book (1985) has an enormous influence on U.S. auction prices. Wines he doesn't rate or mistakenly rates make fabulous bargains."

To U.S. wine buyers this advice may border on the heretical. Here is the reason. Most of the information available about the quality of wine appears in publications that are run by advertisers. Newspaper writers often accept direct and indirect payoffs for touting wines and many knowledgeable consumers are aware of this practice. (After a detailed expose by media reporter David Shaw in the *Los Angeles Times* in the summer of 1987, the *Times* fired its own wine writer!) The result is that there is a market for independent information. Robert Parker, lawyer turned wine writer, has captured that market and the absolute faith of his readers by refusing to accept handouts and payoffs.

What Parker and many other wine writers attempt to do is to infer the likely quality of a red Bordeaux, Burgundy, or California wine when it is 10 or 15 years old from the taste of the wine when it is a few months old. In other words, wine consumers in search of their liquid asset are much the same as oil drillers in search of their own liquid asset. In the future the true value of the asset will be revealed, but meanwhile the consumer must be satisfied with an estimate of its value. What Dennis Foley seemed to be telling me was that U.S. wine consumers were suffering from an extreme version of the winner's curse. Consumers would bid on a wine in his auctions only up to Parker's valuation of it, as if Parker's appraisals could not possibly contain error. It is precisely this kind of failure to make probability judgments that seems to be the cause of the winner's curse found in experiments by Kagel and Levin (1986).

The question is, of course, how to take advantage of the errors of these bidders. As it turns out, the theoretical literature on the information content of auctions suggests a possible way to do this. In a classic paper Wilson (1977) shows that the auction price is a better estimator of the true value of an item as the number of bidders gets larger. Since the volume of wine sold at auction in London is more than ten times the U.S. equivalent, and the number of potential bidders may be greater still, why not use the prices from London's auctions as benchmarks, buying wine in the U.S. auctions only when its price is systematically lower than in London?

If this form of arbitrage works, it will not make you (or anybody else) any money. Unless the wine is shipped to London, no one in the U.S. is likely to buy it for more than you paid for it. But if you buy the wine to drink, you may have purchased a great bargain.

Over the last year or so I have tested this strategy for wine auction buying several times. So far it has worked very well, although there are signs that enough market participants are learning about it so that it may not last a great deal longer. Here is a recent example that you might still run across: 1970 Chateau Brane-Cantenac, a red Bordeaux, sells for about $330 per dozen bottles in London, while it regularly fetches about 20 percent less in both San Francisco and Chicago. I and several colleagues recently sampled this wine and found it to be excellent.[9] Why is this wine so much cheaper in the United States? Well, here is what Parker (1985) says about it: "This is a distressingly poor wine, particularly in view of the vintage. The 1970 has quite a foul aroma and dirty barnyard scent. On the palate, the wine is beginning to fall completely apart. Lacking fruit and concentration, this is a vivid example of a very poorly and sloppily made wine." I can assure you that neither I nor my colleagues detected any barnyard scents in this wine and I do not believe that Parker would either.

Auctioneers and Accurate Information

The theoretical literature about auctions emphasizes that there are good reasons for auctioneers to provide truthful information about the items being sold (Milgrom and Weber, 1982). The basic idea is that revealing information tends to remove uncertainty and make low bidders more aggressive; this puts upward pressure on the bidding of others, which is in the interest of the auctioneer. It may seem surprising to some, but auctioneers do appear to act consistently with this prediction.

For example, auction houses typically go to considerable effort to estimate the price that an item offered for sale will fetch. Predicting the price at which a unique

[9]I am indebted to my colleagues Dwight Jaffee and Richard Quandt for their help in this empirical work and to Burton Malkiel who also supplied the wine.

Table 4

Comparison of Actual and Estimated (by the Auctioneer Prior to the Auction) Sale Price of Impressionist Paintings 1980–1982

Auction House	*Number of Paintings Put up for Auction*	*Percent not Sold*	*Percent Sold at Price Below the "Low Estimate"*	*Percent Sold at Price Above the "High Estimate"*	*Percentage Difference Between Sale Price and Estimated Sale Price*
Christie's London	211	44%	18%	20%	3.9%
Christie's New York	433	30%	21%	24%	2.1%
Sotheby's London	918	34%	21%	24%	1.5%
Sotheby's New York	617	26%	19%	28%	3.6%

Source: Abowd and Ashenfelter (1988).

item will sell requires considerable expertise, so it is of some interest to see just how good these predictions are. The usual practice is for the auctioneer to provide a high estimate and a low estimate in an auction catalogue.

Taking the auctioneer's point estimate to be the midpoint of the high and low estimates, Table 4 contains the results of an empirical study of how well the auctioneers predicted the prices fetched by Impressionist paintings in London and New York in auctions held by Sotheby's and Christie's. Figure 1 provides a scatter plot of the actual prices against the auctioneer's estimates.

These data reveal some important results. First, the auctioneer's price estimates are very highly correlated with the actual prices fetched and they are very close to unbiased. Since the prices fetched are available only for pictures that are actually sold, unbiased estimates averaged over only those pictures who find a buyer will appear downward biased. Although the extent of this selection bias is very small, this is precisely what the data indicate for both auction houses operating in both London and New York. It is also worth observing that, whatever implicit rules the auction houses use for defining their high and low price estimates, the results of these rules lead to very similar points on the empirical frequency function of forecast errors.

In sum, auctioneers do seem to provide genuine expertise in predicting prices. In fact, Abowd and Ashenfelter (1988) find that the auctioneer's price estimates are far better predictors of the prices fetched than any hedonic price function presently available. Perhaps honesty is an auctioneer's most profitable policy rule.

Figure 1
The Relationship Between Predicted and Actual Prices for Impressionist Paintings

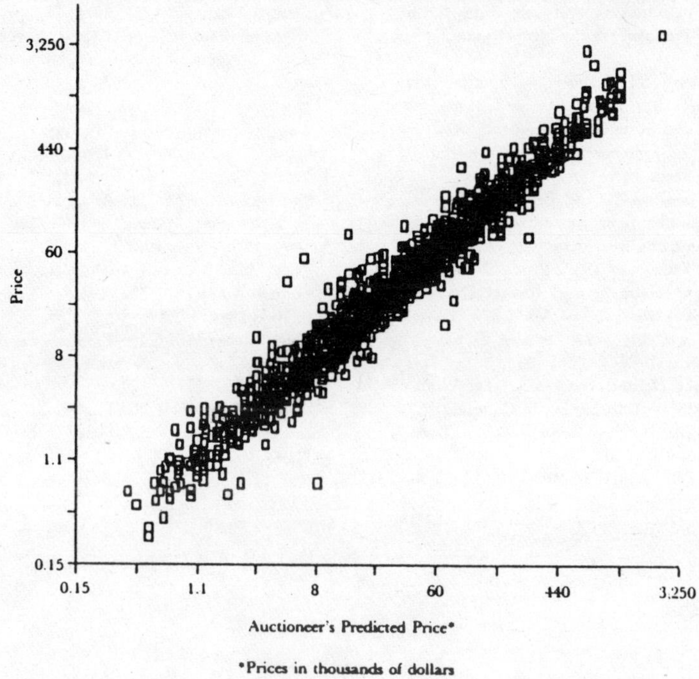

■ *I am deeply indebted to several people in the auction trade who have been very generous in describing the institutions with which they work. Brian Cole, Director of Auctions at Christie's New York, Michael Broadbent, Director of the Wine Department at Christie's, and Bruce Kaiser, Director of the Wine Department at Butterfield and Butterfield, San Francisco have all been exceptionally helpful. I have also received helpful comments on an earlier draft of this paper from David Card, Robert Marshall, Robert Wilson, and the editors of this journal.*

References

Abowd, John, and Orley Ashenfelter, "Art Auctions: Price Indexes and Sale Rates for Impressionist Pictures," unpublished manuscript, 1988.

Burns, Penny, "Experience and Decision Making: A Comparison of Students and Businessmen in a Simulated Progressive Auction," Vol. 3 of *Research in Experimental Economics*. Greenwich, Conn.: JAI Press, Inc., 1985.

Graham, Daniel A., and Robert C. Marshall, "Collusive Bidder Behavior at Single-Object Second-Price and English Auctions," *Journal of Political Economy*, December 1987, *95*, 1217–39.

Hendricks, Kenneth, and Robert H. Porter, "An Empirical Study of an Auction with Asymmetric Information," *The American Economic Review*, December 1988, *78*, 865–83.

Kagel, John H., and Dan Levin, "The Winner's Curse and Public Information in Common Value Auctions," *The American Economic Review*, December 1986, *76*, 894–920.

Maskin, Eric, and John Riley, "Optimal Auction with Risk Averse Buyers," *Econometrica*, November 1984, *52*, 1473–1518.

Milgrom, Paul R., and Robert J. Weber, "A Theory of Auctions and Competitive Bidding," *Econometrica*, September 1982, *50*, 1089–1122.

Mortensen, Dale T., "Job Search, the Duration of Unemployment, and the Phillips Curve," *The American Economic Review*, December 1970, *60*, 847–62.

Parker, Robert M., Jr., *Bordeaux: The Definitive Guide for the Wines Produced Since 1961*. New York: Simon and Schuster, 1985.

Riley, John G., and William F. Samuelson, "Optimal Auctions," *The American Economic Review*, June 1981, *71*, 381–92.

Thiel, Stuart E., "Some Evidence on the Winner's Curse," *American Economic Review*, December 1988, *78*, 884–95.

Wilson, Robert, "A Bidding Model of Perfect Competition," *Review of Economic Studies*, October 1977, *44*, 511–18.

[7]

DESIGNING MORE EFFICIENT MARKETS: LESSONS FROM LOS ANGELES SMOG CONTROL*

VIVIEN FOSTER *and* *ROBERT W. HAHN*
Oxford Economic Research Associates — *American Enterprise Institute*

Abstract

Market-based approaches for environmental protection are beginning to take root around the world. This article attempts to improve our understanding of the performance of environmental markets by constructing and evaluating an information base on trades in Los Angeles, which includes the first detailed data on trading prices. The analysis suggests that trading activity has been shaped by the detailed regulations governing the market. In addition, transaction costs have played a crucial role. We argue that the move toward adopting market-based approaches for environmental protection needs to be accompanied by a vigorous effort to assess the properties of these systems as they are actually implemented.

I. Introduction

Tradeable permits and pollution taxes have received widespread support from economists as cost-effective ways for promoting environmental protection.[1] However, until recently, there has not been a great deal of interest in the use of economic instruments for environmental protection outside of academia.

* Foster was a graduate student in economics at Stanford University when doing this research. She is currently an economic consultant with Oxford Economic Research Associates. Hahn is a Resident Scholar at the American Enterprise Institute and an Adjunct Research Fellow, John F. Kennedy School of Government, Harvard University. The authors gratefully acknowledge the unique contribution of John Palmisano—one of the true pioneers in this field—without whose insights and data this article could not have been written. We also would like to thank Matt Borick, Linda Cohen, David Harrison, Ambrose Lam, Josh Margolis, and Roger Noll for their ideas and feedback and Jonathan Siskin for his excellent research assistance. Support for this research was provided by the National Science Foundation's Decision, Risk and Management Science Program. The views in this article reflect those of the authors and do not necessarily reflect the views of any individuals or institutions with which they are affiliated.

[1] See J. Dales, Pollution, Property and Prices (1968); Allen Kneese & Charles L. Schultze, Pollution, Prices, and Public Policy (1975); and William J. Baumol & Wallace E. Oates, The Theory of Environmental Policy (1975).

[*Journal of Law and Economics*, vol. XXXVIII (April 1995)]

The 1990 Clean Air Act, which contained provisions for reducing acid rain using a tradeable permit approach, heightened general public awareness of market-based approaches. With the passage of the act, there has been a virtual explosion of potential applications for the use of economic instruments for environmental protection.[2] The economics community has moved from the point of doing simulations on hypothetical problems to providing guidance on real-world applications. Examples include the use of credit systems to encourage the scrappage of high-polluting vehicles, reduce acid rain, restore the Everglades, limit greenhouse gas emissions, and help achieve air quality standards in Los Angeles.

The empirical literature on market-based approaches has attempted to keep pace with the heightened interest by providing an ongoing assessment of different policy experiments. However, previous studies of market-based approaches for environmental protection have been hampered by a paucity of data, particularly at the level of individual firm response. Most available information has been highly aggregated. With the exception of case studies,[3] there have been no details of the functioning of specific markets or of the nature of individual trades. A particularly serious problem has been the almost complete absence of price data.

This article attempts to fill in critical gaps in our understanding of the performance of environmental markets by constructing and analyzing the most detailed information base on the emissions trading market in Los Angeles. It is the first to include micro-level data on trading prices. This information base is used to analyze the process of exchange in tradeable permit markets: in particular, how trading patterns are affected by transaction costs and regulations governing exchange. The ease with which trades can be completed is typically overlooked in the theoretical literature; yet, in practice, it is a critical factor in determining the performance of tradeable permits schemes.

The remainder of this article is structured as follows: Section II briefly reviews the literature and provides the institutional context for the market under study. Section III presents the main empirical findings. Broader implications of the analysis for market design are examined in Section IV.

[2] See Project 88: Harnessing Market Forces to Protect Our Environment—Initiatives for the New President (Robert N. Stavins ed. 1988); U.S. Environmental Protection Agency, *Economic Incentives: Options for Environmental Protection* (1991); and Robert Repetto *et al.*, *How a Tax Shift Can Work for the Environment and the Economy* (1992).

[3] Richard A. Liroff, *Reforming Air Pollution Regulation: The Toil and Trouble of EPA's Bubble* (1986).

II. Environmental Markets and Emissions Trading in Los Angeles

The virtues of environmental markets and pollution taxes are well understood in theory.[4] Compared with a centralized solution, markets or taxes have the potential to achieve a given environmental outcome at lower cost. An understanding of how these instruments perform in actual practice is just beginning to emerge.[5] There are three general insights from this literature. First, the rules governing trading can have a dramatic effect on transaction costs and, hence, the efficiency and equity characteristics of the market.[6] Second, politics plays an important role in determining the structure and performance of markets and taxes.[7] Third, the support of the bureaucracy charged with implementing the program is frequently crucial for the success of the program.[8]

The Environmental Protection Agency's (EPA) emissions trading policy, which this study examines, represents the oldest and most far-reaching attempt to implement a marketable permit system. It is therefore one of the most promising sources of insight into the functioning of such schemes. The emissions trading program has afforded many firms greater flexibility in meeting emission limits, resulting in substantial cost savings. Based on available data, total cost savings lie in the range of $0.5–$12 billion.[9] Interestingly, these cost savings have been realized primarily from trading emission reduction credits within particular firms, such as between two generation plants owned by the same utility. Far greater savings could have been realized if there had been more trading between firms.

[4] A. C. Pigou, The Economics of Welfare (4th ed. 1932); W. David Montgomery, Markets in Licenses and Efficient Pollution Control Programs, 5 J. Econ. Theory 395–418 (1972); and Thomas H. Tietenberg, Emissions Trading: An Exercise in Reforming Pollution Policy (1985).

[5] J. B. Opschoor & Hans B. Vos, Economic Instruments for Environmental Protection (1989); John L. Moore *et al.*, Using Incentives for Environmental Protection: An Overview (1989); and Robert C. Anderson, Lisa A. Hoffman, & Michael Rusin, The Use of Economic Incentive Mechanisms in Environmental Management (Research Paper No. 051, American Petroleum Institute, Washington, D.C., June 1990).

[6] See Robert W. Hahn & Roger G. Noll, Designing a Market in Tradeable Emissions Permits, in Reform of Environmental Regulation (Wesley Magat ed. 1982); and Robert Franciosi, Mark R. Isaac, David E. Pingry, & Stanley S. Reynolds, An Experimental Investigation of the Hahn-Noll Revenue Neutral Auction for Emissions Licenses, 24 J. Envtl. Econ. & Mgmt. 1–24 (1993).

[7] Robert W. Hahn, Economic Prescriptions for Environmental Problems: How the Patient Followed the Doctor's Orders, 3 J. Econ. Persp. 95–114 (Spring 1989).

[8] Robert W. Hahn & Roger G. Noll, Environmental Markets in the Year 2000, 3 J. Risk & Uncertainty, 351–67 (1990).

[9] See Robert W. Hahn & Gordon L. Hester, Marketable Permits: Lesson for Theory and Practice, 16 Ecology L. Q. 374 (1989), for more details on cost savings. Estimates are in mid-1980s dollars.

The emissions trading program operates nationwide and covers all significant stationary sources of pollution for five principal air pollutants—hydrocarbons (ROG),[10] nitrogen oxides (NO_x), particulate matter (PM), sulfur oxides (SO_x), and carbon monoxide (CO). The commodity that is exchanged under emissions trading is referred to as an "emission reduction credit" (ERC). Credits can be created as a result of a shutdown either when a plant closes or if a particular piece of equipment is no longer operated. Credits can also be created by lowering emissions below the regulatory standard as a result of a process change, such as burning a cleaner fuel. Emission reduction credits are typically issued in terms of quantity of pollutant reduced per unit time. An ERC could give the holder the right to emit 1 ton per year of the stated pollutant, so long as the ERC is valid.[11] Trades of ERCs typically involve "stationary" sources, such as utilities and refineries, but trading credits with "mobile sources," such as cars, is permitted.[12]

Emissions trading has four distinct elements: netting, offsets, bubbles, and banking. Netting allows a firm that creates a new source of emissions in a plant to avoid the stringent emission limits that would normally apply by reducing emissions from another source in the plant. A firm using netting is allowed to obtain the necessary ERCs only from its own sources. This is called "internal trading" because the transaction involves only one firm.[13]

Offsets allow new sources to locate in "nonattainment areas."[14] New sources are required to "offset" their emissions by reducing emissions from existing sources by even larger amounts. The offsets, or ERCs, could be obtained through internal trading, just as with netting. However, they could also be obtained from other firms directly, which is called

[10] ROG stands for reactive organic gases, which is the acronym currently used in Los Angeles for reactive hydrocarbons.

[11] Note that this does not give the buyer the right to do so in perpetuity as rules can change.

[12] However, the scope is limited to ships and in-plant vehicles. See Rule 1306(h), Regulation XIII, New Source Review, in SCAQMD, Rules and Regulations (1991). The California Air Resources Board, Mobile Source Emissions Reduction Credits: Guidelines for the Generation and Use of Mobile Source Emissions Reduction Credits (Stationary and Mobile Source Divisions 1993), provides guidelines for the generation of mobile source ERCs through activities such as scrappage and low-emission bus programs.

[13] Netting generally involves a reduction in emissions but in some cases can lead to a small increase in emissions.

[14] A nonattainment area is a region that has not met a specified ambient standard. The Clean Air Act specified that no new emission sources would be allowed in nonattainment areas after the original 1975 deadlines for meeting air quality standards passed. Concern that this prohibition would stifle economic growth in these areas prompted the EPA to institute the use of offsets.

"external trading." The offset market is essentially a mechanism for assisting the transfer of emission credits between new sources and sources that are closing down or reducing their emissions.[15] It is not primarily concerned with reducing the aggregate costs of pollution control by providing individual sources with a choice between abatement and the purchase of credits.[16] The offset market does not therefore provide direct evidence on the cost-saving properties of tradeable permits schemes.

Bubbles allow existing sources to trade ERCs. The name derives from the placing of an imaginary bubble over a plant, with all emissions exiting at a single point from the bubble. A bubble allows a firm to sum the emission limits from individual sources of a pollutant in a plant and to adjust the levels of control applied to different sources so long as this aggregate limit is not exceeded.

Banking allows firms to save ERCs. While EPA action was initially required to allow banking, the development of banking rules and the administration of banking programs has been left to the states.

This study examines a variety of aspects of trading and banking. The primary focus of this study is the offset program because the majority of external trades under the emissions trading program have been in offsets. The offset program comes closest to the economist's notion of a market where firms engage in arm's-length transactions. This market, therefore, provides valuable insights into the process of exchanging credits between firms. However, it does differ from an economist's textbook notion of a market in a number of other key respects (see Appendix A).

The Los Angeles basin has had the most active offset market under the EPA's emissions trading program. This degree of activity can be attributed to a combination of factors. First, the rapid economic growth experienced in the South Coast basin, where gross regional product growth has exceeded gross domestic product growth every year in the relevant period, means that there has been a relatively high level of de-

[15] The offset market has evolved from, and continues to be embedded in, a traditional command-and-control regulatory framework, where the level of permitted emissions for each source category is determined by a comprehensive body of source-specific technology-forcing rules that are written into the operating permit required for each individual source. In the case of new sources, the prescribed level is that of Best Available Control Technology (BACT). See Rule 1303, Regulation XIII, New Source Review, in SCAQMD, *supra* note 12.

[16] There is some limited scope for cost savings on the supply side of the market, inasmuch as a selling firm may create an ERC by overcontrol (known as process change), in the hope of being able to sell the credit at a price that exceeds the additional abatement costs incurred. However, on the demand side, a firm is bound to purchase credits to cover its total emissions, as determined in the source-specific limits. It may not increase its emissions beyond this limit by purchasing additional credits.

TABLE 1

OVERVIEW OF EMISSIONS TRADING ACTIVITY
(Number of Transactions)

Year	Offsets	Netting	Total
Pre-1977	...	5	5
1977	...	30	30
1978	...	34	34
1979	...	72	72
1980	...	129	129
1981	...	238	238
1982	...	210	210
1983	...	258	258
1984	...	256	256
1985	7	235	242
1986	27	432	459
1987	24	329	353
1988	55	358	413
1989	30	352	382
1990	53	394	447
1991	2,208	155	2,363
1992	3,678	77	3,755
Total	6,082	3,564	9,646

SOURCE.—SCAQMD, Records of the SCAQMD on Banking, Netting, Community Banking and Priority Reserve (Ambrose Lam comp. 1993).

mand for offsets. Second, the emission thresholds for offsetting have consistently been set significantly lower than those in the rest of the country due to the region's failure to meet the National Ambient Air Quality Standards required by the Clean Air Act. The high level of growth combined with the lower thresholds has resulted in a relatively large number of new sources that each require a relatively large number of ERCs. An additional reason for choosing the Los Angeles market as the focus of this study is that it is planning to implement a more extensive marketable credits program called "RECLAIM."[17] RECLAIM is being designed as this research is undertaken, and we are hopeful that insights developed here could be used in RECLAIM and other similar programs.

Table 1 provides an overview of emissions trading activity in the Los

[17] See Linda Cohen, Marketable Permits for Air Pollution in Los Angeles: Issues for Experimental Economics (unpublished manuscript, University of California, Irvine, 1993). RECLAIM stands for Regional Clean Air Incentives Market. See SCAQMD, Regional Clean Air Incentives Market, Summary Recommendations (Spring 1991).

Angeles basin since the start of the program in 1974. It includes offset and netting activity.[18] From the early 1980s the netting program has involved between 200 and 450 transactions annually. Offsetting activity began in the mid-1980s. The annual number of offset transactions did not exceed 100 until 1991, when it grew dramatically owing to the fact that separate institutions were introduced for "small" trades.[19] The total volume of pollutants exchanged since the beginning of both programs is on the order of 10,000 tons per year. The most commonly exchanged pollutants are NO_x (in the case of netting) and ROG (in the case of offsets). In each case, these pollutants account for over half of the volume traded.

III. Results

This section uses the data from the Los Angeles market to analyze the pattern of trades that took place. As well as uncovering new insights on the functioning of the market, the discussion attempts to test conjectures made in earlier work on this subject before the data required to test them were available. Although the data set provides comprehensive coverage of offset trades in Los Angeles over the period, price data were available only for about a quarter of all trades. This placed significant restrictions on the type of statistical analysis that could be performed. Accordingly, two parallel methodological approaches are adopted in the subsequent discussion.

Initially, the emphasis is on discerning relationships that are visible in the data. Where possible, these relationships are analyzed more rigorously using a variety of nonparametric hypothesis tests. Nonparametric tests are chosen because of the relatively undemanding nature of the maintained assumptions.[20] The results of these tests are footnoted throughout the text. Greater detail about the hypothesis tests is provided in Appendix B. A 5 percent significance level is used to accept or reject the various hypotheses. All prices are in 1992 dollars. The reader is advised to interpret the results of these tests with caution. In some cases, the small number of observations puts considerable strain on their statistical validity. A further objection is that the sample of trades for which prices are available was not obtained in a truly random fashion.

[18] Offset activity includes trading from the bank. There is no precise estimate for bubbles, but one estimate suggests that there were on the order of 200 bubbles over the last decade. SCAQMD, Records of the SCAQMD on Banking, Netting, Community Banking and Priority (Ambrose Lam comp. 1993).

[19] See Table 2 along with the related discussion.

[20] Wayne W. Daniel, Applied Nonparametric Statistics (2d ed. 1990).

The remainder of this section is organized as follows. Section A provides an overview of the information base and explains how it was constructed. Specific findings on the effect of transaction costs and trading rules are examined in Sections B and C, respectively.

A. *The Data*

Trading data are derived from two sources: AER*X, the principal broker in the Los Angeles market, and the South Coast Air Quality Management District (SCAQMD), the regulatory body for the Los Angeles basin. AER*X provides information on the year of the trade, the amount traded of the particular pollutant, whether AER*X acted as an intermediary, and in some cases the price of the trade. The data cover the period from 1985 to 1991. The SCAQMD records ERCs deposited in and traded from the SCAQMD bank.[21] In each case, information is provided on the amount of the particular pollutant, the method by which it was produced, and the dates on which it was deposited and subsequently traded. This information set covers the period 1983–92; however, the information available for the last 2 years is not complete. The analysis, therefore, focuses on the period 1985–91, which follows the Los Angeles market through its most active years. Previous studies have used information only up to 1986.[22]

Table 2 provides a breakdown of offset transactions between general offset trades and withdrawals from two special funds created by the SCAQMD. In the 6-year period 1985–92, over 10,000 tons of pollutants per year have been traded in the offset program, and total expenditure on ERCs is estimated to be on the order of $2 billion. There have been more than 200 trades involving over 100 firms. Most of the trades involve firms that have engaged in at least two exchanges. The two special funds established in 1991 are the Community Bank, which caters to small sources producing less than 2 tons per year, and the Priority Reserve, which secures a source of credits for essential public services. Both funds allocate credits on a monthly basis. In the Community Bank, the allocation of credits is in inverse order to the volume of credits requested, whereas the Priority Reserve rations on the basis of how essential the public service is deemed to be. In the first year of their operation, the volume of pollutants offset from these two special funds significantly exceeded the volume traded in the offset market. Because these special

[21] AER*X, Information on ERC Trades (1992); and SCAQMD, *supra* note 18.

[22] Robert W. Hahn & Gordon L. Hester, The Market for Bads: EPA's Experience with Emissions Trading, 3/4 Regulation 48 (1987); Daniel J. Dudek & John Palmisano, Emissions Trading: Why Is This Thoroughbred Hobbled? 13 Colum. J. Envtl. L. 217 (1988).

TABLE 2

Offset Activity by Number and Volume of Transactions

Year	Trades	Community Bank	Priority Reserve	Total
Number of transactions:				
1985	7	. . .	. . .	7
1986	27	. . .	. . .	27
1987	24	. . .	. . .	24
1988	55	. . .	. . .	55
1989	30	. . .	. . .	30
1990	27	26	. . .	53
1991	31	2,113	64	2,208
1992	14	3,557	107	3,678
Total	215	5,696	171	6,082
Volume of transactions:*				
1985	839	. . .	. . .	839
1986	946	. . .	. . .	946
1987	2,621	. . .	. . .	2,621
1988	2,769	. . .	. . .	2,769
1989	1,292	. . .	. . .	1,292
1990	701	16	. . .	717
1991	1,218	1,171	43	2,432
1992	441	1,886	55	2,832
Total	10,827	3,073	98	13,998

Source.—SCAQMD, Records of the SCAQMD on Banking, Netting, Community Banking and Priority Reserve (Ambrose Lam comp. 1993).
* In tons per year.

funds do not involve exchanges of credits between firms, they are not a central focus of this analysis. The funds do affect the offset market, however, by providing an incentive for some small firms not to participate in the offset market.

Offset trading activity for 1985–92 is summarized in Table 3 for each of the five pollutants. The first part of the table summarizes trading in terms of the number of trades, and the second part summarizes trades in terms of the number of tons of a pollutant that are traded per year. The table shows that from 1986 onward, most of the trades involved ROG. Nearly three-quarters of the trades in these years involve ROG. In terms of the quantity of ERCs traded per year, this same pattern emerges. ROG and NO_x are the only pollutants that are traded in every year of the period.

Table 4 summarizes banking activity. Through 1992, there have been some 60 trades involving banked ERCs, amounting to about 4,100 tons

TABLE 3

COMPOSITION OF POLLUTANTS TRADED, 1985–92

Year	CO	NO_x	PM	ROG	SO_x	Total
Number of trades:						
1985	. . .	5	. . .	2	. . .	7
1986	2	5	2	15	3	27
1987	. . .	2	1	21	. . .	24
1988	2	2	5	45	1	55
1989	. . .	5	. . .	25	. . .	30
1990	. . .	4	1	22	. . .	27
1991	3	6	2	18	2	31
1992	1	3	3	6	1	14
Total	8	32	14	154	7	215
Volume of trades:*						
1985	. . .	776	. . .	63	. . .	839
1986	2	236	11	582	115	946
1987	. . .	43	52	2,526	. . .	2,621
1988	203	896	28	1,640	2	2,769
1989	. . .	258	. . .	1,034	. . .	1,292
1990	. . .	51	6	644	. . .	701
1991	36	68	14	1,091	9	1,218
1992	111	33	9	120	168	441
Total	352	2,361	120	7,700	294	10,827

SOURCES.—AER*X, Information on ERC Trades (1992); SCAQMD, Records of the SCAQMD on Banking, Netting, Community Banking and Priority Reserve (Ambrose Lam comp. 1993).
* In tons per year.

TABLE 4

SUMMARY OF ACTIVITY IN THE SCAQMD BANK: TRADES INVOLVING BANKED ERCs

Year	Number	Quantity (Tons/Year)
Pre-1985	0	0
1985	1	27
1986	1	53
1987	6	1,679
1988	7	399
1989	10	421
1990	3	48
1991	20	1,055
1992	14	441
Total	62	4,123

SOURCE.—SCAQMD, Records of the SCAQMD on Banking, Netting, Community Banking and Priority Reserve (Ambrose Lam comp. 1993).

TABLE 5

SUMMARY OF REAL TRADING PRICES FOR ROG AND NO_x
($ per Ton per Year in 1992 Dollars)

Year	Priced Trades	Average Price*	Standard Deviation	Range
ROG:				
1985	1 of 2	81	. . .	. . .
1986	4 of 15	86	32	46–135
1987	3 of 21	116	37	69–161
1988	5 of 45	90	24	51–116
1989	6 of 25	221	75	67–305
1990	2 of 22	165	97	68–262
1991	7 of 18	339	205	43–711
Total	28 of 148			
NO_x:				
1985	4 of 5	196	81	119–320
1986	3 of 5	185	90	116–312
1987	0 of 2	. . .	. . .	. . .
1988	1 of 2	106	. . .	. . .
1989	1 of 5	111	. . .	. . .
1990	2 of 4	428	10	418–439
1991	3 of 6	435	194	182–655
Total	14 of 29			

SOURCE.—AER*X, Information on ERC Trades (1992).
* Average price = sum of unit prices of each trade per number of trades.

per year. Banked trades represent about 30 percent of the total number of trades carried out through 1990.

Trading prices are known for 48 of the trades. Over 90 percent of all trades for which prices are available were intermediated by AER*X.[23] Average price information is summarized in Table 5 for ROG and NO_x, the two most frequently traded pollutants. Price data are available for 28 ROG trades and 14 NO_x trades. The ROG transactions for which prices are known represent about 20 percent of all external trades in this pollutant. The subsequent analysis focuses primarily on ROG because of the available data on prices and because ROG trades represent three-quarters of all offset trades in Los Angeles.

Prices are stated in terms of dollars per ton per year. The going price represents the price to emit 1 ton per year of the pollutant for as long as

[23] It is possible that this might, in itself, introduce some bias into the price data, particularly since AER*X represents sellers of ERCs almost exclusively. The cost of intermediation might serve to raise the price of AER*X trades. In addition, if buyers were less informed than the intermediary, who presumably knew previous trading prices, this could raise the price, since the intermediary represented sellers.

the regulations are relevant.[24] Average prices weighted by the number of trades are reported here.[25]

The table shows that prices range from less than $100 to over $700 per ton per year for ROG, with a slightly smaller range for NO_x. Prices exhibit wide variation within and across years. For example, the lowest price for ROG in 1991 was $43 while the highest price was $711, and average prices range from $81 in 1985 to $339 in 1991. Two possible explanations for price dispersion can be found in the existing literature.[26] The first explanation is that there is a problem of obtaining early price signals when a market does not have a mechanism, such as a well-designed auction, to elicit prices. Without such a mechanism, there could be considerable initial price dispersion that would gradually diminish as a result of learning effects in the market. Price dispersion, however, does not appear to decrease over time.[27] A second possible explanation is that the degree of price dispersion is inversely related to the volume of activity in the market in any given year. That is to say, prices are less likely to be dispersed in years when a large number of price signals have been generated. However, the evidence from the offset market does not support this view either.[28]

The most plausible explanation for the degree of price dispersion observed in the offset market is the heterogeneity of ERCs as commodities. The credits exchanged in individual transactions differ in a number of important respects. First, there is the issue of whether they have been created by shutdown or process change. The means of credit creation will affect the cost of creating the credit. In some instances, credits may be created as a costless by-product of the decision to close a plant for other economic reasons. In other instances, firms may incur significant increases in annual abatement costs as a result of creating a credit by means of a process change. Second, there is the issue of whether the credits have been deposited in the bank. In order to deposit a credit in the bank, the selling party has to incur the significant costs of bureau-

[24] In actuality, many permits place daily limits on emissions, typically in pounds per day. Tons per year are used here because this is a common unit used in the literature.

[25] Average prices weighted by volume were also computed but are not reported here as there is very little difference between the two. For purposes of the statistical tests reported in Appendix B, the trade is the appropriate unit of analysis.

[26] Hahn & Noll, *supra* note 6.

[27] The particularly wide price dispersion for 1991 is explained by the reforms that took place in 1990. However, the same finding holds even when the data for 1991 are excluded. See Appendix B for a summary of the formal hypothesis test.

[28] See Appendix B for a summary of the formal hypothesis test.

cratic approval in advance of the exchange. Third, there is the degree of geographical separation between trading partners. This separation has important regulatory implications for the terms of exchange, although the nature of geographic restrictions on trades has changed considerably over the period. Fourth, there is the variety in the details of the contract governing the trade. In particular, these differ as to the manner in which risk is allocated between the two trading parties.[29] Given these variations in the characteristics of the commodity exchanged, it would be surprising if there were not significant variation in prices between trades.

Another interesting feature of the price data illustrated in Figure 1 is the fact that the minimum observed market price for ROG stays virtually constant in real terms over the entire period. In spite of credit heterogeneity and changes in regulations over the period, the minimum price falls in the range $40–$70 per ton per year, irrespective of the movements in the maximum price, which ranges from $115 to over $700 per ton per year.[30] This suggests a reservation price that is invariant to market conditions, which may have some connection with the level of transaction costs.

While the minimum price in the market remains stable over time, it seems plausible that the average price at which ERCs trade could be affected by the conditions of the local economy. Good economic conditions will create both a high demand for ERCs and a low supply of ERCs, since more new sources are likely to open and fewer firms will be reducing output or shutting down. Both of these effects would put upward pressure on price. While economic conditions undoubtedly provide an important influence on the market, no statistically significant relationship between average price and regional income levels could be discerned in the data.[31] The particularly sharp rise in average price in 1991 is not related to economic conditions but can be attributed to the increase in demand for ERCs created as a result of significant rule changes that took place in the preceding year.

[29] For example, consider a situation where two trading partners initially agree on a price of $100 for 100 tons per year of NO_x, but where the regulator decides that only 80 tons per year of emissions in fact qualify as having been reduced for the purposes of issuing an ERC. A number of contractual arrangements are possible. If the buyer continues to pay $100, but receives only 80 tons per year of ERC, then he has effectively borne the risk involved in the transaction. If, however, the price were scaled down to $80 for the 80 tons per year exchange, then the seller would be bearing the full risk. Clearly a number of intermediate arrangements are possible where the risk is shared differently between the two parties.

[30] Unfortunately, there is insufficient price data to detect whether the same is true for other pollutants.

[31] See Appendix B for a summary of the formal hypothesis test.

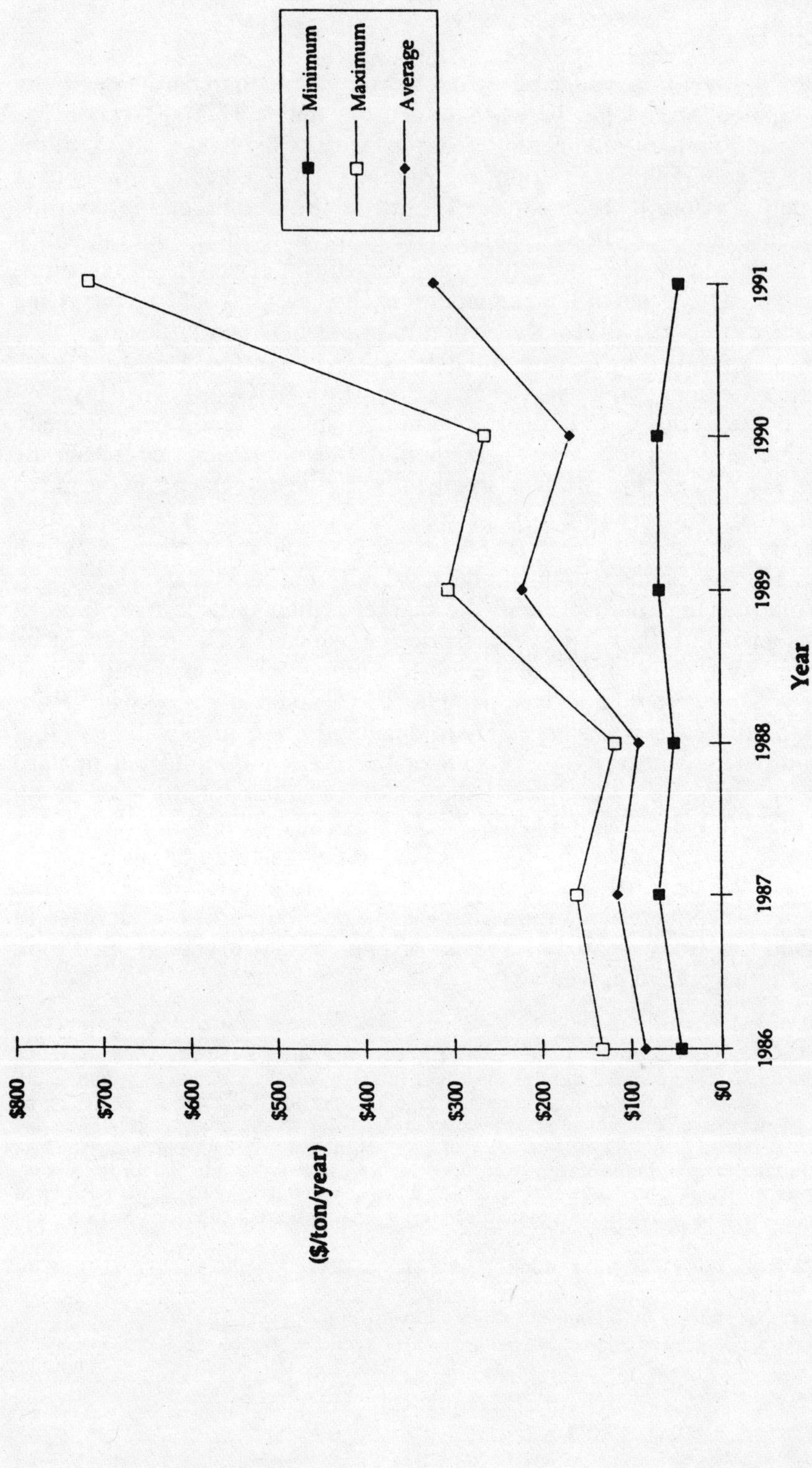

FIGURE 1.—Real annual prices for reactive organic gases (ROG; 1992 dollars)

B. The Effect of Transaction Costs

Earlier literature suggests that the transaction costs of engaging in a trade will be high and may therefore act as a disincentive for participating in the market.[32] High transaction costs are likely to reduce the number of mutually beneficial transactions and thereby reduce the number of trades that take place.[33] An examination of the procedures surrounding exchange in the Los Angeles offset market serves to illustrate the structure and incidence of transactions costs. An analysis of trades indicates that firms have adopted a variety of mechanisms for avoiding or reducing transaction costs.

1. *The Procedures Surrounding an Exchange.* There are two distinct stages involved in completing a trade. The first stage involves identifying a suitable trading partner and can take anywhere from a day to a year and a half. The process is marked by considerable uncertainty. Half of all proposed trades fall through during the negotiation process. Under emissions trading, the problem of identifying a trading partner is compounded by the large number of potential traders relative to the number of trades taking place each year and by the wide range of industries involved. Hahn and Hester attribute part of the success of the lead credit scheme to the fact that all the firms came from the same industry and were therefore accustomed to doing business with each other.[34]

There are, however, a number of devices that firms can use to speed up the process of identifying a trading partner and reduce the risks of the negotiations falling through at an early stage. First, a firm may circumvent the search process altogether by trading internally. About a quarter of all trades in the data set were of this kind. Second, a firm may obtain a list of the credits deposited in the SCAQMD bank and identify a suitable trading partner there. Third, a firm may approach an intermediary. The principal intermediary in the market is the brokering firm AER*X, which was established in 1984 and has dealt with over 40 percent of all trades. In 80 percent of the cases, AER*X represents sellers of ERCs.[35] In addition to AER*X, there are a few attorneys in Los Angeles who act as intermediaries. While reducing search costs, the use of an intermediary

[32] Hahn & Hester, *supra* note 9.

[33] For discussions of how the initial distribution of allowances affects the efficiency of the market in the presence of transaction costs, see Hahn & Noll, *supra* note 6; and Robert N. Stavins, Transaction Costs and the Performance of Markets for Pollution Control (Discussion Paper No. 93-02, Harvard University, Center for Science and International Affairs 1993).

[34] Hahn & Hester, *supra* note 9.

[35] Telephone interview with John Palmisano, president of AER*X, October 10, 1992.

will increase the financial costs of trading. Brokerage fees are levied in proportion to the value of the trade at a rate that can vary between 4 and 25 percent, depending on the complexity of the transaction. Where firms are seeking to exchange a number of different pollutants, a fourth method of reducing search costs is to identify a trading partner with a similar range of needs so that a "multipollutant cluster" of credits may be exchanged. "Multipollutant clusters" are defined as a series of trades between two firms in the same year (or 2 contiguous years) involving more than one pollutant. Such "clustering" avoids the need to find a number of different trading partners, one for each of the pollutants concerned.

Once a suitable trading partner has been identified, the second stage in the exchange process is to obtain bureaucratic approval from the SCAQMD, which usually takes between 5 and 12 months. This stage in the process can entail significant financial costs, which tend to be fixed with respect to the size of the trade. Administrative fees to the regulatory body can amount to $2,900 per trade. Additional administrative fees are levied for certifying ERCs ($1,700), banking them ($900), and reissuing them in smaller units ($900). In addition, firms can incur between $7,500 and $15,000 for the preparation of the substantial supporting documentation required to certify an emissions reduction.[36] Above all, the process of administrative approval introduces a further element of uncertainty into the transaction. Only about 20 percent of all trades that reach this stage are fully approved as proposed. Of the 80 percent of trades not receiving complete regulatory approval, half will be rejected out of hand, and the other half will be subject to a variety of downward revisions. The reason for the large number of unapproved proposed trades is the difficulty associated with certifying the claimed emissions reduction and agreeing on the benchmark against which the reduction is measured. For example, up to 90 percent of the value of the emissions reduction may be discounted to reach compliance with BACT and other source-specific rules.[37] It is this feature of the bureaucratic approval process that necessitates a variety of risk-sharing features to be incorporated into the trading contracts.

Some types of trades may be less vulnerable to these problems than others. For example, the trading of credits in "multipollutant clusters" is likely to reduce the duration of the approval process by permitting a number of trades in different pollutants to be approved simultaneously.

[36] A typical value for the joint financial transaction costs of both partners required to bring about an exchange would be $25,000, with $10,000 as a lower bound. Interview with Josh Margolis, director of trading operations for AER*X, July 1991.

[37] *Id.*

Another example is the exchange of credits through the SCAQMD bank, which considerably reduces the duration and uncertainty associated with the approval process from the buyer's perspective, because the magnitude of the credit has already been certified. However, the seller will have already incurred the cost and delay associated with banking the credit in the first place and, in addition, bears the risk that the value of the credits deposited in the bank will be subsequently devalued by the regulatory authority, as has already occurred on one occasion.[38] The banking of credits thus reallocates transaction costs from buyer to seller. For this reason, one might expect such credits to be exchanged at a higher unit price. There is some evidence that this was indeed the case; however, the small number of observations does not make it possible to draw a very strong conclusion.

A comparison of potential transaction costs with observed credit prices leads to an important finding: the transaction cost of trades may frequently exceed the market value of the credits purchased. For example, a typical trade of 50 tons per year of ROG trading for $150 per ton has an exchange value of $7,500. The total transaction costs of such a trade could easily exceed $10,000. Moreover, a simple financial measure of the costs of trading does not capture the wider costs of delay and uncertainty associated with the exchange process.

2. *Analysis of Trades with High Transaction Costs.* On the basis of the preceding discussion, it is possible to identify two types of trades that would be expected to have relatively high transaction costs. They are exchanges involving thinly traded pollutants and exchanges involving very small volumes of credits. Exchanges of thinly traded pollutants could be expected to involve higher transaction costs because it would be harder to find a suitable trading partner. Exchanges involving very small volumes of credits are likely to be adversely affected by the fixed nature of the transaction costs imposed by the bureaucratic approval process and possibly also by the difficulty of finding suitable trading partners.

It seems plausible that these two types of trades would make disproportionate use of the four transaction-cost-reducing devices identified above—namely, trading internally, from the bank, through an intermediary, or in a multipollutant cluster.

The evidence on thinly traded pollutants is presented in Table 6, which breaks down the trades in each pollutant according to each of these four types. For the purposes of testing this hypothesis, CO, PM, and SO_x are

[38] See Appendix A for a summary of the June 1990 reforms.

TABLE 6

BREAKDOWN OF TRADES FOR EACH POLLUTANT OVER THE PERIOD 1985–91: NUMBER OF TRADES (and Percentage of Total) FOR EACH POLLUTANT

Pollutant	Internal	Clustered	Banked	AER*X	None*	Total
CO	3(43)	2(29)	2(29)	2(29)	1(14)	7
NO_x	4(14)	10(34)	10(34)	13(45)	4(14)	29
PM	6(55)	4(36)	1(9)	1(9)	1(9)	11
ROG	32(22)	6(4)	34(23)	29(20)	61(41)	148
SO_x	3(50)	2(33)	1(17)	2(33)	0(0)	6
Total	48	24	48	47	67	201

NOTE.—Percentages do not sum to 100 and rows do not sum to total because the different types of trades are not mutually exclusive.

* These are trades that are neither internal, nor clustered, nor banked, nor make use of AER*X.

all designated as being "thinly traded," as there are less than 12 trades recorded for each. With close to 150 trades, ROG is clearly not "thinly traded." With about 30 trades, NO_x falls somewhere in between. The data presented in the table suggest that thinly traded pollutants are much more likely to be traded internally or as part of a multipollutant cluster or through an intermediary. However, it is not clear that they are any more likely to be traded through the bank.[39] As far as banking is concerned, the result may partly be attributed to the fact that there are fewer deposits of thinly traded pollutants in the bank from which to choose. A particularly striking result emerges if all of these devices for reducing transaction costs are considered simultaneously (see the penultimate column of Table 6). There are only a small fraction of trades of the thinly traded pollutants that did not make use of at least one of these four devices (no more than 14 percent in the case of any one thinly traded pollutant). It is only in the case of ROG that there were a significant number of trades that did not make use of any of these devices.

The evidence on transaction-cost-reducing behavior for small trades is summarized in Table 7, which examines the extent to which trades of different sizes make use of the four devices identified. For purposes of analysis, a small trade is defined (somewhat arbitrarily) as one below 5 tons per year (or 25 pounds per day) in volume.[40] The results that emerge

[39] These results are formally confirmed by the hypothesis tests that are summarized in Appendix B. There is a statistically significant difference in the number of exchanges of thinly traded pollutants being exchanged internally or as part of a multipollutant cluster or through an intermediary. However, this is not the case when it comes to banking.

[40] This is probably a rather generous definition of a small trade. For the purposes of the SCAQMD Community Bank, a small trade is defined as one below the 2-tons-per-year threshold.

TABLE 7

BREAKDOWN OF TRADES FOR EACH SIZE CLASS: NUMBER OF TRADES (and Percentage of Total) FOR EACH SIZE CLASS

Pounds/Day	Internal	Clustered	Banked	AER*X	None*	Total
<25	7(41)	8(47)	5(29)	3(18)	1(6)	17
26–50	4(21)	0(0)	6(32)	2(11)	7(37)	19
51–100	8(19)	3(7)	9(21)	10(23)	20(47)	43
101–250	15(25)	4(7)	13(22)	14(24)	20(34)	59
251–500	7(16)	8(19)	8(19)	14(33)	15(35)	43
501–1,000	6(55)	0(0)	2(18)	1(9)	3(27)	11
1,001–5,000	1(13)	0(0)	4(50)	3(38)	2(25)	8
>5,000	0(0)	1(100)	1(100)	0(0)	0(0)	1
Total	48	24	48	47	68	201

NOTE.—Percentages do not sum to 100 and rows do not sum to total because the different types of trades are not mutually exclusive.

* These are trades that are neither internal, nor clustered, nor banked, nor make use of AER*X.

from the table are very similar to those found in the case of thinly traded pollutants. Both internal trading and "multipollutant clusters" are significantly more prevalent in the smallest size class of trades. However, for banked trades and trades through intermediaries, the picture is less clear.[41] Once again, considering all of the devices for reducing transaction costs simultaneously gives a much stronger result. For the smallest size class (under 25 pounds per day), there was only one ROG trade that did not make use of one or more of these four devices.

The introduction of the Community Bank in 1991 means that the smallest trades (those less than 2 tons per year in volume) no longer need go through the open trading process. Examining the volume of trades in the Community Bank in 1991 makes it possible to draw some inferences as to the dampening effect of fixed transaction costs on the volume of small trades. The activity in the Community Bank is summarized in Table 2. The Community Bank accounted for over 2,000 transactions in 1991 alone. This dramatic increase in the number of small transactions cannot be solely attributed to the low transaction costs associated with using the Community Bank because the credits obtained from the bank are free, whereas those obtained in the market have a positive price associated with them. (The credits from the Community Bank are allocated on the basis of volume demanded, rather than on the basis of price.) However,

[41] These results are largely confirmed by the hypothesis tests, which identify a statistically significant difference in the case of "multipollutant clusters," but not in the case of banked trades and use of an intermediary. Although the visual evidence for internal trading is quite persuasive, this was not found to be statistically significant. See Appendix B for details.

for a small trade, the cost of purchasing the ERCs would be small relative to the transaction costs. It therefore seems likely that transaction costs were a significant impediment to the trading of small volumes prior to 1991.

In summary, there is some evidence that both internal trading and "multipollutant clusters" may be capable of reducing the transaction costs associated with thinly traded pollutants and small trades.[42] Using the SCAQMD bank and AER*X, in contrast, seems to be more helpful where larger trades of less thinly traded pollutants are concerned. The advent of the Community Bank has led to a huge escalation in the number of small transactions.

C. *The Effect of Regulatory Rules*

The importance of regulatory rules in determining the performance of tradeable permits schemes has been noted in the literature.[43] Trading activity in the Los Angeles offset market is heavily regulated by the SCAQMD. The regulatory environment affecting ERCs in Los Angeles is a dynamic one with frequent rule amendments. For example, Regulation XIII, which governs the exchange of ERCs in the offset market, has seen 59 rule changes over 12 years, with the longest amendment-free period lasting no more than 2 years and 3 months.[44] Undoubtedly, the most significant reform episode experienced in the Los Angeles market took place in June 1990 and came into effect in September of that year. The principal rule changes are summarized in Appendix A and provide the background for the subsequent discussion. The table also highlights the key differences between the Los Angeles market and the textbook conception of a tradeable permits market.

The data indicate that these rule changes had a significant effect on trading activity in the Los Angeles basin. However, they are also of wider interest because of the insights they yield into the importance of the design in ensuring the success of a tradeable permits scheme. The June 1990 reforms in Los Angeles illustrate how the use of the banking facility is affected by regulatory rules. They also permit a comparison of two different ways of incorporating geographical trading restrictions into a market where the spatial location of pollution is important.

[42] There is some correlation between these two categories, since thinly traded pollutants tend to be traded on average in smaller volumes.

[43] Hahn & Noll, *supra* note 6; and Franciosi *et al.*, *supra* note 6.

[44] SCAQMD, *supra* note 12.

1. *The Effect of Regulations on Banking Behavior.* The existence of a banking facility is a key feature of any tradeable permits scheme. Where internal trades are concerned, it gives firms the flexibility to adjust their emissions profiles intertemporally.[45] Where external trades are concerned, banking gives the selling firm the ability to wait until a suitable trading partner emerges or the market price rises to a more attractive level. Moreover, it can reduce the search costs associated with finding a suitable trading partner. It is therefore important to consider how the regulatory framework governing a tradeable permit market affects incentives to make use of the banking facility.

The reforms to the rules governing the Los Angeles offset market in June 1990 provide evidence that regulations had acted to restrain the extent of banking activity in the market. Following the reforms, there was a significant escalation in the number of transactions made from the SCAQMD bank (see Table 4). The data show that both in absolute terms and relative to the overall volume of trading, 1991 was the year with the highest level of trades involving banked ERCs.[46] This high trading level could reflect the increase in the supply of credits brought about by the abolition of the contemporaneous requirement as well as a greater willingness to sell on the part of firms who had recently had their banked deposits devalued.[47]

In addition to the overall dampening affect of the contemporaneous requirement on the use of the SCAQMD bank, an analysis of the pattern of trades in the period prior to the reform indicates how it affected banked and unbanked trades. Two separate effects can be discerned. These concern the extent to which different types of credits were deposited in the bank and then used for trading.

First, a key market participant indicated that the vast majority of unbanked trades involved shutdown-created credits.[48] It is estimated that 74 percent of exchanges of process-change-created ERCs passed through the SCAQMD bank, whereas the corresponding figure for shutdown-

[45] Hahn & Hester, *supra* note 9.

[46] The statistical significance of this difference is confirmed by the hypothesis test that is summarized in Appendix B.

[47] At the time of the June 1990 reforms, over 11,500 tons per year of shutdown-created credits were lying "dormant" in the SCAQMD bank, because they were rendered untradeable by the contemporaneous requirement (see Appendix A). As a result of the abolition of the contemporaneous requirement, and the simultaneous 80 percent devaluation of the credits, some 2,700 tons per year of shutdown-created credits became available for trading.

[48] John Palmisano, *supra* note 35, estimated that at least 95 percent of unbanked trades involved shutdown-created credits.

created ERCs is only 5 percent.[49] The implication is that the existence of the contemporaneous requirement was forcing sellers of shutdown-created credits to circumvent the banking facility. In the case of the offset market, this may not have had any significant effect on the number of credits created by shutdown, since these are largely a by-product of shutdown decisions taken for wider economic reasons. The requirement may, however, have created a price differential between these two types of credits.

Second, once banked, shutdown-created credits were less likely to be traded than those created by process change. Only 24 percent of all banked ERCs created from shutdown were traded, as against 65 percent of all banked ERCs created from process change.[50] The reason for this is that there was less time for shutdown-created trades to take place, once the credits had been banked. Thus, shutdown-created credits were deposited on average for 179 days prior to trade, whereas the corresponding figure for process-change-created credits, unaffected by the contemporaneous requirement, was 409 days.[51] This evidence suggests that the contemporaneous requirement was indeed an effective constraint on the trading of shutdown-created credits once they had been banked.

In summary, the evidence indicates that regulatory rules such as the contemporaneous requirement can constitute a significant impediment to the use of the banking facility. The requirement effectively segmented the market for credits by making it more difficult to trade shutdown-created credits. On the positive side of the balance, the contemporaneous requirement had a benign short-term environmental effect by impeding the purchase of shutdown-created credits; however, its long-term effect on environmental quality is less clear because it may have reduced the rate of environmental innovation.[52]

2. *Different Ways of Regulating the Spatial Distribution of Emissions.* Except in the case of global environmental externalities, such as ozone depletion and global warming, regulators are frequently as much concerned with the spatial distribution of pollution as with its aggregate

[49] These are estimates based on the indication that 95 percent of unbanked trades involved shutdown-created credits. Unfortunately, the exact origin of credits was recorded only in the data set from the SCAQMD bank and not in the larger AER*X data set.

[50] The statistical significance of this difference is confirmed by the hypothesis test that is summarized in Appendix B.

[51] However, this difference in the deposit period was not found to be statistically significant. The details of the hypothesis test are summarized in Appendix B.

[52] The relationship between environmental regulation and innovation is explored in Scott R. Milliman & Raymond Prince, Firm Incentives to Promote Technology Change in Pollution Control, 17 J. Envtl. Econ. & Mgmt. 247 (1989).

level. Market mechanisms for pollution control must therefore be sensitive to the location of emissions. There are essentially two ways of taking spatial considerations into account. The first is to alter trading ratios according to the location of trading partners. Thus, a firm in an environmentally sensitive location may be required to buy more than one credit for every additional unit of emissions it produces. The second is to place absolute restrictions on allowable trades based on the geographic location of the participants. This has the effect of creating a number of geographically segmented markets.

Over the period covered by this study, the Los Angeles offset market made use of both of these approaches to regulating the spatial distribution of emissions (see Appendix A). Before June 1990, trading ratios varied between 1.2:1 and 1.6:1, depending on the geographic location of trading partners.[53] Following the reforms, a single trading ratio of 1.2:1 was used, but the market was segmented into 38 distinct zones, with rules governing exchanges between them. The overall effect of these was to only allow trades of credits from east to west or within each zone.[54] The purpose of the restriction was to prevent deterioration in air quality in the zone in which the emissions reduction was made.

It is difficult to draw any conclusions about the effect of these changes on the number of trades that took place, since there are a number of confounding influences at about the same time. There is however a particularly marked effect on the dispersion of prices, which would appear to be linked to the change in the nature of the spatial restrictions on trades. As illustrated in Figure 1, between 1990 and 1991 there was a threefold increase in the difference between the maximum and minimum price in the market.[55] There are two reasons to believe that this is at least partly attributable to the geographic segmentation of the market. First, by creating a large number of segmented markets, the reform created a variety of different supply and demand conditions in each one, leading to a range of equilibrium prices. Second, the reform converted an already thin market into a set of thinner markets, thus making it less likely that a stable set of prices would emerge for ERCs.

While the move toward geographical segmentation can be justified in

[53] The purpose of keeping the trading ratio greater than one was to ensure that each transaction had an environmentally beneficial effect. Note that such an approach is similar to placing a tax on trading. Robert W. Hahn, Regulatory Constraints on Environmental Markets, 42 J. Pub. Econ. 149 (1990).

[54] Rule 1303(b) and Appendix B of Rule 1303, Regulation XIII, in SCAQMD, *supra* note 12.

[55] However, this result is not found to be statistically significant. See Appendix B for a summary of the hypothesis test.

environmental terms, the consequent effect on price dispersion illustrates the problems that can arise in the operation of a tradeable permits market.

IV. Conclusions and Areas for Future Research

Market-based approaches for environmental protection are beginning to take root across the globe. There are ongoing projects in Eastern Europe, the former Soviet Union, Australia, Europe, and the United States. The federal program for controlling acid rain and the RECLAIM program for Los Angeles are probably the two programs closest to fruition. There has been no dearth of advice from economists on how such programs should be designed.[56] Yet, the design suggestions have tended to rely more on a general understanding of political economy rather than a deeper understanding of the workings of specific environmental markets.

This article takes a step toward providing that deeper understanding by analyzing the arm's-length exchange of credits between firms in the Los Angeles offset market. It therefore provides important evidence on the trading process itself. The ease with which credits can be exchanged is an important determinant of market performance, although it is typically overlooked in theoretical models.

An important finding was the effect that the magnitude and nature of transaction costs have on the incentive to engage in external trades. In many cases, the magnitude of transaction costs exceeded the market value of the credits exchanged. In addition to the financial expenditure involved, transactions are long in duration and subject to considerable uncertainty, leading to the creation of risk-sharing contracts between trading parties. These costs weigh particularly heavily on small trades and exchanges of thinly traded pollutants. Almost all trades of this type made use of one of a number of transaction-cost-reducing devices, such as trading internally, in a "multipollutant cluster," through the banking facility, or through an intermediary.

Banking facilities play an important role in the functioning of a tradeable permits scheme. As well as providing firms with greater intertemporal flexibility, they reduce the search costs and uncertainty associated with exchange. Indeed, there was some evidence that banked credits attracted a price premium in the offset market for these very reasons. However,

[56] Roger G. Noll, Marketable Emissions Permits in Los Angeles (unpublished manuscript, Stanford University, Stanford, Calif. 1990); David Harrison, Jr. & Albert L. Nichols, Market-Based Approaches to Reduce the Cost of Clean Air in California's South Coast Air Basin (1990); and Wallace E. Oates & Albert M. McGartland, Marketable Pollution Permits and Acid Rain Externalities: A Comment and Some Further Evidence, 18 Canadian J. Econ. 668–75 (1985).

regulatory rules may create incentives for firms to avoid using the bank and thereby prevent these benefits from being realized. A particularly insidious problem is the ad hoc devaluation of banked credits.

The data from the Los Angeles offset market indicated that ERC markets are not likely to be in a classical equilibrium with a set of well-defined prices. A striking feature of the market was the range of prices at which ERCs are exchanged at any moment in time. This price dispersion was exacerbated when the market was segmented geographically as a means of regulating the spatial distribution of emissions. The most plausible explanation of price dispersion was the heterogeneity of ERCs. Credits can differ in terms of their method of creation, their geographic location, whether they have been banked, and the risk-sharing arrangements embodied in the exchange contracts. All of these factors are likely to be reflected in the price at which the credit is exchanged.

The analysis presented in this study, while based on the most extensive economic data set to date, still suffers from a marked absence of information. We are concerned that policy makers may not see a payoff to generating the kind of information that would be most needed to improve our understanding of market performance. Those in academia interested in lobbying either for efficiency or for data for publications should take note. The message is simple. Regulators need to spend more resources on gathering appropriate data so the academic community can better assess how programs actually work. The same point about economic data should be made about environmental data. Information on changes in the aggregate-level emissions as well as the regional and temporal pattern of emissions is critical for assessing the environmental effectiveness of market-based programs.

The analysis in this article does not take into account the effect of the political process on system design and performance. In many cases, politics can have an important effect on transaction costs. In Los Angeles, for example, there are very high stakes, in terms of direct economic costs, employment effects, and environmental quality. Some environmentalists said they would not support a market-based system unless the system demonstrated beyond any reasonable doubt that it could deliver environmental gains that exceed those that allegedly would be achieved under a command-and-control regime. At the same time, some members of industry voice concern because they believe that the RECLAIM program would be more onerous than command-and-control, achieving more rapid environmental gains and imposing higher economic costs.[57] With

[57] Some industry officials are supportive of RECLAIM, believing that costs will go down for the business community relative to the command-and-control system. For more detail on interest group perspectives, see Cohen, *supra* note 17, and the references cited therein.

such divergent views about the underlying distribution of property rights, it becomes difficult for programs such as RECLAIM to work effectively.[58] This highly contentious political environment provides a useful laboratory for studying how politics affects the use of economic instruments for environmental protection.

Perhaps the greatest challenge facing the advocates of market-based environmental protection is to have the government make a "credible" commitment to such markets. This requires, among other things, a clear definition of the property right and the conditions under which such rights may be modified. Governments have great difficulties making credible commitments in this area for two reasons: first, in general, it is difficult for elected officials to prevent their successors from undoing new policies if they wish to; second, environmental markets are likely to remain politically contentious for the foreseeable future. Politicians have only recently embraced these markets as a means for meeting the growing demand for environmental quality.

The move toward adopting market-based approaches for environmental protection needs to be accompanied by a vigorous effort to ascertain the properties of these systems as they are actually implemented. There is a great deal more that needs to be learned about environmental markets and taxes—particularly the conditions under which they are likely to be successful. The introduction of policy experiments throughout the world could aid our understanding immensely.

In short, the good news is that the world is beginning to take the ideas of ivory-towered economists seriously in resolving environmental issues. The bad news is that the stock of usable knowledge in this area is a lot lower than we might like. The path to enlightenment is clear: further analysis of the performance of market-based approaches and the political forces that constrain institutional design.

[58] The SCAQMD finds itself caught between these competing interests. In addition, it must satisfy a federal EPA, whose regional office initially opposed market-based reforms in Los Angeles. Yet, there is hope. Officials at the SCAQMD will encourage the introduction of new and improved environmental markets if they believe such behavior will be rewarded. And such behavior is likely to be rewarded, both internally, through cues taken from the head of the agency, James Lents, and externally, through the potential to be a recognized international leader in environmental regulation. Whether these positive incentives are sufficient to overcome bureaucratic inertia and interest group politics remains to be seen.

APPENDIX A

Comparing the Trading Rules for the Offset Market with Those for the "Textbook" Market

Textbook Market	Los Angeles Offset Market Pre–June 1990	Los Angeles Offset Market Post–June 1990
All new emissions must be covered by credit purchases.	Small new sources are exempt from purchasing credits.	All new emissions must be covered by credit purchases. Any previously exempt emissions must be covered retrospectively.
Source-specific emission limits can be avoided by purchasing credits.	Source-specific emission limits cannot be avoided by trading.	Source-specific emission limits cannot be avoided by trading.
Emissions reductions are measured against the current emissions baseline.	Emissions reductions are measured against the current emissions baseline.	Emissions reductions are measured against the emissions that would have resulted if the Best Available Control Technology had been used.
Credits can be banked indefinitely and subsequently traded.	The contemporaneous requirement means that shutdown-created credits can be sold only to firms who filed an application to trade within 90 days of shutdown. Banked shutdown credits are devalued to 20 percent of their face value.	Credits can be banked indefinitely and subsequently traded.
Permits trade at a 1:1 ratio.	Permits trade at a ratio between 1.2:1 and 1.6:1 depending on the location of the trading partners.	Permits trade at a ratio of 1.2:1.
No geographic restrictions on trade.	No geographic restrictions on trade, but distant trades are penalized by the trading ratio.	Region divided into 38 zones and geographic restrictions on trading from east to west.

APPENDIX B

TABLE B1

Summary of Results of Nonparametric Hypothesis Tests

Hypothesis	Test	N	df	Result*
Section A:				
The dispersion of prices decreases with time as the market evolves	Spearman rank correlation test	6	6	Reject
The dispersion of prices is lower in years when the market is relatively active	Spearman rank correlation test	6	6	Reject
Average ROG prices are correlated with regional per capita income	Spearman rank correlation test	6	6	Reject
Section B2:				
Thinly traded pollutants are more likely to be traded in clusters	χ^2 test for homogeneity	153	4	Accept
Thinly traded pollutants are more likely to be traded internally	χ^2 test for homogeneity	201	4	Accept
Thinly traded pollutants are more likely to be traded through the bank	χ^2 test for homogeneity	153	4	Reject
Exchanges of thinly traded pollutants are more likely to involve AER*X	χ^2 test for homogeneity	153	4	Accept
Small trades are more likely to be traded in clusters	χ^2 test for homogeneity	153	7	Accept
Small trades are more likely to be traded internally	χ^2 test for homogeneity	201	7	Reject
Small trades are more likely to be traded through the bank	χ^2 test for homogeneity	153	7	Reject
Small trades are more likely to involve AER*X	χ^2 test for homogeneity	153	7	Reject
Section C1:				
The number of trades making use of banked credits was lower prior to 1991	χ^2 test for homogeneity	201	1	Accept
Once banked, shutdown-created credits were less likely to be traded	χ^2 test for homogeneity	75	1	Accept
When traded, banked shutdown-created credits were deposited for a shorter period	Mann-Whitney test	30	8, 22	Reject

Note.—df = degrees of freedom. ROG = reactive organic gases.
* A 5 percent significance level for formal hypotheses is used to determine "accept" or "reject."

Bibliography

AER*X. *Information on ERC Trades*. Washington, D.C.: AER*X, 1992.

Anderson, Robert C.; Hofmann, Lisa A.; and Rusin, Michael. "The Use of Economic Incentive Mechanisms in Environmental Management." Research Paper No. 051. Washington, D.C.: American Petroleum Institute, June 1990.

Baumol, William J., and Oates, Wallace E. *The Theory of Environmental Policy*. Englewood Cliffs, N.J.: Prentice-Hall, 1975.

California Air Resources Board. "Mobile Source Emission Reduction Credits: Guidelines for the Generation and Use of Mobile Source Emission Reduction Credits." N.p.: California Air Resources Board, Stationary and Mobile Source Divisions, February 1993.

Cohen, Linda. "Marketable Permits for Air Pollution in Los Angeles: Issues for Experimental Economics." Unpublished manuscript. Irvine: University of California, Irvine, January 14, 1993.

Dales, J. *Pollution, Property and Prices*. Toronto: University Press, 1968.

Daniel, Wayne W. *Applied Nonparametric Statistics*. 2d ed. Boston, Mass.: PWS-KENT, 1990.

Dudek, Daniel J., and Palmisano, John. "Emissions Trading: Why Is This Thoroughbred Hobbled?" *Columbia Journal of Environmental Law* 13 (1988): 217–56.

Franciosi, Robert; Isaac, R. Mark; Pingry, David E.; and Reynolds, Stanley S. "An Experimental Investigation of the Hahn-Noll Revenue Neutral Auction for Emissions Licenses." *Journal of Environmental Economics and Management* 24 (1993): 1–24.

Hahn, Robert W. "Economic Prescriptions for Environmental Problems: How the Patient Followed the Doctor's Orders." *Journal of Economic Perspectives* 3 (Spring 1989): 95–114.

Hahn, Robert W. "Regulatory Constraints on Environmental Markets." *Journal of Public Economics* 42 (1990): 149–75.

Hahn, Robert W., and Hester, Gordon L. "The Market for Bads: EPA's Experience with Emissions Trading." *Regulation* 3/4 (1987): 48–53.

Hahn, Robert W., and Hester, Gordon L. "Marketable Permits: Lessons for Theory and Practice." *Ecology Law Quarterly* 16 (1989): 361–406.

Hahn, Robert W., and Noll, Roger G. "Designing a Market in Tradeable Emissions Permits." In *Reform of Environmental Regulation*, edited by Wesley Magat, pp. 119–46. Cambridge, Mass.: Ballinger, 1982.

Hahn, Robert W., and Noll, Roger G. "Environmental Markets in the Year 2000." *Journal of Risk and Uncertainty* 3 (1990): 351–67.

Harrison, David, Jr., and Nichols, Albert L. "Market-Based Approaches to Reduce the Cost of Clean Air in California's South Coast Air Basin." Cambridge, Mass.: National Economic Research Associates, Inc., November 28, 1990.

Kneese, Allen V., and Schultze, Charles L. *Pollution, Prices, and Public Policy*. Washington, D.C.: Brookings Institution, 1975.

Liroff, Richard A. *Reforming Air Pollution Regulation: The Toil and Trouble of EPA's Bubble*. Washington, D.C.: Conservation Foundation, 1986.

Margolis, Josh. Interview. AER*X, Menlo Park, Calif., July 1991.

Milliman, Scott R., and Prince, Raymond. "Firm Incentives to Promote Technological Change in Pollution Control." *Journal of Environmental Economics and Management* 17 (1989): 247–65.

Montgomery, W. David. "Markets in Licenses and Efficient Pollution Control Programs." *Journal of Economic Theory* 5 (1972): 395–418.

Moore, John L., *et al. Using Incentives for Environmental Protection: An Overview*. Document No. 89-360 ENR. Washington, D.C.: Congressional Research Service, June 2, 1989.

Noll, Roger G. "Marketable Emissions Permits in Los Angeles." Unpublished manuscript. Stanford, Calif.: Stanford University, 1990.

Oates, Wallace E., and McGartland, Albert M. "Marketable Pollution Permits and Acid Rain Externalities: A Comment and Some Further Evidence." *Canadian Journal of Economics* 18 (1985): 668–75.

Opschoor, J. B., and Vos, Hans B. *Economic Instruments for Environmental Protection*. Paris: Organization for Economic Cooperation and Development, 1989.

Palmisano, John. Telephone interview. AER*X, Washington, D.C., October 10, 1992.

Pigou, A. C. *The Economics of Welfare*. 4th ed. London: Macmillan & Company, 1932.

Repetto, Robert, *et al. Green Fees: How a Tax Shift Can Work for the Environment and the Economy*. Washington, D.C.: World Resources Institute, November 1992.

SCAQMD (South Coast Air Quality Management District). *Rules and Regulations*. El Monte, Calif.: SCAQMD, February 1991.

SCAQMD. *Regional Clean Air Incentives Market Summary Recommendations*. El Monte, Calif.: SCAQMD, Spring 1992.

SCAQMD. *Records of the SCAQMD on Banking, Netting, Community Banking and Priority Reserve*. Compiled by Ambrose Lam. El Monte, Calif.: SCAQMD, 1993.

Stavins, Robert N., ed. "Project 88: Harnessing Market Forces to Protect Our Environment—Initiatives for the New President." A public policy study sponsored by Senator Timothy E. Wirth and Senator John Heinz, Washington, D.C., 1988.

Stavins, Robert N. "Transaction Costs and the Performance of Markets for Pollution Control." Discussion Paper No. 93-02. Cambridge, Mass.: Harvard University, Center for Science and International Affairs, 1993.

Tietenberg, Thomas H. *Emissions Trading: An Exercise in Reforming Pollution Policy*. Washington, D.C.: Resources for the Future, 1985.

U.S. Environmental Protection Agency. *Economic Incentives: Options for Environmental Protection*. Document No. 21P-2001. Washington, D.C.: U.S. Environmental Protection Agency, March 1991.

[8]

New Physicians: A Natural Experiment in Market Organization

ALVIN E. ROTH

The National Resident Matching Program is a centralized clearinghouse through which new medical graduates in the United States obtain their first positions. The history of this market, from the market failures that the centralized system was designed to address, to the present, is discussed, and a hypothesis about the behavior of such markets is presented. New evidence is then presented from a set of similar centralized markets in the United Kingdom. Because some of these latter markets have failed, while others have succeeded, they provide a natural experiment that permits the hypothesis to be tested. The new evidence also suggests directions in which modifications of existing procedures might be considered.

MEDICAL SCHOOL GRADUATES IN THE UNITED STATES seek their first employment through a centralized labor market called the National Resident Matching Program (NRMP). This centralized market was established in the 1950s in response to persistent failures to organize the market in a timely and orderly way by decentralized means. Similar centralized labor markets, inspired by similar market failures, have been used in some regions of the National Health Service in the United Kingdom, where new medical graduates seek pre-registration positions comparable to U.S. residencies. Because different regions have used different procedures for organizing the market, the British system presents a natural experiment that allows these procedures to be compared with each other and with the U.S. market (*1*). Because some of the centralized procedures used in Britain have failed and been abandoned, whereas others have succeeded, this natural experiment also presents an opportunity to test the hypothesis put forward to explain the success and longevity of the U.S. market (*2*).

The centralized markets discussed here have the same outward form: each student submits a list of positions whose order is intended to reflect his preferences, and the person responsible for filling each set of positions likewise submits a ranked list of students. The markets differ in the algorithms then used to match students to positions—that is, they differ in what matching will be produced for a given set of submitted preference lists. The evidence suggests that these differences have a profound effect on the incentives that agents may have to try to circumvent the centralized market (and on what kinds of preference lists they submit). The differences between the kinds of matchings produced by centralized markets that have succeeded and those that have failed suggest constraints that must be faced in the design of algorithms to perform this kind of market function. (In this respect, this work is on the relatively unexplored interface of economics and operations research.) These differences also permit us to draw inferences about the nature of the matchings achieved in decentralized markets that experience similar success or failure.

The body of theory to which this evidence applies most directly concerns "two-sided matching markets," in which agents of one kind (for instance, workers) are matched with agents of another kind (employers) (*3, 4*). Another two-sided matching market briefly discussed is the process by which sororities recruit members on U.S. college campuses (*5*).

The U.S. Market

From around 1900 to 1945, competition among hospitals for new interns and residents forced the date of appointment ever earlier, until medical students and hospitals were concluding agreements for post-graduation employment up to 2 years before graduation. This was costly in a variety of ways for both students and hospitals, and the date of appointment was finally brought under control in 1945 through intervention by the medical schools. There followed a period in which the market was very disorderly, with students being called upon to make increasingly prompt decisions whether to accept offers. (By 1949, a grace period of 12 hours had been rejected as too long.) The market was characterized by chaotic, last-minute recontracting, with students seeking to improve on the positions they had been firmly offered (and had sometimes accepted) by contacting the hospitals they preferred, and with hospitals sometimes pressuring students into premature decisions in order to be able to contact promptly students on their waiting lists. A centralized clearinghouse was proposed only when other attempts to organize the market had been exhausted.

This centralized market is still in operation (*6*). From 1952, following the introduction of the centralized matching procedure, there was a high degree of voluntary, orderly participation, with about 95% of U.S. medical school graduates entering the match and ultimately being offered and accepting the position with which they were matched. However, beginning in the mid-1970s, with a growing number of married couples in need of two positions in the same vicinity, high percentages of these obtained them outside of the centralized match; thus, the overall rate of participation, while still high, began to drop.

Previously, I proposed a hypothesis (*2*) to account for the transition from chaotic recontracting to orderly voluntary participation that took place in 1952, and the transition from uniformly high rates of participation among medical school graduates prior to the 1970s, to the defection of married couples in the late 1970s and

The author is the A. W. Mellon Professor of Economics at the University of Pittsburgh, Pittsburgh, PA 15260.

early 1980s. To describe the hypothesis, it is first necessary to briefly describe a model phrased in terms of the preferences of each student for positions and of each hospital program for students (*7*).

Because a hospital program typically employs more than one student, a description of a hospital's preferences must include how it evaluates alternative groups of students. For the purposes of this article, it is sufficient to suppose merely that if two groups of students differ only by a single individual, the hospital prefers the group containing the higher ranked individual. A student will be called "unacceptable" to a hospital if the hospital would prefer to keep a position vacant rather than fill it with that student, and a hospital is unacceptable to a student if, rather than accept one of its positions, the student would prefer to remain unmatched (and seek employment in a secondary market).

An outcome of the market is a matching of students and hospitals, such that no hospital is assigned more students than it has positions, and no student is assigned more than one position. A matching is called "unstable" if some student is matched to an unacceptable hospital, some hospital is matched to an unacceptable student, or if some student and hospital who are not matched to one another would both prefer to be matched together (*8*). Notice that an unstable matching gives some agent or pair of agents an incentive to find a different match. A matching that is not unstable in this way is called "stable" (or pairwise stable) (*9*). At a stable matching, each student finds that any hospitals he prefers to the one he is matched with do not return the favor.

The hypothesis proposed previously (*2*) is based on the demonstration that the 1952 matching algorithm produced a stable matching (in terms of any preferences that were submitted), and that the procedure used to assign married couples two jobs in the same vicinity was particularly prone to produce unstable matchings (*10*). Thus, the "stability hypothesis" applied to this market is that the chaotic conditions prior to 1952 reflected the instabilities then present in the market, that the success of the centralized procedure was due to the stability of the matching it produced, and that the decline in participation among married couples in the 1970s was because they once again found instabilities. Note that a student who has been offered or had proposed to him a specific job (or a couple who was matched with a pair of jobs) has only to make a few phone calls to determine if any preferred hospitals would be willing to offer a position, so the problem of determining if there are any exploitable instabilities is not a difficult one.

Of course, even though the stability hypothesis seems to account for the major developments in this market, the real explanations might lie elsewhere; for example, maybe any centralized market organization would have solved the problems experienced prior to 1951, and perhaps the experience of married couples has less to do with instabilities than with the difficulties young couples have in making decisions. Another kind of question about the stability hypothesis concerns the incentives that agents may have to submit rank-orderings that differ from their true preferences. The algorithm used in the U.S. market has the property that opportunities may arise both for students and hospitals to obtain a more preferred matching by submitting a preference list different from their true preferences rather than by submitting their true preferences (*3, 11*). If agents may have reason not to submit their true preferences, the fact that the algorithm produces a matching stable with respect to the submitted preferences does not ensure that the matching is stable with respect to the true preferences (that is, the preferences according to which agents search for and accept alternative opportunities).

One approach to addressing this question is to consider whether the agents in the market have the kind of information about one another's preferences needed to profitably submit rank orderings different from their true preferences. If not, submitted preferences might approximate true preferences sufficiently to produce stable outcomes. And if agents were sufficiently well informed so that they could submit the preference lists that would achieve their best available matches, given the lists submitted by everyone else, then under some circumstances it is possible to demonstrate that the resulting matching would be stable with respect to the true preferences (even though these would differ from the submitted preferences) (*3*). My point in raising these matters here is to indicate that, despite the (mathematical) demonstration of the stability properties of the U.S. system algorithm, and the degree to which stability and its absence seem to explain the major changes in the history of the market, there is room to doubt the stability hypothesis as an explanation of the behavior of the U.S. market. The question remains largely an empirical one, which gives further reason to make additional observations of the kind considered next.

The British Markets

A medical school graduate in Britain is eligible only for provisional registration with the General Medical Council. For full registration a doctor must complete separate medical and surgical pre-registration positions. An outcome of this market is thus a matching of students and consultants (supervising physicians and surgeons) such that no consultant is assigned more students than he has positions, and no student is assigned more than two positions, one medical and one surgical.

Most positions are filled on a regional basis, with graduates of a medical school going to a hospital in the same region (*12*). These regional markets are two orders of magnitude smaller than the U.S. market, ranging from approximately 100 to 300 positions.

That students seek two positions, rather than one as in the United States, makes for some important differences between the U.K. markets and the U.S. market. Both sides of the market must have preferences not just over individuals but over sets; that is, consultants have preferences over groups of students, and students have preferences over pairs of jobs. Thus, agents' preferences cannot be modeled as simple rank orderings, even though, as in the United States, students and consultants are asked to submit rank orderings of one another in these markets. (For example, because of the registration requirements, students prefer one medical and one surgical position to any other combination, regardless of their preferences for individual positions.) Therefore, the mathematical models used to develop the theory of these markets make weaker assumptions about preferences than were appropriate for the U.S. market. The main assumption is that consultants regard students and students regard positions more as substitutes than as complements, in that a consultant who is willing to hire a given student as part of some group of students should remain willing to hire him even if some other member of that group becomes unavailable (*13*). Under this assumption it can be shown (*1*) that the set of stable matchings is nonempty for any preferences, where, as before, a matching is stable if no matches are unacceptable and if no student or consultant who are not matched to one another would both prefer to be matched together (*14*).

The centralized pre-registration markets in Britain arose in reaction to problems that emerged in the 1960s. The markets in the various regions of the National Health Service were previously run in a decentralized way, with students responsible for finding positions on their own, and consultants responsible for filling the positions under their supervision. Competition among students for desirable positions and among consultants for desirable house officers eventually led to these positions being filled earlier and earlier in the students' education, just as had happened in the United States. When a Royal Commission on Medical Education (1965–1968) investigated the problems confronting the pre-registration market, the organization of the U.S. market presented an obvious alternative. Following the Royal Commission's recommendations, many regions introduced centralized matching procedures, but different regions used different algorithms to determine the match from the submitted preferences. (Some, but by no means all, of these centralized schemes were implemented by computer.) It appears that over a dozen regional matching procedures were introduced, but, in contrast to the U.S. experience, only a few survived to the present. Most failed to solve the problems that motivated their introduction and were abandoned.

There are eight matching algorithms for which I have been able to obtain sufficiently precise descriptions to determine whether they produce stable matchings. [All but one (*15*) was computerized.] Two of these always produce stable matchings (*1*), and both of these have controlled the unraveling of appointment dates and survived to the present. The six remaining schemes are based on algorithms that may frequently produce instabilities. Only two of these have survived (and these are in the two smallest markets); the other four have been abandoned. Table 1 summarizes these results and also includes the U.S. market and the "preferential bidding system" used by U.S. sororities (*5*), which are the other two centralized matching procedures whose rules I have so far been able to learn in sufficient detail to determine whether they produce stable matchings (*16*). Of ten matching schemes so far observed, four produce stable matchings, and all four of these are still in use. Six produced unstable matchings, and four of these are no longer in use (*17*).

Table 1. Stable and unstable algorithms.

Market	Stable	Still in use
United States	Yes	Yes
Edinburgh (1969)	Yes	Yes
Cardiff	Yes	Yes
Sororities	Yes	Yes
Cambridge	No	Yes
London Hospital	No	Yes
Birmingham	No	No
Edinburgh (1967)	No	No
Newcastle	No	No
Sheffield	No	No

Because ten is a relatively small sample, and because Table 1 groups together markets that are vastly different in size, and procedures that differ in more ways than the stability of their outcomes, it may be illuminating to briefly describe one of the failed procedures and how it failed.

The scheme introduced in Newcastle in 1967 (*18*) used the product of the student's ranking of the consultant and the consultant's ranking of the student as the basis for a "priority" for that student to be employed by that consultant. The first step of the algorithm was to make all the first priority matches, after which consultants with unfilled positions and students still needing jobs were scanned to identify any second priority matches, and so on. If a consultant and student each ranked one another first [a "(1, 1) match"], they had a priority of 1. If the consultant ranked the student first but the student ranked the consultant second [a "(1, 2) match"], they had a priority of 2, as did a consultant who ranked a student second but was ranked first by the student [a "(2, 1) match"]. Ties were broken in the student's favor (*19*).

For example, consider six consultants, each of whom has only one position to fill, and six students, each of whom needs only one position. (The example does not depend on this simplification.) The rank orderings of the agents are as follows:

C_1: $s_1, \ldots$	s_1: $C_1, \ldots$
C_2: $s_1, s_3, s_2, s_4, s_5, s_6$	s_2: $C_2, C_1, C_3, C_4, C_5, C_6$
C_3: $s_3, s_4, \ldots$	s_3: $C_4, C_3, \ldots$
C_4: $s_4, s_3, \ldots$	s_4: $C_3, C_4, \ldots$
C_5: $s_1, s_2, s_5, s_3, s_4, s_6$	s_5: $C_1, C_2, C_5, C_3, C_4, C_6$
C_6: $s_2, s_5, \ldots$	s_6: $C_5, C_2, \ldots$

The Newcastle algorithm makes the matches: C_1s_1 (1, 1); C_3s_4 and C_4s_3 (2, 1); C_2s_2 (3, 1); C_5s_6 (6, 1); C_6s_5 (2,6). This outcome is unstable because C_5 and s_5 are one another's third choices, but are each matched to their sixth choice.

So far, the example has been analyzed as if the agents all state their true preferences. Before examining the incentives that agents may have to do otherwise, consider the way in which this matching procedure failed and was abandoned. The following description, for example, is from John Anderson, the Postgraduate Dean at Newcastle (*20*): "Shortly before the scheme was discarded we found that in up to 80% of cases students and consultants only used the computer to indicate a first preference. . . . The main reason for the abandonment of the scheme, therefore, was that there were problems in getting students and consultants to participate in an orderly way, and this led to those who rigidly observed the requirements of the scheme to be penalised."

To understand this phenomenon, consider now the incentives which this procedure gives to the agents. To make the above example clear, suppose consultants C_1 through C_5 are in the most desirable teaching hospital, and C_6 is in a much less desirable hospital. Similarly, suppose students s_1 through s_5 are all top graduates, while s_6 has a much less distinguished record.

Then in the example, C_5 is disappointed to learn that his new junior house officer will be s_6, all the more when he learns that s_5, whom he liked better, is unhappy with his own appointment and would have preferred to work for C_5. In a market in which positions could be formally filled by private arrangement (as in the U.S. market), this situation might have led C_5 to decline to hire s_6 and to offer his position instead to s_5. If, in addition, the market were as large and impersonal as the U.S. market, then s_5 might be tempted to accept the offer even if he had already made some sort of preliminary commitment to C_6. This would generally not have been an option in Great Britain, where authority was (and is) more centralized, so that consultants and students would have to abide by the outcome of the matching algorithm once it was completed (*21*).

But suppose C_5 resolves not to suffer the same fate the next year. He, therefore, approaches one of the good students in the next year's class, before the formal match, and suggests that they agree to be matched, which they will accomplish by ranking one another first in the formal match (*22*). The student, mindful of the experience of s_5 the previous year, is receptive. Now consider the situation in the formal match, when a number of positions have been prearranged to be (1, 1) matches. Suppose students t_1, t_2, and t_3 have made such arrangements with consultants C_3, C_4, and C_5, but consultant C_2, not knowing this, submits his true rank ordering, $t_1, t_2, t_3, t_4, t_5, \ldots$, and t_4 submits his true rank ordering $C_3, C_4, C_5, C_2, \ldots$. Although C_2 does not know it, t_4 is his highest ranking student who is actually available, and C_2 is t_4's most preferred available consultant. But since the product of their rankings is 16, C_2 could well end up with his 15th choice student.

Thus, when some matches have been arranged beforehand, other students and consultants stand to do poorly if they do not also prearrange their matches. And matches can be prearranged, even when the rules of employment require students and consultants to participate in the centralized procedure, because a student and consultant who rank one another first will be matched regardless of what anyone else does. This goes a long way toward explaining both why a high percentage of appointments were soon arranged in advance under this system, and why this worked to the disadvantage of those who tried to arrange employment through the formal match procedure.

The Newcastle market is representative in this respect of the four unstable procedures in Table 1 that are no longer in use. Because it produced unstable matchings, some students and consultants had mutual interests in circumventing the formal procedure. And the market environment and matching procedure allowed them to communicate these interests to one another and effectively prearrange matches privately. Furthermore, as more agents went outside the system, the greater was the incentive for other agents to do so, so that the market quickly began to unravel.

If the sample consisted only of the four stable procedures that are still in use and the four unstable procedures that are no longer in use, it would have provided very strong support for the simplest form of stability hypothesis, along the lines of "stable procedures work and unstable ones do not." The two unstable matching procedures that are still in use (Cambridge and London Hospital) are therefore worth special notice, because they suggest that the situation may be more complex. These are the two smallest of the U.K. markets in the sample, and each involve the graduates of a single medical school and the teaching hospital associated with that school. The participants in these two markets may be effectively compelled by social pressure of various sorts (*1*) to comply with the match procedures, and this may be a sufficient explanation for their continued use (*23*). But it is worth noting that of the ten stable and unstable procedures in this sample, these two are the only procedures in which a student and consultant who each rank one another as first choice will not necessarily be matched together. This makes it more difficult for a student and consultant to prearrange a match, and together with the social pressures that can be brought to bear in a small market in which participants know each other, this may be a factor in preventing these unstable procedures from unraveling.

Concluding Remarks

There is now considerable evidence that stable centralized procedures allow markets to be organized more successfully than do unstable procedures. Unstable matchings give some market participants incentives to circumvent the formal procedures. Open questions remain concerning the extent to which there may be unstable procedures that in some environments nevertheless prevent the interested parties from acting on these incentives and whether there may be environments in which even stable procedures are prone to unravel.

Note that the centralized markets studied here do not involve central planning as it is most usually understood, because these markets have been designed to be sensitive to the preferences expressed by the participants, rather than to achieve the independent objectives of a planner. What is centralized is not the objective, but the market mechanism itself. This kind of centralization is something that occurs more often than is generally recognized: for example, the stock market contains institutions like the New York Stock Exchange, governed by explicit rules about how and when trades may be transacted. How such centralized market institutions arise, and the functions they serve, are subjects that deserve more attention than they have so far received in the economics literature, which often treats markets as arising spontaneously.

Another natural question is, what practical lessons about the design of centralized matching markets can we draw from this evidence? It seems clear that a designer of a centralized procedure to replace a decentralized market that has failed for reasons symptomatic of instability would be well-advised to choose a stable procedure. In fact, different stable procedures have different strategic properties (*3*), so more specific advice may be possible. But what, if anything, can we say about modifying existing centralized procedures? This is probably the question that I am asked second most often by participants in the NRMP. (The most often asked question concerns how to approach the existing system strategically.)

Let me state right away that I think that modifications of procedures that are working fairly well should be contemplated with caution, because a procedure like the NRMP is a vast improvement over the chaotic conditions that preceded it, and because we have seen that unstable centralized procedures are themselves prone to unravel. So the first priority should be preserving the stability of the system. [This puts serious constraints on certain kinds of "fine-tuning" that might otherwise seem desirable, for example, to attempt to change the distribution of residents to rural hospitals (*3*).] And modifications that increase stability may become important as instabilities develop (as in the case of married couples).

But beyond this (and here I venture cautiously), one of the features of these markets that is burdensome to many participants is the fact that there are strategic decisions to make in deciding what preference list to submit. Although there are aspects of this that are inevitable consequences of stability (*3*), one issue that arises is that any stable procedure makes it important for hospital programs to be highly ranked by the students they desire (and vice versa). There is thus an incentive for program directors to engage in various activities designed to influence the rank orderings submitted by students. One possibility, regarded as unethical, is for a director to ask a student whether he will rank the program first, and to say that if the student agrees to do so the director will in turn rank the student in his first group of choices (*24*). This is a problem for two reasons. First, although it is arguably justifiable for students to respond to such a breach of conduct by coolly asserting that they will rank the program first (and then proceeding to rank programs as they wish), many students will be understandably reluctant to begin their professional careers with an act of duplicity. And the misinformation introduced in the market when students do change their preference lists causes avoidable distortions. A possible solution is for hospitals' preference lists to be made available to students before they must submit their own. This practice has developed for other reasons at Cardiff, where it does not interfere with the operation of the market (*25*).

In closing, modern economic theory is increasingly game-theoretic in nature, which is to say that it focuses on the rules by which markets are organized. Centralized markets present a natural place to begin an empirical investigation concerned with rules, because important parts of the rules are formally codified, and can therefore be observed with precision. But a natural direction in which to extend this research is to decentralized entry-level labor markets, some of which exhibit the kinds of failures that can now be interpreted as symptoms of instabilities, and others that do not.

It is noteworthy that the simple idea of pairwise stability formulated by Gale and Shapley (*4*) has turned out to have so much empirical power. It is the kind of theoretical work that merits high scientific recognition.

REFERENCES AND NOTES

1. For a more detailed presentation, see A. E. Roth, *Am. Econ. Rev.*, in press.
2. A. E. Roth, *J. Polit. Econ.* **92**, 6 (1984).
3. The modern theory of these markets is described by A. E. Roth and M. A. O. Sotomayor [*Two-Sided Matching: A Study in Game-Theoretic Modelling and Analysis* (Econometric Society Monograph Series, Cambridge University Press, Cambridge, 1990)]. Much of the theory traces its origins to the work of Gale and Shapley.
4. D. Gale and L. Shapley, *Am. Math. Mon.* **69**, 1 (1962).

5. S. Mongell and A. E. Roth, *Am. Econ. Rev.*, in press.
6. Roughly 20,000 positions are now offered annually in the U.S. market, where students each seek one position and hospital programs seek multiple students. After students are interviewed by hospitals, both students and hospitals submit preference lists. (Salaries are part of the job description and are simply one of the factors that determine students' preferences over hospitals.)
7. Because preferences cannot be directly observed, it is desirable to make the weakest assumptions possible about them. (In these markets the preference lists that agents submit are observable, but the matching algorithm may give agents incentives to submit lists that do not faithfully reflect their preferences.) The assumptions made here, although not terribly strong, nevertheless assume that hospitals have preferences over groups of students that bear a certain relation to preferences over individual students. These assumptions can be considerably weakened, and in some cases this is necessary to accommodate choices by students or hospitals that do not reflect an underlying preference over individual students or positions at all (*1*, *3*). Throughout, preferences are assumed to be complete and transitive orderings.
8. Specifically, the hospital must prefer the student to one of the students it is matched with, or, if it has some unfilled positions, it must prefer the student to leaving a position unfilled.
9. The notion of (pairwise) stability was formulated by Gale and Shapley (*4*). In their model of one-to-one matching, pairwise stable matchings have the further property that no larger group of agents can collectively improve their situation, and in that model the set of stable matchings coincides with the set called the "core," which is a standard game-theoretic concept.
10. Prior to the mid-1980s, couples participating in the match were required to specify one of their members as the "leading member," and to submit a rank ordering of positions for each member of the couple; that is, a couple submitted two preference lists. The leading member was then matched to a position in the usual way, the preference list of the other member of the couple was edited to remove distant positions, and the second member was then matched if possible to a position in the same vicinity as the leading member. It is easy to see why instabilities would often result. Consider a couple whose first choice is to have two particular jobs in Boston, and whose second choice is to have two particular jobs in New York. Under the couples algorithm, the leading member might be matched to his or her first choice job in Boston, whereas the other member might be matched to some undesirable job in Boston. If their preferred New York jobs ranked this couple higher than students matched to those jobs, an instability would now exist. Recent changes in the way married couples are handled may somewhat reduce this problem, but when there are married couples in the market, the set of stable matchings may be empty (*2*, *3*).
11. In 1951, an algorithm for the U.S. market was proposed that gave students clear incentives to state rank orderings different from their true preferences. It was replaced for this reason by the 1952 algorithm, which was claimed in the literature distributed to participants never to give such incentives to either students or hospitals. In fact, this property is incompatible with stability (*3*).
12. But in London, where there are many more graduates of local medical schools than local pre-registration positions, medical schools commonly have arrangements with hospitals elsewhere.
13. Even this assumption is sometimes too strong to fit the facts and must be relaxed. For example, at some point in the history of the market operated in Cardiff, students could hold no more than one of their positions at the teaching hospital. So the first choice of some student might be to have his medical position at the teaching hospital and his surgical position elsewhere, but if that medical position were unavailable his second choice might be to have his surgical position at the teaching hospital. That is, he would become unwilling to accept the surgical position that was part of his first choice package, even though it was still available, because the medical position which went with it was no longer available. The role of this kind of assumption was first explored by A. Kelso and V. Crawford [*Econometrica* **50**, 6 (1982)].
14. One important difference between the U.K. and American markets is that in the U.K. markets, even when a matching is (pairwise) stable, so that no student and consultant can together arrange to do better than a given matching, there might be a larger coalition, consisting of many consultants and students, who by rearranging job assignments could obtain preferred assignments for all members [C. Blair, *Math. Oper. Res.* **13**, 619 (1988); (*3*)]. Needless to say, identifying and organizing large coalitions may be more difficult than making private arrangements between two parties, and it will become clear that the set of stable matchings is still of primary concern.
15. Included here is a matching scheme that was tried and subsequently abandoned at Sheffield; it is not included among those formally analyzed in (*1*) because the match was done by a committee, whose exact procedures cannot therefore be determined. But A. D. Clayden and J. Parkhouse [*Brit. J. Med. Ed.* **5**, 5 (1971)] report a computer program designed, in their words, "to mimic the manual allocation," and for my purposes here, I take that to be the system used.
16. The two Edinburgh procedures were adopted sequentially: the unstable procedures were adopted in 1967 and replaced by the stable procedures in 1969. The preferential bidding system used by sororities does not produce a matching for some possible inputs, but on the four campuses studied (*5*), in which the number of interested new members does not exceed the available positions, students have an incentive to submit preference lists containing only their first choice sorority. When students do so (and high percentages of the preference lists in that data do contain only a single choice), the resulting matching is stable.
17. More precisely, the four procedures I have called stable can all be shown to have the property that the matchings they produce are stable with respect to whatever preference lists may be used as the input. The six procedures I have called unstable do not have this property; although they may sometimes produce stable matchings, there are preferences for which they will not.
18. A. G. Leishman and R. P. Ryan, *Lancet* ii, 459 (1970).
19. At least initially—a later modification was to reverse this method of tie-breaking (D. A. Shaw, personal communication).
20. J. Anderson, personal communication.
21. But notice that if C_5 had submitted a preference list on which s_5 was his first choice, they would have been matched, as would also have been the case if s_5 had submitted a preference list on which C_5 was his first choice. So there are incentives for both students and consultants to carefully consider what preference lists to submit, because submitting their true preferences does not always yield the most preferred outcome.
22. In these relatively small markets both parties to such an agreement can be confident it will be carried out, because a consultant with a reputation for not delivering on his promises will soon find it difficult to attract good junior house officers, and a junior physician is reluctant to incur the enmity of a senior physician in the region in which he hopes to practice. The situation may differ in larger, more impersonal markets.
23. Stability as formulated here plays little role in procedures in which the participants can be compelled to accept the resulting match. A familiar example is the procedure by which U.S. football teams draft college players. That procedure is not stable in the sense discussed here, but does not need to be, because players must play for the team that drafts them.
24. There is anecdotal evidence that directors do this and, furthermore, that they do not always live up to their part of the bargain. Although I have not tried to gather systematic evidence on this point, the incentives for just this kind of behavior are large.
25. One way to exercise caution in modifying an existing procedure is to have evidence from another market that the modification does not introduce new problems. In this respect, the emerging tools of experimental economics may be of use in allowing some kinds of modifications to be explored on a small scale under laboratory conditions [A. E. Roth, Ed., *Laboratory Experimentation in Economics: Six Points of View* (Cambridge University Press, Cambridge, 1987)].

26. Supported by the Alfred P. Sloan Foundation and NSF. I am also indebted to numerous British physicians, surgeons, and medical administrators who have taken the time to correspond with me on these matters, and sometimes to unearth old records. I would be remiss not to mention J. Anderson, T. J. Bayley, P. G. Bevan, K. C. Calman, S. C. Farrow, J. Fraser, F. J. Goodwin, T. M. Hayes, K. Johns, J. H. Lazarus, D. McInnes, G. A. Mogey, R. Mulligan, K. M. Parry, R. P. Ryan, D. A. Shaw, D. M. Taylor, H. R. A. Townsend, and N. D. Wright. And I have received helpful comments from S. Mongell, J. Ochs, and J. Prasnikar.

[9]

THE "RUSH TO TRANSPLANT" AND ORGAN SHORTAGES

A. H. BARNETT and DAVID L. KASERMAN*

Normally, economists expect entry to improve industry performance. The effects of entry, however, can become perverse. Here, we examine the causes and effects of observed entry into the transplantation industry. Entry appears to be caused by economic rents created by the shortage of organs resulting from the current policy proscribing payment to organ donors. Under this policy, entry has little effect on the number of transplants performed. Consequently, entry spreads available organs among an increasing number of transplant centers, resulting in both increased costs and lower success rates. Thus, current policy simultaneously encourages entry and perverts its normally salutary effects.

I. INTRODUCTION

For some time now, there has been a severe and growing shortage of cadaveric human organs made available for transplantation. Each year the quantity demanded of kidneys, hearts, livers, lungs, and other organs consistently exceeds the number supplied. The obvious cause of this shortage is the existing public policy which proscribes purchases and sales of cadaveric organs. By forcing price to zero, this policy virtually guarantees a shortage of these organs.[1]

This shortage has persisted for at least the past two decades. It has, however, become increasingly severe in recent years. Technological advances in immunosuppressant drugs have dramatically increased transplant success rates, and expanded insurance coverage has made transplantation affordable to a much larger group of patients.[2] The upshot has been a rapid growth of demand with no corresponding increase in the supply of transplantable organs.

As a result, waiting lists (demand backlogs) are expanding at an accelerating rate, and expected waiting times for potential recipients are increasing commensurately. Delays that were once measured in months now frequently run into years. Over 25,000 patients now appear on official waiting lists in the U.S., and approximately 2,000 of these individuals die each year due to the lack of a suitable donor organ.[3]

Despite the organ shortage, however, the number of hospitals performing transplant operations is increasing at an alarming rate. According to recent figures, the number of heart transplant centers rose from 12 in 1983 to 148 in 1989. In this latter year, 251 hospitals nationwide offered some type of transplant services.[4] Thus, despite the chronic and, in fact, increasing shortage of the primary input required for a transplant operation, entry into this market has occurred rapidly over the past decade.

* Associate Professor and Professor, Auburn University. We are grateful to anonymous referees, the editor, Frank C. Wykoff and our colleague T. Randolph Beard for helpful comments. We are, of course, responsible for any remaining errors.

1. See Blair and Kaserman [1991].

2. See Hull [1990].

3. See Peters [1991]. This figure understates the total number of deaths attributable to the organ shortage because it includes only those individuals who die while on official waiting lists. Many potential transplant recipients are never placed on these lists, because, for a variety of reasons (e.g., age), they are assigned a low priority. Due to this priority and the shortage itself, these patients are denied access to transplantation and, consequently, never appear on the waiting lists.

4. See Winslow [1989].

Economic Inquiry
(ISSN 0095-2583)
Vol. XXXIII, July 1995, 506–515

This proliferation of transplant programs in the presence of a shortage of transplantable organs presents an apparent anomaly for both economists and public policy officials. Specifically, what is the underlying cause of such entry without any corresponding expansion in supply? And what are the implications of such entry for industry equilibrium and performance? In this paper, we explore the likely adverse consequences of excessive entry into the transplant industry for both costs and the quality of patient care (i.e., transplant success rates). In addition, we offer an explanation of the underlying cause of the "rush to transplant organs." Finally, we describe the resulting equilibrium and suggest some public policy implications of our analysis.

II. ADVERSE EFFECTS OF EXCESSIVE ENTRY

Growth in the number of transplant centers has far exceeded growth in the number of organ transplants performed due to the severe shortage of cadaveric organ donations. The number of organs harvested annually from cadavers in the U.S. has remained virtually constant since 1986, despite intense educational and promotional attempts to encourage expanded donation rates.[5] Given a relatively constant quantity of transplantable organs supplied, the rapid entry of new transplant centers translates directly into a corresponding reduction in the average number of transplant operations performed at individual centers.[6]

This entry and reduction in the number of procedures performed at transplant centers is likely to have serious adverse effects on both costs and quality of care in the transplant industry. Two separate effects tend to increase costs. First, operation of a transplant center entails certain fixed costs (associated with relatively indivisible assets) that, in order to achieve efficient utilization, must be spread over a sufficient number of transplants each year. The principal input generating economies of scale is the team of surgeons and associated medical personnel employed by the hospital to perform the transplant operation and provide post-transplant care during the critical period immediately following the operation. It is during this period that the probability of rejection is at its highest level. Here, team production is required, and a minimum efficient scale must be achieved in order to utilize a viable team effectively.[7] As a result, long-run average costs appear likely to decline over a fairly wide range of output as an increasing number of transplant operations allows more efficient team production.

Moreover, the cost-inflating effect of a reduced number of transplants is not confined solely to the smaller transplant programs that have recently entered the industry. To the extent that such programs draw transplants away from the larger pre-existing centers (which, in the presence of a constant number of transplantable organs supplied, they must), the latter's average costs will also increase with entry.[8] Thus, the large number of firms entering this industry tends to raise costs for all transplant centers.

The second way in which entry increases costs in this industry is through

5. See Hull [1990]. Prior to 1986, organ donations had grown fairly steadily at approximately 10 percent per year for many years. The cause of this abrupt change in the historic trend in organ donation is, as yet, unexplained. Apparently, it is not due to exhaustion of the potential supply because we currently collect only about 20–25 percent of potential donations. See Blair and Kaserman [1991].

6. Winslow [1989] reports that in 1988 over 40 percent of all heart transplant centers performed fewer than six transplant procedures. Over 80 percent performed fewer than twenty-one procedures in that year.

7. On the subject of team production, see Alchian and Demsetz [1972].

8. For example, the number of liver transplants performed at the Pittsburgh Medical Center has fallen from a peak of 650 per year to 359 in 1992. See McCartney [1993].

the impact it has on input prices, particularly surgeons' wages. Although the number of transplant operations cannot increase because of the virtually fixed supply of organs, the demand for transplant surgeons, particularly those with good reputations, has risen as additional transplant centers bid for this crucial input.[9] That is, the transplant industry is not characterized by constant costs but, instead, faces an upward sloping supply of at least one major input. As a result, the long-run average cost curve is shifted upward by the entry of additional transplant centers.

With regard to the quality of care delivered, three significant problems may arise. First, due to the Law of Large Numbers, the ability to match human leukocytes antigen (HLA) tissue types and other donor-recipient characteristics is directly related to the size of the transplant program.[10] A center with twenty patients on its waiting list is unlikely to find as good a match for any given donor organ as a center with two hundred patients on the list. As a result, a reduction in the size of transplant programs brought on by the proliferation of such programs will tend to affect adversely the success rate of transplant operations through its impact on the ability to match successfully donor organs to recipients. Second, as an increasing number of transplant centers vie for a fixed number of transplantable organs, existing centers may attempt to maintain prior output levels and new centers may try to reach more efficient scales of production by lowering the quality of the organs deemed acceptable.[11] Blood group lines may be crossed, and size and age criteria may be relaxed to increase the number of transplants performed. Such a decline in quality standards is likely to further erode transplant success rates.

Finally, the third problem concerning quality of care has to do with the learning curve phenomenon.[12] While organ transplant operations are becoming more or less routine, post-transplant patient care is anything but routine and is unlikely to become so in the foreseeable future. The first few weeks following an organ transplant are extremely critical in determining the ultimate success or failure of the transplanted organ. Rejection, infection, and myriad other problems are quite common during this period, and the variation in patients' experiences is extremely large. Administration of the regimen of immunosuppressive and other drugs utilized at this juncture is very important to the ultimate outcome, and appropriate protocols are still under development and subject to extensive research and experimentation. Even drugs that have been used for some time now, such as cyclosporin, perform substantially different across individual patients, and their pharmacological properties are not yet well understood. Moreover, new immunosuppressants (e.g., FK506) are rapidly becoming available. These new drugs require considerable research and experimentation in the way they are administered before their effectiveness can be determined. Well-received standard protocols simply do not exist at this time.

As a result, the quality of care a transplant patient receives in the post-transplant period is directly affected by the joint and cumulative experience of the transplant team responsible for his or her care. Such experience comes only from performing a large number of transplants over a considerable period of time. Pro-

9. McCartney [1993] writes that "hospitals were offering million-dollar signing bonuses to lure coveted transplant surgeons."

10. Due to differing time constraints on transplanting different cadaveric organs HLA tissue typing is performed for kidney transplants only. Nonetheless, blood types must be matched for all organs and body size is also a factor in matching donor organs to recipients.

11. See McCartney [1993].

12. Possai and Goetz [1994] emphasize, inter alia, learning curve effects in organ transplantation.

gram proliferation through excessive entry frustrates the achievement of proficiency in post-transplant care by restricting the ability to obtain the requisite cumulative experience. Again, the quality of patient care and, ultimately, transplant success rates suffer.

Thus, the rapid entry that has been occurring into the organ transplantation industry is likely both to increase costs and to lower success rates. The former effect arises from foregone economies of scale and increased input prices, while the latter occurs from poorer donor-recipient matching, use of inferior organs, and dissipated learning curve effects. These perverse effects of entry on overall industry performance are primarily attributable to the inability of such entry to increase quality-adjusted total industry supply. And this inability to increase supply, in turn, is attributable to the current policy which proscribes payment for cadaveric human organs for use in transplantation. A policy allowing payment for cadaveric organs would increase the number of transplants performed as the market price of organs would be bid up to its equilibrium level.[13]

III. THE ORGAN SHORTAGE AND THE INCENTIVE TO ENTER

As noted above, entry of new centers into the organ transplantation industry adversely affects both cost and quality. We now turn to an analysis of (1) why, in the face of a persistent shortage of transplantable organs and the rising cost of transplantation, firms continue to enter the industry, and (2) the implications of this entry for long-run industry equilibrium and performance.

An important economic reason for the rush of firms into transplantation is rooted in the current legal restriction regarding compensation for organ donors.[14] By prohibiting payment for organ donation, current law effectively mandates a zero price for human organs. But, to state the obvious, laws which prohibit the sale of organs do not make those organs worthless or even less valuable. In fact, since the legally mandated zero price yields a smaller number of organs than would be supplied in a freely functioning market, the zero price actually increases the marginal value (i.e., demand price) of those organs which are supplied.[15]

Reliance upon the present "altruistic" (zero-price) system of cadaveric organ procurement has been shown to be an effective substitute for a successful cartel agreement among organ transplant centers.[16] Such a system leads to a monopoly-like restriction in output while simultaneously preventing cheating by making it difficult, if not impossible, for individual centers to expand the number of transplants performed due to their inability to

13. Payment to donors may be opposed by some on grounds that the quality of organs harvested might deteriorate (i.e., the incidence of diseased organs might increase). Moreover, such opposition might ostensibly be based upon an analogy to U.S. experience with payment for blood and the debate that surrounded that experience. See Titmuss [1972] and the subsequent literature. Such opposition, however, is ill-founded for two reasons. First, the actual impact of positive prices for blood on the quality of blood collected has never been fully resolved as interpretation of the evidence remains ambiguous. There are, in fact, good reasons to believe that the alleged quality problems are not a necessary consequence of the use of the market mechanism for this good. See Eckert and Wallace [1985, ch. 2]. And second, it has been argued persuasively that, whatever the experience with blood, that experience would not carry over to a market for organs. See Cohen [1989, 29–30], Hansmann [1989, 68–69], and Blair and Kaserman [1991, 442–43].

14. Other, noneconomic, reasons for hospitals to enter this industry may exist as well. For example, some have argued that a prestige effect may influence this decision.

15. Because close substitutes for transplantation are generally unavailable and third-party payment is common, the demand for transplants is likely to be extremely price inelastic. As a result, the restriction in the quantity supplied attributable to the zero price policy will exert a very large effect on the demand price of recipients.

16. We are not arguing that a cartel exists. Rather, we argue that the zero-price policy results in a restriction in the supply of transplant operations that causes the industry to perform *as though* a cartel were present. See Barney and Reynolds [1989], Kaserman and Barnett [1991], and Barney and Reynolds [1991].

acquire the organs needed for such expansion. Thus, a cartel-like restriction of output in the transplant industry through enforcement of the zero-price procurement policy lies at the heart of the organ shortage and the associated problems it has engendered. Moreover, the economic consequences of the resulting supply restriction provide a plausible explanation for the medical community's opposition to the formation of organ markets.[17]

Further, because donors are prohibited from receiving payment for the organs they supply, the various other parties involved in the transplant procedure (e.g., the hospitals) may be able to appropriate a portion of the inflated value (or rents) associated with the donated organs.[18] In order to be in a position to appropriate these rents, however, the hospital must first enter the transplant industry. As with organ donors and their surviving family members, the hospitals at which the organs are harvested cannot sell them. Consequently, these hospitals have only two choices for use of the organs they collect: (1) provide them, without compensation, to an organ procurement organization for distribution to a transplant center, or (2) establish a transplant center which can use the harvested organ in a transplant operation, a procedure for which they can receive compensation.

Current federal regulations require hospitals that collect organs to list them on the United Network for Organ Sharing (UNOS) system. These regulations, however, require very little transference of organs across collection regions.[19] For kidneys, unless a perfect (six antigen) tissue match is found on the UNOS network (a rare event), the harvesting hospital is free to transplant the organ to a suitable recipient on its own waiting list. For other organs, for which HLA tissue typing is not used, the hospital may transplant any organ it collects for which it has an acceptable recipient on its waiting list. As a result, the UNOS allocation rules result in the hospital collecting the organ holding a virtual de facto property right in most of the organs it collects. And, as noted above, due to the prohibition on organ sales, exercising that property right requires that the hospital open a transplant center.

In short, the prohibition against compensating organ suppliers creates potentially capturable rents equal to the implicit market value (i.e., shadow price) of the harvested organs. The prospect of capturing some portion of these rents then provides an economic motivation for the observed "rush to transplant."

Because organ donors cannot legally be compensated, the (inflated) market value of the organs used is either captured by participants involved in the transplantation process or it is dissipated in rent-seeking activities. Two groups of participants potentially benefit from the zero price for organs: (1) organ recipients and third parties who pay medical expenses for transplant patients may capture the value of organs in the form of lower prices for the transplantation procedure; and/or (2) sur-

17. Such opposition has ostensibly been founded upon ethical concerns about commercialization of human body parts. Upon close examination, however, these concerns appear to be generally specious. The economic reasons appear, at least to us, to be far more convincing. See Barnett, Beard and Kaserman [1993].

18. While some hospitals claim that organ transplantation is unprofitable, Possai and Goetz [1994] have recently argued that, due to both demand and cost complementarities and learning by doing, these claims are likely to be false. Moreover, Evans [1993] presents empirical evidence which strongly suggests that transplant centers are able to appropriate rents through the fees they charge for organ acquisition.

19. Until 1991, organs listed on the UNOS network were rationed nationally among patients based on established medical criteria. In 1991, a UNOS committee composed of twelve transplant surgeons eliminated the emergency classification from the organ distribution criteria. Under the guidelines established by this committee, available organs are first offered to local transplant centers. Organs are now offered to distant recipients only if local transplant centers do not wish to use them. The effect of this change has been to increase the importance of geographical boundaries and, consequently, increase the viability of new transplant centers. See McCartney [1993].

geons, transplant centers, organ procurement organizations, and other providers of transplant-related services may receive higher compensation for their services than they would receive in the absence of the rents created by this policy.[20]

In all likelihood, both of the above groups benefit in some measure from the organ shortage and the rents it creates. That is, while neither group is likely to be able to appropriate all of the rents created by this policy, both groups are likely to capture some portion of them. The actual allocation of rents between input suppliers (e.g., transplant surgeons and hospitals) and output demanders (e.g., transplant recipients and third-party payers) depends upon the reimbursement rates that are established. For kidneys, the Health Care Financing Administration (HCFA) sets these rates under Medicare Part A for hospitals on the basis of their cost reports. Surgeons' fees, however, fall under Part B and are not cost based. For non-renal transplants, reimbursement rates are established by health insurance companies through negotiation with the centers. Because these companies may exercise less monopsony power than the HCFA in these negotiations, the profitability of non-renal transplants seems likely to be greater.[21] This expectation is supported by the observed pattern of entry into this industry. Specifically, the rate of entry has been much greater for centers performing heart and liver transplants than for those performing kidney transplants.[22]

Consequently, we expect a share of the rents attributable to a zero price for organs to be realized by those who pay for transplantation, and we expect input suppliers to receive compensation somewhat higher than they would otherwise receive. Our expectation that the latter group benefits from this policy is supported both by the observed entry into the transplant business and the strong opposition to organ markets voiced by the medical community.[23] In addition, the empirical evidence reported in Evans [1993] supports this conclusion. We also expect some resources to be wasted in rent-seeking activities as transplant centers compete with each other for the fixed quantity of organs available at the zero price.[24] This waste could occur, for example, as organ procurement agencies or transplant centers devote resources to largely offsetting rivalrous activities, such as advertising or entry, which are designed to procure organs that would otherwise be harvested by another organization.

The situation faced by a representative transplant center experiencing entry is depicted in Figure 1. Let P_0 represent the fixed reimbursement rate paid for an organ transplant. In general, such prices can be taken as parameters for a given center. Let $LRAC_0$ represent long-run average cost at an arbitrarily chosen point in time for an incumbent transplant center. At this point in time, let S_0 represent the supply curve of cadaveric organs to this center,

20. Current Medicare physician payment policy is to reimburse physicians on the Resources Based Relative Value Scale (RBRVS), which is a national resources-used scale. This system is not cost based, though it may have some features of a cost-based scheme. Under this system, reimbursement rates may be subject to manipulation.

21. It should be noted that health insurance companies may also benefit from the organ shortage that the current "altruistic" procurement system creates, because the number of claims (transplants) is reduced under this system.

22. See Winslow [1989].

23. See Barnett, Beard and Kaserman [1993].

24. As pointed out to us by an anonymous referee, this rent-seeking activity is similar to that experienced with some common access resources. Would-be transplanting hospitals are like those who, in trying to harvest oil from a given reserve before it is captured by other oil producers, drill more than an optimal number of oil wells. The result with oil is that resources are "wasted" because less total oil is harvested and the cost of extraction is higher than it might be otherwise. In transplantation, resources are "wasted" because costs are increased and quality is reduced as new transplant centers enter the market in an attempt to stake claim to harvested organs which are drawn from a fixed pool of available organs.

FIGURE 1
Entry into the Organ Transplant Market

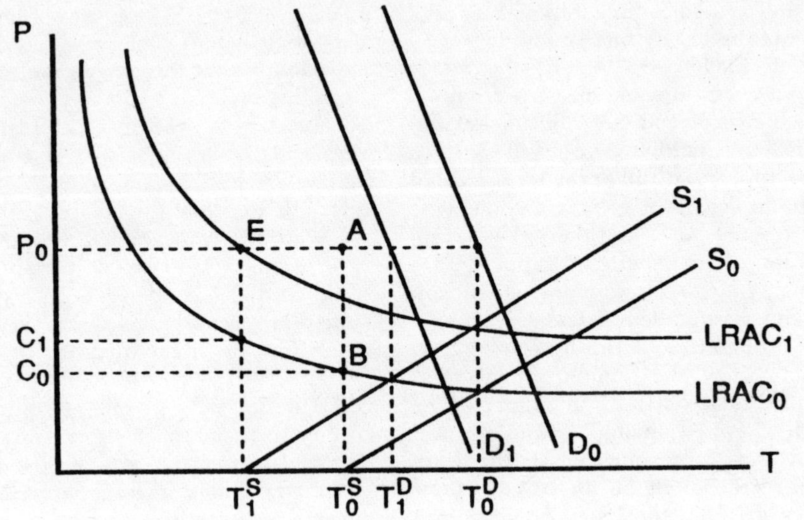

with T_0^S organs supplied at the zero price.[25] This supply fixes the center's output at T_0^S. With price set at P_0, a shortage equal to $T_0^D - T_0^S$ is realized (i.e., the transplant market does not clear). With a price of P_0 and average cost of C_0, however, the center is earning positive economic profits. It is these profits which provide the incentive for entry of new transplant firms.

In traditional economic theory, the entry of new firms into a profitable industry would increase industry supply and drive price down to the competitive level. But, in this case, the legally mandated zero price for organs prevents entry from increasing the number of organs harvested and, therefore, prevents the supply of transplant operations from increasing as well. While an increase in the number of transplant centers might be expected to increase the visibility of organ donation programs and, thereby, minimally increase donations, even this marginal effect has not materialized. Cadaveric organ supply has, in fact, remained constant over recent years. As a result, entry has simply spread a fixed pool of organs over a larger number of transplant facilities.

25. We are able to plot the long-run average cost of transplant procedures and the supply of organs in the same diagram because there is a fixed one-to-one correspondence between organs and transplant procedures.

Prior to entry, the incumbent firm receives a profit of P_0ABC_0. The entry of new firms, however, introduces new "competitors" for an essentially fixed number of organs. Thus, entry has the effect of reducing the supply of organs to the incumbent firm from S_0 to S_1. This reduction in organ supply lowers the firm's output to T_1^S. Assuming that production was occurring at or below an efficient scale prior to entry, it also reduces productive efficiency as average cost increases along $LRAC_0$ from C_0 to C_1.

At the same time, entry increases these costs as input prices are bid upward. Thus, the firm's long-run average costs rise from $LRAC_0$ to $LRAC_1$. Entry also reduces the incumbent firm's demand from D_0 to D_1 as prospective transplant patients are listed with the new centers. This combination of (1) reducing individual centers' output and (2) raising all centers' costs will continue until a "competitive-like" (i.e., zero-profit) equilibrium is established at point *E*.

Two points should be noted regarding this post-entry "equilibrium." First, it is an equilibrium only in the limited sense that no incentive for additional entry exists. That is, the entry of new firms does nothing to reduce or eliminate the organ (and, therefore, transplant) shortage. The number of transplants demanded, T_1^D, still exceeds the number of transplants supplied, T_1^S.

Second, while long-run equilibrium is characterized by zero expected economic profits for new entrants, the well-established incumbent centers may continue to realize positive economic profits. Their ability to sustain these profits could arise from two sources. First, incumbent centers may be able to maintain higher levels of output than entrants. The power of reputation, personal and professional relationships, referring physician or patient knowledge of the correlation between the number of transplants performed and success rates and insurance company practices, inter alia, may allow incumbents to retain a scale advantage.[26] And second, incumbent centers may experience lower costs as a result of the learning-by-doing phenomenon described above.

Of course, the learning (i.e., human capital) acquired by each individual may be capitalized in labor market transactions, thus yielding no long-run cost advantage to the incumbent employer. As noted above, however, the care of transplant patients is team oriented and some of this learning is embodied in the transplant team itself. To the extent there is team learning that cannot be fully capitalized in labor markets by individual team members, incumbent firms may retain a long-run cost advantage. As a result, incumbent centers may be able to sustain some positive profits in the post-entry equilibrium.

In summary, the "rush to transplant" is rooted in an ill-conceived public policy which prohibits payment to organ suppliers. This policy perversely encourages excessive entry by (1) restricting the quantity of organs supplied and, thereby, artificially inflating the rents potentially available from transplantation; and (2) requiring that harvested organs be transplanted by the hospital where they are collected if that hospital is to be able to capture any portion of these rents. In most markets, the entry of new producers would reduce price and lead to a more socially efficient use of resources. But current law does not allow organ markets to respond to the increasing scarcity of transplantable organs through the normal price adjustment process. The consequence of this policy is a market in which entry leads to increased costs and a lower quality of care. The current policy which mandates a zero

26. For example, in a cost cutting move, Prudential Insurance company restricts policy holders to one of a small number of transplant centers based on the experience of surgeons and the number of procedures performed in those centers. See Winslow [1989].

price for cadaveric organs (1) creates an economic incentive for entry to occur, and (2) causes such entry to exhibit perverse detrimental effects on industry performance.[27]

There is a fundamental economic moral to our story. Misallocation of a single resource in a complex economy often leads to distortions or inefficiencies in the allocation of other resources, much as illness or injury in one part of a human body often produces secondary maladies in other parts of the body. In the case of cadaveric organs, the effects of the current policy of prohibiting compensation for those who supply organs are a direct cause of a variety of resource allocation problems in organ transplantation and related activities. The "rush to transplant," with its accompanying waste and reduced quality of care, is but one form of that misallocation.

Finally, we should note that our argument supporting payment to organ suppliers has no direct implications for using the price mechanism to distribute these organs once they are collected.[28] Collection and distribution are separate issues. There is no reason that positive prices to organ suppliers could not be combined with a system which continues to distribute organs to transplant recipients according to medical, instead of market, criteria.

27. As pointed out by an anonymous referee, the increased value of organs and the resulting entry into the transplantation industry, should increase the percentage of harvested organs used at the collection site and reduce the percentage "shared" over the UNOS system. Unfortunately, the data available at this time are ambiguous on this point. Specifically, these data do not allow one to clearly identify the percentage of organs collected at one site and transplanted at another. Thus, it is not possible to test this hypothesis at this time.

28. For a discussion of how a market for cadaveric organs might work, see Barnett and Kaserman [1993], and Schwindt and Vining [1986].

IV. CONCLUSION

Everyone involved in any capacity with organ transplantation is keenly aware of the tremendous social costs of the chronic shortage of cadaveric organs in terms of waiting times and even deaths. But the costs of the shortage do not stop there. By creating economic incentives for transplant programs to proliferate, additional long-run problems arise in terms of (1) higher costs through lost economies of scale, higher input prices, and learning curve effects; and (2) reduced success rates through poorer matching of donor organs to recipients and dissipation of important post-transplant physician experience. Together, the cumulative effect of the declining performance engendered by these problems stands to jeopardize the historical success of this important medical technology.

REFERENCES

Alchian, Armen, and Harold Demsetz. "Production, Information Costs and Economic Organization." *American Economic Review*, 62, December 1972, 777–95.

Barnett, A. H., T. Randolph Beard, and David L. Kaserman. "The Medical Community's Opposition to Organ Markets: Ethics or Economics?" *The Review of Industrial Organization*, 8, December 1993, 669–78.

Barnett, A. H., and David L. Kaserman. "The Shortage of Organs for Transplantation: Exploring the Alternatives." *Issues in Law & Medicine*, 9, Fall 1993, 117–37.

Barney, Dwane L., and R. Larry Reynolds. "An Economic Analysis of Transplant Organs." *Atlantic Economic Journal*, 17, September 1989, 12–20.

______. "An Economic Analysis of Transplant Organs: Reply." *Atlantic Economic Journal*, 19, June 1991, 64–65.

Blair, Roger D., and David L. Kaserman. "The Economics and Ethics of Alternative Cadaveric Organ Procurement Policies." *Yale Journal of Regulation*, Spring 1991, 403–52.

Cohen, Lloyd R. "Increasing the Supply of Transplant Organs: The Virtues of a Futures Market." *George Washington Law Review*, 58, November 1989, 1–51.

Eckert, Ross D., and Edward L. Wallace. *Securing a Safer Blood Supply: Two Views*. Washington, D.C.: American Enterprise Institute for Public Policy Research, 1985.

Evans, Roger W. "Organ Procurement Expenditures and the Role of Financial Incentives." *Journal of the American Medical Association*, 269, 23–30 June 1993, 3113–18.

Hansmann, Henry. "The Economics and Ethics of Markets for Human Organs," in *Organ Transplantation Policy: Issues and Prospects*, edited by James F. Blumstein and Frank A. Sloan. Durham, N.C.: Duke University Press, 1989, 57–85.

Hull, Alan. "U.S. Donor Procurement in 1989: Same Song, Third Verse." *Nephrology News and Issues*, March 1990, 32–35.

Kaserman, David L., and A. H. Barnett. "An Economic Analysis of Transplant Organs: A Comment and Extension." *Atlantic Economic Journal*, 19, 1991, 57–63.

McCartney, Scott. "Agonizing Choices: People Most Needing Transplantable Organs Now Often Miss Out." *Wall Street Journal*, 1 April 1993, A1.

Peters, T. G. "Life or Death: The Issue of Payment in Cadaveric Organ Donation." *Journal of the American Medical Association*, 13 March 1991, 1302–05.

Possai, Kathleen W., and Michael Goetz. "Scope, Learning and Cross-Subsidy: Organ Transplants in a Multi-Division Hospital." *Southern Economic Journal*, 60, January 1994, 715–26.

Schwindt, Richard, and Aidan R. Vining. "Proposal for a Future Delivery Market for Transplant Organs." *Journal of Health, Politics, Policy and Law*, 11, Fall 1986, 483–500.

Titmuss, Richard M. *The Gift Relationship: From Human Blood to Social Policy*. New York: Vintage Books, 1972.

Winslow, Ron. "Hospitals Rush to Transplant Organs." *Wall Street Journal*, 29 August 1989, B1.

Part II
Market Dynamics

[10]

4

Commodity Price Variability

An explanation for the roller-coaster-like behavior of the farm price level has now been developed and sketched. But this is only a part of the price variability problem in agriculture. Individual commodity prices bob around the moving farm price level in all manner of ways: some in an extreme fashion, some in an irregular fashion, some in a periodic fashion, and some hardly at all. So even where there is no price level problem — that is, where the price level is steady and smooth, or even better, gently upsloping — individual commodity prices vary in a variety of ways from that level. It is the task of this chapter to provide an explanation for this second form of price variability in the agricultural sector of the economy.

Since commodity prices and production are what we will be concerned with in this chapter, our unit of inquiry is conveniently defined for us. It is the individual commodity. We should recognize that we are not concerned with any, or all, aspects of commodity prices, however. We are concerned with developing an explanation for deviations of individual commodity prices from the average of all other farm commodity prices. We are concerned, therefore, with *relative prices* — how one farm commodity price varies relative to all other farm commodity prices. The analysis thus joins the main stream of economic theory at this point, for this is the kind of problem with which economic theory has traditionally been concerned: What consequences flow from a change in the price of a single commodity relative to other commodity prices? But again, as we shall see, certain peculiarities of the food and agricultural sector emerge to give the analysis of relative prices and production a special twist.

COMMODITY PRICE VARIABILITY

Commodities To Be Studied

Thinking back to Chapter 2, we will recall that individual commodity price variations around the moving farm price level ranged from very small to very great: whole milk prices varied as little as 6 per cent from year-to-year, and onion prices by as much as 58 per cent from year-to-year, over the long period 1920–55, with the price variability of other commodities falling into a continuum between these extremes. If time and space permitted, it might prove interesting to investigate the causes of price variability for each of the major farm commodities (it might not, too, for a great deal of repetition would be involved). But time and space do not permit, so we will investigate three commodities: potatoes, hogs, and milk. These three commodities represent respectively the different degrees of price variability found among farm commodities – extreme, moderate, and minor.

Year-to-year variations in the prices of potatoes, hogs, and whole milk, where the influence of changes in the price level have been removed, are presented in Figure 12. (Dividing the index of each commodity price by the index of prices received for all farm commodities for each year, converts the price level to a horizontal line at 100 in Figure 12, and commodity price variations to percentage deviations around it.) Some interesting facts emerge from Figure 12. Before 1940 potato prices rocket about the price level in a beautifully clear, but uncertain, cycle of two or three or four years' duration. Hog prices pursue a somewhat less extreme pattern, but a more irregular one, than do potato prices. And whole milk prices roll along like a peaceful sea.

But something happens around 1940 – war and price supports. And commodity price variability around the price level acquires a new look following 1940. During World War II, and in the years immediately after, the degree of price variability for all three commodities is reduced importantly. By 1950 the older patterns of price variability have reasserted themselves, but with potatoes on a new and relatively lower plane.

Our problem is, then, Can we find, or develop, an analysis which provides an adequate explanation of the price behavior of three such diverse commodities as potatoes, hogs and milk? Within limits the answer is yes. That analysis is to be found in part, at least, in the rigorous cobweb theorem, and in part in the degeneration of the cobweb in the real world of food and agriculture.

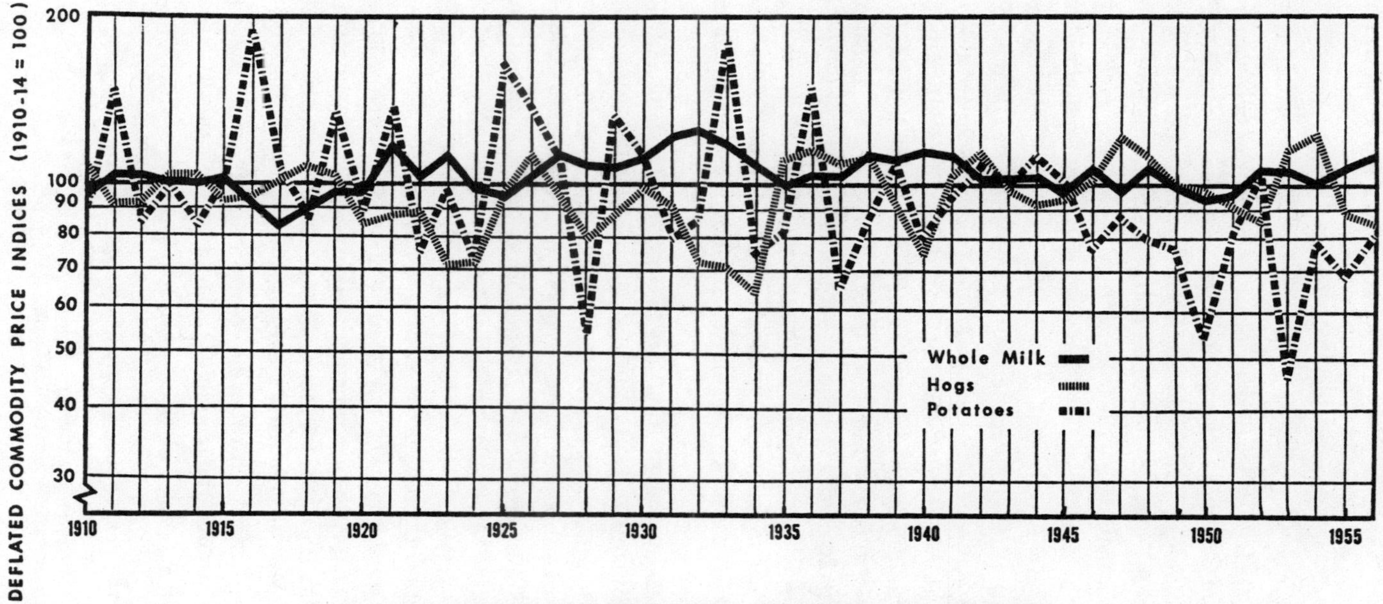

Figure 12. Commodity price indices expressed as percentages of the index of prices received for all commodities, 1910–56.

COMMODITY PRICE VARIABILITY

The Cobweb Analysis

THE CONCEPT

In the late 1930s Mordecai Ezekiel formulated the cobweb theorem to explain commodity price-output sequences in agriculture.[1] This framework of analysis has been employed by many persons since that time to unravel such sequences.[2] The cobweb analysis is an equilibrium type of analysis, making use of the traditional concepts of demand and supply. But, whereas the typical demand and supply analysis is static (e.g., the illustrative model of Figure 10, Chapter 3), the cobweb analysis is semi-dynamic; it is concerned with price-output sequences through time where the relevant demand and supply relations do not shift during the time span under consideration. This partially dynamic analysis facilitates the formulation of an explanation of price-output behavior in agriculture where a *growth period,* often a season in length but perhaps longer, separates the decisions to produce and the decisions to sell a finished product. The working of a distinct and disjointed production period, recurring periodically, into the analysis to correspond to such production periods in agriculture is, no doubt, the novel aspect of the cobweb framework of analysis.

Not so generally recognized, but central to the cobweb analysis, are two different but related concepts of supply. It takes two concepts of supply, related in a time sequence, to make the analysis go. First, we have a supply relation which describes those quantities of a commodity that farmers *plan* to produce at varying prices. It is a planning curve, to which we give the name *schedule of intentions to produce.* Second, we have a supply relation which describes at the close of the growth or production period those quantities of a commodity that farmers stand ready to offer on the market at varying prices. And since it is assumed (1) that most farm products are perishable and (2) that farmers have poor storage facilities, it is further assumed that this second supply relation, to which we give the name *market supply curve,* is severely or perfectly inelastic. Armed with these two concepts of supply, we can now take a trial spin around the cobweb.

[1] "The Cobweb Theorem," *Quarterly Journal of Economics,* February 1938, pp. 255–280.

[2] It provides, for example, the basic framework of analysis for the policy study of the potato industry under price supports by Gray, Sorenson, and Cochrane, *An Economic Analysis of the Impact of Government Programs on the Potato Industry of the United States,* Minn. Agri. Exp. Sta. Tech. Bul. 211, June 1954.

An Analysis of Farm Price Behavior

THE COBWEB ILLUSTRATED

Two cobweb models are presented in Figure 13; later we will draw certain comparisons between these models, but for the present, and for exposition purposes, let us concentrate on model I. To get under way in this analysis we must arbitrarily break into the continuing price-output sequence at some point in time, and this we do at price P_0 in year 0. Price P_0 in year 0 induces farmers to plan to produce quantity Q_1 in year 1. This quantity information we read off the schedule of intentions to produce curve S_I S_I, which describes those quantities of this commodity that farmers intend to produce at varying prices.

Now let us assume that the farmers' intentions to produce are just realized, and that quantity Q_1 is forthcoming in year 1. This quantity comes to market in a rush—is dumped onto the market—since it is assumed that the commodity is perishable and farmers lack adequate storage facilities. Thus, in fact, the market supply curve in year 1 is perfectly inelastic and is described in model I by the line Q_1 S_m. The market supply curve intersects the demand curve for the commodity at price P_1; this intersectional point provides the price solution for year 1. Farmers receive price P_1 for an output of Q_1 in year 1. Price P_1 in year 1 now induces farmers to plan to produce Q_2 in year 2. This quantity sells in turn at a price P_2 in year 2. The cobweb is forming, and will continue until something comes along to break it.

It will be observed that the price-output path of model II differs markedly from that of model I. Model II is convergent; model I is explosive. Now why does the price-output path of model II converge on its equilibrium position, and the price-output path of model I explode? The answer is to be found in the relative slopes of the demand relation and the schedule of intentions to produce. Whenever the slope of the schedule of intentions to produce exceeds (i.e., is steeper than) the slope of the demand relation, the price-output path converges. And, of course, whenever the slope of the demand relation exceeds that of the schedule of intentions to produce, the opposite is true. Finally, in that unlikely case where the slopes of the two curves are identical, the cobweb action goes on endlessly in the same track.

In the world of reality, it seems reasonable to assume that most commodity cobweb patterns are of the model II type. This must be the case; otherwise agriculture would be flying apart. True, price variability is extreme for certain agricultural commodities, but to date agriculture has

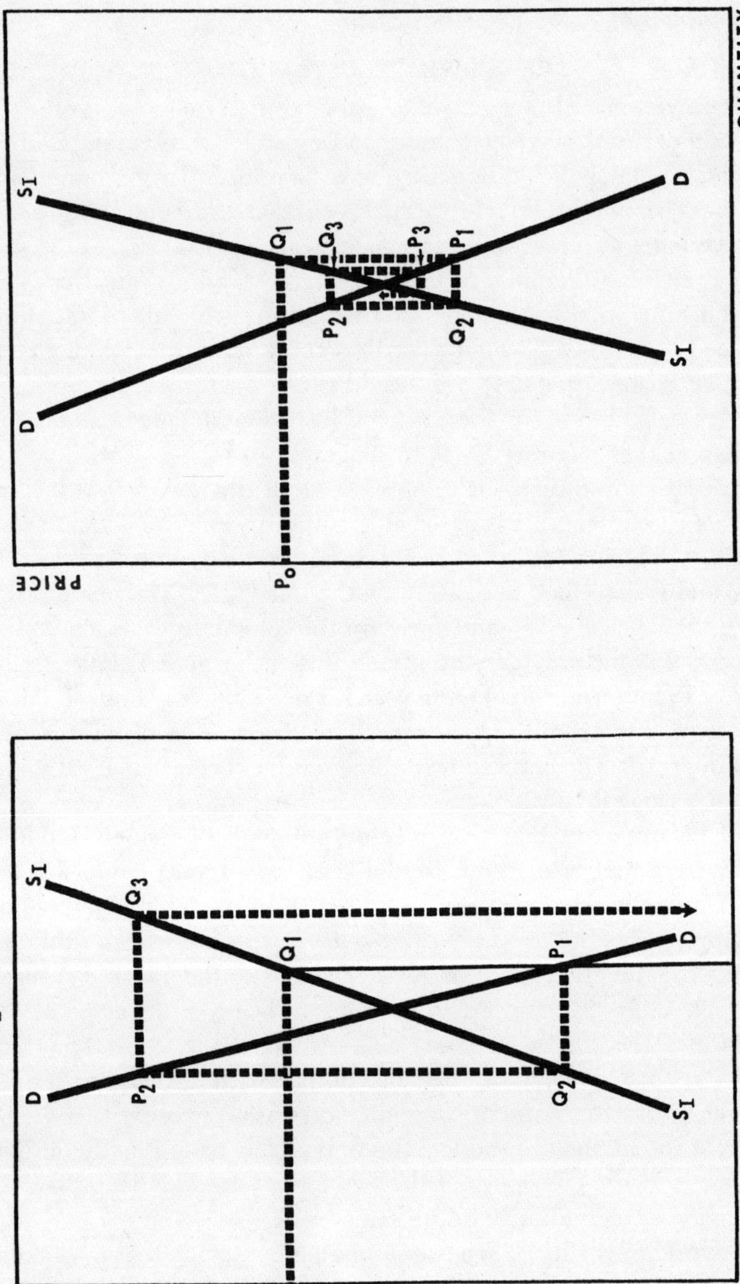

Figure 13. Two cobweb models: one explosive and one convergent.

65

not exploded. And this would be the tendency if commodity patterns were generally of the model I type.

A brief digression on the relation of the cobweb model to the structure of agriculture is perhaps in order at this point. It is probably true that no situation can be found in the real world of food and agriculture which fits perfectly the neat cobweb pattern of either model I or model II of Figure 13. In other words, it would be difficult to find a commodity situation in agriculture where (1) last year's price is always used as the planning price in the current year, (2) actual production always equals intended production, and (3) the conditions are such that the market supply curve is always perfectly inelastic.

But it would be wrong to view the cobweb framework of analysis as a Rube Goldberg contraption concocted by Mordecai Ezekiel in the 1930s and revived by the author in the 1950s to bedevil people trying to understand the workings of the agricultural economy. *The principal features of the cobweb model are inherent in the structure of most of agriculture.* The use of prices received in the past to arrive at current planning prices, the disjointed and recurring growth period in agricultural production, and the tendency for finished agricultural products to come to market in a rush following the growth period—these are all typical structural features of the agricultural economy. Thus, an analysis that purports to explain commodity price-output behavior in agriculture must assume a cobweb form. It must take into account the structural features built into agriculture.

USE OF THE COBWEB IN THIS ANALYSIS

The cobweb analysis is generally used to conceptualize the price-output behavior of a commodity in agriculture, not to generate the actual prices and quantities of that commodity. The latter is generally not attempted because of the difficulties of estimation involved. In order to use the cobweb analysis to generate actual prices and quantities, three relations must be estimated with reasonable accuracy: the demand relation, the schedule of intentions to produce, and the market supply curve. And these relations must be related in a system where they shift through time in accordance with the shifting forces (e.g., personal incomes, farm technological advance) at work in the markets. With present-day data and statistical estimating techniques, the analyst is lucky to derive one such relation in which he has confidence, let alone three; and his chances of replicating the system at work through time for some commodity are slim indeed. In short, with the present state of econometric knowledge, the estimating problems are simply insurmountable; this is why the cobweb is not used to predict actual price-quantity sequences.

The cobweb analysis can, however, be used to conceptualize the price-output behavior of a commodity, and such will be its use here. The cobweb analysis will be used to describe, and in this sense explain, the *degree* or *extent* of commodity price variability around the moving farm price level for potatoes, hogs, and milk. As used here, the cobweb framework is positioned astride the farm price level – the intersection of the demand curve and the schedule of intentions to produce is positioned at the price level. In this context, the price-output behavior generated by the cobweb around the price level becomes an explanation of the degree of commodity price variability around this price level. In other words, it is assumed here that the farm price level is perfectly horizontal (this is the implicit assumption of all orthodox economic theory), and the cobweb framework of analysis is used to explain the extent of relative price deviations from that price level.

Models I and II in Figure 13 cannot, however, be used to describe actual patterns of price variability through dated time. They cannot because price variability patterns result from shifts in the three relations involved as well as the price-output path around the cobweb, and in those semi-dynamic models the demand and supply relations hold fixed positions through time. We will, as a second step in these commodity analyses, however, consider the price variability patterns *and their unpredictable characteristics,* which result from the breakdown of the cobweb models through dated time.

The commodity analyses that follow thus begin with a cobweb model of the commodity. The price-output path around the model describes or explains the extent of price variability from the farm price level for the commodity. The analysis in each case then proceeds to break down the cobweb model, as the cobweb structure of the commodity in the real world might be expected to break down with the passage of time. From this second phase of the analysis we gain insights into the actual patterns of price variability for agricultural commodities.

Estimates of demand elasticity for each commodity analysis were obtained from published studies, and are cited in each instance. The schedules of intentions to produce used in each commodity analysis were estimated for this chapter, and the statistical analyses are presented in Appendix A. It is assumed that the market supply curve is perfectly inelastic in each commodity analysis; this is the conventional assumption, but in reality these market supply curves need not be, and probably are not, completely inelastic. The true elasticities of these market curves defy estimation at the present time, however.

The Cobweb Analysis for Potatoes

THE MODEL

A two-year cobweb model for potatoes is presented in Figure 14. In this model, price P_0 in year 0 induces some quantity Q_1 in year 1; that quantity sells for some price P_1 in year 1; that price in turn induces some quantity Q_2 in year 2; the loop is completed in two years with price P_2. This model is consistent with the growth period in potato production; potatoes are planted, grown, and sold in one year. And it is generally hypothesized that potato prices in the previous year, or the previous two years, cause farmers to produce the quantity of potatoes that they do in the current period. In short, the model appears to fit the facts of the world reasonably well.

The potato cobweb model is positioned astride the farm price level, where that level is equal to 100. Price deviations from 100 represent relative price changes — changes in the price of potatoes relative to the average of all farm prices. The elasticity of demand at the farm level, that is at the point where price equals 100 and quantity equals 100 in Figure 14, is —.28.[3] The elasticity of the schedule of intentions to produce at the point where price equals 100 and quantity equals 100 is .25.[4] With the slope of the demand relation a bit more gentle than the schedule of intentions to produce, the potato model is convergent. Since the slopes of the two relations are nearly the same, however, and both are rather inelastic, the price-output path does converge slowly. And during the slow convergent process the price of potatoes gyrates around the price level in a wide orbit.

Beginning the price-output sequence for potatoes at a relative price of 120 is completely arbitrary. But each of the other commodity analyses

[3] Estimate by Milton Shuffett from *The Demand and Price Structure for Selected Vegetables*, U.S.D.A. Tech. Bul. 1105, and presented by Richard Foote in *Price Elasticities of Demand for Nondurable Goods with Emphasis on Food*, U.S.D.A., AMS–96, March 1956, p. 31.

[4] Refer to Appendix A for a discussion of method and relevant statistical measures.

in this chapter originates at the relative price of 120, too. A comparison of the three analyses makes clear that the price-output orbit for potatoes is wider than for the other commodities. Thus, a logical explanation emerges out of the cobweb analysis for the extreme year-to-year variations in potato prices around the farm price level. Basically the explanation grows out of the low elasticities of demand and of the schedule of intentions to produce, and the assumption of complete inelasticity for the market supply relation. This particular set of relations linked together in a dynamic, recursive system [5] provides a logical explanation for the wide relative price movements for potatoes.

BREAKING THE MODEL AND THE CONSEQUENCES

The potato model presented in Figure 14 would in time converge on the price level and thus eliminate potato price variations around the price level. It might take a long time, but, *if the model remained intact,* it would occur. Further, it might be noted that, if the slopes of the demand relation and the schedule of intentions to produce were identical, the price-output path would fall into an endless, but *regular,* two-year cycle. To such a cycle producers could adjust with certainty; the situation might be likened to that of a wage earner who *regularly* receives a large check on the first of the month and a small check in the middle of the month. He might prefer that the payments were evened out, but he could adjust to this regular but uneven flow of income.

Something, therefore, must be missing from the analysis to this point. The cobweb model of Figure 14 does not generate the pattern of price variability that we find in the real world. Except for the brief World War II period, year-to-year variations in potato prices around the farm price level have not dampened down. Furthermore, historical potato price variations do not fall into a neat, regular, two-year cycle; on the contrary, they fall into unpredictable two-, three-, or even four-year cycles.

The logical construction of Figure 14 is all right as far as it goes; it simply does not go far enough. Over a period of time the cobweb breaks down to yield an irregular pattern of price variability for a number of

[5] The idea of a recursive system is discussed in Appendix A, and it is thoroughly developed by Herman Wold and Lars Jureen in *Demand Analysis* (New York: John Wiley and Sons, 1953), Chapters 2 and 3. In general terms, however, a recursive system is one where events grow out of one another in an orderly and nonreversible progression.

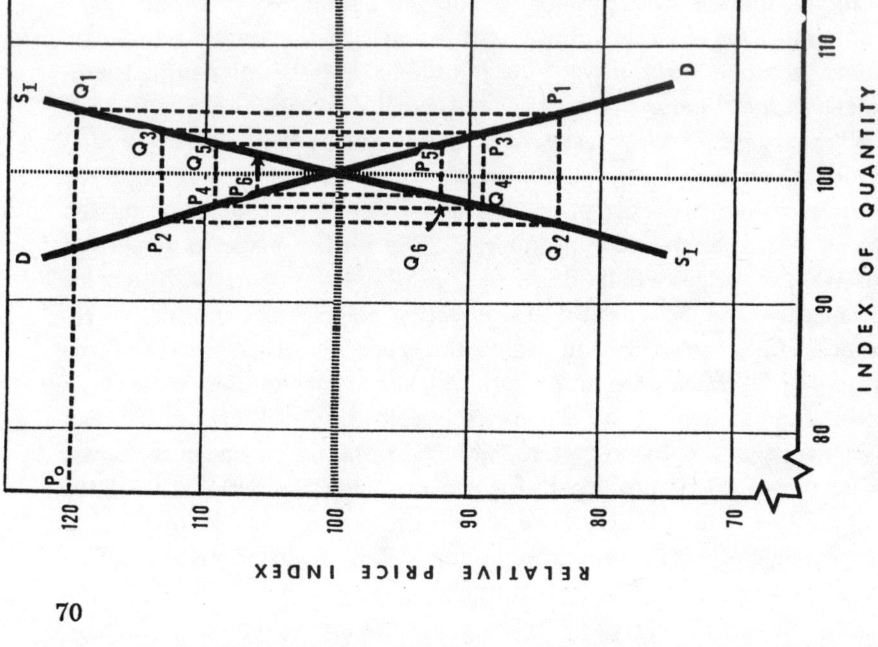

Figure 14. The cobweb model for potatoes.

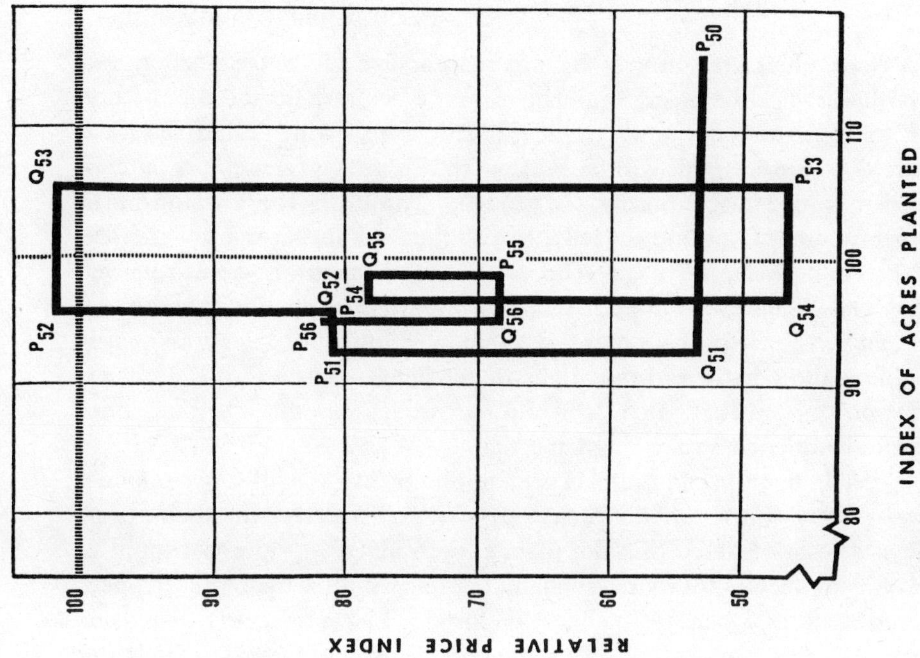

Figure 15. The actual price-output path for potatoes, 1950–56.

reasons. But three broad, generic reasons are given here. First, and probably most common, is a change in the demand for the commodity. If the demand for potatoes changes during the growing period, the regular price-output path will be broken. In Figure 14, for example, a contraction in demand during the growing season of year 1 would mean that quantity Q_1 would not sell at price P_1, but rather at some lower price.

Second, a change in the schedule of intentions to produce from one year to the next, owing perhaps to an important technological advance, breaks the neat cobweb pattern. Again in terms of Figure 14, an expansion in the schedule of intentions to produce between year 1 and year 2 would mean that price P_1 would not induce quantity Q_2, but rather would induce some output greater than Q_2.

Third, up to this point it has been implicitly assumed that the planned quantity of output would in each case be just realized. In other words, it has been assumed that the planned output Q_1 in Figure 3 would in fact be realized. But there are many reasons why this might not happen. And weather is perhaps the most important. Better or poorer than average weather may well upset production plans and give rise to a larger or smaller output than was planned. In short, realized output in any one year may deviate from planned output and break the cobweb pattern. For these general reasons, growing out of a variety of specific causes, the regular price-output path of the cobweb model may be broken. And breaking the regular price-output path brings about a jumbled, irregular pattern of price variability—how jumbled depends upon the circumstances of the breaks.

Where relative prices vary from production period to production period in a wide and unpredictable fashion, uncertainty is created in the minds of producers. Past prices become a poor guide to planning the current year's, or period's, production. The farmer becomes uncertain as to whether prices will hold up, rise, or fall in future periods. The price system ceases to be a useful and effective allocator of productive resources. Highly variable and highly uncertain commodity prices force farmers to fall back on hunches and other arbitrary guides in planning production. So it turns out that price uncertainty itself serves to break down the regular cobweb pattern, and thus produce further uncertainty.

The actual price-output path for potatoes over the period 1950–56 is presented in Figure 15. Here we have a three-year cycle followed by a two-year cycle, with both cycles falling below the farm price level as suggested by the historical data of Figure 12. In the first cycle, relative prices rise from P_{50} to P_{51} to P_{52} and then fall by more than 50 per cent to P_{53}; the price rise from P_{51} to P_{52} must have resulted from an important increase in demand, since production increased in 1952 as would be expected. The price-output path converges sharply in the second cycle, and then begins to expand again in the third and unfinished cycle. Potato producers get precious little information from Figure 15 on which to base price and income expectations.

The events of the real world break down the logical construction presented in Figure 14, but these events do not lessen year-to-year potato price variations. Since the price scales in Figures 14 and 15 are the same, it can be seen that the events of the real world give rise to a wider range of relative price variability than the range suggested by the arbitrary point of origin, price 120, in the cobweb model. In the 1950s, as in the years prior to World War II, relative potato prices (i.e., actual prices deflated for changes in the price level) can change by more than 50 per cent in one year without too much trouble. This is real price variability.

The Cobweb Analysis for Hogs

THE MODEL

A two-year cobweb model for hogs is presented in Figure 16. The price-output sequence of this model does not, however, represent full year units of time. The cycle in Figure 16 relates to the spring pig crop, which goes to market during the period August through January. Thus, the price P_0 is for the period August through January of year 0; this price induces farmers to produce a spring pig crop Q_1 which goes to market during the period August through January of year 1; and so on around the cobweb. This model is probably not absolutely consistent with the time periods involved in producing and marketing the spring pig crop; the prices that influence farmers to breed sows for the spring pig crop may precede the August–January period somewhat, and marketings from the spring pig crop may lap over the end of that six-month period somewhat. But granted some latitude in the facts of the situation, this model fits the time schedule of gestation, animal growth, and marketing peaks reasonably well.

As in the case of potatoes, the cobweb model for the spring pig crop is positioned astride the farm price level where that level is equal to

100. Price deviations from 100 represent relative price changes — changes in the price of fall marketed hogs relative to the average of all farm prices. The elasticity of demand at the farm level, that is at the point where price equals 100 and quantity equals 100, in Figure 16, is —.55.[6] The elasticity of the schedule of intentions to produce a spring pig crop at the point where price equals 100 and quantity equals 100, is .31.[7] With the slope of the demand relation significantly less steeply inclined than the schedule of intentions to produce in this model, the price-output path is strongly convergent.

There is still room for some price variability around the farm price level in this model, but compared with the potato model in Figure 14, it generates a restricted orbit of price variability. This is consistent with the comparative data on relative price variability. It will be recalled from Chapter 2 that the average year-to-year percentage variation in potato prices around the moving farm price level is 49 per cent for the period 1920 to 1955, whereas the average variation is only 15 per cent for hogs for the same period. In sum, the relative elasticities of demand and the schedule of intentions to produce employed in the hog cobweb model ensure some price variability around the farm price level, but considerably less than for potatoes.

BREAKING THE MODEL AND THE CONSEQUENCES

Again the model presented in Figure 16 does not provide an adequate explanation of commodity price variability. Left alone, the price-output path of the cobweb model would converge on the price level, eliminating all further variability. Further, and more important, price variability for hogs does not fall into a regular two-year pattern; a glance at Figure 12 makes this clear. Hog price variability around the farm price level moves through unpredictable patterns of four, five, six, or even seven years' duration.

But this can be explained again in terms of a breakdown of the cobweb model. It is unreasonable to assume that the demand relation and the schedule of intentions to produce in Figure 16 would hold fixed positions over four or five years, thus permitting the price-output path to converge on the farm price level. In the real world of food and agriculture, the demand relation probably shifts every year, and the schedule

[6] Estimate by Elmer Learn, "Estimating Demand of Livestock Products," *Journal of Farm Economics*, Proceedings Issue, December 1956, p. 1488.

[7] See Appendix A for a discussion of method and relevant statistical measures.

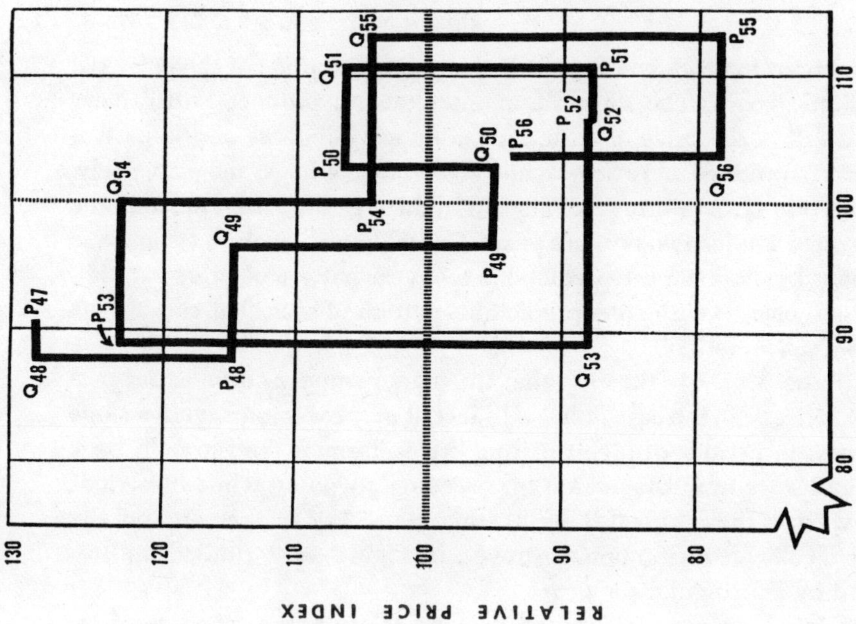

Figure 17. The actual price-output path for the spring pig crop, 1947–56.

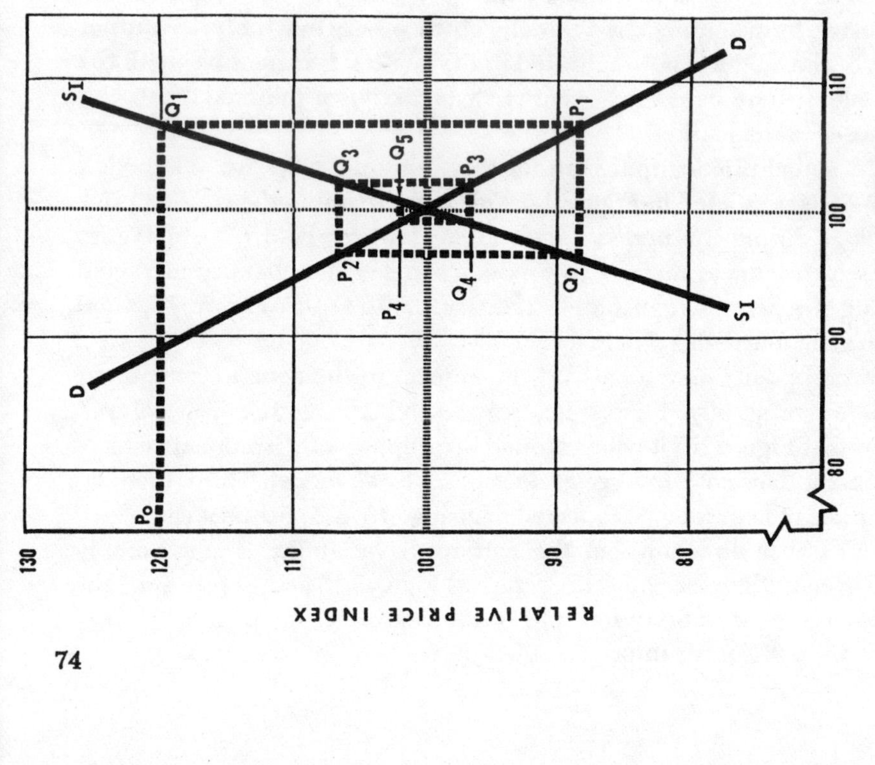

Figure 16. The cobweb model for hogs.

of intentions to produce shifts with changes in the price of the principal hog input — corn. The schedule of intentions to produce will expand with a fall in the price of corn, indicating a willingness on the part of farmers to produce more hogs at any given price of hogs, and conversely. And corn prices, resulting from cycles in the weather, often move in the same direction for two or more years. Consequently, such shifts in these relations break down the predictable two-year pattern of price variability and replace it with an unpredictable pattern of four, five, six, or even seven years' duration.

It is also probably the case that the market supply curve is not perfectly inelastic in the case of hogs. In fact, it may exhibit a negative slope at times: in periods of high or rising prices, farmers tend to hold back gilts and sows from the market for breeding purposes, while in periods of low prices they ship off their breeding stock. For this reason, too, the regular cobweb interaction portrayed in Figure 16 is riddled and replaced by an irregular pattern.

The forces represented by the demand relation, the schedule of intentions to produce, and the market supply curve in the hog cobweb model are all at work in the hog-corn sector, and they are related in the recursive form implied by the cobweb theorem; but the price-output path of the model is not replicated in the market. It cannot be; with the passage of time numerous events that break down the model can and do occur in the market.

The actual price-output path for the spring pig crop over the period 1947–56 is presented in Figure 17. This path describes the relative price for hogs during the period August 1947–January 1948 (P_{47} in Figure 17) which induces farmers to produce and sell the quantity marketed during the period August 1948–January 1949 (Q_{48} in Figure 17), and so on along the realized path.

Several points may be made with respect to the actual price-output path for spring pigs. First, it bears no resemblance to the clear cobweb pattern of Figure 16; it winds around in an apparently irrational fashion. Second, it does not converge as does the cobweb model. Third, the relative price of hogs may be expected to change 10 to 20 per cent each year, and in either direction, but the pattern of variability is considerably less for hogs than for potatoes (compare Figures 15 and 17). In sum, the relative price variability for hogs is not so great as for potatoes, but in some ways it is more unpredictable.

An Analysis of Farm Price Behavior

The Cobweb Analysis for Milk

Milk fits the cobweb framework of analysis least well of the three commodities under consideration. The cobweb analysis assumes a definite growth period in the production process interspersed between the decisions to produce and the decisions to sell, recurring in a periodic fashion; the juxtaposition of these events is what creates the cobweb. But milk production does not occur in distinct and disjointed time periods; it flows endlessly on. Certainly there is seasonality in milk production, but this complicates rather than eases the problem of fitting milk into the cobweb analysis, for seasonality in milk production grows out of the seasons, not out of economic decision-making.

The major question to be answered in constructing a cobweb analysis for milk is what time period to use. If the analyst is thinking in terms of variations in output growing out of variations in numbers of cows, or some sort of a dairy cattle cycle, then the time span must be very long. And the schedule of intentions to produce must be estimated so as to permit cattle numbers to vary. But past efforts in this direction have been fruitless and frustrating.[8] On the other hand, if the analyst is thinking in terms of variations in output (i.e., seasonally adjusted output) growing out of variations in feeding rates, then the time span must be very short – perhaps a month; the assumption here being that the last milk check influences feeding rates. The cobweb analysis developed in this chapter for milk is something of a compromise between these views, but leans toward the latter.

The cobweb model for milk presented in Figure 18 involves a six-month cycle: two periods, each three months in duration. All prices and outputs are seasonally adjusted to remove that complicating and noneconomic factor from the analysis. Price P_0 in the last quarter of year 0, it is assumed, induces farmers to try to produce quantity Q_1 in the first quarter of year 1; quantity Q_1 sells for a price P_1 in the first quarter; this price P_1 induces farmers to try to produce quantity Q_2 in the second quarter, and so on around the cobweb.

There are problems with this model; it is not consistent with some disjointed and periodic production period, since none exists. But it is not useless. In the first place, milk prices in one three-month period must influence output in the next period through feeding rates and culling

[8] Estimates of milk supply relations where numbers of cows are not held constant are as likely to have a negative sign as a positive one.

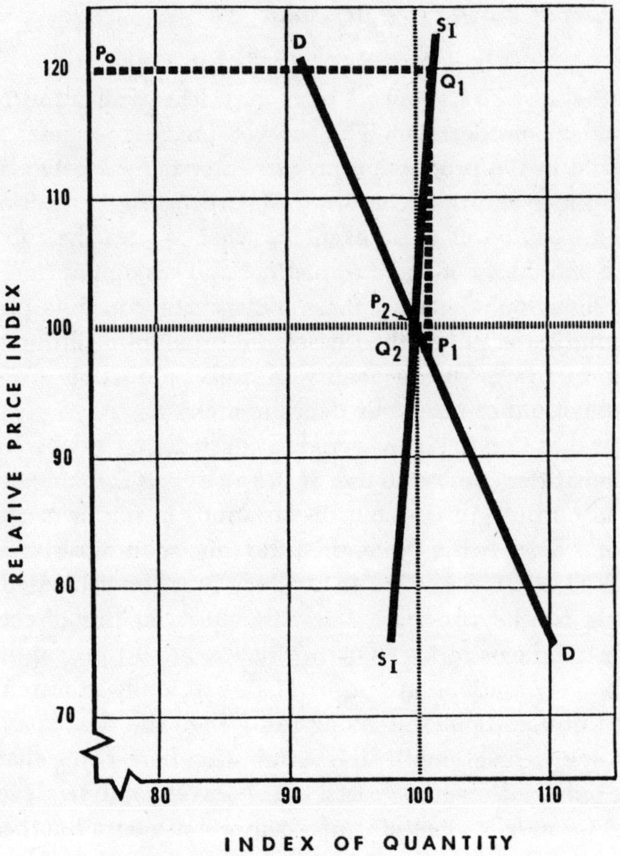

Figure 18. The cobweb model for milk.

rates, if price has any effect on milk production. Second, the idea of a perfectly inelastic market-supply relation makes good sense for a highly perishable commodity like milk. Third, the estimates of the demand relation and the schedule of intentions to produce employed in this model appear, on the basis of past experience, to be reasonable.

As in previous commodity analyses, the milk cobweb model is positioned astride the farm price level where that level is equal to 100. Price deviations from 100 represent relative price changes – changes in the price of milk relative to the average of all farm prices. The elasticity of demand at the farm level, that is at the point where price equals 100 and quantity equals 100, in Figure 18, is —.38.[9] The elasticity of the

[9] Learn, *op. cit.*, p. 1488.

schedule of intentions to produce at the point where price equals 100 and quantity equals 100 is .03.[10] In other words, the demand relation at the farm level is inelastic, but the short-run supply relation, the schedule of intentions to produce, is extremely inelastic. Hence, the slope of the schedule of intentions to produce is extremely steep relative to the slope of the demand relation. Given this set of relations, the cobweb converges on the price level immediately.

It may well be that the time span employed in the milk cobweb model portrayed in Figure 18 is not the proper one. But, if there is a cobweb action of some time span present in milk, and it appears that there is, then we have found an explanation for the tendency for milk prices to converge on the farm price level. This tendency derives out of the cobweb action, where the demand relation is relatively much more elastic than the supply relation. In this set of circumstances, any time that the price of milk increases relative to other farm commodity prices, a unique and powerful set of forces drives it back toward the farm price level. Hence, the year-to-year, or season-to-season, price variations of milk around the moving farm price level are at a minimum.

Economic Implications of the Cobweb Analyses

Inferences and statements have been made in the foregoing commodity analyses to the effect that relative price variability, particularly as uncertainty attaches to it, is undesirable. Now it should be obvious that highly variable prices and highly uncertain prices are harmful to producers. But all relative price changes — that is, changes in one commodity price relative to all others — are not bad. On the contrary, relative price changes are an essential part of economic change and development. Relative price changes guide and direct resources into those productive uses that maximize the total utility of society; relative price changes effect, or induce, wanted changes in the composition of total output.

A relative price increase growing out of an increase in demand resulting in turn from increased consumer preference, which induces farmers to shift resources into the production of that commodity and increase its output, means that the pricing system is properly performing one of the important roles assigned to it by society in a mixed-enterprise, capitalistic economy like ours. Or a relative price decrease growing out of

[10] See Appendix A for a discussion of method and relevant statistical measures.

an increase in supply resulting in turn from a technological advance, which induces farmers to shift some resources out of the production of this commodity and decrease its output, means also that the pricing system is functioning properly. In these examples, relative price changes are facilitating or inducing changes in resource combinations in accordance with the dictates of a changing world. This is what we want from the pricing system.

Thus we should not, and cannot, subscribe to the view that all price changes are undesirable. Relative price changes are indispensable to economic change and development.

But incessant commodity price gyrations around the farm price level, extreme and unpredictable in nature, are undesirable. Extreme and irregular relative price changes create uncertainty — undue uncertainty — in the minds of producers, and this leads to two kinds of inefficiency. First, the producer is handicapped with respect to planning next year's production. Last year's prices are of little or no use to him. He must guess at some most probable set of prices for planning purposes — probably a discounted set of last year's prices — and this set of prices may not reflect the wants of society.

Second, uncertainty in the minds of farm producers leads to an unwillingness on their part to invest in costly new production techniques, or to assume long-term financial commitments associated with new and improved production techniques. Farm businessmen like other businessmen hesitate to invest heavily in risky enterprises; hence the adoption of improved production techniques is often delayed. Price and income risks arising out of price uncertainty have the effect of slowing down technological advance in farming.

Price and income risk arising out of price uncertainty may be viewed as a social cost, but it is a cost that must be borne entirely by the producers of the commodities involved. Such costs have two effects: (1) they distort the allocation of resources and (2) they slow down technological advance. The cost of risk in commodities with highly variable and highly uncertain prices has the effect first of reducing the employment of inputs in that commodity relative to other less risky commodities, and second, increasing the cost of, or reducing the flow of, new capital investments into the enterprise. Thus, we conclude that extreme and irregular relative price changes arising out of a broken cobweb interaction leads to widespread inefficiencies.

An Analysis of Farm Price Behavior

It is difficult to say how important these risk-induced inefficiencies may be. There can be no doubt that they are widespread. Several million farmers in many commodity lines are involved. But what these inefficiencies add up to in the way of reduced real incomes and reduced human satisfaction is impossible to say. Perhaps about all that can be said is that price and income uncertainty results in some annoyance to a great number of farmers, a great deal of annoyance to some farmers, and almost no annoyance to nonfarm people.

The Commodity Parts of the Aggregative Analysis

The relationship of the individual commodity analyses to the aggregative analysis will now be developed. In a way, this has already been done, since the commodity analyses of this chapter describe output changes in response to relative price changes – changes in the price of one commodity relative to all others (i.e., the aggregate). But it may help to construct, so to speak, the aggregative analysis out of the individual commodity parts. In other words, the logical consistency of the general theory of farm prices may be enhanced by a thorough understanding of the relationship of the parts to the whole.

THE CONSTRUCTION PROCESS

The supply relation – the schedule of intentions to produce which describes the intentions of farmers to produce a commodity as its price varies relative to the prices of other commodities – generally exhibits some positive price elasticity. In other words, farmers *plan* to produce more of a commodity when the price of it increases relative to the prices of commodity substitutes, and conversely. And these plans are realized on multiple enterprise units by farmers shifting resources among enterprises, and in agriculture generally by farmers lending, renting, and selling resources among themselves. But the market supply curve, which describes the flow of products to market at the end of the production period, is highly inelastic. The extreme inelasticity of the market supply curve results from the perishable nature of most farm products, and their rush to market at the end of the growing period.

Now let us assume a rapid and important increase in the demand for all food, resulting, say, from a decision on the part of the United States to feed a large part of the world, which is precisely what happened during and following World War II. In such a situation the demand for each food item probably would not increase proportionately, but each would increase and that is the important point for this discussion. Given a sharp and general increase in the demand for food in one year, the relatively elastic schedules of intentions to produce do not describe the output responses to this increase in demand. They cannot, because decisions to produce will have already been translated into actions to produce, and production processes will have been set in motion for the year.

In the short run of the year, the market supply curves describe, commodity by commodity, the nature of the supply response. And they are highly, or perfectly, inelastic. Thus, demand relations, commodity by commodity, will, in this assumed situation, ride up highly inelastic supply relations and drive prices up, commodity by commodity. The result is a higher farm price level and little or no increase in aggregate output. This result is consistent with some things we already know: (1) that the aggregate supply relation for farm products is highly, or perfectly, inelastic in the short run; and (2) that during wide sweeps in the farm price level, individual commodity prices pull together and move in a parallel fashion.

But this intra-year analysis does not go to the heart of the problem. Assuming that this general expansion in the demand for food extends over several years and, to keep our thinking straight, assuming also that there is no technological advance, then the relatively elastic schedules of intentions to produce again fail to describe the output responses of individual commodities to the general increase in demand. The schedules of intentions to produce cannot describe the planned output responses in this situation, *because each describes the planned output response of a commodity on the assumption that only the price of that one commodity is changing (i.e., that we have a relative price change).* But in this assumed situation all farm prices are rising. True, all farm prices may not be rising at the same rate; hence there may be some shifting of resources among enterprises with some change in the composition of total output. But equally true, the output of each enterprise on each farm cannot expand, as described by the relevant schedule of intentions to produce, as all commodity prices rise, unless the total complex of resources used in agricultural production is increased during the period. And the latter is clearly impossible.

Thus, in the short run of several years, the market supply curves once again take over and describe supply behavior, commodity by commodity. And demand relations, commodity by commodity, ride up these highly inelastic market supply relations and drive prices up, commodity by commodity. The consequences of a general increase in the demand for food over several years is thus the same as for one year: a higher farm price level and little or no increase in aggregate output. And this result, too, is consistent with some things we already know: (1) the aggregate supply relation for farm products may hold a fixed and highly inelastic position over several years, and (2) total resources employed in agriculture typically do not expand during good times in agriculture — typically total resource inputs in agriculture hold constant.

Now let us assume another, and very different, situation. Let us assume that the total demand for farm food products is constant, unchanging. And similarly that total supply is unchanging. In other words, changes in the farm price level are assumed away, by assuming away changes in over-all demand resulting from changes in national income or population, and by assuming away changes in over-all supply resulting from changes in total resources employed or in technological advance. But changes within the aggregate may be expected to occur: the demand for a particular commodity may expand or contract because of a change in consumer preferences for it; a crop failure in one commodity may occur alongside a bumper crop in another commodity; or disease control may greatly increase the cost of production of some commodity. Any one of the above causal events could set off a cobweb action for the commodity involved, leading to a relative price change, resource shifts among enterprises, changes in the output of the commodity, then relative price change again, and so on. In other words, in this context the schedule of intentions to produce does describe the planned output responses of farmers, and the schedule of intentions to produce in conjunction with the demand relation for the commodity sets up a cobweb interaction leading to *shifts in the composition of total output and variations in commodity prices around the price level.*

In connection with these two assumed cases, it might prove interesting to refer back to Figure 2 of Chapter 2 (p. 14) and once again observe the tendency for the various farm commodity prices to pull together and move together in times of major movements in the farm price level, and to gyrate around the farm price level during periods of price level stability.

COMMODITY PRICE VARIABILITY

THE SEA OF COMPETITIVE BEHAVIOR

The commodity parts of agriculture flow together into a sea of competitive behavior. The ubiquitous process of substitution — the substitution of cheap for dear food items on the demand side, and the substitution of more profitable for less profitable enterprises on the supply side — works impersonally and endlessly to stabilize commodity prices at sea level within the agricultural aggregate. Whitecaps and troughs dot this sea, which from time to time becomes a little rough; all of this, however, may be explained by the workings of the various commodity cobwebs. But powerful forces — competitive forces involving substitution — are forever leveling the whitecaps and filling in the troughs.

With these competitive forces at work in a great sea like American agriculture, studying one commodity is like studying one whitecap in the Pacific Ocean; it merges into the larger sea in an infinite number of ways, leaving the analyst with nothing to study. The sense of futility which overtakes the analyst and student alike in studying the market behavior of individual commodities in agriculture is evident in this chapter. One can trace the consequences of some event to a commodity through dated time for a brief period, but soon the consequences of this event in the market are lost in the maze of other consequences resulting from numberless other events, all tied together or integrated into a meaningful whole by an infinity of resource and product substitutions. Unraveling the market behavior — the price-output behavior — of a commodity in this seamless web is hopeless.

Within the agricultural sea of competitive behavior the economy operates, with the exception of the cobweb interaction, just about as the classical and neo-classical economists said it does and implied that it *should.* This agricultural sea that we have been talking about differs, however, from the seas that ships sail on and the sea of competitive behavior that the classicals implicitly assumed. The level of the agriculture sea rises and falls, and sometimes sharply, and it can remain low relative to other seas — that is, other sectors of the economy — for extended periods. The price level of this agricultural sea, to push this analogy just a little further, is a stormy one. When it rises it brings prosperity to all farmers, efficient and inefficient alike, and when it falls it brings despair to all farmers and failure to many. Changes in the level of farm prices create income problems ignored and/or assumed away by the classical and neo-classical economists.

An Analysis of Farm Price Behavior

Now changes in the level of farm prices, where they all act together, can be analyzed and explained in terms of the behavior of each individual commodity, as was done in the previous section. But this is a cumbersome procedure. It is easier, much easier, to treat all food as one big commodity, and to relate the demand for all food to the supply of all food. (Here we assume that the aggregate food is synonymous with agriculture; this, of course, is not entirely true, but the tobacco and fiber exceptions do not impair the logic of the argument.)

And there are logical grounds for treating all food as one big commodity. The high degree of product and enterprise substitutability which exists within agriculture, and fuses the commodity parts into a sea of competitive behavior, does not extend across the agricultural sector to other sectors of the economy. Resources transfer across the farm-nonfarm line, but not nearly so easily as among enterprises within agriculture. And the substitution of food items for nonfood items, and conversely, is certainly at a minimum. So it is appropriate to visualize the food and agricultural sector as a self-contained sea, where the substitutional possibilities within the sector are varied and numberless, but the substitutional possibilities across the sector line are limited and restrained.

This was the view taken in the aggregative analysis of Chapter 3. The aggregate demand for the big commodity food was related to the aggregate supply of the big commodity food to explain changes in the food product price level (i.e., the farm price level). And this shall be our general procedure once again in Chapter 5.

APPENDIX A

Supply-Estimating Equations

THROUGHOUT Chapter 4 it was assumed that agricultural commodity prices and outputs are generated in cobweb structures. The cobweb structural conditions are not satisfied perfectly by each agricultural commodity, but the economic structure of most agricultural commodities is of a cobweb form. Now the cobweb structure is a special case of a recursive system — a system in which price gives rise to output, output to price, price to output, and so on through time in an irreversible process.

We are concerned here with estimating one relation, the schedule of intentions to produce, in such recursive systems. And, as Herman Wold has shown,[1] reliable (i.e., reasonably unbiased and efficient) estimates of demand or supply in a recursive system may be obtained through least-squares regression analysis, where the cause variables are treated as independent variables and the effect variable as the dependent variable. Such is our procedure here. We estimate the regression coefficients of the schedules of intentions to produce by least-squares regression techniques, being careful to treat cause variables as independent variables and the effect variable as a dependent variable in the analysis.

All estimates are for the United States, for the periods indicated. Where the regression analyses are in actual numbers, the price elasticity estimates are given for the point of means.

SCHEDULE OF INTENTIONS TO PRODUCE FOR POTATOES (1921–41, 1950–56)

Estimating equation (actual numbers)	$X_1 = 378.791$	$+ .6308X_2$	$- 1.8351X_3$
Standard errors of b's		(.2402)	(.1499)
Level of significance of b's		2%	.1%
Means	283.1	110.5	90.1

$$R^2_{1.23} = .9175$$

Price elasticity = .246

Where

X_1 = Acres planted in current year, as an indication of intentions to produce, 10,000 acres.

X_2 = Potato prices deflated by index of prices received for all crops for years t-1 and t-2, weighted equally, cents per cwt.

X_3 = Yield per acre in current year, cwt.

[1] *Demand Analysis* (New York: John Wiley & Sons, Inc., 1953), Chapter 2.

The X_2 variable, deflated potato prices, in this regression analysis is not completely consistent with the potato cobweb model of Chapter 4. The causative price in the cobweb model is the previous year's price, whereas the causative price in the regression analysis is an average of the previous two years' prices. The use of the previous two years' prices in the regression analysis increases the coefficient of multiple correlation considerably, suggesting that the true cobweb model is somewhat more complex than that portrayed in Figure 14 of Chapter 4. Implied in the schedule of intentions to produce estimated in the above regression analysis and used in the cobweb model is that farmers plan to produce on the basis of an average of the previous two years' potato prices.

SCHEDULE OF INTENTIONS TO PRODUCE FOR SPRING PIGS (1921–56)

Estimating equation (in first differences of logarithms)	$X_1 = -.0019 + .3086X_2$	$- .3497X_3$
Standard errors of b's	(.0754)	(.0618)
Level of significance of b's	.1%	.1%

$$R^2_{1.23} = .5491$$

Price elasticity = .309

Where

X_1 = Number of sows farrowed December 1, year t-1 to June 1, year t, times the trend values of spring pigs saved per litter, as an indication of intentions to produce.

X_2 = Hog prices, average for July through November of year t-1, cents per cwt.

X_3 = Corn prices for September through November of year t-1, cents per cwt.

SCHEDULE OF INTENTIONS TO PRODUCE FOR MILK, BY QUARTERS (1947–56)

Estimating equation (actual numbers) ..	$X_1 = -56.6747$	$+ .0301X_2$	$- .0220X_3$	$+ .0152X_4$	$+ .0033X_5$
Standard errors of b's		(.0847)	(.0208)	(.0021)	(.0009)
Level of significance of b's		...*	...*	.1%	.1%
Means	100	100	337	5433	23787

$$R^2_{1.2345} = .7324$$

Price elasticity = .030

Where

X_1 = Milk production by calendar quarters, seasonally adjusted, percentage of 1947–56 average.

X_2 = Average wholesale milk prices, quarters q and q-1, percentage of 1947–56 average (seasonally adjusted).

X_3 = Dairy ration prices, average for quarters q and q-1, cents per cwt.

X_4 = Production per cow in pounds, annual production in year t used for each quarter in t.

X_5 = Number of cows kept for milk; number on January 1 used for first quarter, numbers for other quarters interpolated from preceding and succeeding January 1 figures.

Again in this regression analysis the X_2 variable, wholesale milk prices, is not completely consistent with the milk cobweb model of Chapter 4. The current quarter's prices are included in the regression analysis, because it was reasoned that current prices must influence current milk production.

* Not significant at the 10% level.

APPENDIX TABLE 1. PROCEDURE FOR CALCULATING THE AVERAGE REALIZED NET INCOME OF COMMERCIAL FARM OPERATORS FROM ALL SOURCES

Description	Year								
	1947	1948	1949	1950	1951	1952	1953	1954	1955
1. Average realized net income of *all* farm operators from farming, including government payment [a]	$2927	$2747	$2389	$2276	$2682	$2660	$2649	$2357	$2268
2. Incomes from line 1 expressed as index numbers (1949 = 100)	122.52	114.99	100.00	95.27	112.26	111.34	110.88	98.66	94.94
3. 1949 average realized net income of *commercial* farm operators from farming [b]	...	...	$3028	...	...	...	...	...	...
4. *Estimated* average realized net income of *commercial* farm operators from farming [c]	$3710	$3482	$3028	$2885	$3399	$3371	$3357	$2987	$2875
5. Estimates of off-farm income [d]	679	716	740	764	825	926	934	910	993
6. Total estimated average realized net income of *commercial* farm operators *from all sources*	$4389	$4198	$3768	$3649	$4224	$4297	$4291	$3897	$3868

[a] *The Farm Income Situation*, July 17, 1956, p. 26, column 7.

[b] *Agricultural Economics Research*, April 1956, p. 53, column 4.

[c] The amounts in line 4 were obtained by multiplying the 1949 average realized net income of *commercial* farm operators from farming by the index number in line 2 for the relevant year and dividing by 100. Thus, the estimates of average realized net income to *commercial* farm operators from farming vary about the base year (1949) by the same proportion as do average realized net incomes to *all* farm operators as given in line 1.

[d] The values in line 5 were obtained by the same general procedure described for line 4. The off-farm income to commercial farm operators (as reported in *Agricultural Economics Research*, April 1956, p. 53, column 7) was adjusted by the index of the average off-farm income to all farmers (1949 = 100). Data for this index were compiled from statistics reported in *The Farm Income Situation*, July 17, 1956, p. 20, column 6, and p. 26, column 1.

APPENDIX TABLE 2. DATA USED IN THE DEMAND ANALYSIS FOR THE PERIODS 1929–42, 1947–56

Year	Index of Per Capita Food Consumption (1)	Retail Food Price Index (Not Deflated) (2)	Index of Per Capita Disposable Income (Not Deflated) (3)	Time (4)	Adjusted Index of Per Capita Food Consumption* (5)
1929	91.1	65.6	55.1	1	97.5
1930	90.7	62.4	48.8	2	98.0
1931	90.0	51.4	41.6	3	98.4
1932	87.8	42.8	31.5	4	97.8
1933	88.0	41.6	29.4	5	98.2
1934	89.1	46.4	33.2	6	98.4
1935	87.3	49.7	37.1	7	95.7
1936	90.5	50.1	41.8	8	97.8
1937	90.4	52.1	44.5	9	97.0
1938	90.6	48.4	40.9	10	97.7
1939	93.8	47.1	43.5	11	100.2
1940	95.5	47.8	46.5	12	101.1
1941	97.5	52.2	56.3	13	101.1
1942	96.7	61.3	70.4	14	97.5
1947	102.0	95.9	94.7	19	97.3
1948	99.1	104.1	103.4	20	92.6
1949	98.9	100.0	101.9	21	92.5
1950	99.9	101.2	109.8	22	91.8
1951	98.1	112.6	118.3	23	88.3
1952	100.4	114.6	122.1	24	89.7
1953	101.5	112.8	126.7	25	89.7
1954	101.4	112.6	126.6	26	89.4
1955	102.8	110.9	132.2	27	89.6
1956	104.0	111.4	137.6	28	89.6

* The data in this column were estimated from the following regression equation for each year, with the influence of change in income from the mean and change in time from the mean removed.

Regression equation .... $X_1 = 88.448 - .131X_2 + .183X_3 + .212X_4$

Standard errors of b's .... (.081) (.082) (.150)

$$R^2_{1.234} = .904$$

Where

X_1 = Index of per capita food consumption.
X_2 = Index of retail food prices.
X_3 = Index of per capita disposable income.
X_4 = Time.

APPENDIX TABLE 3. INCENTIVE INCOME RATIO IN THE UNITED STATES FOR SELECTED YEARS, 1910–55

Year	Net Farm Income (millions)[a] (1)	Adjustment for Retail Valuation of Self Supplies (millions)[b] (2)	Aggregate Wages (millions)[c] (3)	Interest (millions)[d] (4)	Est. Total Net Rent (millions)[e] (5)	Farmers and Family Workers: No. of Man Units[f] (6)	Farm Incentive Income: Aggregate: Cols. (1+2) −(3+4+5) (millions) (7)	Farm Incentive Income: Per Man-Yr.: Col. 7 ÷ Col. 6 (8)	Nonfarm Incentive Income Per Man-Yr.[g] (9)	Incentive Income Ratio Col. 8 ÷ Col. 9 (10)
1910 ……	$ 5,436	$1,041	$ 755	$ 426	$1,659	9,343,000	$ 3,637	$ 389	$ 785	50%
1920 ……	10,626	2,047	1,790	876	2,557	8,934,000	7,450	834	1,517	55
1940 ……	6,340	997	1,029	525	1,904	9,083,000	3,879	427	1,476	29
1947 ……	19,899	2,240	2,808	1,300	6,095	8,157,000	11,936	1,463	2,904	50
1950 ……	17,883	1,608	2,750	1,680	4,831	7,066,000	10,230	1,448	3,312	44
1955 ……	15,910	1,325	2,750	1,840	4;886	6,272,000	7,759	1,237	4,193	30

[a] *The Farm Income Situation*, FIS–159, July 17, 1956, p. 21, column 5.

[b] *Ibid.*, p. 31, column 3 minus page 34, column 6. [c] *Ibid.*, p. 34, column 9.

[d] Interest charged on all non–real estate productive farm assets (livestock, crops excluding Commodity Credit Corporation stocks, machinery, motor vehicles used in production). Data were taken from *Agricultural Statistics 1952*, p. 625, columns 2, 4, 5; *Agricultural Statistics 1954*, p. 432, columns 2, 4, 5; *Agricultural Statistics 1955*, p. 434, rows 2–4; *Balance Sheet of Agriculture 1947*, p. 2; *Balance Sheet of Agriculture 1950*, p. 3; *Balance Sheet of Agriculture 1955*, p. 2. The interest rate is based on estimates made by D. Gale Johnson in "Allocation of Agricultural Income," *Journal of Farm Economics*, Volume XXX, No. 4, November 1948, p. 748, column 2, for years through 1947 and upon data from *Agricultural Statistics 1955*, p. 492, column 10 for 1950 and 1955.

[e] Obtained by dividing "Net Rental to All Landlords" (*Agricultural Statistics 1943*, p. 412, column 3; *Agricultural Statistics 1955*, p. 481, column 3) by "Proportion of All Land Rented" (Johnson, *op. cit.*, p. 746; *1954 Census of Agriculture*, Volume II, Chapter X, General Report, p. 965, columns 2, 7; the 1955 figures are estimated from 1954 figures).

[f] The number of farm operators and family workers was divided by the total number of people employed in agriculture; the same was done for hired labor (*Agricultural Statistics 1952*, p. 637, columns 1, 3, 5; *Agricultural Statistics 1955*, p. 438, columns 1, 3, 5). The number of people 14 years of age or over employed in agriculture (*Statistical Abstract of the United States, 1955*, p. 187, columns 4–6; *Labor Force, Employment and Unemployment in U.S., 1940–1946*, Dept. of Commerce, Series P-50, No. 2, pp. 25–26; *Current Population Reports, Labor Force*, Dept. of Commerce, series P-50, No. 31, p. 16) was then multiplied by the respective percentages described earlier in this footnote to calculate the number of persons 14 or over (a) in the family labor force and (b) in the farm hired labor force.

The total hired farm laborers were added to nonagricultural industry employees to give the "total nonagricultural man units."

Farm operator and family labor figures were adjusted to man units by multiplying the data by the average number of hours worked on the farm and dividing this figure by the average number of hours worked in nonagricultural industries (*Current Population Reports, Labor Force*, Dept. of Commerce, Series P-50, No. 63, p. 1, columns 2, 3).

[g] See Appendix Table 4 for the relevant data and computational steps involved in the nonfarm incentive income estimates.

APPENDIX TABLE 4. NONFARM INCENTIVE INCOME IN THE UNITED STATES FOR SELECTED YEARS, 1910–55

Year	Personal Income (millions)[a]	National Nonfarm Profit-Yielding Assets (billions)[b]	Interest rate[c]	Interest: Col. 2 × Col. 3 (millions)	Farm Income (millions)[d]	Total Nonagricultural Incentive Income: Cols. 1 − (4 + 5) (millions)	No. of Man Units[e]	Nonfarm Incentive Income Per Man Year: Col. 6 ÷ Col. 7
	(1)	(2)	(3)	(4)	(5)	(6)	(7)	(8)
1910	$ 33,252	$ 88.5	6%	$ 5,310	$ 4,681	$ 23,261	29,641,000	$ 785
1920	75,730	252.2	6	15,132	8,836	51,762	34,119,000	1,517
1940	78,680	278.9	5	13,945	5,311	59,424	40,270,000	1,476
1947	190,522	474.7	5	23,735	17,091	149,696	51,554,000	2,904
1950	227,050	653.1	5	32,655	15,133	179,262	54,132,000	3,312
1955	306,100	993.7	5	49,685	13,160	243,255	58,012,000	4,193

[a] Sources: *The Farm Income Situation*, FIS–159, July 17, 1956, p. 22, column 3 (national income figures used for 1910 and 1920); *National Income 1954 Edition. A Supplement to the Survey of Current Business*, pp. 164–165, Table 4, line 20; *Economic Indicators*, March 1957, U.S. Government Printing Office, p. 5, column 1.

[b] Based on January 1 estimates. Sources: R. W. Goldsmith, *A Study of Saving in the United States* (Princeton: Princeton University Press, 1955–56), Vol. III, pp. 14–15, Table W-1, columns 4, 5, 6, 10, 17, 21, 22, 23, 25; and *Statistical Abstract of the United States 1955*, p. 308, columns 4, 5, 6, 10, 11, 14, 21. The 1955 asset figure was extrapolated from 1949, 1950, and 1953 estimates.

[c] Data taken from Johnson, *Journal of Farm Economics*, Vol. XXX, No. 4, p. 748.

[d] Column 1 minus column 3 of Appendix Table 3.

[e] See footnote f, Appendix Table 3.

[11]

DYNAMIC SHORTAGES AND PRICE RISES: THE ENGINEER-SCIENTIST CASE*

By Kenneth J. Arrow and William M. Capron

The frequent and loud complaints of a shortage of engineers and scientists heard over the past eight years or so might be taken as indicating a failure of the price mechanism and indeed have frequently been joined with (rather vaguely stated) proposals for interference with market determination of numbers and allocation. It is our contention that these views stem from a misunderstanding of economic theory as well as from an exaggeration of the empirical evidence. On the contrary, a proper view of the workings of the market mechanism, recognizing, in particular, the dynamics of market adjustment to changed conditions, would show that the phenomenon of observed shortage in some degree is exactly what would be predicted by classical theory in the face of rapidly rising demands.

In this paper we present a model which explains the dynamics of the market adjustment process and apply the conclusions drawn from this analysis to the scientist-engineer "shortage."

Equality of supply and demand is a central tenet of ordinary economic theory, but only as the end result of a process, not as a state holding at every instant of time. On the contrary, inequalities between supply and demand are usually regarded as an integral part of the process by which the price on a market reaches its equilibrium position. Price is assumed to rise when demand exceeds supply and to fall in the contrary case.[1] A shortage, in the sense of an excess of demand over supply, is then the normal concomitant of a price rise.

* This paper is part of an economic analysis of the engineer-scientist market conducted for The RAND Corporation, A. A. Alchian, K. J. Arrow, and W. M. Capron, RM-2190-RC, "An Economic Analysis of the Market for Scientists and Engineers," 6 June 1958.

1. See, for example, Marshall's well-known analysis of the equilibrating process on the corn market, *Principles of Economics*, 8th ed., pp. 332–34. P. A. Samuelson has shown the fundamental importance of the law of supply and demand in stability analysis; see *Foundations of Economic Analysis*, pp. 263, 269–70.

If we assume stability of the market mechanism, the shortage observed during the equilibrating process is transitory and tends to disappear as the price approaches equilibrium. If, however, the demand curve is steadily shifting upward at the same time, the shortage will persist, and the price will continue to rise. We argue that the interaction of rising demand with price movements which do not instantaneously equate supply and demand provides a plausible interpretation of the recent history of the engineer-scientist market in the United States from about 1950 to date. We also suggest a more detailed account of the price-adjustment mechanism than the bare statement that price varies according to the inequality between supply and demand.

I. Shortages and Price Rises

In what follows, we use the terms supply and demand to mean the aggregation of *the choices made by all firms and individuals in equilibrium at a given price* on a given market. Thus for a firm, the quantity demanded or supplied at a given price is that which maximizes profits. The equilibrium of each firm does not, of course, imply the equilibrium of the market, since the aggregate of the decisions of all firms need not lead to equality of supply and demand. At any given moment, the decision made by a firm or individual need not be optimal from its point of view at the given price, since economic agents require time to make decisions and to learn. It is assumed that each agent gradually corrects its errors, but in the process the firm or individual will not, by definition, be on its demand or supply curve. We hold that the process by which an economic agent moves towards its own internal equilibrium is an integral part of the process by which the market as a whole comes into equilibrium.

In Marshall's formulation, two equilibria were distinguished, short-run and long-run. A movement along a long-run demand or supply curve manifests itself as a shift in the short-run curve. Market price at any moment may diverge from *both* equilibrium prices. In comparative static analysis all that is shown is that under certain assumptions about the nature of supply and demand functions, price will tend to move toward both short-run and long-run equilibrium price, given a shift in one or both of these functions. Over short periods of time, in which we are interested, the shift of the short-run demand or supply functions can be taken as exogenous trends, and will be so treated in this paper. Our analysis is, in Marshallian terms, short-run; but it differs from the neoclassical analysis in that we are presenting a model which explains not only the direction of price adjustment (i.e., toward equilibrium) but the rate of adjustment in the face of continued shifts in the short-run functions.

For purposes of comparison we draw the usual price-quantity diagram (see Figure I). If P_1 is the initial price, we expect the existence of a shortage to raise the price gradually to the equilibrium value P. During the process the shortage decreases to zero. The shortage can persist only if the price is held at some value such as

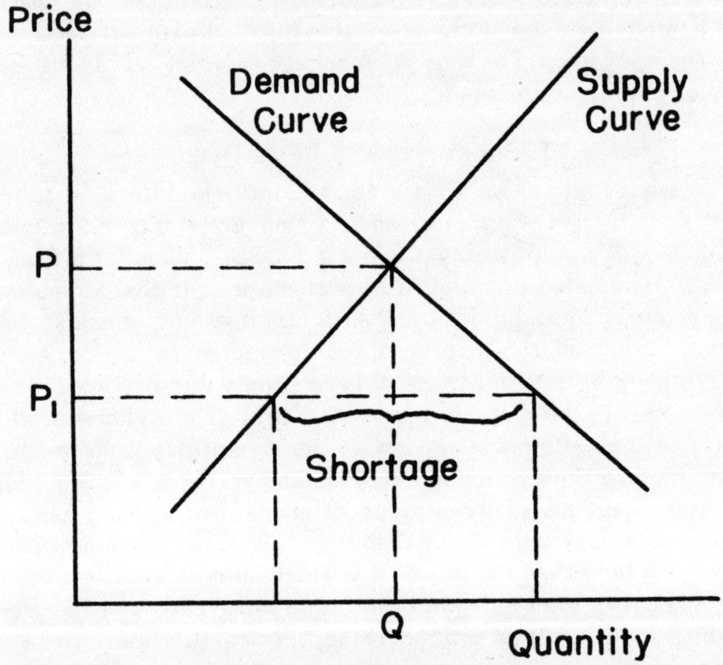

FIGURE I

P_1 by an outside force, such as price control. In that case we have a shortage due to a fundamental imperfection of the market.

Now suppose that we have a market which is initially in equilibrium. For concreteness, we may think of it as the market for engineers and scientists. Suppose further that the price of a commodity that uses engineers in its production has increased. Assume further that each firm producing this commodity was in equilibrium before the increase in the commodity price, that is, that it had as many engineers as it wished to hire at a given salary level. Under the new conditions, the number of engineers that it would pay the firm to hire at the previous salary has gone up, and therefore the market demand has risen. The change from the old situation to the new is illustrated in Figure II. Here D_1 represents the original demand curve for engineers. Curve D_2 represents the new demand arising from some change in external conditions, in this instance the rise in the price of the commodity in whose production the engineers are engaged. Recall that for present purposes we define demand as the amount which the firm would choose to buy after careful calculation.

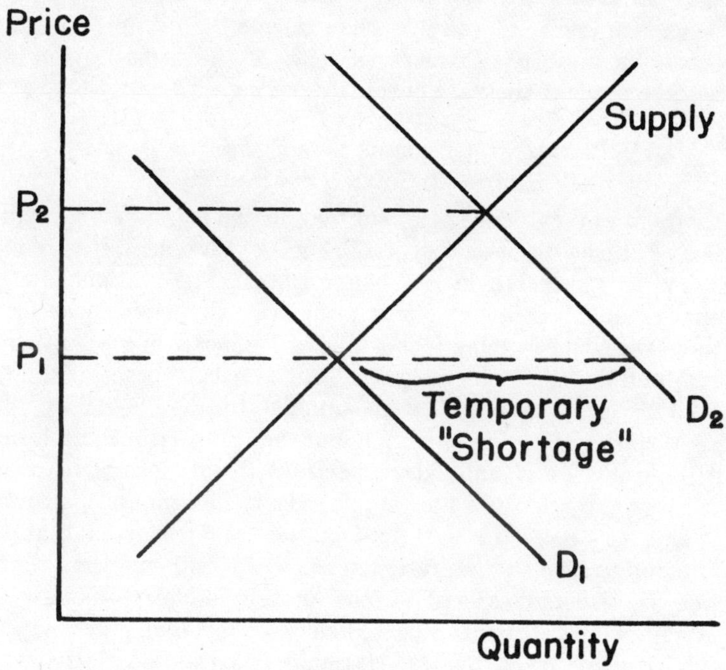

FIGURE II

At any given moment of time the firm may not be fully aware of what its demand (in our sense) is and seek to hire more or fewer engineers. But we do assume that the firm will gradually become aware of any such errors and correct them.

In Figure II, P_1 represents the equilibrium price when the demand curve is D_1. Let us assume that in fact P_1 was the price prevailing just before the shift in the demand curve. After the demand curve has shifted to D_2, the price that would bring supply and demand into equilibrium is P_2. But movement to this price or salary level typically will take time.

Consider the situation of a firm just after the shift of the demand curve to D_2. A comparison of Figures I and II shows a strong analogy, not to say identity. At the moment of the shift, the market is experiencing a shortage, which is in many respects comparable to what it would face under price control. Each firm seeks to hire additional engineers at the price it currently pays, but there are no more engineers available at this price. We do not assume that each firm recognizes fully its demand, that is, how many engineers it would be best to have under the new conditions. All that is required is that each firm realize it wants more engineers than it now has. Then there will be unfilled vacancies so long as the firms do not raise salaries above what they are currently paying.

II. Empirical Evidence of a Shortage in the Engineer-Scientist Market

Is there any evidence of a shortage in the sense just described? In view of all the discussion of the "shortage" problem, it is remarkable how little direct evidence is available. The National Science Foundation in 1953 asked officials in large companies whether or not they were experiencing a shortage of engineers and scientists for research and development purposes,[2] but no clear operational definition of the term "shortage" was supplied to these officials. It is plausible to suppose that a respondent would interpret the term to mean the existence of unfilled vacancies with salaries equal to those of engineers and scientists now employed by the firm and performing equivalent services. At least half of the firms reported that they were unable to hire enough research scientists and engineers to meet their needs, although, except for the aircraft industry, there was no industry in which all firms reported such a shortage.

The picture given by the National Science Foundation study is similar to that given by G. W. Beste in a study of the chemical industry.[3] Referring to the Ethyl Corporation, Beste states, "We employ 370 chemical engineers today but need an additional 39. This 39 represent the accumulated deficiency of the last five years."[4] The meaning of the term "deficiency" is not explained, but it is

2. See National Science Foundation, *Scientific Manpower Bulletin No. 6*, August 1, 1955.

3. G. W. Beste, "A Case Study of the Shortage of Scientists and Engineers in the Chemical Industry," presented at the second meeting of the National Committee for the Development of Scientists and Engineers, June 21, 1956.

4. Actually, this deficiency turns out to be largely the product of the two years, 1955 and 1956. It is typical of the lack of historical perspective in the engineer-scientist shortage discussion that such short-run phenomena are made the basis for discussion of long-run policies.

perhaps fair to assume that it means the inability to fill vacancies at salaries then being paid to employees. If Beste and the respondents to the National Science Foundation's survey have understood the term "shortage" in this way, there is then fragmentary evidence of a shortage as manifested by unfilled vacancies, but this shortage is not large. Such a situation is to be expected when the demand curve has shifted and the price does not immediately rise to the level that would equate supply and demand.

III. The Process of Adjustment in the Market

We will trace briefly the sequence of events that will be observed in the market as a result of the shift in the demand curve from D_1 to D_2. At the moment, any individual firm may not have fully calculated how many more engineers it could profitably hire, but we may suppose that it will be aware of wanting more engineers than it now employs. It will begin by seeking to hire more engineers at the going salary but will find that there are none to be had. Its advertised vacancies find no takers; its offers are refused. The firm becomes aware that in order to hire additional engineers it must pay higher salaries, and it will now have to calculate whether or not the additional product derivable from additional engineers will be sufficient to cover the higher level of salaries. In the situation envisaged, the firm will indeed eventually decide to hire some additional engineers at a higher salary, but the decision will take time. First, there must be recognition of the need for higher salaries, then approval must be obtained from various echelons of management, and finally orders must be issued to hire.

Thus the time lag in the firm's reaction is spent partly in learning about the supply conditions in the market and partly in determining the profitability of additional hiring under the new supply conditions. This, however, is only one step in the process of adjustment. First of all, the firm may not yet have fully adjusted to the new demand curve; it has hired some more engineers than before but possibly not as many as would achieve maximum profitability. But second, even if the firm has hired as many as would be profitable at the new salary level, the market as a whole would still not be in equilibrium, because the firm is now paying a lower salary to its old employees than to the new ones, and there is really more than one price being paid for the identical services rendered by different individuals. The multiplicity of prices is characteristic of disequilibrium situations, but in any well-developed market it cannot persist indefinitely. What happens is that other firms, also experiencing shortages, bid for the services of the engineers belonging to the firm we have been considering. While old employees will probably have some reluctance to move, this reluctance is certainly not absolute and can be overcome by a sufficiently high salary offer. That engineers do change jobs in sufficient numbers to suggest a responsiveness to market forces has been shown by Blank and Stigler.[5] However, we would again expect a lag in information.[6] An employed engineer may not be in touch with current salary offers, and it may take some time before he is aware that the salary he is receiving is below what he might receive elsewhere. We would, however, certainly expect that he will become informed eventually, and that the discrepancy between his actual and his possible salary will tend to be reduced over time. While some individuals will not be tempted to move even in the presence of considerable possible salary increases, many would be willing to do so; either they will in fact move or the hiring firm, to keep them, will raise their salaries to the competitive level. Thus the initial tendency within the firm for new employees to enjoy higher salaries than old ones will gradually be overcome as the salaries of the latter are raised in response to competition.

There is another mechanism which will work to eliminate salary differences within a firm but at the expense of slowing down the firm's willingness to raise salary offers for new personnel. Salary differences within the firm are certain to be a source of morale problems to the extent that they are known, and clearly complete secrecy is out of the question. There will be pressure on the firm to increase the salaries of all its employees (in the same category) to the new higher levels. The lag in adjustment of the salaries of already-employed engineer-scientists is thereby reduced, but on the other hand the firm is more reluctant to increase its salary offers to new employees because it realizes it must incur the increased cost not only for the new employees but also for the old ones. In effect the additional cost of the salary rise is recognized by the firm to be much greater if it has to extend the increase to all employees.

5. David M. Blank and George J. Stigler, *The Demand and Supply of Scientific Personnel* (New York: National Bureau of Economic Research, 1957), pp. 29–30.

6. We might note that in some markets such as the organized exchanges for securities or commodities information is available very quickly, indeed almost instantaneously, but this is clearly accomplished only because it has been found worthwhile for those who buy and sell on these markets to pay the costs of the operation of such exchanges. No such exchange exists for scientists and engineers, and one can understand why: the product is not homogeneous, and each unit of supply is controlled by a different owner (i.e., the individual scientist or engineer himself).

The total lag in the response of salaries to a shortage (in the sense of an excess of demand over supply) is then compounded out of the time it takes the firm to recognize the existence of a shortage at the current salary level, the time it takes to decide upon the need for higher salaries and the number of vacancies at such salaries, and either the time it takes employees to recognize the salary alternatives available and to act upon this information or the time it takes the firm to equalize salaries without outside offers.

IV. A Model of Dynamic Shortages and Price Rises

While there is, strictly speaking, no one market price during the process of adjusting supply to increased demand, a multiplicity of prices being characteristic, we may focus attention on the average price being paid for engineering services. The preceding discussion makes clear that the average price will tend to rise so long as there is an excess of demand over supply, but it will not rise instantaneously to the level that will bring supply and demand into equality (P_2 in Figure II). Further, the forces that induce price rises will clearly operate more strongly the greater the excess of demand over supply. Hence we find it reasonable to accept the usual view that the rate of increase of price per unit of time is greater the greater the excess of demand over supply. As a corollary, price will cease rising when the price is such that demand equals supply. Recall that demand and supply at any given price are defined as the quantities demanded and supplied after complete rational calculation.

Call the ratio of the rate of price rise to the excess of demand over supply the *reaction speed.* Then the amount of shortage will tend to disappear faster the greater the reaction speed and also the greater the elasticity of supply (or demand).[7]

7. Let p be the (average) price, k the reaction speed, D demand, S supply, and t time. The movement of the market over time is determined, in the above model, by the following relations (using linear approximations for the demand and supply functions):

(1) $dp/dt = k(D-S)$,
(2) $D = -ap + c$,
(3) $S = bp + d$.

Equation (1) expresses the assumption in the text about the relation between price rises and the difference between supply and demand; equations (2) and (3) are simple assumptions about the nature of the demand and supply functions, as represented graphically in Figures I and II.

Let X represent the shortage, i.e., $X = D - S$. From (2) and (3),

(4) $X = -(a + b)\,p + (c - d)$.

Differentiate (4) with respect to time; then $dX/dt = -(a + b)\,(dp/dt)$. If we then substitute from (1) and replace $D - S$ by X, we have,

(5) $dX/dt = -k(a + b)\,X$.

We have thus far been sketching a way of looking at the response of the market to a single shift of the demand curve; we have suggested that the price will tend to move to the new equilibrium but with a lag. This analysis has been preliminary to our main purpose, which is to consider a situation of *continuing* change in demand (or supply). We will suggest that this has been the case for engineer-scientists in the period beginning about 1950. If, for example, the demand curve is rising steadily, then as the market price approaches the equilibrium price the latter steadily moves away from the former. There will be a chronic shortage in the sense that as long as the rise in demand occurs buyers at any given moment will desire more of the commodity at the average price being paid than is being offered, and the amount of the shortage will not approach zero. The price will increase steadily and indefinitely but always remain below the price that would clear the market. This condition will continue as long as demand is increasing.[8]

Thus for any given shortage X, the speed of convergence is greater the greater $k(a + b)$. In particular, other things being equal, the smaller the value of b (which is closely related to the elasticity of supply), the slower will be the convergence of the shortage X to zero.

8. The steady upward shift in demand may be represented by adding a trend term to the demand as given by (2) in footnote 7,

(6) $D = -ap + c + et,$

where t represents time and e the rate of increase of demand with time for any given price. Let X be the amount of shortage, i.e., $D - S$. From (3) and (6),

(7) $X = -(a + b)p + (c - d) + et.$

Differentiate all the terms of (7) with respect to time.

(8) $dX/dt = -(a + b)(dp/dt) + e.$

In view of the definition of X, (1) can be written,

(9) $dp/dt = kX.$

Substitute from (9) for dp/dt into (8).

(10) $dX/dt = -(a + b)kX + e.$

Assume that at the beginning, there is no shortage, so that $S = D$, or $X = 0$. Then from (10) we see that $dX/dt > 0$, so that the shortage X starts increasing and must continue to increase (since if dX/dt ever reached zero, it would remain at zero thereafter). It is also easy to see that,

(11) $\lim_{t \to \infty} X(t) = e/(a + b)k,$

so that the shortages tend to a limit which is greater the greater the rate of increase of demand and the slower the speed of adjustment would have been with an unshifting demand schedule.

Let p' be the rate of increase of prices, i.e., dp/dt. Differentiate (9) with respect to time, and then substitute from (8).

(12) $dp'/dt = k\,dX/dt = -k(a + b)p' + ke.$

By the same reasoning as with (10), p' must be increasing over time and approaching a limit. Since it is zero to begin with, it follows that p' must be positive for all t, so that, by the definition of p', the price p must be increasing steadily.

Let p^* be the price at any time which would clear the market, that is, which would make $X = 0$. In view of (7), p^* satisfies the equation,

In the market for engineer-scientists or for any other commodity we expect that a steady upward shift in the demand curve over a period of time will produce a shortage, that is, a situation in which there are unfilled vacancies in positions where salaries are the same as those being currently paid in others of the same type and quality. Such a shortage we will term a *dynamic shortage*. The magnitude of the dynamic shortage depends upon the rate of increase in demand, the reaction speed in the market, and the elasticity of supply and demand. The reaction speed in any particular market depends partly on institutional arrangements, such as the prevalence of long-term contracts, and partly on the rapidity with which information about salaries, vacancies, and availability of personnel becomes generally available throughout the market. In the case of an organized exchange, such as those for securities or certain agricultural products, we should expect the information to be passed on so rapidly that the reaction speed is virtually infinite and dynamic shortages virtually nonexistent.[9] In the following section we will advance evidence for the hypothesis that the engineer-scientist market for the last seven or eight years has shown a dynamic shortage in the sense just defined.

(13) $0 = -(a + b)\, p^* + (c - d) + et.$

Multiply through in (13) by k.

(14) $0 = -k\,(a + b)\, p^* + k\,(c - d) + ket.$

Let q be the excess of the market-clearing price over the actual price, i.e., $q = p^* - p$. Substitute from (7) into (9).

(15) $p' = -k\,(a + b)\, p + k\,(c - d) + ket.$

Subtract (14) from (15) and use the definition of q.

(16) $p' = k\,(a + b)\, q.$

Since p' is positive and increases from zero to a limit, the same must be true of q. Thus the actual price will always remain below the market-clearing price and indeed the gap will actually widen with time, but the two time paths will approach parallelism.

The discussion to this point has dealt with a single market. In the real world there are a number of related markets. Firms in different industries, in different localities, etc., may in any given case compete for the services of engineer-scientists of certain specified skills. Therefore the firms in any one industry will find that the supply available to them depends not only on their own salary offers but on the salary levels in all industries buying similar skills. In short, the demand for engineer-scientists comes from a whole series of interrelated markets. This situation cannot be represented graphically, but the general conclusions just drawn remain valid. See K. J. Arrow, "Price-Quantity Adjustments in Multiple Markets with Rising Demands," The RAND Corporation, P-1364-RC, 7 May 1958, Santa Monica, California; to be published in *Proceedings of the First Stanford Symposium on Mathematical Methods in the Social Sciences* (Stanford, Calif.: Stanford University Press).

9. Thus, in Marshall's example of the corn market (*op. cit.*) the adjustment process took a day. In the market for scientists and engineers the "day" will be much longer — say several weeks or even months.

V. Dynamic Shortage in the Engineer-Scientist Market

The preceding analysis has been very abstract. Though we have referred to the market for engineer-scientists for the sake of concreteness, actually everything said would be equally applicable to any other market. We want to argue here that because of the character of the engineer-scientist market and the demands made on it over the last few years, the magnitude of the dynamic shortage may well have been sufficient to account for a great proportion of the complaints. It should be made clear that we are not arguing that the market is subject to unusual imperfections. Rather the very way in which the market performs its functions leads to the shortage in this particular period.

A dynamic shortage is a possible explanation of the observed tensions in the engineer-scientist market because (1) there has been a rapid and steady rise in demand, (2) the elasticity of supply is low, especially for short periods, and (3) the reaction speed on the engineer-scientist market may, for several reasons, be expected to be slow. The hypothesis stated in the previous section would imply that under such conditions a dynamic shortage could be expected. And we believe that such a shortage would largely explain such reactions as intensified recruiting and attempts at long-range policy changes observable in the industries affected.

(1) The market on which the tensions seem to be focused is not the engineer-scientist market in general but the market for engineers and scientists for research and development purposes. It is a matter of common knowledge that there has been a very rapid increase in demand in this market. During the year 1951 the total number of research engineers and scientists in industry rose from 74,028 to 91,585, an increase of 17,557 or 23.7 per cent.[1] Such an increase is clearly capable of putting a strain on the smooth functioning of almost any market.

The increase in demand is, in turn, to be explained chiefly by the action of the government in contracting for research and development work by private industry. The increase in the number of research engineers and scientists employed on government contracts during the year 1951 was 15,547,[2] so that virtually the whole increase

1. See U. S. Department of Labor, Bureau of Labor Statistics, *Scientific Research and Development in American Industry: A Study of Manpower and Costs*, Bulletin No. 1148, 1953, Tables C-5 (p. 62) and C-11 (p. 68). This source gives the January 1952 employment and the percentage increase; the other figures were calculated from these two.

2. *Ibid.*, Table C-13 (p. 70), shows that the number employed on government contracts in January 1952 was 45,425 and that this figure was an increase

in employment of research engineers and scientists was due to government demand. The importance of the increase in government demand as the chief explanation of shortages has also been stressed by some observers, such as C. B. Jolliffe, of the Radio Corporation of America.[3] Jolliffe also states that the type of research and development done on military contract is more complicated than the usual industrial work. This would imply that there is some differentiation between the markets for engineer-scientists in military and in other research and development, so that the full force of the increased demand would fall on the former.

(2) The elasticity of the supply of engineer-scientists with respect to price changes may be expected to be small but not zero over short periods of time, owing to the length of time it takes to train new personnel. Over longer periods, higher salaries will certainly elicit a greater supply, though again because of the importance of non-economic factors in choosing a career and because of the uncertainty of rewards in the distant future, the responsiveness of supply will be less than for commodities such as manufactured goods. Hence while it would be totally incorrect to deny the influence of price on supply, the responsiveness is sufficiently low to add to the possibility of a dynamic shortage.

(3) There are three reasons why it might be expected that the speed of reaction in the engineer-scientist market would be slower than that in the markets for other commodities, such as manufactured goods, or even than in other labor markets. They are the prevalence of long-term contracts, the influence of the heterogeneity of the market in slowing the diffusion of information, and the dominance of a relatively small number of firms in research and development.

Typically, for the engineer-scientist already employed by the government, a university, or a private industrial firm, there will be no instantaneous adjustment in the price he receives even in the face of demand changes, since contracts are not subject to daily renegotiation. Even in the absence of specific contractual elements of this sort, reaction is slowed down because of the greater job security which comes with long service with a particular employer.

of 52 per cent over that of January 1951. The figure in the text is calculated from these two.

3. C. B. Jolliffe, "Electronics: A Case Study of the Shortage of Scientists and Engineers," delivered to the President's Committee for the Development of Scientists and Engineers, 21 June 1956. In discussing his own company, Jolliffe says, "We could use one thousand more right now without any question. Where could we use them? Mainly on military contracts because it is here — rather than in consumer and industrial electronics — that the pinch is tightest." (p. 6)

Professorial tenure is an extreme and institutionalized form of this phenomenon.

We have remarked earlier that the market for engineer-scientists is not a single one. The heterogeneity of the market may interfere with the diffusion of information because an individual engineer-scientist may not know to which market he belongs. He may be aware that an associate is getting a higher salary, which may suggest that he ought to look around for another position. But he may very well wonder whether the associate's higher salary is perhaps due to superior ability or to the fact that somewhat different skills are being rewarded more highly at the moment. Because of his doubts he may be delayed in ascertaining his alternative opportunities. Thus the length of time before he actually does achieve a higher salary, either from another firm or from his own, will be longer, and the reaction speed will be correspondingly less.

Finally, one special characteristic of the market for engineers and scientists in research and development is that the typical buyer is large; in particular a single buyer, the government, directly and indirectly accounts for about half of total demand.[4] Up to a certain point a large firm with large competitors has an incentive to keep salaries down rather than bid engineer-scientists away from competitors. Any one firm in an industry dominated by a few large ones will fear that increasing salaries in order to attract more scientists and engineers may set off competitive bidding that will end up with no substantial change in the distribution of scientists and engineers among firms but a considerably higher salary bill. This is especially likely to be the attitude of firms if the total supply of the engineer-scientists for which they are competing is not likely to change much in response to higher prices.

The desire to avoid competitive bidding sometimes takes the form of "no-raiding" agreements, drawn up among otherwise competing firms in the same industry. Such a situation is alleged to exist to some extent in the electrical equipment and electronics industries, dominated by General Electric, Westinghouse, and the Radio Corporation of America, and in aircraft, where a handful of firms account for the bulk of the research and development and of output.

But in no case do the large firms dominate the research and development market to such an extent that "no-raiding" agreements

4. Bureau of Labor Statistics Bulletin No. 1148, *op. cit.*, presents some relevant figures for 1951. In that year, seven companies spent 26 per cent of the total expenditures on research and development in industry (p. 21), and the government financed 46.8 per cent of all such expenditures (Table 4) in addition to research performed directly by the government.

or other devices to limit competition in hiring can be effective indefinitely. If nothing else happens, the competition of smaller firms forces the large firms to match their offers. There is no evidence that attempts by large firms to avoid competitive bidding can in the long run prevent the market price from reaching its equilibrium level. But they certainly can slow down the speed with which prices will rise in response to an excess of demand over supply and so, in accordance with the analysis of the preceding section, increase and prolong the dynamic shortage.

VI. Alternate Definitions of a Shortage

It is not our purpose here to present an exhaustive review of alternate concepts of shortage. However, it is appropriate to call attention to the discussion of the alleged shortage of scientists and engineers presented in the recently published, important study of the engineer-scientist market by Blank and Stigler.[5]

After considering several definitions of the term "shortage," the authors settle on the following: "A shortage exists when the number of workers available (the supply) increases less rapidly than the number demanded *at the salaries paid in the recent past.* Then salaries will rise, and activities which were once performed by (say) engineers must now be performed by a class of workers less well trained and less expensive."[6] Blank and Stigler rely primarily on a comparison of the earnings of engineers with the earnings of other professional groups and wage earners in order to test the hypothesis of a shortage of engineers. By definition a shortage exists if the relative earnings of engineers have risen.

The authors look at such data as are available going back to 1929, in more detail at the period since 1939, and in still greater detail at the post-World War II period. They say:

> We may summarize these pieces of information on engineering earnings as follows. Since 1929, engineering salaries have declined substantially relative to earnings of all wage earners and relative to incomes of independent professional practitioners. Especially since 1939 engineering salaries have declined relative to the wage or salary income of the entire group of professional, technical and kindred workers, as well as to the working population as a whole. After the outbreak of the Korean War there was a minor increase in the relative salaries of engineers (and of other college trained workers), but this was hardly more than a minor cross-current in a tide. Relative to both the working population as a whole and the professions as a separate class, then, the record of earnings would suggest that up to at least 1955 there had been no shortage — in fact an increasingly ample supply — of engineers.[7]

5. Blank and Stigler, *op. cit.*, p. 9; Chap. II, p. 2.
6. *Ibid.*, p. 24. Italics by Blank and Stigler.
7. *Ibid.*, pp. 28–29.

The Blank-Stigler conclusion that there has been no significant shortage must be viewed not only in the light of their definition but also in the context of their major concern with long-run trends, not short-run phenomena. It might be pointed out, however, that it is only in the post-Korean era that there have been any complaints of shortages in this market. Therefore even if one is primarily concerned with the broad sweep of events, it seems proper to suggest that the period of real interest as far as possible shortage goes is that of the last few years, and with this interest in mind one may legitimately view "the minor cross-current" as being significant. The reason that Blank and Stigler adduce for dismissing the evidence of a shortage (by their own definition as tested by their own data) in the years since 1950 is that the relative change in salaries of engineers has been so slight that the shortage could not have been serious. But concluding that the market is a free, competitively working market, they do not consider the suggestion put forward here, namely, that even though there may be no obvious imperfections in the market, there may be a considerable lag in the adjustment of salaries in response to changes in demand.

It is worth noting just what the Blank-Stigler data do show. By their definition a shortage exists whenever the price of a given commodity rises. From 1950 to 1956 they show a rise in average starting salaries for college graduates with an engineering degree of 51.5 per cent.[8] Since increases in starting salaries for college graduates in other fields have been roughly comparable (though none are quite so high for this same period), this merely indicates, by their definition, that there has been a shortage of college graduates in general, i.e., a rise in their relative wages. (The same table shows that, for the period 1950–55, starting engineers' salaries increased by 38.0 per cent compared with an increase for manufacturing wage earnings of 31.8 per cent.)

Blank and Stigler acknowledge that there has been considerable talk about a shortage of engineers and scientists, but having concluded that there has not in fact been a "shortage" of the price-rise type of any significance, they make no attempt to explain all the talk except to point to the use of the word "shortage" as embodying some social criterion. It may be their hypothesis that the recent complaints of "shortage" have been based solely on this use of the term.

As we have recognized elsewhere,[9] there are other possible

8. *Ibid.*, Table 14, p. 28.
9. Alchian, Arrow, Capron, *op. cit.*

explanations for at least some of the public concern over the "shortage" of scientists and engineers in recent years. It should be emphasized that many of those who have discussed this problem have been using the term "shortage" in a very different sense from that we have employed here. In particular, careful reading of such statements indicates that the speakers have in effect been saying: There are not as many engineers and scientists as this nation should have in order to do all the things that need doing such as maintaining our rapid rate of technological progress, raising our standard of living, keeping us militarily strong, etc. In other words, they are saying that (in the economic sense) demand for technically skilled manpower *ought* to be greater than it is — it is really a shortage of *demand* for scientists and engineers which concerns them. A somewhat different implicit definition of shortage which has been applied asserts that since we are not producing scientists and engineers at as fast a rate as the Soviet Union we have a "shortage." Still another explanation of the complaints may be found if one recalls the servant shortage of World War II days. In that situation, there is no evidence that the market did not respond to changed supply and demand conditions; alternative opportunities for employment developed for those who had previously been servants; the higher wages in these alternate lines of employment lured many to these occupations so that, *at the price they had been paying for household help*, many families found they could no longer find such people. Rather than admit that they could not pay the higher wages necessary to keep help, many individuals found it more felicitous to speak of a "shortage." There is reason to think that at least some of the complaints of shortage in the scientist-engineer market have the same cause. Indeed, in any market when there is a relatively sudden and dramatic change in either demand or supply which results in large price increases, we may find complaints of a "shortage" while people get used to the fact that the price has risen significantly.

VII. Conclusion

It is our view that the model of dynamic shortage developed in this paper is useful in helping to understand the behavior of the market for scientists and engineers in the past several years. The very rapid increase in demand in the market during this period has led to "shortage" conditions resulting basically from a failure of the price of such services to adjust upward as rapidly and by as large an amount as warranted by the increasing demand, given the supply schedule of such services. This lag in adjustment, so far as we can see, can be attributed to a significant extent, not to any successful overt attempt to control prices artificially, but to certain inherent characteristics of supply and demand conditions and of the operation of the market. While the relative rigidity of supply in the short run is unpleasant (from the buyers' standpoint), and the price rise required to restore the market to equilibrium may seem to be very great, it is only by permitting the market to react to the rising demand that, in our view, it can allocate engineer-scientists in the short run and call forth the desired increase in supply in the longer run.

Stanford University

[12]

SOCIAL AND PRIVATE RATES OF RETURN FROM INDUSTRIAL INNOVATIONS*

EDWIN MANSFIELD
JOHN RAPOPORT
ANTHONY ROMEO
SAMUEL WAGNER
GEORGE BEARDSLEY

I. INTRODUCTION

For many years, economic analysts and policy-makers have been interested in developing and obtaining better and more complete data concerning social and private rates of return from industrial innovations. It has long been recognized that information of this sort is essential if public policy concerning civilian technology is to be formulated rationally. Yet despite the work of Denison, Fellner, Griliches, Mansfield, Minasian, Peterson, Terleckyj, and others, existing knowledge in this area is far too weak to provide a reasonably adequate foundation for analysis and policy.[1] The purpose of this paper is to report the results of seventeen case studies, each of which estimates the social and private rate of return from the investment in a particular industrial innovation. The results of this paper, although subject to obvious limitations and shortcomings, should provide us with a somewhat better understanding of this topic. The studies described

* The work on which this paper is based was supported by a grant to Mansfield from the Office of National R and D Assessment of the National Science Foundation. The bulk of the basic data on which this study is based was collected by Beardsley, Rapoport, Romeo, and Wagner. A preliminary version of this paper was presented by Mansfield at the meetings of the Eastern Economic Association on October 26, 1974; at the National Bureau of Standards; in a paper at the 1975 meetings of the American Economic Association; and in a paper at the First U.S.–U.S.S.R. Symposium; at M.I.T.; at the RAND Corporation; and at the National Science Foundation. Also, he presented some of this material in his Schmookler Memorial Lecture at the University of Minnesota in 1975 on the Economics of Information (which took place in Leningrad in 1975).

1. For a summary of existing knowledge in this area, see E. Mansfield, "Contribution of R and D to Economic Growth in the United States," *Science*, CLXXV (Feb. 4, 1972), 477–86.

here seem to be the first attempts to make direct measurements of this sort in the industrial sector.

II. The Sample of Innovations

Our first step in carrying out this investigation was to contact a number of business firms in the Northeast and to try to persuade them to provide us with data bearing on the social and private returns from innovations that they had carried out. As would be expected, a substantial percentage of those who were contacted refused to cooperate because, despite our assurance that the data would be held in strictest confidence, they felt that such data were too sensitive to show outsiders. Those firms that were willing to cooperate were asked to pick one or more of their recent innovations more or less at random. Then many manweeks were spent gathering data concerning each innovation and its effects from the innovating firm, from firms using the innovation (if it was used by firms), and from other sources. These innovations occurred in a wide variety of industries (described below), and in firms of quite different sizes. Most of them are of average or routine importance, not major breakthroughs. Although the sample cannot be regarded as randomly selected, there is no obvious indication that it is biased toward very profitable innovations (socially or privately) or relatively unprofitable ones. The sample is described in Table I.

III. Estimation of Social Benefits: Product Innovations Used by Firms

As is evident from Table I, the innovations in our sample can be divided into three classes: product innovations used by firms, product innovations used by households, and process innovations. Based on an intensive study of each of the innovations in each of these classes, it appears that the same general kind of model is applicable to all of the innovations in our sample in a particular class. In this and the following sections we describe the model that is used to measure the social benefits in a particular period from product innovations used by firms.

In each case these new products resulted in a potential saving to users. For example, the product innovation in the primary metals industry resulted in a potential saving to makers of household appliances. Thus, each of these innovations could shift downward the supply curve of the industry using the innovation. How far downward

TABLE I

CHARACTERISTICS OF SAMPLE OF SEVENTEEN INNOVATIONS

Industry producing the innovation	Type of innovation	Nature of innovation	Type of user	Approximate date of innovation
1. Primary metals	New product	New type of metal that reduced cost of appliances	Firms	Late 1950's
2. Machine tools	New product	New computer controls	Firms	Early 1970's
3. Control systems	New product	New type of component	Firms	Late 1960's
4. Construction	New product	New material that cut cost of building	Firms	Mid 1950's
5. Drilling	New product	Reduced cost of drilling wells	Firms	Mid 1960's
6. Industrial equipment	New process	New type of drafting	Firms	Early 1960's
7. Paper	New product	New paper product that cut costs of users	Firms	Mid 1960's
8. Thread	New product	New type of thread that cut costs of garment makers	Firms	Early 1960's
9. Industrial controls	New product	New mechanism for doors	Firms	Early 1970's
10. Electronics	New product	New device that reduced costs of certain video tape operations	Firms	Early 1970's
11. Chemicals[a]	New product	New product that reduced costs of users	Firms	Late 1960's
12. Chemicals[a]	New process	Reduced costs of production	Firms	Mid 1960's
13. Chemicals[a]	New process	Reduced cost of certain aromatic chemicals	Firms	Late 1960's
14. Chemicals[a]	New process	Major process improvement	Firms	Early 1960's
15. Household cleaners	New product	New product that reduced cost of cleaning floors	Households	Early 1960's
16. Stain removers	New product	New stain remover	Households	Mid 1960's
17. Dishwashing liquids	New product	New product that cut costs of operating dishwashers	Households	Early 1960's

a. Chemicals are defined to include petroleum refining.

this supply curve will shift depends, of course, on the pricing policy of the innovator. If the innovator charges a relatively high price for the new product, the supply curve may shift only slightly. Indeed, if the innovator charges a high enough price, the supply curve will not shift downward at all.

Suppose that the innovator decides to set a price for its new product that yields a profit[2] to the innovator equivalent to r dollars per unit of output of the industry using the innovation (for example, r dollars per appliance in the case of the new type of metal). Also, suppose that the industry using the innovation is competitive and that its supply curve is horizontal in the relevant range. In particular, assume that, before the advent of the innovation, this supply curve was S_1 in Figure I, and the price charged by the industry using the innovation was P_1. After the advent of the innovation, this supply curve is S_2, and the price is P_2.

Under these circumstances, the social benefits from the innovation can be measured by the sum of the two shaded areas in Figure I. The top shaded area is the consumers' surplus due to the lower price (P_2 rather than P_1) resulting from the use of the innovation.[3] In addition, there is a resource saving, and a corresponding increase in output elsewhere in the economy, due to the fact that the resource

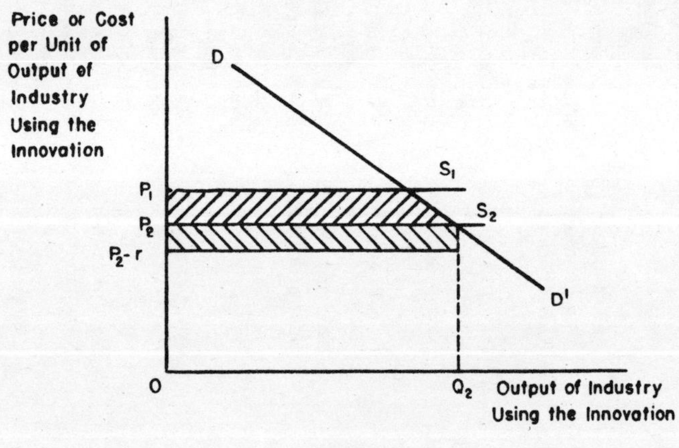

FIGURE I
Social Benefit from Product Innovation That Reduces the Costs of the Industry Using It

2. Profit here is defined to be gross of any depreciation on the investment in the innovation. Basically, it is a cash flow concept.

3. Of course, one problem in any model of this sort is that the concept of consumers' surplus is a controversial one. But as so many writers have pointed out, it is hard to do applied work in this area without adopting some such concept. See, for example, J. Currie, J. Murphy, and A. Schmitz, "The Concept of Economic Surplus and Its Use in Economic Analysis," *Economic Journal*, LXXXI (Dec. 1971), 741–99.

costs of producing the good using the innovation—including the resource costs of producing the innovation—are less than P_2Q_2. Instead, they are P_2Q_2 minus the profits of the innovator from the innovation, the latter being merely a transfer from the producers of the good using the innovation to the innovator. Thus, besides the consumers' surplus arising from the price reduction, there is a resource saving amounting to the profits of the innovator.[4]

However, two adjustments must frequently be made in this estimate corresponding to the lower shaded area in Figure I. First, if the innovation replaces another product, the resource saving cited in the previous paragraph does not equal the profits of the innovator (from the innovation), but these profits less those that would have been made (by the innovator or other firms) if the innovation had not occurred and the displaced product had been used instead. This is the correct measure of the resource saving. Second, if other firms imitate the innovator and begin selling the innovation to the industry that uses it, their profits from the sale of the innovation must be added to those of the innovator to get a full measure of the extent of the resource saving due to the innovation.

Based on this model, an estimate was made of the social benefit in each period from the investment in each of these innovations. For each innovation, the top shaded area in Figure I equals

$$(P_1 - P_2)Q_2\,(1 - 1/2\,Kn), \tag{1}$$

where $K = (P_1 - P_2)/P_2$, and n is the price elasticity of demand (in absolute value) of the product of the industry using the innovation. To estimate $P_1 - P_2$, we obtained as much information as we could concerning the size of the unit cost reduction due to the innovation in the industry using the innovation. Based on interviews with executives of the innovating firm, executives of a sample of firms using the innovation, and reports and studies made by these firms for internal purposes, it was possible to obtain reasonably reliable estimates of $(P_1 - P_2)$.[5] And once we had an estimate of $(P_1 - P_2)$, it was simple

4. To put matters somewhat differently, the sum of the two shaded areas in Figure I can easily be shown to equal the social value of the extra output of the product (as measured by the area under the demand curve) plus the value of the resources saved.

5. We assume that the cost reduction experienced by the industry using the innovation is passed on to consumers. In view of the market structures of the industries in question, this seems to be a reasonable assumption. Also, the available evidence seems to support this assumption. But it is important to note that, if the cost reduction were kept by the industry using the innovation, the social benefit would equal this industry's cost saving due to the innovation plus the innovator's (adjusted) profits. Since the industry's cost saving must be greater than our measure of the upper shaded area in Figure I, our measure of social benefit would be conservative.

to compute K. Also Q_2 was generally available from published records. Rough estimates of n were obtained from published studies and from the firms. Since K is generally very small, the results are not sensitive to errors in n. Indeed, the expression in equation (1) can be approximated quite well in most cases by $(P_1 - P_2)Q_2$, which is the total savings to consumers due to the lower price, if they buy Q_2 units of the product of the industry using the innovation.

To estimate the additional resource saving from the innovation, which equals the bottom shaded area in Figure I (if the adjustments described in the paragraph before the last are unnecessary), the innovator's profit from the new product was obtained from detailed discussions with the firm's executives, as well as study of relevant financial records. For each year, the costs of marketing and producing the innovation, as well as the costs of carrying out the innovation (R and D, plant and equipment, manufacturing start-up, and marketing start-up),[6] were deducted from the innovator's revenues from the innovation. Note that the R and D costs were adjusted to allow for the fact that the innovator invested R and D resources in uncommercialized R and D projects. To make this adjustment, we obtained estimates from each of the innovating firms of the average number of dollars spent on uncommercialized R and D projects per dollar spent on a commercialized R and D project during the relevant period. Then we multiplied the innovator's R and D outlays (in each year) on the innovation by this number in order to get an estimate of the total R and D investment, including a prorated allowance for uncommercialized projects. In cases where the adjustments described in the paragraph before the last were necessary, estimates of the foregone profits from displaced products were deducted, and the profits of imitators were added, to the innovator's profits. These estimates were obtained from the relevant firms.

IV. Parallel Innovative Efforts, Time Horizon, and Rates of Return

In calculating the social rate of return, we must recognize that, besides the innovator, other firms or research organizations in the United States[7] may have invested resources (prior to the introduction

6. For discussions of the cost categories involved, see E. Mansfield and J. Rapoport, "The Costs of Industrial Product Innovations," *Management Science*, XXI (Aug. 1975), 1380–86; and E. Mansfield, J. Rapoport, J. Schnee, S. Wagner, and M. Hamburger, *Research and Innovation in the Modern Corporation* (New York: Norton, 1971).

7. We are concerned here only with the costs and benefits arising within the United States. Thus, we ignore the fact that some of these innovations resulted in significant

of the innovation in question) in R and D and related innovative activities aimed at innovations of essentially the same kind as this one. Clearly, it is not easy to obtain data on the extent of such investments, but fortunately the difficulties seem to be less than they might appear, for two reasons. First, only a limited number of organizations could reasonably have been expected to be doing R and D in the relevant area, and if they had been devoting any substantial amount of resources to such work in the relevant time frame, it is inconceivable that the current executives of these organizations (and all their competitors) would have been unaware of it. Second, since these innovations occurred some time ago, firms generally are quite willing to discuss whether they were carrying out work of the relevant kind at that time. Moreover, and this is particularly fortunate, our results are quite insensitive to errors in the estimated investment in R and D carried out by others. Even if the true social research expenditures were ten times our estimate, and the true social development expenditures were double our estimate, the results change remarkably little.

Based on interviews with executives of the innovating firm, as well as with other firms that could reasonably be expected to do (and be aware of) R and D of the relevant kind, it appears that, in most of the cases in our sample, no other firm or research organization was doing work aimed at roughly the same kind of innovation. Thus, in these cases, the private investment seems to be a good approximation to the social investment. In the remaining cases, other firms or individuals were engaged in R and D aimed at the same kind of innovation. In the cases where this R and D was *unsuccessful,* we obtained as accurate an estimate as possible of the cost of this unsuccessful R and D, and added this figure to the R and D costs described in the previous section to get an estimate of the total social cost of the relevant R and D carried out by the innovator and others.[8]

---

social benefits in other countries, and we do not attempt to include whatever costs may have been incurred in other countries in an attempt to produce innovations of roughly the same kind. Also, each rate of return estimated here is on the investment in the innovation in question, given that previous investments in basic science, education, and so forth had already occurred. Clearly, the rates of return on the investments considered here were dependent on these previous investments.

8. Of course, some of the unsuccessful R and D directed at one innovation may be part of the uncommercialized R and D carried out by the innovator in the case of another innovation. Really, the social cost of an innovation should include a prorated share of the cost of uncommercialized R and D carried out by the innovator, excluding the cost of its uncommercialized R and D aimed at innovations where other firms beat it to the punch. But there is no way to estimate the latter cost, and our procedure clearly biases the social rates of return downward.

In the one case (among product innovations used by firms) where other firms or individuals were engaged (prior to the introduction of the innovation in question[9]) in R and D aimed at roughly the same kind of innovation, and where this R and D was *successful*, we must recognize that the innovator's investment resulted only in the innovation's availability at an earlier point in time, not in all of the social benefits from the innovation date up to the relevant time horizon. In other words, the proper comparison is between what would have occurred if the innovator had not carried out the innovation (but other firms were free to do so) and what in fact occurred. In this case, we obtained as accurate an appraisal as we could of the date when the innovation would have appeared if the innovator had not carried out the innovation, and we calculated the social benefits only during the period between the date when the innovation occurred and the date when it would have appeared if the innovator had done nothing.[10] Of course, it frequently is very difficult to estimate when the innovation would have occurred if the innovator had not carried it out. But in this particular case a realistic (if perhaps somewhat conservative) estimate is that the second firm to produce the innovation would have come up with it when in fact it did so, regardless of whether the innovator preceded it or not.

For most innovations these calculations were carried out for each year from the beginning of work on the innovation until 1973. Thus, our estimates of the social benefits are conservative, since all benefits after 1973 are ignored. But in some cases, this would introduce a serious distortion, since the innovation is relatively new. In these cases, forecasts were made of the consumers' surplus and the innovator's profits (adjusted for imitators' profits and for profits on older products) in each year up to 1980. These forecasts are based on firms' expectations concerning $(P_1 - P_2)$, Q_2, and the relevant profits in the next few years. They are intentionally very conservative, so whatever bias there is in the resulting rates of return should be downward.

Finally, having made the calculations described in this and the previous section for each year, we have an estimate of the net social benefits from the innovation for each year. Then we can compute the

9. Work of this sort that occurs after the innovation takes place is of a different kind. It is directed at *imitating* or *improving on* the innovation, and is not properly regarded as part of the work *producing* the innovation.

10. Note that this procedure assumes that, once the innovator is joined by another firm producing the innovation, they adopt a pricing policy that is just the same as the other firm would have adopted if it were the sole producer of the innovation. Needless to say, this may not be true, since there may be advantages stemming from competition between the two firms. However, we adopt this assumption because it results in a conservative estimate of the social rate of return and because any other assumption would have to be based largely on speculation.

internal social rate of return, the interest rate that makes the present value of the net social benefits equal to zero. In other words, it is the interest rate i that results in the following equality:

$$B(t) + \frac{B(t+1)}{1+i} + \frac{B(t+2)}{(1+i)^2} + \cdots + \frac{B(t+n)}{(1+i)^n} = 0, \quad (2)$$

where $B(t)$ is the net social benefit year in t, t is the first year in which the net social benefit is nonzero, and $(t + n)$ is the last year in which the net social benefit is nonzero.

Finally, we also compute the private rate of return from the innovator's investment in each innovation. To do so, we calculate the cash flow to the innovator from the innovation during each year. This calculation involves the subtraction of all costs incurred by the innovator to carry out, produce, and sell the innovation (including the allowance described in the previous section for R and D on uncommercialized projects) from the innovator's revenues from the innovation. Also, profits that the innovator would have earned on products displaced by the innovation must be subtracted as well.[11] The time period over which these computations were made was generally up to 1973, but in some cases (as in the case of the social rate of return) it extended to 1980. Again, the forecasts in the latter cases are decidedly conservative. The net private benefits in each year, like the B's in equation (2), were deflated. The Consumer Price Index, which generally was used, is not ideal, but it seems very unlikely that the results will be affected in an important way by this choice of a deflator.

V. Product Innovations Used by Households

In this section we turn to the model used to calculate the social benefits for product innovations used by households. Since all of the innovations of this type in our sample are meant to reduce the cost of some particular household activity, basically the same model will apply. Suppose that the demand curve for this activity is DD' in Figure II and that the innovation reduced the price of performing this activity from P_1 to P_2. Suppose too that the innovator makes a profit

11. In all but one case, it is assumed that the profits from the displaced product would have continued (up to the time horizon indicated below) at their previous level if the innovation had not occurred. This seems reasonable, based on the facts. But in the one remaining case, there is reason to believe that, if the innovation had not occurred, another innovation superior to this one would have occurred at a particular point in time afterward. Thus, we assume that the innovator would have earned nothing on the displaced product after this point in time. Of course, it also earned nothing on the innovation after this point.

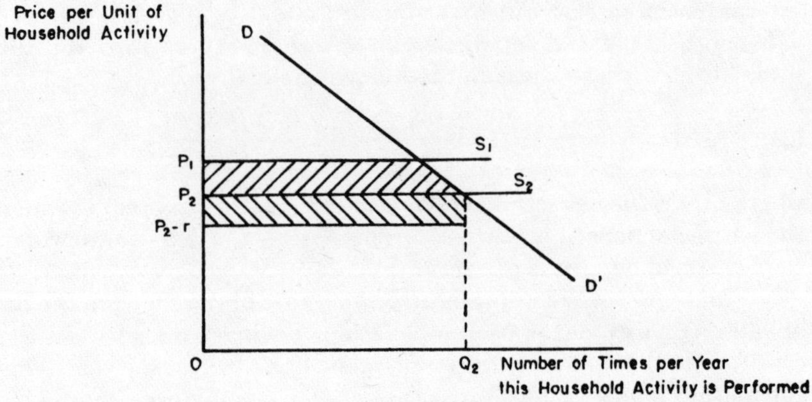

FIGURE II
Social Benefit from Product Innovation That Reduces the Price of a Household Activity

of r dollars every time this activity is performed using the product innovation. Then the social benefits from the innovation can be measured by the sum of the two shaded areas in Figure II. These two areas are exactly analogous to those in Figure I, and the methods used to estimate them are similar to those described above, except that no interviews were carried out with users. Instead, the results are based entirely on the estimates and findings of the firms. As in the previous sections, it is necessary to correct the R and D costs for uncommercialized projects, to estimate R and D costs incurred by firms and organizations other than the innovator, to deduct the profit from displaced products from the innovator's profit, and to include the profits of imitators.

However, not everything is the same as in previous sections. For one thing, one of these innovations, the stain remover, resulted in some environmental costs, since it increased the amount of a certain chemical that is put into our water supplies. As a rough measure of these costs, we used an estimate (obtained from an official of the Environmental Protection Agency) of the cost of removing a unit of this chemical from water, given that it occurs in a particular concentration. Then we multiplied this cost times the number of units of the chemical that is deposited in the water, given that consumers use the innovation to perform the relevant household activity Q_2 times per year. Finally, this estimate was deducted from the social benefit to correct, at least roughly, for the environmental costs. Note that this was the only innovation in our entire sample that resulted in any substantial environmental costs, so far as we could determine.[12]

In all but one of these cases, there is no reason to believe that, if the innovator had not introduced the new product, any other firm would have done so in the relevant time frame. But in the remaining case, a competitor introduced a similar new product only a short while after the innovator introduced its new product. In this case, we obtained estimates from the relevant firms concerning the quantity of its new product that the competitor would have sold each year if the innovator had not developed and introduced its new product. Then we deducted this amount from the actual combined sales of both new products to get the extra amount that was used each year because the new product was introduced earlier than it otherwise would have been, due to the innovator's actions. Then we calculated the consumers' surplus based on this extra amount. Also, we calculated the innovator's profit less the profit that would have been earned by the competitor on the share of the innovator's sales that the competitor would have gotten if the innovator had not introduced its product (and less the profit on products displaced in the remainder of cases). Based on these calculations, we computed the social rate of return.

Finally, as in the case of product innovations used by firms, we computed private as well as social rates of return. The calculations are entirely analogous to those described in the previous section. In all cases the calculations end with 1973.

VI. PROCESS INNOVATIONS

Next, let us turn to the model underlying our calculation of the social benefits from process innovations. In the case of three of the four process innovations included in our sample, there was no apparent effect on product prices. By lowering the costs of the innovators, these process innovations increased the innovator's profits. Also, since they were imitated (or used at nominal cost) by other firms, they soon increased the profits of other firms as well. The total decrease in costs (which equals the increase in profits) of all of the relevant firms is a measure of the social benefit of each of these innovations in a particular period. It equals the social saving in resources due to the innovation. For each of these innovations, we estimated the total reduction in costs on the basis of interviews with the relevant firms

12. Note that some of these innovations had positive environmental effects. However, since these benefits are hard to measure, we ignore them. Of course, whatever bias this introduces results in our estimates of the social rate of return being conservative.

and of studies and reports concerning the cost reductions due to the innovations and the extent of their utilization.

In the case of the fourth process innovation (the innovation in industrial heating equipment), the situation was different. In this case, the innovator shared the gains with its customers. As shown in Figure III, it reduced the price of its product from P_1 to P_2. Thus, the social

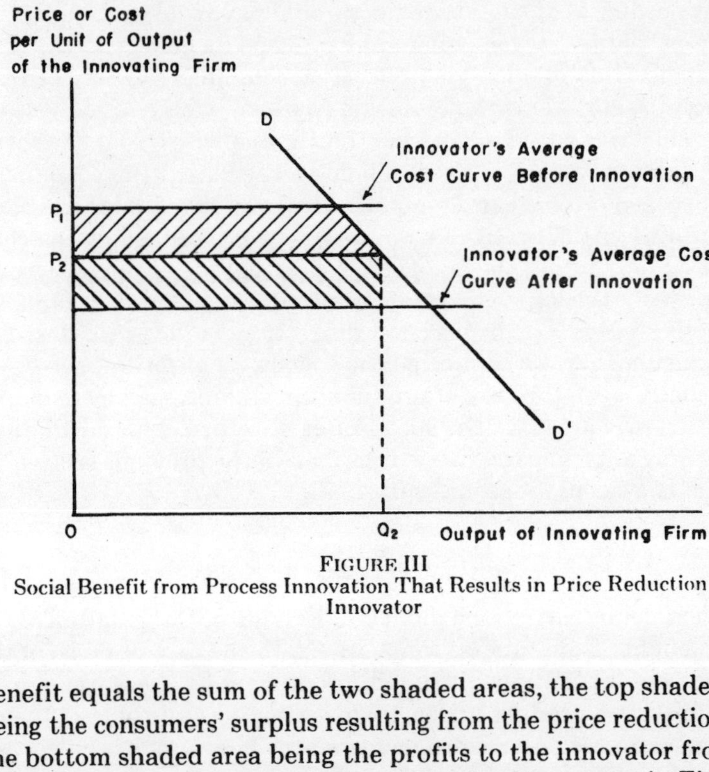

FIGURE III
Social Benefit from Process Innovation That Results in Price Reduction by Innovator

benefit equals the sum of the two shaded areas, the top shaded area being the consumers' surplus resulting from the price reduction, and the bottom shaded area being the profits to the innovator from the innovation. The situation is almost exactly the same as in Figures I and II.

For one of the process innovations, it was necessary to estimate the length of time that the innovator hastened the appearance and introduction of the new process. (In the other cases, there is no reason to believe that if the innovator had not introduced the innovation in the relevant time period, any other firm would have done so.) In this case other firms were doing R and D along somewhat similar lines, and there was some feeling among knowledgeable engineers and managers that the new process might have been developed and introduced about four years later than in fact occurred if the innovator had not done so. In this case we assume that the diffusion of the new process would have begun four years later (but that it would have proceeded at the same rate) if the innovator had not developed and introduced it. Then the social and private savings are computed by comparing the actual extent of use of the innovation with what it would have been under this assumption. In addition, the social rate of return based on the entire industry's investment in this sort of innovation is estimated, this estimate having the advantage that it is free of any such assumption about how quickly competitors of the innovator would have developed and introduced the innovation.[13] (The latter estimate, which is the lower of the two, is shown in Table II.)

TABLE II

SOCIAL AND PRIVATE RATES OF RETURN FROM INVESTMENT IN SEVENTEEN INNOVATIONS

	Rate of return (percent)	
Innovation	Social	Private
Primary metals innovation	17	18
Machine tool innovation	83	35
Component for control system	29	7
Construction material	96	9
Drilling material	54	16
Drafting innovation	92	47
Paper innovation	82	42
Thread innovation	307	27
Door control innovation	27	37
New electronic device	Negative	Negative
Chemical product innovation	71	9
Chemical process innovation	32	25
Chemical process innovation	13	4
Major chemical process innovation	56[a]	31
Household cleaning device	209	214
Stain remover	116	4
Dishwashing liquid	45	46
Median	56	25

a. Based on investment of entire industry. See Section VI.

VII. SOCIAL AND PRIVATE RATES OF RETURN

The results, shown in Table II, seem to have at least three implications. First, they indicate that the social rate of return from the

13. For two of the processes the calculations end with 1972 or 1973; for the other two, forecasts are used up to 1980 (and in one case, beyond).

investments in these seventeen innovations has been very high. The median estimated social rate of return is about 56 percent. Moreover, for a variety of reasons, these estimates are likely to be conservative lower bounds.[14] To put these results in perspective, recall that Griliches found that the internal social rate of return from hybrid corn—a very successful innovation—was 37 percent.[15] Clearly, the investments that have been made in industrial innovations have, on the average, yielded handsome social returns, if these innovations are at all typical.

Second, the results indicate that the private rates of return from the investments in these innovations have been much lower than the social rates of return.[16] The median private rate of return (before taxes) was about 25 percent. In interpreting this number, it is important to recognize the riskiness of this kind of investment (and the fact that these are pretax figures). This riskiness is evidenced by the enormous variation in the private rates of return in Table II. In the case of six innovations the private rate of return (before taxes) was less than 10 percent, while for five innovations, it was more than 40 percent.

14. For example, in many cases, we ignore all post-1973 benefits from the innovations. Throughout this study, we have tried to use estimates and procedures that, if biased at all, would be biased in this direction.

15. See his "Research Costs and Social Returns: Hybrid Corn and Related Innovations," *Journal of Political Economy*, LXVI (Oct. 1958), 419–31. The models used in Sections III and IV are in the same spirit as the one applied by Griliches. The principal differences are that we have extended the analysis to include the pricing policies of the innovator, the effect on displaced products, and the costs of uncommercialized R and D and of R and D done outside the innovating organization. Another noteworthy study of this kind is W. Peterson, "Returns to Poultry Research in the United States," *Journal of Farm Economics*, XLIX (Aug. 1967), 656–69. This study concludes that the average rate of return from the investment in poultry research was 18 percent.

16. Note that there is nothing in our procedures that makes it inevitable that an innovation's social rate of return exceeds its private rate of return. For a variety of reasons (such as investments in R and D by organizations other than the innovator, and the transfer of profits from the producers of displaced products to the innovator), the social rate of return can be less than the private rate of return—and in fact this turns out to be the case for four of the innovations in our sample. For a study of some of the factors associated with a firm's probabilities of success in R and D, see E. Mansfield and S. Wagner, "Organizational and Strategic Factors Associated with Probabilities of Success in Industrial R and D," *Journal of Business*, XLVIII (April 1975), 179–98.

One of the innovations was developed by a nonprofit organization. In this case the private rate of return is defined to be the rate of return to this organization and the licensees that produced and marketed the innovation.

When we compute a confidence interval for the proportions of innovations where the social rate of return exceeds the private rate of return, we find that the probability is 0.90 that this percentage lies between 60 percent and 92 percent. Thus, if we could treat our sample as randomly chosen, we could be quite confident that the social rate of return exceeds the private rate of return in the majority of cases. Also, a t-test indicates that the mean difference between social and private rates of return, which is 47 percent, differs significantly from zero at the 0.01 level. And so does a sign test, which does not assume normality.

Third, the results indicate that, in about 30 percent of the cases, the private rate of return was so low that no firm, with the advantage of hindsight, would have invested in the innovation, but the social rate of return from the innovation was so high that, from society's point of view, the investment was well worthwhile. We would also like to estimate the extent to which innovations with favorable social rates of return have anticipated rates of return that are so low that they are not carried out. Unfortunately, Table II cannot provide much information on this score for the obvious reason that all of these innovations were carried out. Also, expected and actual private rates of return may differ considerably.[17]

VIII. Factors Associated with the Gap Between Social and Private Rates of Return

Economists have long been interested in the sorts of innovative activity where the gap between social and private rates of return, if it exists, is particularly large. There has been considerable speculation on this score, but it seems fair to say that the current state of knowledge in this regard is extremely limited. Economic theorists have generally singled out three factors as being of considerable importance in determining the extent of the gap between the social and private rates of return from an innovation. The first of these factors is the market structure of the innovator's industry. If the innovator is faced with a highly competitive environment, it is less likely that it will be able to appropriate a large proportion of the social benefits than if it has a secure monopoly position or if it is part of a tight oligopoly. Of course, the extent to which the innovator is subjected to competition, and how rapidly, may depend on whether the innovation is patented. Moreover, another consideration of at least equal importance is how expensive it is for potential competitors to "invent around" the innovator's patents, if they exist, and to obtain the equipment needed to begin producing the new product (or using the new process). In some cases, like DuPont's nylon, it would have been extremely diffi-

17. However, a limited amount of evidence can be given on this score. We could obtain data for nine of the innovations concerning the approximate private rate of return expected from the innovation by the innovator when it began the project. In five of the nine cases, the expected private rate of return was less than 15 percent, indicating that these five projects were quite marginal; yet the average social rate of return of these five projects was over 100 percent! Unless there is a marked discontinuity of some sort, it would appear from this that there may be many projects where the expected private rate of return was a bit lower (with the result that they were not carried out), but where the social rate of return would have been quite high. (The rank correlation between the expected private rate of return and the social rate of return does not differ significantly from zero in this sample.) However, the very small sample and the crudeness of the analysis should be borne in mind.

cult to imitate the innovation (legally). In other cases, a potential competitor could obtain and begin producing a "me too" product (or using a "me too" process) at relatively little cost.

A second factor that economists have emphasized as a determinant of the size of the gap between social and private rates of return is whether the innovation is major or minor. (A reasonable measure of an innovation's importance (at least in our sample) might be the annual net social benefits derived from it.) According to R. C. O. Matthews, the "degree of appropriability is likely to be less . . . in major innovations than in minor ones. . . ," [18] since major innovations are more likely, in his view, to be imitated quickly. Similarly, on the basis of a model stressing the indivisibility of information, Kenneth Arrow concludes that "the inventor obtains the entire realized social benefit of moderately cost reducing inventions but not of more radical inventions." [19]

A third factor that is sometimes cited is whether the innovation is a new product or process. Thus, Matthews thinks that the degree of appropriability may be less for process innovations than for product innovations. On the other hand, Nelson, Peck, and Kalachek stress that new processes can often be kept secret and that it frequently is difficult for one firm to find out what processes another firm is using.[20] This, of course, suggests that the gap between social and private rates of return might be greater for products than for processes. Neither Matthews nor Nelson, Peck, and Kalachek present any evidence on this score.

Although most of these hypotheses seem quite plausible, the truth is that none of them have been subjected to any sort of systematic empirical tests. Based on the results presented in the previous section, it is possible for the first time to attempt some empirical tests of these hypotheses. These tests are made in two steps. First, we divide the sample into two groups, processes and products, to see whether the average difference between the social and private rates of return is different in one group than in the other. Second, looking at products alone (since there are too few processes to support such an analysis),

18. R. C. O. Matthews, "The Contribution of Science and Technology to Economic Development," in B. Williams, ed., *Science and Technology in Economic Growth* (London: Macmillan, 1973), p. 14.

19. K. Arrow, "Economic Welfare and the Allocation of Resources for Invention," in National Bureau of Economic Research, *The Rate and Direction of Inventive Activity* (Princeton: Princeton University Press, 1962), p. 622. Arrow's model bears a resemblance to ours in Section III, but he was interested in a somewhat different set of questions, and no attempt was made to use it as a basis for empirical work.

20. R. Nelson, M. Peck, and E. Kalachek, *Technology, Economic Growth, and Public Policy* (Washington: Brookings Institution, 1967), p. 161.

we assume that

$$D_i = \alpha_0 + \alpha_1 S_i + \alpha_2 P_i + \alpha_3 I_i + z_i, \quad (3)$$

where D_i is the difference between the social and private rates of return for the ith innovation, S_i is the annual net social benefit (in thousands of dollars) from the ith innovation three years after its initial introduction (a crude, but reasonable, measure of the innovation's importance), P_i is a dummy variable that equals 1 if the innovation is patented and 0 otherwise, I_i is an estimate of the minimum amount of money (in thousands of dollars) it would have cost any of the innovator's competitors to imitate legally and introduce the ith innovation, and z_i is a random error term. According to the hypotheses stated above, one would expect α_1 to be positive and α_2 and α_3 to be negative. Ordinary regression techniques were used to determine whether this was the case.

The results suggest that the difference between the social and private rates of return tended to be higher for products than for processes. (The average value of D_i was about 57 percent for products and about 21 percent for processes.) But this difference is not statistically significant. Turning to the estimation of the α's, we obtained data concerning I_i for each innovation.[21] Then, combining these data with the information concerning D_i, P_i, and S_i (which stems from the work in previous sections), we used least squares to estimate the α's, the resulting equation being

$$\underset{}{D_i} = \underset{(0.46)}{12.4} + \underset{(4.34)}{0.0313 S_i} - \underset{(1.87)}{0.0509 I_i}, \; (R^2 = 0.67), \quad (4)$$

where the t-statistic of each of the regression coefficients is shown in parentheses, and P_i is excluded because its regression coefficient is not even close to being statistically significant. Despite the relatively small sample size, the estimate of α_1 is highly significant, and the estimate of α_3 is significant at the 0.05 level. Both have the expected signs.

Thus, the results seem to support the hypothesis that the gap between social and private rates of return tends to be greater for more important innovations and for innovations that can be imitated relatively cheaply by competitors. Apparently, when the cost of imitating

21. These estimates were obtained from the innovating firms. In each case executives of the innovating firm were asked to estimate the minimum amount that it would have cost a competitor to imitate the innovation (legally). In some cases the estimate of I_i was as high as \$2 million; in other cases, it was as low as \$3,000. Although these estimates are rough, the executives seemed to think that they were not very wide of the mark.

the innovation is held constant, it makes little or no difference whether the innovation is patented—which seems reasonable because whether or not a patent exists is of relevance largely (perhaps only) because of its effects on the costs of imitation. It is important to note that S_i and I_i can explain about two-thirds of the observed variation in this gap among the product innovations in our sample.[22] However, at the same time, it is important to bear in mind the smallness of the sample and its nonrandom character.

IX. Unemployment, Repercussions on Other Markets, and Future Changes in Technology

Before concluding, we must take up several additional factors that have not been mentioned explicitly in previous sections. First, new technology can, of course, result in prolonged and serious unemployment of particular kinds of labor. Recognizing this fact, we tried to determine whether there was any substantial unemployment (or change in job content) resulting from each innovation described in Section II. In no case could we find any evidence of an appreciable change of this sort: although labor requirements sometimes were reduced by the innovation, growth in output offset these reductions. Thus, in this sample at least, this factor does not seem of substantial importance. Obviously, however, it can be of importance in other cases; and in situations where it is of importance, one must adjust the social benefits, as calculated in previous sections, for the fact that (for a certain period of time) some of the resources saved by the innovation do not find employment elsewhere.[23]

Second, new technology can, of course, have an effect on other industries and markets besides the ones directly involved. For example, by reducing the cost and price of the product using an innovation, the innovation affects the outputs of goods that are substitutes or complements of this product. However, so long as the prices of these and other goods (other than the product using the innovation) are not materially affected, the effects of these output changes are already included in the measures specified above.[24] In our sample there is no

22. One innovation had to be excluded from the regression (and the t-test in note 16) because its private rate of return was incalculable, since the private net benefit in each year was negative. Note too that the ratio of I_i to the innovator's cost in carrying out the ith innovation was tried as an additional explanatory variable in equation (4), but it was not close to being significant. Apparently, the absolute, not relative, cost is what matters most.

23. See A. Schmitz and D. Seckler, "Mechanized Agriculture and Social Welfare: The Case of the Tomato Harvester," *American Journal of Agricultural Economics*, LII (Nov. 1970), 569–77.

24. See E. Mishan, *Economics for Social Decisions* (New York: Praeger, 1972), Ch. 6.

evidence that any of these innovations had any appreciable impact on any price other than that of the good using the innovation (in Section IV) or of the household activity in question (in Section V) or of the good based on the one relevant process (in Section VI). Also, one must assume that inputs that were displaced from industries producing goods competing with the product using the innovation readily found employment elsewhere. There is no evidence that this was not the case.

Third, new technology can, of course, play an important role in suggesting and prompting further innovations. Without question, practically all of the innovations in our sample had this effect. Thus, since each of these innovations is instrumental in bringing about future innovations, each results in social benefits above and beyond what we have measured. However, each of these innovations may have been suggested, prompted, or aided by previous innovations, and there is no feasible way to estimate the extent to which there is a net understatement of benefits.

X. Conclusion

As everyone who writes on this subject is quick to point out, very little is known about the social and private returns from industrial research and technological innovation. The need for measurement in this area is acute and widely recognized. For example, the Council of Economic Advisers, in its 1972 Annual Report, stressed the need for further analysis "to show the benefits, costs, and processes associated with R and D." [25] Our purpose in this study has been to measure, as best we can, the social and private rates of return from a sample of innovations.[26] We believe that our results go far beyond anything heretofore attempted in this area. (Also, to check and extend our results, we obtained very rich and detailed data concerning the returns from the innovative activities from 1960 to 1972 of one of the nation's largest firms. The results bear out our present findings.[27])

25. Economic Report of the President, 1972, pp. 127–28.

26. Griliches, Mansfield, Minasian, and Terleckyj have estimated rates of return from nonagricultural R and D based on econometric studies where R and D is inserted into production functions. Where the results of these studies can be compared with this one, the results are quite similar. For example, see N. Terleckyj, *Effects of R and D on the Productivity Growth of Industries: An Exploratory Study* (Washington: National Planning Association, 1974).

27. For each year, this firm has made a careful inventory of the technological innovations arising from its R and D and related activities, and it has made detailed estimates of the effect of each of these innovations on its profit stream. We computed the average rate of return from this firm's total investment in innovative activities during 1960–1972, the result being 19 percent, which is not too different from the

Of course, proper caution should be exercised in interpreting our results. For a host of reasons, they can tell us little about the extent to which there is an underinvestment (or whether an underinvestment exists) in innovative activities of various kinds.[28] Our sample of innovations is not a random sample, the data sometimes are rough, and for a few of the innovations they are based partly on forecasts. Further, the models that we use are simplified in many respects.[29] For these and other reasons, our results should be treated with considerable caution. The measurement of social and private rates of return from investments in new technology is an extremely difficult business, which is one good reason why so few such measurements have been attempted. Nonetheless, it is important that we make the best estimates we can.

UNIVERSITY OF PENNSYLVANIA
MOUNT HOLYOKE COLLEGE
UNIVERSITY OF CONNECTICUT
TEMPLE UNIVERSITY
CALIFORNIA POLYTECHNIC STATE UNIVERSITY

median private rate of return in Table II. Also, we computed lower bounds for the social rate of return from the firm's investment, and found that they were about double its private rates of return. For further discussion of this study, see G. Beardsley's Ph.D. thesis, University of Pennsylvania; E. Mansfield, J. Rapoport, A. Romeo, E. Villani, S. Wagner, and F. Husic, *The Production and Application of New Industrial Technology* (New York: W. W. Norton, 1977); and E. Mansfield, "Comments on Returns to R and D Expenditures in the Private Sector," Conference on Research in Income and Wealth, November 1975.

28. See E. Mansfield, "Federal Support of R and D in the Private Sector," *Priorities and Efficiency in Federal Research and Development*, Joint Economic Committee of Congress, October 29, 1976; his testimony before the House Committee on Science and Technology, published in *Federal Research and Development Expenditures and the National Economy* (Washington: Government Printing Office, 1976); and G. Eads, "U. S. Government Support for Civilian Technology: Economic Theory vs. Political Practice," *Research Policy* (1974).

29. An important point to bear in mind is that the models used here cannot cope with innovations whose effects cannot be regarded as a form of cost reduction. This limitation is likely to be much more important for very major innovations than for lesser ones.

Part III
Intervening in Competitive Markets

[13]

THE
QUARTERLY JOURNAL
OF
ECONOMICS

AUGUST, 1946

REFLECTIONS ON PRICE CONTROL

SUMMARY

Introduction, 475.—I. Prewar undervaluation of price control by economists as an instrument of emergency policy, 476. — II. Relation of market structure to informal rationing by the seller, 478. — III. Relation of market structure to enforcement, 480. — IV. Price inflexibility as an aid to price control, 481. — V. Conventional pricing as a further aid, 483. — VI. The period of grace between price-fixing and shortage, 484. — VII. Constant and decreasing costs in relation to price control, 485. — VIII. Concluding disclaimer, and comment on administration, 488.

The time, happily, is perhaps near when economists can consider the implications for their subject of some of the questions with which they have been occupied during the war years. It is unlikely in this exercise that price control will be overlooked. Not only did control of prices in the second World War produce an unprecedented and dramatic reordering of market phenomena, but it was also an enterprise with which a sizable minority of the country's economists were associated.

There is some danger, however, that the experience of OPA may be reëxamined too narrowly in its relation to the exigent wartime task of preventing inflation. This would be to the neglect of another opportunity — that of examining the price system in an artificially static context that peculiarly illuminates some aspects of its behavior. During the war years, if the analogy be permitted, the price system was not a living organism but a cadaver. While physiological study has been advanced by the examination of healthy specimens, it has also been immeasurably aided by dissection. So perhaps with markets.

The pages that follow make no pretense to being a final theoretical judgment on price phenomena as illuminated by price control. They are preliminary judgments and their standing, if standing they have, is partly that they are based on notes and reflections contemporary with my service with OPA.

I

One of the more intriguing problems in the revaluation of price theory suggested by the price control experience can perhaps best be introduced by this question: why did economists before the war rather generally undervalue the efficiency of price control as an instrument of emergency policy?

That prewar doctrine led to the conclusion that price fixing was an instrument of limited utility can hardly be doubted. Though it is always a risky enterprise for one economist to attempt a consensus of his colleagues, perhaps it would have been agreed before the war that price-fixing was a useful first step in establishing special equilibria at a given price. If sugar prices were rising because supply promised to be insufficient at the ruling price, then sugar prices might usefully be fixed. But many, if not most, would have argued that the fixed price, to be effective and permanent, would have to be supported rather promptly by some system of consumer allocation or rationing. To fail to support the fixed price by such controls was to attempt to regulate prices "in a vacuum," This was a naive or even an abhorrent act, the impossibility of which politicians were always learning anew. And few economists would have advised using price control except selectively for commodities and services which war-time demand or supply had made peculiarly scarce. With the exception of Mr. Baruch[1], whom it must be said few professional economists took seriously, price control was not considered an appropriate instrument vis-à-vis general disequilibrium of supply and demand. If aggregate demand exceeded supply at ruling prices, the only effective way of maintaining a stable price level was an appropriate curtailment of demand. Merely to fix price ceilings would be to invite a large-scale conspiracy between sellers who would willingly receive and consumers (or producers) who would willingly pay more than established prices. The price-fixer would be left pathetically helpless amidst wholesale violation of his orders. But if by

1. I remember my own mild shock when, during the summer of 1941, I encountered the first professional economist of my own acquaintance — it was Professor Alvin H. Hansen — who was urging that economists give more serious consideration to the "Baruch Plan."

some magic he should succeed in holding prices, some (and I for one) would have argued that he would only have succeeded in ruining the machinery by which the economy distributes resources and rations scarce goods without providing a substitute. The cost of formal stability of prices would be a malfunctioning economy and perhaps even chaos.

These views which, justifiably or not, I have attributed to economists in general were certainly held by the economists associated with price control in its earliest days.[2] Indeed, many feared that popular pressure might force too extensive use of price ceilings and so discredit a regulatory device of definite but limited serviceability. Those fears had not been dispelled by the spring of 1942 when the General Maximum Price regulation was issued — even though Germany appeared to have had some success with a general price "stop," and the Canadian government had just initiated a highly convenient and seemingly promising experiment in blanket price control. The General Maximum Price Regulation — by all odds the most important single step in war-time price policy — was to some extent an act of desperation. By the time the Emergency Price Control Act was finally passed, early in 1942, Congress and the country believed, or had been led to believe, that vigorous administration of the law would insure reasonably stable prices. Price control, many of us felt, had been oversold. In the early months of 1942 there was a steady and sustained increase in prices. The procedures that had been devised for selective price-fixing contemplated slow and deliberate action and they were not easily redesigned. And even prompt action on many individual prices promised to take too much time and be too difficult of equitable administration. There was no prospect of taxes or compulsory savings high enough to bring aggregate demand into balance with aggregate supply, and some of us were just beginning to suspect what many have since concluded — that price stability achieved through tax and saving policies was a rainbow one might chase indefinitely. The overall ceiling was thus the only hope.

2. Mr. Henderson took a position along these lines before the House Banking and Currency Committee during hearings on the Emergency Price Control Act of 1942. In early 1941 I suggested that the appropriate sphere of war-time price control was limited to special commodity situations in a generally non-inflationary context. (Review of Economic Statistics, May, 1941, p. 82.)

The *Statement of Considerations* accompanying the GMPR, the most carefully drafted and edited document of the early OPA, shows that the authors were not sanguine — in fact several sections can now be read as rather engaging hedges against eventual failure of the Regulation. At one point the *Statement* says: "There can be no effective price control while at the same time there is so large an amount of excess purchasing power."[3] And again it states: "Without [adequate taxation, savings and wage stabilization] the ceiling would in the long run become *administratively unenforceable and socially harmful*."[4] Those statements were made partly in the hope of stimulating collateral action on taxes and wages, partly as a warning against what was deemed to be excessive reliance on price-fixing and partly, perhaps, to protect the professional reputations of the authors of the regulation.

The simple fact is that price control has worked. If it hasn't worked well, it has at least worked to the extent of preventing a wholesale deterioration of values. And prices have been fixed in the context of a large and continuing excess of aggregate demand over supply. The concept of the "inflationary gap," as it was used in the early months of the war, was not as subtle as one might have wished and some of the arithmetic was bad. Nevertheless a gap existed; since 1942 purchasing power has exceeded the supply of goods, shortages have been widespread and there has been a good deal of involuntary saving forced by shortages. For only part of the period and for only part of the total stock of goods has demand been adjusted to supply by rationing or its equivalent. Prices, withal, have been comparatively stable. This is the disequilibrium at legislated prices that needs to be explained.

II

Rationing as an explanation of the success of price control merits specific comment. It has, of course, the well-explained effect of paring down demand and establishing a special equilibrium that is wholly stable. With reasonable enforcement, stable prices for rationed consumer goods and allocated producers goods present no mystery. Admittedly, price control has worked better for rationed than for unrationed commodities. But it has also

3. The General Maximum Price Regulation Bulletin No. 1, April 28, 1942, p. 24.

4. Ibid. Italics added.

worked moderately well for unrationed commodities. It was moderately effective for primary metals, coal, and petroleum before or after they were rationed or allocated, for houseroom throughout the war, and for scores and hundreds of other producer's and consumer's goods from (latterly) farm machinery to breakfast foods, when there were no formal controls. For these some further explanation is in order.

The core of the explanation is to be found, without much doubt, in market structures which readily permit of informal controls by the seller. Monopolistically competitive or imperfect markets lend themselves readily to these informal controls, and price control was effective because these markets are rather more common than was conventionally assumed before the war. In the purely competitive market, individual buyers and sellers are anonymous; no seller, for example, can have a specified group of buyers identified as *his* customers. All buyers and all sellers are fluidly participant in "the market." But when the number of buyers is relatively small, or the number of sellers relatively small, or both conditions obtain, the semi-abstraction of the market disappears. Then sellers and buyers are no longer anonymous; they deal with each other as individuals. It is possible for sellers (or vice versa, the buyers) to allocate scarce supplies to specific customers. If the established price is below the equilibrium price, it is possible and even rather easy for sellers to give large, habitual, or otherwise favored buyers, preference rights to what is available. In such markets, in other words, price-fixing is accompanied, pari passu, by allocation or rationing. Or, to put it another way, when the government fixes prices it delegates to sellers in imperfect markets the power to ration their customers. From some points of view this delegation of power and the possibility of its abuse might be disturbing. For present purposes it is sufficient that it was an effective buttress for price control.

The efficiency of private rationing depends, first of all, on how sharply customers are identified with the seller—if there are not too many of them, if their past purchases are a matter of record, and if the seller knows their needs and the reliability of their claims, he can ration rather effectively. The identification of buyer with seller becomes increasingly indistinct the more competitors the seller has. Then any one seller becomes less able to assume responsibility for fair distribution. One customer by luck, diligence or wile is certain to get more than a fair share; others, who for that reason get less, have a powerful motive to bribe another seller into breaking the ceiling. It was commonplace in OPA experience that the primary metal markets, where sellers were few, were relatively easy to control without formal allocation. The secondary metal markets, with numerous sellers, were far more difficult to control without allocation. Even in areas or at times of substantial shortage, control of milk prices, invariably (at retail) a market with few sellers, was effective without formal rationing. An effort to control fresh vegetable markets in the spring of 1943, when there was a substantial disequilibrium at the fixed prices and where sellers are numerous, was far richer in experience than results.

III

Although the prevalence of a sympathetic market structure is the most important explanation of successful price control, there is obviously a good deal more to be explained. For one thing, while it is possible for sellers to ration their customers, this is not their most profitable course of action. It is more profitable for them simply to raise prices and break the law — and the price-fixer as well. The simple circumstance that sellers *could* charge and buyers *would* pay more than the established prices, the law notwithstanding, presumably was what broke nearly all price-fixers of record.

Without doubt the present generation of price administrators has had a more law-abiding generation of businessmen with which to deal than their even less happy predecessors. And a community that has come to regard war as a tragedy stigmatizes illegal profiteering as a more heroic age did not. The freebooting merchants who supplied the Continental or Union armies of the Civil War would be distressed at the restraints which public opinion has imposed on their descendants. Also, for the first time under OPA, price regulations have been carefully tailored to fit the practices and convenience of individual industries and even of individual firms. Price control has been a meticulously planned operation, the fruit of a sound and adult subject matter of which economists can be proud. (This was also an effort, I can't help pointing out and with some residue of feeling, that necessitated lengthy regulations and which was for that reason profoundly and unfairly misinterpreted by superficial critics.) Finally, it was realized from the beginning that price control required enforcement. In the past, as indeed today in a number of South American countries, much price control consisted of a series of decrees from a remote central government and, since there was no machinery for enforcement, the violator was all too obviously secure in any violation.

But enforcement of price control is also easier in the imperfect than in the purely competitive market. It is obviously easier to police a few firms than many, but this is not all. In the perfectly or purely competitive market (I use the terms interchangeably to connote perfect elasticity of demand for the individual seller), the initiative in violation is, in principle, quite as likely to be taken by the buyer as the seller, just as the initiative in any legitimate price change is as likely to lie with one side as the other.

In the imperfect market, at least in those characterized by small numbers, the initiative to violate will almost always be taken by the seller, for the initiative in price changes almost always rests with him. In such markets the buyer, since he is not a party to the crime (or is unlikely so to consider himself), is more likely to report the offender. If small numbers are associated with individual firms of large size, there are other reasons why the seller must be circumspect. He has more employees, and employees that are more impersonal, to report his violations. The aberrations of a large concern have more news value than those of a small one. The large seller also has lawyers and public relations counselors to tell him to obey the law. Withal, one of the unsuspected war-time virtues of monopoly or oligopoly has been its special vulnerability to price control.

IV

Apart from its susceptibility to informal controls and to enforcement, there is one other major respect in which the imperfect or monopolistically competitive market aids the price-fixer. That is by the tendency for prices to become inflexible and even institutionalized in such markets. Where the seller has control over his prices, as by definition he has in some measure in every imperfect market, he has good reason for minimizing the frequency of change. In some instances, market control — the *entente* between sellers — can be maintained only if prices are stable; the understanding may not be sufficiently subtle or durable to survive too many ups-and-downs. In other cases, customers (or the Department of Justice) may have become accustomed to stable prices and may be aroused if prices change. Changes in prices may also be costly either in money or administrative convenience.[5] So the perfectly wise and rational seller in an imperfect market may maximize his profits by keeping prices constant over substantial periods — to attempt to have them always at a maximum would reduce returns over time.

The phenomenon of inflexible prices had been well-observed before the war,[6] but so far as I am aware, and for good enough reasons, no one had observed that this inflexibility would greatly facilitate war-time control. Not only had buyers and sellers become accustomed to the level of the price, but they had also become familiar with the differentials, discounts, special deals and all the other appurtenances of the price structure. It is infinitely easier to continue and enforce such a settled and familiar structure than to check the upward surge of a more nearly competitive market. And there, because differentials and discounts, like the level of prices itself, change in day-to-day bargaining, no price schedule will ever conform as neatly to a past structure. So, precisely at the time when sellers or market operators lose the prospect of higher prices or speculative gains, they must alter their business to conform to rules laid down in some not very engaging government prose. For such sellers, as compared with those who have been selling at infrequently changing prices, the discomforts of price control are great. The Office of Price Administration controlled the prices of all steel mill products with far less man-power and trouble than was required for a far smaller dollar volume of steel scrap. Handlers of farm products complained with especial bitterness of OPA regulations, perhaps partly because that is their nature, but partly because their difficulties were greater. To the extent that small firms are more competitive than large ones, they had reason to be especially aggrieved by price

5. For this latter observation and phrase I am indebted to Dean Robert D. Calkins, who suggests that a surprisingly large number of decisions in both business and government are governed by this cost. He is undoubtedly right.

6. "Price Inflexibility," Review of Economic Statistics, May, 1938, by Edward S. Mason. Gardiner C. Means, The Structure of the American Economy, Part I, National Resources Planning Board, June, 1939. "The Nature and Meaning of Rigid Prices, 1894–1933," Journal of Political Economy, October, 1937, by Donald D. Humphrey and others. I venture to refer also to a paper of my own, "Monopoly Power and Price Rigidities," this Journal, May, 1936.

control. I am tempted to enunciate a rule that is all too self-evident in this discussion: it is relatively easy to fix prices that are already fixed!

V

Infrequent changes in prices may best serve the long-run earnings position of a firm or industry. There is also a strong element of convention in price-making, which works on the side of infrequent change, and which does not directly serve the goal of maximum return. Traditionally (or in textbooks, at least) custom or convention has been considered an exceptional or off-type factor. The experience of OPA, I believe, would indicate its general importance. It, too, helped the price fixer.

The stronghold of conventional or customary pricing is the resale market, namely, wholesale and retail selling. For a large proportion of all retailers and a rather smaller proportion of all retail trade, the price or toll charged for the service is a strictly conventional mark-up or "mark-on." Sometimes this is the mark-up suggested by the supplier; sometimes it is conventional with the store or trade for that particular merchandise. In either case, price control was applied to a market which had ceased to look upon price-setting as one of the exploitive or profit-making decisions on which the revenues of the business depended. Accordingly, as shortages developed, it seemed perfectly normal procedure to the radio dealer, the refrigerator dealer, or even the cigarette vendor, that he sell off his limited stock at his accustomed mark-up. Quite often he eliminated, sometimes illegally, his accustomed concessions or "markdowns," which he had looked upon as vaguely abnormal. But he did not think of exacting the new and higher markup that the market would have allowed. Had retailers attempted this on any considerable scale, as I, for one, often supposed they might, OPA enforcement would have been nearly helpless.

This whole phenomenon of customary or conventional pricing perhaps deserves more analysis than it has received. Indeed the very terms "custom" and "convention" may be deceptive. That many sellers neglect the opportunities inherent in pricing cannot be doubted. They follow the easier rule of charging what they have charged before or what someone else is charging. Pricing by custom, in this case, is a clear-cut atrophy of market motivations; it can properly be termed a decadent alternative to what economists once called *rational* behavior. But I suspect that what is called custom is more often an indispensable simplification of what otherwise would be an inordinately complex task. The small retailer — and often the larger one — has neither the information nor the capacity to adjust his margins commodity by commodity, week by week, or season by season, so as to maximize his returns. It is of special significance, I think, that resale markets *are* the stronghold of customary pricing. Here the individual seller typically dispenses a large number of items. To arrive at a theoretically right price or margin for each would require that he solve a formidable array of simultaneous equations. He lacks the capacity for any such ideal price policy; its mental, if not its monetary, cost would be exorbitant. So he relies on rule-of-thumb. To put it another way, in the manner of many sophomores similarly situated in relation to price theory, the retailer attempts to resolve an inordinately complex problem by memorizing a few simple maxims.

VI

Another unsuspected aid to the price fixer is the margin of time that elapses between an increase in price in an uncontrolled market and the ensuing shortage of goods, if that price increase is prevented. Obviously the price-fixer is not in trouble when he fixes a price, so long as supply is sufficient at the fixed price. One clear conclusion from the experience of the Office of Price Administration is that this interlude may be considerable. Repeatedly the agency was able to forestall strong upward thrusts in prices and hold these prices, while for several months, sometimes a year or two, supply remained abundant. This period of grace was invaluable. While it lasted, the machinery for control could be perfected — a simple "freeze" translated into a workable price schedule. Enforcement was not difficult.

This experience would suggest, to speak somewhat elliptically, that the supply-demand equilibrium is a loose-jointed concept — that, in the jargon of an earlier discussion, it is "indeterminate." But some analysis is possible. In disturbed times the demand function, viewed as an independent variable, is not intimately related to current consumption. In the immediate prewar years and the early years of the war, there was much anticipatory buying

— far more than in a similar upswing of peacetime activity; for, especially after the war began, advance buying was no longer speculative in the ordinary sense — indeed, it was partly a form of insurance. Where this buying was in anticipation of price increases, i.e. where the buyer sought to avoid higher costs later or hoped to realize on increasing inventory values, price control had a remedial aspect, for it partly eliminated the motive. In the early stages of this war, business men, guided by their recollections of the last war, undoubtedly bought in anticipation of higher prices, rather than to protect themselves against absolute shortages. Price control, needless to say, does not reduce demand where the motive for advance buying is fear of shortages. It was, therefore, a more important restraint on anticipatory buying in this war than it would ever be in the future. It will be the shortages for which this war will be remembered.

I am not sure that this period of grace is peculiar to any class of market. It was noticeable in commodities — coffee, wheat, sugar, cocoa and pepper — as well as for industrial goods. Without doubt, however, it is also most markedly a phenomenon of imperfect markets, where price changes are few and the related market imperfection is oligopoly. Routine shifts in demand must ex hypothesi be accommodated at the going price. The result is some margin of excess capacity. In an inflationary context, the decision to increase prices will usually be taken before the excess capacity has been exhausted by increasing demand. If the increase is forestalled, the industry's reserve capacity will enable it to supply its markets perhaps for a considerable time. As early as December of 1941 the American Tobacco Co. initiated a sizable increase in the price of Lucky Strikes. Presumably the other majors would have soon followed suit. The increase was disallowed and, in spite of a steady increase in current consumption, there was no shortage even of individual brands for over two years.

VII

Finally, price control has been aided by an unsuspected cost behavior under conditions of expanding output. Many if not most of the economists actively associated with price control in its early phases consciously or implicitly assumed that, where large increases in production would be required, it would be at increasing cost. Some certainly had in mind the bulk-line cost curves of the first

World War (it is significant that the term has gained currency in this war) and the presumption of increasing cost implicit in these arrays.[7] For as large an industrial expansion as has occurred, they would have predicted rather general increases in prices or else the widespread use of subsidies and differential prices to compensate for higher (marginal) costs.

In retrospect, except for agriculture, the number of industries that were expanded for war purposes at increasing cost seems small. Certainly the number of manufacturing industries expanded at increasing cost was extremely small. During the early months of price control, a strenuous effort was made to gain acceptance for the principle of using subsidies to offset higher "marginal" costs in increasing-cost industries. This was successful[8], and such subsidies have been notably useful in maintaining prices of copper, other non-ferrous metals, petroleum and a number of other commodities. In a miscellany of other situations, the same result has been achieved through differential pricing. Nevertheless, the area where these policies proved appropriate was relatively small, and in the main it was the extractive industries. It is a fair conclusion that most industrial expansion during the war has been at constant or decreasing cost.

Decreasing costs may be partly attributed to the methods by which war-time capital expansion was financed. Where, for example, the government supplied plant or equipment through the Defense Plant Corporation, the existing supply of fixed plant ceased to be a factor shaping the supply curve. Provided the factors were supplied at constant cost, only the diseconomies of scale — an increasingly unfavorable combination of management with other factors — could be the cause of increasing costs, even in the short run.

In principle this question of whether war-time expansion was obtained at increasing, constant or decreasing cost has only a

7. Notably in Taussig's "Price-Fixing as seen by a Price Fixer," this Journal, February, 1919, p. 205. While there may have been others, the only industry group with an acute recollection of these bulk-line cost curves that I encountered during my service with the OPA was, appropriately enough, the anthracite producers. Members of the industry informally but urgently recommended adherence to the principle that prices be set to cover (full) costs of the highest-cost *necessary* producer. Taussig notes that the anthracite industry was a rich beneficiary of the bulk-line principle.

8. Credit for this achievement and for saving the government many millions of expenditure belongs primarily to Dr. Donald H. Wallace.

derived relation to the problem of price control. The main problem of price control and the main task of the price-fixer is to administer the disequilibrium of demand and supply. Price increases to cover the cost of high-cost output at the margin are not, in the strict sense, inflationary. They contribute to inflation only to the extent that bulk-line firms have more income to dispose which, especially if it becomes the target of wage demand, adds to the aggregate of excess demand.

In practice, however, avoidance of these price increases was most important. The community does not discriminate between price increases in an increasing cost industry and price increases that are in response to redundant demand. Any increase is, in some measure, a precedent for others.[9] In a period of general expansion of output a tendency toward constant or diminishing costs was, therefore, notably helpful.[1]

The unity of decreasing costs with market imperfection, particularly oligopoly, provided another aid for the price-fixer. Even where price covers cost by a substantial margin, it is by no means certain, especially in the short-run context of war economics, that supply will be forthcoming. Supplementary negotiation is essential to obtain the supply, i.e. to keep supply price in normal relation to cost. Such negotiation is only practical where the number of firms is relatively small. This inability to supplement price control with negotiation accounts in part for the relative ineffectiveness of price control for agricultural products. The Department of Agriculture did use propaganda on behalf of increased production with considerable success. And during 1943 proposals for entering contracts with individual farmers for expanded production were seriously debated. But, in general, increased farm production was obtained by assuming that his supply price for the quantity wanted (the "goal") was high. The prices so set have borne no relation to costs. While this course of action could be defended on grounds of expediency, it is only fair

9. Although I am inclined to believe that the fear of precedent was exaggerated. In fact, experience suggests that a superficially discriminatory, but fundamentally logical, differentiation in price policy as between firms or industries can be explained to principals and even to the Courts.

1. For a large number of military items, initial contract prices were very high. As manufacturers gained experience, both in technique and in costing, prices declined spectacularly. While this phenomenon was also generally helpful to the price-fixer, it represents a secular movement not properly a part of this discussion of cost behavior.

to add that some of its authors in the Department of Agriculture would have approved it without any visible justification.

VIII

Two final observations may be in order. If it be allowed that a good many economists miscalculated the potential efficiency of price control, it is clear that the fault was less in analysis than in application. The experience of the OPA does not suggest that price control would have been effective, had it generally operated in vacuo in markets shared by the numbers of buyers and sellers commonly associated with the notion of pure or perfect competition. But if imperfect markets are assumed, then the comparative effectiveness of price control can be explained and presumably it could have been foreseen. I suppose there were few economists before the war who had much real faith in the applicability of the conventional opening chapters on the competitive market. But it is equally clear that some (myself included) had not fully accepted the implications of their apostasy.

In exploring why price control has been possible I am a little uneasy lest I appear to argue that price control has been easy. That is a conclusion which no participant is likely to reach; it is one which my own former colleagues in the enterprise would assuredly not forgive. For if a kind Providence simplified part of the task, a stern one made other parts more difficult than anyone could reasonably have expected. Certainly few guessed how adept and compelling would be the pressures brought to bear on the price-fixer. As economists for several centuries have suspected, the desire for money is one of the strongest of human motives. And as students of government have long assumed, the urge to reëlection, in its own sphere, is also potent. The price-fixer must thwart both of these aspirations — either individually or in a mighty coalition. Where price control failed — for farm products, as all too clearly suggested by the current inflation of farm land values, or in relating prices to quality standards — the failure is traceable most directly to this coalition. In both instances, the technical problems were considerable; but there is no reason to doubt that they could have been overcome.

At least as inhibiting to effective price control as politics are the administrative difficulties of the task. An approximation to equal standards for treatment had to be formulated and made applicable to a thousand and one different industries. A staff had to be assembled and trained in a relatively subtle subject matter for the almost infinite variety of products. A large and complex piece of administrative machinery had to be built and it had to perform a difficult and diverse task at the same time. That combination of administrative and policy design and operation will always be recalled, by those responsible, as a task that looked possible only in retrospect. To anyone associated with price control during the second World War, one of the most disconcerting recollections will always be the glib dismissal by outsiders of the whole issue of administrative difficulty. Businessmen, Members of Congress and even other Executive agencies were equally inclined to wave it aside. Yet one could say of overall price control that, while it proved itself a rugged instrument of war-time economic policy, it also proved that, if initiated *de nouveau*, it is administratively all but impossible.

J. K. Galbraith.

Washington, D. C.

[14]

COMMUNICATIONS

A Geometrical Analysis of Black-Market Behavior

In many of today's economies which continue the use of price controls abidance by the laws and regulations seems to be rather imperfect, and "black markets" develop for many commodities. The behavior of these markets is of great importance in these economies, not only for those who take an active part in it, as buyers or sellers, but also for those who obey the law, and for the authorities that make and administer the law.

It is the purpose of the present paper to develop, in diagrammatic form, an analysis of price determination in the black market. However, it will be convenient first to examine briefly two earlier analyses of the problem.

Boulding, apparently the first to give a diagrammatic representation of price determination in the black market, used the diagram shown as Figure 1.[1] *S* and *D* are the supply and demand curves for a product in a competitive industry. *OR* is the official price, fixed below *NP*, the equilibrium price in a free market. *RH* is the amount supplied at the official price. S_b and D_b are drawn by assuming that there are special legal and moral obstacles that tend to restrict entry into black-market operations. The effect is that, at any black-market price, the combined amount supplied by the official and black markets is smaller than the amount that would be supplied in a free market at the same price; demand is affected in a similar way. The black-market price, determined by the intersection of S_b and D_b, may be anywhere between *OR*, the official price, and *OG'*, the price at which the quantity demanded in the black market is zero.

On the demand side, this presentation implicitly assumes that the legally sold quantity is purchased only by those who would normally bid the highest prices for it in a free market. We can hardly expect, however, that this is the case when formal rationing by the government accompanies the price control. It would be unlikely even without official rationing.[2]

Boulding's black-market supply curve, as it is presented in Figure 1, implies that the supply to the black market consists only of those units of the commodity that are produced at a marginal cost higher than the official price. This in turn implies that the goods that would have been supplied in the free market, had the free-market price been equal to the established official price, would, under price control, always be sold at this price. This, however, is highly improbable. We know that there is some shifting of supply from the official to the black market, a movement which increases with the widening gap between the prices in the two markets.[3]

[1] K. E. Boulding, "A Note on the Theory of the Black-Market," *Canadian Jour. Econ. Pol. Sci.*, Feb. 1937, XIII, 115-18. Most of the note is reproduced in the revised edition of *Economic Analysis* (New York, 1948), pp. 153-55.

[2] This has been pointed out earlier by A. F. W. Plumptre, "The Theory of the Black Market: Further Considerations," *Canadian Jour. Econ. Pol. Sci.*, May 1947, XIII, 280-282.

[3] Boulding does not overlook this possibility in his forementioned note, and he attempts

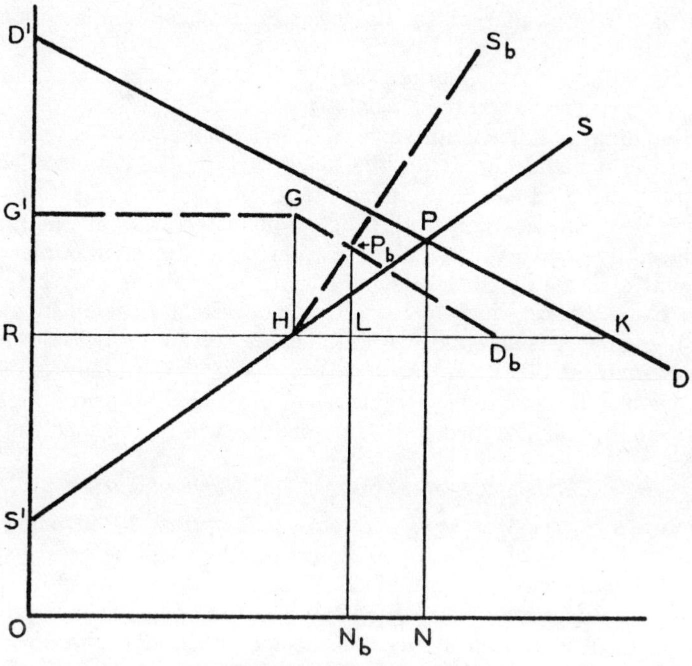

FIGURE 1

Bronfenbrenner used a different diagrammatic presentation of the black market.[4] On the supply side, he suggests, total supply (in both legal and black markets combined) is the same as the quantities supplied in the legal market when no black market exists. Only the distribution of this total supply between the official and black markets will shift in response to a change in price in the latter.

In his construction of the black-market demand curve, Bronfenbrenner regards the excess of quantity demanded over quantity supplied in the official market as the maximum amount demanded in the black market. As to the form of rationing, Bronfenbrenner assumes "neutrality," *i.e.*, a (formal or informal) rationing system that does not discriminate between the more and the less well-off. On this assumption he concludes that the black market demand will be a fraction of the free-market demand, determined by the ratio between excess demand and total demand at the official price.[5]

At this point, however, there appears to be an inconsistency. While the con-

to incorporate it into his black-market supply curve. He was, however, not successful, as he apparently himself recognized by omitting this part when he reproduced most of the note in the revised edition of his *Economic Analysis*.

[4] M. Bronfenbrenner, "Price Control under Imperfect Competition," *Am. Econ. Rev.*, Mar. 1947, XXXVII, 107-20.

[5] *Op. cit.*, p. 112. We shall later see that the assumption of "neutrality" alone is not enough to provide us with this black-market demand curve.

struction of the black-market supply curve is based on the assumption that an increase in the black-market price will bring an enlarged leakage of supply from the official to the black market, the black-market demand curve implies an unchanged excess demand at the official price.[6]

Both Boulding and Bronfenbrenner thus fail to take into account, in constructing their demand curves for the black market, the double effect of the black-market price on demand. In addition, Boulding's presentation of the supply side does not incorporate shifting of quantities from one market to the other induced by changes in the black-market price; Bronfenbrenner does not take account of those portions of supply which are induced only by the existence of a black market, and thus would not be available at all in the official market. The analysis suggested in the following section proposes to overcome these shortcomings. Since the term "black market" is usually applied to a market in which a commodity (or service) is traded at prices *higher* than some *maximum* predetermined price, the analysis will be confined to this case.

I. *The Black-Market Supply and Demand Curves*

The analysis is based on the four main assumptions listed below. In the last section the effects of removing these assumptions will be briefly surveyed. (1) We deal with only one commodity, the market for which is perfectly competitive. (2) The commodity has little weight in consumers' budgets; *i.e.*, changes in its price have no noticeable income effect. (3) The imposition of price control has no psychological or speculative effects on the supply of and demand for the commodity; *i.e.*, the supply and demand schedules are not changed by the mere knowledge that the commodity is excessively demanded. (4) Buyers in the official market do not resell the commodity in the black market. As we proceed with the construction of the black-market curves, auxiliary assumptions will be added, but these may be changed without affecting the main body of the analysis.

We shall define the "inhibited-supply curve" as the schedule of quantities offered at each price higher than the official one (after the decree of price control). It shows the rise in total supply (in the official and black markets combined) called forth by an increase in the black-market price. The "inhibited-demand curve" is the schedule of quantities that would be demanded at each black-market price, should everyone suppose that nothing is available in the official market.

In Figure 2, *DD* and *SS* are the free-market supply and demand curves. An official price, OP_o is now fixed, below the equilibrium price Q_eP_e. The inhibited supply and demand curves become Q_oS' and DD', respectively; DD' is to the left of *DD*, reflecting the additional costs, both monetary and moral, involved in making black-market purchases. For the same reason, Q_oS', the inhibited-supply curve, is to the left of *SS*. P_oQ_o is the amount supplied in the legal market at the official price OP_o. This, however, is true only in the ab-

[6] An earlier comment on this point may be found in J. A. Nordin and Wayne R. Moore, "Bronfenbrenner on the Black Market," *Am. Econ. Rev.*, Dec. 1947, XXXVII, 933-34.

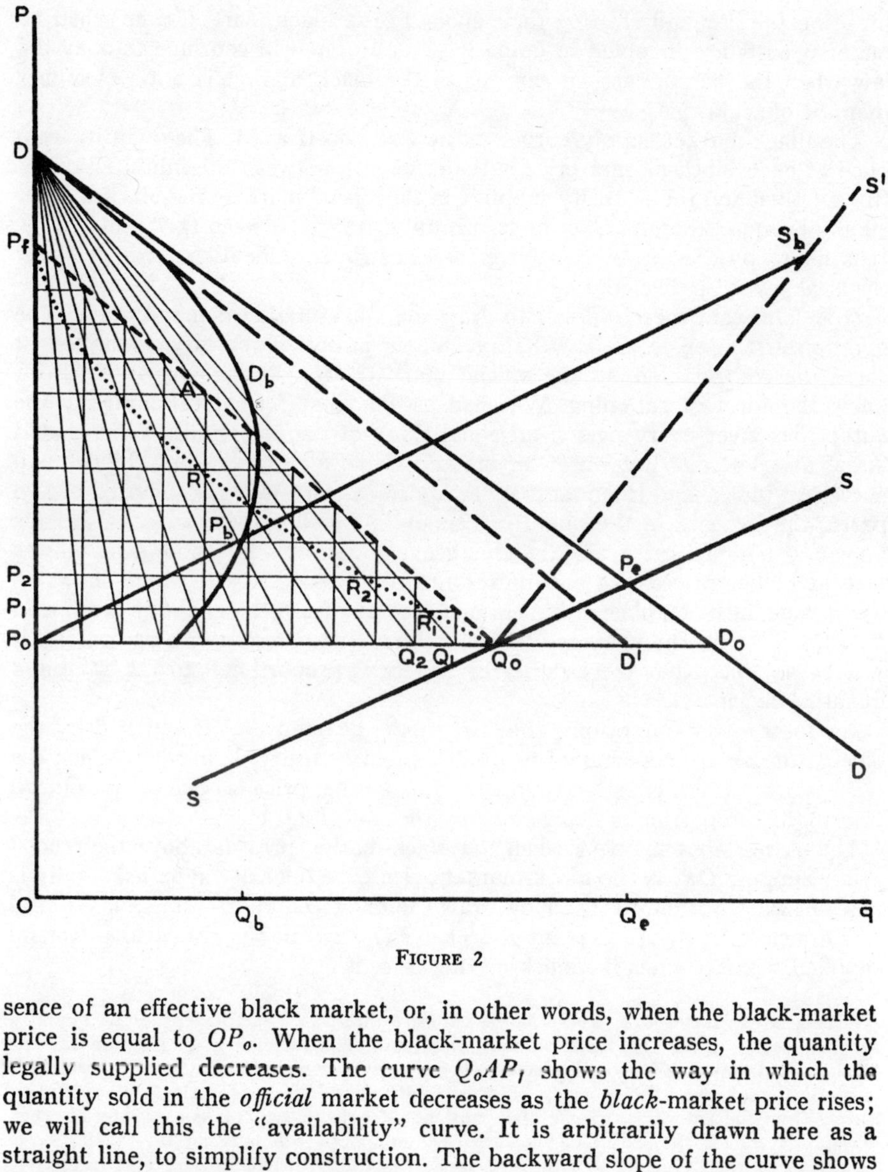

FIGURE 2

sence of an effective black market, or, in other words, when the black-market price is equal to OP_o. When the black-market price increases, the quantity legally supplied decreases. The curve Q_oAP_f shows the way in which the quantity sold in the *official* market decreases as the *black*-market price rises; we will call this the "availability" curve. It is arbitrarily drawn here as a straight line, to simplify construction. The backward slope of the curve shows how a rise in the black-market price overcomes, to an increasing extent, the cost differentials between selling in each of the two markets: differentials created by possible penalties, the necessity of clandestine transaction of black-market business, the difficulties of withdrawing the commodity from the official market without attracting the attention of the authorities, etc. The price rise, we may also assume, progressively offsets lingering ethical objections. Few suppliers may regard a premium of 5 per cent as sufficient compensation for breaking the law and shifting their goods to the black market, even when no material costs are involved in doing it; equally few will continue to obey the law when the net price they can get in the black market is 5 times higher than the official price.[7]

The black-market supply curve can now be constructed. The quantity supplied at each black-market price is the difference between the inhibited quantity supplied and the quantity supplied in the official market; the black-market supply is equal, therefore, to the horizontal distance between Q_oS' and Q_oAP_f. It is shown by the line P_oS_B. Above the price P_f, it is identical with Q_oS', for the legal supply is then zero.

It is somewhat more difficult to draw the black-market demand curve. The question first to be asked is: What part of the inhibited quantity demanded, at each price, is satisfied by the official market? In order to answer we must know the form of rationing. We shall assume that formal rationing by the authorities gives every person an equal share of the commodity.[8] We should know, also, the distribution of buyers and would-be buyers along the demand curve. An increase in the quantity demanded as price falls is composed of two parts: the increase in the quantity demanded by those who would also have bought at a higher price, and the emergence of new buyers, whose demand was zero at higher prices. We are interested in this second part, which shows us the change in the number of buyers prepared to absorb the quantity demanded at each price. In the absence of specific knowledge (or better assumption) it will be assumed that the number of buyers is proportional to the inhibited quantity demanded.[9]

On these two assumptions, the part of the demand that is satisfied by the official market is proportional to the inhibited quantity demanded. When the black market is not effective (and the black-market price is equal to the official price), this proportion is determined by the ratio P_oQ_o to P_oD'.

Let us see what happens when the black-market price is above the official price. Suppose OP_1 is the black-market price. The quantity supplied legally is now not P_oQ_o but only P_oQ_1. Now draw the line Q_1D, intersecting a horizontal line drawn from P_1 at the point R_1. Then P_1R_1 will be the part of the demand supplied officially when the black-market price is OP_1.

[7] There is one factor that works in the opposite direction, *i.e.*, to increase the quantity supplied legally when the black-market price rises: The increase in production for the black market, associated with the increase in price, will often be accompanied by some increase in the amount offered legally, since it is difficult to hide the additional product completely from the authorities; some of it must be offered legally. This is especially so when new producers are the source of the increased supply, since it is easier for existing firms to increase production secretly than for new firms to hide their existence. This factor will cause the availability curve, Q_oAP_f, to be steeper than it would otherwise be. It also will cause Q_oS' to be steeper since the difference between the marginal cost of these units that are offered at the official market, and the (low) price received for them, is an additional cost of the added output produced for the black market.

[8] Instead of formal rationing, Bronfenbrenner's "neutral assumptions" could be used to achieve the same results.

[9] This assumption (as the previous one) is by no means essential to the analysis; alternative assumptions can serve as well.

In a similar way we can find the points R_2, R_3 . . . up to R_f, which is necessarily zero and coincides with P_f. The curve Q_oRP_f, which combines these points, shows that part of the demand which is satisfied legally and will be referred to as the rationing curve. By deducting it from the inhibited-demand curve, DD', we obtain the black-market demand curve, shown in Figure 2 by DD_b.[10] It is identical with the inhibited-demand curve above the price OP_f. At OP_o, the official price, it is equal to Q_oD', the "inhibited excess-demand." Under the circumstances depicted by Figure 2, the black-market price will be Q_bP_b, and the quantity transacted illegally will be OQ_b.

The black-market supply curve is necessarily less steep than the inhibited-supply curve, while its slope may be less than, greater than, or equal to, that of the free-market supply curve. This is due to the fact that every increase in the black-market price will increase the quantity sold illegally, not only by inducing new production for the black market, but also by increasing the transfer of supplies from the official market. On the other hand, the rise in the quantity produced is smaller than it would be in a free market, because of the additional costs, etc, involved in black-market operations. One cannot say which of these two effects will dominate; but certainly the stricter the control is, the steeper will be the black-market supply curve, since stricter control steepens both the inhibited-supply curve and the availability curve.

The black-market demand curve represented in Figure 2 is a rather unusual demand curve—in one part it is positively sloped. The reason for this is that a rise in the black-market price has two effects working in opposite directions on the quantity demanded in the black market: on the one hand, this quantity decreases because the inhibited quantity demanded is reduced; on the other, it is increased because the part of demand supplied legally decreases.[11] Whenever the second factor happens to be the stronger one, the black-market demand curve will be positively sloped. As in Figure 2, we can see that this demand curve will be less steeply sloped negatively and less likely to be positively sloped, the steeper is the rationing curve. The slope of the latter, on the other hand, is positively related to that of the availability curve.

One simple relation between the last-mentioned two curves should be kept in mind, for it will play some part later. The two extreme points of each are

[10] By using this procedure we implicitly assume that the inhibited-demand curve is independent of the rationing curve Q_oRP_f, *i.e.*, changes in the fraction of an inhibited quantity demanded that is satisfied by the legal source do not affect this quantity itself. This, in turn, implies the presumption that the marginal extra costs involved in black-market purchases are constant for the individual consumer. The inhibited-demand curve of the individual, based on this suggestion, is parallel (vertically) to his free-market demand curve. The increasing distance between the two curves as the black-market price drops, in Figure 2, is explained by the increased number of individuals who enter the market when the price declines.

The reader should recall our initial assumption 2, which allows us to abstract from income effects. The average price of the commodity is, therefore, irrelevant at this point, and all we are concerned about is the marginal price.

[11] Underlying this demand curve is a rather special *ceteris paribus* assumption: among the things that are given and unchanged there is not one specific amount of supply to the legal market, but rather a whole schedule of such amounts, related to changes in price in the black market.

coincident (Q_o and P_f), but at any intermediate price the rationing curve must be to the left of the availability curve, or at most tangent to it. The reason for this is that the availability curve shows the total quantity supplied in the official market (at various black-market prices), and the part of the demand supplied by the official market *cannot exceed it*. The two curves will be identical in the improbable case where the quantity supplied legally is sold to those who would be the highest bidders in a free market.

Since the relation between the slopes of the inhibited-demand curve and of the rationing curve determines the slope of the black-market demand curve, the latter will be positively sloped when the first of these two is greater, and negatively sloped in the opposite case. The peculiar shape of the black-market demand curve suggests the paradox that even a case where there is no "inhibited excess-demand" at the official price (*i.e.*, where the inhibited quantity demanded at a black-market price equal to P_o, the official price, is equal to the quantity supplied officially), does not necessarily insure that an effective black market would not prevail. A sufficient degree of discrimination of the rationing system in favor of the less eager demanders, combined with relatively inelastic inhibited supply and demand curves, would insure that the slope of the black-market demand curve, in this section, would be positive and smaller than that of the black-market supply curve. There would be, then, in addition to P_o, another point of intersection of the two curves, at a higher price; of the two possible black-market equilibrium prices (one equal to the official price, the other one higher), the higher one would be in stable equilibrium. In general, the possibility of a black-market demand curve which is positively sloped, suggests that the amount transacted in the black market may be greater than the inhibited excess-demand at the official price.

II. *Equilibrium Prices in the Black and Free Markets*

Interesting results can now be derived by using the tools constructed in the last section. The most important one is probably the following proposition: If the additional costs of operating in the black market are no greater for buyers than they are for sellers, the black-market equilibrium price will be higher, or at least no lower, than the free-market equilibrium price.

To prove it, let us assume momentarily that the inhibited demand and supply curves are identical with the corresponding free-market curves. In Figure 3, *SS* and *DD* are the free-market supply and demand curves, with Q_eP_e the equilibrium price, OP_o the official price, Q_oAP_f the availability curve, and Q_oRP_f the rationing curve. At a black-market price Q_eP_e, the quantity illegally supplied would be AP_e, and the quantity demanded RP_e. As was seen before, R must be to the left of A, or at most identical with it. Thus, RP_e must be greater than AP_e, or at least equal to it. The price Q_eP_e is, therefore, either below the black-market equilibrium price or equal to it. The latter will occur only when either the rationing curve is identical with the availability curve (or is tangent to it at the price Q_eP_e), or when the availability curve is so flat that it will meet the price axis below the price Q_eP_e. In this case the official market will not exist at all, that is, all transactions would be conducted in the black market.

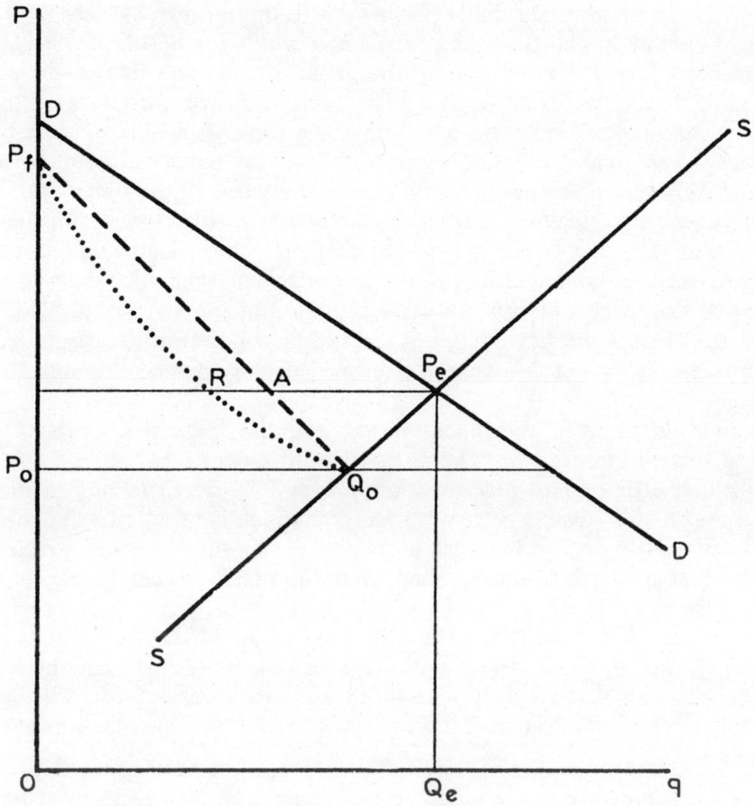

FIGURE 3

To complete the proof we have to replace the assumption momentarily made (the identity of the total supply and demand curves with the corresponding free-market curves) by another one, namely, that at the free-market equilibrium price Q_eP_e, the deviation of the inhibited-demand curve from the free-market demand curve is not greater than the deviation of the inhibited-supply curve from the free-market supply curve. On this assumption, the quantity demanded at the black-market price Q_eP_e is still greater than, or at least equal to, the quantity supplied.

This assumption is, apparently, well in accordance with reality. It is always easier for the authorities to control production and sales than the activities of consumers. It is immensely troublesome to catch the consumer in the act of buying in the black market, or to search consumers' homes for illegally purchased goods. Moreover, the seller in the black market is subject to stronger public criticism than the buyer. Plumptre even tells of a city in which during wartime buying in the black market was something of which to be proud;[12]

[12] *Op. cit.*, p. 282.

the present writer suspects that this was the feeling in many places, and even more widespread in the postwar period. The seller in the black market is a "war-profiteer," one who profits by the general suffering; the buyer, on the other hand, is acquitted, in his own and the public's view, because he "must" buy the scarce commodity, he just "can't manage without it"—be it bread, cigarettes, shoes, cars, or washing machines. The assumption made above seems, therefore, not to narrow significantly the scope of the proposition.

This proposition seems a rather important one. Intuitively it is usually believed that the black-market price is higher than that which would prevail in a free market.[13] Boulding stated that "The black market price may easily be lower than the price which would have obtained in the absence of all regulation."[14] Bronfenbrenner assumed, but did not prove, that in the case of imperfect competition the black-market price "will usually exceed the uncontrolled . . . price."[15]

The relation between the black-market and the free-market prices is not merely a matter of curiosity. The authorities in a controlled economy usually devote much attention to black-market prices. They are anxious to know if they represent the "true" or "real" prices, by which is usually meant the free-market price. Often controlled prices are changed in order to make them more "realistic." It is worth knowing, then, that *the black-market price is not the "real" price but its upper limit.*

Although the black-market price will usually exceed the free-market price, the total quantity produced (for both legal and black market) may be smaller than the quantity that would be produced for a free market; this will happen if the extra costs (material and moral) of producing for the black market are relatively high.

III. *Possible Results of Generalizing the Analysis*

Finally, it is desirable to consider the extent to which the analysis is affected by relaxing the original assumptions. First we may relax Assumption 2, concerning the relative budgetary unimportance of the commodity. If we allow an income effect to exist, the inhibited-demand curve will have to be higher than the one discussed before; instead of having only deductions from the free-market demand curve (caused by material and moral costs), we should also add now the rise in the demand curve brought about by the increase in real income of those served at the cheap official price.[16]

[13] Bronfenbrenner tells how sensational was once the news that, after decontrolling the price of meat, it rose above the previous black-market price. *Op. cit.*, p. 112, fn. 5.

[14] *Op. cit.*, p. 117. Plumptre commented that "black market demand and black market prices are likely to be higher than [Boulding's] note might lead us to believe" (*op. cit.*, p. 280). Plumptre's reasons were mainly that the legal supply does not satisfy the more vigorous demanders first and, in addition, that buyers have a low degree of respect for the law.

[15] *Ibid.*, p. 112.

[16] By incorporating the necessary assumptions regarding the effects of changes in real income on the free-market demand curve, it would be possible to derive the inhibited-demand curve that allows for income effects. The procedure is very similar to the one followed in the construction of the rationing curve Q_oRP_f (Figure 2). This inhibited-demand

Turning to Assumption 3, concerning psychological and other effects on supply and demand, the most important of such effects to be considered are expectations of price increases and fears of more severe shortages in the future arising out of the establishment of price control. Expectations of this sort tend to raise the inhibited demand and decrease the inhibited supply. Such effects seem to be more important immediately after control is established than after price control has existed for some time. There is another significant psychological effect on demand—the creation of a feeling of "shortage," which tends to raise the marginal utility schedule of individuals. People may rush to buy, even in the black market, commodities that are completely useless to them, not because they expect to resell, or to have some need of them in the foreseeable future, but just because of a vague feeling that the commodity must be "worth having" if it is scarce.[17] This response contributes also toward an increase in the inhibited demand curve.

Removal of Assumptions 2 and 3 thus does not seem to damage the main conclusion of the analysis, namely, that the black-market equilibrium price is, in a stated condition, higher than that of the free market. If anything, it rather tends to reinforce the plausibility of the proposition.

Elimination of Assumption 4, that purchasers in the official market will not resell in the black market, would make the construction of the black-market curves exceedingly complicated, but would not appreciably affect the conclusions of the analysis. One may treat the reselling either as an addition to the black-market supply or as a subtraction from the black-market demand. If we follow the latter procedure, we shall have an unchanged black-market supply; on the demand side, however, the rationing curve will be pushed closer to the availability curve, since a greater portion of what was originally available at the legal market is sold to the high bidders. The rationing curve, however, will now have a slightly different meaning, namely, it will show the part of the demand satisfied by *other sources than sales of original suppliers to ultimate buyers in the black market*. Although the black-market price will thus be lower than without reselling, the rationing curve must still be to the left of the availability curve, or at most tangent to it at some or all points; hence the aforementioned proposition will still hold.

Assumption 1, which confines the analysis to the case of a single commodity, the market for which is perfectly competitive, seems to be the most difficult to remove. The shift from one to many industries would involve us in an

curve would be to the right of the one that abstracts from income effects. Moreover, since at lower black-market prices more will be available at the (low) official price, the income effect will be greater the lower the black-market price. The inhibited-demand curve would thus tend to be less concave (or even convex), viewed from the origin, in cases where it was concave when the income effect was neglected; likewise, it will tend to be convex or more convex, respectively, where it was straight line or convex. Consequently, the black-market demand curve would not only be higher than otherwise, but would also be less likely to be positively sloped.

[17] "That peculiar craze for buying which grips people in situation of severe shortage, so that it is a great satisfaction 'to have got hold of something' even if there is no sensible use for what has been bought." Bent Hansen, *A Study in the Theory of Inflation* (London, 1951), p. 128.

aggregative analysis, which is beyond the scope of this paper. Regarding the assumption of perfect competition, it seems to the writer that the analysis presented above could well be extended to include cases of oligopoly or monopoly. The writer does not venture, however, to make the extension. There are reasons to believe that the existence of a black market is less likely where competition is very imperfect; such grounds are suggested by Galbraith,[18] who supports his reasoning by his experience in the OPA during the war. It may be concluded that the analysis presented above, even if we cannot claim general validity for it, probably applies in a great number of practical cases.

MICHAEL MICHAELY*

[18] John Kenneth Galbraith, "Reflections on Price Control," *Quart. Jour. Econ.*, Aug. 1946, LX, 475-89, and *A Theory of Price Control* (Cambridge, 1952), especially Chapters 2 and 3.

* The author is a graduate student at The Johns Hopkins University. He is indebted to Professors Fritz Machlup and Carl F. Christ, for their helpful criticism and suggestions, and to Mr. R. W. Richardson, whose patient attention to argument and style made the paper readable. Any surviving deficiencies in content and exposition are, of course, the sole responsibility of the author.

[15]

PRICE STABILIZATION AND WELFARE *

BENTON F. MASSELL

I. INTRODUCTION

Some time ago Frederick Waugh demonstrated that, with a negatively sloped demand curve, assuming consumers to be price-takers, and starting from a given price, consumers gain more from a price decline than they lose from an equal price rise.[1] They thereby gain from price fluctuations, and accordingly lose from price stabilization. More recently, Walter Oi demonstrated that, with a positively sloped supply curve, and assuming producers to be price-takers, producers also gain from price fluctuations and hence lose from price stabilization.[2] Oi was apparently unaware of Waugh's much earlier work. But, having seen Oi's paper, Waugh restated his argument.[3] Unfortunately, in doing so, he stopped short of integrating the consumer and producer sides of the picture.

It is the purpose of the present paper to integrate the Waugh and Oi results and to consider the welfare effects of price stabilization in a model containing both producers and consumers. Following Waugh and Oi, we shall use as a measure of gain: (a) for producers, the expected value of producer surplus; and (b) for consumers, the expected value of consumer surplus. We thus ignore the effect of price stabilization on the variances of the variables involved. One interpretation of our model is that it assumes individuals to be indifferent to risk. A more palatable interpretation is that we assume the commodity under discussion to form a sufficiently small part of

* I am indebted to Professor R. M. Parish (University of New England, Armidale, Australia) for contributing actively to the formulation of some of the ideas contained in this paper and for stimulating comments on three earlier drafts. I also wish to thank the referee for helpful suggestions concerning the organization of the paper.

1. Frederick V. Waugh, "Does the Consumer Benefit from Price Instability?", this *Journal*, LVIII (Aug. 1944), 602–14.

2. Walter Oi, "The Desirability of Price Instability Under Perfect Competition," *Econometrica*, Vol. 29 (Jan. 1961), pp. 58–64.

3. Frederick V. Waugh, "Consumer Aspects of Price Instability," *Econometrica*, Vol. 34 (April 1966), pp. 504–8.

total producer sales and consumer purchases that a change in its price leaves the marginal utility of money unchanged.

We begin, in the following section, with a review of the results obtained by Waugh and Oi. Then, in Section III, we consider a market consisting of producers and consumers, and examine the gains from price stabilization to each group individually and to society as a whole. It is assumed that the price fluctuations are due to parallel shifts in the demand or supply curves. Following Waugh and Oi, the analysis is presented geometrically, permitting the price to assume only a limited number of values. The assumption of costless storage, made in Section III, is relaxed in Section IV, and the results modified accordingly. In Section V we formulate the model algebraically, with price as a continuously distributed random variable, and consider the gains from price stabilization to producers and consumers jointly. Section VI continues with a discussion of the distribution of the gains between producers and consumers. Then, in Section VII, we extend the analysis to the case of an individual producer or consumer. Section VIII notes the relationship between price stabilization and quantity destabilization.

In Sections II–VIII, stabilization is referred to the arithmetic mean of the price; in Section IX, we indicate how the results can be modified to permit stabilization about a trend. Section X presents some concluding remarks.

II. The Waugh-Oi Results

Waugh's result can be seen in Figure I, where it is assumed that consumers are faced with either of two competitively determined prices: p_1 or p_2.[4] Each price occurs with .5 probability. Using a cardinal measure of utility, consumer surplus, C, can be written

$$(1) \qquad C=\begin{cases} a+b+c+d+f, & p=p_1 \\ f, & p=p_2 \end{cases}.$$

Then the expected value of consumer surplus, $E(C)$, is given by

$$(2) \qquad E(C)=f+\frac{1}{2}(a+b+c+d).$$

Now consider that consumers are given as an alternative a single price, $\mu=\frac{1}{2}(p_1+p_2)$, which obtains with certainty. At this price, the expected value of consumer surplus equals

4. Waugh, this *Journal, op. cit.*

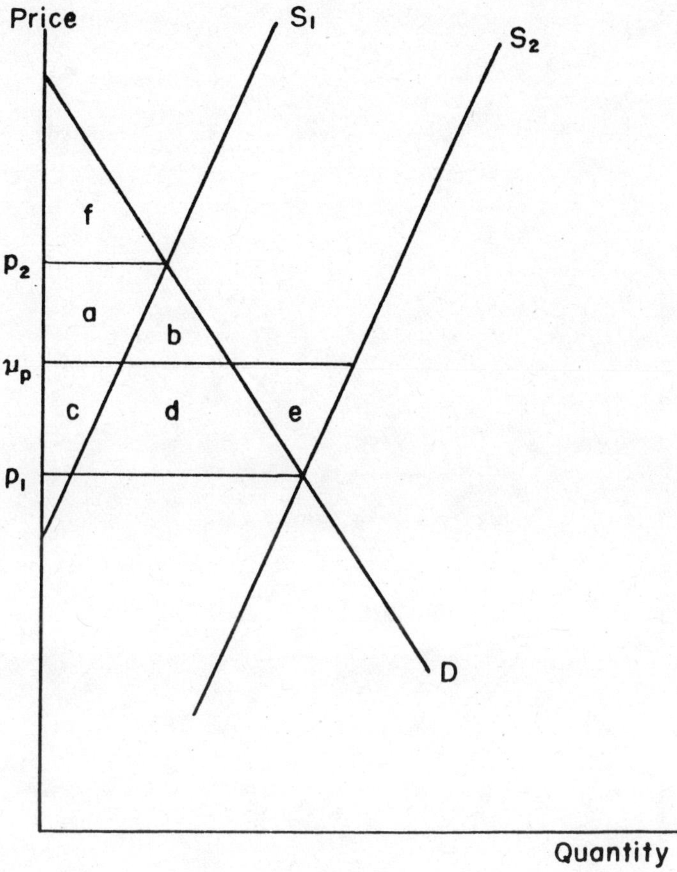

FIGURE I

$$(3) \qquad E(C) = a+b+f.$$

Compared with the prestabilization regime, the consumers stand to lose an amount equal to areas $c+d$ when the market price is p_1 and to gain $a+b$ when the price is p_2. Provided the demand curve is negatively sloped, and subject to the assumption that the marginal utility of money is constant with respect to a change in the price of the item, $c+d>a+b$, so that stabilization provides a net loss, measured in terms of consumer surplus; i.e., $E(C)$ is less in equation (3) than in equation (2).

Oi's argument is formally equivalent to the above.[5] In Figure II, producers are confronted with two prices, each with .5 probabil-

5. Oi, *op. cit.*

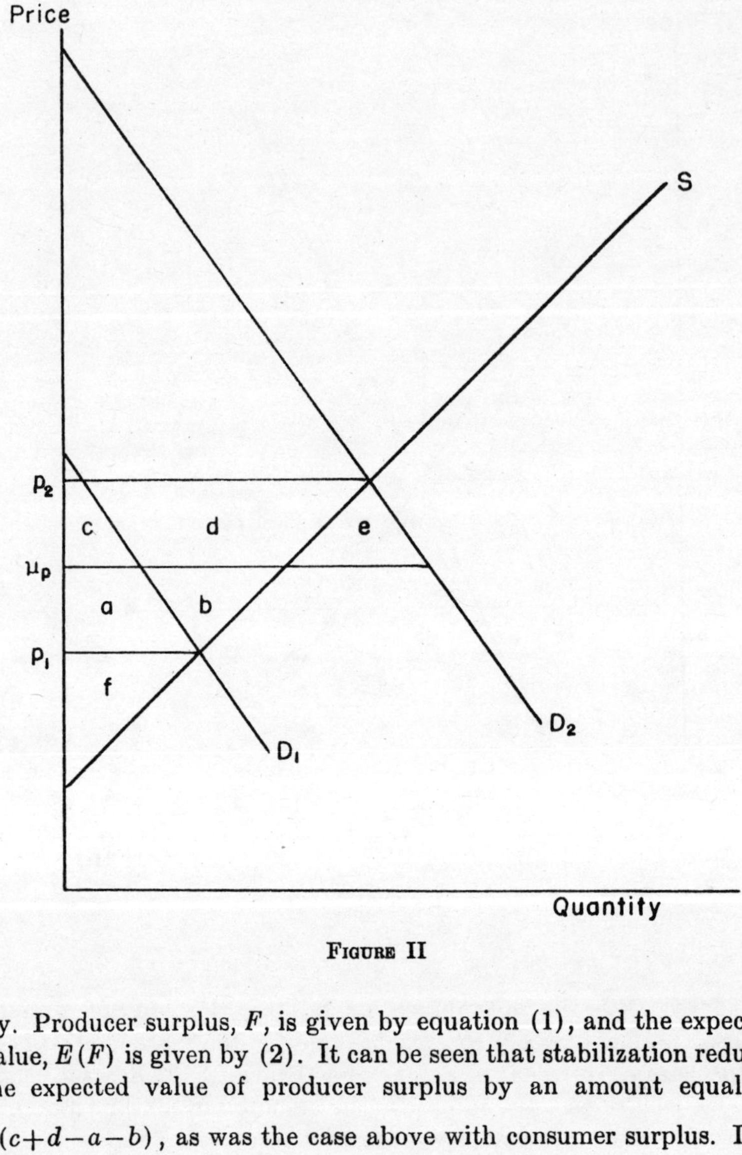

FIGURE II

ity. Producer surplus, F, is given by equation (1), and the expected value, $E(F)$ is given by (2). It can be seen that stabilization reduces the expected value of producer surplus by an amount equal to $\frac{1}{2}(c+d-a-b)$, as was the case above with consumer surplus. It is necessary to assume, as above, that the supply curve is positively sloped and that the marginal utility of money remains constant as producers move along this curve.[6]

6. For a further discussion of this point see: Clem Tisdell, "Uncertainty, Instability, Expected Profit," *Econometrica*, Vol. 31 (Jan.-Apr. 1963), pp. 243-47. Walter Oi, "Rejoinder," *Econometrica*, Vol. 31 (Jan.-Apr. 1963), p. 248.

In Waugh's analysis, consumers gain from a fluctuating price because they can adjust quantity purchased to the price. Thus they are able to buy more at a low than at a high price. If the price is stabilized not at μ_p but at a price p^*, defined

$$(4) \qquad p^* = \frac{q_1 p_1 + q_2 p_2}{q_1 + q_2}$$

where q_1 and q_2 are the quantities demanded at p_1 and p_2 respectively, then consumer welfare is not reduced through stabilization. A corresponding argument holds for producers.[7]

Oi's results depend on the assumption, not made explicit in his analysis, that there is a zero covariance between shifts in the supply curve and changes in the price. His analysis is based on a stationary supply curve, in which case the covariance is trivially zero. Thus, price changes are due solely to shifts in demand.

A similar condition holds for Waugh's results. His analysis implicitly assumes that the demand curve is stationary, so that price changes arise solely from shifts in supply. In this sense, the two sets of results cannot both hold simultaneously.

III. A Model with Producers and Consumers

Consider a market consisting of atomistic consumers and producers. In this market, price fluctuations can arise from shifts in either supply or demand or both. The case of a supply shift is depicted in Figure I and a demand shift in Figure II; in both cases, the curves are assumed to be linear and the shifts to be parallel.

In Figure I we have assumed that the price fluctuations are due to shifts in supply, with S_1 and S_2 each obtaining with .5 probability. The price μ_p is an alternative that can be achieved through a costless storage activity.[8] A buffer stock is set up, with a buying and

Albert Zucker, "On the Desirability of Price Instability: An Extension of the Discussion," *Econometrica*, Vol. 33 (April 1965), pp. 437–41. Oi's result was obtained independently, at about the same time, by Richard R. Nelson, "Uncertainty, Prediction, and Competitive Equilibrium," this *Journal*, LXXV (Feb. 1961), 41–62, in a slightly different context. Nelson's paper draws on this result to build an interesting model of the value of information to the firm. Oi's result was also obtained by H. G. Grubel. "Foreign Exchange Earnings and Price Stabilization Schemes," *American Economic Review*, LIV (June 1964), 378–85. A somewhat less sophisticated presentation of this point appeared earlier in Ragnar Nurkse, "Trade Fluctuations and Buffer Policies of Low-Income Countries," *Kyklos*, XI (Fasc. 2, 1958).

7. Zucker, *op. cit.*

8. In the discussion by Waugh and Oi it is unnecessary to specify how price stabilization is achieved. Here, however, it is necessary. We shall assume that stabilization is brought about by a buffer stock.

selling price equal to μ_p, thereby establishing the market price at this level.

Raising the price from p_1 to μ_p involves a gain to producers of $c+d+e$, and a loss to consumers of $c+d$. If we subtract the consumers loss from the producers gain, there is a net gain equal to area e. Reducing the price from p_2 to μ_p benefits consumers by $a+b$ and costs producers only a; thus again there is a net gain of b. On balance, stabilizing the price at μ_p provides a net gain to producers of $c+d+e-a$, and a net loss to consumers of $c+d-(a+b)$, and therefore a net gain of $b+e$ to consumers and producers jointly. Although this analysis involves the addition of producer and consumer surplus,[9] and thus raises sticky welfare questions, one can argue that producers are able to compensate consumers so as to leave both groups better off. Given costless storage, the stabilization authority breaks even by buying and selling equal amounts at the same price, μ_p.[1]

In Figure II, price fluctuations are caused by shifts in the demand schedule, with D_1 and D_2 each obtaining with .5 probability. By an argument analogous to that above, it can be shown that there is a net gain to consumers of $c+d+e-a$, a net loss to producers of $c+d-(a+b)$, and a net gain to the two groups jointly of $b+e$.

The case considered by Waugh is that shown in Figure I, whereas Oi's results relate to the situation in Figure II. Waugh (Oi) is correct that price stabilization makes consumers (producers) worse off if the source of the instability is shifts in the supply (demand) schedule. However, this is only half of the story. If the instability is due to shifts in demand (supply), then consumers (producers) as a whole gain from a buffer stock scheme that stabilizes the price at μ_p. And the gain to consumers (producers) is sufficiently large to permit compensation, leaving both parties better off.[2]

9. This assumption is made by J. E. Meade "Degrees of Competitive Speculation," *Review of Economic Studies,* XVII (3), 1949–50, No. 44, 159–67, in his analysis of the welfare effects of speculation. Meade's gains from speculation are (not surprisingly) similar to our gains from stabilization.

1. An alternative would be to stabilize the price at $p^* = \dfrac{p_1q_1+p_2q_2}{q_1+q_2}$. In this case areas a and b would be larger and $c+d$ smaller, so that $a+b=c+d$. Consumers would then be indifferent to stabilization while producers would gain. However, the price p^* would not be an equilibrium price, as there would be on balance an excess demand providing pressure for the stabilization authority to raise the price.

2. Viewed differently, whereas the Waugh (Oi) results implicitly assume zero correlation between demand (supply) shifts and price changes, the analysis of the present section assumes perfect correlation.

IV. A Positive Storage Cost

A positive storage cost can easily be accommodated in the model. Figure III corresponds to Figure I, except that here the stabilization authority has set a buying price of $p_1' > p_1$ and a selling price of $p_2' < p_2$. As in Figure I producers and consumers jointly gain $e+b$ from stabilization, although these areas are smaller here than in Figure I. The stabilization authority makes a gross return of $p_2' - p_1'$ on each unit of the product handled. The pegged prices can be set so that $p_2' - p_1' = J$, the unit cost of storage. Stabilization will always afford a gain if $J < p_2 - p_1$.

V. The Gains from Price Stabilization: A More General Analysis

This section presents a more general analysis of the gains from price stabilization. Here the supply and demand curves each have a shift factor that is a continuously distributed random variable. Consider a competitively priced commodity with supply and demand curves of the form

$$S = \alpha p + x \qquad (\alpha \geqslant 0) \tag{5}$$

$$D = -\beta p + y \qquad (\beta \geqslant 0) \tag{6}$$

where S = quantity supplied, D = quantity demanded, p = price, α and β are constants, and x and y are jointly distributed random variables with means μ_x and μ_y, variances σ_{xx}, and σ_{yy} covariance $\sigma_{xy} = 0$.

By assuming that $\sigma_{xy} = 0$, we are in effect postulating a market in which shifts in demand and shifts in supply are influenced by different sets of forces. Shifts in demand may be related to changes in income and tastes, and in the prices of substitutes and complements; whereas shifts in supply may be related to changes in factor costs and technology. In the case of agricultural commodities, there are typically large shifts in supply because of factors related to the weather,[3] which are unrelated to the factors influencing demand.[4]

The equilibrium price and quantity traded are given by

$$p = \frac{y - x}{\alpha + \beta} \tag{7}$$

3. We are using "supply" here in an *ex post* sense, and not in the conventional *ex ante* sense. Thus the weather does not affect planting decisions (*ex ante* supply), but does affect the harvest (*ex post* supply).

4. If $\sigma_{xy} > 0$, the gains from stabilization are reduced but not eliminated.

$$q=\frac{\alpha y+\beta x}{\alpha+\beta} \tag{8}$$

where $\alpha+\beta>0$, $p\geqslant 0$, and $q\geqslant 0$.

Consider that the mean price, μ_p, is known, and that a decision is made to eliminate price fluctuations by establishing a buffer stock authority that stands ready to buy or sell at μ_p. Stocks held by the authority are stored at zero cost. In any one year, producers gain

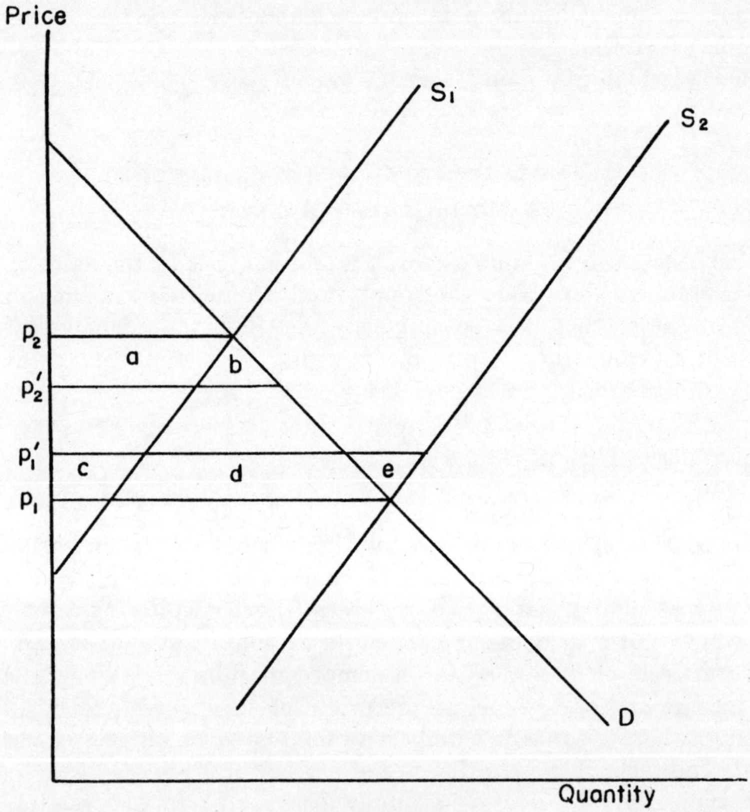

FIGURE III

an amount corresponding to $c+d+e$ in Figure I or $a+b$ in Figure II.[5] Algebraically, letting G_p = the gain to producers (i.e., the increase in producer surplus), we can write [6]

5. This amount may be negative.

6. Geometrically, this gain is the sum of the areas of a rectangle and a triangle. The area of the rectangle is given by the product $(\mu_p-p)[S(p)]$,

$$G_p = \frac{1}{2}(\mu_p - p)[S(p) + S(\mu_p)] \tag{9}$$

where

$$\mu_p = \frac{\mu_y - \mu_x}{\alpha + \beta}. \tag{10}$$

Substituting (5), (7), and (10) into (9), and simplifying,

$$G_p = \frac{1}{2}\left[\frac{\mu_y - \mu_x - (y - x)}{\alpha + \beta}\right]\left[2x + \frac{\alpha(\mu_y - \mu_x + y - x)}{\alpha + \beta}\right]. \tag{11}$$

Integrating over x and y, the expected value of the gain can be written [7]

$$E(G_p) = \frac{(\alpha + 2\beta)\sigma_{xx} - \alpha\sigma_{yy}}{2(\alpha + \beta)^2}. \tag{12}$$

Next, consider the effect of price stabilization on consumer welfare, measured as the expected value of the change in consumer surplus. Denoting the gain from price stabilization by G_c, we can write [8]

$$E(G_c) = \frac{(2\alpha + \beta)\sigma_{yy} - \beta\sigma_{xx}}{2(\alpha + \beta)^2}. \tag{13}$$

To derive the total gain, G, we add the gains to consumers and to producers:

$$G = G_p + G_c. \tag{14}$$

Substituting (12) and (13) into (14), and simplifying,

$$E(G) = \frac{\sigma_{yy} + \sigma_{xx}}{2(\alpha + \beta)} \tag{15}$$

which is necessarily nonnegative and is positive if either σ_{yy} or σ_{xx} is. Thus those gaining from stabilization can compensate those losing, leaving everyone better off. This is then a generalization of the conclusions presented in Section III.

It can be seen that the price variance is given by

$$\sigma_{pp} = \frac{\sigma_{yy} + \sigma_{xx}}{(\alpha + \beta)^2} \tag{16}$$

thus

and the area of the triangle can be written $\frac{1}{2}(\mu_p - p)[S(\mu_p) - S(p)]$. Equation (9) is the sum of these two expressions.

7. Remember it is assumed that $\sigma_{xy} = 0$.

8. G_c is given by the areas $a+b$ in Figure I, $c+d+e$ in Figure II. The derivation of the algebraic expression for G_c is analogous to that for G_p, above.

$$(17)\qquad E(G)=\left[\frac{a+\beta}{2}\right]\sigma_{pp}\,.$$

It follows that the gains from price stabilization will tend to be greater the greater the degree of price instability. From (15) we see that $E(G)$ is greater the larger are the demand and supply variances and the steeper the two curves.

VI. The Distribution of Gains Among Producers and Consumers

In deriving expression (15) for the total gains, we obtained expressions for the gains to producers and consumers individually. Although there is necessarily a total net gain, it is possible for one group to gain at the expense of the other. It is correspondingly of interest to consider the conditions under which each group gains from stabilization.

From equation (12) we see that

$$(18)\qquad E(G_p)>0 \text{ if } \frac{\sigma_{yy}}{\sigma_{xx}}<\frac{2\beta}{a}+1\,.$$

Producers are more likely to gain the larger the supply variance relative to the demand variance. Further, the likelihood of gain is greater the steeper the supply curve relative to the demand curve. In the limiting case of either a vertical supply curve or a zero demand variance, producers cannot lose from price stabilization.

The factors that influence the likelihood of a gain are nearly (but not exactly) the same as the factors that influence the magnitude of the gain. By differentiating (12) with respect to σ_{xx}, σ_{yy}, a, and β, we find that the magnitude of the gain to producers is a decreasing function of the demand variance and an increasing function of the supply variance and of the steepness of the supply curve. The relationship between $E(G_p)$ and the demand slope is more complex. It can be shown that

$$(19)\qquad \frac{\partial E(G_p)}{\partial\beta}>0 \text{ if } \frac{\beta}{a}<\frac{\sigma_{yy}}{\sigma_{xx}}\,.$$

Thus, beyond some point, further increases in the demand slope reduce the gain to producers. This results from the fact that the denominator of (12) increases faster than the numerator. In the limiting case of a horizontal demand curve, the price is stable even without a buffer stock, so the problem is irrelevant.[9]

9. In an important sense, this result is built into the model, by specifying

The gain to consumers was given by (13). A condition for this expression to be positive is

$$E(G_c) > 0 \text{ if } \frac{\sigma_{xx}}{\sigma_{yy}} < \frac{2a}{\beta} + 1 . \tag{22}$$

This expression is analogous to that for producers. Consumers are more likely to gain, the larger the demand variance relative to the supply variance, and the steeper the demand curve relative to the supply curve. In the limiting case of a vertical demand curve, consumers cannot lose from price stabilization. Similarly, consumers cannot lose from stabilization if the supply variance is zero. The results of the present section can be viewed as an extension of the results obtained in Section III.

VII. Gains to Individual Producers and Consumers

Although producers as a whole may benefit from price stabilization, some producers may gain at the expense of others. It is of interest to consider the conditions under which the gains are positive to an individual producer — or a subset of producers. The notion of a subset of producers has particular real-world relevance if one wishes to consider whether an individual producing-country gains from an international buffer stock. For expository convenience we shall refer only to a single producer, but the analysis of this section can equally well apply to a subset of producers. We shall also discuss the gains to an individual consumer.

Consider an individual producer with supply curve

$$s = \gamma p + z \qquad (\gamma \geqslant 0) \tag{23}$$

where $s =$ the firm's output and z is a random variable with mean and variance, μ_z and σ_{zz}. It is assumed that the producer is sufficiently small to be a price-taker. By the same method used in Section V, we may obtain the gain to the producer, g_p. Write

the demand shift as linear in the quantity (rather than price) variable. Strictly speaking, the demand curve shifts perpendicularly to the horizontal axis. The effect of a demand shift on the price diminishes as the demand curve becomes flatter, and becomes zero when the demand curve is horizontal. This assumption is acceptable if it is understood that one is discussing only demand curves that are fairly steep.

An alternative formulation would be to write

$$D = -\beta p + y[\lambda + \beta(1-\lambda)] \qquad (0 \leqslant \lambda \leqslant 1). \tag{20}$$

Here, the demand curve shifts relative to both axes. The analysis can be generalized by substituting (20) for (6). It can be shown that, with this formulation,

$$\lim_{\beta \to \infty} \sigma_{pp} = \sigma_{yy}(1-\lambda)^2, \tag{21}$$

which is positive if $\sigma_{yy} > 0$ and $\lambda < 1$.

$$(24) \qquad g_p = \frac{1}{2}(\mu_p - p)\,[s(p) + s(\mu_p)]\,.$$

Substituting; integrating over x, y, and z; and simplifying, the expected value of the gain can be written

$$(25) \qquad E(g_p) = \frac{1}{\alpha+\beta}\left[\sigma_{xz} - \frac{\gamma}{2(\alpha+\beta)}(\sigma_{yy} + \sigma_{xx})\right]$$

where it is assumed that $\sigma_{yz}=0$. It can be seen that

$$(26) \qquad E(g_p) > 0 \text{ if } \frac{2\sigma_{xz}}{\sigma_{yy}+\sigma_{xx}} > \frac{\gamma}{\alpha+\beta}\,.$$

If the individual producer's supply curve is influenced by some of the same forces that affect the industry's supply curve, then $\sigma_{xz}>0$. Whether the producer gains from stabilization will then depend on the values of the parameters in inequality (26). He will be more likely to gain — and the gain will be greater — the larger is the covariance between his and the industry's supply curve, relative to the industry supply and demand variances. An intuitive interpretation of this result is that the industry will tend to be in a Section III rather than a Section II situation. He is also more likely to gain the steeper is his supply curve relative to the industry supply and demand curves. In the limiting case, where his supply curve is vertical (assuming $\sigma_{xz} \geqslant 0$), he cannot lose from stabilization.

Consider next the effect of price stabilization on consumer welfare, measured as the expected value of the change in consumer surplus. Let the individual consumer's demand curve be written

$$(27) \qquad d = -\delta p + v \qquad (\delta \geqslant 0).$$

Denoting by g_c the gain from price stabilization we can write

$$(28) \qquad E(g_c) = \frac{1}{\alpha+\beta}\left[\sigma_{yv} - \frac{\delta}{2(\alpha+\beta)}(\sigma_{yy} + \sigma_{xx})\right]$$

assuming $\sigma_{xv}=0$. Thus

$$(29) \qquad E(g_c) > 0 \text{ if } \frac{2\sigma_{yv}}{\sigma_{yy}+\sigma_{xx}} > \frac{\delta}{\alpha+\beta}\,.$$

The reader will note the similarity between (29) and (26). A consumer is most likely to gain if the covariance between his and the industry's demand curve is large relative to the industry demand and supply variances, and if his demand curve is steep relative to the industry demand and supply curves.[1]

1. An interpretation of the Oi-Waugh results is that they relate not to producers (consumers) as a whole but to an individual producer (consumer). In the case considered by Oi, it is then implicitly assumed that $\sigma_{xz}=0$, and $\gamma>0$, so that (26) does not hold, and the producer loses from stabilization.

VIII. Quantity Destabilization

If producers benefit from price stabilization, a likely result is the destabilization of the quantity sold. Denote by σ^*_{SS} and σ_{SS} the variance in producers' sales with and without price stabilization. Then let $\triangle\sigma_{SS}=\sigma^*_{SS}-\sigma_{SS}$. Now

$$\text{(30)} \quad \sigma_{SS}=E[a(p-\mu_p)+(x-\mu_x)]^2 = \frac{a[a\sigma_{yy}-(a+2\beta)\sigma_{xx}]}{(a+\beta)^2}+\sigma_{xx}$$

$$\text{(31)} \quad \sigma_{SS}^*=\sigma_{xx}.$$

Thus, subtracting (30) from (31), and substituting (12),

$$\text{(32)} \quad \triangle\sigma_{SS}=2aE(G_p).$$

Therefore, if $a>0$, then $\triangle\sigma_{SS}>0$ if and only if $E(G_p)>0$, establishing the link between producer gain and quantity destabilization.[2]

It is easy to show for consumers, as we did for producers, that if price stabilization increases consumer surplus, it must destabilize the quantity purchased, assuming the demand curve to be negatively sloped.

Assuming that neither the supply nor the demand curve is vertical, then either the quantity purchased by consumers or the quantity sold by producers must be destabilized. If consumer purchases are destabilized, then consumers gain; and if producer sales are destabilized, then producers gain. This suggests some scope for empirical research on particular stabilization schemes. In the absence of stabilization, $\sigma_{DD}=\sigma_{SS}$. Thus if $\sigma^*_{DD}>\sigma^*_{SS}$, it follows that $\triangle\sigma_{DD}>0$. Similarly, if $\sigma^*_{SS}>\sigma^*_{DD}$, then $\triangle\sigma_{SS}>0$. Therefore, if under stabilization, the variance in consumer purchase exceeds the variance in producer sales, then consumers have necessarily gained. Alternatively, if the variance in producer sales exceeds the

Similarly, with Waugh's implicit assumption that $\sigma_{yv}=0$ and $\delta>0$, (29) does not hold and the consumer also loses from stabilization. Although the Waugh and Oi results cannot both hold for consumers and producers as a whole, it is certainly possible for individual consumers and producers to lose from stabilization, if σ_{xz} and σ_{yv} are sufficiently small.

One can no doubt find the isolated producer whose *ex post* supply curve shifts in a way that is independent of shifts in the total supply curve for the product. This would be the case for a good whose supply curve shifts mainly in response to changes in the weather, and with respect to a producer situated in a climatically atypical area. However, it is a very special assumption, even for an individual producer and is less likely to hold for a group of producers. Similarly, the factors influencing shifts in demand are likely to affect large groups of consumers in roughly the same way. This is particularly the case for the derived demand by firms — for example, for materials for further processing.

2. If $a=0$, then $\Delta\sigma_{SS}=0$.

variance in consumer purchases, producers have necessarily gained. This method permits us to determine that one group has gained. It does not permit us to say whether the other group has gained or lost. However, the more nearly equal are the two variances, and the more nearly equal are the slopes of the two curves, the greater the likelihood that both groups have gained.

IX. Time Trend

Our analysis has proceeded thus far on the implicit assumption that there is no time trend in either demand or supply, and therefore in price or quantity traded. Clearly, if there is a trend, then stabilization of price about the mean would make little sense, and would produce some odd results.

Consider that both the demand and supply curves shift linearly to the right over time, not necessarily at the same rate. If the demand curve shifts faster (slower) than the supply curve, there will be an upward (downward) linear trend in price; only if the two curves shift at the same rate, will price contain no time trend. The reader can easily verify that the analysis of Sections V–VII holds if price is stabilized about the trend instead of about the mean. The stabilization authority is then assumed to know the expected value of price as a function of time.[3]

X. Conclusions

The present paper has tried to reconcile the analyses presented by Walter Oi and Frederick Waugh, concerning the gains to producers and consumers resulting from a stable as compared with a fluctuating price. Using the expected value of the change in producer and consumer surplus as a measure of gain, we have shown that price stabilization, brought about by a buffer stock, provides a net gain to producers and consumers taken together.

It is tempting to argue from this that a buffer stock is a desirable policy measure. However, one should bear in mind the simplifications underlying the analysis. First, we assumed storage to be costless. Taking the cost of storage into account would reduce the gains from price stabilization.

3. If storage operations stabilize price about a trend, the storage authority will no longer earn zero profits: instead, profits will be positive or negative depending on whether the price trend is rising or falling.

Second, we ignored the effect of price stabilization on the variance of producers' and consumers' incomes. This is particularly serious with respect to producers, because income from the commodity produced is likely to form a large part of total income. If price stabilization increased the expected value of producers' income but also increased the variance, then producers might on balance suffer a welfare decline. A more complete analysis would consider this aspect of the problem as well.

Third, we have assumed that μ_p was known so that the price could be stabilized at this level. It goes without saying that one of the chief difficulties of a price stabilization scheme is to predict the changes in the equilibrium market price.

FOOD RESEARCH INSTITUTE
STANFORD UNIVERSITY

[16]

CHAPTER FOUR

Economic Effects of Voluntary Export Restrictions

FRED MANNERING and CLIFFORD WINSTON

IN 1981, under the pressure of record financial losses in the automobile industry and the near bankruptcy of Chrysler Corporation, the U.S. government negotiated voluntary export restrictions with the Japanese government that limited total annual sales of new Japanese cars to 1.68 million vehicles (1980 Japanese retail passenger car sales in the United States had been 1.90 million vehicles).[1] In 1984 the restrictions were extended for another year, but the quota was raised to 1.85 million vehicles. Record profits in 1984 seemed to testify to the health of the U.S. industry, and the government allowed the restrictions to expire in March 1985. But apparently fearful of fanning the flames of protectionist sentiment in the White House and the Congress, the Japanese government decided in 1985 to limit the sales to 2.3 million vehicles. In 1987 the Japanese government announced that Japanese automakers would abide by the agreement until March 31, 1988.

The object of the restrictions has been to provide the U.S. automobile industry with time to retool and meet the Japanese challenge, thereby saving American jobs. The actual effects on consumers, automakers, and automobile workers, however, call into serious question the effectiveness of the restrictions in achieving their objective.

Conceptual Framework

Our discussion uses the automobile demand models presented in chapter 3 to assess whether consumers would have been economically

1. Motor Vehicle Manufacturing Association of the United States, *MVMA Motor Vehicle Facts & Figures '86* (Detroit: MVMA, 1986), p. 16.

better off with or without the restrictions.[2] Our analysis improves upon previous work by taking into account the effect of the restrictions on the prices of used vehicles, changes in vehicle quality mix and macroeconomic conditions, and shifts in consumers' choice of vehicle type in response to price changes induced by the restrictions.[3]

The first step in the comparison is calculating the prices of new and used U.S. and Japanese cars both with and without the restrictions. The prices of new cars with the restrictions are simply market prices in 1981–84; the prices of used cars for this period are estimated by the market

2. Formally, the change in welfare attributable to the restrictions is measured by compensating variations that indicate how much money a consumer would have to be given after a change in price or quality or both to be as well off as he was before the change. Given the logit automobile demand models presented in chapter 3, the compensating variations can be calculated using the formula presented by Kenneth A. Small and Harvey S. Rosen, "Applied Welfare Economics with Discrete Choice Models," *Econometrica*, vol. 49 (January 1981), pp. 105–30:

$$CV = -1/\lambda \left[\ln \sum_{i=1}^{n} \exp(V_i) \right]_{P_o}^{P_f},$$

where CV is the compensating variation, λ is the marginal utility of income, V_i is the mean (indirect) utility based on the vehicle type-choice specification given in appendix A to chapter 3 (which permits welfare calculations because it satisfies the condition that the demand for vehicle types is given by Roy's Identity), n is the number of vehicle types, and the square brackets indicate the difference in the expression inside when evaluated at prices of new and used U.S. and Japanese cars with no restrictions, P_O, and at prices of new and used U.S. and Japanese cars with restrictions, P_f.

In a logit model, the term in brackets equals the expected maximum utility obtainable from the available choices. The difference in utility from initial to final points is multiplied by the inverse of the marginal utility of income (that is, the dollars per unit of marginal utility) to yield a dollar value of the change in consumers' utility from the restrictions. Given our choice specifications for vehicle types (using Roy's Identity), the marginal utility of income, λ, equals minus the capital cost coefficient divided by household income.

3. Among the previous studies of the economic effects of the restrictions are José A. Gomez-Ibañez, Robert A. Leone, and Stephen A. O'Connell, "Restraining Auto Imports: Does Anyone Win?" *Journal of Policy Analysis and Management*, vol. 2, no. 2 (1983), pp. 196–219; David G. Tarr and Morris E. Morkre, *Aggregate Costs to the United States of Tariffs and Quotas on Imports: General Tariff Cuts and Removal of Quotas on Automobiles, Steel, Sugar, and Textiles*, Bureau of Economics staff report to the Federal Trade Commission (Government Printing Office, December 1984); Robert C. Feenstra, "Voluntary Export Restraints in U.S. Autos, 1980–81: Quality, Employment, and Welfare Effects," in Robert E. Baldwin and Anne O. Krueger, eds., *The Structure and Evolution of Recent U.S. Trade Policy* (University of Chicago Press, 1984); and Junichi Goto, "A General Equilibrium Analysis of Trade Restrictions under Imperfect Competition Theory and Some Evidence for the Automotive Trade," World Bank discussion paper no. DRD 130 (July 1985).

Table 4-1. Percentage Reduction in New Car Prices If Japanese Imports Had Not Been Restricted, 1981–84

Year	*Japanese autos*	*U.S. autos*[a]
1981	−0.1	0
1982	3.3	1.3
1983	17.3	6.9
1984	20.0	8.0

Source: Authors' calculations based on Robert W. Crandall, "Assessing the Impacts of the Automobile Voluntary Export Restraints upon U.S. Automobile Prices," paper presented to the Society of Government Economists, New York, December 1985.

a. Based on Crandall's estimate of conjectural elasticity of 0.4.

equilibrium model presented in chapter 3.[4] Calculations of what the prices of new U.S. and Japanese cars would have been in 1981–84 without the restrictions are based on an analysis by Robert Crandall.[5] Crandall developed a model to predict what new Japanese car prices in the United States would have been without restrictions, controlling for Japanese factor prices, exchange rates, vehicle option mix, and U.S. regulations on emissions. He then calculated the percentage increase in new Japanese car prices that could be attributed to the restrictions. Percentage increases in new U.S. car prices attributable to the restrictions were made by estimating the U.S. manufacturers' response to the Japanese car price increases—an elasticity of 0.4. The restrictions led to substantial price increases by both U.S. and Japanese automakers (table 4-1). By 1984 Japanese prices were roughly 20 percent higher than they would have been without the restrictions.

Estimates of what new car prices would have been if the restrictions had not been instituted can be made by reducing the actual new car prices in 1981–84 by the percentages given in table 4-1.[6] From these estimated prices, the equilibrium model estimates what used car prices and aggregate sales of U.S. and Japanese vehicles would have been without the restrictions. These predictions of average vehicle prices and total sales with and without the restrictions make it possible to calculate the change in U.S. and Japanese automakers' profits.

4. For new car prices see *Automotive News*, various issues 1981–84. Used car prices are predicted rather than actual to maintain consistency with the used car prices we must estimate for conditions not subject to restraints.

5. Robert W. Crandall, "Assessing the Impacts of the Automobile Voluntary Export Restraints upon U.S. Automobile Prices," paper presented to the Society of Government Economists, New York, December 1985.

6. Due to the absence of disaggregate estimates, we must assume these percentages apply uniformly to all vehicle types.

Estimates of the effects of the restrictions on U.S. automobile industry employment can be made using the U.S. labor demand function estimated in chapter 2. Because labor demand depends upon automobile output, these effects can be predicted by using output levels generated with and without the restrictions.

Results

Although international trade theory predicts that restricting free trade in imperfectly competitive industries, such as the automobile industry, will cause both domestic and foreign firms to raise their prices, it does not predict unambiguously what will happen to domestic firms' output.[7] One explanation is that trade restrictions allow domestic firms to raise prices because they know they will not lose sales to foreign firms. Thus the restrictions make the domestic firms' residual demand curve less elastic and induce them to equate marginal revenue and marginal cost at a higher price and a lower output than they would under free trade.[8] Alternatively, restrictions could cause an increase in domestic firms' residual demand, leading to an equilibrium at a higher price and higher output. In theory, then, trade restrictions can either increase or decrease domestic firms' output.

The estimated effect of the voluntary restrictions accepted by Japan has been a reduction in U.S. industry output from the levels that would have existed under unrestricted trade. As estimated in table 4-2, by 1984 industry output was reduced by roughly 300,000 vehicles.[9] Although cutting production at the very time Japanese competitors have agreed to curb sales may seem counterintuitive, the response is explained by the

7. See, for example, Kala Krishna, "Trade Restrictions as Facilitating Practices," Woodrow Wilson School discussion paper 55 (October 1983); and David Kreutzer, "Negative Output Response to Quota Protection" (unpublished paper, James Madison University, July 1985).

8. Because a change in elasticity will not influence domestic firms' output decisions under perfect competition, this explanation assumes an imperfectly competitive industry structure.

9. Although the price elasticities obtained from the logit type-choice models are reasonable (see appendix B to chapter 3), they do not reflect household changes in the number of vehicles owned in response to price changes and thus understate household total demand elasticities. The impact of quota-induced price increases on industry output is underestimated because for such increases output would fall further with more elastic demands.

Table 4-2. U.S. and Japanese Vehicle Sales and Average Prices with and without Trade Restrictions, 1982–84
Prices in current dollars

Item	*1982*	*1983*	*1984*
U.S. sales			
Restricted	5,803,632	6,703,788	7,548,168
Unrestricted	5,878,909	6,929,536	7,851,302
U.S. average new vehicle prices			
Restricted	9,742	10,248	10,713
Unrestricted	9,555	9,659	9,599
Japanese sales			
Restricted	1,848,329	1,922,937	1,912,249
Unrestricted	1,886,549	2,084,803	2,164,096
Japanese average new vehicle prices			
Restricted	7,952	8,462	9,574
Unrestricted	7,639	7,044	7,001

Source: Authors' calculations.

change in U.S. industry profits attributable to the restrictions. We estimate that by 1984 the restrictions led to an $8.9 billion increase in U.S. producers' profits, virtually all of the industry's record profits that year.[10] But the U.S. automakers were not alone in harvesting the benefits. Substantial vehicle price increases enabled the Japanese to earn at least an additional $3 billion in revenues by 1984.[11]

Estimates of the deadweight cost of the restrictions, that is, the difference between the loss to household vehicle owners and the gain in profits by automakers, are striking. By 1984, when the restrictions were binding very tightly, the welfare cost to household vehicle owners was roughly $14 billion, while automakers increased profits nearly $9 billion.[12]

10. The change in profits is determined by taking the estimated output response and the U.S. cost function in chapter 2 to determine the change in costs and by taking the estimated output and price response to determine the change in revenues.

11. The theoretical possibility of this result is discussed in Krishna, "Trade Restrictions as Facilitating Practices." The figure reported here represents a lower-bound gain in profits because total Japanese costs were reduced by the lower output. The Japanese automakers probably used the additional capacity caused by the restrictions for additional domestic or other foreign sales. Thus we cannot calculate the effect of the restrictions on Japanese industry profits in the same manner as we did for the U.S. industry.

12. Estimates of the cost to vehicle owners were obtained by the Small-Rosen formula using the household as our unit of measurement. This unit is used because the demand model estimated the vehicle purchasing decisions of households. In addition,

Table 4-3. Estimated Change in U.S. Automobile Employment Attributable to Voluntary Export Restrictions, 1982–84

Year	*Number of workers*	*Average industry wage (dollars)*
1982	−7,265	34,323
1983	−23,448	35,473
1984	−31,754	37,007

Source: Authors' calculations.

Thus the deadweight loss to U.S. society from the restrictions approached $5 billion; it was less than $2 billion when more than $3 billion in revenue gains to the Japanese are accounted for.[13]

This result may be somewhat disturbing to policymakers, but not so disturbing as the impact of the restrictions on automobile employment. As table 4-3 shows, the fall in U.S. automakers' output caused by the increased vehicle prices associated with restrictions led to an estimated loss in employment of more than 30,000 workers by 1984.[14] At the average industry wage, such a cut would amount to more than a $1 billion reduction in the total wage bill. To be sure, the average industry wage has probably increased because of the restrictions, and workers who were able to share the U.S. industry profits have received a benefit that partially offsets this overall loss to labor. Further, increasing numbers

because the demand model is a probabilistic choice model, we must include all households regardless of vehicles chosen or ownership levels. Aggregate estimates were obtained by estimating the cost per household by ownership level and multiplying this figure by the number of households in that ownership level. The cost of the restrictions for all ownership levels was then tabulated. For households with no vehicles or with three or more, we used the average welfare cost for one- and two-vehicle households, then explored alternative welfare cost assumptions and found no significant qualitative changes in our findings. Finally, this analysis assumes that households do not change ownership levels in response to quota-induced price changes. This assumption is reasonable given the relatively constant share of ownership levels during the past decade. For example, the largest change in each ownership level from 1977 to 1983 was less than 2.2 percent. The change in the number of households that do not own a vehicle was 1.9 percent. See MVMA, *Motor Vehicle Facts & Figures '86*, p. 42.

13. Using a different methodology, Goto estimates the deadweight loss to U.S. society from the restrictions to be $5.5 billion in 1984 dollars. See "General Equilibrium Analysis of Trade Restrictions," p. 48. Because we do not account for the additional gain to Japanese producers from lower costs, $2 billion represents an upper bound on the U.S.-Japan deadweight loss. A world deadweight loss would have to include profits to European producers generated by the restrictions.

14. As indicated in note 9, the loss in employment is actually understated by our logit type choice models.

of Japanese automobile plants in the United States mean increasing U.S. automobile employment in some regions of the country, but this also means decreasing U.S. automobile employment in other regions of the country.[15] Thus these gains probably do not directly offset the losses.

Policy Implications

The object of the voluntary export restrictions was to help the U.S. automobile industry get back on its feet and to preserve American jobs. The restrictions may partially have succeeded because they enabled the industry to earn record profits, some of which may be used for investments that improve productivity and technology. But the restrictions have not saved American jobs, and American consumers have paid a heavy price. Worse, as argued in chapter 3, domestic firms may be hurt in the long run because foreign firms responded to trade protection by increasing their U.S. production capacity.

Although the current restrictions are not as tightly binding as the original sales limits, they nonetheless contribute to a deadweight loss and provide further incentives for Japanese firms to expand their U.S. production capacity. Ultimately, U.S. workers, consumers, and producers are likely to be hurt by the continuation of any form of automobile sales restraints.

15. Japanese firms have built most of their U.S. plants far from Detroit. Thus the additional employment generated will not accrue to people who were laid off because of the restrictions or who may be laid off because of increased competition.

[17]

11 The Political Economy of Protectionism: Tariffs and Retaliation in the Timber Industry

Joseph P. Kalt

11.1 Introduction

11.1.1 A Brief Military History

The United States is in the middle of a trade war—or at least a skirmish—with its largest trading partner and one of its closest allies. The most important battle of this conflict is being fought over lumber. The first confrontation came in June 1986 when President Reagan imposed ad valorem duties of up to 35 percent on imports of wooden shakes and shingles, which are primarily supplied by Canada.[1] The Canadians retaliated almost immediately with duties on a hodgepodge of imports from the United States, including Christmas trees, computers, semiconductors, and books.

The shakes and shingles industry is relatively small, with annual U.S. sales of only $80 million and Canadian imports of $50 million per year. On October 16, 1986, however, the U.S. Department of Commerce issued a preliminary finding that Canada was subsidizing its softwood (construction) lumber imports at the rate of 15 percent of their value. This finding followed an initial determination by the International Trade Commission (ITC) that U.S. lumber producers were being materially harmed by Canadian imports. This set the stage for the United States to impose a 15 percent countervailing duty on issuance of a final Commerce Department finding of subsidy (due December 30) and a final ITC determination of material injury (due by February 1987). Pending these expected final determinations, importers

Joseph P. Kalt is professor of political economy at the Kennedy School of Government, Harvard University.

of Canadian lumber were required to post bonds equivalent to 15 percent of the value of their shipments (subject to refund should the United States eventually drop its countervailing duty action).

The softwood lumber industry is important to both countries. Sales in the United States total approximately $10 billion per year, and Canadian imports amount to $3 billion per year. In Canada, softwood lumber is a $5 billion per year industry and is larger than metals, agriculture, fisheries, and autos combined. Lumber accounts for approximately 4 percent of both Canadian GNP and Canadian exports to the United States. Canadian imports hold roughly 30 percent of the U.S. market and provide over 99 percent of the foreign lumber supplied to the United States.

A week prior to the October 16 announcement of the U.S. softwood lumber decision, Canada's minister for international trade had called U.S. producers' lobbying for tariff protection "total harassment" and explicitly warned of retaliation.[2] On November 7, with support from liberals and conservatives in Parliament, the Canadian government imposed a 67 percent countervailing duty on U.S. corn exports to Canada. Within two weeks, as tensions over the U.S. lumber duty mounted, the U.S. secretary of state (then embroiled in the Iran-Contra scandal) was in Ottawa attempting to find grounds for U.S. backtracking on the lumber duty. With the 15 percent U.S. duty scheduled to become permanent on December 30, Canadian and U.S. negotiators reached an agreement on December 31 that implemented a 15 percent Canadian export duty in exchange for the U.S. lumber industry dropping its duty action. As of 1987, the corn retaliation remained in place.

In terms of the size of the import sector and the anticipated domestic price effects, the U.S. lumber duty was the largest countervailing/antidumping action that the country has ever taken against a specific trading partner under the terms of GATT. The Canadian corn retaliation represented the first countervailing duty ever imposed on the United States and one of the few times Canada has imposed such a duty on any nation. Within Canada, the eventual lumber export tax has been assailed by the timber industry as "bizarre" and "sickening,"[3] and opposition parties had urged the Mulroney government to reject any negotiated settlement and to mount its opposition to U.S. protectionist measures through U.S. and international judicial proceedings. The negotiated settlement, they argue, puts Canada in a defensive posture and establishes precedents that leave "any major Canadian export . . . subject to this kind of action by the United States."[4] The Mulroney government, meanwhile, defends itself on the grounds that U.S. domestic political pressures could not possibly have been deflected by Canada, and that it is better that Canada collect the revenues from a lumber duty than have the revenues flow to the United States. But even Canada's trade minister laments that "today it's lumber—tomorrow it could be any number of issues. This is not the way to conduct business between the world's largest trading partners. There must be a better way."[5]

Interestingly, the timber trade war is taking place in the middle of high-level negotiations aimed at reaching a general free trade arrangement between the United States and Canada. The future and direction of the free trade negotiations, however, have been threatened by the lumber controversies. Public support in Canada for an agreement has declined markedly over the last year, as opinion polls show rising distrust of U.S. motives and promises, declining faith in the abilities of Canadian negotiators, and a general waning of the faith that free trade will improve the Canadian economy. In the face of these sentiments, even Prime Minister Mulroney has noted (specifically within the context of the lumber affair) that it is "extremely difficult for anyone, including Canadians, to be friends with the Americans."[6]

11.1.2 Can the United States Win a Trade War?

It goes without saying that there is much concern or hope, depending on one's viewpoint, that protectionist "sentiments" are on the rise in the United States and that a major change in the direction of U.S. trade policy may be in the offing. I suspect that among economists the protectionist trends afoot are viewed with apprehension. New theoretical developments and a certain amount of playing to the public's heightened nationalistic predilections may have softened the profession's traditional, if not downright doctrinaire, preaching of free trade, but most economists appear to continue to worry that protection that leads to cycles of confrontation and retaliation is nationally and globally harmful.

The U.S.-Canadian rift over lumber trade provides a potentially revealing example of one of the paths that the nascent changes in trade policy can take. On the face of it, the circumstances of the timber trade war do not appear extraordinary. The U.S. industry has been in the employment and output doldrums for a number of years; prospects for sharp improvement are not particularly encouraging; and import market shares have been on the rise. On the Canadian side, the lumber industry is an important industry in the economy—overwhelming, in fact, to certain regions of the country. It is unrealistic to think that Canada would not respond in some substantive way to attempts to limit its access to export markets.

The political origins and economic consequences of the timber trade war are the focus of this study. The former appear to lie in a combination of a well-organized and forceful group of beneficiaries (that is, U.S. lumber producers) and a serendipitous timing of congressional pressures on the White House. The outcome, to date, of the timber trade war has, indeed, been an improvement in the lot of domestic producers, as they have realized a rise in the price of lumber. From the broader perspective of nationalistic aggregate welfare, the United States appears to have started, but ultimately lost, the war. What began as a large-country, monopsony tariff directed against Canada has become a large-country, monopoly tariff directed against the United States.

11.2 The U.S. Countervailing Duty Decision

U.S. restrictive action against the importation of softwood lumber from Canada originated with a 1982 petition to the Department of Commerce and the International Trade Commission. This petition was filed by the Coalition for Fair Lumber Imports (CFLI), a lobbying association of 350 U.S. forest products companies and each of the eight major lumber and timber trade associations. The Coalition requested that the United States impose countervailing duties against Canadian softwood imports under the terms of the (amended) Tariff Act of 1930. The Coalition argued that countervailing duties were warranted because Canadian federal and provincial governments were subsidizing the production of softwood lumber, and subsidized production was materially injuring U.S. lumber producers.

The 1982 case ended in May 1983 when the Department of Commerce failed to rule in favor of the U.S. lumber industry. In essence, the Commerce Department found that there was ample evidence that Canadian governmental policy was subsidizing lumber production through below-market pricing of trees sold by public forest authorities, but that these subsidies were "generally available" and not specifically targeted at lumber producers. In the view of the Department of Commerce, this lack of specificity disqualified the Canadian subsidies as actionable under the countervailing duties provisions of the 1930 Tariff Act.

A reading of the record of the 1982 case leaves the very strong impression that the Commerce Department (or, more realistically, the White House) was squirming to find a technicality under which it could reject the Coalition's petition. Under the "general availability" criterion, the Commerce Department found that below-market-price trees were available to a number of parties beyond construction lumber producers, including manufacturers of pulp and paper, plywood and veneer, furniture, turpentine, and food additives. Within months of the lumber decision, however, the Commerce Department was enunciating a "dominant use" standard in order to provide protection to the domestic steel industry, which was requesting countervailing duties against imports of Brazilian steel made with subsidized iron ore (which has uses, albeit minor, beyond steel production). Under this standard, a subsidy could be generally available (in other words, to sectors other than the export industry of concern), but still qualify for countervailing duties, if the dominant user of the subsidized inputs if found to materially injure U.S. competitors. In the case of Canadian softwood trees, the lumber industry is by far the dominant user.

The broadening of the qualifications for countervailing duties prompted the Coalition for Fair Lumber Imports, with strong support from a number of members of the House and Senate, to again petition for protection. The resulting 1986 petition found the Commerce Department boxed in by the new precedent of its "dominant use" standard and the strong possibility that a negative decision would be overridden by federal legislation. The White House, in deciding whether to back the adoption of a countervailing duty, faced this second constraint as well as the fact that five Republican senators from major lumber-producing states (Washington, Oregon, Idaho, Georgia, and Alabama) were facing reelection challenges. Thus, with virtually the same substantive record before it (and, if anything, a slightly improved domestic industry), the Commerce Department reversed its 1983 decision and determined that purported Canadian lumber subsidies did meet the requirements of the Tariff Act.

11.2.1 The Case before the ITC and the Commerce Department

The basic substantive argument of the U.S. lumber industry before the Department of Commerce is succinctly summarized in table 11.1. Over 95 percent of Canadian softwood timber lands are publicly owned, compared to only 28 percent in the United States. The various Canadian governmental authorities sell the rights to remove trees from public forests to private logging companies (including lumber producers). The price at which the right to remove a tree is sold is known as the

Table 11.1 **U.S. and Canadian Stumpage Prices**

	United States	Canada	Canada as % U.S.
1977	$96.41	$10.16	10.5%
1978	$118.76	$21.59	18.2%
1979	$134.37	$30.96	23.0%
1980	$122.16	$27.48	22.5%
1981	$140.98	$12.09	8.6%
1982	$93.57	$10.57	11.3%
1983	$105.99	$11.63	11.0%
1984	$104.16	$11.84	11.4%

Source: U.S. ITC 1985.
Note: US$/per 1000 board feet (mbf).

"stumpage price." In most Canadian provinces, stumpage fees are based on mechanistic (if not totally arbitrary) formulas that work back from a selected end-market value, subtracting administratively determined forest-to-market costs to arrive at a value of trees on the stump. By contrast, rights to harvest timber on U.S. public lands are sold through a bidding process (with problems of its own) that is designed to recover full market value.

As indicated in table 11.1, the Canadian and U.S. systems for determining stumpage prices produce dramatically different results. U.S. prices are commonly many times higher than Canadian prices, and this holds even after adjustments for quality, transportation differentials, and production costs. This evidence that Canadian stumpage policy results in much lower Canadian stumpage prices has formed the central argument for protection before the ITC, the Commerce Department, Congress and, most recently, U.S.-Canadian negotiators.[7]

Evidence of the type presented in table 11.1 has been employed by interested parties to establish the existence of a Canadian lumber subsidy. ITC standards, however, require that any purported subsidy must be shown to cause material injury to domestic producers before countervailing duties may be imposed. The standards of "material injury" are problematic for the ITC. Economic criteria might be quick to equate "injury" with reduced profitability. Virtually any industry facing import competition will satisfy this criterion. The patterns of ITC cases, however, suggest that "material injury" commonly is interpreted as giving protection a bailout role. The criteria for determining the extent to which an industry is in need of protection under this definition of material injury, as revealed by ITC practice, include the existence of negative profits, declining employment, plant closings, and declining prices.

It is not sufficient (at least not according to the ITC's legislative mandate) that an industry seeking countervailing protection be able to show that it is experiencing hard times. The industry must demonstrate that it is materially injured by reason of the subsidized imports. To determine whether subsidized imports are the cause of material injury to a petitioning industry, the ITC's reports reveal that it explicitly examines such factors as the depth of any foreign sector subsidies, offsetting U.S. subsidies, exchange rates, macroeconomic growth and other general economic conditions, foreign-domestic price differentials, and the market share of imports.

The Coalition for Fair Lumber Imports emphasized four primary pieces of evidence regarding the extent and cause of the lumber industry's distress in its 1986 case before the ITC: (1) the market share of Canadian imports had risen steadily over the last decade (table 11.2); (2) sawmill capacity (and associated employment) in the United States

Table 11.2 **Imports, Exchange Rates, and Prices**

	Canadian Share of U.S. Lumber Consumption	Real Exchange Rate (US$/Can$; 77 = 100)	Real U.S. Lumber Prices (1984$/mbf)
1975	18.7%		
1976	21.9%		
1977	25.3%	100.0	$302.81
1978	27.6%	94.7	$323.81
1979	27.3%	93.6	$343.66
1980	28.1%	93.2	$295.97
1981	28.6%	91.9	$276.27
1982	29.2%	92.8	$204.06
1983	30.1%	94.9	$202.17
1984	30.7%	91.7	$214.87
1985	33.2%	89.8[a]	
1986	33.0%[a]		

Sources: U.S. ITC 1985; Coalition for Fair Lumber Imports 1986b.
[a]Estimated.

had declined over 1977–82, with only minor recovery since the end of the early-1980s recession (fig. 11.1); (3) profitability in the 1980s had deteriorated sharply (fig. 11.2); and (4) despite some recovery in demand since the early 1980s (fig. 11.1), real U.S. lumber prices showed little improvement and remained far below historic highs (table 11.2). This last point was played particularly hard by the Coalition. It provided the tactically important argument that "something is not right" with the workings of supply and demand and, by implication, the free trade views of neoclassical economists, since recovering demand did not pull up prices; the "something" that was not "right" was Canadian stumpage policy (Coalition 1986b). This argument was eventually endorsed by the ITC.

The ITC (U.S. ITC 1985) examined a number of indicators of relative competitiveness, but these showed little evidence of a strong Canadian advantage. As shown in table 11.3, the Canadians reveal a moderate advantage in unit labor costs, owing to higher productivity (that is, Canadian hourly wages actually exceed U.S. wages). Effective Canadian tax rates, however, are higher than U.S. rates in the lumber industry, and average total costs of U.S. and Canadian lumber production hardly differ at all.

This last observation is a reflection of the efficiency of the Canadian log market. That is, it might be thought that low Canadian stumpage prices should show up as low Canadian lumber prices. But the stumpage price is the price of removing a log from its forest, and, once removed,

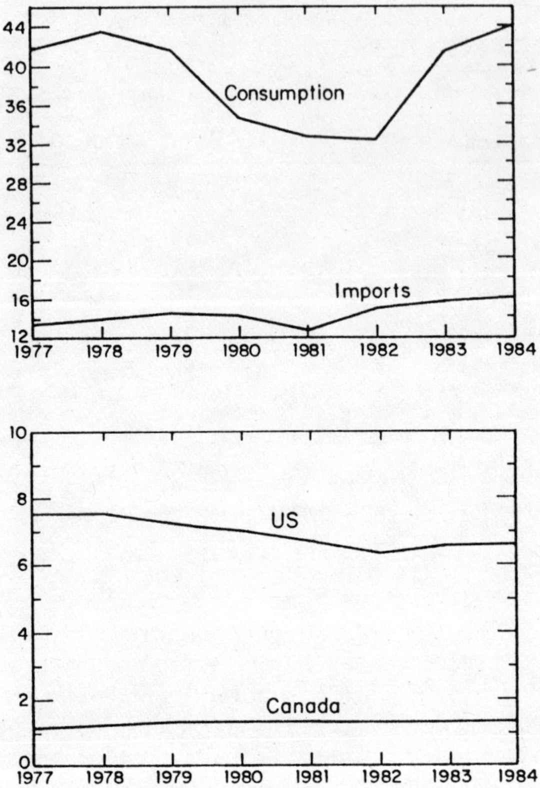

Fig. 11.1 Softwood lumber consumption and imports (billions of board feet) and number of sawmill establishments (1000s).

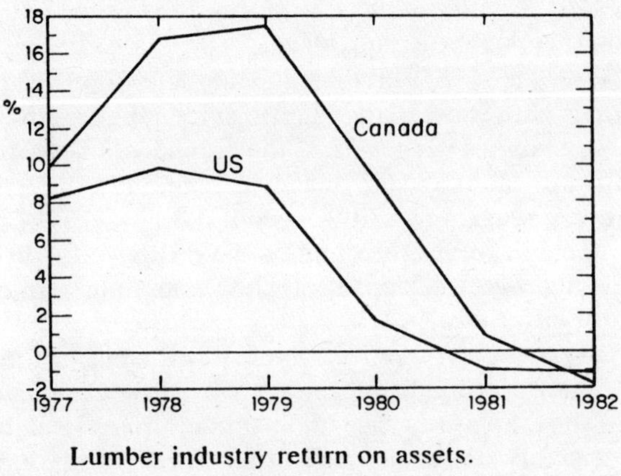

Fig. 11.2 Lumber industry return on assets.

Table 11.3 Determinants of Production Costs in the Softwood Lumber Industry

	Average Total Cost (US$ per mbf)		Unit Labor Cost (US$ per mbf)	
	U.S.	Canada	U.S.	Canada
1977	$180	$162	$67	$56
1978			$69	$61
1979	$278	$193	$73	$65
1980			$77	$67
1981	$240	$188	$79	$74
1982	$204	$206	$86	$78
1983	$221	$207	$85	$71
1984	$213	$205	$81	$65

	Average Hourly Wage (US$)		Labor Productivity (board feet/year)	
	U.S.	Canada	U.S.	Canada
1977	$5.14	$6.76	208,405	292,276
1978	$5.79	$6.75	206,718	285,679
1979	$6.07	$7.29	199,399	277,892
1980	$6.36	$8.15	185,418	285,207
1981	$6.80	8.79	185,061	269,209
1982	$8.27	$9.60	206,719	299,478
1983	$8.77	$9.98	243,640	365,979
1984	$9.26	$10.24	239,200	382,814

	Effective Tax Rates	
	U.S.	Canada
1977	26.4%	40.6%
1978	24.4%	36.1%
1979	21.6%	36.8%
1980	33.1%	29.4%
1981		23.1%

Source: U.S. ITC 1985.

logs are marketed by logging firms on the open market to Canadian lumber producers. Market-clearing log prices paid by lumber producers are roughly uniform, after accounting for quality differentials and transportation costs (FTC 1986). Canadian prohibitions on log (as opposed to lumber) exports do keep in-Canada log prices to lumber mills somewhat lower than U.S. prices, although differences turn out to be minor (U.S. ITC 1985; FTC 1986).

Thus, the vehicle by which the Canadian stumpage system could subsidize lumber exports is *not* through direct subsidization of lumber production. Rather, Canadian stumpage policy is alleged to subsidize lumber exports by subsidizing Canadian loggers, resulting in increased timber production turned into increased output from the Canadian lumber industry (Coalition 1986b). In the absence of the prohibition on Canadian log exports, an increase in Canadian timber production would tend to depress log prices evenly throughout North America—to the benefit of both Canadian and U.S. lumber mills. In the presence of restrictions on log exports, however, log prices tend to be levelized through an expansion of the Canadian sellers of log *products* (such as lumber). The result is that more of North America's sawmill capacity comes to be located in Canada than would otherwise be the case—to the displeasure of the U.S. Coalition.

11.2.2 The Economics of the ITC's Decision

Upon perusal of the kind of information available to the ITC and shown in tables 11.1–11.3 and figures 11.1–11.2, it is tempting to try to apply a more rigorous analysis to see if, in fact, Canadian stumpage prices (table 11.1) are the cause of the upward trend in the market share of imports (table 11.2), the soft prices in the North American lumber market (table 11.2), or depressed industry profitability. Do the data indicate changes in Canadian stumpage that correspond to changes in Canadian lumber export performance or lumber price levels? And what other explanations (such as exchange rate movements and recession) are there for the relative performance of the U.S. and Canadian lumber industries? These are, of course, the kinds of analyses that we might hope the ITC would perform in a systematic (for instance, econometric) fashion. However, there is a much more fundamental issue regarding the effects of below-market stumpage pricing in Canada.

The Federal Trade Commission, in its legal role as a guardian of consumer interests and in its de facto role as a proponent of free international trade, intervened in the 1982 and 1986 lumber proceeding before the ITC (FTC 1986). In its challenge to the Coalition's request for tariff protection, the FTC argues that the Canadian stumpage subsidy is entirely inframarginal; it has no effect on the level of forest harvest and, hence, no effect on Canadian lumber output. With appropriate references to Adam Smith, David Ricardo, Paul Samuelson, and Joan Robinson, the FTC asserts that

> the stumpage fee represents that portion of the trees' value, or economic rent, that is captured by the landowner. By definition, an economic rent does not affect the quantity of a factor supplied. Characterization of stumpage fees as part of economic rent rather than a cost that affects the quantity supplied follows from the fact that the

> [Canadian] government, which decides how much land will be made available for logging, would make the land available for harvesting and loggers would harvest the logs regardless of where the stumpage fee is set, so long as it is within the range between zero and the amount by which the value of the logs exceeds the cost of harvesting them. (FTC 1986, 22–23)

The FTC's interpretation of the Canadian below-market stumpage prices as gifts of rent to loggers is founded on two observations. First, the stumpage prices do not even come close to clearing the market and are far exceeded by the market-clearing prices received on resale by loggers. That is, once cut, Canadian logs fetch prices that leave logging firms with unit revenues that exceed logging expenses and stumpage charges. Second, and most fundamentally, Canadian harvest (or "cut") levels on public lands are set administratively without reference to the stumpage price. By law, Canadian public cut levels are set (as they are on U.S. public lands) according to fundamentally noneconomic, biological criteria dealing with the physical sustainable yield, the age of the trees, and the species mix of the forest. Although specifics vary from province to province, the Canadian procedure for establishing a cut level begins with official determination of how much acreage to be allotted to tree harvesting and when to allocate that acreage to loggers. The right to remove timber from cuttable acreage is determined by an administrative process that awards long-term cut licenses to selected logging firms without charge and on the basis of explicitly noneconomic criteria. The licensee then submits a cut plan requiring approval on the basis of its conformation with sound logging practice. Loggers are permitted flexibility to vary their efforts at any point in time as market price and cost conditions vary, subject to the overall cut limit over the full term of the license. The stumpage price the licensee is charged on the removal of timber is determined through an administrative formula that arrives at the stumpage value as a net-back from the administratively calculated log value (FTC 1986).

In short, the Canadian cut of timber is not determined by reference to the price that public authorities receive for timber. Formally, the supply response of the Canadian cut to the stumpage price is zero. This conclusion leads directly to the FTC position that the Canadian stumpage system has no adverse effect on the U.S. lumber industry. The FTC's conclusion is based, however, on a combination of a priori economic theory and a reading of the literal content of Canadian cut policies. The FTC notes that there is an alternative hypothesis regarding the responsiveness of Canadian timber supply to the below-market stumpage system: "The Canadian stumpage fee systems could lead to an increase in the quantity of timber harvested if the timber companies successfully lobbied the Canadian federal or provincial governments to expand the quantity of cutting permitted *because the increased economic rents they would earn by cutting additional trees at the low stumpage fee*" (FTC 1986, 30–31, n. 38; emphasis in original). If true, this hypothesis provides support to the Coalition's assertions that U.S. lumber companies have been harmed by Canadian stumpage practices.

To test whether the Canadian supply of timber is responsive to the stumpage subsidy, we might directly estimate the supply of Canadian logs as

$$Q_c^s = Q_c^s\,(P,\ SUBSIDY,\ X_c), \tag{1}$$

where Q_c^s is Canadian timber production, P is the price received for cut logs, $SUBSIDY$ is the stumpage subsidy, and X_c represents Canadian input cost and productivity variables (such as labor costs). The view of Canadian stumpage subsidies as entirely inframarginal implies that the effect of $SUBSIDY$ on Q_c^s is zero, while the U.S. lumber industry's assertion is that this effect is positive.

In reacting to the possibility that Canadian timber supply responds positively to stumpage subsidies, the FTC puts forth the possibility that the Canadian stumpage system might even discourage supply. The FTC argues that the noncompetitive process of license awards makes the Canadian system particularly likely to allocate harvesting to inefficient firms for whom some market-cuttable tracts are unprofitable. Raising stumpage fees worsens the fate of such firms and may cause a reduction in cut.

The FTC further notes that the arbitrary Canadian stumpage system may typically produce inframarginal rents, but it can also lead to the overpricing of some tracts of cuttable land for which market-determined levels of Ricardian rent are less than the stumpage fees. Such lands will go unharvested under the Canadian system; in effect, a rise in stumpage has no impact on tracts for which the stumpage fee is less than the associated Ricardian rent, but pushes some tracts and their supply out of the market. Both of these hypotheses amount to the observation that the Canadian stumpage system can reduce supply if and when fees are raised above market levels on particular tracts of forest, but should be entirely inframarginal when set below market levels.

The Canadian logging activity described in equation (1) is plausibly determined by the simultaneous action of supply and demand for timber. The indigenous Canadian demand for timber can be expressed as

$$Q_c^d = Q_c^d\,(P,\ Z_c), \tag{2}$$

where Z_c represents determinants of timber demand, such as housing starts or aggregate income. Of course, Canadian timber markets are linked through trade in forest products to international markets. This really means U.S. markets, as transocean shipping costs effectively limit broader trade; only about 5 percent of North American timber output leaves the continent and most of these exports are specialty and high-grade products. Thus, there are corresponding supply and demand schedules for the U.S. that, together with equations (1) and (2), describe the market for timber in which Canadian loggers find themselves. Using u subscripts to denote the United States, this market can be described by equation (1) and the residual demand left over for Canadian suppliers after U.S. loggers have put their output on the market.[8] This demand is

$$(3) \qquad Q^d_{c,u} = Q^d_c + Q^d_u - Q^s_u = Q^d_{c,u}\,(P, X_u, Z_c, Z_u),$$

with s and d continuing to signify supply and demand.

Expressions (1) and (3) now constitute a two-equation system that we can estimate with available (albeit limited) data.[9] I have collected data for the six Canadian logging regions that produce all but a minute amount of the country's timber (Coastal B.C., Interior B.C., the Prairie Provinces, Quebec, Ontario, and the Maritime Provinces) over 1977–84. These data provide 48 sample points on prices (P) of logs (in real US$/mbf), annual harvest levels (Q^s_c), and stumpage prices. *SUBSIDY* is measured by the difference between the price received by loggers and the stumpage fee.[10] To capture determinants of the cost of logging in Canada (X_c), we have data on industry labor costs and productivity.[11] Corresponding measures are used to capture X_u for the United States. The demand determinants reflected in Z_c and Z_u are measured by housing starts per year. The supply schedule in equation (1) is estimated using the pooled data and utilizing two-stage least squares, instrumental variables techniques that allow the separation of supply factors from demand influences on Canadian timber prices and quantities.

The estimated Canadian timber supply function is shown in table 11.4. A log-log (no pun intended, just lucky) specification is employed and produces elasticities of supply with respect to the indicated variables. My econometric "fishing" was restricted to the endogeneity/exogeneity of *SUBSIDY* and labor productivity, and the inclusion/exclusion of the lagged value of the dependent variable (Q^s_c). Results were not sensitive to these choices, including the magnitude and sign of the effect of *SUBSIDY*. Although confidence is weak, the elasticity of Canadian timber supply with respect to the price received by loggers appears to be of the same magnitude that others have reported when estimating U.S. supply functions (e.g., Adams, McCarl, and Homayounfarrokh 1986). It appears that the data allow the detection, with fairly good confidence, of the supply effects of costs and productivity factors.

Table 11.4 indicates that the elasticity of Canadian timber supply with respect to official stumpage prices has a point estimate of −0.13. There is moderate confidence suggested for this result, but I believe

Table 11.4 Does the Canadian Stumpage System Subsidize Lumber Exports?

The Canadian Timber Supply Function

Variable	Expected Sign	Elasticity	2-Tail Signif.
Stumpage subsidy	+ (Lobbying for +Q)	−0.13	0.27
	0 (Inframarginal rents)	(−1.13)	
Price	+	+0.23	0.46
		(.75)	
Labor Costs/HR	−	−2.03	0.04
		(−2.09)	
Labor Productivity	+	+0.68	0.003
		(3.14)	
Intercepts			0.10–0.00

Notes: Standard error = 0.11; F-statistic = 307.14; D.W. = 1.84; and number of observations = 48.

the most that can really be said is that the approach and data employed here have produced no evidence that the Canadian system of stumpage subsidies results in an increase in Canadian timber supply. In this negative sense, my results are supportive of the view that the ITC incorrectly ruled that the Canadian timber pricing system constituted an export subsidy to the lumber industry that warranted countervailing U.S. duties.

This is not to say that, had the ITC seen table 11.4 (or understood the FTC's argument about inframarginalism), it would have ruled any differently. My reading of the record of the case is that the ITCs decision turned on a combination of (1) evidence that, for whatever reason, the U.S. lumber industry finds itself in poor condition, and (2) irresistible domestic, election-year political forces. Indeed, from the Administration's point of view, it must have seemed far preferable to have protection for the lumber industry emanate from the Commerce Department and the ITC, rather than from congressional legislation. The former leaves the Administration in control of both the level of duties and negotiations with the Canadians regarding remedial measures.

11.3 The Welfare Consequences of Protection

Even if there were compelling evidence that the Canadian stumpage system for timber effectively subsidized the expansion of the Canadian lumber industry, the existence of a subsidy, by itself, would provide little economic justification for tariff protection of the U.S. lumber industry. Indeed, taking the sum of consumers' and producers' surplus as our yardstick of aggregate national welfare, the ITC might be instructed to send a note of gratitude to the Canadians, rather than impose a tariff against them. If Canada would like to tax other sectors of its economy (through resource diversion into timber and lumber production) to subsidize the production of goods for which the United States is a large net consumer, the United States benefits.

This (neo)classic response to the importation of products subsidized by foreign governments, of course, needs to be qualified. For example, were Canadian lumber subsidies part of a predatory strategy to drive the U.S. industry under in anticipation of a subsequent exercise of monopoly power, the United States might appropriately respond with protective tariffs. Successful predation, however, has as its first requirement the ability of the predator to drive its victim's capital out of production and to keep that capital out of production. This is hard to imagine in the timber or lumber industries. In the former, the basic capital stock on which production is based just keeps on growing if taken out of production, and the lumber industry's mills are extremely long-lived and highly specific to lumber production.[12] At any rate, figure 11.1 indicates that capital has been (re)entering the U.S. industry since the bottom of the early-1980s recession.

Other, nonpredatory justifications for countervailing against a subsidy to Canadian shipments of lumber are also difficult to defend. The Canadian industry is quite competitively structured and hardly presents an oligopolistic front to the United States. The lumber industry, in general, is low on the list of industries likely to produce beneficial technological spillovers if protected against subsidized imports. Strategic, national defense justifications for protecting an indigenous softwood (construction) lumber industry are equally unconvincing, since the probability of a military interdiction that cuts off supplies from Canada seems so farfetched. In fact, the Coalition for Fair Lumber Imports is notable, if not commendable, among lobbyists seeking protection for its *not* waving the national security banner.

11.3.1 The United States as an Import Monopsonist

If there is a nationalistic (that is, national welfare) justification for tariffs on imported lumber, it lies in the observation that the United States is a large-country importer of softwood products. As noted above, North America is virtually a closed market. The United States annually buys more than 60 percent of Canadian lumber production, and other outlets for Canada are subject to very high transportation costs and tend to be restricted to specialty products. Moreover, the elasticities of Canadian lumber supply, both for total production and exports, are quite low.[13] In short, Canada's very large neighbor to the south is its primary market, and the economics of forestry and milling are such that production levels are not especially sensitive to price. Policies such as U.S. import duties have the potential of depressing lumber and timber prices in Canada, and the country is an easy target for monopsonistic U.S. trade policies that improve the U.S. terms of trade—unless it can credibly retaliate.

Canada has, however, considerable scope for defending itself against an aggressive, monopsonistic United States. Canada is, for all intents and purposes, the sole foreign supplier of lumber to a country with a very inelastic demand.[14] In 1984, for example, the United States imported 12.995 billion board feet of softwood lumber. Fully 99.6 percent (12.947 billion board feet) of this total came from Canada.

The current trade wars in the timber industry, then, are being played out in a setting in which both trading partners have significant market power. Each might like to exercise its respective ability to act as a price maker, but the danger that a move away from the traditional free trade equilibrium will force the other country to exercise its market power is very real.

The stakes that the United States and Canada face, if not the game-theoretic optimal strategies each could play, can be quantified through the application of existing information on supply and demand responses in the lumber industry. From the U.S. perspective, an import duty on lumber from Canada has the potential of depressing the price of Canadian imports. Domestic producers stand to gain as the duty-inclusive price of imports is driven up. U.S. lumber consumers may not be pleased by having to pay higher prices, but the U.S. Treasury can collect the tariff wedge between U.S. and Canadian lumber prices. Depending on the height of the duty relative to the optimal monopsony tariff, the gains to U.S. producers and the Treasury can outweigh the losses of domestic consumers, and in that sense raise aggregate national welfare.

To estimate winners' gains and losers' losses from U.S. lumber duties, I have parameterized a simple three-sector model of North American lumber trade, employing the estimates of supply and demand elasticities provided by researchers who have specialized in modeling lumber markets. This model is used to simulate alternative tariff policies and measure the associated incidence and welfare effects. There are two supply sectors to be captured: the U.S. supply (Q^s_u) and the supply of imports from Canada (Q^i_c). These supplies must be priced to clear the U.S. market, given U.S. demand for lumber (Q^d_u). The two supply schedules and one demand schedule are taken to have constant elasticity functional forms over the relevant range, such that $Q = \alpha P^{\epsilon}$ where ϵ represents the elasticity.[15] When a duty of t percent is imposed on imports, the import supply schedule as perceived by the United States becomes:

$$Q_c^i = \alpha_i\,[(1 + t)P^i]^{\epsilon^i}$$

where P^i refers to the duty-exclusive delivered price of Canadian lumber and $P = (1 + t)p^i$. Solution of $Q_u^s + Q_c^i = Q_u^d$ for P then yields equilibrium prices and quantities. The model's results are clearly partial equilibrium results in the sense that no feedback effects to the macroeconomy or close substitutes and complements are calculated.

The elasticity of U.S. lumber supply is taken to have a value of .42, which is the three-region weighted (1985 quantities) average of supply elasticities reported by Adams, McCarl, and Homayounfarrokh (1986). Domestic demand elasticity is set at −.15, which accords with estimates reported by Spelter (1985) and Adams, McCarl, and Homayounfarrokh (1986). The most important of the elasticity values is the value for the elasticity of import supply from Canada. This elasticity fundamentally determines the extent of any U.S. monopsony power vis-à-vis Canada. This elasticity reflects both the elasticity of Canadian demand and the elasticity of Canadian supply:

$$\epsilon^i = \epsilon_c^s(Q_c^s/Q_c^i) - \epsilon_c^d(1 - Q_c^s/Q_c^i). \tag{4}$$

Adams, McCarl, and Homayounfarrokh (1986) estimate a value of .917 for ϵ^i and this value is employed here. This is close to the estimate of 0.89 reported by Boyd and Krutilla (1987). While an import supply elasticity of less than one may seem small, it also accords with direct calculation of equation (4). Employing 1984 values for the quantities in equation (4), assuming that Canadian consumers have the same demand elasticity as U.S. consumers, and taking a value of $\epsilon_c^s = .23$ from table 11.4 produces an import supply elasticity of approximately 0.9. Any value in this range suggests a very high degree of monopsony power for the United States.

The Effects of a 15 Percent Countervailing Duty

Under the foregoing parameterizations, table 11.5 reports the calculated incidence and welfare effects of a 15 percent U.S. countervailing

Table 11.5 **Welfare Consequences of a 15 Percent U.S. Lumber Duty (millions of 1986 dollars)**

	Gains	Losses
U.S. lumber producers (labor, capital, land)	$416.8	
U.S. lumber users (intermediate and final)		$556.9
U.S. government (tariff revenues)	$340.5	
Net U.S.	$200.4	
Net Canada		$223.0
Net U.S. and Canada		$22.5

duty on Canadian lumber imports. Table 11.6 shows the corresponding price and quantity impacts on the North American lumber market. In each table, it is assumed that Canada does not respond with retaliation of any form. A 15 percent duty raises domestic lumber prices (by approximately 5 percent). Through the monopsony effect, however, the duty also depresses Canadian lumber prices. U.S. lumber producers are unambiguously better off—by an estimated $400 million per year. The U.S. Treasury also realizes a gain from tariff revenues totaling $340 million annually. These benefits are in contrast to the negative effects of a 15 percent duty on U.S. lumber consumers. Consumers suffer a burden of over $550 million per year.

The gains of U.S. lumber producers and the Treasury are large enough to more than offset consumers' losses. In this sense, a 15 percent duty raises national welfare. The duty effectively transfers some of the rents that otherwise accrue to Canadian lumber producers to U.S. producers and to U.S. governmental revenue collections. As a result, Canada in its role as a net producer of lumber is worse off. Canadian losses are on the order of $220 million (US$) per year. The $20 million excess of Canadian losses over U.S. gains is the deadweight "world" loss as a result of the exercise of U.S. monopsony in the international lumber market.

The "Optimal" Tariff

If the United States benefits, on net, from a 15 percent lumber duty, how far could it push the duty and still see rising benefits? How high is the optimal tariff? This question is addressed in tables 11.7 and 11.8. *Assuming no Canadian policy response,* table 11.8 indicates that the optimal duty is roughly 50 percent. A duty of this magnitude has very large impacts on the lumber market. The optimal duty would drive domestic lumber prices up sharply, severely depress Canadian prices, cut imports by close to 40 percent, and raise domestic production by 10 percent.

Table 11.6 Market Effects of a 15 Percent U.S. Timber Duty (1986 dollars)

	% Change from No Tariff	Price/Quantity Impact
Tariff	15	$29/mbf
Change in U.S. Price	5	$13/mbf
Change in Canadian price	−9	−$18/mbf
Change in U.S. production	2	698mmbf
Change in imports	−8	−1026mmbf
Change in U.S. consumption	−1	−328mmbf

Table 11.7 Welfare Consequences of an "Optimal" U.S. Lumber Tariff (millions of 1986 dollars)

	Gains	Losses
U.S. lumber producers (labor, capital, land)	$2,249.0	
U.S. lumber users (intermediate and final)		$2,910.2
U.S. government (tariff revenues)	$1,119.9	
Net U.S.	$458.7	
Net Canada		$890.0
Net U.S. and Canada		$431.2

The optimal, unopposed tariff would be a great boon to domestic lumber producers, who would realize a gain of over $2.2 billion per year. Similarly, the Treasury would see tariff revenues of more than $1.1 billion. These gains are in contrast to the $3 billion loss that would be experienced by domestic consumers. This burden would manifest itself in higher home construction costs and higher prices of homes, apartments, and commercial buildings. The gains of U.S. lumber producers and revenue collectors from an optimal tariff would outweigh the losses of consumers, by the definition of optimal. The net gain to the nation would be on the order of $450 million per year.

An optimal tariff would hit Canada extremely hard. As indicated in table 11.7, Canada would suffer a loss of almost $900 million per year. For an economy of the size of Canada's, this sum is hardly trivial and could be expected to engender a vociferous response designed to exploit Canada's monopoly power. The net international deadweight loss of $430 million, however, would presumably go unnoticed by anyone.

As previously discussed, the central parameter determining the degree of U.S. monopsony power in the lumber market is the elasticity of import supply. Not only is there the usual statistical uncertainty

Table 11.8 Market Effects of an "Optimal" U.S. Lumber Tariff (1986 dollars)

	% Change from No Tariff	Price/Quantity Impact
Tariff	53	$140/mbf
Change in U.S. price	26	$65/mbf
Change in Canadian price	−41	−$85/mbf
Change in U.S. production	10	3408mbf
Change in imports	−38	−4929mbf
Change in U.S. consumption	−3	−1521mbf

about this parameter, but an optimal tariff as large as indicated by table 11.8 would severely depress Canadian lumber prices. This could be expected to open up very significant trans-Pacific and trans-Atlantic trade for the Canadians, and would effectively move the United States into a much more elastic portion of the Canadian import supply function. To provide some indication of the sensitivity of welfare implications to the import supply elasticity, figure 11.3 graphs the net national U.S. welfare gains from an optimal tariff over alternative values of the import supply elasticity (again assuming no policy response by Canada). Cutting the import supply elasticity to .5 would imply an increase in U.S. monopsony power, and the net gain from an optimal tariff would exceed $700 million annually. Doubling the initial value of the import supply elasticity to 1.8 cuts the optimal tariff; the associated net welfare gains would be less than $200 million per year.

11.3.2 Canada as an Export Monopolist

Optimal duties approaching 50 percent are primarily of academic interest. The vehement response of the Canadians to the October actions in support of a 15 percent import duty provides an indication of the intolerance that would meet an even higher duty—and that would invalidate the calculations in tables 11.7 and 11.8. Moreover, the U.S. political and administrative process provides no indication that it con-

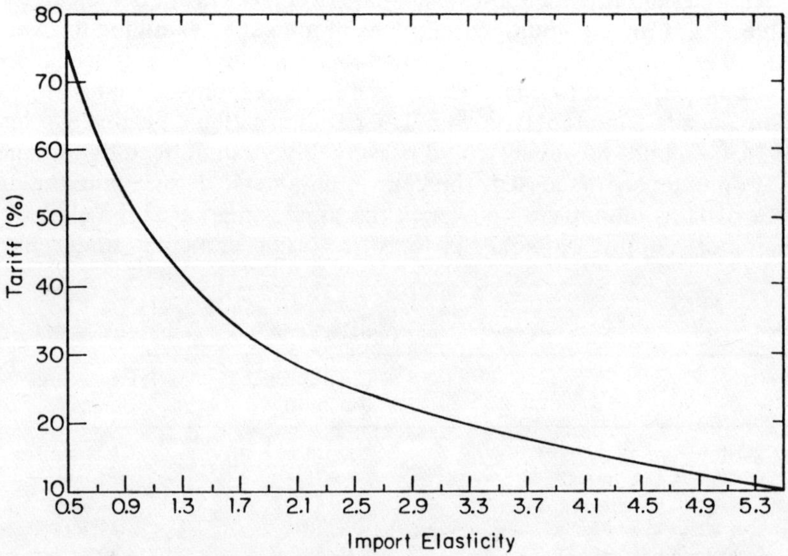

Fig. 11.3 Optimal U.S. timber tariff.

siders an optimal duty within the realm of possibility. The U.S. lumber industry's most aggressive demands have been in the range of 25–28 percent.

More relevant than the matter of an optimal tariff is whether the kinds of distributional payoffs to the domestic lumber industry and/or the associated net national impacts of the magnitudes shown in table 11.5 were worth putting the United States' broader relationships with Canada at risk of significant deterioration. The end result, after all, is that the negotiations regarding a general free trade agreement have been set back, and the December 30, 1986 lumber accords have left the United States subject to a monopolistic Canadian export tariff.

Table 11.9 shows estimates of the incidence and welfare effects of the Canadian 15 percent export duty, relative to the previous free trade regime.[16] The Canadian export duty raises delivered lumber prices in the United States and depresses prices in Canada. In fact, news reports out of the timber- and lumber-producing regions of Canada are already reporting output and employment cutbacks, as well as the attendant public outcry against the Canadian government for agreeing to the export duty. The export duty, however, permits Canada to exercise its monopoly power vis-à-vis the United States—although it is apparently no consolation that the resulting monopoly rents accrue to the Canadian treasury rather than to the Canadian timber and lumber industries. On net, Canada appears to gain roughly $120 million per year from the 15 percent lumber export duty.

The U.S. lumber industry cares little if its prices are raised by a U.S. import tariff or an equivalent Canadian export tariff (table 11.9). (In fact, this observation probably carries the heart of the political economy of the timber trade war.) U.S. lumber consumers are equally indifferent to the reason the prices they face are going up. At the national level, the

Table 11.9 **Welfare Consequences of a 15 Percent Canadian Export Duty (millions of 1986 dollars)**

	Gains	Losses
U.S. lumber producers (labor, capital, land)	$416.8	
U.S. lumber users (intermediate and final)		$556.9
U.S. government (tariff revenues)	$0.0	
Net U.S.		$140.1
Net Canada	$117.6	
Net U.S. and Canada		$22.5

primary economic difference between the countervailing duty and the ultimate Canadian export tax that has been adopted is found in which government gets to collect the tariff revenues. The move from a U.S. import duty to a Canadian export duty has caused a transfer from the U.S. Treasury to the Canadian treasury. Relative to the pre-October free trade regime, the United States now finds itself $140 million per year worse off. From a national perspective, the war has not gone well.

11.4 Conclusion

11.4.1 Observations on the Conduct of U.S.-Canadian Trade Relations

What began in October 1986 as a monopsonistic action against Canada has ended with a breakdown of free trade in lumber and the imposition of a monopoly tariff against the United States. While the economic logic of this is troubling, the political rationale does not seem hard to fathom. The U.S. lumber industry appears to have pulled off a classic case of industry capture of the political process.

It is fashionable to criticize simple industry "capture" theories of economic policy-making (e.g., Kalt and Zupan 1984), and in some sense it would be nice if there were a more complicated and less traditional story to tell here. In this case, however, the capture theory holds considerable appeal: the U.S. lumber industry was able to organize itself into a highly effective lobby group that was able to organize virtually all timber and lumber producers, suppress free-rider factionalism, produce technical legal and analytic submissions to the relevant administrative agency, and enlist particularly important congressional support in its appeals to the White House, the Commerce Department, and the ITC. In Washington, Oregon, Idaho, Georgia, and Alabama, the November elections for the U.S. Senate provided the catalyst that forced the political process to focus on the lumber industry. The finding, three weeks prior to the elections, that Canada was subsidizing lumber production and was subject to countervailing duties may have angered the Canadians, but within two months a negotiated settlement was reached that left the U.S. lumber industry and Canada better off than if no intervention had occurred. This helped the Administration preserve, or at least partially salvage, its relations with Canada while supplying the benefits to the domestic sector that put forth the most compelling political demand. In classic Stigler-Olson fashion (that is, more concentrated groups are more effective at political organization), the U.S. consumers of lumber products were so diffuse and faced such low per capita stakes relative to lumber producers that they had (and continue to have) little ability to block moves to raise the prices they pay.

From the Canadian perspective, the prospect of a countervailing duty imposed by the United States created sharp strategic choices: fight the ITC and Commerce Department findings through the courts or negotiate a settlement. The former path suggests a strategy designed to convince the United States of Canadian toughness in opposing monopsonistic U.S. tariffs, but why take this stand? The negotiated settlement, after all, offered the prospect of a net gain for Canada—a victory in the timber trade war. To imply, however, that the Canadians adopted the negotiations approach because they were pursuing the Net Canada entry in table 11.7 is to beg the question of why the Canadian political process would be driven less by capturing private interests and more by considerations of net national economic welfare than is the policy process in the United States. The Canadian lumber and timber industries would appear to be no less powerful relative to consumers than their counterparts in the United States, and they have not benefited from the timber trade war. The reality seems to be that Canada really was put in a defensive posture when the United States launched its import duty, and the negotiated settlement was explicitly justified internally in Canada by the argument that, if there is going to be a duty on lumber, it is better that Canada collect the sizable tariff revenues than let these monies accrue to the U.S. government.

It remains to be seen whether the timber trade war is completely over. If it is rekindled, the impetus will come from Canada. Only within Canada is there significant, continuing unrest and distress over the current state of affairs. Layoffs have begun in the Canadian timber and lumber industries, and nationalistic sentiments have been piqued by a sense of having been put on the defensive by the United States. The global solution may still ride on the fate of ongoing attempts to establish a general free trade agreement. The lumber incident, however, has probably reduced the prospects of a broad agreement. In the United States the lumber and timber industries now have vested interests in opposing a return toward free trade, and in Canada mistrust of the United States runs high.

11.4.2 Observations on the Conduct of Protectionist U.S. Trade Policies

The U.S.-Canadian lumber dispute forcefully demonstrates that the realms in which trade wars are fought are not solely the economic marketplaces. The outcome of the lumber dispute has hinged significantly on broader geopolitical, foreign policy concerns. For, at the core, the outcome of the timber trade war refllects a combination of (1) the domestic political necessity of transferring wealth to the U.S. forest products industry, while (2) trying to keep the Canadians "happy." The essence of the negotiated settlement of December 1986 (and table 11.9) is that to accomplish the former, the United States had to raise the amount it pays for the latter—by $117.6 million per year (table 11.9).

This interpretation of the timber trade war explains why the U.S. political system ended up at table 11.9—a Canadian monopoly export tariff—rather than a table 11.5—a U.S. monopsony import tariff. If the path to protection for the U.S. industry was a U.S. import duty, Canada was going to be harmed—table 11.5. The prospect of direct economic harm, as well as the fueling of Canadian nationalism, was demonstrably going to reduce the supply of an important ally's cooperation in the conduct of U.S. foreign policy. As Prime Minister Mulroney noted (threatened?), it is "extremely difficult for anyone . . . to be friends with the Americans."

This kind of Canadian response was unacceptable to the White House and, especially, to the State Department. But if protection had to be delivered, the congressional, legislative route to protection for the U.S. lumber and timber industries was the *least* appealing course: it would be extremely difficult and time-consuming to repeal tariff legislation and replace it with a policy that transferred wealth back to Canada. The alternative result of a temporary U.S. duty replaced by a negotiated Canadian export tariff was far more appealing, the Net U.S. loss of $140.1 million per year from table 11.9 is the price the nation has paid to satisfy the domestic political demands of the timber and lumber industries while ensuring continued Canadian cooperation and allegiance in the conduct of foreign policy. This sum really is a net loss for the United States: the country now pays a higher price to Canada for no more, and probably less, Canadian contribution to U.S. foreign policy.

The path of protectionism that this case reveals is sobering. It is not a picture of the United States engaged in strategic moves to improve the national welfare. It is not even a picture of the United States and its trading partners engaging in mutually destructive rounds of economic retaliation. Rather, it is a picture of the United States pushed into protectionist measures by powerful domestic political interests and then, through the foreign policy branches of government, having to find ways to quickly halt the resulting trade war and appease the affected foreign nations.[17] The United States must act in this way because, as the dominant member of its alliances, it is forced to bear the brunt of the responsibility for maintaining those alliances. Thus, this case suggests that, at least when it affects allies, protectionism can raise the cost and inhibit the conduct of foreign economic and political policy.

Notes

The author would like to thank David Butler and Eric Press for their valuable research assistance. The author has also benefited from comments by workshop participants at the Canadian Studies Conference (Duke University), the Conference on Trade Issues (National Bureau of Economic Research), the Hoover Institution, and the Energy and Environmental Policy Center (Harvard University). Special thanks are due Robert Baldwin, Henry Lee, Arye Hillman, Irwin Stelzer, and Raymond Vernon for their detailed remarks.

1. The shakes and shingles duties arose out of a section 201 case before the International Trade Commission. Section 201 cases allow for import protection of a domestic industry when the ITC is satisfied that imports have been shown "to be a substantial cause of serious injury." This criterion makes no reference to unfair trading practices by foreign competitors and is generally regarded as outside the intent of GATT provisions for countervailing duties.

2. *New York Times*, October 9, 1986.

3. *New York Times*, January 1, 1987.

4. Ibid.

5. *New York Times*, October 17, 1986.

6. *MacClean's*, January 5, 1987, 38.

7. The coalition's filings before the ITC predictably include a list of additional Canadian subsidies that allegedly harm U.S. lumber producers. This list includes preferential tax treatment, loan guarantee programs, and public reforestation programs. At least the first of these does not appear to be substantiated by the data (see table 11.3), and reading the coalition's discussion of these other subsidies, it is hard to resist the impression that the list of U.S. preferential programs for the forestry industry could be made to seem as extensive as the Canadian list.

8. After adjustment for transport costs and exchange rates. This formulation assumes that the process of log-price equalization through trade in log products works within the period of observation (one year in the data used below). Available data require this approach.

9. The basic limitation is disaggregated stumpage fees that can be matched to appropriate measures of logging output. All data employed here are from U.S. ITC 1985.

10. Data that would permit a more accurate accounting for the market-clearing stumpage price and the actual price are not available on a comparable basis.

11. The latter, in particular, may be endogenous since its measurement involves Q^s_c. Results reported below treat labor productivity as an endogenous variable. Results are not sensitive to this.

12. The human capital in the lumber industry is not particularly high skilled, with low-skill labor dominating the work force (see, e.g., the wages in table 11.3). It is also notable for its unwillingness to relocate.

13. See, for example, Adams and Haynes 1981; Adams, McCarl, and Homayounfarrokh 1986; and Boyd and Krutilla 1987.

14. Adams, McCarl, and Homayounfarrokh 1986, for example, estimates the elasticity of U.S. lumber demand to be in the range of $-.15$ to $-.17$.

15. The α's are explicitly calculated by parameterization of ϵ and insertion of actual values of Q and P.

16. The price and quantity effects are as indicated in table 11.8.

17. The United States–Japan dispute over Japanese auto imports followed the same general course: U.S. quota restrictions were superseded by Japanese voluntary export restraints that leave the rents from trade restriction in Japan.

References

Adams, Darius M., and Richard Haynes. 1981. U.S.-Canadian lumber trade: The effects of restrictions. In Roger A. Sedjo, ed., *Issues in U.S. international forest products trade*. Research Paper R-32. Washington D.C.: Resources for the Future.

Adams, Darius M., Bruce A. McCarl, and Lalehrokh Homayounfarrokh. 1986. The role of exchange rates in Canadian-U.S. lumber trade. Center for International Trade in Forest Products, College of Forest Resources, University of Washington, Seattle.

Boyd, R., and K. Krutilla. 1987. The welfare implications of U.S. trade restrictions against the Canadian softwood lumber industry: A spatial equilibrium analysis. *Canadian Journal of Economics* 20(1):17–35.

Coalition for Fair Lumber Imports. 1986a. *Lumber fact book: The facts, issues and policies behind the Canada/U.S. lumber trade problems*. Washington, D.C.

———. 1986b. *Petition for the imposition of countervailing duties pursuant to the Tariff Act of 1930, as amended, in the matter of: Certain Softwood Lumber Products from Canada*. Vol. 1. Washington, D.C.

Federal Trade Commission. 1983. *Prehearing brief by the Federal Trade Commission in the matter of: Certain Softwood Lumber Products from Canada, countervailing duty proceeding*. USITC.

———. 1986. *Post-conference brief of the Federal Trade Commission in the matter of: Certain Softwood Lumber Products from Canada*. No. 701-TA-274 (Preliminary). USITC.

Kalt, J. P., and M. A. Zupan. 1984. Capture and ideology in the economic theory of politics. *American Economic Review* 74 (June): 279–300.

Spelter, H. 1985. A product diffusion approach to modeling softwood lumber demand. *Forest Science* 31(3):685–700.

U.S. International Trade Commission. 1982. *Determination of the commission in investigation no. 701-TA-197 (preliminary) under section 703 (a) of the Tariff Act of 1930, together with the information obtained in the investigation, softwood lumber into the U.S.* USITC Publication 1320.

———. 1985. *Report to the president on investigation no. 332-210 under section 332 of the Tariff Act of 1980, conditions relating to the importation of softwood lumber into the U.S.* USITC Publication 1765.

Comment Arye L. Hillman

Joseph Kalt has presented us with a most interesting case study of the political economy of protection. Kalt's study confirms the appropri-

Arye L. Hillman is professor of economics in the Department of Economics and Business Administration, Bar-Ilan University, Israel.

ateness of the political-influence models of protection in explaining the formulation of international trade policy and reveals how approaches to the determination of trade policy that presume a benevolent government pursuing efficiency objectives assume motivations for intervention that tend to be of little importance in the political arena wherein trade policy decisions are made. A particularly interesting aspect of the study is the revelation that whereas initially pleas for protection went unheeded, once the loophole had been found that provided a legal basis for protection, competition arose between the executive and legislative branches of government to become the provider of protection. This competition is clearly understood in political economy terms. Given that protection could now be provided, both the executive and legislative branches of government sought to reap the benefits attendant on being the agents dispensing increases in rents to the residual claimants in the domestic import-competing industry. Presumably the transaction is not one way; protection is provided against an offsetting return. The political competition was to designate the beneficiary of the return.

The economic theory underlying political-support-maximizing choice of trade policy is based on the principle that policymakers trade off the political costs and benefits of intervention; the costs are the loss of political support from the losers from intervention and the benefits are the gains via the political support from the beneficiaries. Kalt shows us that complex linkages can underlie this cost/benefit calculation. The United States instigated protection for the domestic lumber industry. But such protection in the form of an import tariff has associated political costs that either are absent or at least can be diminished if the same protection were seen to be the consequence of a trade-restricting policy by a foreign government, in this case, Canada. Hence, if one asks why the U.S. government insisted that the Canadians impose an export tax to replace the U.S. import duty, thereby transferring $220 million of revenue annually to Canada, the answer can only be that the political benefits to the United States of casting Canada as the interventionist government were at least equal to the present value of the revenue stream.

Of course, the ITC's position was that intervention in this case corrected for a market distortion rather than created one. Kalt's econometrics confirm that the assignment of rights to Canadian trees is a story about rents rather than subsidies. Rent-seeking activities of Canadian loggers could have evoked an output response, but Kalt's estimates indicate that the supply of Canadian logs is determined administratively, and thus, from an economic perspective, inelastically with respect to the price of logs. Thus the ITC's reasoning went the wrong way around: the difference between the payments made for logs in Canada and the United States does not affect Canadian output of logs, but administratively determined Canadian output establishes the value of the residual rents available to the recipients of the rights to fell Canadian trees.

Thus, rents are assigned in Canada via rights to trees, presumably to individuals who are adept rent-seekers. And a restriction of Canadian lumber exports increases the rents available in the U.S. lumber industry. The list of gainers, not taking into account more complex general equilibrium interdependencies, consists of the claimants to rents in the U.S. lumber industry, the Canadian federal government as the recipient of the revenue from the export tax, and Canadian consumers who presumably benefit from lower domestic lumber prices via the output-substitution effect of the export tariff on domestic Canadian producers' market allocation decisions; one must infer that the gainers also include the U.S. government, which initiated the interventionist process in the first place. Missing from this list are U.S. consumers of lumber, whose loss from intervention Kalt quantifies, and the Canadian logging industry.

The absence of the Canadian logging industry from the list of gainers from intervention is somewhat of a puzzle. After all, the Canadian loggers appear sufficiently politically astute and well organized to be the beneficiaries of the substantial rents from below-market-price access to Canadian trees. But enter a new set of actors: the Canadian provincial authorities who assign the right to log and thereby allocate the rents from logging. The Canadian export tax on lumber therefore effected a transfer from the beneficiaries of administrative allocation decisions made by the provinces to the Canadian federal government. The Canadian provinces lost and the Canadian federal government gained via discretionary assignment of rents and revenues.

There is one final step in tracing through the transfer of rents. The Canadian federal government has announced that revenue from the export tax is to be transferred to the provincial authorities, who, we recall, exercise the discretion to determine the assignment of rents from access to trees. Thus, somewhat circuitously, the Canadian provincial authorities have secured a share of the rents accruing from Canadian timber production. Of course, the provincial authorities could directly secure access to these rents if they could directly sell the right to trees. But the right to trees is "given away" at prices below market value. The export tax permits the Canadian provincial authorities to secure natural resource rents that otherwise are allocated via the interaction between provincial officials and loggers.

We have not been told how the Canadian federal government, the Canadian provincial authorities, and Canadian loggers decide on the mechanism for sharing Canadian natural resource timber rents. Nor do we know the sharing rule for the monopoly rents from restriction of Canadian supply. However, the Canadian rent recipients together have more rents to share subsequent to the intervention, because of the exercise of monopoly power. Taking the Canadian rent recipients into consideration, the list of losers from the United States–Canada lumber intervention reduces to one—domestic U.S. consumers. And this is what the political economy approach to explaining government intervention would predict. The diffused domestic U.S. consumers of the import-competing goods are the source of the rents for the more cohesive U.S. and Canadian industry-specific interests and for the Canadian authorities. "Rational ignorance" or perhaps "rational apathy" of the U.S. consumer facilitates this outcome.

Joseph Kalt is to be complimented for unraveling all of this for us, and for showing us how good applied economic theory and econometrics can be put to use to demonstrate that even though governments may frame their interventionist motives in efficiency terms, considerations of political support and income distribution, and not efficiency, more often explain governments' interventionist decisions. Indeed, in this case, since both governments appear to have gained, Kalt has shown us how international economic policy can well be collusive. The U.S. government can claim that it had no choice but to react to the Canadian "subsidy"; the Canadian federal government can claim that given the options it was presented by the U.S. government, it had no choice but to implement the export tax transferring the revenue to Canada for discretionary spending. And the Canadian provincial authorities, who also appear to be ultimate beneficiaries of the rent transfers, can claim to have been passive agents throughout the entire affair.

Kalt computes estimates of the Harberger efficiency costs of government intervention. But to these costs of intervention one could add the value of the real resources expended in contesting the rents created and assigned at government discretion. Direct computation of the cost of rent-seeking activity is not possible in this instance because we are not in a position to observe the various rent-seeking outlays that have been made. However, we are able to observe the values of the rents assigned and transfers made as the consequence of intervention, and procedures (for example, reviewed in Hillman 1988) can be proposed for inferring the value of the resources expended in a rent-seeking quest from the observed value of the rent being contested. The addition of the real resource cost of rent-seeking activity would result in an increase over the estimates of social loss based on Harberger efficiency costs alone.

Finally, a straightforward application of a basic theorem from the theory of international trade demonstrates a difficulty with the initial basis of the U.S. timber industry's claim of "unfairness" in international trade practices. The U.S. timber industry complained that it was "unfair" that it did not have access to "cheap" Canadian lumber because of the Canadian government's ban on the export of logs. However, the factor-price equalization theorem suggests that in a free trade equilibrium there would be no difference in price between Canadian and U.S. lumber, notwithstanding the Canadian export ban on logs. Kalt reports labor costs in the Canadian and U.S. timber industries to be more or less the same. Given a common technological coefficient on log/lumber, the price of logs is then equalized internationally if there is free trade in lumber. The complaint of the U.S. timber producers was therefore presumably not that they were denied access in the free trade equilibrium to "cheap" Canadian logs but that they were barred from access to competition for the rents associated with the assignments of rights to Canadian trees. The United States–Canada lumber intervention then proceeded to provide compensating rents for the U.S. domestic industry, and indeed it would appear there are gains all around, except for U.S. consumers.

References

Hillman, A. L. 1988. *The political economy of protection*. In the series, Fundamentals of pure and applied economics. New York: Harwood Academic Publishers.

Part IV
The Economics of Cartels and Monopoly

[18]

A THEORY OF OLIGOPOLY

GEORGE J. STIGLER[1]
University of Chicago

No one has the right, and few the ability, to lure economists into reading another article on oligopoly theory without some advance indication of its alleged contribution. The present paper accepts the hypothesis that oligopolists wish to collude to maximize joint profits. It seeks to reconcile this wish with facts, such as that collusion is impossible for many firms and collusion is much more effective in some circumstances than in others. The reconciliation is found in the problem of policing a collusive agreement, which proves to be a problem in the theory of information. A considerable number of implications of the theory are discussed, and a modest amount of empirical evidence is presented.

I. THE TASK OF COLLUSION

A satisfactory theory of oligopoly cannot begin with assumptions concerning the way in which each firm views its interdependence with its rivals. If we adhere to the traditional theory of profit-maximizing enterprises, then behavior is no longer something to be assumed but rather something to be deduced. The firms in an industry will behave in such a way, given the demand-and-supply functions (including those of rivals), that their profits will be maximized.

The combined profits of the entire set of firms in an industry are maximized when they act together as a monopolist. At least in the traditional formulation of the oligopoly problem, in which there are no major uncertainties as to the profit-maximizing output and price at any time, this familiar conclusion seems inescapable. Moreover, the result holds for any number of firms.

Our modification of this theory consists simply in presenting a systematic account of the factors governing the feasibility of collusion, which like most things in this world is not free. Before we do so, it is desirable to look somewhat critically at the concept of homogeneity of products, and what it implies for profit-maximizing. We shall show that collusion normally involves much more than "the" price.

Homogeneity is commonly defined in terms of identity of products or of (what is presumed to be equivalent) pairs of products between which the elasticity of substitution is infinite. On either definition it is the behavior of buyers that is decisive. Yet it should be obvious that products may be identical to any or every buyer while buyers may be quite different from the viewpoint of sellers.

This fact that every transaction involves two parties is something that economists do not easily forget. One would therefore expect a definition of homogeneity also to be two-sided: if the products are what sellers offer, and the purchase commitments are what the buyers offer, full homogeneity clearly involves infinite elasticities of substitution between both products and purchase

[1] I am indebted to Claire Friedland for the statistical work and to Harry Johnson for helpful criticisms.

commitments. In other words, two products are homogeneous to a buyer if he is indifferent between all combinations of x of one and (say) $20 - x$ of the other, at a common price. Two purchase commitments are homogeneous to a seller if he is indifferent between all combinations of y of one and (say) $20 - y$ of the other, at a common price. Full homogeneity is then defined as homogeneity both in products (sellers) and purchase commitments (buyers).

The heterogeneity of purchase commitments (buyers), however, is surely often at least as large as that of products within an industry, and sometimes vastly larger. There is the same sort of personal differentia of buyers as of sellers—ease in making sales, promptness of payment, penchant for returning goods, likelihood of buying again (or buying other products). In addition there are two differences among buyers which are pervasive and well recognized in economics:

1. The size of purchase, with large differences in costs of providing lots of different size.
2. The urgency of purchase, with possibly sufficient differences in elasticity of demand to invite price discrimination.

It is one thing to assert that no important market has homogeneous transactions, and quite another to measure the extent of the heterogeneity. In a regime of perfect knowledge, it would be possible to measure heterogeneity by the variance of prices in transactions; in a regime of imperfect knowledge, there will be dispersion of prices even with transaction homogeneity.[2]

The relevance of heterogeneity to collusion is this: It is part of the task of maximizing industry profits to employ a price structure that takes account of the larger differences in the costs of various classes of transactions. Even with a single, physically homogeneous product the profits will be reduced if differences among buyers are ignored. A simple illustration of this fact is given in the Appendix; disregard of differences among buyers proves to be equivalent to imposing an excise tax upon them, but one which is not collected by the monopolist. A price structure of some complexity will usually be the goal of collusive oligopolists.

II. THE METHODS OF COLLUSION

Collusion of firms can take many forms, of which the most comprehensive is outright merger. Often merger will be inappropriate, however, because of diseconomies of scale,[3] and at certain times and places it may be forbidden by law. Only less comprehensive is the cartel with a joint sales agency, which again has economic limitations—it is ill suited to custom work and creates serious administrative costs in achieving quality standards, cost reductions, product innovations, etc. In deference to American antitrust policy, we shall assume that the collusion takes the form of joint determination of outputs and prices by ostensibly independent firms, but we shall not take account of the effects of the legal prohibitions until later. Oligopoly existed before 1890, and has existed in countries that have never had an antitrust policy.

The colluding firms must agree upon the price structure appropriate to the transaction classes which they are prepared to recognize. A complete profit-maximizing price structure may have

[2] Unless one defines heterogeneity of transactions to include also differences in luck in finding low price sellers; see my "Economics of Information," *Journal of Political Economy*, June, 1961.

[3] If the firms are multiproduct, with different product structures, the diseconomies of merger are not strictly those of scale (in any output) but of firm size measured either absolutely or in terms of variety of products.

almost infinitely numerous price classes: the firms will have to decide upon the number of price classes in the light of the costs and returns from tailoring prices to the diversity of transactions. We have already indicated by hypothetical example (see Appendix) that there are net profits to be obtained by catering to differences in transactions. The level of collusive prices will also depend upon the conditions of entry into the industry as well as upon the elasticities of demand.

Let us assume that the collusion has been effected, and a price structure agreed upon. It is a well-established proposition that if any member of the agreement can secretly violate it, he will gain larger profits than by conforming to it.[4] It is, moreover, surely one of the axioms of human behavior that all agreements whose violation would be profitable to the violator must be enforced. The literature of collusive agreements, ranging from the pools of the 1880's to the electrical conspiracies of recent times, is replete with instances of the collapse of conspiracies because of "secret" price-cutting. This literature is biased: conspiracies that are successful in avoiding an amount of price-cutting which leads to collapse of the agreement are less likely to be reported or detected. But no conspiracy can neglect the problem of enforcement.

Enforcement consists basically of detecting significant deviations from the agreed-upon prices. Once detected, the deviations will tend to disappear because they are no longer secret and will be matched by fellow conspirators if they are not withdrawn. If the enforcement is weak, however—if price-cutting is detected only slowly and incompletely—the conspiracy must recognize its weakness: it must set prices not much above the competitive level so the inducements to price-cutting are small, or it must restrict the conspiracy to areas in which enforcement can be made efficient.

Fixing market shares is probably the most efficient of all methods of combating secret price reductions. No one can profit from price-cutting if he is moving along the industry demand curve,[5] once a maximum profit price has been chosen. With inspection of output and an appropriate formula for redistribution of gains and losses from departures from quotas, the incentive to secret price-cutting is eliminated. Unless inspection of output is costly or ineffective (as with services), this is the ideal method of enforcement, and is widely used by legal cartels. Unfortunately for oligopolists, it is usually an easy form of collusion to detect, for it may require side payments among firms and it leaves indelible traces in the output records.

Almost as efficient a method of eliminating secret price-cutting is to assign each buyer to a single seller. If this can be done for all buyers, short-run price-cutting no longer has any purpose. Long-run price-cutting will still be a serious possibility if the buyers are in competition: lower prices to one's own customers can then lead to an expansion of their share of their market, so the price-cutter's long-run demand curve will be more elastic than that of the industry. Long-run price-cutting is likely to be important, however, only where sellers are providing a major cost component to the buyer.

There are real difficulties of other sorts

[4] If price is above marginal cost, marginal revenue will be only slightly less than price (and hence above marginal cost) for price cuts by this one seller.

[5] More precisely, he is moving along a demand curve which is a fixed share of the industry demand, and hence has the same elasticity as the industry curve at every price.

to the sellers in the assignment of buyers. In general the fortunes of the various sellers will differ greatly over time: one seller's customers may grow threefold, while another seller's customers shrink by half. If the customers have uncorrelated fluctuations in demand, the various sellers will experience large changes in relative outputs in the short run.[6] Where the turnover of buyers is large, the method is simply impracticable.

Nevertheless, the conditions appropriate to the assignment of customers will exist in certain industries, and in particular the geographical division of the market has often been employed. Since an allocation of buyers is an obvious and easily detectible violation of the Sherman Act, we may again infer that an efficient method of enforcing a price agreement is excluded by the antitrust laws. We therefore turn to other techniques of enforcement, but we shall find that the analysis returns to allocation of buyers.

In general the policing of a price agreement involves an audit of the transactions prices. In the absence or violation of antitrust laws, actual inspection of the accounting records of sellers has been employed by some colluding groups, but even this inspection gives only limited assurance that the price agreement is adhered to.[7] Ultimately there is no substitute for obtaining the transaction prices from the buyers.

An oligopolist will not consider making secret price cuts to buyers whose purchases fall below a certain size relative to his aggregate sales. The ease with which price-cutting is detected by rivals is decisive in this case. If p is the probability that some rival will hear of one such price reduction, $1 - (1 - p)^n$ is the probability that a rival will learn of at least one reduction if it is given to n customers. Even if p is as small as 0.01, when n equals 100 the probability of detection is .634, and when n equals 1000 it is .99996. No one has yet invented a way to advertise price reductions which brings them to the attention of numerous customers but not to that of any rival.[8]

It follows that oligopolistic collusion will often be effective against small buyers even when it is ineffective against large buyers. When the oligopolists sell to numerous small retailers, for example, they will adhere to the agreed-upon price, even though they are cutting prices to larger chain stores and industrial buyers. This is a first empirical implication of our theory. Let us henceforth exclude small buyers from consideration.

The detection of secret price-cutting will of course be as difficult as interested people can make it. The price-cutter will certainly protest his innocence, or, if this would tax credulity beyond its taxable capacity, blame a disobedient subordinate. The price cut will often take the indirect form of modifying some nonprice dimension of the transaction. The customer may, and often will, divulge price reductions, in order to have them matched by others, but he will learn from experience if each disclosure is followed by the withdrawal of the lower price offer. Indeed the buyer will frequently

[6] When the relative outputs of the firms change, the minimum cost condition of equal marginal costs for all sellers is likely to be violated. Hence industry profits are not maximized.

[7] The literature and cases on "open-price associations" contain numerous references to the collection of prices from sellers (see Federal Trade Commission, *Open-Price Trade Associations* [Washington, 1929], and cases cited).

[8] This argument applies to size of buyer relative to the individual seller. One can also explain the absence of higgling in small transactions because of the costs of bargaining, but this latter argument turns on the absolute size of the typical transaction, not its size relative to the seller.

fabricate wholly fictitious price offers to test the rivals. Policing the collusion sounds very much like the subtle and complex problem presented in a good detective story.

There is a difference: In our case the man who murders the collusive price will receive the bequest of patronage. The basic method of detection of a price-cutter must be the fact that he is getting business he would otherwise not obtain. No promises of lower prices that fail to shift some business can be really effective—either the promised price is still too high or it is simply not believed.

Our definition of perfect collusion, indeed, must be that no buyer changes sellers voluntarily. There is no competitive price-cutting if there are no shifts of buyers among sellers.

To this rule that price-cutting must be inferred from shifts of buyers there is one partial exception, but that an important one. There is one type of buyer who usually reveals the price he pays, and does not accept secret benefices: the government. The system of sealed bids, publicly opened with full identification of each bidder's price and specifications, is the ideal instrument for the detection of price-cutting. There exists no alternative method of secretly cutting prices (bribery of purchasing agents aside). Our second empirical prediction, then, is that collusion will always be more effective against buyers who report correctly and fully the prices tendered to them.[9]

It follows from the test of the absence of price competition by buyer loyalty—and this is our third major empirical prediction—that collusion is severely limited (under present assumptions excluding market-sharing) when the significant buyers constantly change identity. There exist important markets in which the (substantial) buyers do change identity continuously, namely, in the construction industries. The building of a plant or an office building, for example, is an essentially non-repetitive event, and rivals cannot determine whether the successful bidder has been a price-cutter unless there is open bidding to specification.

The normal market, however, contains both stability and change. There may be a small rate of entry of new buyers. There will be some shifting of customers even in a regime of effective collusion, for a variety of minor reasons we can lump together as "random factors." There will often be some sharing of buyers by several sellers—a device commending itself to buyers to increase the difficulty of policing price agreements. We move then to the world of circumstantial evidence, or, as it is sometimes called, of probability.

III. THE CONDITIONS FOR DETECTING SECRET PRICE REDUCTIONS

We shall investigate the problem of detecting secret price-cutting with a simplified model, in which all buyers and all sellers are initially of equal size. The number of buyers per seller—recalling that we exclude from consideration all buyers who take less than (say) 0.33 per cent of a seller's output—will range from 300 down to perhaps 10 or 20 (since we wish to avoid the horrors of full bilateral oligopoly). A few of these buyers are new, but over moderate periods of time most are "old," although some of these old customers will shift among suppliers. A potential secret price-cutter has then three groups of customers who would increase their patronage if given secret price cuts: the old customers of rivals;

[9] The problem implicitly raised by these remarks is why all sales to the government are not at collusive prices. Part of the answer is that the government is usually not a sufficiently large buyer of a commodity to remunerate the costs of collusion.

the old customers who would normally leave him; and new customers.

Most old buyers will deal regularly with one or a few sellers, in the absence of secret price-cutting. There may be no secret price-cutting because a collusive price is adhered to, or because only an essentially competitive price can be obtained. We shall show that the loyalty of customers is a crucial variable in determining which price is approached. We need to know the probability that an old customer will buy again from his regular supplier at the collusive price, in the absence of secret price-cutting.

The buyer will set the economies of repetitive purchase (which include smaller transaction costs and less product-testing) against the increased probability of secret price-cutting that comes from shifting among suppliers. From the viewpoint of any one buyer, this gain will be larger the larger the number of sellers and the smaller the number of buyers, as we shall show below. The costs of shifting among suppliers will be smaller the more homogeneous the goods and the larger the purchases of the buyer (again an inverse function of his size). Let us label this probability of repeat purchases p. We shall indicate later how this probability could be determined in a more general approach.

The second component of sales of a firm will be its sales to new buyers and to the floating old customers of rivals. Here we assume that each seller is equally likely to make a sale, in the absence of price competition.

Let us proceed to the analysis. There are n_0 "old" buyers and n_n new customers, with $n_n = \lambda n_0$ and n_s sellers. A firm may look to three kinds of evidence on secret price-cutting, and therefore by symmetry to three potential areas to practice secret price-cutting.

1. *The behavior of its own old customers.*—It has, on average, n_0/n_s such customers, and expects to sell to $m_1 = pn_0/n_s$ of them in a given round of transactions, in the absence of price cutting. The variance of this number of customers is

$$\sigma_1^2 = \frac{(1-p)pn_0}{n_s}.$$

The probability of the firm losing more old customers than

$$\frac{(1-p)n_0}{n_s} + k\sigma_1$$

is given by the probability of values greater than k. The expected number of these old customers who will shift to any one rival is, say,

$$m_2 = \frac{1}{n_s - 1}\left[\frac{(1-p)n_0}{n_s} + k\sigma_1\right],$$

with a variance

$$\sigma_2^2 = \frac{n_s - 2}{(n_s - 1)^2}\left[\frac{(1-p)n_0}{n_s} + k\sigma_1\right].$$

The probability that any rival will obtain more than $m_2 + r\sigma_2$ of these customers is determined by r. We could now choose those combinations of k and r that fix a level of probability for the loss of a given number of old customers to any one rival beyond which secret price-cutting by this rival will be inferred. This is heavy arithmetic, however, so we proceed along a less elegant route.

Let us assume that the firm's critical value for the loss of old customers, beyond which it infers secret price-cutting, is

$$\begin{aligned}\frac{(1-p)n_0}{n_s} + \sigma_1 &= \frac{(1-p)n_0}{n_s}\left[1 + \sqrt{\left(\frac{p}{1-p}\frac{n_s}{n_0}\right)}\right] \\ &= \frac{(1-p)n_0}{n_s}(1+\theta),\end{aligned}$$

that is, one standard deviation above the mean. Any one rival will on average attract

$$m_2 = \frac{1}{n_s - 1}\left[\frac{(1-p)n_0}{n_s} + \sigma_1\right]$$

of these customers, with a variance of

$$\sigma_2^2 = \frac{n_s - 2}{(n_s - 1)^2}\left[\frac{(1-p)n_0}{n_s} + \sigma_1\right].$$

Let the rival be suspected of price-cutting if he obtains more than $(m_2 + \sigma_2)$ customers, that is, if the probability of any larger number is less than about 30 per cent. The joint probability of losing one standard deviation more than the average number of old customers and a rival obtaining one standard deviation more than his average share is about 10 per cent. The average sales of a rival are n_0/n_s, ignoring new customers. The maximum number of buyers any seller can obtain from one rival without exciting suspicion, minus the number he will on average get without price-cutting ($[1 - p]n_0/n_s\ [n_s - 1]$), expressed as a ratio to his average sales, is

$$\frac{[\theta(1-p)n_0/(n_s-1)n_s + \sigma_2]}{n_0/n_s}.$$

This criterion is tabulated in Table 1.

TABLE 1

PERCENTAGE GAINS IN SALES FROM UNDETECTED PRICE-CUTTING BY A FIRM

Criterion I: $\frac{1}{(n_s-1)}\left[\theta(1-p) + \sqrt{\frac{n_s(n_s-2)(1-p)(1+\theta)}{n_0}}\right]$ $\qquad \theta = \sqrt{\frac{p}{1-p}\frac{n_s}{n_0}}$

Probability of Repeat Sales (p)	No. of Buyers (n_0)	No. of Sellers					
		2	3	4	5	10	20
p=0.95	20	6.9	11.3	11.3	11.4	11.8	12.7
	30	5.6	8.9	8.8	8.8	9.0	9.6
	40	4.9	7.5	7.4	7.4	7.5	7.9
	50	4.4	6.6	6.5	6.4	6.5	6.8
	100	3.1	4.4	4.3	4.3	4.2	4.4
	200	2.2	3.0	2.9	2.8	2.8	2.8
	400	1.5	2.1	2.0	1.9	1.8	1.8
p=0.90	20	9.5	14.8	14.7	14.6	14.8	15.7
	30	7.8	11.7	11.5	11.4	11.4	12.0
	40	6.7	10.0	9.7	9.6	9.5	9.9
	50	6.0	8.8	8.6	8.4	8.3	8.6
	100	4.2	6.0	5.8	5.6	5.4	5.5
	200	3.0	4.1	3.9	3.8	3.6	3.6
	400	2.1	2.8	2.7	2.6	2.4	2.4
p=0.80	20	12.6	19.3	18.9	18.7	18.6	19.4
	30	10.3	15.4	15.0	14.7	14.5	15.0
	40	8.9	13.1	12.7	12.5	12.2	12.5
	50	8.0	11.6	11.2	11.0	10.6	10.8
	100	5.7	8.0	7.7	7.4	7.1	7.1
	200	4.0	5.5	5.3	5.1	4.8	4.7
	400	2.8	3.8	3.6	3.5	3.2	3.2
p=0.70	20	14.5	22.3	21.8	21.5	21.2	21.9
	30	11.8	17.8	17.3	17.0	16.6	16.9
	40	10.2	15.2	14.8	14.5	14.0	14.2
	50	9.2	13.5	13.1	12.8	12.3	12.4
	100	6.5	9.3	9.0	8.7	8.2	8.2
	200	4.6	6.5	6.2	6.0	5.6	5.5
	400	3.2	4.5	4.3	4.2	3.8	3.7

The entries in Table 1 are measures of the maximum additional sales obtainable by secret price-cutting (expressed as a percentage of average sales) from any one rival beyond which that rival will infer that the price-cutting is taking place. Since the profitability of secret price-cutting depends upon the amount of business one can obtain (as well as upon the excess of price over marginal cost), we may also view these numbers as the measures of the incentive to engage in secret price-cutting. Three features of the tabulation are noteworthy:

a) The gain in sales from any one rival by secret price-cutting is not very sensitive to the number of rivals, given the number of customers and the probability of repeat sales. The aggregate gain in sales of a firm from price-cutting—its total incentive to secret price-cutting—is the sum of the gains from each rival, and therefore increases roughly in proportion to the number of rivals.

b) The incentive to secret price-cutting falls as the number of customers per seller increases—and falls roughly in inverse proportion to the square root of the number of buyers.

c) The incentive to secret price-cutting rises as the probability of repeat purchases falls, but at a decreasing rate.

We have said that the gain to old buyers from shifting their patronage among sellers will be that it encourages secret price-cutting by making it more difficult to detect. Table 1 indicates that there are diminishing returns to increased shifting: The entries increase at a decreasing rate as p falls. In a fuller model we could introduce the costs of shifting among suppliers and determine p to maximize expected buyer gains. The larger the purchases of a buyer, when buyers are of unequal size, however, the greater is the prospect that his shifts will induce price-cutting.

In addition it is clear that, when the number of sellers exceeds two, it is possible for two or more firms to pool information and thus to detect less extreme cases of price-cutting. For example, at the given probability levels, the number of old customers that any one rival should be able to take from a firm was shown to be at most

$$(1-p)\frac{n_0(1+\theta)}{n_s-1},$$

with variance

$$\frac{(n_s-2)(1-p)(1+\theta)}{(n_s-1)^2}\,n_0.$$

At the same probability level, the average number of old customers that one rival should be able to take from T firms is at most

$$\frac{T(1-p)n_0}{n_s-T}\left(1+\frac{\theta}{\sqrt{T}}\right),$$

with the variance

$$\frac{(n_s-T-1)}{(n_s-T)^2}(1-p)\left(1+\frac{\theta}{\sqrt{T}}\right)n_0T.$$

Each of these is smaller than the corresponding expression for one seller when expressed as a fraction of the customers lost by each of the firms pooling information.

There are of course limits to such pooling of information: not only does it become expensive as the number of firms increases, but also it produces less reliable information, since one of the members of the pool may himself be secretly cutting prices. Some numbers illustrative of the effect of pooling will be given at a later point.

2. *The attraction of old customers of other firms is a second source of evidence of price-cutting.*—If a given rival has not cut prices, he will on average lose $(1-p)$ (n_0/n_s) customers, with a variance of σ_1^2. The number of customers he will retain with secret price-cutting cannot exceed

a level at which the rivals suspect the price-cutting. Any one rival will have little basis for judging whether he is getting a fair share of this firm's old customers, but they can pool their information and then in the aggregate they will expect the firm to lose at least $(1 - p)(n_0/n_s) - 2\sigma_1$ customers, at the 5 per cent probability level. Hence the secret price-cutter can retain at most $2\sigma_1$ of his old customers (beyond his average number), which as a fraction of his average sales (ignoring new customers) is

TABLE 2

OLD CUSTOMERS THAT A SECRET PRICE-CUTTER CAN RETAIN, AS A PERCENTAGE OF AVERAGE SALES

Criterion II: $2\sqrt{\frac{p(1-p)}{2}}\frac{n_s}{n_0}$

Probability That Old Customer Will Remain Loyal (p)	No. of Old Customers per Seller (n_0/n_s)			
	10	20	50	100
0.95	13.8	9.7	6.2	4.4
.90	19.0	13.4	8.5	6.0
.85	22.6	16.0	10.1	7.1
.80	25.3	17.9	11.3	8.0
.75	27.4	19.4	12.2	8.7
.70	29.0	20.5	13.0	9.2
.65	30.2	21.3	13.5	9.5
.60	31.0	21.9	13.9	9.8
.55	31.5	22.2	14.1	10.0
0.50	31.6	22.4	14.1	10.0

$$\frac{2\sigma_1}{n_0/n_s} = 2\sqrt{\frac{(1-p)pn_s}{n_0}}.$$

This is tabulated as Table 2.

If the entries in Table 2 are compared with those in Table 1,[10] it is found that a price-cutter is easier to detect by his gains at the expense of any one rival than by his unusual proportion of repeat sales. This second criterion will therefore seldom be useful.

3. *The behavior of new customers is a third source of information on price-cutting.*—There are n_n new customers per period,[11] equal to λn_0. A firm expects, in the absence of price-cutting, to sell to

$$m_3 = \frac{1}{n_s}\lambda n_0$$

of these customers, with a variance of

$$\sigma_3^2 = \left(1 - \frac{1}{n_s}\right)\frac{\lambda n_0}{n_s}.$$

If the rivals pool information (without pooling, this area could not be policed effectively), this firm cannot obtain more than $m_3 + 2\sigma_3$ customers without being deemed a price-cutter, using again a 5 per cent probability criterion. As a percentage of the firm's total sales, the maximum sales above the expected number in the absence of price cutting are then

$$\frac{2\sigma_3}{n_0(1+\lambda)/n_s} = \frac{2}{1+\lambda}\sqrt{\frac{(n_s-1)\lambda}{n_0}}.$$

We tabulate this criterion as Table 3.

Two aspects of the incentive to cut prices (or equivalently the difficulty of detecting price cuts) to new customers are apparent: the incentive increases rapidly with the number of sellers[12] and the

[10] For example, take $p = .95$. The entry for 10 customers per seller is 13.8 in Table 2—this is the maximum percentage of average sales that can be obtained by price reductions to old customers. The corresponding entries in Table 1 are 6.9 (2 sellers, 20 buyers), 8.9 (3 and 30), 7.4 (4 and 40), 6.4 (5 and 50), 4.2 (10 and 100), etc. Multiplying each entry in Table 1 by $(n_s - 1)$, we get the maximum gain in sales (without detection) by attracting customers of rivals, and beyond 2 sellers the gains are larger by this latter route. Since Table 1 is based upon a 10 per cent probability level, strict comparability requires that we use 1.6 σ, instead of 2 σ, in Table 2, which would reduce the entries by one-fifth.

[11] Unlike old customers, whose behavior is better studied in a round of transactions, the new customers are a flow whose magnitude depends much more crucially on the time period considered. The annual flow of new customers is here taken (relative to the number of old customers) as the unit.

[12] And slowly with the number of sellers if customers per seller are held constant.

incentive increases with the rate of entry of new customers. As usual the incentive falls as the absolute number of customers per seller rises. If the rate of entry of new buyers is 10 per cent or more, price-cutting to new customers allows larger sales increases without detection that can be obtained by attracting customers of rivals (compare Tables 1 and 3).

Of the considerable number of directions in which this model could be enlarged, two will be presented briefly.

The first is inequality in the size of firms. In effect this complication has already been introduced by the equivalent device of pooling information. If we tabulate the effects of pooling of information by K firms, the results are equivalent to having a firm K times as large as the other firms. The number of old customers this large firm can lose to any one small rival (all of whom are equal in size) is given, in Table 4, as a percentage of the average number of old customers of the small firm; the column labeled $K = 1$ is of course the case analyzed in Table 1.

The effects of pooling on the detection of price-cutting are best analyzed by

TABLE 3

MAXIMUM ADDITIONAL NEW CUSTOMERS (AS A PERCENTAGE OF AVERAGE SALES) OBTAINABLE BY SECRET PRICE-CUTTING

$$\textit{Criterion III: } \frac{2}{1+\lambda}\sqrt{\frac{\lambda(n_s-1)}{n_0}}$$

Rate of Appearance of New Buyers (λ)	No. of Old Buyers (n_0)	No. of Sellers					
		2	3	4	5	10	20
1/100	20	4.4	6.3	7.7	8.9	13.3	19.3
	30	3.6	5.1	6.3	7.2	10.8	15.8
	40	3.1	4.4	5.4	6.3	9.4	13.6
	50	2.8	4.0	4.8	5.6	8.4	12.2
	100	2.0	2.8	3.4	4.0	5.9	8.6
	200	1.4	2.0	2.4	2.8	4.2	6.1
	400	1.0	1.4	1.7	2.0	3.0	4.3
1/10	20	12.9	18.2	22.3	25.7	38.6	56.0
	30	10.5	14.8	18.2	21.0	31 5	45.8
	40	9.1	12.9	15.8	18.2	27.3	39.6
	50	8.1	11.5	14.1	16.3	24.4	35.4
	100	5.8	8.1	10.0	11.5	17.2	25.1
	200	4.1	5.8	7.0	8.1	12.2	17.7
	400	2.9	4.1	5.0	5.8	8.6	12.5
1/5	20	16.7	23.6	28.9	33.3	50.0	72.6
	30	13.6	19.2	23.6	27.2	40.8	59.3
	40	11.8	16.7	20.4	23.6	35.4	51.4
	50	10.5	14.9	18.3	21.1	31.6	46.0
	100	7.4	10.5	12.9	14.9	22.4	32.5
	200	5.3	7.4	9.1	10.5	15.8	23.0
	400	3.7	5.3	6.4	7.4	11.2	16.2
1/4	20	17.9	25.3	31.0	35.8	53.7	78.0
	30	14.6	20.7	25.3	29.2	43.8	63.7
	40	12.6	17.9	21.9	25.3	38.0	55.1
	50	11.3	16.0	19.6	22.6	33.9	49.3
	100	8.0	11.3	13.9	16.0	24.0	34.9
	200	5.7	8.0	9.8	11.3	17.0	24.7
	400	4.0	5.7	6.9	8.0	12.0	17.4

comparing Table 4 with Table 1. If there are 100 customers and 10 firms (and p = 0.9), a single firm can increase sales by 5.4 per cent by poaching on one rival, or about 50 per cent against all rivals (Table 1). If 9 firms combine, the maximum amount the single firm can gain by secret price-cutting is 28.9 per cent (Table 4). With 20 firms and 200 customers, a single firm can gain 3.6 per cent from each rival, or about 30 per cent from 9 rivals; if these rivals merge, the corresponding figure falls to 14.0 per cent. The pooling of information therefore reduces substantially the scope for secret price-cutting.

This table exaggerates the effect of inequality of firm size because it fails to take account of the fact that the number of customers varies with firm size, on our argument that only customers above a certain size relative to the seller are a

TABLE 4

PERCENTAGE GAINS IN SALES FROM UNDETECTED PRICE-CUTTING BY A SMALL FIRM

Criterion IV:

$$\frac{1}{n_s - K}\left[\theta(1-p)\sqrt{K}+\sqrt{\frac{n_s K(1-p)(n_s-K-1)(1+\theta/\sqrt{K})}{n_0}}\right]$$

$$\theta=\sqrt{\frac{p}{1-p}\frac{n_s}{n_0}}$$

Probability of Repeat Sales (p)	No. of Firms (n_s-K+1)	Buyers per Small Seller (n_0/n_s)	Size of Large Firm (K)			
			1	2	5	9
p=0.9	2	10	9.5	13.4	21.2	28.5
		30	5.5	7.7	12.2	16.4
		50	4.2	6.0	9.5	12.7
	3	10	11.7	15.8	23.9	31.4
		30	6.3	8.7	13.3	17.6
		50	4.8	6.6	10.2	13.5
	4	10	9.7	13.1	19.7	25.7
		30	5.2	7.1	10.9	14.4
		50	4.0	5.4	8.3	11.0
	10	10	5.4	7.2	10.7	14.0
		30	2.9	3.9	5.9	7.7
		50	2.2	2.9	4.5	5.9
p=0.8	2	10	12.6	17.9	28.3	37.9
		30	7.3	10.3	16.3	21.9
		50	5.7	8.0	12.6	17.0
	3	10	15.4	21.0	32.1	42.3
		30	8.4	11.6	18.0	23.9
		50	6.4	8.9	13.8	18.4
	4	10	12.7	17.3	26.3	34.7
		30	6.9	9.5	14.7	19.5
		50	5.3	7.3	11.3	15.0
	10	10	7.1	9.5	14.4	18.9
		30	3.8	5.2	8.0	10.6
		50	2.9	4.0	6.1	8.1

feasible group for secret price-cutting. The small firm can find it attractive to cut prices to buyers which are not large enough to be potential customers by price-cutting for the large seller.

The temporal pattern of buyers' behavior provides another kind of information: What is possibly due to random fluctuation in the short run cannot with equal probability be due to chance if repeated. Thus the maximum expected loss of old customers to a rival in one round of transactions is (at the 1σ level)

$$\frac{n_0}{(n_s-1)n_s}(1-p)(1+\theta),$$

but for T consecutive periods the maximum expected loss is (over T periods)

$$\frac{T}{n_s-1}(1-p)\frac{n_0}{n_s}[1+\theta\sqrt{T}],$$

with a variance of

$$\sigma_5{}^2=\frac{(n_s-2)}{(n_s-1)^2}T(1-p)\frac{n_0}{n_s}[1+\theta\sqrt{T}].$$

This source of information is of minor efficacy in detecting price-cutting unless the rounds of successive transactions are numerous—that is, unless buyers purchase (enter contracts) frequently.

Our approach has certain implications for the measurement of concentration, if we wish concentration to measure likelihood of effective collusion. In the case of new customers, for example, let the probability of attracting a customer be proportional to the firm's share of industry output (s). Then the variance of the firm's share of sales to new customers will be $n_n s(1-s)$, and the aggregate for the industry will be

$$C=n_n\sum_{1}^{r}s(1-s)$$

for r firms. This expression equals $n_n(1-H)$, where

$$H=\Sigma s^2$$

is the Herfindahl index of concentration. The same index holds, as an approximation, for potential price-cutting to attract old customers.[13]

The foregoing analysis can be extended to non-price variables, subject to two modifications. The first modification is that there be a definite joint profit-maximizing policy upon which the rivals can agree. Here we may expect to encounter a spectrum of possibilities, ranging from a clearly defined optimum policy (say, on favorable legislation) to a nebulous set of alternatives (say, directions of research).[14] Collusion is less feasible, the less clear the basis on which it should proceed. The second modification is that

[13] A similar argument leads to a measure of concentration appropriate to potential price-cutting for old customers. Firm i will lose

$$(1-p)n_0s_i$$

old customers, and firm j will gain

$$(1-p)n_0\frac{s_is_j}{1-s_i}$$

of them, with a variance

$$(1-p)n_0\frac{s_is_j}{1-s_i}\left(1-\frac{s_j}{1-s_i}\right).$$

If we sum over all i ($\neq j$), we obtain the variance of firm j's sales to old customers of rivals

$$(1-p)n_0s_j(1+H-2s_j),$$

to an approximation, and summing over all j, we have the concentration measure,

$$(1-p)n_0(1-H).$$

The agreement of this measure with that for new customers is superficial: that for new customers implicitly assumes pooling of information and that for old customers does not.

[14] Of course, price itself usually falls somewhere in this range rather than at the pole. The traditional assumption of stationary conditions conceals this fact.

the competitive moves of any one firm will differ widely among non-price variables in their detectability by rivals. Some forms of non-price competition will be easier to detect than price-cutting because they leave visible traces (advertising, product quality, servicing, etc.) but some variants will be elusive (reciprocity in purchasing, patent licensing arrangements). The common belief that non-price competition is more common than price competition is therefore not wholly in keeping with the present theory. Those forms that are suitable areas for collusion will have less competition; those which are not suitable will have more competition.

TABLE 5

RESIDUALS FROM REGRESSION OF ADVERTISING RATES ON CIRCULATION*

No. of Evening Papers	n	Mean Residual (Logarithm)	Standard Deviation of Mean
One	23	0.0211	0.0210
With morning paper	10	− .0174	.0324
Without morning paper	13	.0507	.0233
Two	30	−0.0213	0.0135

* The regression equation is

$$\log R = 5.194 - \underset{(.620)}{1.688} \log c + \underset{(.063)}{.139} (\log c)^2 ,$$

where R is the 5 M milline rate and c is circulation.

Source: American Association of Advertising Agencies, *Market and Newspaper Statistics*, Vol. VIIIa (1939).

IV. SOME FRAGMENTS OF EVIDENCE

Before we seek empirical evidence on our theory, it is useful to report two investigations of the influence of numbers of sellers on price. These investigations have an intrinsic interest because, so far as I know, no systematic analysis of the effect of numbers has hitherto been made.

The first investigation was of newspaper advertising rates, as a function of the number of evening newspapers in a city. Advertising rates on a milline basis are closely (and negatively) related to circulation, so a regression of rates on circulation was made for fifty-three cities in 1939. The residuals (in logarithmic form) from this regression equation are tabulated in Table 5. It will be observed that rates are 5 per cent above the average in one-newspaper towns and 5 per cent below the average in two-newspaper towns, and the towns with one evening paper but also an independent morning paper fall nearly midway between these points. Unfortunately there were too few cities with more than two evening newspapers to yield results for larger numbers of firms.

The second investigation is of spot commercial rates on AM radio stations in the four states of Ohio, Indiana, Michigan, and Illinois. The basic equation introduces, along with number of rivals, a series of other factors (power of station, population of the county in which the station is located, etc.). Unfortunately the number of stations is rather closely correlated with population ($r^2 = .796$ in the logarithms). The general result, shown in Table 6, is similar to that for newspapers: the elasticity of price with respect to number of rivals is quite small (−.07). Here the range of stations in a county was from 1 to 13.

Both studies suggest that the level of prices is not very responsive to the actual number of rivals. This is in keeping with the expectations based upon our model, for that model argues that the number of buyers, the proportion of new buyers, and the relative sizes of firms are as important as the number of rivals.

To turn to the present theory, the only test covering numerous industries so far devised has been one based upon profitability. This necessarily rests upon company data, and it has led to the exclusion of a large number of industries for which the companies do not operate in a well-defined industry. For example, the larger steel and chemical firms operate in a series of markets in which their position ranges from monopolistic to competitive. We have required of each industry that the earnings of a substantial fraction of the companies in the industry (measured by output) be determined by the profitability of that industry's products, that is, that we have a fair share of the industry and the industry's product is the dominant product of the firms.

Three measures of profitability are given in Table 7: (1) the rate of return on all capital (including debt), (2) the rate of return on net worth (stockholders' equity); (3) the ratio of market value to book value of the common stock.

In addition, two measures of concentration are presented: (1) the conventional measure, the share of output produced by the four leading firms; and (2) the Herfindahl index, H.

The various rank correlations are given in Table 8. The various concentration measures, on the one hand, and the various measures of profitability, on the other hand, are tolerably well correlated.[15] All show the expected positive relationship. In general the data suggest that there is no relationship between profitability and concentration if H is less than 0.250 or the share of the four largest firms is less than about 80 per cent. These data, like those on advertising rates, confirm our theory only in the sense that they support theories which assert that competition increases with number of firms.

Our last evidence is a study of the prices paid by buyers of steel products in 1939, measured relative to the quoted prices (Table 9). The figure of 8.3 for hot-

TABLE 6

REGRESSION OF AM SPOT COMMERCIAL RATES (26 TIMES) AND STATION CHARACTERISTICS, 1961

(n = 345)

Independent Variables*	Regression Coefficient	Standard Error
1. Logarithm of population of county, 1960	.238	0.026
2. Logarithm of kilowatt power of station	.206	.015
3. Dummy variables of period of broadcasting:		
a) Sunrise to sunset	−.114	.025
b) More than (*a*), less than 18 hours	−.086	.027
c) 18–21 hours	−.053	.028
4. Logarithm of number of stations in county	−.074	0.046
	R^2 = .743	

* Dependent variable: logarithm of average rate, May 1, 1961 (dollars).

Source: "Spot Radio Rates and Data," *Standard Rate and Data Service, Inc.*, Vol. XLIII, No. 5 (May 1961).

[15] The concentration measures have a rank correlation of .903. The profitability measures have the following rank correlations:

	Return on All Assets	Ratio of Market to Book Value
Return on net worth	.866	.872
Ratio of market to book value	.733	....

TABLE 7

PROFITABILITY AND CONCENTRATION DATA

INDUSTRY*	CONCENTRATION (1954)		AVERAGE RATE OF RETURN (1953–57)		RATIO OF MARKET VALUE TO BOOK VALUE (1953–57)
	Share of Top 4	H†	All Assets	Net Worth	
Sulfur mining (4)	98	0.407	19.03	23.85	3.02
Automobiles (3)	98	.369	11.71	20.26	2.30
Flat glass (3)	90	.296	11.79	16.17	2.22
Gypsum products (2)	90	.280	12.16	20.26	1.83
Primary aluminum (4)	98	.277	6.87	13.46	2.48
Metal cans (4)	80	.260	7.27	13.90	1.60
Chewing gum (2)	86	.254	13.50	17.06	2.46
Hard-surface floor coverings (3)	87	.233	6.56	7.59	0.98
Cigarettes (5)	83	.213	7.23	11.18	1.29
Industrial gases (3)	84	.202	8.25	11.53	1.33
Corn wet milling (3)	75	.201	9.17	11.55	1.48
Typewriters (3)	83	.193	3.55	5.39	0.84
Domestic laundry equipment (2)	68	.174	9.97	17.76	1.66
Rubber tires (9)	79	.171	7.86	14.02	1.70
Rayon fiber (4)	76	.169	5.64	6.62	0.84
Carbon black (2)	73	.152	8.29	9.97	1.40
Distilled liquors (6)	64	0.118	6.94	7.55	0.77

* The number of firms is given in parentheses after the industry title. Only those industries are included for which a substantial share (35 per cent or more) of the industry's sales is accounted for by the firms in the sample, and these firms derive their chief revenues (50 per cent or more) from the industry in question.

† *H* is Herfindahl index.

TABLE 8

RANK CORRELATIONS OF MEASURES OF PROFITABILITY AND MEASURES OF CONCENTRATION

MEASURE OF CONCENTRATION	MEASURE OF PROFITABILITY		
	Rate of Return on All Assets	Rate of Return on Net Worth	Ratio of Market Value to Book Value
Share of output produced by four largest firms	.322	.507	.642
Herfindahl index (*H*)	.524	.692	.730

TABLE 9

PRICES OF STEEL PRODUCTS, 1939, AND INDUSTRY STRUCTURE, 1938

PRODUCT CLASS	PRICES, 2D QUARTER, 1939 (PER CENT)		HERFINDAHL INDEX	OUTPUT IN 1939 RELATIVE TO 1937
	Average Discount from List Price	Standard Deviation		
Hot-rolled sheets	8.3	7.3	0.0902	1.14
Merchant bars	1.2	4.5	.1517	0.84
Hot-rolled strip	8.5	8.3	.1069	0.56
Plates	2.6	4.8	.1740	0.85
Structural shapes	3.2	4.3	.3280	0.92
Cold-rolled strip	8.8	9.8	.0549	0.88
Cold-rolled sheets	5.8	5.0	.0963	1.14
Cold-finished bars	0.9	3.4	0.0964	0.83

Source: Prices: "Labor Department Examines Consumers' Prices of Steel Products," *Iron Age*, April 25, 1946; industry structure: 1938 capacity data from *Directory of Iron and Steel Works of the United States and Canada*; output: *Annual Statistical Report, American Iron and Steel Institute* (New York, 1938, 1942).

rolled sheets, for example, represents an average of 8.3 per cent reduction from quoted prices, *paid by buyers*, with a standard deviation of 7.3 per cent of quoted prices. The rate of price-cutting is almost perfectly correlated with the standard deviation of transaction prices, as we should expect: the less perfect the market knowledge, the more extensive the price-cutting.

In general, the more concentrated the industry structure (measured by the Herfindahl index), the larger were the price reductions. Although there were no extreme departures from this relationship, structural shapes and hot-rolled strip had prices somewhat lower than the average relationship, and cold finished bars prices somewhat higher than expected, and the deviations are not accounted for by the level of demand (measured by 1939 sales relative to 1937 sales). The number of buyers could not be taken into account, but the BLS study states:

> The extent of price concessions shown by this study is probably understated because certain very large consumers in the automobile and container industries were excluded from the survey. This omission was at the request of the OPA which contemplated obtaining this information in connection with other studies. Since a small percentage of steel consumers, including these companies, accounts for a large percentage of steel purchased, prices paid by a relatively few large consumers have an important influence upon the entire steel price structure. Very large steel consumers get greater reductions from published prices than smaller consumers, often the result of competitive bidding by the mills for the large volume of steel involved. One very large steel consumer, a firm that purchased over 2 pct of the total consumption of hot and cold-rolled sheets in 1940, refused to give purchase prices. This firm wished to protect its suppliers, fearing that "certain transactions might be revealed which would break confidence" with the steel mills. However, this company did furnish per-cent changes of prices paid for several steel products which showed that for some products prices advanced markedly, and in one case, nearly 50 pct. The great price advances for this company indicate that it was receiving much larger concessions than smaller buyers.[16]

These various bits of evidence are fairly favorable to the theory, but they do not constitute strong support. More powerful tests will be feasible when the electrical equipment triple-damage suits are tried.[17] The great merit of our theory, in fact, is that it has numerous testable hypotheses, unlike the immortal theories that have been traditional in this area.

[16] See "Labor Department Examines Consumers' Prices of Steel Products," *op. cit.*, p. 133.

[17] For example, it will be possible to test the prediction that prices will be higher and less dispersed in sales on public bids than in privately negotiated sales, and the prediction that price-cutting increases as the number of buyers diminishes.

APPENDIX

The importance of product heterogeneity for profit-maximizing behavior cannot well be established by an a priori argument. Nevertheless, the following simple exposition of the implications for profitability of disregarding heterogeneity may have some heuristic value. The analysis, it will be observed, is formally equivalent to that of the effects of an excise tax on a monopolist.

Assume that a monopolist makes men's suits, and that he makes only one size of suit. This is absurd behavior, but the picture of the sadistic monopolist who disregards consumer desires has often made fugitive appearances in the literature so the problem has some interest of its own. The demand curve of a consumer for suits that fit, $f(p)$, would now be reduced because he would have to incur some alteration cost a in order to wear the suit. His effective demand would therefore decline to $f(p + a)$. Assume further that the marginal cost of suits is constant (m), and that it would be the same if the monopolist were to make suits of various sizes.

The effect on profits of a uniform product—uniform is an especially appropriate word here—can be shown graphically (Fig. 1). The decrease in quantity sold, with a linear demand curve, is

$$MB = \tfrac{1}{2} a f'(p) \, .$$

The decrease in the price received by the monopolist is

$$DN = \frac{MB}{f'(p)} - a = -\frac{a}{2} ,$$

so if π is profit per unit, and q is output, the relative decline in total profit is approximately

$$\frac{\Delta\pi}{\pi} + \frac{\Delta q}{q} ,$$

or

$$\frac{MB}{OB} + \frac{ND}{AD} .$$

Since

$$OB = \frac{f(m)}{2}$$

$$AD = -\frac{p}{\eta} ,$$

where η is the elasticity of demand, the relative decline of profits with a uniform product is

$$\frac{a f'(p)}{f(m)} + \frac{a\eta}{2p} = \frac{a\eta}{2p} + \frac{a\eta}{2p}$$

$$= \frac{a\eta}{p} .$$

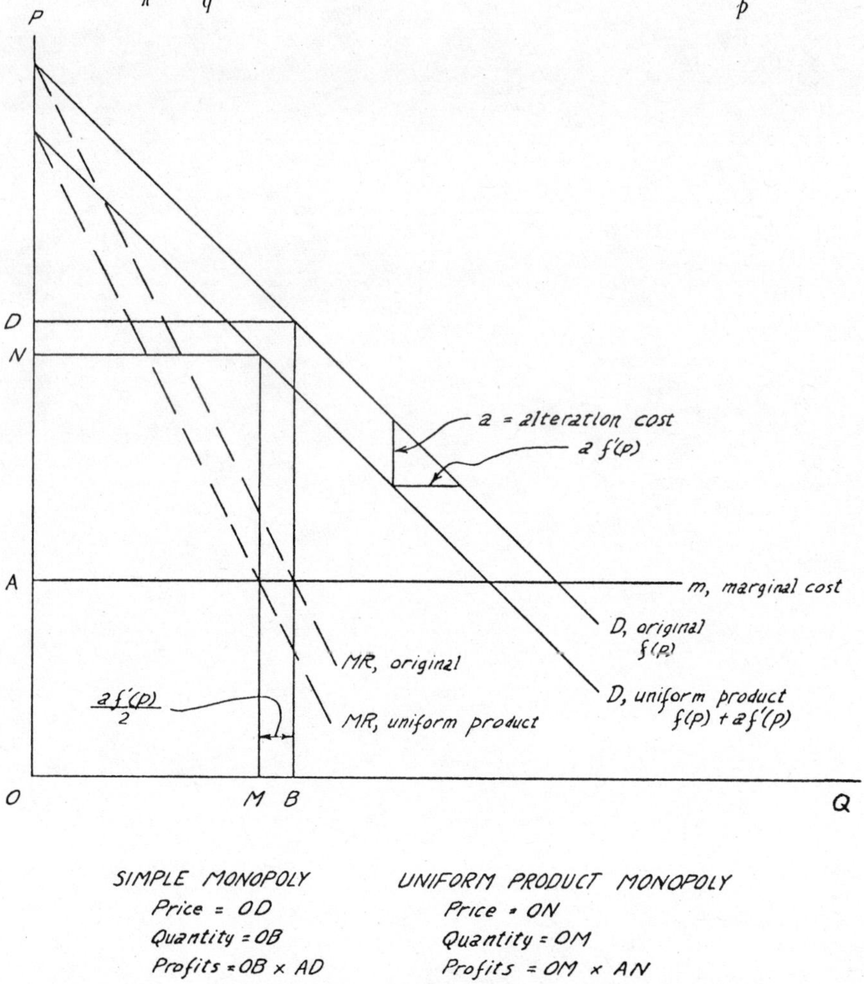

FIG. 1

The loss from imposed uniformity is therefore proportional to the ratio of alteration costs to price.

Our example is sufficiently unrealistic to make any quantitative estimate uninteresting. In general one would expect an upper limit to the ratio a/p, because it becomes cheaper to resort to other goods (custom tailoring in our example), or to abandon the attempt to find appropriate goods. The loss of profits of the monopolist will be proportional to the average value of a/p, and this will be smaller, the smaller the variation in buyers' circumstances.

Still, monopolists are lucky if their long-run demand curves have an elasticity only as large as -5, and then even a ratio of a to p of 1/40 will reduce their profits by 12 per cent. The general conclusion I wish to draw is that a monopolist who does not cater to the diversities of his buyers' desires will suffer a substantial decline in his profits.

[19]

THE ECONOMIC JOURNAL

JULY 1993

The Economic Journal, 103 (*July*) 833–848. Published by Blackwell Publishers, 108 Cowley Road, Oxford OX4 1JF. UK and 238 Main Street, Cambridge MA 02142, USA.

COLLUSIVE EQUILIBRIUM IN THE GREAT SALT DUOPOLY*

Ray Rees

This paper sets out to test two interesting lines of recent development in oligopoly theory. The first, arising out of the analysis of infinitely repeated games, suggests conditions under which collusive outcomes can be supported as non-cooperative equilibria by appropriate threat strategies. The second considers the nature of equilibrium in a homogeneous duopoly in which firms set prices subject to fixed capacity constraints. Both these bodies of theory are discussed more fully in the next section.

The data used for the tests are given in a report on the UK Monopolies and Merger Commission (MMC) inquiry into price behaviour in the UK market for white salt.[1] In this market two firms produce an essentially homogeneous commodity with blockaded entry and fixed capacities. The report provides detailed data on prices, outputs and (marginal) costs as well as a great deal of more qualitative information which is valuable in interpreting these data. The information in the report is derived directly from the working of a real-world oligopoly. Its main drawback is that it relates only to five years, and does not allow standard econometric methods to be applied, in particular to the estimation of a demand function.

Nevertheless, this paper hopes to demonstrate that some quite strong conclusions can still be drawn, in particular on the extent to which the various possible equilibrium concepts proposed by the theoretical literature can explain the apparent nature of the equilibrium in this case. The wealth of detail given in the report seems too good to ignore, even if it cannot support a standard econometric investigation.

There is a correspondence between the two types of model with which this paper is concerned and the positions taken by the MMC and the firms that

* Earlier versions of this paper have been presented at seminars at the Universities of Birmingham, Bristol, East Anglia, and Swansea, the European University Institute, Florence, the Institute of Economics and Statistics, University of Oxford, and Northwestern University, Evanston, Ill. I am grateful to participants in those seminars for many helpful comments, as well as to James Friedman, Rolf Färe, Shawna Grosskopf, Dan Kovenock, Val Lambson, Venk Sadanand, Mike Waterson and two referees. None of these of course bears responsibility for the final version.

[1] 'White salt: A Report on the Supply of White Salt in the United Kingdom by producers of such salt', H.M.S.O. London 1986. This is subsequently referred to as MMC (1986). Though the present author was at the time a member of the MMC he was not involved in this particular inquiry, and all the information used in this paper was derived solely from the published report.

were the subject of the inquiry. The theory of price-setting duopoly under capacity constraints assumes that firms act non-cooperatively, making no attempt, whether tacit or explicit, to agree upon their choice of prices. The firms in the MMC inquiry claimed that they had in fact not colluded, and that the market outcome was fully consistent with 'competitive' behaviour. By examining whether the predictions of the price-setting model match what happened in this market, we have simultaneously a test of the model and also of whether the firms' claims can be accepted.

While skating carefully around the word 'collusion', the MMC concluded that the firms had 'severely restrained price competition'.[2] The basis for this judgement appears to have been some evidence on communication between the firms, the fact that over a long period prices had been virtually identical and changed more or less simultaneously, and finally a view of what the outcome should have been had the firms in fact competed. This view was not based on the predictions of the models considered here, and it is indeed questionable that it could be supported by any generally accepted positive model of the market, but later in this paper we argue that the MMC's judgement was essentially correct.

Given then that the behaviour of the firms can be taken to be collusive, the question arises of whether this can be explained by recent developments in the analysis of repeated games. In the next section we present brief outlines of the relevant theories and identify the sense in which they will be tested in this paper.

I. THEORETICAL BACKGROUND

Consider a market with two firms producing homogeneous outputs in a single time period, and independently choosing prices subject to equal, constant marginal costs and exogenously given capacity constraints. Edgeworth (1897) showed that if each firm's capacity is less than market demand at a price equal to the given marginal cost, the Bertrand result that equilibrium price equals marginal cost no longer holds. If the market situation is repeated over a sequence of periods, price will vary cyclically between well-defined upper and lower limits, p_h and p_l. The upper limit p_h is the price which maximises a firm's profit *given* that it is undercut by its competitor. The firm with the lower price produces at capacity, the higher-priced firm is then faced with a residual demand with respect to which it finds the most profitable price p_h. The lower limit p_l is the price which yields a firm the same profit π^* when it is the lower-priced firm and produces to capacity, as when it is the higher priced firm and sets p_h. In general p_l exceeds marginal cost. If, however, we insist that the analysis must relate to only one time period, i.e. to a 'one-shot game', then Edgeworth essentially shows that no equilibrium price exists in this model.

Shubik (1959) gave this result a game-theoretic reinterpretation: in this game there is no equilibrium in pure price strategies, but there is an

[2] Para. 9.10, MMC (1986).

equilibrium in mixed strategies. Beckman (1965) and Levitan and Shubik (1972) derived these equilibrium mixed strategies for specific examples of the model, the main difference between them being in the assumptions made about the rationing process. When the firms set different prices, some assumption must be made as to how the residual demand facing the higher-priced firm is determined, or equivalently, how buyers wishing to be supplied by the lower-priced firm are rationed. Beckman assumed a form of random rationing. Levitan and Shubik assumed *efficient rationing*: the lower-priced firm supplies those buyers with higher willingness to pay.[3] For concreteness, we focus here on this latter case. Then the equilibrium outcome in this type of market is predicted to be as follows: there is a given interval of prices which is defined by the Edgeworth upper and lower bounds p_h and p_l. Firms choose prices randomly from this interval, and the equilibrium probability distributions regulating these choices are such that each firm has the same expected profit π^* whatever the price pair chosen. It follows that there is a zero probability that the firms will choose equal prices, and that if the market situation is repeated after a period, each firm's price changes randomly (within the given interval) over time.[4]

An interesting extension of these results with particular relevance to the market studied in this paper has recently been made by Deneckere and Kovenock (1992). They allow the (still exogenously given) capacity levels of the firms, as well as their (constant) marginal costs, to differ, and consider the question of the endogenous non-cooperative determination of the identity of a price leader in this model. That is, firms engage in a game of timing of price announcements, and the equilibrium of the game determines which firm is the price leader and which the follower. Their result is that the firm with larger capacity will be the price leader, while the smaller firm will follow with a price just below that of the leader, and will produce at full capacity. Thus the price set by the leader is p_h, the upper bound of the Edgeworth interval, and it earns the same profit π^* as in the mixed strategy equilibrium. On the other hand the smaller firm earns higher profit under price leadership than under simultaneous choice of (mixed strategy) prices, since it is producing to capacity at a price greater than p_l.

The theories then give quite definite testable predictions about the kind of price behaviour we should observe in this type of market. It is argued in the next section that the market for white salt is the type of market for which these models can apply, and therefore can be used to test these theories.

[3] For a thorough discussion of the economics of these rationing schemes see Dixon (1987).

[4] Capacity is here taken to be exogenous. Kreps and Scheinkman (1983) allow capacity levels to be chosen endogenously, in a two stage game. At the second stage firms play a price-setting game with fixed capacities. At the first stage they choose capacities in the light of their effects on the equilibrium at the second stage. The interesting result is that capacities are chosen to be such that outputs and price are precisely those given by the Cournot equilibrium of the model. This result is further generalised by Osborne and Pitchik (1986). Unfortunately, as Davidson and Deneckere (1986) show, this striking reconciliation of the results of quantity-setting and price-setting duopoly models is not robust to relaxation of the 'efficient rationing' assumption. Moreover, as we show below, its prediction that both firms will produce at capacity is not confirmed in the market being considered. However, this is probably not a fair test of the theory, since capacity in this market is best taken as exogenous over the period to which the observations relate.

The models just discussed are essentially 'one-shot games': they are concerned with deriving a Nash equilibrium in a single play of the price-setting game. However, if we move to the empirically more relevant view of the market as an infinitely repeated game, then it is well-known that repeated plays of the one-shot Nash equilibrium also represent a Nash equilibrium of the repeated game. However, the important point is that other Nash equilibria are possible, and in particular those that yield the firms more profitable outcomes than those in the one-shot non-cooperative equilibrium. The basic idea underlying the work of Friedman (1971), Abreu (1986, 1988) and Fudenberg and Maskin (1986) among others, is that these more profitable outcomes in the one-shot game may be sustained as non-cooperative Nash equilibria of the repeated game by threats of appropriate punishments for deviation. The intuition is clear. If a firm deviates from an agreement to collude in one period, it could be punished in later periods, and the threat of this *ex ante* may be enough to sustain collusion. However, going beyond intuition, a number of issues have to be considered. What form can or should punishment take and will it be sufficient in fact to offset these gains since it causes future losses which have to be discounted to be comparable with immediate gains from deviating? Moreover, since punishment will often hurt the punishers, for example a punitive price war reduces profits to all firms, will threats to carry out such punishment in fact be credible?

A formal answer to these questions is given by Abreu's theory of 'simple penal codes', which has been applied to the case of price-setting capacity-constrained oligopoly by Lambson (1987, 1991). Suppose that firms agree, tacitly or explicitly, on a particular price and allocation of outputs for each period. They also agree on a time path of prices that will be applied as a punishment for a deviation from the agreed price by a firm, where this punishment path may depend on exactly which firm deviates. A punishment path is credible if it is in each firm's interest not to deviate from it in the event that it has to be imposed. An agreed price and output allocation is sustainable if it would not pay any firm to deviate from it given the credible punishment path that would then be imposed. An interesting aspect of the punishment path is its 'stick and carrot' nature. In the first stage of punishment, price is cut to inflict loss of profit, but this is followed by a second stage of reversion to the more profitable price and output allocation. It then pays a firm that has just deviated to accept its punishment, since failure to do so leads to reimposition of the punitive phase of the punishment path and postponement of the return to the more profitable cooperative phase. If a firm that did not deviate originally refused to participate in punishing the firm that did, then it itself would become a deviant and have the appropriate punishment path inflicted on it. In this theory the requirement of credibility is formally embodied in the concept of subgame perfect equilibrium. The strategy of adhering to the agreed price and output allocation as long as no firm deviates, and adhering to the prescribed punishment path immediately following any deviation, is shown to induce a Nash equilibrium for every possible subgame of the infinitely repeated game. Of course, if the cooperative agreement *is* sustainable, we would not actually observe implementation of the punishment strategies – the observed market equilibrium would be the agreed price and output allocation.

Any particular price and output allocation may or may not be sustainable by Abreu's punishment strategies or simple penal code. This depends on the firms' discount factors and the structure of the market – the demand and cost functions the firms face. Those determine the extent of the gains from deviation, the losses of profit that can be inflicted through punishment, and the present value of future losses relative to immediate gains from deviation. For our present purposes, we are interested in the question: if we were to accept that firms in the white salt market behaved collusively, whether tacitly or explicitly, is this consistent with the models of Abreu and Lambson? We would conclude that it was, if the actual allocation turned out to be sustainable by Abreu-type punishment strategies, while if the actual allocation turned out to be not sustainable (at reasonable discount rates), we would have to reject the theory and look for some alternative explanation of collusion. Note that this is a one-sided test of the theory. It would also be interesting to find a market in which collusion did not take place, and to examine whether more profitable allocations than the actual one would be sustainable, in which case we could again reject the theory.[5] This will however have to be left for further work.

II. THE MARKET FOR WHITE SALT

This section sets out briefly some salient facts about the salt market.[6]

Production. Salt production in the United Kingdom consists essentially of the extraction and processing of a non-renewable natural resource. However, reserves are so large relative to consumption that the resource rent is effectively zero and we can regard salt as a manufactured commodity. Water is pumped down into salt strata lying underground, this dissolves the salt to form brine, which is then pumped to the surface and transported through a pipeline to, initially, a purification plant. Here chemicals are added to remove unwanted minerals, then the purified brine is pumped to an evaporation plant. Six large boilers, known as effects, are arranged in sequence, brine is pumped into the first, the water is boiled off and the salt precipitated, and the waste steam is passed into the second effect where it is used to heat more brine, and so on. After the evaporation process 'undried salt' is produced, with the consistency of wet sand. Part of this output is shipped immediately to chemical plants, mainly for use in production of caustic soda and chlorine. The remainder is dried, and then shipped, in bulk or in bags, again to chemical plants for use in

[5] To put this more precisely, consider the set of all markets, and the subsets of markets (*a*) which satisfy Abreu's conditions for the sustainability of an agreed allocation by credible threats, and (*b*) in which collusion is observed. I interpret Abreu's theory to say that these subsets are equal. All that this paper can do, in considering just one market, is to show that their intersection is not empty, if Abreu's conditions are satisfied; or that the sets are not equal, if the conditions are not satisfied. In this latter case the set in (*a*) could still be a subset of that in (*b*), in which case Abreu's conditions would be sufficient but not necessary for collusion.

[6] A fuller description, together with a complete set of the data on which the later discussion is based, is given in Rees (1991).

production of sodium and chloride, but also to food manufacturing and animal feed preparation plants, and tanning and dyeing works. Less than 10% of total salt output is sold for cooking or table use.

Concentration. There are effectively just two producers: British Salt, (BS), a self contained but wholly-owned subsidiary of an industrial engineering and contracting group, Stavely Industries; and ICI Weston Point, (WP), a small part of the Mond division of the large chemicals conglomerate ICI. Fortunately for this study WP is a self-contained accounting unit selling less than 5% of its output to other ICI plants. Imports and a number of very small salt works account for around 3% of the market and so in the rest of this study will be ignored. We treat BS and WP as single-plant profit maximising firms. BS takes on average about 55% of the UK market and WP the remainder.

Capacity. Each firm is subject to a maximum capacity constraint, which is 824 kilotonnes (kte) pa for BS and 1095 kte pa for WP. Over the years 1980–4 there was considerable excess capacity: BS averaged less than 75% capacity utilisation, while WP's UK sales alone amounted only to 45% of capacity, on average, though its export sales, made at a much lower profit, brought its capacity utilisation rate up to around 65%. The degree of excess capacity appears to have been caused by an unanticipated decline in demand since the capacity was first installed in the early 1970s.

Entry. Though salt strata suitable for extraction are common in the United Kingdom, a combination of planning controls and high transport costs seems to rule out production outside the Cheshire area in which both BS and ICI's plants are located. The main users are located quite closely to the salt plants, while at the prevailing prices imports were not regarded as a threat because of the high cost of transport and transshipment relative to value. The major salt strata in Cheshire are owned by the incumbent firms. Moreover, there are significant economies of scale and as we have just seen significant excess capacity in the market. In the rest of this study therefore we assume that the market behaviour of the incumbents has been influenced by the threat of new entry only to the extent that the possibility of imports places an upper bound on the price that can be set.

Costs. The MMC report suggested that variations in output by BS can be achieved without significantly affecting energy usage per unit of output (para 4·10, MMC (1986)) and, since this is the main variable input, we translate this into the assumption that over the relevant range of outputs average variable cost of production (*avc*) is constant as output varies and so equals marginal production cost. WP, which has a somewhat different technology than BS, has a more complex cost structure. Reductions in output below capacity are most efficiently coped with by reducing the number of effects in operation, and this raises *avc* in a stepwise way.[7] See Fig. 1. The MMC report gives an indication

[7] As Fig. 1 shows, fixed production costs are assumed not to depend on the number of effects in operation. The total cost function jumps discontinuously at an output level (here 400 kte pa and 800 kte pa are chosen for purposes of illustration) at which it becomes efficient to change the number of effects in operation. Essentially, however, we are interested only in the middle step, which corresponds to the actual operations, and costs in the neighbourhood of WP's capacity output.

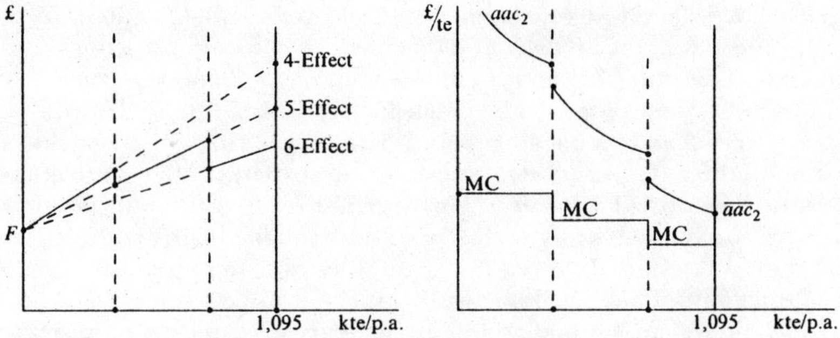

Fig. 1. Cost Structure for WP.

of the heights of these steps but does not give the precise output levels at which the steps occur. In the period under study WP operated along the middle step.

In addition to production cost, the other component of variable cost is distribution cost, consisting mainly of transport costs. We assume these are constant per unit of output. Marginal cost *MC* is then the sum of *avc* and average distribution cost. Finally, we define as average avoidable cost (*aac*) a firm's *MC* plus 'fixed production costs' per unit of output. The latter, consisting mainly of labour, management and maintenance costs, do not vary with output, but are incurred if and only if the plant is operating: *aac* is therefore zero if output is zero and the plant is shut down. $\overline{aac}_1$ denotes BS's *aac* at its capacity output, and similarly $\overline{aac}_2$ is WP's capacity *aac* and takes into account WP's lower average variable production cost at capacity, due to six-effect operation. Since all these costs play an important role in what follows, it is useful to summarise the full range of information in Table 1.

Table 1

Firms' Marginal and Average Avoidable Costs

		Year			(£/te)	
		1980	1981	1982	1983	1984
avc	*BS*	6·30	8·07	8·12	9·21	9·07
	WP	6·02	7·39	9·49	10·82	11·47
mc	*BS*	9·81	12·11	12·03	13·67	13·36
	WP	12·77	14·22	14·74	16·77	16·14
$\overline{aac}$	*BS*	12·61	15·07	14·72	17·07	17·01
	WP	14·46	15·68	16·28	18·49	17·72

Source: MMC (1986).

The data in Table 1, interpreted here as the actual values of marginal and average avoidable costs firms would have used in their decision-taking, are one of the most valuable contributions of the MMC report, given the concerns of this paper. We should at this point therefore enter a qualification. We shall throughout conduct the analysis as if there is only one output. However, there are at least three: undried and dried salt sold in bulk, and dried salt sold in bags. The last two outputs must be somewhat costlier to produce because of the additional drying and/or bagging costs. It is impossible to disaggregate the cost data among these three outputs (for example no separate figures are given on bulk and bagged dried salt sales). However, for each firm the proportions of total output accounted for by each type of salt remained fairly stable over this period. For WP, undried salt varied apparently randomly between 35% and 41% of total output and for BS between 30% and 37%. Thus we assume that no significant systematic bias results from treating output as homogeneous. This is helped by the fact that, as we see below, the two firms made identical percentage increases in the prices of all types of salt over this period.

Prices. In a fascinating section of the report (paras 5·25–5·41, MMC (1986)), the MMC lists the dates and amounts of the seventeen changes to list prices made by the two firms between January 1974 and January 1984. The increases are always either exactly or virtually identical. From 1980 each firm made the same percentage increases across all grades of salt, prior to this increases varied across grades. In each case one firm announced its price increases and the second firm followed within a month and usually within two weeks. Of the 13 price increases announced from 1974–80, BS led 8 times and WP led 5 times. In each of the years 1981–4, WP was the leader. Typically the leader would inform the follower of its planned price increase a month before it came into effect, and the latter would then inform the leader of its proposed (identical) price change within that period (Table 5·8 of MMC (1986)).

In their evidence to the MMC on this matter, the firms denied collusion[8] and the exchange of any information other than of proposed price changes[9] (paras 8·8–8·17, 8·56–8·74, MMC (1986)). They made the point that in a competitive market prices would be identical and would move closely together. They also argued that it is not enough to consider only list prices, since there is widespread discounting to buyers and so actual prices paid could well have moved differently. To test this latter point the MMC examined the discount structure of each seller. Until 1980 the rebate scales of the firms had been identical. Furthermore, for the majority of buyers discounts have been insignificant, amounting to less than 1% of the list price. For a few very large buyers, BS's discount structure after 1980 implied a price per tonne of roughly 0·25% below that of WP. Moreover, the MMC sampled a group of buyers to identify the values of differences in prices they had been quoted by the two sellers. These differences average about 0·5% of the price, with the highest at

[8] Prior to the Restrictive Practices Act, 1956, a formal agreement to set common ex works and delivered prices for producers and common resale prices for merchants had been in force for more than twenty years. There was also an aggregated rebate scheme under which buyers received a discount based on aggregate purchases from all sellers. The Act required such agreements to be registered with the Registrar of Restrictive Practices, following which they could be challenged in the Restrictive Practices Court. The salt agreement was discontinued and not registered.

[9] The firms explained that this was done because each bought salt from the other and it was usual to notify buyers in advance of price increases.

Table 2
Capacity Utilisation, Market Share, Prices and Profits

	Year				
	1980	1981	1982	1983	1984
I. Capacity utilisation (%)					
BS	85	71	79	69	67
WP (U.K. output/capacity)	54	47	43	40	41
WP (total output/capacity)	75	60	65	59	64
II Shares of U.K. market (%)					
BS	54	53	58	57	55
WP	46	47	42	43	45
III. ROC (%)					
BS	46	45	53	52	53
WP	33	32	30	24	24
IV. Rate of Price Increase (%)	19·4	7·5	14	8	5
Firm initiating	BS	WP	WP	WP	WP

Source: MMC (1986).

2·2% and the modal value close to zero (Table 5·14, MMC (1986)). The proposition that buyers perceived price uniformity is supported by the fact that around 78% of buyers had not changed their sources of supply over the five years previous to the enquiry (para 5·13, MMC (1986)).

Profits. The accounting rates of return on capital employed (ROC), net of depreciation, and at historic cost, are shown for the two firms in Table 2, which also gives some other important market information. Over the same period, the comparable rate of return for all large quoted companies varied between 9% and 13%, and of companies in the chemicals and man-made fibres industries between 7% and 16%. However, in the remainder of this paper we consider only profits defined as revenues less variable and fixed production and distribution costs. The reason is of course that the capital costs were essentially sunk and did not vary either with the level of output or the shutdown decision. Profits are the short run quasi-rents which the firms are assumed to maximise.

III. COMPETITION, PRICE LEADERSHIP, COLLUSION AND JOINT PROFIT MAXIMISATION

The data on costs, capacities and prices given by the report we take to be 'hard data'. Though they are subject to interpretation, the numbers themselves are those the firms themselves would have had to work with. We can give reasonably firm answers, on the basis only of these data and, in some cases, general assumptions on demand, to the three questions with which we are concerned. Did the firms behave non-cooperatively as in the Edgeworth–Levitan–Shubik (ELS) or Deneckere–Kovenock models? If not, does an Abreu-Lambson type of explanation of collusion hold? Did they maximise joint profits? We consider these in turn.

From the results summarised in Section I, we know that the one-shot non-cooperative equilibrium involves firms operating at below capacity and choosing mixed strategies in prices.[10] Clearly, both firms were producing at less than capacity. If they had been choosing prices according to mixed strategies, then the probability that every time they chose prices those prices would be identical, is zero. Yet on each of the 17 times prices were set in the period 1974–84 prices were in fact identical. Thus we could reject the ELS model, even if we had no knowledge of the extent to which the firms actually exchanged information on proposed price changes, and thus could be said to be correlating strategies.

A somewhat stronger case could be made for the Deneckere–Kovenock theory of price leadership. The theory predicts that the larger firm would be the price leader. This was true in each year 1981–4. In the seven years previous to that, leadership varied between the two firms, but we have cost data only for 1980–4. In the Deneckere–Kovenock model, the smaller firm could be price leader if its marginal cost is sufficiently higher than that of the larger firm, and only in 1980 can we certainly say that this was not true, so that BS's price leadership in that year contradicts the theory. The theory also predicts that the follower will price 'just below' the leader, and, though this is not consistent with the data on list prices, the evidence on discounts given by the MMC could perhaps be interpreted as just consistent with this. However, the crucial mismatch is in respect of capacity utilisation. In the Deneckere–Kovenock price leadership equilibrium, the follower sells at full capacity. This was clearly not the case in the white salt market.

Thus, in this market at least, the predictions of the ELS and Deneckere–Kovenock theories are not confirmed. The main reason, we would claim, is that they are derived from one-shot non-cooperative equilibria.

In its evidence to the MMC, BS stated that 'if it raised prices by a lesser amount than [WP], and [WP] failed to lower its own price to the same level, there would be an immediate transfer of business to itself... This would lead to a long-term retaliation by [WP] who would seek to take customers from British Salt'. (MMC (1986), para 28·11). This statement shows that the firms clearly share the intuition underlying the idea of collusive equilibrium supported by the threat of retaliation, which is hardly surprising, simple as it is.

We now have to see if the outcome in this market is consistent with the more formal theory. We assume that the actual prices and profits in each of the years 1980–4 correspond to collusive allocations, and we wish to test whether these can be sustained by credible threats. Following Lambson (1987), we have the criteria for:

(i) *Sustainability:* Let π_i^C denote the one-period profit firm $i = 1, 2$ earns under the agreement, π_i^R the maximum profit it can earn by reneging on this agreement, τ_t a punishment path of prices that will be imposed in the period

[10] In fact there are two other equilibrium possibilities, each of which can be ruled out in the salt market. Where firms' capacities are sufficiently large, we would have the Bertrand equilibrium with price equal to marginal cost. This was clearly not the case here. Alternatively, if each firm's capacity is less than or equal to its Cournot output in this market each would produce at capacity and price would clear the market. Since both firms produced below capacity we can also rule out this as a possible equilibrium.

following a violation of the agreement by firm i, $V_i(\tau_i)$ the present value at the date punishment begins of profits to firm i along this path, $r > 0$ the per-period interest rate and $\delta = (1+r)^{-1}$ the discount factor. Then the agreed allocation is sustainable if at each time t

$$\pi_i^R - \pi_i^C \leqslant \pi_i^C/r - \delta V_i(\tau_i) \quad i = 1, 2. \tag{1}$$

This says that the one-period gain from deviating at time t is less than the present value at t of the future loss of profit from having the punishment path inflicted next period rather than enjoying the collusive profit forever. Provided the punishment path is credible, satisfaction of (1) ensures that the threat of future punishment will deter a one-shot violation of the agreement.[11]

(ii) *Credibility*: Let π_i^P denote the profit in some given period t that firm i will make on a prescribed punishment path[12], π_i^{RP} the maximum profit it could make at t if it reneged on the punishment path in that period, and V_i^L the present value at $t+1$ of profit the firm would earn from adhering to that prescribed punishment path from $t+1$ onward. Then that punishment path is credible if

$$\pi_i^{RP} - \pi_i^P \leqslant \delta[V_i^L - V_i(\tau_i)] \quad i = 1, 2. \tag{2}$$

The right-hand side of (2) gives the present value at t of the difference in profits between continuing along the prescribed punishment path from $t+1$ on, and having a punishment path for a deviation imposed at $t+1$ from its beginning. The left-hand side gives the one-shot gain from deviating from the prescribed punishment path. If this inequality is satisfied, it does not pay firm i to deviate from the prescribed punishment path and so the threat of imposing that path is credible.[13]

To test whether these conditions can be satisfied in the market under study we first need to specify a time period and associated interest rate. We take 3 months and 10% respectively as reasonable assumptions.[14] Next we need to specify the exact nature of the punishment price paths. In general, a path which can satisfy (1) and (2) for some set of interest rates is not unique, but the following specification has some intuitive appeal:

If either firm deviates, in the following three periods both firms set price at aac_2 and then they revert to the initial allocation.

Since on this (symmetric) punishment path price falls to WP's actual *aac*, it makes no profit in the punishment phase, while BS makes a small profit because its *aac* is somewhat lower. The punishment strategy corresponds to a 'price

[11] Abreu (1988) shows that if deviation is unprofitable for one period it will never be profitable.

[12] Strictly we should write π_{itj}^P, $t = 1, \ldots, j = 1, 2$ since profits may well vary along a punishment path, and the path may depend on which firm deviated, but no confusion should result from keeping the notation uncluttered here.

[13] Simply rearranging the condition as $\pi_i^{RP} + \delta V_i(\tau_i) \leqslant \pi_i^P + \delta V_i^L$ shows that we could equivalently interpret the condition as saying it is better to continue along the given punishment path than to deviate this period and have punishment begin anew next period.

[14] The longer the time period, the more profitable does reneging become, since the longer the period for which additional profit is earned and the further into the future retaliation takes place. Assuming a period of one year does not change the conclusion that for reasonable interest rates the cooperative allocations in this market were sustainable by credible threats, though to assume that one firm would take an entire year to react to open price-cutting by the other is extreme. A quarterly interest rate of 10% is equivalent to an annual rate of 46%, which again seems to be a reasonable upper bound.

war' in which prices are slashed to the break-even level (at actual output) for the higher cost firm.

To quantify the effects of punishment on the firms' profits as well as the gains from one-shot deviations from the punishment path we require some assumption about market demand. As a first approximation, we assume zero elasticity of demand at any prices below the agreed price. Since, if this were true at prices above the agreed price, the latter could not be profit maximising, we are implicitly assuming a kink in demand at the actual price, possibly due to the threat of imports.

Finally, we need to assume how total market demand will be shared between the firms along a punishment path. Since they set the same prices, it seems reasonable to assume that their market shares are as in the actual allocation. Thus, effectively we assume that along a punishment path the firms would produce the same outputs as those they actually produced, but at much lower prices and profits. For each of the years 1980–4, we then calculate the values of the quantities entering into conditions (1) and (2), given the punishment strategies just described. The results[15] are given in Table 3, and show that the specified punishment path was credible in each year, and could sustain the actual allocation.

Table 3

Gains and Losses from Deviation and Punishment

(£000)

	$\pi_t^R - \pi_t^C$		$(\pi_t^C/r) - \delta V_t$		$\pi_t^{RP} - \pi_t^P$		$\delta(V_t^L - V_t)$		
	BS	WP	BS	WP	BS	WP	BS	WP	
1980	367	2,015	3,347	3,759	256	1,068	1,012	1,136	(17%)
1981	964	2,901	4,172	4,148	376	636	1,260	1,254	(116%)
1982	800	3,340	5,143	4,006	276	735	1,554	1,211	(80%)
1983	1,377	3,397	5,041	3,621	494	948	1,524	1,094	(26%)
1984	1,631	3,633	6,035	3,645	468	819	1,824	1,101	(49%)

Thus for example if in the first quarter of 1984 BS (WP) had undercut the agreed price slightly,[16] it would have gained just over £1·6 m. (£3·63 m.) in additional profit in that quarter, but would have lost just over £6 m. (£3·65 m.) in present value of profit from the ensuing three quarter long price war, relative to the agreed allocation.[17] On the credibility of the punishment path, if BS reneged on the first quarter's punishment, by setting price slightly below the agreed level of WP's *aac* and producing to capacity, then it would have made a net gain of close to £½ m., but would have lost over £1·8 m. in present value of profit from postponing the time of reversion to the agreed

[15] Space limitations preclude presentation of the detailed calculations here. An appendix presenting these was supplied to the referees and is available from the author upon request.

[16] The numerical calculations assume a price cut resulting in a 1% fall in 'net sales value', i.e. revenue minus distribution cost per unit.

[17] In fact a punishment phase lasting only one quarter would have been sufficient to deter BS from reneging on the agreed allocation. However this would not have been sufficient to deter BS from reneging on the first period of a punishment path following a deviation by WP.

allocation by one period. In WP's case, in 1980 and 1982 it was more profitable to renege on the punishment path by setting price at the actual level and allowing itself to be undercut by BS. Market demand in those years was sufficiently high that its residual output was large enough to give it more profit than if it undercut the punishment price slightly and produced at capacity. In the other years market demand was so low that the latter was the better means of reneging. In no year however did it pay WP to renege on punishment. The figures in brackets are the quarterly interest rates at which condition (2) for WP is just satisfied as an equality. Condition (2) for BS, (as well as condition (1)), could be satisfied at far higher interest rates even than these. Thus we conclude that on our assumptions conditions (1) and (2) were satisfied and cooperation in this market was consistent with the Abreu–Lambson theory.

This then raises the question of how to explain the collusive allocation. The solution most usually considered in the literature is that of joint profit maximisation. On the face of it, this would immediately be rejected as an explanation of the actual equilibrium in this market, since we would expect it to imply that the firm with the lower marginal cost, in this case BS, would produce to capacity, leaving the higher marginal cost firm to meet residual demand. The fact that both firms produced well below capacity is then not consistent with this. However, some care must be taken in drawing this conclusion in the present instance, because two important non-convexities in the cost functions complicate the analysis. First, as Fig 1 showed, at low levels of output WP has to switch to 4-effect operation, resulting in a significant increase in unit production cost (MMC(1986) para. 4·37). It may actually minimise total production costs to keep WP's output high enough for it to maintain 5-effect working, therefore. Secondly, for each firm there is a large fixed production cost which is avoidable if the plant shuts down. In order to identify the output allocation which minimises total avoidable costs, therefore, we consider four sets of costs:

A. the variable and fixed production costs actually incurred in producing total market output;
B. the cost resulting when BS produces to capacity in each year, with WP meeting residual demand, on the assumption that 5-effect working could be maintained and WP operates at the corresponding (actual) marginal cost;
C. the costs resulting when BS produces to capacity and WP meets residual demand with 4-effect working;
D. the costs resulting when WP produces to capacity and BS meets residual demand[18] at its actual marginal cost.

Table 4 gives the results. The figures in brackets show the percentage deviation of the given cost figure from the actual cost figure for that year.

Thus we see that total costs could have been around 2% to 5% lower if BS had always produced to capacity, but only if WP would have been able to

[18] Only in 1980 was total market output significantly greater than WP's capacity of 1095 kte pa. In 1983 and 1984 total output was less than this, and in 1981 and 1982 was greater by 4 kte and 30 kte respectively. In neither of these two latter cases would it have been worth incurring the fixed production cost to open up the BS plant.

Table 4
Total Cost Comparisons

	Output (kte)	A	B	(£000) C	D
1980	1,294	19,455	19,095 (−1·9)	19,884 (+2·2)	20,103 (+3·3)
1981	1,099	19,479	18,399 (−5·5)	19,546 (+0·3)	17,170 (−11·8)†
1982	1,125	20,074	19,598 (−2·4)	20,393 (+1·6)	17,827 (−11·2)‡
1983	1,007	21,352	20,567 (−3·7)	21,117 (−1·1)	18,730 (−12·3)
1984	1,003	21,031	20,281 (−3·6)	20,852 (−0·8)	18,054 (−14·2)

† The market would have been undersupplied by 4 kte.
‡ The market would have been undersupplied by 30 kte.
Figures in parentheses are % deviation of cost of B, C and D from A. A, B, C and D are defined above in the text.

maintain 5-effect working. If this had not been the case then overall there would have been no cost advantage in doing this. The interesting result however is that in every year except 1980, because market output was close to or below WP's capacity, the cost-minimising policy was clearly to close BS's plant and meet market demand only from WP. Although, even at full capacity (6-effect) working WP's marginal cost was above that of BS, the latter's capacity was too small to meet market demand, and the saving in fixed production costs from shutting down BS more than offsets the higher variable production costs from switching production to WP. Thus we can conclude that the actual production allocation between BS and WP did not minimise total costs, and therefore did not maximise joint profit. An explanation for the non-maximisation of joint profit is of course that side-payments would have been required, and these would have been clear evidence of collusion.

IV. CONCLUSIONS

The first conclusion of this paper is that the type of market behaviour predicted by the non-cooperative one-shot game models of Edgeworth, Levitan and Shubik, and Deneckere and Kovenock was not observed in the white salt market. The predictions of these models call into question the standard defence of oligopolists (also used by the salt producers) that identical prices which change (virtually) simultaneously by identical amounts is evidence of 'competitive' behaviour. Of course we cannot expect 'perfectly competitive' outcomes in these markets, and the only feasible requirement for 'competitive' behaviour is that it be non-cooperative. But in a market for which these models are appropriate, namely a homogeneous, price-setting duopoly with exogenous capacity constraints, non-cooperative behaviour does not result in identical prices.[19] For this reason, we would support the MMC's conclusion that the salt duopolists 'acted to restrain competition'.

[19] This is not to say that there are no non-cooperative duopoly models which predict identical prices – homogeneous quantity-setting duopoly is obviously one. The point is rather that non-cooperative behaviour may well not result in identical prices.

The second conclusion is that the intuitive idea, apparently shared by the firms, that deviation from the (possibly tacitly) agreed prices could not pay, is fully borne out by application of the more formal analysis of Abreu and Lambson. Taking a time period and interest rate which err on the side of favouring deviation, we show that the gains from deviating from the actual prices were easily outweighed by the losses from credible, relatively short-lived punishments. Because of its lower degree of capacity utilisation, the higher cost firm WP had the greater incentive to deviate, but a short price war in which price was cut to its average avoidable cost was a credible deterrent to this deviation. On the one hand this tells us that it is not difficult to explain collusion in this market, and on the other that behaviour in the market was consistent with the theory of Abreu and its extension by Lambson.

Finally, we conclude that the actual allocation did not correspond to joint profit maximisation, because the output allocation did not minimise the (avoidable) production costs of total output. The apparent cost minimising allocation would have BS, the firm with lower marginal cost, producing to capacity. However, given the fairly small residual output, this may well have caused a jump in WP's marginal production cost and, our calculations show, total cost may not have been lower as a result. In fact, given that aggregate output was about or below WP's capacity, the cost minimising allocation would involve shutting down BS, thus saving its fixed production costs, and meeting total output requirements from WP. The general point is that the non-convexities in the cost structures of the two firms make marginal cost-based comparisons potentially misleading.

If side-payments between the firms are ruled out then there is no compelling reason to expect the agreed allocation to be joint profit maximising. This is reinforced in the present case by the extreme nature of the joint profit maximising solution. This still leaves open the question of how to explain the observed prices and outputs in this market. That appears to be a fruitful subject for further study.

University of Guelph

Date of receipt of final typescript: October 1992

References

Abreu, D. (1986). 'Extremal equilibria of oligopolistic supergames.' *Journal of Economic Theory*, vol. 39, pp. 191–225.

Abreu, D. (1988). 'On the theory of infinitely repeated games with discounting.' *Econometrica*, vol. 56, pp. 383–96.

Beckman, M. J. (1965). 'Edgeworth–Bertrand duopoly revisited.' In *Operations Research-Verfahren*, III (ed. R. Henn), Meisenheim am Glan: Hain.

Davidson, C. and Deneckere, R. (1986). 'Long-run competition in capacity, short-run competition in price and the Cournot model.' *Rand Journal of Economics*, vol. 17, pp. 404–15.

Deneckere, R. and Kovenock, D. (1992). 'Price leadership.' *Review of Economic Studies*, vol. 59, pp. 143–62.

Dixon, H. (1987). 'The general theory of household and market contingent demand.' *The Manchester School*, vol. 55, pp. 287–304.

Edgeworth, F. Y. (1897). 'La teoria pura del monopolio.' *Giorn. Econ. Ser.*, vol. 15, pp. 13–31, 307–20, 405–14. (English translation 'The pure theory of monopoly.' In *Papers Relating to Political Economy*, (ed. F. Y. Edgeworth), vol. 1, pp. 11–142. London: Macmillan.

Friedman, J. W. (1971). 'A non-cooperative equilibrium for supergames.' *Review of Economic Studies*, vol, 38, pp. 1–12.

Fudenberg, D. and Maskin, E. (1986). 'The folk theorem in repeated games with discounting or with incomplete information.' *Econometrica*, vol. 54, pp. 533–54.

Kreps, D. M. and Scheinkman, J. A. (1983). 'Quantity precommitment and Bertrand competition yield Cournot outcomes'. *Bell Journal of Economics*, vol. 14, pp. 326–37.

Lambson, V. (1987). 'Optimal penal codes in price-setting supergames with capacity constraints.' *Review of Economic Studies*, vol. 54, pp. 385–98.

Lambson, V. (1991). 'Optimal penal codes in asymmetric Bertrand supergames.' Brigham Young University Working Paper, 91–03.

Levitan, R. and Shubik, M. (1972). 'Price duopoly and capacity constraints.' *International Economic Review*, vol. 13, pp. 11–122.

Osborne, M. J. and Pitchik, C. (1986). 'Price competition in a capacity-constrained duopoly.' *Journal of Economic Theory*, vol. 38, pp. 238–60.

Rees, R. (1991). 'Collusive equilibrium in the great salt duopoly.' University of Guelph Discussion Paper, 1991–15.

Shubik, M. (1959). *Strategy and Market Structure*. New York: Wiley.

[20]

THE JOURNAL OF INDUSTRIAL ECONOMICS

Volume XXXI March 1983 No. 3

ANATOMY OF A PRICE LEADERSHIP CHALLENGE: AN EVALUATION OF PRICING STRATEGIES IN THE AUSTRALIAN NEWSPAPER INDUSTRY

WILLIAM J. MERRILEES*

THREE companies (John Fairfax and Sons, Herald and Weekly Times and News Limited) completely dominate the daily Australian newspaper industry, with takeovers having played a spectacular part in the pursuit of dominance. Product differentiation has also been an important competitive weapon. However, here we wish to concentrate on another strategic weapon, namely price. Historically price competition has not played a vital role in inter-firm rivalry in the newspaper industry. This position changed dramatically in the 1975–80 period in one of the key sectors of the industry—the Sydney market—where rivalry between News Limited and John Fairfax and Sons intensified.

In this study we aim to explore the causes of this intensified price competition and evaluate the relative merits of the marketing strategies employed by the two companies involved. Despite an obsession with price as a key decision variable in most economics and management textbooks, very little is known about pricing tactics in real world oligopolistic industries. For a few overseas exceptions see Stigler [20], Nichols [13] and Fog [4].

The analysis proceeds in terms of informal models of strategic thinking. However, existing formal models of strategic thinking, such as game theory, have little to say about prolonged periods of disequilibrium associated with mistakes by management. Price wars and related phenomena can be analysed with game theory models, but this assumes rational, reasonably informed decisions by managers. Consequently we use more discoursive models of strategic thinking to analyse the pricing tactics used by each firm. Part of this analysis draws upon the concept of cross elasticity of demand.

The effect of time in particular segments the morning and evening markets. This adds an interesting dimension to our study because the competitive tactics used by News Limited and John Fairfax and Sons Limited differ between the two markets. Although we will be concentrating on the evening market, it is useful to make cross references to the morning market. Our emphasis is on cover prices, but corresponding data are also available on

* I would like to thank the two Sydney based newspaper firms for their cooperation and especially Mr Jim McPherson, General Manager of Mirror Newspapers (interviewed 18/8/76) and Mr Noel Hodges, Chief Circulation Manager of the Sun (interviewed 22/4/80). The sales figures were kindly supplied by the non-government body, Audit Bureau of Circulation. Useful comments on the paper were made by a colleague John Stuckey. An anonymous referee greatly contributed to the final shape of the article, providing invaluable ideas in relation to advertising rates and promotional outlays in particular.

advertising rates. The evolution of (cover) pricing policies can be broken up into chronological epochs and it is more meaningful and interesting if presented as such.

THE RELATIONSHIP BETWEEN ADVERTISING REVENUE AND CIRCULATION REVENUE

Our analysis of price competition refers explicitly to cover price competition. This is where most public attention is focused. However, circulation revenue (cover price times circulation) is only about a third of total revenue, with two-thirds coming from advertising revenue (advertising rate times volume of advertising). Therefore, it would be misleading to ignore advertising rate setting prices in our discussion of this industry. Fortunately we do have fairly good data on advertising rates by company (though for nominal rather than for transaction prices—discounts are not known) over time, with more fragmented data on advertising volume and revenue.

Despite the size of the media industries, very little work has been carried out on the determinants of media prices in Australia. At this stage, it is difficult to say whether newspaper advertising rates and other media rates are market-determined (with readership mix, circulation and media competition being important) or monopolistically-determined (a small number of dominant, large firms are conglomerates across several media types).

A superficial impression from studying the media industries for several years is that the market model rather than the monopoly model better describes inter-media price setting. The print media generally (mainly newspapers and magazines) are very conscious of competition from television. For example, in response to the arrival of colour television in 1976, they have brought out colour supplements and advertisements (in newspapers) and glossier paper (in magazines). This competitive response occurred despite considerable overlap in the ownership of print and television media firms.

Within the newspaper media group, we can assume that other media influences affect each firm equally. Therefore, in comparing inter-firm advertising rate differentials within the newspaper industry, we can effectively ignore other media competition. We have already noted readership-mix and circulation as possible determinants of inter-firm advertising rates. In the first instance, we might associate affluence as the key readership characteristic enhancing advertising rates. This is consistent with the Sydney morning newspaper market, where the advertising rate for News Limited's *Daily Telegraph* is only marginally ahead of Fairfax's *Sydney Morning Herald,* despite a substantial lead in circulation. It is widely believed that the *Herald* readers are more discerning and more affluent. However, this is not consistent with the Sydney evening newspaper market, where News Limited's *Daily Mirror* has persistently achieved a higher advertising rate over Fairfax's *Sun,* even when the circulations have been equal. The *Sun*'s readers come mainly from the more affluent Northern and Eastern suburbs, so affluence *per se* is not the dominant characteristic of reader enabling higher advertising rates. Thus advertisements in the *Mirror* may be more effective (from the advertiser's point of view) because *Mirror* readers are more gullible or alternatively more price conscious. Retail advertising could be an area where the *Mirror* has an advantage. In general, newspapers attempt to specialize in particular areas (retail, national, classifieds and components thereof) which, if successful, enables a lift in advertising rate for a given level of circulation.[1]

As an initial approximation, we assume that the *comparative* effectiveness of advertising between the *Sun* and the *Mirror* is unchanged during the time period under review. This would then leave changes in relative circulation as the main determinant of changes in relative advertising prices between the *Sun* and the *Mirror*. This is consistent with the data. Prior to mid-1975, the *Mirror*'s advertising rate was a few percent above the *Sun*'s reflecting an historical advantage in advertising effectiveness. During 1975–76, the *Mirror*'s relative circulation rose 7 percent. Also during 1975–76, the *Mirror*'s advertising rate rose by 15 percent and the *Sun*'s by 8 percent; i.e. by 7 percent in relative terms. This makes commercial sense: 7 percent more messages commands 7 percent more price. This wider circulation differential persisted over the 1975–78 period, as did the higher than usual relative advertising price of the *Mirror*. When circulations swung back towards equality in 1978–80, the relative advertising price of the *Mirror* also moved back to historical levels; in November 1980 the premium was 3 percent.

There is therefore a very close relationship between changes in relative circulation and changes in relative advertising rates over the 1974–80 period in the evening newspaper market. To double-check this phenomenon, there was no tendency, for instance, for the companies' own promotional campaigns to raise their relative advertising prices.

Analytically we can formulate the relationship between advertising revenue and circulation revenue as:

(1) $$\Pi = PQ + RA - C$$

(2) with $$R = f(Q)$$

(3) in addition to $$P = g(Q) \text{ and } C = h(Q)$$

where Π is profit, P is cover price, Q is circulation, R is the advertising rate, A is advertising volume and C is total cost.

Equation (2) has several important implications. For one, it may *justify* profit-maximizing monopolists (duopolists) rationally setting a price level corresponding to an inelastic part of their demand curve. In the absence of equation (2), this would have entailed negative marginal revenue and would

[1] It would seem that in the Sydney morning market the *Herald* has had more success in specializing (notably in classifieds), while in the evening market, the *Mirror* has been more successful.

have been irrational. Secondly, we now see why newspaper cover prices are often relatively low, perhaps below marginal costs. There are offsetting benefits in terms of advertising revenue. Indeed equation (2) is imperative for an understanding of the cover price decisions of the *Mirror* in the analysis below.

STAGE 1. 1941–73: AN ERA OF PRICE COLLUSION?

Prior to 1941, the market was monopolised by Associated Newspaper's *Sun*. Mirror Newspapers entered with the *Mirror* in May 1941 and simply adopted the same price as the *Sun*. In 1953 John Fairfax and Sons, well established in the morning market with their *Sydney Morning Herald*, took over Associated Newspapers and the *Sun* with it. In 1959 the *Mirror* was taken over for a brief period by a company friendly to John Fairfax and Sons, but was sold in 1960 to News Limited.[2] No further ownership changes have occurred since. None of these ownership changes seemed to make any difference to the infrequent pattern of price changes, as can be seen in Table I. Nor did the ownership changes alter the salient fact that between 1941 and 1973 the prices of the *Sun* and the *Mirror* were identical to the day.

Identical prices over time are consistent with either an overt, collusive agreement or with advance signalling tacit price coordination. From the consumer's perspective it probably does not matter which price system is causing identical prices. From a behavioral perspective the difference is noteworthy, while from a legal perspective the difference is controversial. Currently collusive agreements are illegal while the legality of 'non-collusive' parallel pricing is obscure. Just as identical prices do not prove collusion, nor do unequal prices disprove collusion. Fog [4, p. 156] gives an example of three Danish firms whose collusive oral agreement stipulates that agreed price increases were not to be made simultaneously so that it would look as if there were no mutual agreement.

Price agreements were very common in Australia in the 1950s and 1960s and were legal in most cases. There is some evidence[3] that newspapers was one of the many industries where collusive agreement flourished. Further to substantiate this view, I checked the announcement dates of price increases for the *Sun* and *Mirror* over the 1964–74 period. Both papers gave *simultaneous* notice of two, five and four days for the 1964, 1970 and 1974 price increases. This can only be construed as joint announcements of mutual agreements.

Instead of price competition, the emphasis had been on non-price policies.

[2] This is an interesting phase in the history of the *Mirror*. As of 1959 *Mirror Newspapers* was in danger of bankruptcy and the eventual takeover by News Limited was seen as a means of revitalising the company. Fairfax's brief control of the *Mirror* via O'Connell Pty Ltd's purchase in January 1959 was to ensure that the *Mirror* did not fall into the hands of the Melbourne-based *Herald* and *Weekly Times*. It is ironic that Fairfax saw the Melbourne Herald group as a greater threat than News Limited. Twenty years later, Fairfax and the Melbourne Herald group are allied, while News Limited is the common adversary. For information on the 1959 takeover, see *Jobson's Investment Digest*, [8, May 26, 1960, p. 28].

[3] See Hunter [7] and Sheridan [18, p. 14].

TABLE I
COVER PRICES IN THE SYDNEY EVENING NEWSPAPER INDUSTRY, 1930–81

Date of Change	*Price of the Sun (Cents)*	*Price of the Mirror (Cents)*
1930, Aug. 4	1.3	—
1940, Feb. 5	1.7	—
1941, May 12		1.7 (entry)
1949, Sept. 12	2.5	2.5
1951, Mar. 12	3.3	3.3
1956, Oct. 8	4.2	4.2
1964, Sept. 14	5.0	5.0
1970, Mar. 31	7.0	7.0
1974, Jan. 21	8.0	8.0
1974, Sept. 30	9.0	—
1974, Oct. 1	—	9.0
1974, Nov. 25	10.0	—
1974, Dec. 10	—	10.0
1975, July 7	12.0	
1979, Jan. 15	10.0	
1979, Nov. 1	15.0	15.0*
1980, July 7	20.0*	20.0
1981, Sept. 21	25.0	25.0*

Note: * Denotes price leader in terms of the first firm to announce a price rise, effective on the same date for both firms.

Sources: John Fairfax and Sons, Mirror Newspapers, and Mitchell Library, Sydney.

Each evening paper has come out with all sorts of innovations and style changes (using sporting celebrities, competitions, racing form liftout guides, etc.) and the other has usually been quick to imitate.

STAGE 2. 1974–75: FROM PRICE COLLUSION TO PRICE LEADERSHIP

While the notion of 'collusive agreement' is likely to be construed in terms of a clear, predictable and watertight system of industry price control, there are well known reasons why cartel-type agreements break down. Conflict between members of a co-operative agreement occurs for all sorts of reasons: different cost structures, different objectives, power struggles, etc.

Although a bargaining process underlies collective agreements, it seems likely that one firm plays a dominant firm in the newspaper price agreement. As of the mid-1960s it was probably John Fairfax and Sons. Fairfax dominated the Sunday market, had an equal share of the evening market and was well represented in the morning market. No other firm was in all three markets. The *S.M.H.* (Fairfax) led the *Telegraph* (Packer) in the 1964 market price change.

The arrival of the *Australian* in 1964 and News Limited's 1972 takeover of the *Telegraph* radically changed the status quo. There are clear signs that

Rupert Murdoch (News Limited) had become the dominant member of the price alliance in the 1973–74 period; as revealed in the morning and Sunday markets.

Although News Limited seemed to be the dominant member of the price alliance, it was nevertheless Fairfax which made the first application to the Prices Justification Tribunal in July 1974 for price increases in the *Sun* and *S.M.H.* This does not necessarily indicate conflict within the alliance. It is likely that it was in the interests of News Limited to allow John Fairfax and Sons to make the first application to the P.J.T. since the newsprint cost increase was known to be greater for Fairfax and therefore would provide a stronger justification for a price rise (based on the increase in unit production costs). The cause of the greater newsprint cost increase is discussed below. The need to provide a strong case for a price rise reflected the need to deal with a more experienced and assertive P.J.T. compared to an earlier (December 1973) application. In retrospect, the expectations of the two newspaper firms proved correct. In contrast to the uncomplicated granting of the December

TABLE II
PRICE ROUNDS IN THE SYDNEY MORNING NEWSPAPER MARKET, 1970–81

Price Level	*Price Leader*	*Price Follower*	*Lag (weeks)*
7 cents	Telegraph May 11, 1970	S.M.H., June, 1970	4
8 cents	Telegraph April 23, 1973	S.M.H., June 25, 1973	8
9 cents	S.M.H.* Sept. 30, 1974	Telegraph Sept. 30, 1974	0
10 cents	S.M.H. Jan. 13, 1975	Telegraph Feb. 17, 1975	5
12 cents	S.M.H. June 2, 1975	Telegraph July 28, 1975	7
13 cents	Telegraph Dec. 20, 1976	S.M.H. July 11, 1977	29
14 cents	Telegraph Mar. 21, 1977	S.M.H. Feb. 27, 1978	49
15 cents	Telegraph Oct. 3, 1977	S.M.H. Sept. 25, 1978	51
20 cents	Telegraph* Feb. 8, 1980	S.M.H. Feb. 8, 1980	0
25 cents	Telegraph* Oct. 12, 1981	S.M.H. Oct. 12, 1981	0

Notes: * Prices effective the same date, but earlier announcement. The *Australian* newspaper represents about 6% of the Sydney market. If included it led the price rises to 10 cents (9/12/74), 15 cents (11/9/76) and 20 cents (July 1977).

Sources: As in Table I.

1973 price application, the July 1974 price application was subjected to a prolonged public inquiry. Ironically, the P.J.T. Report on this inquiry indicates that the additional newsprint cost increase for Fairfax was unusual and potentially unjustifiable, but was allowed in the end for extraneous reasons (its support of the local newsprint industry).

More or less simultaneously with the price round associated with the P.J.T. newspaper public inquiry, there emerged the tougher 1974 Trade Practices Act which made price agreements illegal. By default, this left price leadership as the only effective means of price coordination. As can be seen in Tables I and II, Fairfax was the price leader in both the morning and evening markets from mid-1974 to mid-1975.

STAGE 3. MID-1975: THE FIRST SHOTS OF A PRICE WAR

On July 7, 1975, after 34 harmonious years, price coördination collapsed in the evening market. The *Sun* increased its price from 10 to 12 cents, but the *Mirror* did not follow. What sparked off this price war?

Discovering the cause of the price war is complicated by the difficulty of assigning the initiating role to a particular firm. Ostensibly the *Sun* made the first move by raising its price to 12 cents. Yet by not following this rise, the *Mirror* was effectively cutting price. At least this is true in an inflationary milieu when inaction amounts to a price cut in real terms. Our difficulty in identifying an initiator to the price war is echoed in my interviews with managers of the two newspapers. The *Mirror* manager saw their role as purely passive, with the *Sun* initiating the price differential, while the *Sun* manager saw the *Mirror* as the aggressor.

Although the *Sun* did create the initial price differential, it is clear that it did so in a non-threatening way. Indeed, few if any price increases are threatening in the way price cuts can be. Moreover, the ultimate price retreat by the *Sun* suggests that it originally believed the *Mirror* would follow the rise to 12 cents. The *Sun*'s expectations in this regard were confirmed in my interview; the whole industry (including the *Sun*, newsagents, etc.) expected the *Mirror* would quickly follow to 12 cents. Thus we need to seek out the *Mirror*'s motivation in initiating price competition. The fact that the *Mirror* manager denied initiating the price war made it difficult to pursue this line of thought directly with the *Mirror*. We are therefore forced to proceed indirectly, with four hypotheses checked for plausibility. The first hypothesis is the least plausible, the next two hypotheses acted as catalysts in the price war while the fourth hypothesis is seen as fundamental.

(a) It has been argued (Wiltshire and Stokes, [22]) that the editorial quality of a newspaper tends to be higher, the greater the relative contribution from circulation revenue to total revenue. Given the tendency of the *Sun* to play up its image as a quality paper relative to the *Mirror*, it is possible that the *Sun* is more concerned with a higher cover price to raise circulation revenue (given inelastic demand). This hypothesis is rejected outright. In its July 1974 P.J.T. submission, John Fairfax requested a higher percentage rise in advertising rates compared to cover price. Additionally, in the interview, the *Sun* manager did not rank the issue of any importance.

(b) The introduction of the 1974 Trade Practices Act provided a fillip to price experimentation. Several quick and punitive Trade Practice decisions made it clear to all firms that the rules of the game had changed. No doubt many firms reframed their attitude to competition.

(c) The failure of the *Mirror* to match the July 1975 price rise could reflect the uniqueness of the *Sun*'s production cost changes, or at least the magnitude of such. Newsprint is a major component of the cost of newspapers. In Australia A.N.M. (Australian Newsprint Mills) has a monopoly of newsprint production, though with low rates of duty, imports are important. Most major newspaper publishers, including Fairfax, were vertically integrated backwards into A.N.M. as of 1972–73. However, from 1972, News Limited did not have a holding in A.N.M.

In June 1966 A.N.M. began ten-year contracts with its customers, which provided for small annual increments in prices. With the acceleration of inflation in the early 1970s, these long-term contracts placed A.N.M. in a desperate financial situation. In 1972–73 A.N.M.'s customers voluntarily agreed to pay more for their newsprint, to ensure the survival of A.N.M. and hence the continuity of future supplies. The fact that most customers were also owners no doubt further prompted this gesture. News Limited, as a non-owner customer, did not join in with a voluntary price rise to A.N.M. to the displeasure of the rest of the industry. Apart from pecuniary motive, Murdoch's non-altruistic behaviour was no doubt influenced by a long standing rift between the *Mirror* and A.N.M.

Thus the costs of newsprint for the *Sun* (and other Fairfax papers) rose much faster than those of the *Mirror* (and other News Limited papers) over the 1973–76 period. The saving to News Limited over this period amounted to about $6 million, spread over all papers including the *Mirror*.[4] The windfall cost differential between the *Sun* and the *Mirror* provided useful leverage for Murdoch to conduct his pricing strategy.

(d) In our previous section (Stage 2), the discussion suggested that, as of mid-1974, News Limited was the dominant member of a collusive price agreement in the Sydney newspaper markets. In the evening market, the *Mirror* had a marginal edge over the *Sun*. In the morning market, News Limited's *Telegraph* had a substantial lead over Fairfax's *S.M.H.*, with another paper (the *Australian*) in support. In the Sunday market, the combined sales of the *Sunday Telegraph* and *Sunday Mirror* greatly exceeded those of the *Sun Herald*. Yet from mid-1974 to mid-1975, John Fairfax and Sons had been elevated to price leader.

[4] For further discussion, see Davidson and Stewardson [3, especially pp. 142–46].

There is little doubt that News Limited was unhappy about being forced into a followship role, especially given the all embracing marketing aspirations of Rupert Murdoch. We have argued that News Limited acquiesed in the July 1974 price leadership initiative by Fairfax. Presumably News Limited intended to assert their inter-firm bargaining power in the next round of price increases. However, Fairfax moved unexpectedly fast in initiating further price increases in both the evening and morning markets. One sign that News Limited was unhappy with such action came in November 1974. The *Mirror* delayed over two weeks before increasing its price in line with the *Sun*, which was a long delay in light of previous experience. It could be regarded as a warning of the impending price war which began seven months later. Similar, though less clear, "warnings" were also made in the morning market.

It is instructive at this stage to consider reasons why firms seek price leadership. If both (all) firms charge the same price, then it could be argued that it does not matter who is the price leader. In terms of profit this may be true, but in terms of the utility of owner-managers, it may not be. When, say, two firms are evenly balanced in economic strength and carrying out similar routine operations day after day, a large weight may attach to being in control of infrequent strategic decisions including price policies. Certainly Murdoch would attach value to strategic control and Fairfax may do likewise as a reflection of its "historic rights" in this area. This suggests that both firms would be prepared to sacrifice profits in order to retain or retrieve price leadership.

Apart from kudos or utility effects, it is possible that possession of price leadership could benefit profits and related objectives for the holder. If the two firms have different price objectives, then clearly the price leader is in a position to edge price changes closer to its target. Of course, if the price objectives are wide apart and the price leader moves too far from a centre position, then a leadership challenge is possible. In our context there is the possibility that News Limited was uneasy about the frequency and magnitude of price rises initiated by Fairfax during 1974–75. Perhaps News Limited felt that newspapers needed to moderate price increases in order to compete against other media sectors. This hypothesis is dismissed as unlikely because of the very low own-price elasticity of newspapers, opposite actions by News Limited in the morning market during 1976–81, and opposite actions by News Limited in the evening market during 1979–81.[5]

We therefore emphasize the utility-augmenting effects of price leadership. Given Rupert Murdoch's desire to regain the price leadership title, it is certain that he carefully considered the questions of *when*, *how*, and *where* the challenge should take place. The question of 'when' to challenge was presumably 'as soon as possible'.

[5] For discussion of a price leadership challenge based on conflict in pricing objectives, see Merrilees [12].

'How' to challenge a price leader involves three pricing options: initiating a price rise, initiating a price cut or by not following the established price leader. The first option could backfire if the 'price leader' (Fairfax as of mid-1975) did not match the move, forcing a retreat by the rebellious 'follower'. The second option is limited by potential resistance from newsagents in the retail market. With newsagents' gross margin proportional (usually 25%) to the cover price, they could have hampered distribution of the *Mirror* if its price were too low. At least one low price paper (the *Melbourne Daily Morning Post,* 1925–27) had been killed off by a newsagents' boycott. This leaves the third option as the preferred tactic and is the one chosen by Murdoch; when the price of the *Sun* went up in July 1975, he did not follow.

'Where' to strike was essentially a choice between the morning and evening markets. The evening market was preferable for two reasons. First, it seemed likely that the cross elasticity of demand was greater in the evening market because of a higher casual/contract sales ratio and because product differentiation seemed less than in the morning newspapers. As of mid-1975 this was an untested hypothesis because the absence of a price differential in the previous 34 years prevented empirical measurement of cross demand elasticities. Secondly, traditionally there had been a minimal (if any) lag between changes in the prices of the *Sun* and *Mirror*, whereas in the morning market a lag of two or three months had been common. Therefore, a policy of not following a Fairfax price lead would have had the quickest impact in the evening market. Within a few weeks after the *Sun*'s price rise on July 7, 1975 it was clear that News Limited was not following, whereas it would have taken months after the *Herald*'s price rise on June 2, 1975 to get the same message across. The time, means and place had been successfully plotted for a leadership challenge.

In summary, an attempt to regain the price leadership position from Fairfax seems to have been the overriding motivation behind the 1975 price war. However, News Limited's move received encouragement from the 1974 Trade Practices Act and a temporary windfall in the cost of newsprint.

STAGE 4. 1975–79: THE BATTLE; ITS EFFECT ON MARKET SHARES

The price war lasted more than $3\frac{1}{2}$ years, from July 1975 to January 1979. The *Mirror*'s price of 10 cents lasted five years, from November 1974 to November 1979. Both of these figures are quite amazing when one considers that inflation averaged 10% p.a.

Like most oligopolistic price wars, it was not a case of price changing continuously. Rather there was one discrete change which was then maintained. This pattern is similar to recent price wars in the margarine industry, with prices taking one or two downward moves, reaching a zero or negative profit situation very quickly. Notwithstanding, in the *Sun-Mirror* case, the prolonged nature of the conflict could lead one to interpret the price cutting process as continuous for *both* the *Mirror* and *Sun*; at least in real terms.

TABLE III
SALES AND MARKET SHARES IN THE SYDNEY EVENING NEWSPAPER INDUSTRY, 1973-81

Six-monthly Period Ending:	*Average Sales of Mirror*	*Average Sales of Sun*	*Mirror's Market Share* (%)
March 1973	349,522	347,437	50.2
September 1973	361,549	352,709	50.6
March 1974	304,317	301,017	50.3
September 1974	369,153	364,288	50.3
March 1975	358,836	356,994	50.1
September 1975	379,081	340,434	52.7(a)
March 1976	371,944	326,990	53.2
September 1976	389,078	341,754	53.2
March 1977	375,107	318,370	54.1
September 1977	377,508	328,731	53.5
March 1978	361,615	318,558	53.2
September 1978	391,393	331,530	54.1
March 1979	387,173	338,511	53.4(b)
September 1979	399,450	374,726	51.6
March 1980	361,520	342,284	51.4
September 1980	358,907	348,715	50.7
March 1981	345,917	342,244	50.3
September 1981	387,868	358,825	51.9

Notes: (a) Half of this six month period involved a newly established price differential; (b) The last two months of this six month period involved the elimination of the price differential.
Source: Sales figures from *Audit Bureau of Circulation* [1].

In analysing the economic effects of the price war, most interest focuses on changes in market shares. In this regard we are fortunate to have reliable (audited) data by firm on a continuous (six-monthly) basis. Table III records the changes in firm sales and market shares over the 1973–80 period.

Prior to the July 1975 price changes, the sales of the two evening newspapers moved in a near parallel fashion, with market shares virtually constant. Minor fluctuations in market shares can be attributed to publishing problems (industrial relation problems), distributional problems (petrol or transport strikes), random distributions in front page stories between the two papers and inter-firm variations in promotion.

In fact, given the virtual constancy of market shares prior to July 1975, one is tempted to attribute most of the post-July 1975 market share variations to the emergence of a price differential. Thus, as a first approximation, the price differential appears to have increased the *Mirror*'s market share from 50.1% in the period ending March 1975 to 54.1% in the six months period ending March 1977; about four percentage points. While this method is crude, it seems reasonable in light of prior market share behaviour in the industry. Moreover the method is indistinguishable from the 'experimental approach' underlying Reekie's [16] U.K. results.

Adding to the plausibility of the crude method is the apparent symmetry between the creation and removal of the price differential. Thus nine months after the establishment of the price differential, the *Mirror*'s market share increased by 3.1 percentage points. Eight months after the price differential was removed, the *Mirror*'s market share decreased by 2.5 percentage points.

These estimates can be checked using more refined empirical tests. The availability of price and market share time series data enables us to use regression analysis. With a relatively small sample there is no guarantee that the more sophisticated regression technique is more reliable than our crude method. However, our hypothesis that recent variations in market shares are dominated by one systemmatic influence (relative product prices) and many random influences, makes regression analysis a particularly attractive tool.

Apart from price, an attempt was made to include more salient aspects of promotional and innovational activity. Minor stylistic changes (such as the use of sporting celebrities to write columns) were not included as these changes were quickly imitated by the other firm. This imitative behaviour is explicable in terms of either Hotelling's [6] spatial variety model or simply in terms of game theory (either constant or non-constant sum models). Quite often, as with the bingo competition promotion initiated in July 1981, the rival's response came within a couple of days. However, as detailed below, the bingo example eventually involved differential strategies and so we have included it in the regression analysis. It therefore is an exception to the rule of imitation.

Data on general promotional (advertising) expenditure are not available on a time series basis by firm. We do have knowledge of peak promotional spending, which is included as a simple dummy variable for each firm. Thus the *Sun*'s advertising expenditures peaked in the six months ending September 1976, while the *Mirror*'s expenditures peaked in the following six months. There is a tendency to "cannibalize" (*cf.* Scherer, [17]) the other firm's advertising expenditure by matching them in amount. Assuming equal effectiveness of the advertisements, this "cannibalizing" policy prevents any firm elevating its market share via advertising expenditure. Given a short. response lag, much of the *Mirror*'s response to the *Sun*'s peak outlay occurred in the same period as the *Sun*'s peak; that is, cannibalization was partly operative. It is therefore virtually impossible to identify a period where promotional outlays differed much by firm. We are therefore not hopeful that our peak outlay variables will be significant.

A variety of price lag structures were tried, but the best results were obtained by adding one lagged term to the current price term. Thus we get for 1971-I to 1981-II (with standard errors in brackets):

$$\begin{aligned} MS_{Mt} = & -0.32 + 0.129 \log(P_S/P_M)_t + 0.051 \log(P_S/P_M)_{t-1} \\ & \quad (0.068) \quad (0.026) \qquad\qquad\qquad (0.026) \\ & -0.006 \text{ ADS} + 0.003 \text{ ADM} + 0.014 \text{ Bingo} \qquad (4) \\ & \quad (0.005) \qquad\quad (0.005) \qquad\quad (0.005) \\ & \bar{R}^2 = 0.902 \qquad \text{D.W.} = 1.75 \qquad n = 20 \end{aligned}$$

where MS_{Mt} is the *Mirror*'s market share, P_S/P_M is the relative cover price of the *Sun* to the *Mirror*, ADS is the *Sun*'s peak advertising outlay (which takes on a value of one for 1976-II and zero otherwise), ADM is the *Mirror*'s peak advertising outlay (which takes on a value of one for 1977-I and zero otherwise) and bingo is a product variety variable emphasized more by the *Mirror* than the *Sun* (and it takes on value of one for 1981-II and zero otherwise).

From a statistical viewpoint the results are quite good, with more than 90 percent of the 1971–81 variations in market shares in the evening newspaper market explained. This high explanatory power together with the satisfactory Durbin-Watson statistic suggest that omitted influences are minor and fairly random. Relative prices is the key explanatory variable.

The sum of the price coefficients is 0.18, which means that a doubling of relative prices would add 18 percentage points to the *Mirror*'s market share (*ceteris paribus*).

Thus a 20 percent increase in the *Sun*'s relative price would raise the *Mirror*'s market share by 3½ percentage points, not greatly different from our "eyeball" estimate. Nearly three-quarters of the market adjustment occurs within the first six months of a relative price change, with effectively all of the adjustment completed within a twelve-month period.

The bingo competition emphasized by the *Mirror* appears to have raised its market share by 1.4 percentage points in 1981-II. Future observations, especially the next release of market share data, will help confirm this phenomenon. The bingo term is highly significant—at the one percent level.

Neither of the peak advertising outlay coefficients (relating to ADS and ADM) are particularly large and neither is significant at the 5 percent level. At least the signs are as expected. The *Sun*'s advertising outlays seem to be slightly more effective, but the difference is not significant. We are unable to say whether the lack of significance of these outlay terms is due to cannibalization by the other firm or simply because advertising has little impact on consumer preferences in this sector.

A similar market share analysis has been carried out for the morning market. No lagged effect is evident here and relative prices explain very little of the 1971–81 variations in market shares. The price coefficient is at best marginally significant from zero and only a tenth of the size of the corresponding coefficient in the evening market. Clearly the two morning newspapers are segmented from each other, while the two evening newspapers are reasonably close substitutes with each other.

In summary, the relatively lower price of the *Mirror* over the 1975–79 period apparently raised its market share by about 3½ percentage points (i.e. 7 percent). In the morning market the relatively lower price of the *S.M.H.* apparently raised its market share by about half a percentage point (i.e. one percent) over the 1976–78 period.

STAGE 4. 1975–79: THE BATTLE; ITS EFFECT ON PROFITABILITY

We will concentrate on the effects of the price war on relative profitability for the year 1975–76. Profits of the two companies altered greatly in 1975–76 compared to the preceding year, while the 1976–77, 1977–78 and 1978–79 profit picture was very similar to 1975–76.

With some trepidation I have attempted to construct the change and composition of profits for the two companies in Table IV. Profit data always have to be treated with caution. In our case a full account of the *Sun*'s operations is not available separate from Fairfax's other newspapers, with fewer problems in the case of measuring the *Mirror*'s profits.

Table IV is quite revealing. If we exclude the special effects of higher newsprint prices paid by Fairfax and additional promotional expenses, then profits fell by $1.3 million in 1975–76. In contrast, News Limited's profits rose by $1.6 million. Thus the profit effects of events in 1975–76 were close to a zero sum game, with News Limited winning what Fairfax lost.

The compositional breakdown of these changes is interesting. It is clear that

TABLE IV
INCREMENTS IN COMPANY PROFITS 1974–75 TO 1975–76
($ MILLION)

	Mirror	*Sun*
Increment to Revenue		
Circulation Revenue	+0.4[1]	+0.8[1]
Advertising Revenue	+4.4[2]	+0.3[2]
Total	+4.8	+1.1
Increment to Costs		
Mirror's Cost	+3.2[4]	+3.2[5]
Higher Newsprint Prices for Sun		+0.3
Higher Promotional Costs for Sun		+0.1
Lower Production Costs for Sun		−0.8[6]
Total	+3.2	+2.8
Increment to Gross Profit	+1.6[2]	−1.7[4]

Notes: [1] Based on wholesale *net* prices and circulation data from Tables I (adjusted from gross price) and III.

[2] Company annual report.

[3] *Mirror* source. Checked in part by *Thompson Publication* [21] Australian Advertising Rate and Data Service Newspaper Edition. This confirms advertising price component.

[4] Residual.

[5] The *Mirror*'s increment in costs are taken as a numeraire and adjusted for differential factors.

[6] The lower production costs for the *Sun* arise because of a reduced production volume, while the *Mirror*'s production volume rose. Each aspect amounts to $0.4 million given that marginal production costs are about equal to marginal circulation revenue. The latter information came from my interview with the *Mirror* management and is consistent with data in the 1974 P.J.T. report on John Fairfax and Sons.

Fairfax outperformed News Limited in terms of circulation revenue. With demand price inelastic the increased price of the *Sun* increased circulation revenue. With a constant price and increased circulation, the *Mirror* also increased its circulation revenue, but not as much. Reinforcing these gains is the effect on operating costs. The *Mirror*'s operating costs *rose* $0.4 million because of increased production volume (marginal costs about equal to marginal circulation revenue), while the *Sun*'s operating costs *fell* by a corresponding $0.4 million because of decreased production volume. The sum of these production cost changes and cover price changes puts the *Sun* ahead by $1.2 million. However, we now have to bring equation (2) into effect. About half of the *Mirror*'s increased advertising revenue shown in Table IV is attributable to the equation (2) effect, that is, to greater circulation increasing its relative advertising rate. Greater advertising volume explains the remainder of the increased advertising revenue. No doubt some of the increased advertising volume can be attributed to increased circulation, though this component is more fickle; year to year changes reflect changes in the mix of advertising, economic activity, etc. *Excluding* advertising volume changes, the increase in the *Mirror*'s relative circulation via equation (2) added $1.7 million to its *relative* profit, which exceeds the *Sun*'s gains, noted above, by $0.5 million. This can be taken as the *minimum* annual volume of the price war game to News Limited, somewhat larger if advertising volume effects were also related to circulation. Over a four year period, the price war netted News Limited about $2 million and cost Fairfax the same.

STAGE 4 CONTINUED. 1975–79: TACTICS DURING THE BATTLE

The *Mirror*'s tactics over the 1975–79 period concentrated on price competition in the evening market, backed up by discontinuous bursts of advertising which emphasized price. As we saw above, this pricing strategy added about seven percent to the *Mirror*'s sales in relatively quick time. We have also shown that this pricing strategy was very profitable, adding at least $0.5 million annually to News Limited's gross profits.

The advantage of delineating the Sydney newspaper market becomes clear when we discover that News Limited simultaneously employed the opposite strategy in the morning and Sunday markets. In these markets, from late 1976 (see Table II), News Limited led John Fairfax in increasing prices. Several factors underlie this opposite strategy. First, as of mid-1976, the *Australian* newspaper had been operating at heavy losses ($3 million p.a.) which required special attention, namely hefty cover price increases. Secondly, the strategy fits the objective of News Limited to regain the overall price leadership.

With prices deadlocked in the evening market, News Limited had an open hand to initiate changes in the morning market. Thirdly, the opportunity cost to News Limited from pushing price in the morning market was minimal in light of the likely small own and cross price elasticity of demand. Fourthly, another factor stems from the uncertainty in which the evening newspaper price was couched. News Limited lacked experience in price experimentation, so the morning market provided a useful hedge in case events did not go to plan.

The *Sun*'s tactics were altogether different. Its early competitive response to the *Mirror*'s attack was not the orthodox price matching move, but rather an intensified advertising campaign. Presumably Fairfax was not in a hurry to relinquish its price leadership role and therefore resisted surrendering to Murdoch's challenge. This proved to be a costly mistake, with heavy declines in circulation, advertising volume and advertising revenue, which were only partially offset by the gain in circulation revenue (a 20% increase in price and a 7% loss in sales volume). The *Sun* lost at least $0.5 million in profit annually because of its higher relative price. Other factors compounded this loss.

In a subtle way, the *Sun*'s advertising response can be interpreted as a pricing strategy. Many oligopolistic firms employ product segmenting techniques whereby brands are differentiated on the basis of real or imagined quality. Frequently the brand price structure reflects or even identifies the segmented range of brands. Given that the *Sun*'s advertising extolled its quality, we have some basis for interpreting this as part of a product-price segmentation tactic. As we have shown in the previous section, the *Sun*'s promotional campaign was not particularly successful. The lack of success by the *Sun* in this area was caused partly by cannibalization and perhaps partly by the general ineffectiveness of advertising in the newspaper industry. For the former the Hotelling or game theoretic models provide an explanatory framework.

Although the *Sun*'s emphasis on advertising rather than price in the evening market was a strategic error, so too was its emphasis on price in the morning and Sunday markets. As can be seen in Table II, the *Telegraph* led the *S.M.H.* in price rises to 13, 14, 15 and 20 cents. For the first three of these, the lag in Fairfax's response was 7, 11 and 12 months respectively. This is most puzzling. What was Fairfax trying to do? It would seem that Fairfax was playing the Murdoch game with a slightly different slant; by following the *Telegraph* with an increasingly long lag, the *Herald* offered the threat that one day it might not follow at all. It certainly seems a cumbersome, though intriguing alternative to what Murdoch did with the *Mirror* after July 1975. Unfortunately, as we have now confirmed, the morning and evening markets are quite different. The lower *S.M.H.* price over the 1976–78 period cost the *Telegraph* less than one percent of its sales volume and equally little advertising volume or revenue.

STAGE 5. 1979–80: THE END OF THE BATTLE BUT NOT THE WAR

On January 15, 1979, backed by a large $500,000 advertising campaign the *Sun* retreated to 10 cents. This signalled a tactical victory to Murdoch. Until the *Mirror* had been appeased, the *Sun* was unable to increase its price beyond

12 cents. Thus Fairfax's price move to 12 cents proved abortive and indeed the next round of price increases to 15 cents in November 1979 were led by News Limited.

In the previous section we have criticised Fairfax's tactics. Three and a half years was a long time to retreat on price. The emphasis on advertising was criticised as being ineffective in raising market share and also for inappropriately deploying funds which could have been used to finance a price war. In recent margarine price wars, by contrast, most firms severely trimmed their advertising budgets during the peak of the war.

In retrospect one might have anticipated that the price war would have ended much earlier, say in late 1976 or early 1977. By that time there was apparently sufficient evidence of the cross elasticity of demand with respect to price and of the effect of increased promotional expenditures upon circulation.

One suspects that an important element in the long delay by Fairfax relates to the conglomerate media interests of Fairfax in Sydney: in television (Channel 7), radio (2GB), magazines and other specialised papers (including the *Financial Review* and *National Times*). These other media outlets provided a means of cross-subsidizing the *Sun*. There is also the possibility of internal transfer pricing manipulation, whereby the *Sun* could have paid a price below the market rate to Fairfax's other media outlets. Such manipulation is usually discussed in an international context, where differences in company tax rates between countries could make such schemes profitable on an after-tax basis. Within Australia fully owned subsidiaries are treated as separate tax paying units, so there is some scope for internal transfer pricing arrangements. But would they be profitable if both the parent and the subsidiary pay the same company tax rate? The answer is yes because modified transfer prices can *defer* tax payments, which in present-value terms is a benefit in the same way as accelerated depreciation allowances are. Having said all this, there are *limits* on the ability of companies to manipulate internal transfer prices for taxation purposes under the Companies Tax Act. To the extent that the *Sun* did take advantage of lower media charges by other Fairfax media organizations, then its true loss would be even greater than shown in Table IV!

If instead the *Sun* paid *market* rates for its use of other Fairfax media services, it could be argued that the opportunity cost was below the price charged for similar advertising time to outside organizations. Under what conditions would this be true? Last minute cancellations of advertising time on 2GB or Channel 7 would create vacant time slots in which advertisements for the *Sun* could be run. This suggests a novel advantage of diversified firms, which may be unique to media industries. However this practice may not be *flexible* enough to accommodate a planned large increment of advertising by the *Sun* in desired times of the year or day, especially when there is high demand for television time, as in the mid-1970s.

In summary, the ability of the *Sun* to operate within a conglomerate media network and either pay less than market price for other media services, or market prices, but at reduced opportunity cost, goes a long way in explaining the slow response by Fairfax in ending the price war. However, cheaper prices for other media services simply makes Fairfax's tactics less irrational; it does not make them rational. Even if the cost of other media services were zero it still cost Fairfax half a million dollars in profits in having higher relative cover prices. Similarly, Fairfax was earning less than maximum profits in the morning newspaper market because its prices were too low!

There is no escaping the conclusion that Fairfax was determined to retain its price leadership in the evening newspaper market and was prepared to sacrifice profits in the process. Perhaps Fairfax thought that the *Mirror*'s price freeze would be short-lived, ending, say, in June 1976 when News Limited's windfall newsprint cost advantage ended.[6] In turn, Fairfax may have underestimated the importance of price leadership to Murdoch. The Trade Practices Act must be partly credited for engendering confusion on the price setting front, with price leadership proving to be an imperfect substitute for collusion in the formative years of establishing leadership.

Although the 1975–79 price battle was won by News Limited, who demonstrated their newly won price leadership in initiating the November 1979 price increase, events in 1980 made it clear that the struggle was not over. On June 30, 1980 John Fairfax gave a week's notice that the price of the *Sun* was to rise to 20 cents. The *Mirror*'s counterpart announcement followed two days later. With the convenience of 'one coin shopping' and ground lost to inflation since 1974, there was perhaps little doubt about whether the *Mirror* would match the move to 20 cents. As things stand, Fairfax cleverly sneaked back in as price leader in the evening market. Moreover, the *Sun* cemented its newly found dominant position by leading the November 1980 advertising rate increases. Similarly in the Sunday newspaper market, Fairfax led the May 1981 round of cover price increases.

STAGE 6. 1981–82: A NEW NON-PRICE BATTLE

With both firms vying for power, it would be surprising if Fairfax's initiatives in 1980 ushered in a new era of stability. In fact, an unusually aggressive bout of non-price competition began in July 1981 and continues as of mid-1982. The *Mirror* initiated the bingo competition ploy, but was quickly matched by the *Sun* with a slightly different version of the competition. The Australian fever in the area trails England's Fleet Street events by about a month. In the

[6] Over the longer term, Fairfax could have been hoping for a newsagent's boycott in light of the temporal decline in the real value of the *Mirror*. Money illusion may have partly avoided such action. Moreover the case noted in our Stage 3 discussion, the Melbourne *Daily Morning Post*, was 50 percent cheaper than its rivals (compared with 20 percent in the case of the *Mirror*); there was more choice of newspapers in the 1925–27 case (three rivals, not one) and the *Morning Post* did not have News Limited's overall bargaining power in the publishing industry. For these reasons, a boycott would have required a much greater cover price differential than the actual figure of 20 percent.

U.K. the cost of running bingo games in newspapers is expected to be £15 million for prizes alone in 1981–82 (Garcia [5]). Distribution costs are additional. Circulation, especially for Express Newspapers' *Daily Star* and Murdoch's *Sun* are up dramatically, but so are costs, so there has been little change in profitability. This pattern on a smaller scale is repeated in the Sydney evening newspaper market.

In the U.K., with the exception of the "quality" nationals, the move into bingo competition has been across the board. The same was true in the initial phases in the Sydney evening market. Again these imitative strategies are explicable in terms of Hotelling or game theoretic models. Initially the Sydney *Sun* accelerated the pace of the bingo promotion by raising the prize money compared to what the *Mirror* offered initially. However, shortly after, the *Sun* scaled down its involvement and has since withdrawn altogether from bingo competition while the *Mirror* continues. This is a calculated risk for the *Sun*. To refrain from a popular promotional strategy when a rival is aggressively implementing such a strategy, spells doom in a game theoretic framework. At least in terms of market share, there are clear short-term gains for the *Mirror* (*cf.* Table III and also equation (4)). The *Sun*'s management (Garcia, [5]) believes that these gains may be temporary—which may include the prospect of the bingo novelty wearing out. As well, there is a presumption that circulations increased by bingo competitions will not be attractive to advertisers because such additional sales may be by people who do not read the rest of the paper. Readership and circulation volumes would diverge.

The *Sun* is hoping that the *Mirror* will haemorrhage from a cost squeeze, at which time it can assert its power aspirations. Similarly the *Mirror* is trying to move into a position of strength. In the current intermediate phase, neither company is as yet ready to take a firm resolve for leadership. As a result, initiatives on price setting in recent years have oscillated from one company to the other, as shown in Table I. This may continue until one company feels it is in a favoured position. As with New York and London, only one evening newspaper might survive such an encounter.

CONCLUSIONS

The emergence of a competitive price struggle in this industry is particularly interesting because it is preceded by three decades of identical prices. Government policy designed to facilitate competition in the economy can learn much from cases such as this one. While more cases will enrich our understanding of the competitive process, one point already seems especially clear. Even in what appear to be very stable oligopolies, there is always a latent power struggle between the major firms. The theory of games emphasizes the inherent conflict between firms which can only artificially and temporarily be resolved by collusive price leadership or similar practices. It is up to government agencies to exploit this latent conflict.

One by-product of this research is the idea that theories of cartel behaviour need to be modified to incorporate the possibility of a dominant firm. The role of Saudi Arabia in the OPEC Cartel is a case in point. As such the role is very similar to that of a price leader, except most of the assertion of power is behind closed doors. In the Australian newspaper case the dominant firm switched in the early 1970s from Fairfax to News Limited. We know very little about this switchover. Why was it so smooth? Why didn't Fairfax resist and spark off a price war?

The other theme looked at in this paper is the quality of management in forming appropriate marketing strategies. We have generally praised News Limited's tactics in both the morning and evening markets, which effectively exploited the differing cross elasticities of demand and correctly judged other aspects of the challenge to Fairfax's price leadership. There is no doubt that Fairfax used inappropriate strategies in both the evening and morning markets; advertising was an ineffective instrument in the evening market and price an ineffective instrument in the morning market. Perhaps the desperate struggle for leadership induced these irrational actions by John Fairfax and Sons. None the less, better use of economic theory and practice could have averted the worst of these management mistakes and conserved resources for a more informed counter-attack on the Murdoch empire at a later date.

William J. Merrilees
Department of Economics,
The University of Sydney,
New South Wales 2006,
Australia.

ACCEPTED MAY 1982

REFERENCES

[1] AUDIT BUREAU OF CIRCULATION, 'Six Monthly Circulation Data', available on request and published in *Australian Financial Review, passim.*

[2] COMANOR, W., 'Market Structure, Product Differentiation and Industrial Research', *Quarterly Journal of Economics,* 81, **1** (November 1967), pp. 639–57.

[3] DAVIDSON, F. and STEWARDSON, B., *Economics and Australian Industry* (Longman, Melbourne, 1979).

[4] FOG, B., *Industrial Pricing Policies* (North Holland, Amsterdam, 1960).

[5] GARCIA, L., 'Who are the Winners in the Bingo War,' Article in the *Sydney Morning Herald,* December 12, 1981.

[6] HOTELLING, H., 'Stability in Competition', *Economic Journal,* 39, **153** (March 1929), pp. 41–57.

[7] HUNTER, A., 'Restrictive Practices and Monopolies in Australia,' *Economic Record,* 37, **77** (March 1961), pp. 25–52.

[8] JOBSON'S INVESTMENT DIGEST, 'Spotlight on Mirror Newspaper Ltd.', 41, **10** (May 26, 1960), p. 290.

[9] JONES, R., 'The Sydney Newspaper Industry', in C. Terry (ed.) *Australian Microeconomics* (Prentice Hall, Sydney, 1980).

[10] LIPSEY, R., *Positive Economics* (Wiedenfeld and Nicolson, London, 1979).

[11] MAYER, H., *The Press in Australia* (Lansdowne Press, Melbourne, 1964).
[12] MERRILEES, W., 'Price Competition in the Magazine Industry', in K. Heys and B. Langworthy (eds.) *ECTA Readings in Economics* Volume 3 (Economic Commercial Teachers' Association of N.S.W., Sydney, 1982), pp. 143–50.
[13] NICHOLLS, W., *Price Policies in the Cigarette Industry* (Vanderbilt Press, Nashville, 1951).
[14] PORTER, M., 'Consumer Behaviour, Retailer Power and Market Performance in Consumer Goods Industries', *Review of Economics and Statistics*, 56, **4** (November 1974), pp. 419–36.
[15] PRICES JUSTIFICATION TRIBUNAL, 'Report on John Fairfax and Sons Limited', September 13, 1974.
[16] REEKIE, W., 'The Price Elasticity of the Demand for Evening Newspapers', *Applied Economics*, 8, **1** (March 1976), pp. 69–79.
[17] SCHERER, F., 'The Welfare Economics of Product Variety: An Application to the Ready-to-Eat Cereals Industry', *Journal of Industrial Economics*, 28, **2** (December 1979), pp. 113–34.
[18] SHERIDAN, K., *The Firm in Australia*, (Thomas Nelson, Melbourne, 1974).
[19] STEINER, P., 'Monopoly and Television in Television: Some Policy Issues', *Manchester School of Economics and Social Sciences*, 29, **2** (May 1961) pp. 107–31.
[20] STIGLER, G., 'The Kinky Oligopoly Demand Curve and Rigid Prices', *Journal of Political Economy*, **55** (October 1947), pp. 432–49.
[21] THOMSON PUBLICATIONS, 'Australian Advertising Rate and Data Service: Newspaper Edition', *passim*.
[22] WILTSHIRE, K. and STOKES, C., *Government Regulation in the Printed Media Industry* (Committee for Economic Development of Australia, Melbourne 1977).

EXPLORATIONS IN ECONOMIC HISTORY 15, 341–367 (1978)

Predatory Price Cutting: The Standard Oil of New Jersey Case Revisited*

RANDALL MARIGER

Harvard University

INTRODUCTION

Standard Oil Company and its founder John D. Rockefeller are invariably associated with monopoly and all of its undesirable attributes. It is generally believed that during the period 1870 to 1911 Standard practiced a host of unfair business methods; among them were industrial espionage,[1] bribery of state legislative members,[2] operation of bogus independent companies soliciting the trade of individuals opposed to monopoly,[3] and engaging in predatory pricing in markets where it faced competition.[4]

This last accusation is of special interest since the facts brought out in the dissolution case of 1909 and 1911[5] in this regard were of substantial influence in framing the prohibitions against price discrimination as drafted in the Clayton Act of 1914 and later in the Robinson Patman Act of 1936. These acts have been criticized. Some have conjectured that these statutes, contrary to their intended purpose, have actually resulted in a lessening of competition.

The Robinson Patman Act prohibits price discrimination which has the effect of injuring competition and which cannot be justified by (1) a difference in selling costs or (2) the meeting of an equally low price of a competitor.[6] In regard to the problems with this act a noted authority on the subject states:

* Requests for reprints should be sent to Randall Mariger, Littauer Hall, Room 122, Harvard University, Cambridge, Mass. 02138.

[1] Nevin (1953), Vol. II, p. 40, and Tarbell (1904), p. 40.

[2] Hidy and Hidy (1955), p. 205.

[3] U. S. Department of Justice (1909), Brief of Facts and Argument for Petitioner, Vol. II, pp. 150–357.

[4] *Ibid*., pp. 4–115.

[5] United States vs Standard Oil of New Jersey, 173 F 177 (1909); and Standard Oil Co. of New Jersey vs United States, 221 U. S. 1 (1911). The original dissolution suit was filed in Missouri, in 1906, and the decision against Standard came in 1909. The case was appealed to the Supreme Court which, in 1911, upheld the lower court's finding.

[6] Gellhorn (1976), pp. 366–368.

0014-4983/78/0154-0341$02.00/0

> The concern is that selective price discrimination could be used to eliminate competitors, give the discriminating seller (or favored buyer) monopoly power which will then be followed by raising prices to a monopoly level. This scenario will work, however, only if the subsequent monopoly profits exceed the costs of driving out competitors. And this depends generally on the existence of effective barriers to easy market entry by others or re-entry by those driven out. Because such predatory price discrimination is not likely to be profitable, it is possible,—indeed probable—that the price discriminator is not acting with a predatory intent but rather with a desirable (ie. competitive) purpose—to increase its sales, market shares, and profits. In other words, the careless or over vigorous application of section 2(a) may lead to uniformity and may dampen rather than enhance competition.[7]

The latest precedent established on the subject of geographical price discrimination is that of Utah Pie vs Continental Baking Co. (1967)[8] in which one of the defendants was found guilty of discriminatory prices set with a predatory intent. About the implications of the decision the authority cited above comments:

> The result, it would seem, is that under Utah Pie a national firm will be inhibited from seeking to enter a market through price cutting for fear that a competitor who is thereby injured can recover treble damages.[9]

In light of these considerations it seems appropriate to investigate whether there really is a tendency toward predatory pricing behavior on the part of a monopolist. The natural place to begin such an inquiry is with the most famous case of alleged predatory pricing behavior, the case of the Standard Oil Company.

Before proceeding a brief outline of the remainder of the paper will be presented. In section I, predatory pricing is explicitly defined. Section II gives a brief discussion of the economic forces involved in shaping the behavior of a "dominant" firm in its dealings with its smaller competitors. Here the dominant firm model of industrial organization is mentioned as a plausible alternative to the predatory pricing hypothesis. Section III presents a cursory sketch of the evidence given in the Standard Oil of New Jersey court case of 1909 and shows that, on the whole, the evidence is not inconsistent with profit maximizing behavior given the assumptions of the dominant firm model. We then turn to the problem of devising an empirical test to determine if the dominant firm model is inconsistent with

[7] *Ibid.*, p. 369.

[8] Utah Pie vs Continental Baking Co, 386 U. S. 685. In 1958 Utah Pie had 67% of the Salt Lake City area market in frozen pies. Pet Milk Co., a national company, entered the market at this time with a lower price, lower than the price at which it sold the same pies in California, the place of processing. Utah Pie followed the price cuts but by 1961 it had its market share cut to 45%. It sued under the Robinson Patman Act (for treble damages under section four of the Clayton Act) charging geographic price discrimination. It went to the Supreme Court where the original jury decision of guilty as charged was upheld.

[9] Gellhorn (1976), p. 372.

Standard's pricing behavior. Section IV presents the simple dominant firm model which is adapted in Appendix I to the circumstances of the petroleum industry in the early twentieth century. It is pointed out that if the model correctly explains Standard's pricing behavior then Standard's marginal revenue less marginal transportation costs must be equal in all markets. A procedure to test this prediction, given the available data, is then developed. Section V contains the empirical findings and section VI is a summary and conclusion.

I. PREDATORY PRICING DEFINED

Since predatory pricing is presumedly done so as to maximize the present value of present and future profits it is apparent that predatory pricing is a special case of profit maximizing behavior. The distinction we wish to make, however, is between profit maximizing behavior where the competitive environment is an instrument of policy and where it is not. In the models of perfect competition and simple monopoly the firm does not tamper with its environment; it takes it as given and operates accordingly. This, of course, is not the case with a predatory pricing model.

In view of this distinction, we define a predatory pricing policy as one where the predating firm sets a price too low to afford maximal profits *if* its competitive environment were to remain unchanged.

II. PREDATORY PRICING, AN OPTIMAL STRATEGY?

In a well-known article published in 1958 John S. McGee attacked, from a theoretical vantage point, the assertion that Standard Oil implemented a policy of predatory pricing.[10] He argued that it would have been more profitable for Standard to have bought out its competitors at, or slightly above, a competitive market price than to have engaged in wasteful price competition. Essentially the argument is that cutthroat price competition is not Pareto optimal with respect to Standard and the competitor; it results in a smaller total combined wealth of the two firms. It follows, then, that there is an alternative cooperative arrangement which will result in both parties being better off. McGee also pointed out that Standard, with from 70 to 90% of the market sales, loses a great deal more when the price is cut than do all the competitors combined. This is especially apparent when it is considered that in order to cut price Standard must supply a greater amount of oil, while the competitors supply less.

McGee also argues that the existence of different prices in different markets is not prima facie evidence of a predatory pricing policy. Differing prices can be explained (in the context of a dominant firm model

[10] McGee (1958).

presented below) with differing demand elasticities and/or differing degrees of competition.

In his analysis McGee glosses over an important consideration. He recognizes that Standard may be able to influence the price at which it can buy the competing firm by causing it to make losses but thinks this influence to be small since the artificially low retail oil price would clearly be temporary and the competitor could meanwhile cease operation. The problem with this argument is that the low price is not necessarily temporary. McGee ignores that there are other potential competitors observing Standard's policies; it therefore may be true that losing money in markets where there is competition will, by discouraging potential competitors, be profitable in the long run. Judging from Standard's slowly deteriorating domestic market position in the decade prior to 1911, it appears as if barriers to entry were not overly pervasive.[11] It seems plausible, therefore, that in markets where competition existed Standard would set predatory prices which it was prepared to maintain as examples to ward off would-be competitors.

This same argument would lead one to believe that Standard would be reluctant to pay lucrative prices for competitor plants as this would encourage others to construct new plants with the intention of selling them to Standard and sharing in the monopoly profits. Evidently this occurred quite often.[12] The exemplifying evidence which follows is the text of a letter to Rockefeller from a Mr. S. W. Hall of Philadelphia dated December 28, 1883:

> Dear Sir—I have leased the Sea Board Oil Co.'s works as you will see by this heading. Would it be to your interest to have it run or not run as you might suggest. If so could I have an interview with you in New York on next Wednesday and at what hours, please address me on a plain envelope—marked personal 51-N-6st—Phila.[13]

The fact that such blackmailing schemes were not uncommon would indicate that Standard did occasionally pay remunerative prices for competing refineries. But it is also true that Standard was not always receptive to such blackmail schemes as is indicated by the following letter from Rockefeller to an associate:

> They will be sick unto death now having failed in their wicked scheme. A good sweating will be healthy for them and they ought to have it, and it is not money lost for us to have other people see them get it. Our chances of fair play in the future will be better.[14]

[11] Williamson, Andreano, Daum, and Klose, (1963), p. 216. Standard's declining market position is referred to in section II.

[12] Nevin (1953), Vol. II, p. 56.

[13] *Ibid.*, p. 56.

[14] *Ibid.*, p. 56.

From the tone of the letter it appears that this was not a case in which a cooperative arrangement was made.

A final criticism of McGee's argument is that it hinges on the assumption that the cost to Standard and a competitor of making a mutually beneficial agreement was zero. To the contrary, it is inevitable that there would be dickering as to how the proceeds derived from such an agreement would be divided and therefore negotiations could break down completely. When transactions costs are considered the noncooperative price cutting outcome no longer seems so unreasonable.

I am led to conclude that it is not clear from a theoretical point of view what would be the optimal strategy of a dominant firm in dealing with smaller competitors. It can be said that the stronger the barriers to entry in the industry, the more likelihood that there would be a cooperative outcome. But even with complete barriers to entry, transactions costs may be such that an agreement cannot be reached and a noncooperative outcome is achieved.

III. EVIDENCE PRESENTED IN THE DISSOLUTION CASE

The evidence presented in the Standard Oil of New Jersey court case of 1909 and heard in the United States district court in Missouri was not necessarily indicative of predatory price cutting by the Standard Oil Company.[15] There was some evidence that threats of severe price cutting were made by Standard salesmen and in some cases were carried out. But in general the evidence presented was that of correlation between the degree of competition and the market price of illuminating oil. As will be shown in section IV, this is consistent with profit maximization of the type implied by the dominant firm model and does not imply that Standard was attempting to injure the competition.

The evidence presented by the Petitioner in regard to price cutting was of two kinds; statistical data secured from Standard and the testimony of 16 individuals connected with independent refining operations purporting to have suffered the effects of Standard's predatory pricing methods.

III. A. Statistical Data

In making its case against Standard, The Prosecution seemed to rely most heavily on price and market share data for various cities in the United States. These data show a definite positive relationship between the market price and Standard's market share.[16] Following are the results

[15] Neither the Missouri District Court or the Supreme Court considered the evidence on Standard's unfair business practices in arriving at their respective decisions. Simply stated, it was ruled that the trust agreement of 1899 gave Standard the power to restrict interstate commerce and this alone rendered the trust agreement illegal.

[16] U. S. Department of Justice (1909), Brief of Facts and Argument for Petitioner, Vol. II, p. 9.

of a regression run with price depending on Standard's market share and a constant for 31 cities in New England, Pennsylvania, Connecticut, and New York for the year 1904 (data are presented in Appendix II, cities 1–31).

$$\text{Cents/gallon} = \underset{(1.55)}{6.895} + \underset{(1.75)}{3.341} * \text{Share.}$$

Standard errors are in parentheses. Such a correlation is neither a necessary nor a sufficient condition for proving that Standard had a predatory pricing policy. However, if we were to assume some regularity in the elasticities of demand and competitive supply in the different markets we would expect to observe such a correlation in the case of predatory price cutting. But I would like to emphasize that, assuming the same regularity conditions and ruling out pathological cases (described in section IV), dominant firm profit maximizing on the part of Standard implies the existence of this same correlation.

The Prosecution also signaled out several specific instances as examples of Standard's predatory pricing policy. For example, the price of a gallon of Standard's illuminating oil in Springfield, Massachusetts, was 11.5¢ in late 1903 but, when new competition entered the market in early 1904, fell to 8¢. The government presented this fact as clear evidence of Standard's predating policy. But, as is stated above, the dominant firm model predicts this same type of pricing behavior.

III. B. Oral Testimony

For the most part the oral testimony was no more illuminating than the raw statistical data. Questions pertaining to who cut the price first were given a great deal of emphasis. It should be noted that this line of questioning could either prove Standard's innocence or nothing at all. If Standard led in the reductions in price it does not indicate that those cuts were designed to eliminate competition (as opposed to a dominant firm profit maximizing response to a declining market share) whereas a finding that Standard followed price cuts would be prima facie evidence of its innocence. As it was, with few exceptions, Standard claimed to have followed price cuts and the competitors claimed it had led.

There was some testimony that Standard's salesmen had threatened store owners who carried the product of a Standard competitor with a drastic reduction in the price of oil sold to the store owners' competitors unless they switched to Standard's product. In at least one instance this strategy was alleged to have been successfully carried out. The salesman responsible was said to have pointed out the instance to other retailers as an example of the seriousness of his threats.[17]

[17] *Ibid.*, p. 104.

TABLE 1

Standard's Relative Decline in the Refining Industry in the Decade prior to Dissolution

	1897		1906
Share of domestic illuminating oil produced	.889		.848
Share of domestic naptha produced	.912		.861
	1900		1906
Share of illuminating oil exports	.908		.863
	1899		1909
Number of refinery establishments	67		147
Change in number of refineries		80	
Change in Standard's number of refineries		7	

Source: U. S. Department of Justice (1909), Brief for Defendants on the Facts, Vol. I, p. 238; Hidy and Hidy (1955), p. 417.

III. C. Standard's Defense

In its defense Standard pointed out that if it had used predatory pricing to keep down competition then the policy was clearly ineffective. This is shown in Table 1. Many of the witnesses testifying against Standard admitted that they increased their volume of sales and had operated profitably in spite of price competition with Standard.[18]

Standard denied the charge that it had forced the sale of competing refineries. It was pointed out that, of the more than 100 refineries purchased by Standard from its inception to the time of the trial, only two of the former owners charged that the sales were brought about by unfair business practices on the part of Standard and in neither of these instances was Standard accused of predatory price cutting.[19]

In short, the evidence that was presented in regard to predatory pricing is not at all conclusive. It is not clear that Standard cut prices with the intention of either driving the competition to bankruptcy or to a nonremunerative sale.

Since the prosecution emphasized the market data on shares and prices in making its case against Standard it seems appropriate to attempt an alternative explanation of this data. The alternative explanation we will

[18] Hidy and Hidy (1955), p. 469; U. S. Department of Justice (1909), Petitioner's Testimony Vol. IV, pp. 1844–1844.

[19] U. S. Department of Justice (1909), Brief for Defendants on the Facts, Vols. I–III, pp. 151–152.

consider, and for which we will attempt an empirical test, is the dominant firm model of Standard Oil's pricing behavior.

IV. THE DOMINANT FIRM MODEL OF PRICING BEHAVIOR

IV. A. Explanation of Model

The dominant firm model of industrial organization is designed to explain the price-making policy of a single large firm who is competing with any number of smaller competitors. The characteristic which distinguishes the large firm from the small firms is that its output decisions affect the market price whereas the output decisions of any one of the small competitors does not.

The model assumes that the large firm subtracts its estimate of the joint supply curve of the competitors from the market demand curve, takes the residual as its demand curve, and sets price as would a simple monopolist. The competitors take this price as given and produce in accordance with their supply curves. The dominant firm produces and sells the difference between the market demand at this price and the quantity supplied by its competitors.

Note that the model *does not* assume that the dominant firm ignores potential entry of new firms when it makes its pricing decision. This factor is taken into account by defining the competitive supply curve to be that which applies in the long run. It may be thought that when allowance is made for potential entry to affect the dominant firm's price the dominant firm model includes predatory pricing as a special case. But this is not so, since a predatory price is designed to eliminate the competitive supply curve completely (after which price is raised), whereas the dominant firm model implies that the large firm treats the competitive supply curve as given and permanent and sets price accordingly.

Note too that the dominant firm, which presumedly makes abnormally large profits, must have some advantage(s) over its competitors if it is to retain its dominant position. Some possible advantages are scale economies, the availability of internal financing, better access to capital markets, and/or a superior entrepreneurial staff.

Figure 1 is a graphical representation of the model.

Before the model can be used for analyzing the early petroleum industry we must generalize it by (1) introducing many separate selling markets, (2) allowing for jointly produced products, and (3) allowing for a multiplant dominant firm. The reason for the first added complication is obvious; we wish to investigate the reasons for prices differing in different localities. The second complication is necessary since crude oil yields many different products in variable proportions, depending on the method used in refining. During the first years of the twentieth century the primary products were illuminating oil (kerosene), naptha (gasoline), and lubricating oils. The third consideration is warranted because Standard con-

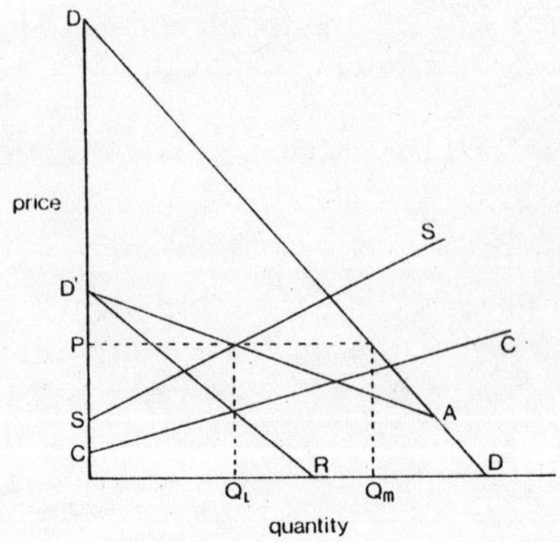

FIG. 1. The dominant firm model of pricing behavior for one output and one selling market. *DD*, Market demand; *D'AD*, large firm's demand; *D'R*, large firm's marginal revenue; *CC*, large firm's marginal cost; *SS*, competitive supply; Q_L, large firm's output; Q_M, market output; $Q_M - Q_L$, competitors' output; *P*, market clearing price.

trolled many separate refineries during this period of time. In 1899 Standard controlled 18 separate plants; by 1911 its holdings expanded to 26 plants.[20]

Unfortunately the generalized model, which is developed fully in Appendix I. A, does not reduce to a model of simple monopoly as does the simpler model described above. The reason is that, in the case of jointly produced products, a change in the price charged by the dominant firm for one product, say product A, not only causes a change in the competitors' quantities supplied of product A but also in their quantities supplied of the other jointly produced products, say Ã. This, in turn, changes the quantities demanded from the dominant firm of Ã at the existing prices.

A rather lengthy discussion in Appendix I. A, however, demonstrates that these joint product effects are probably small in the case of the early petroleum industry and, for the purpose of formulating a test of the dominant firm model, can safely be ignored. This is due to small and offsetting cross elasticities of supply as well as the fact that the sale of kerosene (the product on which we will focus our attention) generated nearly 60% of Standard's total revenue during the period of time we will consider.[21]

The introduction of many selling markets and a multiplant dominant firm is discussed in section IV. C and does not change any of the conclusions stated in reference to the simpler model. Therefore, the graphical analysis of the dominant firm model, as well as the discussion which precedes it, is the appropriate framework for analyzing Standard Oil's pricing

[20] Hidy and Hidy (1955), pp. 410–412. This fact may seem to contradict the fact stated previously that Standard had, between 1870 and 1906, bought out more than 100 competitors. Standard was constantly consolidating its holdings, however, and dismantled many plants.

[21] U. S. Department of Commerce and Labor, Bureau of the Census (1908), p. 571.

decisions in one of its many selling markets. The linkage between these markets is the topic of section IV. C.

Our graphical analysis having been vindicated, we may look back to it to explain the observed positive correlation between Standard's market share and its price. Here it is seen that an outward shift in the competitive supply curve results in Standard's demand curve shifting downward. Only in the seemingly perverse case where this shift is accompanied by a *substantial* reduction in the absolute value of Standard's demand elasticity (made more inelastic) at quantities in the neighborhood of the old equilibrium will this result in an increased price. In such a case Standard's output would be cut drastically in order to facilitate the fall in market output (increase in price) in spite of the increased competitive supply. Such a state of affairs would be pathological indeed. It is much more likely that an outward shift in the competitive supply curve would result in a decreased price along with a decrease in Standard's share of the market sales. Therefore the observed positive correlation between Standard's share of market sales and the equilibrium price can easily be explained in the context of the dominant firm model.

IV. B. Naiveté of the Model: Only an Approximation

Not all the assumptions of the dominant firm model held true in the early years of the petroleum industry. Perhaps the most serious divergence between the model and reality comes with the assumption of a homogeneous product and the corollary of a single price in each market. In the court testimony there were brought out numerous instances of competitive firms charging different prices in the same market, in some cases for extended periods of time.[22]

The quality of refined products of the same rated grade did vary considerably for different suppliers during the period of time considered here. Although competitors frequently charged Standard with marketing an inferior product it is apparent that Standard's products were superior or equal in quality to those of its competitors.[23] Perhaps Standard's greatest attribute was its marketing services. All but the largest of Standard's competitors shipped oil to retailers in wooden barrels which were hard to handle and could be depended on to leak from 5 to 8% of their contents. In addition retailers were forced to buy in 42-gal lots. Standard, on the other hand, had an elaborate network of bulk storage stations across the country, 3573 of them in 1906, from which, in most cases, oil was delivered by tank wagon and sold by the gallon.[24] In 1906, 70% of Standard's business was done by tank wagon.[25]

[22] U. S. Department of Justice (1909), Brief for Defendants on the Facts, Vols. I–III, pp. 622–623.

[23] Tarbell (1904), p. 33; Williamson *et al.* (1963), p. 213.

[24] Nevin (1953), Vol. II, p. 45.

[25] Hidy and Hidy (1955), p. 463.

Counteracting this advantage of Standard's was the growing dislike for monopoly which the competition did its best to exploit. Some of the names chosen by competitors are indicative of this sentiment, names such as Independent Oil Company and the Anti-Trust Oil Company.[26] Perhaps to improve its public image Standard's advertising expenditures grew rapidly in the early 1900s.[27]

In short, it is recognized that the dominant firm pricing model assumption of a homogeneous product does not correctly characterize the conditions which prevailed in the early years of the petroleum industry. It was chosen, however, because it is tractable to analysis, it captures most of the essential features of optimal price setting, and it was suggested by McGee as an alternative to the predatory pricing hypothesis.

IV. C. A Testable Implication of the Model

IV. C. 1. Once the competitive supply curve has been subtracted from the market demand curve the dominant firm model reduces to one of simple monopoly. It is well known that a simple monopolist selling its product in several markets equates marginal revenue less marginal transportation costs in all markets. This conclusion is still valid in the more complicated case of a multiplant monopolist provided that either: (1) all selling markets considered have at least one supply plant in common and that the transportation charge be from such a plant, or (2) that the transportation cost be the same between any given market and all plants supplying the markets considered. This is the prediction of the dominant firm model which we will test.

IV. C. 2. Expressing the prediction in terms of elasticities and available data. In what follows we will deal with only one product, kerosene. The marginal revenue of the dominant firm (henceforth referred to as Standard) for kerosene in a given market is

$$MR = P_0 * (1 + (1/e_s)), \tag{2}$$

where MR = Standard's marginal revenue when price is P_0; e_s = elasticity of Standard's demand at price P_0; and P_0 = market price. The demand function for Standard's kerosene in the given market is

$$Q^s = f(P_0,\mathbf{P},\mathbf{Y}) - g(P_0,\mathbf{P},\mathbf{T}),$$

where Q^s = quantity of Standard's kerosene demanded; $\mathbf{P}$ = vector of all other prices; $\mathbf{Y}$ = vector of personal incomes in the market; $\mathbf{T}$ = vector of variables describing competitors' technology; $f(\cdot) = Q^D$ = the market demand for kerosene; and $g(\cdot) = Q^C$ = the competitive supply of kerosene.

[26] *Ibid.*, p. 471.
[27] *Ibid.*, p. 462.

It follows that:

$$e_s = \frac{P_0}{Q^s} * \frac{df}{dP_0} - \frac{P_0}{Q^s} * \frac{dg}{dP_0}.$$

But

$$Q^s = s * Q^D = s/(1 - s) * Q^C$$

where s = Standard's market share and $1 - s$ = competitors' market share. Therefore,

$$e_s = e/s - (1 - s)/s * n, \qquad (3)$$

where e = elasticity of the market demand curve and n = elasticity of the competitive supply curve. Giving all the parameters subscripts to specify the market (city), eliminating the 0 subscript on the price of kerosene (since there can no longer be any confusion with **P**), and inserting the above expression (3) into expression (2) we have:

$$MR_i = P_i * (1 - s_i/(e_i + (1 - s_i) * n_i)),$$

where e_i is now defined to be the negative of the demand elasticity and should therefore be positive.

For markets i and j we have the following condition:

$$MR_i - t_i = MR_j - t_j,$$

where t_i and t_j are the per unit transportation charges to markets i and j, respectively.

Substituting for MR_i and MR_j from above:

$$P_i * (1 - s_i/(e_i + (1 - s_i) * n_i)) - t_i = P_j * (1 - s_j/(e_j + (1 - s_j) * n_j)) - t_j. \qquad (4)$$

With some manipulation we arrive at the following relation:

$$\begin{aligned} e_i = [&n_i * e_j * (1 - s_i) * (P_j - t_j - P_i + t_i) \\ &+ n_i * n_j * (1 - s_i) * (1 - s_j) * (P_j - t_j - P_i + t_i) \\ &+ e_j * s_i * P_i + n_j * s_i * P_i * (1 - s_j) + n_i * s_j * P_j * (1 - s_i)]/ \qquad (5) \\ [&e_j * (P_i - t_i - P_j + t_j) + n_j * ((1 - s_j) * \\ &(P_i - t_i - P_j + t_j)) + P_j * s_j] = F\{n_i, n_j, e_j / s_i, s_j, t_i, t_j, P_i, P_j\}. \end{aligned}$$

The variables to the right of the slash in the list of arguments are variables for which we have data.

If the dominant firm model correctly describes Standard's pricing strategy (5) must hold for all market pairs. The most straightforward method of determining whether this is the case would be to estimate the demand and supply elasticities for a few selected cities. These estimates in conjunction with the price and market share data and available transportation cost data would allow us to determine whether (5) held for the markets considered. The problem with this approach is that it requires quantity data for well-defined marketing areas for which price, income, and population data are also available. I was only able to find quantity data for 14 cities for two separate month-long periods, one in 1906 and the other in 1907. But I was able to obtain price data for only 4 of these cities and only for the month in 1906. Clearly such a few number of observations does not allow for robust estimates. Furthermore, being limited to cross-sectional data, it would be necessary to assume demand and supply elasticities not to vary from one city to another in order to make estimates.

Given the severe data limitations it was decided that the best approach would be a simulation. Eleven New England cities and the year 1904 were chosen for the analysis. From prior expectations and after a consideration of the particular circumstances of the petroleum industry in the early twentieth century, ranges of plausible values for the demand and supply elasticities for illuminating oil in each of the 11 cities were chosen. These chosen bounds define a subset of a 22 dimensional space. The question we ask is, is there a subset of this subset of values for the 22 parameters for which equation (5) is satisfied for the 11 cities? If there is then we cannot reject the dominant firm model on the basis of the market data considered.

The following section describes the method used to answer the question posed above.

IV. C. 3. The simulation procedure described. Equation (5) applied to all the 11 cities in all possible pairwise combinations constitutes 10 independent relations. Boston (city 1) was chosen as the market to be compared (this is a poor term but was used for want of a better one; its meaning will become clear below) with each of the other 10 cities (cities 2 through 11). In other words, in equation (5) i is set equal to 1 (Boston) for the entire analysis and j is varied from 2 to 11 depending on which city is being compared with Boston. When a particular city is being compared with Boston it shall be referred to as the "comparee."

Now consider the jth comparee. Let each point of a three-dimensional space define three values; Boston's supply elasticity, the comparee's demand elasticity, and the comparee's supply elasticity. Suppose that the chosen bounds of the elasticities for this particular comparee (the jth) are $e_{jL} < e_j < e_{jH}$ and $n_{jL} < n_j < n_{jH}$ and for Boston are $e_{1L} < e_1 < e_{1H}$ and $n_{1L} < n_1 < n_{1H}$. These bounds define a subset of the three-dimensional space described above (henceforth referred to as the "subset"). The range of permissible values of Boston's supply elasticity is marked off into discrete intervals of .2 pure number units. A planar slice of the subset is associated with each value of Boston's supply elasticity thus defined. Such a planar slice is illustrated in Figure 2. This planar slice will serve as the domain of expression (5) given the discretely chosen value of Boston's supply elasticity. Over this domain there exists a maximum and a minimum for Boston's demand elasticity. In fact, it is apparent from inspection of (4) that expression (5) is monotonically increasing in e_j and n_j given n_i. Therefore the maximum over the domain occurs at the corner

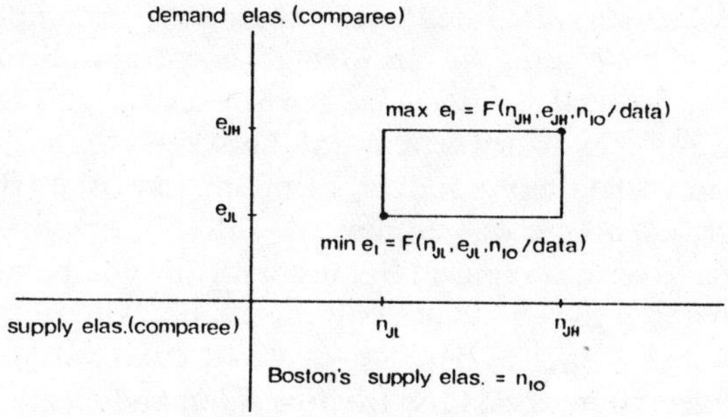

FIG. 2. The planar slice.

point (e_{jH}, n_{jH}) and the minimum occurs at the corner point (e_{jL}, n_{jL}). A continuum of points (a level curve) are contained in the slice for which Boston's demand elasticity takes on any intermediate value between the minimum and maximum found above. This is true because (5) is continuous in e_j and n_j given n_i and the planar slice is closed and convex. In this way we may define an interval for Boston's demand elasticity (the interval between the minimum and the maximum) for a given value of Boston's supply elasticity (n_{10}) which is consistent with the dominant firm pricing model and with the bounds placed on the comparee's demand and supply elasticities.

Notice that the minimum and maximum values of Boston's demand elasticity occur where the comparee's demand elasticity is at its lower and upper bounds, respectively. This is comforting since our interval will not depend on an implausible divergence between Boston's demand elasticity and that of the comparee. Unfortunately this needn't be so in the case of supply elasticities. The minimum and maximum value of Boston's demand elasticity occur where the comparee's supply elasticity is at its lower and upper bounds, respectively, regardless of the value of

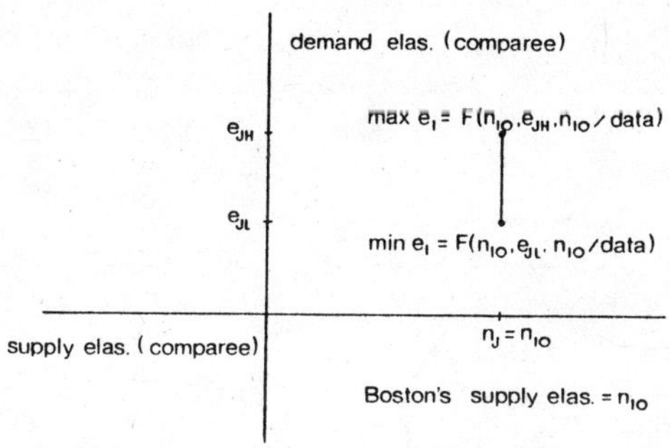

FIG. 3. The planar slice reduced to a line. Supply elasticities constrained to be equal.

Boston's supply elasticity. Since some regularity in supply elasticities across markets is desirable, we decided to constrain all market supply elasticities to be identical. In this case the subset reduces to a plane and the planar slice reduces to a vertical line between e_{jL} and e_{jH} where the comparee's supply elasticity equals that of Boston (n_{10}) (Figure 3). The procedure described above was employed with this dimension reduction.

Thus far we have only compared Boston with one comparee. This whole procedure is repeated for all 10 cities, but possibly with different demand elasticity intervals for each. Then, for this particular value of the supply elasticity, we have 10 intervals for Boston's demand elasticity which are consistent with our restrictions for each city taken separately. The intersection of these 10 intervals along with the acceptable interval for Boston's demand elasticity then defines a new interval for Boston's demand elasticity which is consistent with the given supply elasticity and with the restrictions placed on all 11 cities *simultaneously*. This procedure is then repeated for all the discretely chosen values for the supply elasticity. We then have an interval of acceptable values for Boston's demand elasticity for each chosen value of the supply elasticity. Since all these supply elasticities are acceptable the union of all these intervals then defines the interval of values for Boston's demand elasticity which is consistent with all the restrictions imposed. The larger this interval is the more credible is the dominant firm pricing model.

Below is an example for three comparees and two discretely chosen values for the supply elasticity. The interval (−1.4, −.6) was used as the acceptable interval for the demand elasticities of Boston and the comparees.

Example 1: Simulation Procedure*

	Boston's Demand Elasticity							
	Brockton		Fall River		Lowell		Intersections	
Supply elasticity	Min	Max	Min	Max	Min	Max	I	II
1.4	.36	1.04	.37	1.00	.42	1.03	.42–1.0[a]	.6–1.0[b]
3.0	.18	.86	.19	.82	.28	.88	.28–.82[c]	.6–.82[d]
Union = .6–1.0[e]								

[a] (.42 − 1.0) = (.36 − 1.04) ∩ (.37 − 1.0) ∩ (.42 − 1.03).
[b] (.6 − 1.0) = (.42 − 1.0) ∩ (.6 − 1.4).*
[c] (.28 − .82) = (.18 − .86) ∩ (.19 − .82) ∩ (.28 − .88).
[d] (.6 − .82) = (.28 − .82) ∩ (.6 − 1.4).*
[e] (.6 − 1.0) = (.6 − 1.0) ∪ (.6 − .82).
* Demand elasticities are presented as absolute values.

IV. C. 4. The elasticity bounds. In 1904 the kerosene lamp was the primary source of artificial illumination, particularly among the lower income classes. Artificial gas was much more expensive than kerosene and its use as illuminating fuel was restricted to high-income homes.[28] Electricity, on the other hand, was cheap (once wiring and fixtures were installed) and was growing fast in popularity. The number of electricity meters on consumption circuits for lighting rose from 582,689 in 1902 to 3,837,518 in 1912.[29] In tandem with this increase Standard's sales of illuminating oil declined absolutely after 1903.[30] It can be safely concluded that the demand for illuminating oil was falling due to the increasing use of electricity.

However, it does not follow that since electricity was an available alternative to illuminating oil, the demand for kerosene was elastic; on the contrary, a more careful analysis indicates the opposite. It was inevitable that the demand for illuminating oil would shift down due to the superior services provided by the electric light bulb. It is not clear that the price of illuminating oil, in the relevant range, would appreciably affect the rate at which this demand shift occurred. As it was, electric light was cheaper than light from a kerosene lamp.[31] It was the installation of wiring and electric fixtures, as well as the limited rate at which the supply of generated electricity could be expanded, that slowed the switchover to electricity. And these things were much less influenced by the price of illuminating oil than they were by other factors. We therefore conclude that the demand elasticity for illuminating oil was quite small.

Our first inclination is to specify a common interval for the demand elasticity in all 11 cities. But this is incorrect since it ignores the fact that the demand elasticity is endogenous depending on, among other things, the price of illuminating oil and thus on Standard's actions. In particular, Standard will not produce where the absolute value of its demand elasticity is less than 1. Otherwise Standard could not possibly be maximizing profits.

Because of this, our strategy is to set a lower bound on Standard's demand elasticity ("Low") rather than on the market demand elasticity. The value of Low must be at least 1 to be consistent with the dominant firm model (demand elasticities are expressed as absolute values and are assumed negative). Since Standard's demand elasticity in a particular city depends on its market share, the competitive supply elasticity, and the market demand elasticity (see section IV. C. 2), it follows that, for a

[28] *Ibid.*, p. 452.
[29] *Ibid.*, p. 452.
[30] *Ibid.*, p. 473.
[31] *Ibid.*, p. 452.

particular value of the supply elasticity, a given value of Low puts a minimum value on the market demand elasticity. This value is taken to be the lower bound on the market demand elasticity for each city, given the supply elasticity and a value of Low. An upper bound on the market demand elasticity is obtained by adding a value "Spread" to the lower bound.[32]

We consider small values of Low because of our conclusion that the market demand elasticity was small. The values considered in the analysis are 1.0, 1.2, and 1.4. The lower bound to the market demand elasticity, given the supply elasticity and a value for Low, is computed as follows:

$$\text{Lower Bound} = (\text{Standard's share}) * \text{Low} - (1 - \text{Standard's share}) * \text{supply elasticity}.$$

If the lower bound as computed above is less than 0.6, then 0.6 is used as the lower bound. The values of Spread considered are 0.6 and 0.8.

The competitive supply elasticity is more difficult to specify. The demand for petroleum products in general was expanding very rapidly in the early twentieth century, and it is evident that the supply was lagging behind. The rate at which refinery working capacity was utilized has been estimated to have been 94% during the period 1895 to 1897 and 105% in 1906.[33] Presumably the corresponding figure for 1904 was somewhere in between. One reason capacity was overworked was to produce more gasoline, a joint product of kerosene.[34] But this is of little consequence since, as the discussion in Appendix I indicates, the existing technology did not allow for transforming kerosene into gasoline. These considerations indicate that, at the margin of production, the short-run supply elasticity was quite small.

A simple model which ignores the joint product nature of refining gives a more moderate estimate of the short-run supply elasticity. Suppose that there is a fixed ratio of crude oil input to refined kerosene output and that, given sufficient crude oil input, the production technology is described by a Cobb–Douglas production function in capital and labor. Under these assumptions Appendix I. B. shows that the short-run (capital fixed) supply elasticity for kerosene is:

[32] The reader may be wondering why we don't just specify intervals for Standard's demand elasticities and forget about their determinants. This would not be equivalent, however, since "Spread" is added to the *market* demand elasticity lower bound, not to "Low." Our procedure also allows us to analyze the implications a given value of Standards demand elasticity has for the underlying market demand and supply elasticities so that we may assess their plausibility.

[33] Andreano (1960), p. 350.

[34] Hidy and Hidy (1955), p. 445.

$$n = \frac{1}{1 - c} * \frac{(1 - a)}{a} = 2.2,$$

where c = proportion of the value of kerosene accounted for by the cost of materials = 0.7 and a = capital's share in value added = 0.6. It should be kept in mind that this estimate is crucially dependent on the assumption that the elasticity of substitution between labor and capital (σ) was one for the refining process. This is probably a bit high: a more realistic value for σ would result in a smaller supply elasticity. On the other hand, this estimate assumes capital to be totally fixed, whereas Standard would be perceptive of a longer run supply elasticity. Relaxing this assumption leads to a higher supply elasticity. We conclude that the supply elasticity is highly uncertain, but was probably in the neighborhood of 2.2, the interval chosen being 1.4 to 3.0.[35]

Note that these intervals for the demand and supply elasticities were deliberately chosen to be quite restrictive. There are certainly plausible values for the elasticities which lie outside of these intervals, but it is our feeling that the intervals do not include any unacceptable values. In this way we add an additional measure of robustness to any finding in favor of the dominant firm model.

Before the simulation results are presented, we must establish that our test of the dominant firm model is indeed valid for the 11 New England cities considered. Recall that, for this to be true, it is sufficient that the transportation charge be the same between any given market and all refineries. This fact is easily established since the 11 New England cities chosen were all supplied from Standard's New York and Philadelphia refineries. From these refineries illuminating oil was shipped by tanker to large bulk receiving and distributing stations at Wilson Point, Connecticut; New London, Connecticut; East Providence, Rhode Island; and East Boston, Massachusetts. The additional per unit cost of traveling by ship the extra distance from Philadelphia was trivial and can safely be ignored.[36]

V. SIMULATION RESULTS

The simulation results are presented in Tables 2 and 3. Since the true value of the supply elasticity is very uncertain the results are tabulated for supply elasticities of 0.8 to 3.0 in intervals of 0.2. The union operation giving the final acceptable interval for Boston's demand elasticity is left to the reader who may make his own judgements as to what interval for supply elasticities and which values of "Low" and "Spread" are appropriate. The numbers in parentheses will be explained below.

[35] Our ignorance of how the supply elasticity varies with price causes us to specify a common supply elasticity interval for all cities.

[36] U. S. Department of Commerce, Bureau of Corporations (1906), pp. 148–149.

TABLE 2

Boston Demand Elasticity Interval with New London Included

Supply elasticity	Low = 1.0 Spread = .8	Low = 1.2 Spread = .8	Low = 1.4 Spread = .8	Low = 1.0 Spread = .6	Low = 1.2 Spread = .6	Low = 1.4 Spread = .6
0.8	.93–1.19	.95–1.26	1.11–1.33	.93–1.10	.95–1.18	1.11–1.26
	(9)	(10)	(15)	(7)	(9)	(13)
1.0	.97–1.16	.97–1.24	1.09–1.31	.97–1.08	.97–1.16	1.09–1.24
	(9)	(10)	(14)	(8)	(9)	(12)
1.2	1.01–1.14	1.01–1.22	1.06–1.29	1.01–1.05	1.01–1.14	1.06–1.21
	(9)	(11)	(13)	(8)	(9)	(12)
1.4	1.05–1.12	1.05–1.19	1.05–1.26	∅	1.05–1.11	1.05–1.19
	(10)	(11)	(12)		(10)	(11)
1.6	1.09–1.10	1.09–1.17	1.09–1.24	∅	1.09–1.09	1.09–1.17
	(10)	(11)	(13)		(10)	(11)
1.8	∅	1.12–1.15	1.12–1.22	∅	∅	1.12–1.14
		(12)	(13)			(12)
2.0	∅	∅	1.16–1.19	∅	∅	∅
			(14)			
2.2–3.0	∅	∅	∅	∅	∅	∅

The results with New London included (Table 2) are not nearly as favorable for the dominant firm model as the results obtained when excluding New London (Table 3). The dominant firm model is rejected for any values of the supply elasticity greater than 2.0 when New London is included. When New London is excluded the dominant firm model is rejected only when the supply elasticity is 3.0, "Low" is 1, and "Spread" is 0.6. For either table the results do not appear overly sensitive to assumptions about "Low" and "Spread."

Our results indicate that plausible demand and supply elasticities do exist for which Eq. (5) holds when applied simultaneously to all 11 cities. In fact, for any given supply elasticity and any Boston demand elasticity contained in the corresponding intervals shown in Tables 2 and 3, there exists a unique solution to this system of 10 simultaneous equations. Example solutions, for various supply elasticities and the midpoints of the corresponding Boston demand elasticity intervals ("Low" = 1.0, "Spread" = 0.6), are tabulated in Table 4. Table 2 was used for supply elasticities of 0.8 and 1.2 and Table 3 was used for larger supply elasticities. The solutions presented in Table 4 appear reasonable and are not in conflict with our prior expectations (see Footnote *a* to Table 4; the problem of New London is discussed at the conclusion of this section).

Finally we turn our attention to the case of Springfield, Massachusetts. Recall that Springfield was singled out as a market where Standard was particularly vicious in its reaction to new competition. The numbers in parentheses in Tables 2 and 3 are the percentage loss in market share which Standard must have suffered in Springfield in order to reconcile the drop in its price of illuminating oil in that market with the dominant firm

TABLE 3

Boston Demand Elasticity Interval with New London Excluded

Supply elasticity	Low = 1.0 Spread = .8	Low = 1.2 Spread = .8	Low = 1.4 Spread = .8	Low = 1.0 Spread = .6	Low = 1.2 Spread = .6	Low = 1.4 Spread = .6
0.8	.81–1.19 (6)	.95–1.26 (10)	1.11–1.33 (15)	.80–1.10 (5)	.95–1.18 (9)	1.11–1.26 (13)
1.0	.79–1.16 (6)	.93–1.24 (10)	1.09–1.31 (14)	.77–1.08 (5)	.93–1.16 (8)	1.09–1.24 (12)
1.2	.77–1.14 (6)	.91–1.22 (9)	1.06–1.29 (13)	.79–1.05 (5)	.91–1.14 (8)	1.06–1.21 (12)
1.4	.80–1.12 (6)	.89–1.19 (8)	1.04–1.26 (12)	.80–1.03 (5)	.89–1.11 (7)	1.04–1.19 (11)
1.6	.81–1.10 (6)	.86–1.17 (8)	1.02–1.24 (11)	.81–1.01 (5)	.86–1.09 (7)	1.02–1.17 (10)
1.8	.82–1.07 (6)	.84–1.15 (7)	.99–1.22 (11)	.82– .99 (5)	.84–1.07 (6)	.99–1.14 (10)
2.0	.83–1.05 (6)	.83–1.13 (7)	.97–1.19 (10)	.83– .96 (5)	.83–1.05 (6)	.97–1.12 (9)
2.2	.84–1.03 (6)	.84–1.10 (7)	.95–1.17 (10)	.84– .94 (5)	.84–1.02 (6)	.95–1.10 (9)
2.4	.85–1.01 (6)	.85–1.08 (7)	.93–1.15 (9)	.85– .92 (5)	.85–1.00 (6)	.93–1.08 (8)
2.6	.86– .98 (6)	.86–1.06 (7)	.90–1.13 (9)	.86– .90 (5)	.86– .98 (6)	.90–1.05 (8)
2.8	.87– .96 (6)	.87–1.04 (7)	.88–1.10 (8)	.87– .87 (5)	.87– .96 (6)	.88–1.03 (7)
3.0	.88– .94 (6)	.88–1.01 (7)	.88–1.08 (8)	∅	.88– .93 (6)	.88–1.01 (7)

TABLE 4

Example Solutions

Supply elasticity	Demand elasticities					
	$n = .8$	$n = 1.2$	$n = 1.6$	$n = 2.0$	$n = 2.4$	$n = 2.8$
Boston	1.01	1.03	.91	.90	.89	.87
Brockton	1.32	1.39	1.30	1.34	1.38	1.42
Fall River	1.35	1.44	1.33	1.38	1.42	1.47
Lowell	1.33	1.41	1.29	1.32	1.35	1.38
Lynn	1.33	1.41	1.31	1.36	1.40	1.43
Springfield	.98	1.00	.78	.75	.72	.69
Worcester	1.37	1.48	1.30	1.35	1.40	1.44
Hartford	.91	.91	.72	.68	.63	.59
New Haven	1.14	1.19	1.03	1.03	1.04	1.04
New London[a]	.64	.58	.40	.31	.23	.14
Providence	1.31	1.39	1.29	1.33	1.37	1.42

[a] For supply elasticities of 1.6 and greater the demand elasticities computed for New London are outside the acceptable range.

model's prediction, presuming: (1) that Boston's demand elasticity fell at the midpoint of the respective intervals, and (2) that Springfields's demand and supply elasticities remained unchanged. This last assumption is admittedly unrealistic, but could not be avoided. The results indicate that a loss of as little as 5% of the market could explain the observed drop in Standard's price.

The problem of New London is of some interest. This city does tend to stand out. Interestingly, the reason is that in New London the price was too high given that the competitive suppliers had a greater share of the market sales than they had in any of the other 10 cities (see data, Appendix II, cities 1–11). The failure of New London to fit into the scheme well does not lend any support to the predatory pricing hypothesis.

VI. SUMMARY AND CONCLUSION

It has been argued that the evidence presented in the Standard Oil of New Jersey case of 1909, which attempted to show predatory pricing behavior, was, for the most part, consistent with the dominant firm pricing model. That model was developed and a necessary condition for inter-market relationships was derived. Without sufficient data to do proper estimates, a simulation was carried out. It was found that there are some very plausible demand and supply elasticity combinations for the various markets which entirely explain the variations in price across markets. It was also found that a sudden drop in Standard's price at Springfield, Massachusetts, alleged to have been carried out with a predatory intent, could be explained as a dominant firm profit maximizing response to as little as a 5% drop in market share. It thus was shown that the statistical data for these cities are also consistent with the dominant firm model of Standard Oil's pricing behavior. The model, therefore, cannot be rejected on the basis of the available evidence. Insofar as the dominant firm model is shown to be a viable alternative to the predatory pricing hypothesis, our results cast some doubt on the traditional interpretation of Standard Oil's pricing behavior.

APPENDIX I

A. The Magnitude of the Joint Product Effects

We will focus our attention on one market and the case of three joint products: kerosene (Q_1), lubricating oils (Q_2), and gasoline (Q_3). The marginal revenue for kerosene in this market can be written

$$MR_1 = P_1 * (1 + 1/e_{11}{}^s + A_2(A_1 * e_{12}{}^s) + A_3(A_1 * e_{13}{}^s)),$$

where $e_{1i}{}^s = \partial Q_1/\partial P_i * (P_i/Q_1)$, $i = 1, 2, 3$; A_i = product i's share of total revenue, $i = 1, 2, 3$; and Q_i = quantity of good i sold by Standard,

$i = 1, 2, 3$. We will now derive expressions for $e_{1i}{}^s$, $i = 1, 2, 3$. The market inverse demand function for product i can be written

$$P_i = P_i\{Q_i + q_i\}, \qquad i = 1, 2, 3, \tag{A1}$$

where q_i = competitors' quantity supplied of good i, $i = 1, 2, 3$. In the case of joint products the competitive supply of product i is a function of the price of all the joint products as well as those of the factors of production. Therefore (A1) can be written

$$P_i = P_i\{Q_i + q_i[\tilde{\mathbf{P}},\mathbf{W}]\}, \qquad i = 1,2,3, \tag{A2}$$

where $\tilde{\mathbf{P}} = (P_1,P_2,P_3)$ and $\mathbf{W} = (w_1,w_2, \ldots ,w_n)$ = prices of the factors of production. Differentiating this system with respect to Q_1 and solving the resulting system of three equations for $\partial\tilde{P}/\partial Q_1$, we obtain the following solutions:

$$e_{11}{}^s = e_{11}/s_1 - (1 - s_1) * n_{11}/s_1 - ((1 - s_1) * n_{12} * C_{12})/(s_1 * C_{11})$$
$$- ((1 - s_1) * n_{13} * C_{13})/(s_1 * C_{11}).$$

$$e_{1j}{}^s = (e_{11}/s_1 - (1 - s_1) * n_{11}/s_1) * C_{11}/C_{1j} - (1 - s_1) * n_{1j}/s_1$$
$$- ((1 - s_1) * n_{1k} * C_{1k})/(s_1 * C_{1j}),$$

$$j = 2, 3,$$
$$k = 3 \quad \text{if } j = 2,$$
$$k = 2 \quad \text{if } j = 3,$$

where:

e_{ii} = market demand elasticity for good i, $i = 1, 2, 3$;
n_{ij} = competitive cross (own)-supply elasticity, $i, j = 1, 2, 3$;
s_i = Standard's share of the market for good i, $i = 1, 2, 3$;

$$C_{11} = (1 - s_2) * (1 - s_3) * (n_{22} * n_{33} - n_{23} * n_{32})/e_{22} * e_{33} - (1 - s_3) * n_{33}/e_{33}$$
$$- (1 - s_2) * n_{22}/e_{22} + 1; \text{ and}$$

$$C_{1j} = ((1 - s_j)/e_{jj}) * (n_{j1} + ((1 - s_k)/e_{kk}) * (n_{jk} * n_{k1} - n_{kk} * n_{j1})),$$

$$j = 2, 3,$$
$$k = 3 \quad \text{if } j = 2,$$
$$k = 2 \quad \text{if } j = 3.$$

These expressions for the elasticities are monstrous, to say the least. A much needed simplification is achieved if the joint product effects can be ignored because, in this case, all the cross-supply elasticities are zero and:

$$e_{11}{}^s = e_{11} - (1 - s_1) * n_{11}/s_1;$$

$$1/e_{12}{}^s = 0; \quad \text{and}$$

$$1/e_{13}{}^s = 0.$$

We now argue that this simplification is warranted in the case of the early petroleum industry because all reasonable values of e_{11}, e_{22}, e_{33}, n_{11}, n_{22},

n_{33}, n_{12}, n_{13} and n_{23} in conjunction with the market share data, result in negligible joint product effects on marginal revenue.[37] The strategy will be: (1) to specify intervals of reasonable values for these different parameters to obtain an acceptable parameter space (APS), (2) to systematically choose parameter points from the APS so that all regions of the APS are represented, (3) to evaluate marginal revenue, with and without joint product effects, at each of the parameter points so chosen, and (4) to determine the percentage error at each parameter point due to ignoring joint product effects. If all the errors are small we are justified in ignoring these effects.

We first seek to specify probable signs and magnitudes of the cross-supply elasticities. Not surprisingly, general theory is no help in determining the sign, much less the magnitude, of cross-supply elasticities (n_{ij}). This is because there are offsetting influences on n_{ij}. First, there is a substitution effect. When the price of kerosene rises, it becomes more profitable, on the margin, to produce kerosene relative to the other joint products. Refining techniques may be changed to produce more kerosene out of a given amount of crude oil, at the expense of the other joint products, than was produced before the price rise. This effect tends to make n_{ij} negative. Countering this is the output effect. The price rise makes it profitable to process more crude oil, the partial effect being to cause an increase in the production of all the joint products. Clearly the relative strengths of these two effects depend on the degree of output substitutability in production.

During the early years of the petroleum industry refining technology was such that the yield of gasoline per unit of crude oil input could not be altered, whereas there was some substitutability between kerosene and lubricating oils. It was possible to "crack," by extreme heat, the heavier distillates made up of large hydrocarbon molecules (lubricating oils) into smaller hydrocarbon molecules which made up kerosene.[38] Late in the nineteenth century the average yield of kerosene from Pennsylvania and Ohio crude oil of specific gravity .79 could be increased from 50 to 54% to 70% by cracking. A yield of 17.5% lubricating oil and 2% paraffin wax was, in the process, reduced to just 2% residuum which could be converted into heavy lubricating oils. Cracking also resulted in an additional 1.5% waste.[39]

[37] Note that $dq_i/dP_j = dq_j/dP_i$ and $n_{ij} = A_j * n_{ji}/A_i$. Therefore, for every reasonable value of n_{ij} there is a corresponding reasonable value for n_{ji}. This result is analogous to the symmetry of (compensated) Slutsky substitution effects in consumer demand theory. In production theory there are no income effects and no compensation is required for this result to hold.

[38] "Cracking" was not adapted to the production of gasoline until after 1910.

[39] "Petroleum." In *Encyclopaedia Britannica, A Dictionary of Arts, Sciences, and General Literature*, p. 719.

This indicates than the sign of n_{12}, while being a bit dubious, was probably negative. The signs of n_{13} and n_{23} are unambiguously positive since, for gasoline, there were no substitution effects operating.

A cross-supply elasticity, "normalized" so as to be comparable to an own supply elasticity, is probably no larger than .5 in absolute value. By "normalized" we mean that the cross-supply elasticity is adjusted so as to take account of the contribution each product makes to total revenue. So, since gasoline contributes one-fifth as much as kerosene to total revenue, a value of 0.1 for n_{13} is comparable to an own supply elasticity of 0.5. Likewise, since lubricating oils contributed one-third as much to total revenue as did kerosene, a value for n_{12} of $-.17$ is comparable to an own supply elasticity of -0.5. The same logic indicates that a value of 0.3 for n_{23} is comparable to an own supply elasticity of 0.5. In this way we obtain the following acceptable intervals for the cross-supply elasticities.

$$-0.2 < n_{12} < 0.0. \quad \text{(A3)}$$

$$0.0 < n_{13} < 0.1. \quad \text{(A4)}$$

$$0.0 < n_{23} < 0.3. \quad \text{(A5)}$$

We concluded in section IV. C. 4 of the text that the demand elasticity for kerosene was quite small. The same arguments lead to this conclusion for gasoline and lubricating oils. Therefore, we set the interval for all demand elasticities at $(-1.4, -.6)$. The acceptable interval for the supply elasticity of kerosene was set at (1.4,3.0) in the text. We use this same interval for the supply elasticities of gasoline and lubricating oils.

The task of specifying acceptable intervals for the various parameters is now complete and the acceptable parameter space (APS) is defined. In selecting parameter points within the APS, step sizes of 0.4, 0.2, and 0.1 were used for own supply elasticities, demand elasticities, and cross-supply elasticities, respectively. To cut down on the number of function evaluations necessary, the three demand elasticities were constrained to be equal at any given parameter point. The same is true for the three own supply elasticities. These constraints are not crucial since e_{22}, e_{33}, n_{22}, and n_{33} do not play important roles in the determination of marginal revenue for kerosene.

Marginal revenue, with and without joint product effects, was computed at more than 1000 selected parameter points. The result was that for any parameter point which yielded a marginal revenue greater than 1.1 (recall that price was about 10¢ for kerosene) the percentage error in calculating marginal revenue due to ignoring joint product effects was no greater than 10% and was usually much less.

B. The Supply Elasticity: A Ballpark Estimate

The production model described in the text can be summarized as:

$$Q = \text{Min}\,(A * K^{a} * L^{(1-a)}, b * C),$$

where: Q = quantity of kerosene produced; K = capital input; L = labor input; C = crude oil input (gasoline and lubricating oils removed); $b = Q/C$ = constant. Efficient production requires that $A * K^a * L^{(1-a)} = b * C = Q$. Given this constraint the firm maximizes:

$$\text{Profit} = \bar{P} * A * K^a * L^{(1-a)} - w * L - r * K,$$

where $\bar{P} = P_0 - P_C/b$; P_0 = price of kerosene—given to competitive firms; P_C = price of crude oil (gasoline and lubricating oils removed); and w, r = factor prices. This is a simple Cobb–Douglas maximization problem with price $\bar{P}$. It is a well-known result that with capital fixed,

$$n' = \partial Q/\partial \bar{P} * \bar{P}/Q = (1-a)/a = \frac{(1 - \text{capitals share of value added})}{\text{capitals share of value added}} = 2/3,$$

and the short-run supply elasticity of kerosene is

$$n = (P_o/\bar{P}) * n' = (10/3) * (2/3) = 2.2.$$

For the entire refining industry capital's share of value added was approximately 0.6 in 1905 and the cost of crude oil (materials) accounted for about 70% of the price of petroleum products (10/3 = 1/(1 − 0.7)).[40] But since Standard dominated the industry and Standard was a near monopoly we would expect capital's share in the industry to be an upward biased estimate of capital's share for competitive firms. So this simple model gives us a lower bound of 2.2 for the short-run supply elasticity.

APPENDIX II: RAW DATA

All data pertains to illuminating oil in the year 1904. Price and transportation costs are in cents per gallon.

City	Price	Standard's share	Transportation cost
1. Boston	11.0	.887	0.2
2. Brockton	11.0	1.0	0.5
3. Fall River	10.5	1.0	0.6
4. Lowell	10.5	.968	0.9
5. Lynn	11.0	1.0	0.6
6. Springfield	8.0	.783	0.6
7. Worcester	8.0	.950	0.5
8. Hartford	9.0	.783	0.6

[40] U. S. Department of Commerce, Bureau of the Census (1908), p. 567. "Barrels, cases, tin cans" and "Cooper's, carpenters, and tinners materials" were excluded from the category of materials for two reasons: (1) Much of the packaging material was reused (barrels) and can be treated as part of the capital stock, and (2) most of the domestic kerosene trade was done in bulk and packaging was not needed, indicating that a disproportionate share of the packaging costs was for the other joint products or, perhaps, for exports.

APPENDIX II: (*Continued*)

City	Price	Standard's share	Transportation cost
9. New Haven	9.0	.886	0.5
10. New London	10.0	.711	0.2
11. Providence	10.0	1.0	0.2
12. Albany	10.0	.899	
13. Binghamton	9.5	.609	
14. Buffalo	10.0	.866	
15. Elmira	10.0	.732	
16. New York	11.0	.914	
17. Syracuse	10.0	.894	
18. Yonkers	11.0	.925	
19. Altoona	11.0	1.0	
20. Chambersburg	9.5	.972	
21. Chester	8.5	.791	
22. Harrisburg	10.5	.897	
23. Philadelphia	8.0	.824	
24. Reading	9.5	.733	
25. Scranton	9.0	.925	
26. Williamsport	10.0	.865	
27. Wilmington	8.5	.935	
28. Camden	9.5	.901	
29. Newark	11.0	.814	
30. Trenton	9.5	.876	
31. Jersey City	10.9	.925	

Sources: Prices, and market shares, U. S. Department of Justice (1909), Brief of Facts and Argument for Petitioner, Vol. II, p. 9; transportation costs, U. S. Department of Commerce, Bureau of Corporations (1906), pp. 741–742.

ACKNOWLEDGMENT

I would like to express my sincere gratitude to Professor Robert Fogel for unselfishly giving me his encouragement and support. I would also like to thank the participants of the 1978 Cliometrics Conference for their many helpful suggestions.

REFERENCES

Andreano, R. L. (1960), *The Emergence of New Competition in the American Petroleum Industry before 1911*. Unpublished dissertation. Evanston, Ill.: Northwestern Univ.

Areeda, P. (1974), *Antitrust Analysis, Problems, Text, Cases*, 2nd ed. Boston: Little, Brown.

Gellhorn, E. (1976), *Antitrust Law and Economics*. St. Paul, Minn.: West.

Hidy, M. E., and Hidy, R. R. (1955), *History of Standard Oil Co. (New Jersey)—Pioneering in Big Business 1882–1911*. New York: Harper.

McGee, J. S. (1958), "Predatory Price Cutting: The Standard Oil (N. J.) Case." *Journal of Law and Economics*, October, 1958.

Nevin, A. *Study in Power—John D. Rockefeller, Industrialist and Philanthropist*, Vols. I & II. New York: Schribner's.

"Petroleum." Encyclopaedia Britannica, *A Dictionary of Arts, Sciences, and General Literature*, 10th ed. Vol. XVIII, pp. 712–720.

Tarbell, I. (1904), *The History of the Standard Oil Co.*, Vol. II, New York: McClure, Phillips.

U. S. Department of Commerce, Bureau of the Census (1908), *Manufactures 1905*, Part IV: *Special Report on Selected Industries*. Washington, D. C.: Government Printing Office.

U. S. Department of Commerce, Bureau of Corporations (1907), *Report of the Commissioner of Corporations on the Petroleum Industry* Part I—*The Position of Standard Oil Co. In the Petroleum Industry*; Part II—*Prices and Profits*. Washington, D. C.: Government Printing Office.

U. S. Department of Commerce, Bureau of Corporations (1906), *Report of the Commissioner of Corporations on the Transport of Petroleum*, House of Representatives Document No. 812. Washington, D. C.: Government Printing Office.

U. S. Department of Justice (1909), *United States of America*, petitioner, v. *Standard Oil of New Jersey et al., defendants*. Vol. II: *Brief of Facts and Argument for Petitioner's*; Vol. IV: *Petitioner's Testimony*; Vols. VIII, X: *Petitioner's Exhibits*; Vol. XII: *Defendant's Testimony*; Vols. I–III: Brief for Defendants on the Facts. Washington, D. C.: Government Printing Office.

Williamson, H. F., Adreano, R. L., Daum, A. R., and Klose, G. C. (1963), *The American Petroleum Industry 1899–1959. The Age of Energy*. Evanston, Ill.: Northwestern Univ. Press.

Williamson, H. R., and Daum, A. R. (1959), *The American Petroleum Industry 1859–1899. The Age of Illumination*. Evanston, D. C.: Northwestern Univ. Press.

[22]

GAINS TO PRODUCERS FROM THE CARTELIZATION OF EXHAUSTIBLE RESOURCES

Robert S. Pindyck*

I. Introduction

It has been suggested that one reason for OPEC's formation and later success in maintaining itself as a cohesive cartel is that the gains from cartelization in the world oil market are so large. Indeed, looking at the historical success record of various cartels (or attempts at cartelization), a case could be made that those cartels were most successful for which potential monopoly profits were the greatest.[1] After all, there are significant costs associated with cartelization—political costs, cost of coordination of output and price, and, for each producer, costs associated with the risk of being undercut and losing significant short-term profits. Bearing these costs would not be worthwhile if the expected resulting gains were not at least as large. It is therefore important to know what the potential gains from cartelization are.

Often the analysis of producer gains from cartelization is based on a simple static computation of the potential monopoly profit in a particular market, given elasticity estimates for demand and for supply from those producers who would not be likely to join the cartel. Such a static analysis might be realistic and quite sufficient for such markets as bananas, coffee, and sugar, where demand and supply can adjust quickly to price, and where resource exhaustion is not a determinant of, nor constraint on, production. A static analysis might be misleading, however, for such markets as petroleum, copper, or bauxite. First, the process of reserve depletion for these resources might have an important impact on monopoly pricing decisions and on the potential gains from cartelization. Second, the markets for these resources are characterized by demands and supplies that adjust only slowly to changes in price, so that a cartel might have the potential for large short-term monopoly profits by taking advantage of adjustment lags.

The problem of measuring the potential gain from the cartelization of a particular exhaustible resource can be put quite simply. Given reserve levels and the dynamic structure of demand and cost, and given that the objective of each producer is to maximize the sum over time of discounted profits, what are the optimal price trajectories under competition and under cartelization, and how much larger is the sum of discounted profits as a result of cartelization? We assume that the (potential) cartel in question is able to behave as a perfect monopolist that knows the structure of demand and cost. In addition, we do not address the issue of how the gains from cartelization are to be divided up among the cartel members.

To measure these potential gains we turn to the theory of exhaustible resource pricing. It was Hotelling (1931) who first demonstrated that if extraction costs are constant, under competition, price minus marginal cost should rise at the rate of discount, while in a monopolistic market, rents (marginal revenue minus marginal cost) should rise at the rate of discount.[2] It can be shown that under conditions of constant demand elasticity and zero extraction costs, the price trajectories will be the same in both the monopoly and

Received for publication August 13, 1976. Revision accepted for publication May 4, 1977.

* Massachusetts Institute of Technology.

This work was supported by the National Science Foundation under Grant No. SIA75-00739, and is part of a larger project to develop analytical models of the world oil market. The author would like to express his appreciation to Esteban Hnyilicza, who developed the computer program used for this work and provided assistance in obtaining computational solutions, and to Steve Martin, who pointed out an error in an earlier draft of this paper. Considerable thanks are also due to Ross Heide and Kai Wong for their excellent research assistance, and to M. A. Adelman, Michael Athans, James Burrows, Partha Dasgupta, Dermot Gately, Richard Gilbert, Henry Jacoby, Dale Jorgenson, David Kendrick, Edwin Kuh, Alan Manne, Robert Solow, and Joseph Stiglitz for their comments, criticisms, and suggestions.

[1] A historical summary of the experience of some international cartels is given in Eckbo (1975).

[2] For another derivation and interpretation of Hotelling's results, see Herfindahl (1967) and Gordon (1967). For further discussion, see Solow (1974) and Banks (1974).

competitive cases.[3] However, if extraction costs are positive and/or the elasticity of demand is rising, the monopoly price will initially be higher (and later be lower) than the competitive price, i.e., the monopolist will be relatively "conservationist."[4]

The relevant question, however, is *to what degree* will the price trajectories in the two cases differ? Stiglitz (1976) claims that in general "there is a very limited scope for the monopolist to exercise his monopoly power." This may be the case for some exhaustible resources, but not for others. It will depend in part on the particular way in which demand elasticities change and production costs increase as the resource reserve base is depleted. It will also depend on the ability of the monopolist to take advantage of adjustment lags in the demand for his output.

This paper attempts to calculate optimal monopolistic and competitive price trajectories for several exhaustible resource cartels, and thereby to determine the potential gains to producers from cartelization. Our model of cartelization is rather simple; we treat the cartel as a pure monopolist holding a known quantity of reserves and facing a "net demand" function (total world demand minus supply from "competitive fringe" producers who are not members of the cartel). We ignore such potential problems as differences in production costs for different members, differences in objectives, need for output rationalization, etc.[5] The approximate analysis is still useful, however, since if the gains to the pure monopolist are not large, we would not expect the more "realistic" cartel to remain stable over a long period of time, while if the gains are quite large, there should be sufficient incentive for the producers to overcome the problems typical of cartelization.

We limit ourselves here to three cartels that have already identified themselves as politically (if not economically) feasible realities. In particular, we consider OPEC in the case of petroleum, CIPEC (International Council of Copper Exporting Countries) in the case of copper, and IBA (International Bauxite Association) in the case of bauxite. It is clear that OPEC has already demonstrated its ability to enjoy large monopoly profits, and here we calculate the potential profits that it might enjoy in the future. The argument has been made, however, that OPEC is an exception to the rule, and that CIPEC, IBA, and other real or imagined natural resource cartels do not have the potential for any significant monopoly profits.[6] Here we explore this argument quantitatively.

In the next section we present the basic optimal pricing model for an exhaustible resource cartel facing a dynamic "net demand" function, and explain how optimal price trajectories for both the monopoly and competitive cases can be obtained. Then, the basic model is applied to OPEC and the world oil market, and is used to calculate optimal price trajectories for OPEC and measure OPEC's potential monopoly gains. Next we turn to the bauxite and copper markets, fitting the basic model to each in an attempt to measure the potential gains that IBA and CIPEC might realize by following optimal pricing rules. We conclude with some remarks about actual and potential cartel behavior.

II. An Optimal Pricing Model for an Exhaustible Resource

The basic model is specified to account for differences between short-run and long-run price elasticities both in demand and supply from "competitive fringe" countries. Total demand (TD) for the resource in question would be of the form

$$TD_t = f_1(P_t, Y_t, TD_{t-1}) \tag{1}$$

where P_t is real price and Y_t is the measure of aggregate income or product. This specification of the demand function takes into account the substitution of other materials for this resource (e.g., coal for oil or aluminum for copper), and since we assume that the prices of competing materials are fixed, they need not be included explicitly in (1).

[3] A nice demonstration of this is given by Stiglitz (1976).
[4] This is examined by Stiglitz (1976) and Sweeney (1975).
[5] The effects of these problems on pricing and output policy for OPEC are examined in Hnyilicza and Pindyck (1976).

[6] See, for example, Krasner (1974) and Smart (1975). For opposing views see Bergsten (1973, 1974) and Mikdashi (1974).

Net demand facing the cartel is

$$D_t = TD_t - S_t \tag{2}$$

where S_t is the supply function for the "competitive fringe," and is given by

$$S_t = f_2(P_t, S_{t-1}). \tag{3}$$

Resource depletion might be as significant a factor for the competitive fringe as it is for the cartel, in which case we can modify the supply function so that it moves to the left (rising marginal and average cost) in response to cumulative production CS:

$$S_t = f_2(P_t, S_{t-1}) \cdot (1+\alpha)^{-CS_t/\bar{S}} \tag{3'}$$

with

$$CS_t = CS_{t-1} + S_t, \tag{4}$$

and $\bar{S}$ is average annual competitive production and α is a parameter that determines the rate of depletion.

An accounting identity is needed to keep track of cartel reserves, R:

$$R_t = R_{t-1} - D_t. \tag{5}$$

The objective of the cartel is to pick a price trajectory $\{P_t\}$ that will maximize the sum of discounted profits:

$$\max W = \sum_{t=1}^{N} (1/(1+\delta)^t)[P_t - m/R_t]D_t \tag{6}$$

where m/R_t is average production cost (so that the parameter m determines initial average cost), δ is the discount rate, and N is chosen to be large enough (40–60 years) to approximate the infinite-horizon problem.[7] Since average costs become infinite as the reserve base R_t approaches zero, the resource exhaustion constraint need not be introduced explicitly.[8] As a result, we have a classical, unconstrained discrete-time control problem for which numerical solutions can be obtained easily.[9]

The solution to the above problem yields an optimal price trajectory $\{P_t^*\}$ and optimal sum of discounted profits W^* for the monopolist. We would like to compare these with the optimal price trajectory and sum of discounted profits that would result if the cartel dissolved (or never formed), and its member producers behaved competitively. We say "optimal" because competitive producers must still manage an exhaustible resource, balancing profits this year against profits in future years.

Although competitive producers cannot collectively set price, they each determine output given a price. We show in the appendix that the rate of output should be such that the competitive price satisfies the difference equation

$$P_t = (1+\delta)P_{t-1} - \delta m/R_{t-1}. \tag{7}$$

If this were not the case, larger profits could be obtained by shifting output from one period to another. In addition, the initial price must be such that two constraints hold. First, the resulting price and output trajectories $\{P_t\}$ and $\{D_t\}$ must both satisfy, at every point in time, net demand as given by equations (1), (2), and (3), i.e., supply and demand must be in market equilibrium. Second, as the price rises monotonically over time, profits must become zero at the same time that net demand goes to zero.[10] If demand becomes zero before profits do,

[7] Note that we are treating the fringe and the cartel asymmetrically. We might expect members of the fringe to set output optimally, as does the cartel, with the same price foresight that the cartel has. Including this consideration, however, would considerably complicate the computational solution.

[8] A constraint on the production capacity of the cartel can be introduced implicitly by rewriting the objective function as

$$\max W = \sum_{t=1}^{N} (1/(1+\delta)^t)[P_t - m/R_t - a\exp(bD_t^c)] \tag{6'}$$

where c is large enough so that the added expression is close to zero when D_t is just below the capacity constraint and very large when D_t is just above. Typically, c equal to 20 or 30 (with a and b chosen appropriately) is sufficient. In the applications of this model that follow, however, the capacity constraint is never even approached (i.e., it is always optimal for the cartel to produce at below capacity), so that (6′) need not be used.

[9] We use a general nonlinear optimal control algorithm developed by Hnyilicza (1975). Using that algorithm, optimal pricing policies can be derived in a classical control theoretic framework for any model in implicit state-variable form:

$$g(x_t, x_{t-1}, P_{t-1}, z_{t-1}) = 0$$

where g is a vector of nonlinear functions in the set of state variables x_t (endogenous and lagged endogenous variables, together with state variables defined for P and elements of z occurring with lags longer than one period), the price (control) variable P_t, and a set of exogenous variables z_t. The objective function can also be general in form.

[10] We are assuming here that the net demand curve indeed intersects the vertical axis. If this were not the case, price would rise indefinitely with demand asymptotically approaching zero and exhaustion occurring at $t=\infty$.

some of the resource is wasted and yields no profits; profits would be greater if the resource were depleted more rapidly (at a lower price). If profits become zero before demand becomes zero, depletion is occurring too rapidly and should proceed more slowly.[11]

The computation of the optimal price trajectory for the competitive case is thus straightfoward. Pick an initial P_0 and *simulate* (i.e., solve over time) equation (7) together with equations (1), (2), (3), and (5). Repeat this for different values of P_0 until D_t and R_t become zero simultaneously.

III. Petroleum—The Gains to OPEC

The basic model described above is parameterized for the world oil market so that it is consistent with the reserve, production, and elasticity estimates of OECD (1974), and with crude elasticity estimates obtained from aggregate time series data.[12] The equations of the model are as follows:

$$TD_t = 1.0 - .13P_t + .87TD_{t-1} + 2.3(1.015)^t \tag{8}$$

$$S_t = (1.1 + .10P_t)\cdot(1.02)^{-CS_t/7} + .75S_{t-1} \tag{9}$$

$$CS_t = CS_{t-1} + S_t \tag{10}$$

$$D_t = TD_t - S_t \tag{11}$$

$$R_t = R_{t-1} - D_t \tag{12}$$

$$\max W = \sum_{t=1}^{N} ((1+\delta)^t)^{-1}[P_t - 250/R_t]D_t \tag{13}$$

where

TD_t = total demand for oil (billions of barrels (bb) per year)
D_t = demand for cartel oil (bb/yr.)
S_t = supply of competitive fringe (bb/yr.)
CS_t = cumulative supply of competitive fringe (bb)
R_t = reserves of cartel (bb)
P_t = price of oil (\$ per barrel) in constant 1975 dollars.

The linear demand equation (8) is based on a total demand of 18 billion barrels per year at a price of \$6 per barrel; at that price the short-run price elasticity is 0.04 and the long-run elasticity is 0.33 (with a Koyck adjustment), while at a \$12 price the short-run and long-run elasticities are 0.09 and 0.90, respectively. The last term in equation (8) provides an autonomous rate of growth in demand of 1.5% per year, corresponding to a long-run income elasticity of 0.5 and a 3% real rate of growth in income. (The use of an isoelastic instead of linear demand function allows for somewhat higher cartel prices, but as we find empirically, the difference is small.)

At a \$6 price competitive supply is about 6.5 billion barrels per year. The supply equation (9) implies short-run and long-run elasticities of 0.09 and 0.35, respectively, at the \$6 price, and 0.16 and 0.52, respectively, at a \$12 price. Depletion of competitive fringe reserves pushes the supply function to the left over time. After a cumulative production of 210 billion barrels (e.g., 7 bb/yr. for 30 years) supply would fall (assuming a fixed price) to 55% of its original value.[13] We assume that no "backstop technology" (e.g., shale oil) would add significantly to competitive supply at prices below \$20.

Note that the average cost of production for the OPEC cartel rises hyperbolically as R_t goes to zero. The initial reserve level is taken to be 500 billion barrels, and initially average cost is 50¢ per barrel.[14]

In calculating optimal price policies we take as initial conditions $TD_0 = 18.0$, $S_0 = 6.5$, and $CS_0 = 0$. Price trajectories are calculated over a forty-year horizon, with discount rates of 0.05

[11] Note that if the autonomous rate of growth in net demand is greater than the discount rate δ, the optimal price will be such that output is always infinitesimally small, since then it always pays to postpone *all* production into the future.

[12] Cremer and Weitzman (1976) and Kalymon (1975) have recently constructed similar optimal pricing models for OPEC. Those studies, however, do not account for adjustment lags. Non-optimizing simulation models of OPEC behavior have also been constructed; see, for example, Blitzer et al. (1975), and Fischer et al. (1975).

[13] Note that there is no fixed upper bound on cumulative production by competitive fringe countries; there is always *some* price at which additional supplies would be forthcoming. For example, after 210 billion barrels have been produced, a price of \$18.5 would be needed to maintain production at 6.5 bb/yr., while after 420 billion barrels have been produced a \$43 price would be needed to maintain the 6.5 bb/yr. production level.

[14] 500 billion barrels represents a rough estimate of *proved* reserves for OPEC (source: *Oil and Gas Journal*, Dec. 1975). Potential reserves would be greater, but we assume that the more conservative number would be used by OPEC to plan a long-term price policy.

and 0.10.[15] Optimal prices for both the monopolistic and competitive cases are shown graphically for the first 25 years in figure 1, and prices, total demand, OPEC production, OPEC reserves and discounted profits are shown for the longer horizon in table 1.

FIGURE 1.—OPTIMAL OIL PRICE TRAJECTORIES
(M = monopoly, C = competition)

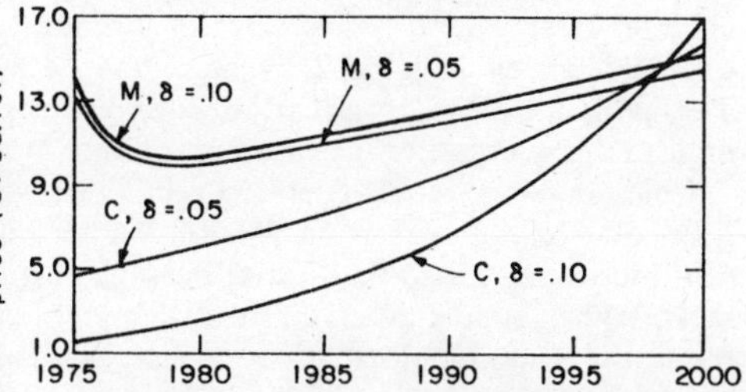

Observe that the optimal monopoly price is $13 to $14 in the first year (1975), declines over the next five years to around $10, and then rises slowly. This price pattern is a characteristic result of incorporating adjustment lags in OPEC's net demand function. If total demand and competitive supply had been modelled as static functions of price, the optimal monopoly price, like the competitive price, would rise monotonically. With adjustment lags, however, it is optimal for OPEC to charge a higher price initially, taking advantage of the fact that net demand can adjust only slowly. Of course, in the competitive case price will still rise monotonically, even with adjustment lags, since the competitors cannot together restrict output to take advantage of the initially inelastic demand.

Observe also that with the smaller discount rate the initial competitive price is higher. With a large discount rate producers pay less attention to the future, so that their output decisions more closely approximate those that would be made without accounting for resource depletion, i.e., they more closely approximate the static competitive solution. When the discount rate is low producers must be more "conservationist," so that initial output levels

TABLE 1.—PETROLEUM

	P	TD	D	R	Π_d
		Monopoly: $\delta = .05$			
1975	13.24	17.24	9.94	488.5	126.5
1976	11.19	16.88	9.23	478.6	93.8
1977	10.26	16.72	8.94	469.3	78.9
1978	9.90	16.66	8.87	460.4	71.7
1979	9.82	16.66	8.91	451.5	67.9
1980	9.88	16.69	9.00	442.6	65.7
1985	10.84	16.96	9.67	396.3	60.6
1990	11.98	17.32	10.40	346.3	56.3
1995	13.18	17.74	11.15	293.0	51.8
2000	14.46	18.22	11.91	235.7	47.1
2005	15.92	18.75	12.66	174.6	42.5
2010	20.29	18.67	12.55	110.5	41.0
		Monopoly: $\delta = .10$			
1975	14.08	17.13	9.75	488.5	132.3
1976	11.75	16.71	8.94	478.8	91.2
1977	10.70	16.52	8.61	469.8	72.4
1978	10.28	16.44	8.52	461.2	62.3
1979	10.19	16.42	8.54	452.7	56.2
1980	10.26	16.43	8.61	444.1	51.8
1985	11.28	16.62	9.21	399.9	37.8
1990	12.51	16.90	9.87	352.6	27.9
1995	13.80	17.24	10.53	301.9	20.3
2000	15.18	17.63	11.20	248.0	14.6
2005	16.72	18.06	11.86	190.7	10.5
2010	20.52	18.05	11.88	130.5	7.9
		Competitive: $\delta = .05$			
1975	4.62	18.36	11.92	488.5	46.64
1976	4.85	18.68	12.29	476.6	48.22
1977	5.09	18.96	12.62	464.3	49.62
1978	5.35	19.20	12.90	451.7	50.90
1979	5.62	19.42	13.14	438.8	52.00
1980	5.90	19.60	13.35	425.6	52.92
1985	7.53	20.19	13.99	357.3	55.87
1990	9.60	20.30	14.04	287.1	56.15
1995	12.26	19.96	13.55	217.6	54.04
2000	15.65	19.13	12.48	151.8	49.15
2005	19.97	17.69	10.71	92.6	40.76
2010	25.48	15.46	8.07	44.0	27.59
		(depletion occurs in 2019)			
		Competitive: $\delta = .10$			
1975	1.55	18.76	12.63	488.5	11.92
1976	1.71	19.43	13.59	475.9	13.31
1977	1.88	20.03	14.40	462.3	14.49
1978	2.06	20.56	15.10	447.9	15.49
1979	2.27	21.04	15.70	432.8	16.50
1980	2.50	21.46	16.20	417.1	17.38
1985	4.02	22.87	17.74	332.4	20.32
1990	6.47	23.49	17.93	242.8	21.23
1995	10.43	22.64	16.74	154.9	19.94
2000	16.79	20.49	13.65	76.5	15.49
2005	27.05	15.98	7.72	18.7	5.50
2010					
		(depletion occurs in 2008)			

[15] With a discount rate of 0.02 or less the initial *competitive* price is over $10. With autonomous growth in net demand (resulting from autonomous growth in total demand and depletion of competitive fringe reserves) the optimal production rate will approach zero if the discount rate is small enough. Pre-OPEC oil prices were never in the vicinity of $10, which means that competitive producers either used higher discount rates or else used a low discount rate but produced at a very sub-optimal rate. The presence of risk (regarding potential reserves, changes in market conditions, etc.) would make it most reasonable to use a discount rate of 0.05 or higher, and so we use 0.05 and 0.10.

are reduced and prices are closer to those that would be set by a monopolist. As can be seen in the results, resource exhaustion by competitive producers occurs earlier at the higher discount rate, since prices begin low and then rise more rapidly in later years when the discount rate is large. The competitive solution —as given by equation (7)—is such that a lower discount rate, implying a lower rate of increase in price, will restrict initial output so that initial price is higher and closer to the monopoly price. With a 10% discount rate the competitive price is $1.55 in the first year, which is in the vicinity of actual pre-1974 Persian Gulf prices. We might thus assume that prior to 1974, OPEC producers set output levels competitively using a high discount rate.

The relative gains from cartelization are summarized in table 2. Note that these gains are largest during the first five years, particularly when the discount rate is large, since it is during this period that a monopoly can take advantage of adjustment lags and reap large short-term profits. Even over the longer term, however, the sum of discounted profits is 50% to 100% larger under cartelization. The incentive for maintaining the cartel is thus considerable.

TABLE 2.—PETROLEUM: RELATIVE PROFITS (ratio of NPV^a for monopolist (M) to NPV for competitors (C))

	$NPV = \sum \Pi_d$ (1975 until exhaustion or 2015)
$\delta = .05$	$NPV_M / NPV_C = 2092/1362 = 1.54$
$\delta = .10$	$NPV_M / NPV_C = 1078/556 = 1.94$
	$NPV = \sum \Pi_d$ (first five years)
$\delta = .05$	$NPV_M / NPV_C = 438.8/247.4 = 1.77$
$\delta = .10$	$NPV_M / NPV_C = 414.4/71.7 = 5.78$

[a] NPV = net present value of profits.

Obviously these results are dependent on the particular model and parameter values described earlier. However, changing the model's parameters has only a small effect on the numerical results. For example, if the elasticities (short- and long-term) of total demand are *doubled*, optimal monopoly and competitive prices decrease by less than 20%. Doubling the elasticity of competitive supply results in a decrease in price of about 10%. Replacing the total demand and competitive supply equations with isoelastic equations (using the $6 elasticities from the linear equations) or doubling the length of the lag response in total demand results in price trajectories that are at all times within 15% of those reported in table 1.[16] Doubling or halving OPEC's initial average production cost has less than a 5% effect on monopoly price and less than a 20% effect on competitive price. None of the aforementioned changes affects the ratios of sums of discounted profits reported in table 2 by more than 10%. The gains to OPEC from cartelization are thus high under a broad range of assumptions.

Changing the initial level of OPEC reserves from 500 billion barrels to 800 billion barrels (but increasing M, so that initial average cost is still 50¢) has almost no effect (less than 10%) on the optimal monopolistic price trajectories, but it does have a significant effect on the competitive solutions. Using the higher reserve estimate, initial competitive prices for $\delta = 0.05$ and 0.10 are $3.06 and $0.65, respectively. These prices are lower because there is less need to conserve (exhaustion occurs after 43 years at the high discount rate and 54 years at the low rate, as compared to 33 years and 44 years in table 1), so that prices are closer to those that would result from competitors making static output decisions (i.e., setting output one period at a time, ignoring future periods). Since competitive prices and discounted profits are lower, the use of a higher initial reserve estimate means *greater potential gains from cartelization* (NPV_M / NPV_C is 2.42 for $\delta = 0.05$ and 3.05 for $\delta = 0.10$). The 800 billion barrel figure represents proven reserves plus "highly likely" potential reserves, and thus might be a more realistic number to use in setting price or output over time. We chose the 500 billion barrel figure in part because it better dramatizes the effects of depletion on price and output dynamics.

IV. Bauxite—The Gains to IBA[17]

There are no published econometric studies of the world bauxite market that can be tapped

[16] Note that net demand for OPEC oil will *not* be isoelastic.

[17] IBA countries in 1974 included Australia, Jamaica, Surinam, Guyana, Guinea, Yugoslavia, and Sierra Leone, and accounted for 74% of non-Communist world bauxite production.

for elasticity estimates, and therefore our competitive supply equation must be somewhat speculative. A total demand equation, however, can be derived from the demand for aluminum and from cost data on the production of alumina from bauxite and from alternative aluminum-bearing ores. Data on costs, reserves, and production are available from the U.S. Bureau of Mines (1974b, 1975). The equations of the model are listed below:

$$TD_t = [1.048 - .131P_t + 13.1(1.03)^t] \times e^{-(.0641P_t)^{10}} + .80TD_{t-1} \quad (14)$$

$$S_t = (-1.69 + .4225P_t)\cdot(1.005)^{-CS_t/17} + .90S_{t-1} \quad (15)$$

$$CS_t = CS_{t-1} + S_t \quad (16)$$

$$D_t = TD_t - S_t \quad (17)$$

$$R_t = R_{t-1} - D_t \quad (18)$$

$$\max W = \sum_{t=1}^{N} ((1+\delta)^t)^{-1} \times [P_t - (55{,}000/R_t)]D_t \quad (19)$$

FIGURE 2.—BAUXITE: LONG-RUN DEMAND FUNCTIONS

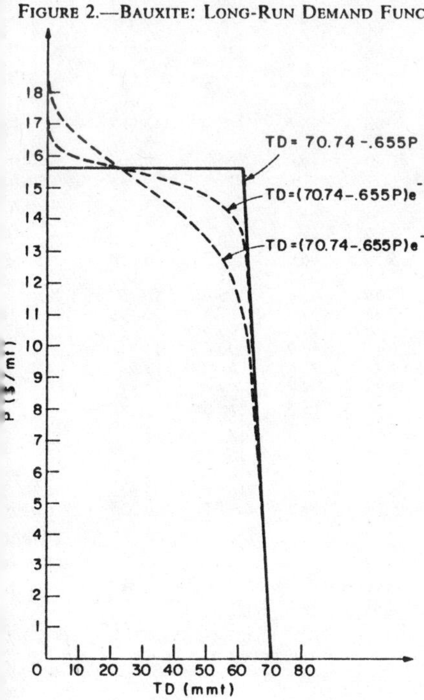

where

TD_t = total demand for bauxite (millions of metric tons per year (mmt/yr.))
S_t = supply from competitive fringe (mmt/yr.)
CS_t = cumulative supply of competitive fringe (mmt)
D_t = net demand for IBA bauxite (mmt/yr.)
R_t = reserves of cartel (mmt)
P_t = price of bauxite ($/mt) in *constant 1973 dollars*.

For a range of prices up to about $15.60 the demand for bauxite is quite inelastic, but at higher prices it becomes economical to produce alumina from sources other than bauxite, so that the demand for bauxite becomes almost infinitely elastic.[18] In the inelastic region the demand for bauxite depends on the demand for aluminum. At a bauxite price of $8 per ton, bauxite itself represents about 8% of the cost of producing aluminum. Using short- and long-run price elasticities of aluminum demand of −0.2 and −1.0, respectively, the corresponding price elasticities for bauxite would be −0.016 and −0.08. The income elasticities should be the same as those for aluminum; we use 0.2 and 1.0 for the short-run and long-run, respectively. The term $(1.03)^t$ in equation (14) builds in the assumption of 3% annual real growth in income.

At a price of around $15.60 we would expect the demand for bauxite to fall rapidly to zero.

[18] Other sources of alumina (Al_2O_3) include high-alumina clays, dawsonite, alumite, and anorthosite, all of which are in great abundance in the earth's crust. The most economical alternative to bauxite is to produce alumina from high-alumina clays using the hydrochloric acid–ion exchange process. In this process there is an operating cost of $74.5 per ton, of which $5.02 is the cost of clay at $1 per ton. In addition, the fixed capital cost of a 1,000 ton per day plant is $108 million. Assuming a 10% cost of capital and 350 operating days per year, and ignoring replacement costs, and/or maintenance, capital cost becomes $30.85 per ton of alumina, so that the total cost of producing alumina through this process is $105 per ton. Producing alumina from bauxite using the Bayer process would not be this expensive unless the price of bauxite rose to $15.60 per ton. At that price operating costs would be $86 per ton, of which $40 would be the cost of bauxite (about 2.5 tons of bauxite for every ton of alumina). The cost of a 1,000 ton per day plant is $66 million, so that the capital cost is $19 per ton, for a total cost of $105 per ton. (*All prices in 1973 dollars.*) Source of data: U.S. Bureau of Mines (1974a).

FIGURE 3.—OPTIMAL BAUXITE PRICE TRAJECTORIES (M = monopoly, C = competition)

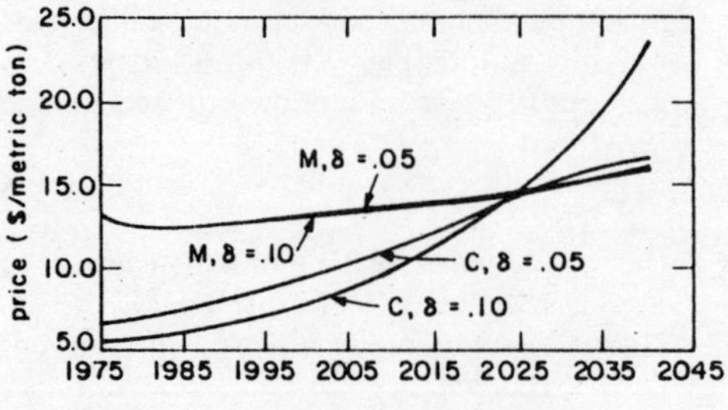

For this reason the exponential term is included in equation (14). By choosing a large enough exponent for $0.0641P_t = P_t/15.60$, we can achieve an arbitrarily close approximation to a piecewise linear demand function. In fact, we would expect demand to start falling off at prices somewhere below $15.60 (if for no other reason than anticipation of future price increase), and demand to be small but not zero at higher prices, so we choose 10 as the exponent. The long-run demand function is plotted in figure 2.

The supply function for the competitive fringe is straightforward and is given by equation (15). At a price of $8 the short-run and long-run elasticities are 0.2 and 2.0, respectively. Since there is considerable uncertainty as to what the true *long-run* elasticity

TABLE 3.—BAUXITE

	P	TD	D	R	Π_d[a]		P	TD	D	R	Π_d[a]
	Monopoly: $\delta = .05$						Competitive: $\delta = .05$				
1975	13.03	62.9	43.9	10,956	352.1	1975	6.43	65.7	49.5	10,950	70.3
1976	12.79	61.6	40.8	10,915	302.9	1976	6.50	66.3	50.6	10,900	71.3
1977	12.62	61.0	38.8	10,876	267.0	1977	6.58	67.1	51.9	10,848	71.4
1978	12.49	61.2	37.7	10,839	240.9	1978	6.65	68.2	53.4	10,795	71.7
1979	12.40	61.7	37.2	10,801	223.4	1979	6.73	69.4	55.1	10,740	72.9
1980	12.34	62.7	37.2	10,764	210.4	1980	6.81	70.9	56.8	10,683	73.9
1985	12.37	70.2	41.7	10,567	183.5	1985	7.27	80.1	66.7	10,370	80.5
1990	12.56	80.0	50.1	10,334	174.3	1990	7.80	91.9	78.2	10,002	86.5
1995	12.79	91.1	60.5	10,053	167.0	1995	8.42	105.9	91.1	9,573	92.0
2000	13.03	103.3	72.6	9,715	158.1	2000	9.15	122.1	105.8	9,075	96.7
2005	13.27	116.6	86.1	9,312	146.6	2005	9.98	140.5	122.2	8,497	99.2
2010	13.53	130.6	100.4	8,839	133.0	2010	10.92	160.7	140.2	7,832	99.8
2015	13.82	144.8	114.9	8,293	117.3	2015	11.96	181.1	158.2	7,077	94.1
2020	14.14	157.9	128.4	7,677	98.6	2020	13.07	196.7	171.1	6,243	81.1
2025	14.50	168.0	138.8	7,002	80.4	2025	14.18	198.0	169.9	5,383	58.7
2030	14.92	172.1	143.2	6,291	60.4	2030	15.20	176.6	146.1	4,596	32.3
2035	15.38	167.4	138.6	5,585	41.0	2035	16.00	138.1	105.9	3,983	12.5
2040	15.82	153.6	124.9	4,930	24.4	2040	16.51	101.2	67.8	3,572	3.2
2045	16.20	134.9	106.4	4,360	12.5	2045	16.76	78.6	44.8	3,309	0.2
							(depletion occurs in 2066)				
	Monopoly: $\delta = .10$						Competitive: $\delta = .10$				
1975	13.09	62.8	43.8	10,956	321.7	1975	5.45	65.8	50.0	10,950	22.0
1976	12.84	61.4	40.6	10,915	288.3	1976	5.50	66.5	51.6	10,898	21.3
1977	12.65	60.9	38.6	10,877	242.8	1977	5.54	67.4	53.4	10,845	20.7
1978	12.52	61.0	37.5	10,839	210.2	1978	5.59	68.6	55.3	10,790	20.5
1979	12.42	61.6	37.0	10,803	185.2	1979	5.64	69.9	57.3	10,732	20.2
1980	12.36	62.5	37.0	10,766	166.1	1980	5.70	71.4	59.4	10,673	20.2
1985	12.35	70.2	41.7	10,569	114.9	1985	6.02	80.9	70.6	10,343	19.1
1990	12.51	80.2	50.3	10,335	86.6	1990	6.42	92.8	83.0	9,953	17.8
1995	12.71	91.7	61.3	10,052	66.0	1995	6.94	106.9	96.7	9,497	16.5
2000	12.91	104.5	74.0	9.708	49.5	2000	7.62	123.4	112.0	8,969	15.4
2005	13.12	118.7	88.5	9,295	36.5	2005	8.48	142.3	129.1	8,358	14.1
2010	13.34	134.1	104.3	8,806	26.3	2010	9.58	163.8	148.1	7,656	12.6
2015	13.59	150.2	120.8	8,235	18.4	2015	10.97	187.1	168.1	6,805	10.7
2020	13.90	165.8	136.9	7,582	12.5	2020	12.66	205.7	182.8	5,836	8.1
2025	14.28	178.6	150.0	6,857	8.0	2025	14.61	194.9	167.5	4,877	4.8
2030	14.76	184.1	155.7	6,085	4.7	2030	16.75	129.5	97.3	4,205	1.9
2035	15.32	176.4	148.0	5,324	2.4	2035	19.38	52.6	15.2	3,817	0.2
2040	15.94	152.2	123.6	4,650	1.0	2040					
2045	16.46	118.8	90.1	4,133	0.4	2045					
							(net demand becomes zero in 2038[b])				

[a]Millions of 1973 dollars.

[b]The optimal initial competitive price is somewhere between $5.44 and $5.45; at that price net demand would become zero at exactly the point that depletion occurred. The $5.45 initial price is our closest approximation to the true optimal, and because it is slightly higher than the true optimal, net demand becomes zero before depletion occurs. This approximation has almost no effect, however, on the sum of discounted profits.

is, we must examine the sensitivity of our results to these parameter values. Bauxite is quite abundant; reserves for the competitive fringe can sustain production for nearly 300 years at current levels. Our competitive fringe supply function moves to the left only slowly as cumulative production increases—after a cumulative production of 1,700 million tons (e.g., 17 mmt/yr. for 100 years), supply would fall to 61% of its original value.

Equation (19) is the objective function for IBA. Initial reserves are 11,000 mmt (225 years of production at current levels), and initial production costs are $5 per ton. Initial conditions for the other variables are $TD_0=65.5$, $S_0=16.9$, and $CS_0=0$.

Optimal monopoly and competitive price trajectories are again calculated for discount rates of 0.05 and 0.10, but this time over an eighty-year horizon, since proven reserves are large. Optimal price trajectories are shown graphically in figure 3, and prices, total demand, IBA production, IBA reserves, and discounted profits are presented in table 3.

Observe that the optimal monopoly price has the typical characteristic of dropping for about five years and then rising slowly. The price fluctuates, however, over a small range, and at all times is within a few dollars of the "limit price" at which production of alumina from other ores becomes economical. The initial competitive price is again higher for the lower discount rate, but the difference in the initial percentage mark-ups above average cost for the two discount rates is much smaller, and the mark-ups themselves are much lower, than was the case for petroleum.[19] This is because the reserve base for bauxite is large (depletion in the competitive case takes at least 75 years) so that there is little incentive for competitive producers to withhold production in earlier years. In both the monopoly and competitive cases depletion plays only a small role in the determination of price during the first thirty years. Monopoly pricing is essentially "limit pricing" for a produced good; except for the effects of lag adjustments during the first five years, price can almost be chosen at the profit-maximizing "limit" each period, ignoring future periods.

The relative gains from cartelization are summarized in table 4. Again the relative gains are largest during the first five years, and are dependent on the discount rate. For either discount rate, however, the relative gains are larger than was the case for petroleum. Over the long term, cartelization of bauxite markets results in a 60% to 500% increase in the sum of discounted profits. This should be sufficient incentive for maintenance of the International Bauxite Association.

TABLE 4.—BAUXITE: RELATIVE PROFITS
(ratio of *NPV* for monopolist to *NPV* for competitors)

$NPV=\sum \Pi_d$ (1975 until exhaustion or 2050)	
$\delta=.05$	$NPV_M/NPV_C=7857/4835=1.63$
$\delta=.10$	$NPV_M/NPV_C=3904/789=4.95$
$NPV=\sum \Pi_d$ (first five years)	
$\delta=.05$	$NPV_M/NPV_C=1386/358=3.87$
$\delta=.10$	$NPV_M/NPV_C=1248/105=11.89$

Because of the "limit pricing" characteristic of the monopoly solution, our results are not very sensitive to the elasticity assumptions that were used. Doubling the long-run elasticity of supply (which is the parameter about which we are most uncertain) results in optimal monopoly and competitive price trajectories that are always within 10% of the numbers reported in table 3.

It should be pointed out that IBA is currently selling bauxite at slightly above what we have calculated to be the optimal monopoly price. *In 1973 dollars*, bauxite is now selling in the range of $15 to $20. The actual limit price is probably higher than the $15.60 that we have calculated due to energy costs that have risen more rapidly than the general price index. We might thus expect the cartel to maintain its current price (in real terms) over the next twenty to thirty years.

V. Copper—The Gains to CIPEC[20]

Our model for copper draws heavily from the econometric model of the world copper market

[19] For bauxite $(P_0-AC_0)/AC_0$ is 0.28 for $\delta=0.05$ and 0.09 for $\delta=0.10$ in the competitive case. For petroleum the corresponding numbers are 8.06 and 2.04.

[20] CIPEC countries include Chile, Peru, Zambia, and Zaire, and in 1974 accounted for 32% of non-Communist world copper production.

constructed by Fisher, Cootner, and Baily (1972), and in fact can be viewed as an aggregated version of their model. We also draw upon the work of Banks (1974), and obtain updated reserve and production data from the U.S. Bureau of Mines (1974b, 1975). The equations of the model are as follows:

$$TD_t = .405 - .78P_t + .90TD_{t-1} + .91(1.03)^t \quad (20)$$

$$SP_t = (-.190 + .8613P_t)\cdot(1.015)^{-CSP/4} + .88SP_{t-1} \quad (21)$$

$$CSP_t = CSP_{t-1} + SP_t \quad (22)$$

$$SS_t/K_t = .00940 + .005733P_t - .37(SS_{t-1}/K_{t-1}) \quad (23)$$

$$K_t = .98K_{t-1} + TD_t - SS_t \quad (24)$$

$$S_t = SP_t + SS_t \quad (25)$$

$$D_t = TD_t - S_t \quad (26)$$

$$R_t = R_{t-1} - D_t \quad (27)$$

$$\max W = \sum_{t=1}^{N} \frac{2204}{(1+\delta)^t}\left[P_t - \frac{67.5}{R_t}\right]D_t \quad (28)$$

where

TD_t = total demand for copper (mmt/yr.);
SP_t = primary supply from competitive fringe (mmt/yr.);
SS_t = secondary supply from scrap ("old" secondary) from competitive fringe (mmt/yr.);
CSP_t = cumulative primary supply of competitive fringe (mmt);
S_t = total supply from competitive fringe (mmt/yr.);
K_t = stock of copper in product form (mmt);
R_t = reserves of cartel (mmt);
P_t = price of copper (\$ per pound) in constant 1974 dollars.

The demand equation (20) explains total demand for refined copper *net of "new" secondary production*.[21] The reason for excluding "new" secondary production will become clear shortly. Corresponding to average figures for 1974, total demand is 7.3 million metric tons at a price of \$0.75 per pound.[22] At this price the short-run price elasticity is 0.16 and the long-run elasticity is 0.80. These elasticities correspond to a weighted average (weighted by consumption levels) of the regional demand elasticities estimated by Fisher, Cootner, and Baily.[23] The last term in equation (20) provides an autonomous rate of growth in demand of 3.75% per year, corresponding to a long-run income elasticity of 1.25 and a 3% real rate of growth in income.[24] The major substitute for copper is aluminum, but since we assume a fixed price for aluminum, an aluminum price need not be included explicitly in (20).

Primary supply from the competitive fringe is 3.8 mmt/yr. at a price of 75¢, with short-run and long-run elasticities of 0.20 and 1.6, respectively. Thus, although in the long-run supply is quite elastic, the adjustment time is considerable.[25] Depletion of competitive fringe reserves pushes the primary supply function to the left over time. After a cumulative production of 160 mmt (e.g., 4 mmt/yr. for 40 years), primary supply would fall (assuming a fixed price) to 55% of its original value.

Secondary supply includes only "old" secondary production, i.e., production from scrap, and thus depends on the stock of copper products available to be converted into scrap. The stock-adjustment effect will result in a price elasticity that is larger in the short run than in the long run. We follow Fisher,

[21] "New" secondary copper is produced from shavings and other wastage that result in the process of milling copper and producing finished copper products, while "old" secondary copper is produced from scrap; i.e., from recycled copper products.

[22] We assume that the same price prevails in all regions, and ignore differences between the U.S. producer price and the London Metal Exchange (LME) price. There have been periods during which the U.S. price was below the LME price, with rationing by U.S. producers. McNicol (1975) argues that rationing is profitable for partially integrated producers since it allows them to achieve the effects of price discrimination. The effect is therefore not that of undercutting a world market price to expand market share, and there would be no impact on the demand for cartel copper.

[23] Regional demand (and supply) equations for which price was statistically insignificant were not included in the average.

[24] The income elasticity is again an average of the Fisher, Cootner, Baily estimates.

[25] Again, this is based on the Fisher, Cootner, Baily estimates. More recent estimates by Banks (1974) indicate elasticities that are somewhat lower—around 1.0 in the long run.

Cootner, and Baily in using the primary price rather than the scrap price since the two prices are very highly correlated, and we apply their elasticity estimates for the United States (0.43 in the short run and 0.31 in the long run) to the rest of the world.[26] The stock of copper products available for scrap is simply last year's stock, minus losses of 2%, plus primary production this year; secondary production is not included since it adds to the stock of products but depletes the stock by the same amount.

As mentioned above, we exclude "new" secondary production from the model. The shavings and other "wastage" that provide the input to "new" secondary production come from the milling of copper sheet as well as the later transformation of sheet into a variety of copper products. Thus a good part of "new" secondary production is just a transformation of the output of primary production, and including it in total demand would involve some double counting. More important, although almost all secondary production occurs in the consuming countries, part of the input to "new" secondary production comes from CIPEC countries, so that including it would result in a misleading understatement of CIPEC's role in the world market.

The model is completed with equation (28), which specifies the maximization of the sum of discounted profits. The initial CIPEC proven reserve level is 135 mmt, and initial average cost is 50¢ per pound. The multiplication by 2,204 is to convert pounds to metric tons.

In calculating optimal price policies we take as initial conditions $TD_0 = 7.3$, $SP_0 = 3.8$, $SS_0 = 1.2$, $CSP_0 = 0$, and $K_0 = 120$. These numbers correspond to 1974 data. We use a forty-year horizon in the monopoly case, with discount rates of 0.05 and 0.10. Optimal monopoly and competitive prices are shown graphically in figure 4, and prices, total demand, competitive

[26] Outside of the United States data for secondary supply are not broken down into "new" and "old," and the determinants of "new" secondary supply are quite different. We obtain an estimate of the level of "old" secondary supply by applying the U.S. ratio of "old" secondary to total secondary outside the United States. Equation (17) represents a stock-adjustment model, so that the long-run elasticity is smaller than the short-run elasticity.

TABLE 5.—COPPER

	P	TD	SP	SS	D	R	Π_d[a]
			Monopoly: $\delta = .05$				
1975	1.23	6.92	4.22	1.43	1.28	133.8	2031
1976	0.78	6.97	4.19	1.14	1.64	132.2	964
1977	1.02	6.86	4.38	1.50	0.98	131.2	998
1978	0.73	6.99	4.29	1.20	1.50	129.7	657
1979	0.98	6.95	4.43	1.55	0.97	128.7	801
1980	0.75	7.13	4.36	1.28	1.50	127.2	570
1985	1.01	7.67	4.69	1.74	1.25	120.7	762
1990	0.97	8.59	5.03	1.78	1.78	112.8	701
1995	1.15	9.64	5.60	2.20	1.85	103.8	768
2000	1.20	10.99	6.20	2.42	2.38	93.0	735
2005	1.36	12.59	6.94	2.90	2.75	80.0	724
2010	1.49	14.47	7.77	3.36	3.34	64.4	590
			Monopoly: $\delta = .10$				
1975	1.06	7.06	4.06	1.41	1.59	133.4	1962
1976	0.75	7.11	4.03	1.17	1.91	131.5	957
1977	0.94	7.04	4.17	1.44	1.42	130.1	1112
1978	0.71	7.18	4.09	1.22	1.86	128.2	565
1979	0.94	7.16	4.22	1.52	1.42	126.8	876
1980	0.73	7.33	4.15	1.28	1.90	124.9	493
1985	1.02	7.85	4.52	1.79	1.54	116.4	576
1990	0.89	8.77	4.86	1.70	2.21	106.8	301
1995	1.17	9.74	5.52	2.27	1.94	96.9	300
2000	1.24	11.00	6.22	2.50	2.27	85.9	210
2005	1.38	12.48	7.06	2.93	2.48	74.0	147
2010	1.58	14.18	8.07	3.48	2.62	61.0	97
			Competitive: $\delta = .05$				
1975	0.79	7.27	3.83	1.23	2.21	132.8	1372
1976	0.80	7.26	3.88	1.28	2.10	130.7	1250
1977	0.82	7.26	3.93	1.32	2.02	128.7	1193
1978	0.83	7.28	3.98	1.36	1.94	126.7	1098
1979	0.85	7.32	4.05	1.41	1.87	124.9	1049
1980	0.87	7.37	4.12	1.45	1.81	123.1	1005
1985	0.95	7.83	4.55	1.67	1.61	114.7	788
1990	1.05	8.56	5.09	1.91	1.56	106.8	691
1995	1.16	9.52	5.74	2.19	1.59	99.0	632
2000	1.29	10.71	6.51	2.53	1.68	90.8	598
2005	1.44	12.14	7.39	2.94	1.81	82.0	569
2010	1.61	13.84	8.40	3.44	2.01	72.4	544
			(depletion occurs in 2031)				
			Competitive: $\delta = .10$				
1975	0.66	7.37	3.72	1.14	2.51	132.5	833
1976	0.68	7.45	3.67	1.22	2.56	129.9	823
1977	0.69	7.53	3.63	1.25	2.65	127.3	771
1978	0.71	7.63	3.62	1.31	2.70	124.6	750
1979	0.73	7.72	3.62	1.35	2.75	121.8	728
1980	0.75	7.83	3.64	1.40	2.79	119.0	698
1985	0.85	8.45	3.93	1.65	2.87	104.8	502
1990	0.96	9.21	4.45	1.93	2.83	90.5	320
1995	1.09	10.16	5.14	2.24	2.78	76.5	189
2000	1.23	11.37	5.88	2.57	2.91	63.4	65
2005	1.34	13.05	6.50	2.89	3.66	50.5	2
2010	1.25	15.08	6.51	2.94	5.63	24.8	0
			(depletion occurs in 2014[b])				

[a] Millions of dollars.

[b] The optimal initial competitive price is between 0.66 and 0.67. The 0.66 initial price is our closest approximation to the true optimal, and because it is slightly below the true optimal, price begins to decline and profits go negative before depletion occurs. The approximation has almost no effect, however, on the sum of discounted profits.

FIGURE 4.—OPTIMAL COPPER PRICE TRAJECTORIES (M = monopoly, C = competition)

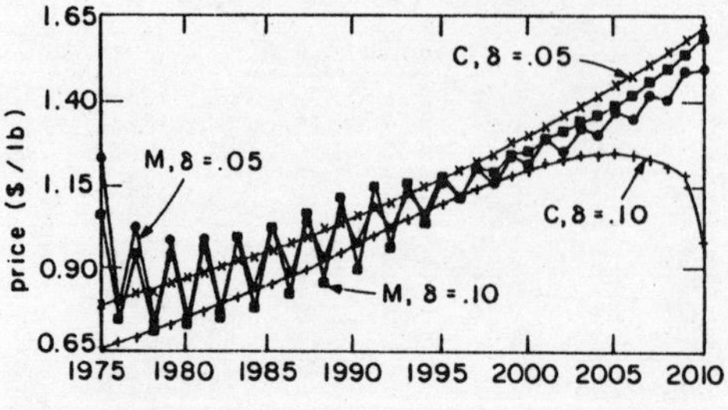

supply, CIPEC production, reserves, and discounted profits are presented in table 5.

We observe that the optimal monopoly price oscillates, and this occurs because of the stock adjustment effect in the secondary supply equation.[27] The envelope of the monopoly price, however, follows the same pattern as the monopoly petroleum and bauxite prices, dropping during the first several years (after taking advantage of lag adjustments in total demand and secondary supply), and then rising slowly as depletion of the resource base nears. Again the initial competitive price is higher for the lower discount rate. Resource exhaustion plays a more significant role in the determination of copper prices than was the case with bauxite; using U.S. Bureau of Mines figures for proven reserves, exhaustion in the competitive case occurs after 56 years at the 0.05 discount rate and after 39 years at the 0.10 discount rate.

TABLE 6.—COPPER: RELATIVE PROFITS
(Ratio of NPV for monopolist to NPV for competitors)

	$NPV = \sum \Pi_d$ (1975 until exhaustion or 2015)
$\delta = .05$	$NPV_M / NPV_C = 28988/26792 = 1.08$
$\delta = .10$	$NPV_M / NPV_C = 14772/11278 = 1.31$
	$NPV = \sum \Pi_d$ (first five years)
$\delta = .05$	$NPV_M / NPV_C = 5453/5962 = 0.91$
$\delta = .10$	$NPV_M / NPV_C = 5472/3905 = 1.40$

[27] The long-run price elasticity of secondary supply is smaller than the short-run elasticity. Price is set high in 1975 to take advantage of lag adjustments in total demand and primary supply, but this results in a large increase in secondary supply. If the 1975 price were maintained in 1976, secondary supply would fall because of the stock adjustment, but primary supply would rise further; dropping the price in 1976 results in a still larger drop in secondary supply.

As can be seen in table 6, the relative gains from cartelization are not large. Over the long term, cartelization of copper markets results in only an 8% to 30% increase in the sum of discounted profits. Furthermore, the increased profits require fluctuations in price (and in profits) that cartel members would probably wish to avoid, and that consuming countries could anticipate and counteract through stockpiling.[28] It would thus appear that there is little incentive for closely coordinated pricing and output policies on the part of the CIPEC cartel. This is consistent with recent history; so far CIPEC countries have not managed to significantly increase their copper revenues through cartelization.

VI. Concluding Remarks

We began this paper by asking whether the owners of exhaustible resources might accrue significant monopoly profits through cartelization. The answer would appear to be yes in the cases of petroleum and bauxite, and no in the case of copper. The reasons for this, however, have little to do with the fact that the resources are exhaustible, and more to do with market share and short-term lag adjustments. OPEC and IBA account for around two-thirds of non-Communist world petroleum and bauxite production, while CIPEC accounts for only one-third of copper production. Demand and competitive supply of petroleum and bauxite adjust only slowly to changes in price, allowing large short-term gains to a cartel, while secondary copper supply responds quickly to price changes.

Resource exhaustion, however, does have a significant effect on the pattern of pricing and output in both the monopoly and competitive cases, and tends to reduce the percentage increase in profits from cartelization when the discount rate is low. As competitive producers pay more attention to future depletion, they tend to restrict present output, raising prices closer to the monopoly level. The fact that pre-cartel oil, bauxite, and copper prices were close to marginal cost could mean that

[28] If the optimal monopoly price trajectory is smoothed out, the increase in profits from cartelization is reduced to only 3%–10%.

producers had large discount rates (which is reasonable at least for bauxite and copper), or that producers made output decisions either ignoring depletion or else assuming that large reserve additions would be discovered in the future.

In estimating the gains to producers from cartelization we have ignored a number of issues that could be important. Competitive fringe producers might form price expectations that would make their supply response different from that of equation (3) and would reduce cartel profits (alternative models of price expectations could easily be introduced into our framework by modifying equation (3)). Consuming countries might form a cartel of their own in an attempt to weaken the producer cartel; the behavior of price for such a bilateral monopoly could be analyzed in a dynamic game-theoretic framework, and would depend on the response assumptions made for each player. Producers—monopoly or competitive—might (and should) take uncertainty about reserves into account in making their price or output decisions, and this could alter cartel gains. The extent to which these issues would affect the conclusion of this paper will be determined from future research. Here we offer only a first approximation to the measurement of increased profits that could accrue to monopoly cartels in three exhaustible resource markets.

APPENDIX

The Competitive Price Trajectory with Rising Production Costs

We show here that equation (7) is a discrete-time approximation to the competitive price trajectory. Assume average cost is a function only of cumulative output x. Then, in continuous time, the competitive firm chooses output q_t to maximize

$$W=\int_0^T[q_tp_te^{-\delta t}-C(x_t)q_te^{-\delta t}]dt \qquad (A.1)$$

with price p taken as given. This is subject to the constraints

$$\dot{x}_t=q_t \qquad (A.2)$$

and

$$x_t\leqslant R_0. \qquad (A.3)$$

Using the Maximum Principle, the Hamiltonian is

$$H=qpe^{-\delta t}-C(x)qe^{-\delta t}+\lambda q \qquad (A.4)$$

and the Lagrangian is

$$L=H+\mu(R_0-x_t) \qquad (A.5)$$

with $\mu \geqslant 0$ and $\mu(R_0-x)=0$, so that μ is zero until exhaustion occurs at time T. We have

$$\dot{\lambda}=C'(x)qe^{-\delta t}+\mu. \qquad (A.6)$$

The optimal production trajectory q_t^* maximizes H, but since H is a linear function of q_t the problem is singular, so that H is maximized by $q_t=0$ or ∞ (or some upper limit q_M), depending on whether $pe^{-\delta t}-C(x)e^{-\delta t}+\lambda$ is negative or positive. λ is always negative (as we would expect, since it is the marginal discounted profit to go resulting from an additional unit of cumulative output) since $\dot{\lambda}$ is positive and λ approaches zero as exhaustion nears. Thus the decision to produce nothing or at the upper limit will depend on the price p. Then the market demand function will ensure that

$$pe^{-\delta t}-C(x)e^{-\delta t}+\lambda=0. \qquad (A.7)$$

At the price that satisfies (A.7), producers will just be indifferent between producing nothing or everything, so that just enough will be produced to satisfy market demand. From (A.7) we have

$$\dot{\lambda}=C'(x)qe^{-\delta t}-\delta C(x)e^{-\delta t}+\delta pe^{-\delta t}-\dot{p}e^{-\delta t}. \qquad (A.8)$$

Combining this with (A.6) and rearranging, we get

$$dp/dt=\delta[p-C(x)]. \qquad (A.9)$$

This is the price solution to the continuous time problem. As a discrete-time approximation to this solution we use

$$p_t=(1+\delta)p_{t-1}-\delta C(x_{t-1}). \qquad (A.10)$$

This equation, together with the boundary condition that exhaustion occurs at the same time that demand becomes zero, can be used to determine the competitive price path.

REFERENCES

Banks, Ferdinand E., "A Note on Some Theoretical Issues of Resource Depletion," *Journal of Economic Theory* 9 (Oct. 1974), 238–243.

———, *The World Copper Market* (Cambridge, Mass.: Ballinger, 1974).

Bergsten, C. F., "The Threat from the Third World," *Foreign Policy* 11 (1973), 102–124.

———, "The Threat is Real," *Foreign Policy* 14 (1974), 84–90.

Blitzer, Charles, Alex Meeraus, and Ardy Stoutjesdijk, "A Dynamic Model of OPEC Trade and Production," *Journal of Development Economics* 2 (Fall 1975), 319–335.

Burrows, James C., Testimony before the Joint Economic Committee, Subcommittee on Economic Growth, July 22, 1974.

Cremer, Jacque, and Martin Weitzman: "OPEC and the Monopoly Price of World Oil," *European Economic Review* 8 (Aug. 1976).

Eckbo, Paul L., "OPEC and the Experience of Some Non-Petroleum International Cartels," M.I.T. Energy Laboratory Report, June 1975.

Fischer, D., D. Gately, and J. F. Kyle, "The Prospects for OPEC: A Critical Survey of Models of the World Oil Market," *Journal of Development Economics* 2 (1975).

Fisher, Franklin M., Paul H. Cootner, and Martin N. Baily, "An Econometric Model of the World Copper Industry," *Bell Journal of Economics and Management Science* 3 (Autumn 1972), 568–609.

Gordon, R. L., "A Reinterpretation of the Pure Theory of Exhaustion," *Journal of Political Economy* 75 (1967), 274–286.

Herfindahl, Orris C., "Depletion and Economic Theory,"

in M. Gaffney (ed.), *Extractive Resources and Taxation* (Madison: University of Wisconsin Press, 1967).

Hnyilicza, Esteban, "OPCON: A Program for Optimal Control of Nonlinear Systems," MIT Energy Laboratory Report, May 1975.

Hnyilicza, Esteban, and Robert S. Pindyck, "Pricing Policies for a Two-Part Exhaustible Resource Cartel: The Case of OPEC," *European Economic Review* 8 (Aug. 1976), 139–154.

Hotelling, Harold, "The Economics of Exhaustible Resources," *Journal of Political Economy* 39 (Apr. 1931), 137–175.

Kalymon, Basil A., "Economic Incentives in OPEC Oil Pricing Policy," *Journal of Development Economics* 2 (1975), 337–362.

Krasner, S. D., "Oil is the Exception," *Foreign Policy* 14 (1974), 68–84.

McNicol, David L., "The Two Price System in the Copper Industry," *Bell Journal of Economics* 6 (Spr. 1975), 50–73.

Mikdashi, Z., "Collusion Could Work," *Foreign Policy* 14 (1974), 57–68.

Organization for Economic Cooperation and Development, *Energy Prospects to 1985*, Paris, 1974.

Smart, Ian, "Uniqueness and Generality," *Daedalus* (Fall 1975), 259–281.

Solow, Robert M., "The Economics of Resources or the Resources of Economics," *American Economic Review* 64 (May 1974), 1–14.

Stiglitz, Joseph E., "Monopoly and the Rate of Extraction of Exhaustible Resources," *American Economic Review* 66 (Sept. 1976), 655–661.

Sweeney, James L., "Economics of Depletable Resources: Market Forces and Intertemporal Bias," Federal Energy Administration Discussion Paper OES-76-1, Aug. 1975.

U.S. Bureau of Mines, Information Circular No. 8648, "Revised and Updated Cost Estimates for Producing Alumina from Domestic Raw Materials," by F. A. Peters and P. W. Johnson, Washington, D.C., 1974a.

———, *Minerals Yearbook*, Washington, D.C., 1974b.

———, *Commodity Data Summaries*, Washington, D.C., 1975.

[23]

COMMODITY BUNDLING AND THE BURDEN OF MONOPOLY*

WILLIAM JAMES ADAMS AND JANET L. YELLEN

I. INTRODUCTION

Firms often sell their goods in packages: sporting and cultural organizations offer season tickets, restaurants provide complete dinners, banks offer checking, safe deposit, and travelers' check services for a single fee, and garment manufacturers sell their retailers clothing grab bags comprised of assorted styles, sizes, and colors. We shall refer to the practice of package selling as commodity bundling. A firm that sells goods only in package form has adopted a *pure* bundling strategy. A firm that sells the same goods separately as well as in packages has adopted a *mixed* bundling strategy.

Commodity bundles sometimes include goods that cannot be sold separately in the market place. For example, an automobile can be interpreted as a package of luxury and transport services. The transport services could be offered without luxury (in the form of a stripped down car), but luxury must be sold in conjunction with motive power. Similarly, aspirin can be sold with or without a well-known brand name, but the brand name cannot be sold alone. In general, firms offering several incarnations of the same product, differing in either real or perceived quality, practice mixed bundling.

Commodity bundling also occurs when firms sell the same physical commodity in different container sizes. For example, toothpaste, detergent, and cereal are sold in small and large packages. In such cases, a bundle consists of multiple units[1] of the same commodity. Offering both sizes constitutes mixed bundling, while offering just the large size constitutes pure bundling.[2]

Why is commodity bundling such a prevalent marketing strategy? Some observers focus on the cost savings in production, trans-

* We are indebted to Richard Caves, Jerry Green, Zvi Griliches, Rachel McCulloch, and Steven Shavell for their comments, Yellen's research was financed by the National Science Foundation via Grant SOC74-19459.

1. Whenever a commodity is infinitely divisible, the choice of a "standard unit" is essentially arbitrary.

2. Thus, a telephone company that offers local calling only for a fixed monthly fee is engaged in pure bundling. A telephone company that offers local calling on both a fee for service and a monthly basis is engaged in mixed bundling.

actions, and information associated with package selling.[3] Others dwell on the complementarity in consumption of bundle components. We shall demonstrate that commodity bundling can be profitable even when these motivations are absent. In particular, we show that the profitability of commodity bundling can stem from its ability to sort customers into groups with different reservation price characteristics, and hence to extract consumer surplus.[4] We choose to emphasize this rationale for commodity bundling for several reasons.

First, in the real world firms cannot always resort to conventional forms of price discrimination in order to extract consumer surplus: reservation prices of specific customers are typically unknown; even if they were known, laws like the Robinson-Patman Act might prevent a seller from using them in an overtly discriminatory scheme. Commodity bundling can overcome these two practical problems associated with conventional price discrimination. We demonstrate this in Section II. In some circumstances, bundling is just as profitable as Pigouvian price discrimination of the first degree. In most circumstances, it is more profitable than simple monopoly pricing.[5]

Second, bundling motivated by price discrimination has dis-

3. This is one implication of the transaction cost literature. See, for example, R. Coase, "The Problem of Social Cost," *Journal of Law and Economics*, III (Oct. 1960), 1–44; and H. Demsetz, "The Cost of Transacting," this *Journal*, LXXXII (Feb. 1968), 33–53.

4. This view was first articulated in G. Stigler, "United States v. Loew's Inc.: A Note on Block Booking," in P. Kurland, *The Supreme Court Review: 1963* (Chicago: University of Chicago Press, 1963), 152–57. See also R. Markovits, "Tie-Ins, Reciprocity and Leverage Theory," *Yale Law Journal*, LXXVI (June 1967), 1397–1472. Several recent papers illustrate the relevance of this phenomenon in a variety of institutional and market settings: R. Parks, "The Demand and Supply of Durable Goods and Durability," *American Economic Review*, LXIV (March 1974), 37–55; S. C. Salop, "The Noisy Monopolist: Imperfect Information, Price Dispersion and Price Discrimination," unpublished manuscript, 1973; J. K. Salop and S. C. Salop, "Self-Selection and Turnover in the Labor Market," paper presented to the Econometric Society Meetings, Toronto, 1972; A. M. Spence, *Market Signaling* (Cambridge, Mass.: Harvard University Press, 1974); A. M. Spence, "Time and Communication in Economic and Social Interaction," this *Journal*, LXXXVII (Nov. 1973), 651–60; and J. Stiglitz, "Monopoly and Imperfect Information: the Insurance Market," unpublished manuscript, 1973. Commodity bundling is not the only sophisticated strategy a monopolist can use to enhance profit and complicate welfare judgments. The most similar practices are full-line forcing and all-or-none offers, although conventional price discrimination, the multipart tariff, and product differentiation are all related. See, respectively, M. Burstein, "The Economics of Tie-In Sales," *Review of Economics and Statistics*, XLII (Feb. 1960), 68–73; and R. Markovits, *op. cit.*; R. Baldwin, "Equilibrium in International Trade," this *Journal*, LXII (Nov. 1948), 748–62; E. Clemens, "Price Discrimination and the Multiple Product Firm," *Review of Economic Studies*, XIX (Jan. 1951), 1–11; W. Oi, "A Disneyland Dilemma: Two-Part Tariffs for a Mickey Mouse Monopoly," this *Journal*, LXXXV (Feb. 1971), 77–96; and E. Chamberlin, *The Theory of Monopolistic Competition* (Cambridge, Mass.: Harvard University Press, 1933).

5. Simple monopoly pricing involves setting those prices for each component that maximize profit. In general, the monopolist must take account of any interdependencies among product demand curves in his computation of these prices. This point is developed in M. Bailey, "Price and Output Determination by a Firm Selling Related Products," *American Economic Review*, XLIV (March 1954), 82–93.

tinctive normative consequences. On the one hand, bundling could lead monopolists to oversupply as well as undersupply specific commodities: equilibrium output could fall on *either* side of ideal output. On the other hand, bundling could lead monopolists to sell whatever output is produced to the wrong people, in the sense that potential gains from trade among cusumers would exist in equilibrium. Hence the conditions for distributive efficiency as well as those for allocative efficiency might be violated. Neither Pigouvian first-degree price discrimination nor simple monopoly pricing results in either of these problems. These findings are discussed in Section III.

Third, the existence of commodity bundling seriously complicates public appraisal of monopoly, for it impairs the validity of major tools of applied welfare economics, such as consumer-producer surplus analysis and hedonic price indices. Finally, prohibition of bundling in monopolistic markets, without elimination of monopoly, can either increase or decrease the deadweight loss arising in the relevant markets. This reinforces the desirability of a structural, as opposed to conduct, attack on market power. We discuss these implications of commodity bundling in Section IV.

II. The Model: Positive Properties

Consider a model with the following characteristics. Technology is such that A1 holds.

A1. (Technology) The marginal cost of supplying each good separately (c_1, c_2) is invariant with respect to output, and the marginal cost of supplying the two goods in a bundle is the sum of the component costs ($c_B = c_1 + c_2$). There are no fixed costs.

Tastes are such that for all individuals A2 and A3 hold.

A2. (Indivisibility) The marginal utility of a second unit of either commodity is zero.

A3. (Independence) The reservation price for a package comprised of one unit of each commodity (r_B) is equal to the sum of their separate reservation prices (r_1, r_2).[6]

By assumption, therefore, this model excludes both economies in the bundling process and complementarity in consumption. If bundling is found to be profitable, it cannot be explained by these phenomena.

If the monopolist knows the reservation price of each consumer for each commodity, his profit-maximizing strategy is simply Pi-

6. We assume here that any individual would be indifferent between consuming both goods 1 and 2 and a package consisting of these two goods. In other words, a package is identical to the sum of its component parts from the consumer's point of view.

gouvian first-degree price discrimination with respect to each commodity separately. If the monopolist knows only the distribution of reservation prices in the population, however, or if he is legally prevented from engaging in pure price discrimination, then his ideal pricing strategy is more difficult to establish. Three options open to him are as follows.

1. Set the single price on each commodity separately, (p_1^*, p_2^*), which yields the greatest profits. We call this a pure components strategy, or simple monopoly pricing.

2. Offer the two commodities for sale only in a package comprised of one unit of each at the price p_B^* chosen so as to maximize profits. This is the pure bundling strategy.

3. Combine strategies one and two by offering each commodity separately and a package of both, at a set of prices (p_1^*, p_2^*, p_B^*), which maximizes overall profits. This is the mixed bundling strategy. Since the value of a bundle to consumers is no greater than the value of its components, mixed bundling is a distinct strategy only if the package is sold at a discount relative to its components.

Each of these strategies is easily represented in diagrammatic form.

The reservation price of each consumer for each commodity can

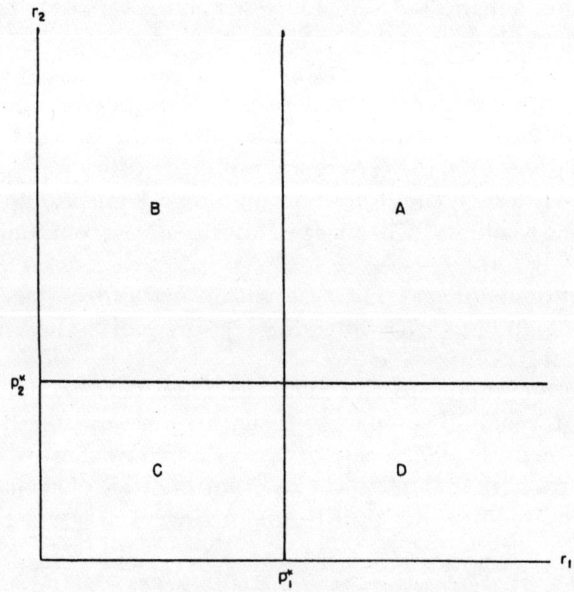

FIGURE I

be represented as a point in Figure I. If the monopolist adopts the pure components strategy, and sets component prices p_1^* and p_2^* (Figure I), the population is sorted into four groups: individuals with reservation prices at least equal to market prices for both commodities (Area *A* in Figure I), individuals with reservation prices less than market prices for both commodities (Area *C*), and individuals with reservation price at least equal to market price for one but not the other commodity (Areas *B* and *D*). Those in Area *A* purchase both goods, those in Areas *B* and *D* purchase goods 2 and 1, respectively, and individuals in Area *C* purchase neither good.

If instead the monopolist adopts the pure bundling strategy, the population is sorted into only two groups: those whose reservation price for the bundle ($r_B = r_1 + r_2$) is at least equal to the bundle's market price, and those for whom the opposite is true. In Figure II the

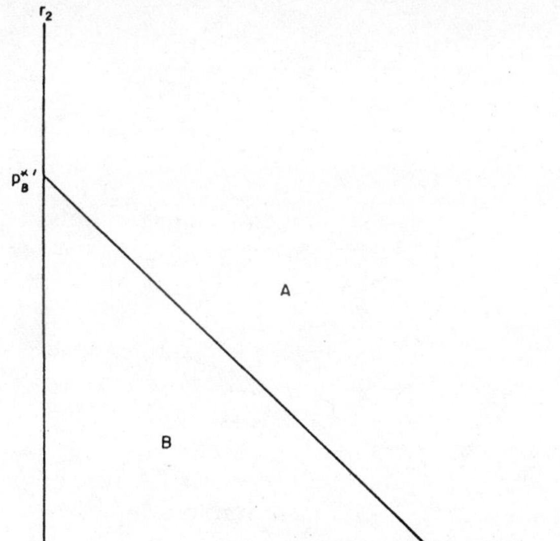

FIGURE II

bundle price appears in reservation price space as a straight line with both intercepts equal to the bundle price p_B^* and hence with a slope of minus one. Those in Area *A* buy the bundle and hence consume both goods. Those in Area *B* do not buy the bundle and hence consume neither good.[7]

7. The sorting of consumers depicted in Figure II assumes that resale of components is impossible.

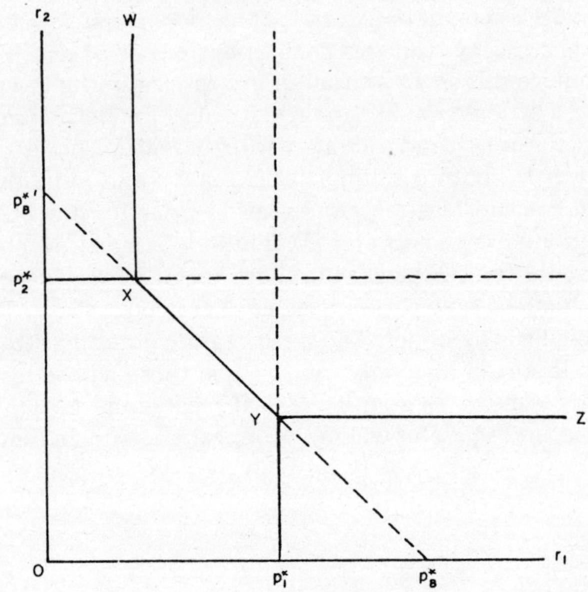

FIGURE III

Finally, if the monopolist adopts the mixed bundling strategy, customers are again sorted into four groups. These appear in Figure III. Individuals in Area $Op_2^*XYp_1^*$ consume nothing. They are characterized by $r_1 \le p_1^*$, $r_2 \le p_2^*$, and $r_B \le p_B^*$. Individuals southeast of p_1^*YZ consume only good 1. They are characterized by $r_1 \ge p_1^*$ and $r_2 \le p_B^* - p_1^*$. The reason is that $(p_B^* - p_1^*)$ represents the implicit price of good 2 to an individual already prepared to buy good 1.[8] For similar reasons those northwest of p_2^*XW consume only good 2. They are characterized by $r_2 \ge p_2^*$ and $r_1 \le (p_B^* - p_1^*)$. The last group comprises those northeast of $WXYZ$, who consume the bundle. They are characterized by $r_1 + r_2 \ge p_B^*$, $r_1 \ge (p_B^* - p_2^*)$, and $r_2 \ge (p_B^* - p_1^*)$. In words, the bundle is consumed by those who not only derive positive consumer surplus from purchase of the bundle but also derive more surplus from the bundle $(r_B - p_B^*)$ than they would from purchase of either component separately $(r_i - p_i^*, i = 1, 2)$.

The profit-maximizing monopolist chooses among these sorting mechanisms by calculating the most remunerative configuration of prices under each strategy and then by comparing the resulting profits. The relative profitability of the three strategies depends on

8. Note that $p_1^*p_B^*$ must equal p_1^*Y, since the slope of $p_B^*p_B^{*\prime}$ is -1.

the distribution of consumers in reservation price space and the structure of costs. Each conceivable ranking of the three is in fact possible.[9] The reason is that each strategy has both strengths and weaknesses vis à vis its rivals.

In order to assess the virtues and defects of each strategy, a benchmark is required. Since pure price discrimination is known to be the most remunerative pricing strategy available to a firm, it provides a benchmark for appraising the profitability of other pricing schemes. In the context of our model pure price discrimination satisfies three conditions:

C1. (Complete Extraction) No individual realizes any consumer surplus on his purchases.

C2. (Exclusion) No individual consumes a good if the cost of that good exceeds his reservation price for it.

C3. (Inclusion) Any individual whose reservation prices for a good exceeds its cost in fact consumes that good.

To what extent does simple monopoly pricing, or bundling in some form, also satisfy these conditions?

The pure components strategy never violates Exclusion because within the framework of our model prices in component markets are never set below cost.[10] As we show below, this virtue of simple monopoly pricing is not shared by its bundling rivals. On the other hand, the pure components strategy violates Extraction or Inclusion as long as customers are distributed in reservation price space such that the monopolist faces downward-sloping demand curves in both component markets: the finite elasticity of demand curves implies that monopolists cannot extract all consumer surplus on a particular good without preventing some individuals with valuation in excess of cost from consuming it. This violates Inclusion.

If the bundle demand curve is extremely elastic while the component demand curves are not, pure bundling avoids excessive violation of Inclusion and Extraction. This proposition is illustrated in Figure IV. The four consumers—A, B, C, and D—are distributed in reservation price space along a straight line with slope minus one. The value of the bundle is the same to all customers so that the bundle demand curve is perfectly elastic. The relative value of the components differs among customers, however, so that each component demand curve is downward-sloping. If the monopolist knows the

9. An appendix to this effect is available upon request from the authors.

10. This follows from assumption A3. If an individual's reservation price for one good depends on the amount of the other he consumes, the profit-maximizing pure components strategy might involve violation of Exclusion. The loss leader is a classic case of this proposition.

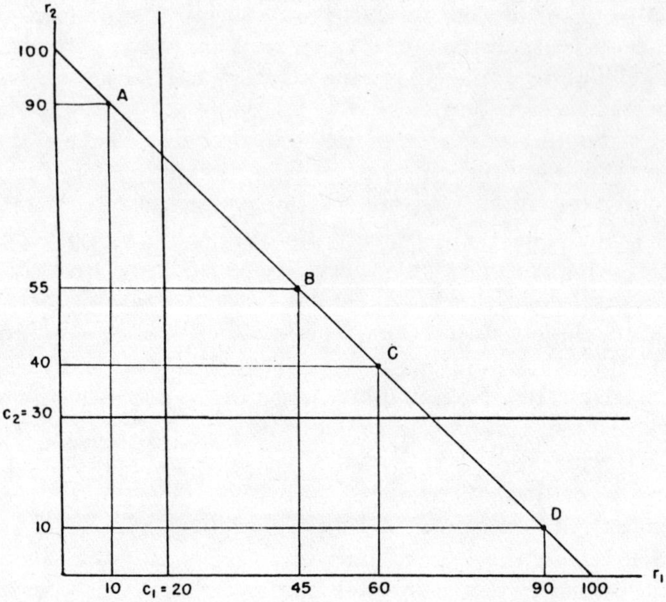

	p_1^*	p_2^*	p_B^*	Profits
Pure Components Strategy	60	90	—	140
Pure Bundling Strategy	—	—	100	200
Mixed Bundling Strategy	90	90	100	230

FIGURE IV

common valuation of the bundle by his customers, he can satisfy the extraction and inclusion requirements simultaneously by charging each customer a price equal to that amount for the bundle.[11]

The chief defect of pure bundling is its difficulty in complying with Exclusion. The greater the cost of supplying either good, the greater the possibility of supplying some individuals with commodities for which reservation price falls short of cost. In Figure IV, *A* and *D* are individuals with $r_i < c_i$ for some commodity. Thus, pure bundling

11. The pure bundling strategy is analytically equivalent to an all-or-none offer. In both cases a package of commodities is offered to the consumer on a "take it or leave it" basis.

is preferred to simple monopoly pricing only if the greater profits accruing from more complete extraction or inclusion are not outweighed by the lower profits due to less complete exclusion. The more negligible are costs relative to reservation prices, the less of a problem this poses for pure bundling.

The mixed bundling strategy is more profitable than its pure counterpart whenever Exclusion is violated in the pure bundling equilibrium. The reason is that creation of separate component markets adds two categories into which the monopolist can sort his customers. In Figure IV, for example, he can charge prices $p_1^* = 90$ and $p_2^* = 90$ in the component markets, thereby inducing individuals A and D to cease consuming the good they value below cost but continue consuming the good they value above cost. In general, *whenever the exclusion requirement is violated in a pure bundling equilibrium, mixed bundling is necessarily preferred to pure bundling.*[12] That mixed bundling satisfies Exclusion more completely than does pure bundling, however, does not mean that mixed bundling avoids the problem altogether. Rarely does a monopolist find it profitable to exclude every individual whose reservation price for a good falls short of its cost. The reason is apparent in Figure V, which is identical to Figure IV except for the presence of consumers E and F. Mixed bundling is still the most profitable strategy, but Exclusion is unfulfilled in the cases of E and F. To exclude them from the bundle market proves too costly in terms of consumer surplus foregone on A and D. Another way of putting this is that the component demand curves are downward-sloping and hence successive price reductions on a given component usually reduce total revenue in that component market. Like pure bundlers, therefore, mixed bundlers face a trade-off between more complete extraction and more complete exclusion. The dilemma is simply less pronounced in the case of mixed bundling.

If customers are distributed in reservation price space such that people with high reservation prices for the package exhibit small variance in their valuations of the components, and vice versa, then mixed bundling has another virtue relative to pure bundling: it fa-

12. The proof of this assertion proceeds as follows. Assume that the monopolist adopts a pure bundling strategy and sets a price of p_B^*. Assume further that there exists some consumer i for whom $r_1 + r_2 \geq p_B^*$ and $r_2 < c_2 - \epsilon$, where $\epsilon > 0$. If the monopolist now adopts a mixed bundling strategy, with prices p_B^* and $p_1 = p_B^* - c_2 + \epsilon$, he necessarily earns more profits than under pure bundling: profits are unchanged on individuals for whom $r_1 + r_2 \geq p_B^*$ and $r_2 > p_B^* - p_1$, since they consume the bundle in both cases. Profits are increased, however, on individuals for whom $r_1 + r_2 > p_B^*$ and $r_2 < p_B^* - p_1$, since they bring in $p_1 - c_1 = p_B^* - c_B + \epsilon$ apiece instead of just $p_B^* - c_B$. Profits are also increased on individuals for whom $r_1 + r_2 < p_B^*$ and $r_1 \geq p_1$, since they previously consumed nothing but now generate $p_1 - c_1$ in profits apiece. All other individuals consume nothing in both cases.

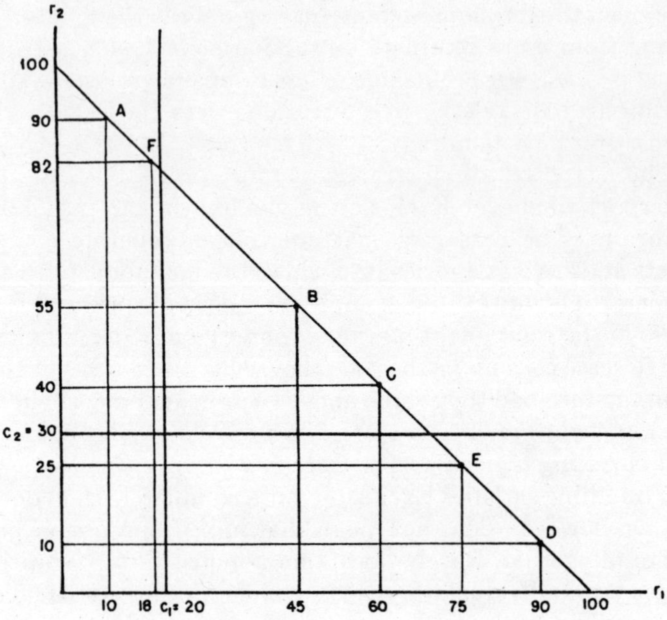

	p_1^*	p_2^*	p_B^*	Profits
Pure Components Strategy	60	82	—	224
Pure Bundling Strategy	—	—	100	300
Mixed Bundling Strategy	90	90	100	330

FIGURE V

cilitates the monopolist's attempts to extract the consumer surplus of individuals with high reservation prices for both goods. The reason is that a mixed bundler can charge a high bundle price and yet extract via separates markets the consumer surplus associated with customers valuing one but not both goods highly. This is illustrated in Figure VI. The bundle is priced to extract all the surplus of *B* and *C*, while the separates markets are used to extract the surplus of *A* and *D*. If the distribution of consumers in reservation price space is the opposite of that assumed here, however, pure bundling could be preferred to its mixed counterpart.[13]

13. For example, if $c_1 = c_2 = 0$ and consumers *A, B, C,* and *D* have reservation prices equal to (30, 90), (40, 60), (60, 40), and (90, 30), respectively, the pure bundling strategy generates profits of 400, while the mixed bundling strategy yields profits of 340. Hence pure bundling could be preferred to mixed bundling.

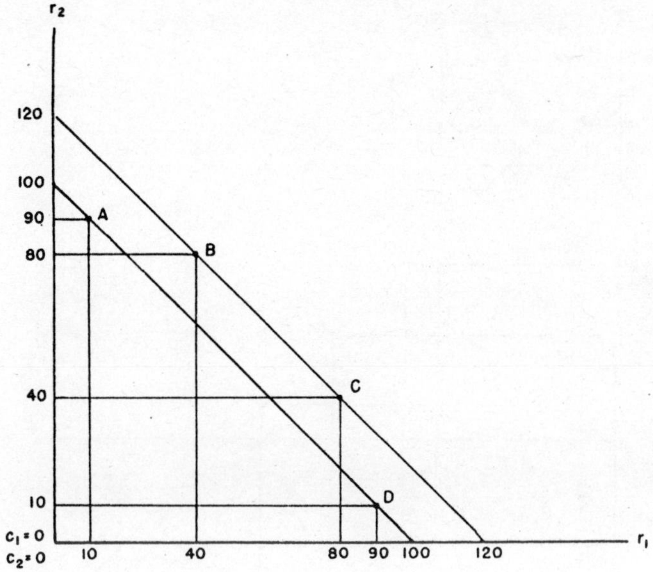

	p_1^*	p_2^*	p_B^*	Profits
Pure Components Strategy	80	80	—	320
Pure Bundling Strategy	—	—	100	400
Mixed Bundling Strategy	90	90	120	420

FIGURE VI

Turning to comparison of mixed bundling with simple monopoly pricing, if the correlation coefficient linking an individual's valuation of one good to his valuation of the other good is not strongly positive, we can see that the mixed bundling strategy is better able to satisfy Extraction and Inclusion simultaneously. This is possible in Figure VII. The monopolist adopting a pure components strategy sets $p_1^* = p_2^* = 10$ in this situation, earning 40 in profits. If he then offers a bundle at $p_B = 16$, without changing the component prices, he entices people currently consuming nothing (i.e., E), as well as people currently consuming just one good (i.e., D, F), to purchase the bundle, while retaining other customers (i.e., A, B, C, G, H, I) in the separates markets. More generally, strong negative correlation helps the mo-

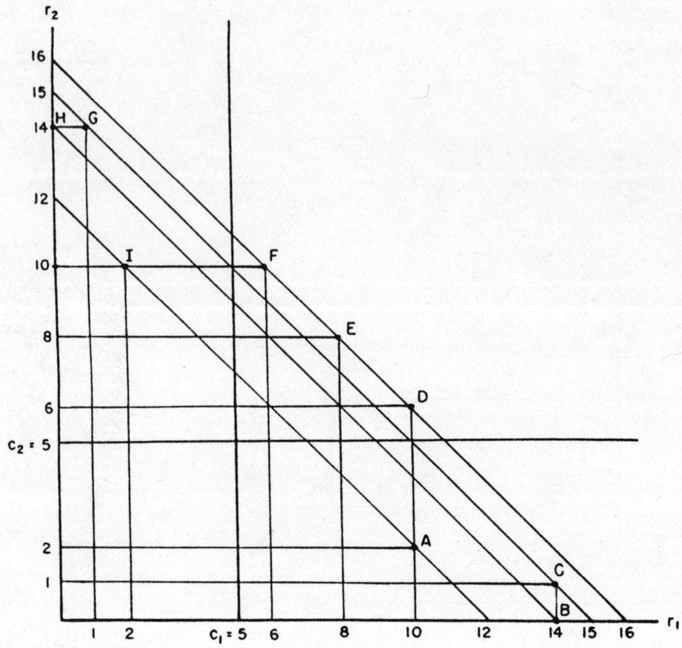

	p_1^*	p_2^*	p_B^*	Profits
Pure Components Strategy	10	10	—	40
Pure Bundling Strategy	—	—	14	28
Mixed Bundling Strategy	14	14	16	54

FIGURE VII

nopolist to achieve greater Inclusion by insuring that numerous individuals like *F*, *E*, and *D* exist. In the case at hand, simply adding the bundle at a price of 16 generates profits of 48 rather than 40. Profits are not maximized, however, by leaving component prices at their prebundle level. The bundle option permits the monopolist to raise prices in component markets, in pursuit of more complete extraction, without driving as many customers entirely out of the market. In Figure VII, for example, introduction of a bundle at a price of 16 makes it profitable to raise each component price from 10 to 14. This involves sacrifice of customers at *A* and *I*. Without the bundle,

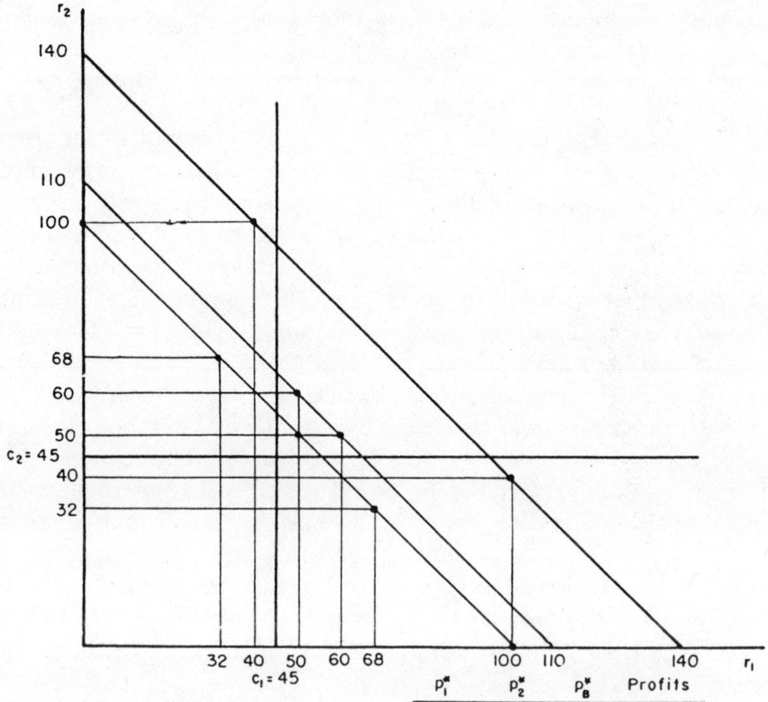

	p_1^*	p_2^*	p_B^*	Profits
Pure Components Strategy	100	100	—	220
Pure Bundling Strategy	—	—	140	100
Mixed Bundling Strategy	100	100	110	190

FIGURE VIII

however, *D* and *F* would also exit from the market. On balance, introduction of a bundle, when coupled with elevation of component market prices, permits achievement of 54 in profits. These are the highest attainable under any of the three strategies. In effect, negative correlation guarantees the existence of individuals with extreme tastes (e.g., *B*, *C*, *G*, *H*) who realize substantial consumer surplus in pure components equilibrium.

A major defect of mixed bundling vis à vis simple monopoly pricing is its difficulty in accomplishing Exclusion and Complete Extraction simultaneously. In Figure VIII, for example, if costs are $c_1 = c_2 = 45$, exclusion is such an important desideratum that pure components pricing is more profitable than mixed bundling. If $c_1 = c_2 = 30$, by contrast, so that exclusion is no longer a serious problem, simple monopoly pricing is less profitable than mixed bundling. This illustrates the general proposition that pure components pricing is a more desirable strategy the greater the cost of violating Exclusion.[14]

In sum, each of the three pricing strategies has both advantages and disadvantages in relation to the other two. Whether one generates more profits than another depends on the prevailing level of costs and on the distribution of customers in reservation price space. In numerous experiments with plausible cost structures and continuous distributions of reservation prices, we found some form of bundling to be more profitable than simple monopoly pricing.[15] Thus, commodity bundling can be expected to occur in the real world under more than the highly particular circumstances discussed here.[16]

We are now in a position to understand why a restaurant might offer complete dinners as well as an à la carte menu. Some people value an appetizer relatively highly (soup on a cold day), others may value dessert relatively highly (Baked Alaska, unavailable at home), but all might wish to pay roughly the same amount for a complete dinner. The à la carte menu is designed to capture consumer surplus from those gastronomes with extremely high valuations of particular dishes, while the complete dinner is designed to retain those with lower variance in their reservation prices.

With slight changes in interpretation, our model can be used to explain why products like toothpaste are sold in multiple container sizes. The horizontal axis in such cases measures an individual's reservation price for a first unit of the good, while the vertical axis measures his reservation price for an additional unit of the same good, given that he consumes a first unit. These definitions guarantee that

14. It is also possible, although less probable, that taste considerations alone render pure components pricing more profitable than mixed bundling. This is illustrated by the following example. Assume that five consumers—A, B, C, D, and E—have reservation prices of (80, 80), (75, 75), (45, 45), (75, 5), and (5, 75). Assume that $c_1 = c_2 = 0$. The pure components strategy with $p_1^* = p_2^* = 75$ generates profits of 450. Although a bundle could be offered at a price of 90 in order to induce C to enter the market, gains from the inclusion of C would be outweighed by the loss of revenue on sales to A and B. Furthermore, increasing prices in components markets in conjunction with introduction of a bundle would not increase profits either. The point of this example is to suggest that there exist some distributions of tastes consistent with any strategy ranking as long as Exclusion is violated by none of the options.

15. To demonstrate this, we explored the profitability of bundling when individual reservation prices for the two components follow the joint normal distribution. Our experiments covered a wide range of parameters of the taste distribution and a wide range of cost structures. Suffice it to say that, for every characterization of tastes we studied, bundling in some form was preferred to pure components pricing for some cost conditions. Less complete explorations of tastes following the uniform and chi-square distributions were consistent with this result.

16. Using attendance data on first-run movies for various cities, Stigler attempted to show that real world tastes are such that the block booking practice of movie distributors can be explained by a model of this type. See Stigler, *op. cit.*

assumptions A1–A3 can be satisfied.[17] Note, however, that what comprises "one unit" of a good is inherently arbitrary. Moreover, customers must lie below the 45-degree line in reservation price space so as to comply with the law of diminishing marginal rates of substitution. Finally, the monopolist must charge the same price in both separates markets. Whenever mixed bundling occurs in toothpaste-type situations, the monopolist is engaging in price discrimination by offering quantity discounts. Individuals with high reservation prices for the first ounce and low reservation prices for the second ounce have lower price elasticities of demand than do those with more equal valuations of successive units. Offering both one- and two-ounce containers thus induces individuals with inelastic demand to pay a high unit price in the component market, while individuals with elastic demand pay a low unit price in the bundle market.[18]

Our model also provides a plausible explanation of why automobile manufacturers add luxury to at least some of their vehicles. If the horizontal axis of reservation price space is defined as valuation of transport services, while the vertical axis is defined as the valuation of added luxury, assumptions A1–A3 can be satisfied.[19] In such situations the monopolist could offer just a basic car, just a luxury car, or both. Since the last strategy is equivalent to mixed bundling, it is usually the most profitable of the three.[20] That explains why consumer

17. Note how this incarnation of the model can be used to treat divisible goods, even though they appear to be excluded by assumption A2. In the limiting case of perfect divisibility, bundling is equivalent to imposing nonlinear budget constraints on consumers. The nonlinearity stems from the fact that the average unit price of toothpaste depends on the quantity of toothpaste consumed. The important point here is that bundling can be profitable in a world of divisible commodities for exactly the reasons set forth here.

18. This point is made in Salop, *op. cit.*

19. Note how this incarnation of the model can be used to treat complementarity even though it appears to be excluded by Assumption A3. Two goods are complements in consumption if an individual's reservation price for a unit of one depends on the quantity consumed of the other. By this definition luxury and transport services are complements in our model, since we assume that no individual would pay anything for luxury if he does not consume transport. Hence, by defining the vertical axis as we have, it is possible to analyze complementary goods.

20. In this situation it is rarely in the monopolist's interest to offer only a basic car. The reason is that as long as some consumer values luxury in excess of cost, profits can be increased by offering a luxury, as well as a basic, car. The proof is as follows. Assume that the monopolist offers a basic car at price p_1^*. Assume further that there exists an individual with $r_1 \geq p_1^*$ and $r_2 > c_2 + \epsilon$, $\epsilon > 0$. If the monopolist introduces a luxury car with price $p_B = p_1^* + c_2 + \epsilon$, all consumers with $r_1 \geq p_1^*$ and $r_2 \leq p_B - p_1^*$ continue to purchase only good 1. Profits on these sales are unchanged. All consumers with $r_1 \geqslant p_1^*$ and $r_2 > p_B - p_1^*$ now purchase the bundle instead of the basic car. Profits on these sales rise from $(p_1^* - c_1)$ to $(p_B - c_1 - c_2 = p_1^* - c_1 + \epsilon)$. In addition, individuals with $r_1 < p_1^*$ and $r_1 + r_2 > p_B$ now consume the bundle instead of nothing. Since $p_B > c_B$, greater profits are earned on these individuals. In situations of the car variety pure bundling is likely to be more profitable relative to mixed bundling than in cases of the restaurant type. However, the existence of any consumer in pure bundling equilibrium with $r_2 < c_2$ still suffices to guarantee the superiority of mixed bundling.

goods' manufacturers typically sell their product in both differentiated and undifferentiated form.[21]

In conclusion, we have shown that commodity bundling is more profitable than simple monopoly pricing in a wide variety of circumstances. The reason is that it often permits more complete extraction of consumer surplus than is possible under a pure components strategy. Price discrimination is another technique designed to achieve that result. What are the relative merits of these two schemes? Package selling has two virtues when compared with price discrimination. First, it requires far less information to implement. For example, Pigouvian first-degree price discrimination could be practiced only if the monopolist knows the reservation prices of each individual for each commodity. Needless to say, individuals have a strong incentive to conceal such information whenever possible. Commodity bundling, on the other hand, can be practiced even if the monopolist knows only the joint distribution of reservation prices in the population. Such information is sufficient to calculate the most profitable bundle and component prices. In a bundling context the price structure is such that individuals automatically sort themselves into distinct reservation price groups and thereby reveal truthful information concerning their tastes. In this sense commodity bundling serves as a self-selection device.[22]

Second, since each person pays the same price for what he consumes as do all others purchasing the same market basket, price discrimination laws based on price differentials alone are not violated. Unlike pure price discrimination, therefore, commodity bundling leaves its practitioner immune from prosecution.

III. The Model: Normative Properties

Two requirements of Pareto optimality in the model of Section II are that commodities be distributed among consumers in such a way that no mutual gains from trade are possible, and that output of

21. In the industrial organization literature it is usually argued that product differentiation is profitable because it raises barriers to new competition. Our results suggest that product differentiation might be profitable even if entry barriers are unaffected. On the market structure explanation see W. Comanor and T. A. Wilson, "Advertising, Market Structure and Performance," *Review of Economics and Statistics*, XLIV (Nov. 1967), 423–40.

One major class of automobile-type situations, sometimes discussed in other contexts, involves bundling of a good and a bad. The bad cannot be disembodied from the package. The bad could be the search costs or waiting time required to purchase a commodity. See, respectively, Salop, *op. cit.;* and Spence, "Time and Communication in Economic and Social Interaction."

22. See Spence, "Time and Communication in Economic and Social Interaction;" and Salop and Salop, *op. cit.*

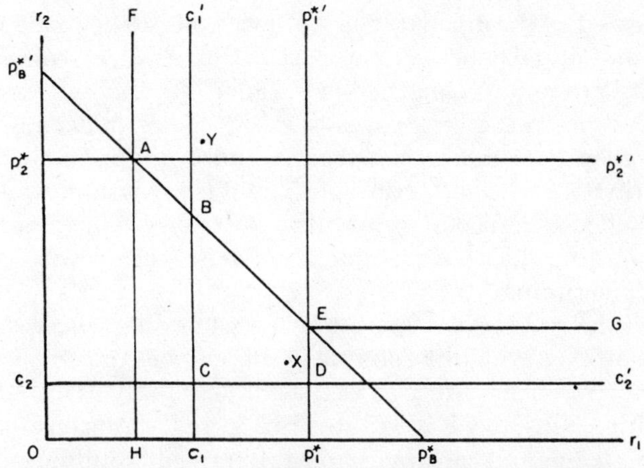

Group	Actually Consumes Good 1	Should Consume Good 1	Actually Consumes Good 2	Should Consume Good 2
Oc_2Cc_1	no	no	no	no
Southeast of $c_2'Dp_1^*$	yes	yes	no	no
Northwest of p_2^*AF	no	no	yes	yes
$c_1'BEG$	yes	yes	yes	yes
$c_2p_2^*ABC$	no	no	no	yes
$c_1CDp_1^*$	no	yes	no	no
$GEDc_2'$	yes	yes	no	yes
$FABc_1'$	yes	no	yes	yes
CBED	no	yes	no	yes

FIGURE IX

each commodity be just sufficient to supply all consumers with reservation prices at least equal to the marginal cost of that commodity. It is well-known that simple monopoly pricing violates the second but not the first of these requirements. Commodity bundling can violate either or both. Since the precise defects of bundling depend on which case—restaurant, toothpaste, or car—is under consideration, we shall discuss the normative consequences of each case separately.

In cases of the restaurant type, where each component can in principle be disembodied from the bundle, package selling typically results in distributive inefficiency. This is illustrated in Figure IX.[23]

23. The prices and costs depicted in Figure IX were selected to permit simultaneous illustration of all potential sources of welfare loss under commodity bundling.

Consumers located in the area AHp_1^*E, for example, do not consume good 1, while individuals northeast of $FAEp_1^{*\prime}$ do. And yet, some individuals in the former area (e.g., X) value good 1 more highly than do some individuals in the latter area (e.g., Y). Thus, mutual gains from trade of good 1 for money between X and Y are possible, violating the distributive efficiency criterion. The same reasoning applies to distribution of good 2. Insofar as it leads to distributive inefficiency, commodity bundling shares certain normative properties with (imperfect) price discrimination.[24]

In cases of the restaurant type commodity bundling also results in allocative inefficiency. Unlike simple monopoly pricing, however, bundling can lead to oversupply as well as undersupply of either or both commodities. This, too, is illustrated in Figure IX. All consumers located east of c_1c_1' should consume good 1. In mixed bundling equilibrium, though, it is individuals northeast of $FAEp_1^*$ who in fact consume good 1. If $FABc_1'$ contains more customers than does $c_1BEp_1^*$, then good 1 is oversupplied. If not, the reverse is true. Economically, a necessary if insufficient condition for oversupply of good 1 is that equilibrium prices bear the relationship $p_B^* - p_2^* < c_1$ so that the shadow price of good 1 when consumed in bundles is less than its opportunity cost. By similar reasoning the necessary and sufficient[25] conditions for undersupply of good 1 are $p_1^* > c_1$ and $p_B^* - p_2^* > c_1$. Since the same logic prevails in analyzing good 2, commodity bundling can lead to oversupply of both commodities, undersupply of both commodities, or oversupply of one and undersupply of the other. Figure V illustrates the first possibility, Figures VI and VII illustrate the second, while Figure IX could be used to illustrate the last.[26] That monopolists can produce too much as well as too little output implies that the conventional view of monopoly output lacks general validity.

The welfare implications of bundling of the toothpaste variety are identical to those of the restaurant variety: both distributive inefficiency and allocative inefficiency typically occur, and equilibrium output might exceed optimal output. Therefore, no separate treatment of this case is required.

Bundling of the automobile variety, however, does possess distinctive normative characteristics. These can be illustrated in Figure

24. Whenever bundling occurs, the shadow price an individual faces for one commodity depends on his reservation price for the other commodity. Hence shadow prices on particular goods typically differ among consumers. This is what can lead to distributive inefficiency.

25. Sufficient as long as the mixed bundling equilibrium violates Inclusion in any way.

26. In Figure IX good 1 can be either oversupplied or undersupplied, but good 2 must, by construction, be undersupplied.

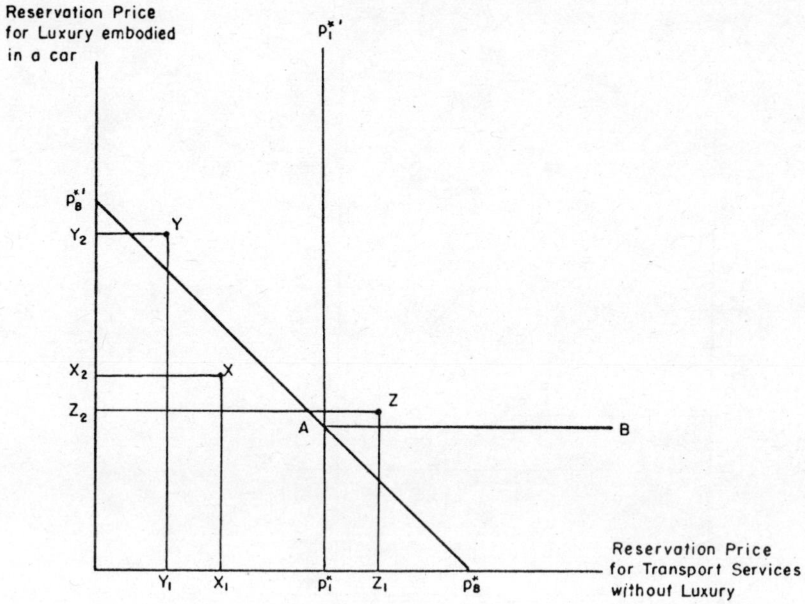

FIGURE X

X. If both the basic car and the luxury car are offered at prices p_1^* and p_B^*, respectively, individuals in the area southeast of p_1^*AB consume the basic car, and individuals northeast of $p_B^{*\prime}AB$ consume the luxury car. Because luxury is valued only by those who also consume transport services, no mutually beneficial trades among potential customers are possible, even though some who do not consume a commodity value it more highly than others who do. For example, X values transport more highly than does Y, and luxury more highly than does Z. Nevertheless, Y would not sell the transport services of his car to X at a price of Y_1, even if he could retain the luxury (e.g., in the form of chrome).[27] For the same reason, X would be unwilling to pay X_2 for the chrome of Z's car if that chrome were disembodied from the vehicle. Thus, no distributive inefficiency results from bundling in the car-type situation.

Allocative inefficiency is possible, however, even if some components cannot be disembodied from the bundle. This can be illustrated in Figure XI. In this situation A, B, and C should consume a luxury car, while D, E, and F should consume a basic car. The mo-

27. This follows from our assumption that no individual has a positive reservation price for chrome when disembodied from transport services.

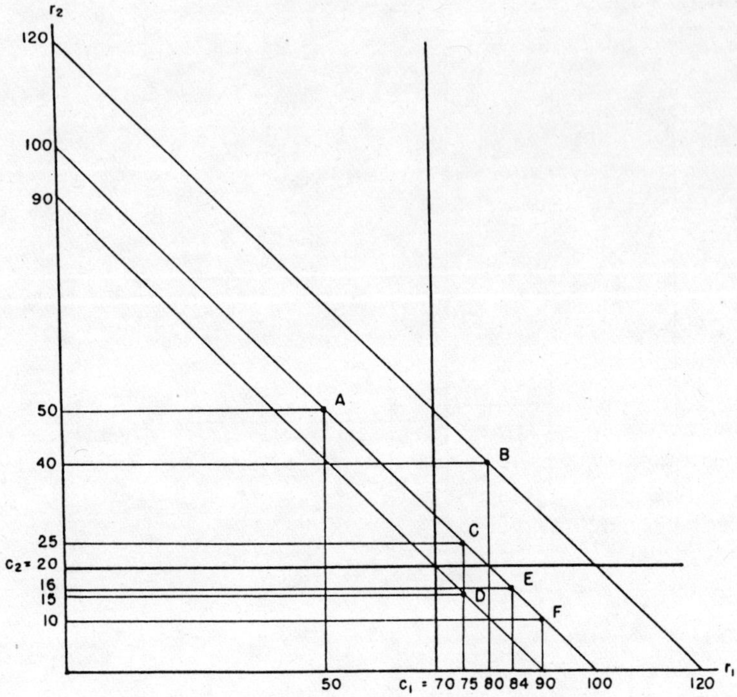

	p_1^*	p_2^*	p_B^*	Profits
Pure Component Strategy (Sale of good 1 alone)	80	—	—	30
Pure Bundling Strategy	—	—	100	50
Mixed Bundling Strategy (Sale of bundle + good 1 alone)	90	—	100	60

FIGURE XI

nopolist's profit-maximizing strategy, however, results in *A*, *B*, *C*, and *E* consuming the luxury car, *F* consuming the basic car, and *D* consuming nothing. Hence luxury is oversupplied, while transport services are undersupplied by the firm. More generally, in cases of the automobile type basic transport is never oversupplied, although the production of luxury can either exceed or fall short of ideal output.

In sum, commodity bundling generally leads to welfare losses when compared with perfect competition. But this does not imply that banning package selling per se decreases the burden of monopoly. In

Figure V, for example, mixed bundling is the most profitable strategy. The associated deadweight welfare loss is 7.[28] If bundling were prohibited and the monopolist forced to adopt a pure components strategy, the associated welfare loss would be 60 instead. Thus, prohibition of bundling without more might make society worse off. In fact, within the framework of our model, whenever mixed bundling is equivalent to pure price discrimination, it is Pareto optimal. Simple monopoly pricing never is. The possibility that mixed bundling is Pareto optimal is illustrated in Figure IV.

The deadweight loss associated with bundling might also exceed the corresponding loss associated with simple monopoly pricing. This possibility is illustrated in Figure VII. The profit-maximizing strategy for a monopolist is mixed bundling. And yet, the deadweight loss associated with that strategy (i.e., 10) exceeds that associated with the most profitable pure components strategy (i.e., 8). In this case, therefore, inability to bundle on the part of the monopolist would decrease the burden of monopoly.

IV. Implications and Conclusion

In the movie *Five Easy Pieces,* Jack Nicholson enters a diner to purchase some toast and coffee. The waitress informs him that toast alone is not available, even though both bread and toaster are on the premises. Nicholson is forced to order a chicken salad sandwich without chicken, lettuce, or mayonnaise.

Our purpose here has been to explain this and other forms of commodity bundling, such as vacation packages, chrome on cars, and quantity discounts. We have demonstrated that a monopolist's urge to charge customers their reservation prices for each of his products could lead to package selling. We have also demonstrated that bundling is inefficient by Pareto standards: it can lead to oversupply or undersupply of particular goods, and it can lead to the wrong people consuming each good. In this section we present some implications of commodity bundling for public policy analysis.

The first step in social appraisal of monopoly is to ascertain the sources and magnitude of the welfare loss it generates. That is the function of certain tools of applied welfare economics, such as consumer-producer surplus analysis and hedonic price indices. Unfortunately, the reliability of both such tools is seriously jeopardized when monopolists practice commodity bundling.

28. We calculated welfare loss as follows: the total loss is equal to the difference between consumer surplus in pure competition and the sum of consumer surplus and profits in the monopoly equilibrium.

Looking first at consumer-producer surplus analysis, we estimate the burden of monopoly as

$$\Delta W = \int_0^{z^*} \sum_i D_i(z) \frac{\partial x_i}{\partial z} dz, \tag{1}$$

where D_i represents the excess of marginal social benefit over marginal social cost per unit level of activity i, x_i represents the number of units of activity i, and z denotes the extent of monopoly power. In effect, this formula measures the excess of consumer surplus lost over producer surplus gained from simple monopoly, as compared with competitive, pricing.

Where monopolists practice commodity bundling, equation (1) has two defects. First, it focuses exclusively on allocative inefficiency, ignoring the distributive inefficiency characteristic of the situation. Second, the formula is inaccurate even in its estimation of allocative inefficiency. To take the simplest and most dramatic example, assume that individuals are uniformly distributed in reservation price space along the line $r_1 + r_2 = 1$, and that both component costs are positive. Suppose also that the monopolist adopts a pure bundling strategy.[29] The profit-maximizing price is $P_B^* = 1$, and all individuals consume the package. Resource misallocation exists, since some consumers have reservation prices below cost for one component, while other consumers have reservation prices below cost for the other component. No distributive inefficiency exists. Yet as long as equation (1) is applied at the bundle level, $\partial x_i / \partial z = 0$, so that estimated welfare loss is zero. This follows from the fact that the bundle demand curve is completely inelastic at prices below unity; hence the usual "triangle" measuring the deadweight loss vanishes entirely. In this example the formula not only underestimates welfare loss but fails even to detect its presence.

These defects of the consumer-producer surplus approach have two implications for public policy analysis. First, society may be unaware of the true extent of the burden of monopoly.[30] Second, even if society knows the extent of welfare loss, it may fail to pinpoint its source.[31] This could set governments on the wrong policy track, since

29. Mixed bundling generates more profits in this situation, but its appraisal via equation (1) is more complicated.

30. The Harberger formula provides neither a floor nor a ceiling to the true burden of monopoly; it can be shown that in situations where bundling is profitable, deadweight loss can be overestimated or underestimated by equation (1).

31. Conceptually, the loss associated with allocative inefficiency should be measured as the net gain in producer and consumer surplus that results from increasing (decreasing) component outputs to their optimal levels, given the correct distribution of output among individuals. The loss associated with distributive inefficiency should be measured as the net gain in consumer surplus that results from redistribution of existing output.

distributive inefficiency requires social intervention of a sort different from that designed to eliminate resource misallocation.

Commodity bundling also affects certain conclusions that may be drawn from hedonic price indices. The reason is that practitioners of that art often discuss whether consumers are willing to pay for the quality change they consume. The standard treatment is to suggest that consumers either are willing to pay for improvements they consume, or else are not fully understanding of the costs they bear.[32] Bundling analysis suggests a third explanation of why quality might be consumed. Some people value it highly; others do not. The seller finds it profitable to offer quality in a bundle with characteristics consumers uninterested in quality wish to have. As a result, not everyone who buys quality is willing to pay for it. The normative interpretation of quality indices would accordingly seem ambiguous.

Once the sources and extent of welfare loss have been ascertained, the second step in policy analysis is to determine whether public intervention can reduce the loss. If goods sold in the market place cannot be decomposed for separate purchase, for example, government is powerless to stop the evils of bundling.[33] To the extent that package goods can be decomposed, however, it becomes possible to guarantee that shadow prices on all components are the same for all customers. Hence the distributive inefficiency of bundling could be prevented. Moreover, pure components selling could reduce the waste associated with individuals consuming commodities for which they are unwilling to pay cost. Hence at least some of the allocative inefficiency of bundling could also be prevented.

What specifically, then, should governments do? Clearly they must embark on policies that achieve competitive supply of each

32. Consider, for example, the stance adopted in F. Fisher, Z. Griliches, and C. Kaysen, "The Costs of Automobile Model Changes Since 1949," *Journal of Political Economy,* LXX (Oct. 1962), 433–51. In discussing consumer expenditures on automobile model changes, they assert that "the model changes of the last decade seem to have been largely those desired by the consuming public, at least until the last years of the horsepower race. There are thus grounds for believing that car owners (at the time of purchase) thought model changes worth most of the cost. The general presumption of consumer sovereignty thus implies that these model changes *were* worth their cost" (p. 450). But they also aver that "the fact that model change costs for the late 1950's (about $700 in the purchase price per car, or more than 25 percent, and $40 per year in gasoline expenses) will probably seem surprisingly high to consumers is an indication that the costs in question were not fully understood by the consuming public" (p. 450).

33. Where no component can be sold separately, bundling is equivalent to the Lancaster formulation of consumer theory. See K. Lancaster, "A New Approach to Consumer Theory," *Journal of Political Economy,* LXXIV (April 1966) 132–57. Apart from the differences in normative interpretation, our model can be distinguished from Lancaster's in the sense that we provide some explanation for the range of products firms choose to offer in the market place. Our model integrates consumer and producer behavior.

decomposable good separately. As some have long, if unpopularly, argued, this might reduce rather than increase the output of firms with market power. The argument that modern industrial societies produce too much product differentiation need not rest on the hypothesis that advertising changes consumer tastes.

In any event public policy must take account of the fact that prohibition of commodity bundling without more may increase the burden of monopoly. This is consistent with the general theorem of second best: when one distortion exists (e.g., monopoly), elimination of other distortions (e.g., bundling) may either enhance or diminish social welfare. The implication is that monopoly itself must be eliminated to achieve high levels of social welfare.

UNIVERSITY OF MICHIGAN
HARVARD UNIVERSITY

[24]

THE ELECTRIC LAMP MONOPOLY AND THE LIFE OF ELECTRIC LAMPS

S. J. Prais*

BACKGROUND

The life of the commonly-used electric light bulb has been fixed at a standard of 1000 hours for over 50 years. Bulbs with a longer life can be manufactured at much the same cost, but at a loss in lighting efficiency, that is with a lower light-output per unit of electricity consumed. It has often been suggested that a longer length of life has not been chosen because manufacturers would lose in sales; and that manufacturers have been in a position to fix a shorter life as a result of national and international agreements. The manufacturers' answer given to the Monopolies Commission (embodied in their *Report* of 1968, paras. 578–84, and Appendix 7) was to the effect that the life-span chosen was calculated to be the best compromise from the point of view of the user, that is to say, if a longer life were chosen the loss in lighting efficiency would outweigh the saving in replacement costs of bulbs.

After looking at the calculations it seems to me that the Monopolies Commission should not have accepted the answer proffered; on correcting certain errors in the calculations it appears that consumers' interests would generally be better served by a bulb of much longer life—perhaps of 3000 hours, if we are to have a single standard. Long-life bulbs are manufactured in this country and sold for export (bulbs of 2500 hours life are made for Norway) and to certain large industrial customers (for example, 2000-hour bulbs are made for the Coal Board). The Monopolies Commission correctly recommended (1968, para. 101) that ordinary domestic consumers should be given the opportunity of buying these lamps in the usual retail shops, and while trade representatives insist that the 'double-life' bulbs made by Crompton are available, they are not widely available.[1]

* In preparing this note for publication I have benefited from comments on an earlier draft made by my colleagues at the Institute (especially by its Director, Mr. G. D. N. Worswick, and by Dr. G. Fane). I have also benefited from discussion with members of the trade but, for fear of associating them with views to which they may not subscribe in whole or in part, I trust this general expression of thanks will suffice.

[1] Readers of *Which* will know that British Home Stores and Curry's stock long-life bulbs; but my own enquiries at a wide range of stores in London (including the nationalized Electricity Board's shops) indicate that elsewhere they are very difficult to obtain.

From time to time the industry says that it offers 2000-hour bulbs to wholesalers who show 'no interest'. This happened in 1962 and, I gather, again in 1970. As the Monopolies Commission said (*Report* 1968, para. 97), 'In the absence of any advertising to the public, the reaction of wholesalers is not surprising'. Asking the industry to offer an alternative bulb which will lose the industry half its replacement sales is unlikely to meet with a wholehearted response on the part of industry; that is why, in my view, it is necessary to change the standard.

THE CORRECT FORMULA FOR LENGTH OF LIFE

The optimum life of a bulb depends on the ratio of the cost of replacing the bulb to the cost of running it per unit of time, such that the greater is this ratio, the longer is the optimum length of life. The Appendix to this note sets out the mathematical argument from which it follows that the optimum life is given by approximately *nine* times the replacement/running cost ratio. In the paper submitted to the Monopolies Commission, the multiple was put at only *six* times; the difference arose partly from a mathematical slip in the original paper, and partly from the neglect of an important relation between the wattage and lighting efficiency of a bulb (further details will be found in the Appendix).

If we accepted the relevance of the other assumptions made in the original paper we would conclude, at this stage of the argument, that the optimum length of life should be higher than the previously-accepted 1000 hours by a factor of 9 : 6, that is we would standardize the life of a bulb at 1500 hours. But, as we shall see, there are other considerations that raise the optimal life further.

THE INCONVENIENCE-COSTS OF REPLACING A BULB

It is easiest to proceed in terms of an example, by calculating the optimal life of a 60-watt bulb. The present (1973) retail price of such a bulb varies between 8p and 12p; let us take it as 10p. Domestic current is 1p per kW so that the cost of running it is 0·06p an hour. According to the formula, this implies an optimum life of $8{\cdot}75 \times 10 \div 0{\cdot}06 \simeq 1500$ hours. But if we are to be realistic in assessing the full replacement cost of a bulb, we must add to the out-of-pocket cost of a bulb, the value of the time spent in buying it and fixing it, including the time spent in removing and replacing the lampshade, the risk of breaking it and of bodily injury, and the cost of replacing a fuse which occasionally blows when the bulb burns out; and we must also include an allowance for the *annoyance* of finding yourself without light when the bulb burns out; and for the time lost of other persons who may be in the room, and whose work or leisure activity may be interrupted until a new bulb is fixed. Of course, this figure varies according to circumstances: for retired persons in good health, it may even be a pleasure to change a bulb;[2] for old people, climbing up a ladder is something to be avoided at all costs. Whatever single figure we choose will to some extent be arbitrary, but it is unlikely to be zero. A plausible average figure for the work and the annoyance seems to me to be of the order of 10 minutes; and I propose to value it at the present average wage in manufacturing of 75p an hour; this adds 12·5p to the cost of replacement, making a total of 22·5p. The optimum life

[2] This is not my view; but it is the kind of argument that has been put to me in seriousness by persons associated with the trade.

of a 60-watt bulb, according to the corrected formula is then extended to 3300 hours.

Some Further Examples

If we consider the commercial or industrial context, and allow for overheads (time of office and supervising staff, etc.), it may well be appropriate to allow a higher figure for the value of the time spent in replacement, and perhaps 20p may yet be conservative. If we take a 100-watt bulb costing, after commercial discount, also 10p, the total cost would be 30p—and the optimum length of life calculated from the formula would be 2600 hours.

If we consider special purpose bulbs, which are sold at high prices, very much longer optimal lives emerge. For example, internally silvered 100-watt floodlamps, of the kind used in modern commercial and some domestic fittings, retail at 87p; allowing for fitting costs, we come to a total of nearly £1. The optimal length of life would then be 9000 hours, or nine times as long as the nominal manufactured life; it seems particularly absurd that expensive bulbs of this sort should be made with a short life.

The most frequently used domestic bulbs are 40, 60 and 100 watts (which it will be assumed, can be bought at 8, 10, and 12p respectively); I have calculated a possible range of optimal lives that warrant consideration according to whether the inconvenience and time spent in replacing a bulb is low or high. For the 'low' estimate, I have taken 5 minutes and valued it half the average wage-rate assumed above; and for the 'high' estimate I have taken 10 minutes (as previously) and valued it at double the average wage-rate. The results are as follows:

Bulb	*Optimal length of life*
40 watts	2300–7200 hours
60 watts	1800–5100 hours
100 watts	1300–3200 hours

If in the interests of standardization it is necessary to choose a single compromise length of life, it seems clear enough that there is nothing to be said for choosing 1000 hours as that compromise. Since different filaments are in any case used for each wattage, there is nothing to be lost in terms of production costs in having a particular standard life for each wattage; if that were accepted (and I have not heard any serious arguments against it), one might choose something like 5000 hours for a 40 watt, 3000 hours for a 60 watt, and 2000 or 2500 hours for a 100 watt (the higher life would be appropriate if the price of the bulb were to be raised).

If, nevertheless, the trade insisted on a single optimum for bulbs of all wattages, 3000 hours might be chosen. A decision to accept a single standard life for all wattages would however warrant close scrutiny.

COSTS AND BENEFITS OF A LONGER LIFE BULB

A reduction in the number of replacement bulbs bought to about a third (or even a half) of the present level would amount to a very great increase in convenience to the consumer; it would also require very great changes in the industry, in that substantial resources would be released for other uses. The many consequential problems need not be considered in this note. It is, however, right to remind the reader that the convenience of fewer replacement bulbs will be paid for, to some extent, by higher electricity consumption; and this may be illustrated again in terms of our earlier example of a 60-watt bulb.

The cost of running a standard 1000-hour bulb over its lifetime would be 60p for current, *plus* 10p for the bulb, making 70p in all (the money value of inconvenience costs is ignored for the moment, but will be considered below). If this is replaced by a bulb with a 3000-hour life, we must allow the consumer to purchase a bulb of a higher rated wattage so that the same degree of illumination is achieved: in practice it may be that in some locations the consumer will be content with a lower illumination, and will retain a 60-watt bulb; but in others he may find it not quite bright enough, and will move to the next higher available wattage. For the purposes of a calculation of this type it seems adequate to take into account a notionally precise compensation by the choice of a higher average wattage; calculation suggests that a 68-watt bulb would be required.[3] The cost of running such a bulb for 1000 hours of its life would be 68p for current, *plus* about 3·3p for the amortized out-of-pocket cost of the bulb (=10p/3); if we ignore inconvenience costs this makes 71·3p in all. The consumer is therefore out of pocket by 1·3p, being the difference between an additional 8p spent on electricity and a saving of 6·7p in bulb costs; in proportionate terms, he has incurred an additional 2% in out-of-pocket costs for the convenience of reducing the number of his bulb-replacements by two-thirds.

But if we take into account also the value of the notional inconvenience costs of replacing a bulb, which we put at 12·5p above, the total costs of running a 1000-hour standard bulb are 82·5p; and those for running the longer-life bulb are 75·4p per 1000 hours. There is thus a notional saving of 7·1p, or 9% of the costs.

The above is an illustrative calculation for a standard 60-watt bulb. The savings for other types of bulb would vary: for standard bulbs of higher wattages the savings would be smaller; for standard bulbs of lower wattage the savings would be greater; and for special bulbs which sell at a premium the savings would be considerably greater.

[3] This follows from equation (2) in the Appendix; for a given degree of illumination, the required wattage is proportional to the length of life raised to the power 0·114 (= 1/8·75). It may be advantageous for long-life bulbs to be made for higher standard wattages to yield the same degree of illumination as the corresponding short-life bulb; but we need not go into this here.

There is therefore a case of abolishing the single 1000-hour standard life, in favour of a greater variety of lives, and requiring that they be made widely available to the public.

NATIONAL INSTITUTE OF ECONOMIC AND SOCIAL RESEARCH, LONDON

Mathematical Appendix[4]

The problem of finding the optimum length of life of a light bulb, in formal terms, is the familiar one of finding a minimum subject to a constraint (indeed, it provides a practical illustration of something that is treated in a generalized way in textbooks of mathematical economics). The cost per hour of running a bulb of wattage w, having a replacement cost of b pence, a length of life of t hours, and with current costing c pence per watt-hour, is

$$M = b/t + cw. \tag{1}$$

This has to be minimized subject to the technical relation between the light output of a bulb, measured in lumens, its wattage and its designed length of life, which may be written in general terms as

$$L = kt^{-\alpha}w^{1+\beta} \tag{2}$$

where k, α and β are constants. We are told that α may be taken as approximately 1/7 (Strange, p. 253), that is to say, a 10% lengthening in designed life is accompanied by a reduction in light-output of approximately $10/7 = 1{\cdot}4\%$. We find from published data (in the Monopolies Commission *Report*, 1968, p. 270) on the relation between light-output and wattage for a given length of life, that β may be taken as about 1/4; that is to say, a 10% increase in the wattage of the bulb is accompanied by a 12½% increase in light-output. (This is an average relation holding approximately in the range 40–150 watts for coiled-coil lamps: a slightly higher value may be appropriate at the lower end, and a slightly lower value at the upper end; for single-coil lamps $\beta \simeq 1/3$.) We need not concern ourselves with the constant k which does not affect the result.

To carry out the minimization we may proceed in one of two ways. The more elementary is to use (2) to express w in terms of t and L; and to substitute this expression for w in (1); we then differentiate M with respect to t. The alternative is to use a Lagrangean multiplier, and to differentiate (1) with respect to both t and w subject to the constraint (2). Both methods of course lead to the same result, which is that the optimum length of life is related to the wattage by the expression

$$T = \frac{1+\beta}{\alpha} \cdot \frac{b}{cw}. \tag{3}$$

Inserting the values of the constants noted above, this is approximately equal to $8{\cdot}75\ b/cw$ (for coiled-coil lamps; and $9{\cdot}33\ b/cw$ for single-coil lamps).

The essence of the method used in the paper submitted to the Monopolies Commission by Dr Strange is the same as the above; but there are the following differences. First, no notice is taken in that paper of the relation between light-output and wattage, which is equivalent to setting $\beta = 0$ in the expression above. This is not legitimate since the crux of the problem is to know how much greater is the required

[4] The technical and mathematical aspects summarized in this Appendix are considered at greater length in a companion Note (to appear in *Lighting Research and Technology*).

wattage of the bulb when we use one that has a longer life. By ignoring the higher efficiency of the higher wattage bulb, we overstate the costs (in terms of wattage) of increasing the designed life of the bulb, and therefore obtain a result which gives a too low length of life. On the assumption that $\beta = 0$, the optimum length of life can be seen from (3) above to be given by

$$T' = \frac{1}{\alpha} \cdot \frac{b}{cw} \simeq 7\ b/cw. \tag{3'}$$

Secondly, however, there is an error in the mathematics of Dr. Strange's paper which leads him not to (3′) but to the result

$$T'' = \left(\frac{1}{\alpha} - 1\right) \cdot \frac{b}{cw} \simeq 6\ b/cw. \tag{3''}$$

The error arises because at a certain stage in the minimization (equation (8) on page 253 of his paper) he treats w as a constant; but this is not legitimate. (I appreciate of course, that the problem of finding the optimum value of t for a given w is not without interest as an abstract problem; but that is not the problem that we are interested in here.) The consumer, in principle, must be presumed to be able to vary both w and t in order to achieve his desired level of L at minimum cost per hour.

The difference between (3) and (3″) is approximately as 8·75 : 6 (for coiled-coil lamps): that is, our method gives a 46% longer life (for single-coil, the excess is 56%).

The third difference is related not to the logic, but to the facts, and depends on how we define b, the cost of replacing a bulb. In my view a realistic allowance has to be made for the value of the time spent in buying and fixing the bulb. This aspect is discussed in the main paper.

REFERENCE

STRANGE, J. W., 'A technical paper on the economic life of incandescent lamps', Appendix 7 to the *Second Report on the Supply of Electric Lamps* by the Monopolies Commission (H.M.S.O., 1968).

Part V
Increasing Returns and Natural Monopoly

On the Proper Cost Tests for Natural Monopoly in a Multiproduct Industry

By WILLIAM J. BAUMOL*

The literature is generally somewhat vague on the circumstances in which monopoly offers cost advantage over production by a multiplicity of firms. The sense of the discussion seems to be that monopoly will be "natural,"[1] that is, it can provide outputs at lower social costs, when and only when the industry has economies of scale. Perhaps the most unexpected finding of this paper is that *scale economies are neither necessary nor sufficient for monopoly to be the least costly form of productive organization.* Rather, the critical concept is (by definition) strict subadditivity of the cost function, meaning that the cost of the sum of any m output vectors is less than the sum of the costs of producing them separately. Since subadditivity is a mathematical concept whose properties do not seem to have been explored fully, a good part of our task will be the characterization of subadditive cost functions and their relation to more conventional concepts such as declining average costs (which, as we will see, it is inaccurate to equate to scale economies).

I

My discussion will begin with the single product firm. For these we will show that evidence of scale economies is always *sufficient* but *not necessary* to prove subadditivity. That is, it is (much) too demanding a test of natural monopoly to require evidence of scale economies or declining average costs, *even in the neighborhood of current output levels.* Nevertheless, if anything, our analysis makes it harder to prove that a particular monopoly is natural, even in the single product case. For it turns out that proof of subadditivity requires a *global* description of the shape of the *entire* cost function from the origin up to the output in question, thus calling for data that may lie well beyond the range of recorded experience.

When we turn to the multiproduct case we will find that sufficient conditions for subadditivity must include some sort of complementarity in the production of the different outputs of the industry which corresponds to a type of convexity to be specified in the next section.

Our discussion will proceed on the assumption that the menu of available techniques is fixed (no technological change), that exactly the same menu of techniques is available to the monopolist and to each of its potential competitors, *and that all input prices are fixed.*[2]

*Professor of economics, Princeton and New York universities. This paper was prepared under the sponsorship of the Division of Science Information of the National Science Foundation as part of a study of scale economies and public good elements in information transfer. The writing of this paper was very much a group undertaking with the most critical contributions made by Elizabeth Bailey and Dietrich Fischer. Important suggestions were also made by M.I. Nadiri, Janusz Ordover, Thijs ten Raa, Michael Rothschild, and Robert Willig as the analysis gradually evolved.

[1]For an interesting discussion of the origins of the concept and the term see Edward Lowry.

[2]Since we assume all input prices, w, to be constant, the cost function $C(y, w)$ can be written simply as $C(y)$, where y is the vector of outputs. Input prices are taken to be constant because an industry may be a natural monopoly at one set of input prices and not at another. For example, where capital is cheap relative to labor, single firm production may be cheapest, while the reverse may be true where low wages call for production techniques that are not capital intensive. Therefore, it seems to me that the appropriate test to determine whether an industry is *now* a natural monopoly must indicate whether it is the least costly market form at (or in the neighborhood of) current input prices. To require this to be true for all input prices would be far too restrictive.

II. Definitions[3]

A rather tedious section on definitions is unavoidable because some of the concepts have not been used widely in the literature and the extension of others to the n-product case is not entirely straightforward.

There seems to be some ambiguity in the term "natural monopoly" which is used to refer to one or both of two circumstances:[4]

a) An industry in which multifirm production is more costly than production by a monopoly (subadditivity of the cost function).

b) An industry to which entrants are *not* "naturally" attracted, and are incapable of survival even in the absence of "predatory" measures by the monopolist (sustainability of monopoly).

This article deals exclusively with the first of these concepts, leaving the issue of sustainability to other papers. (See Faulhaber 1975a; Baumol, Bailey, and Willig; John Panzar and Willig 1975b.)

Accordingly, we begin our formal definitions with our basic criterion of natural monopoly which is given by

DEFINITION 1: *Strict and Global Subadditivity of Costs.* A cost function $C(y)$ is strictly and globally subadditive in the set of commodities $N = 1, \ldots, n$, if for any m output vectors $y^1, \ldots, y^m$ of the goods in N we have

$$C(y^1 + \ldots + y^m) < C(y^1) + \ldots + C(y^m)$$

This is clearly the necessary and sufficient condition for natural monopoly of any output combination in the industry producing (any and all) commodities in N, for subadditivity means that it is always cheaper to have a single firm produce whatever combination of outputs is supplied to the market, and conversely.

Of course, it is possible that for some output vectors an industry will be a natural monopoly while for others it will not. In such a case we have output-specific subadditivity, meaning that the pertinent output vector y^* is produced more cheaply by one firm than by any combination of smaller firms.

We must also define precisely the other pertinent cost attributes, all of which acquire somewhat novel features in an n-product firm or industry. We begin with

DEFINITION 2: *Strict Economies of Scale* in the production of outputs in N are present if for any initial input-output vector $(x_1, \ldots, x_r, y_1, \ldots, y_n)$ and for any $w > 1$, there is a feasible input-output vector[5] $(wx_1, \ldots, wx_r, v_1y_1, \ldots, v_ny_n)$ where all $v_i \geq w + \delta, \delta > 0$.

This definition in effect tests for scale economies by considering any w-fold expansion in all input quantities, and requiring that it permit *at least* a $w + \delta$-fold proportionate increase in each output. Note that if the production function is not homothetic *the firm may not wish to expand its input usage proportionately*, and depending on demand relationships, it certainly may not want to increase its *outputs* proportionately. Thus, our criterion of scale economies is expressed entirely in terms of hypothetical increases in input and output quantities along rays in input and output spaces, respectively.

Declining average costs, a concept usually associated with scale economies, is not so readily extended to a multiplicity of outputs. The problem, of course, is that if outputs do *not* expand proportionately we do not know how to define an index of aggregate output by which to divide total cost, nor do we have any way of apportioning

[3] For a fundamental article covering ground related to much of the substance of this paper see Peter Newman. For illuminating discussions of some of the definitional problems in this area and some related matters see also Giora Hanoch (1970, 1975) and also W. W. Sharkey and L. G. Telser.

[4] See, for example, Richard Posner. Gerald Faulhaber (1975a) has shown with the aid of ingenious and illuminating counterexamples that the two conditions are not equivalent; specifically that condition a) does not imply satisfaction of condition b). Baumol, Elizabeth Bailey, and Robert Willig have demonstrated the converse—that b) does imply a).

[5] I write v_i rather than v to allow for the case where *proportionate* expansion of outputs is not possible. If we assume free disposal then there is no need to do so, since if the percentage increases in some outputs were to exceed $w + \delta$ we could simply get rid of the excess.

joint and common costs so as to calculate an average cost, item by item.[6] For our purposes, however, it will suffice to deal only with the special case in which output quantities all happen to vary proportionately *but input quantities follow the least-cost expansion path*, which in general does not involve proportionate changes in input quantities. Accordingly, we formulate

DEFINITION 3: *Ray Average Costs* (*RAC*) are *strictly declining* when

$$(1)\quad C(vy_1,\dots,vy_n)/v < C(wy_1,\dots,wy_n)/w \text{ for } v > w$$

where v and w are measures of the scale of output along the ray through

$$y = (y_1,\dots,y_n)$$

As Definitions 2 and 3 clearly show, scale economies and declining average costs in the sense we have used it, are both ray-specific properties. We will use one other ray-specific property:

DEFINITION 4: *Ray Concavity*. A cost function $C(y)$ is strictly output-ray concave (marginal costs of output *bundles* everywhere decreasing) if

$$(2)\quad C[kv_1y + (1-k)v_2y] > kC(v_1y) + (1-k)C(v_2y)$$

for any

$$v_1, v_2 \geq 0, \qquad v_1 \neq v_2, \qquad 0 < k < 1$$

This definition can be extended in an obvious way to m rather than two output vectors. The parameters v_1 and v_2 simply assure us that v_1y and v_2y are two output vectors that lie on the same ray (their outputs are proportional). The parameter k plays its usual role in the standard definition of concavity.

In the n-output case we must also have a way of characterizing the behavior of costs as output *proportions* vary. One pattern of such "transray" behavior will prove critical for our analysis. This concept is perhaps best described as a new formal interpretation of the phenomenon of complementarity in the production of the various goods and services supplied by the firm. We call a cost function *transray convex* at output vector $y = (y_1,\dots,y_n)$ if along at least one hyperplane through y, $\Sigma w_iy_i = w$, a weighted average of the costs of producing separately any two output vectors on this hyperplane is no less than the cost of producing any weighted average of those two outputs *together*. That is, in geometric terms, a total cost function is transray convex at y if along some negatively sloping cross section through y in output space, costs are lower (no higher) toward the interior of the cross section than they are toward its edges (curve $C^*C^{*\prime}$ in Figure 4b), so that it is no more expensive to produce goods in combination rather than separately. More formally:

DEFINITION 5: *Transray Convexity*. A cost function $C(y)$ will be called transray convex through $y^* = (y_1^*,\dots,y_n^*)$ if there exists any set of positive constants $w_1,\dots,w_n$, such that for every two output vectors $y^a = (y_{1a},\dots,y_{na})$, $y^b = (y_{1b},\dots,y_{nb})$ lying in the same hyperplane Σw_iy_i through y^*, that is, for which $\sum_i w_i y_{ia} = \sum_i w_i y_{ib} = \sum_i w_i y_i^*$, we have

$$(3)\quad C[ky^a + (1-k)y^b] \leq kC(y^a) + (1-k)C(y^b)$$

for any k, $\quad 0 < k < 1$

This concept is closely related to what Panzar and Willig have named "economies of scope," in contradistinction to economies of scale.

Together, the concepts of strictly declining ray average costs and that of transray convexity turn out to be an extremely powerful combination offering us a new characterization of a cost function that is well behaved for a number of analytical purposes. We will see later (Proposition 12) that they are sufficient for subadditivity of costs. Moreover, in a closely related paper (Baumol, Bailey, and Willig), it is shown

[6]However, there is a natural extension of the concept of declining average *variable* cost of one individual product to the multioutput case. See the author (1976).

that these go far toward giving us conditions sufficient for the existence of some monopoly prices that are sustainable against entry. It may be suspected that they will prove to have many other analytical implications.

III. Some Interrelationships Among the Cost Concepts

Having completed the tedious task of definition of our concepts, I can now summarize their relationships briefly, indicating which of them implies which. This is done in outline in Figure 1 which shows that global scale economies and decreasing ray average costs imply subadditivity along a ray, but that the former are not necessary for the latter. Moreover, they are neither sufficient nor necessary either for strict and global subadditivity, or for strict and output-specific subadditivity, the requirements for natural monopoly in an n-product industry.

We now proceed to prove some of the propositions underlying Figure 1. Before turning to the central issue of subadditivity we must explore briefly a few relationships among scale economies, ray concavity, and declining ray average costs. Among these cost concepts, scale economies occupies a position by itself, because all the others assume that inputs adjust optimally to output changes, that is, inputs are taken to follow along the expansion path of least costs. On the other hand, the concept of scale economies requires inputs to change proportionately, and in general, this will not minimize the cost of an expansion. (See, for example, Hanoch, 1975.) Thus, if unit cost decreases when inputs are increased *proportionately*, they must certainly decrease along the least cost expansion path. This should at least suggest the logic of a result which I have proven elsewhere (1976):

PROPOSITION 1: *Strict economies of scale are sufficient but not necessary for ray aver-*

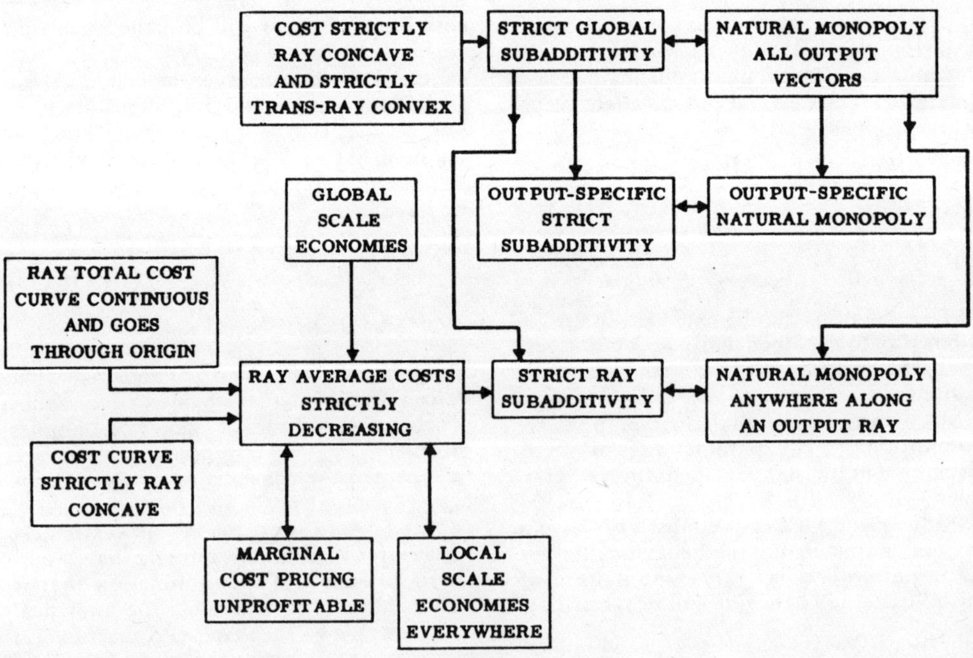

FIGURE 1

age cost to be strictly declining.

We also have a relation between strict concavity and ray average costs:

PROPOSITION 2: *Strict ray concavity (declining marginal cost) of the cost function $C(y)$ and $C(0) = 0$ after subtraction of any fixed costs, are sufficient but not necessary for ray average costs to decline.*

PROOF:
By the definition of strict ray concavity we have by (2) for $v_1 = 1, v_2 = 0$,

(4) $C(ky) > kC(y)$ for $0 < k < 1$

which is criterion (1) of declining ray average cost.

Since it is well known that average costs can fall even when marginal costs are rising (nonconcavity in total cost), the result follows.

IV. Ray Subadditivity and its Relation to Other Cost Attributes[7]

Since subadditivity is the defining attribute of a natural monopoly, the heart of our task consists in the analysis of this property and its relation to the other cost attributes. The next few sections deal with scale behavior—subadditivity along a ray—leaving the true multiproduct case until later. First we prove

PROPOSITION 3: *Strictly declining ray average cost implies strict ray subadditivity.*

PROOF:
Consider the n output vectors $v_1 y, \ldots, v_n y$ along the same ray, all $v_i > 0$. By the definition of ray average costs that are strictly declining

(5) $C(\Sigma v_j y)/\Sigma v_j < C(v_i y)/v_i \qquad (i = 1, \ldots, n)$

Consequently, $C(\Sigma v_j y)/\Sigma v_j$ is less than a weighted average of the $C(v_i y)/v_i$, i.e.,

$$\frac{C(\Sigma v_j y)}{\Sigma v_j} < \sum \frac{v_i}{\Sigma v_j} \frac{C(v_i y)}{v_i} = \frac{\Sigma C(v_j y)}{\Sigma v_j}$$

which immediately yields our subadditivity result

$$C(\Sigma v_j y) < \Sigma C(v_j y)$$

It also follows from Propositions 2 and 3 that strict ray concavity, along with $C(0) = 0$, is sufficient for strict ray subadditivity. However, as I will show now, the converse does not hold—ray subadditivity is *not* sufficient either for ray concavity, or for declining ray average cost.

It is easy to produce the necessary counterexamples to prove this negative result—cost functions that are strictly ray subadditive and yet not ray concave throughout, and for which ray average cost does not decline throughout. An extreme case is shown in Figure 2a—the piecewise-linear cost function $OABDC$. This is clearly *not* concave, as is shown by the portion of the cost curve which lies below line segment WS. Similarly, average cost *increases* along part of the cost curve: output y_s is greater than y_r, yet the slope of ray OS is greater than the slope of OR so that ray average cost at y_s is greater than ray average cost at y_r.

To complete the argument I must now show that the cost function is strictly subadditive. A moment's consideration shows why this is so. In the case depicted, total cost for any output produced by one firm alone cannot exceed $OA + BD$. Similarly, total cost of any output produced by two or more firms in any way cannot be less than $2(OA)$, the fixed costs of two firms together. Since in our cost function $OA > BD$, we have: total cost of any output by a single firm $\leq OA + BD < 2(OA) \leq$ total cost of production by more than one firm.

We have thus proved by counterexample our desired result:

PROPOSITION 4: *Neither ray concavity nor ray average costs that decline everywhere are necessary for strict subadditivity.*

We may note also that while the extreme case shown in Figure 2a makes the proof

[7]A number of results in this section were first derived by Faulhaber (1975b).

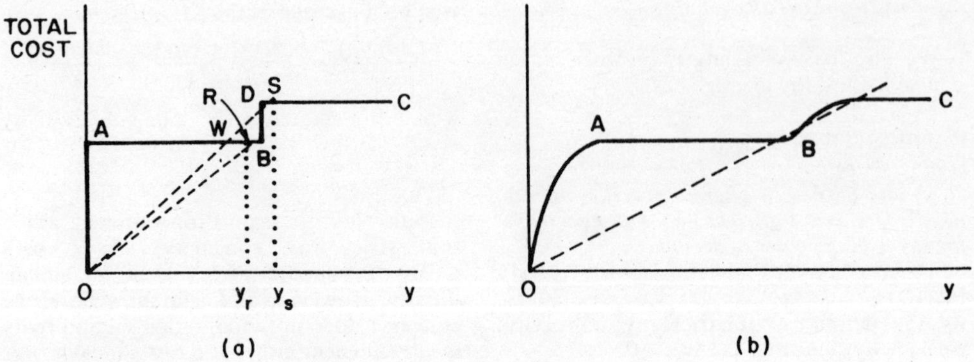

FIGURE 2

easier, less restrictive counterexamples are easy to supply. By including a series of steps in the graph of the cost function instead of the single step of Figure 2a, one can clearly produce a subadditive cost function in which average costs are rising at a number of intervals. Moreover, as Figure 2b illustrates, intervals of rising ray average costs are compatible with a completely smooth cost function that is strictly subadditive.

From Propositions 3 and 4, and since by Proposition 1 economies of scale are sufficient for decreasing ray average costs, we immediately have the following key result:

PROPOSITION 5: *Global scale economies are sufficient but not necessary for (strict) ray subadditivity, the condition for natural monopoly in the production of a single product or in any bundle of outputs produced in fixed proportions.*

V. On Characterization of Ray Subadditivity

Before going further it is appropriate to say something about the characteristics of subadditive (cost) curves. We have seen that they need not be concave, nor need they exhibit declining average costs. What then do they look like in general? Three necessary conditions for subadditivity in a two-dimensional graph may offer the reader some of the pertinent flavor. First we have

PROPOSITION 6: *Strict subadditivity along a ray implies that for any output vector, y, in that ray, $C(y) < vC(y/v)$ for v any integer ≥ 2. That is, for any such integer v, ray average cost must on the average decrease over the interval between y/v and y.*

This result follows from the definition of subadditivity which requires, for example, for $v = 3$, that $C(y) < C(y/3) + C(y/3) + C(y/3) = 3C(y/3)$ and a similar expression obviously holds for any other integer value of v. Thus, in Figure 3a the height of our cost curve at output y^* is C^*. This gives us $C^*/2$, $C^*/3$, $C^*/4$, etc., as respective *floors* for total costs for outputs $y^*/2$, $y^*/3$, $y^*/4$, etc., as indicated by the heights of the vertical line segments. If the cost function is to be subadditive, then at output level $y^*/2$ total cost must be represented by some point such as D which is *above* $C^*/2$, and the analogous observation applies to points B and A.

PROPOSITION 7: *If a function $C(y)$ is strictly subadditive, nonnegative and increasing in value along a ray, then either $c(0) > 0$ or the function must be strictly concave for y in the neighborhood of the origin.*

For suppose $C(0) = 0$, writing $k = 1/v < 1$ in Proposition 6 we have $kC(y) < C(ky)$ in the neighborhood of $k = 0$. But $kC(y) \equiv (1 - k)C(0) + kC(y)$ and $C(ky) \equiv C[(1 - k)0 + ky]$. Consequently, in the limit as k approaches zero we must

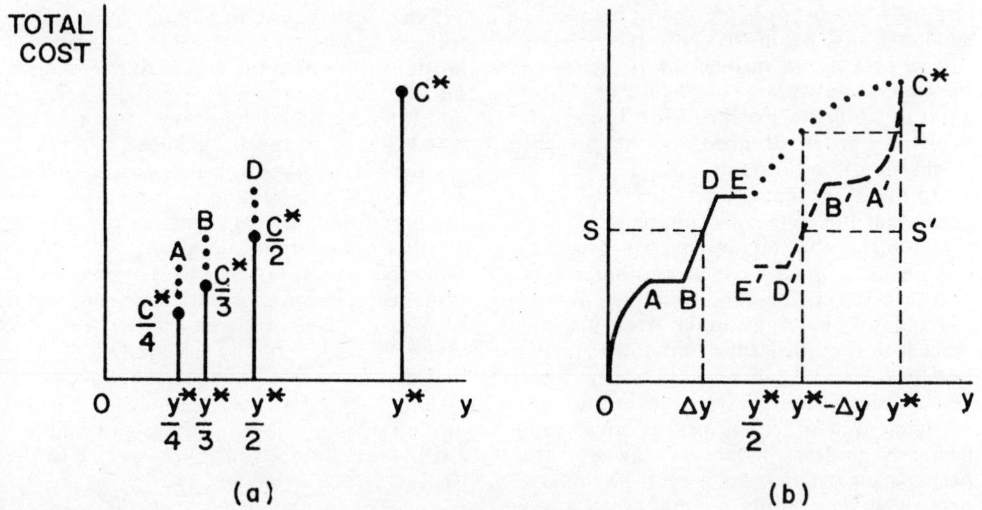

FIGURE 3

satisfy the requirement of strict concavity

$$(1 - k)C(0) + kC(y) < C[(1 - k)0 + ky]$$

A third necessary condition for subadditivity is given by

PROPOSITION 8 (Dietrich Fischer): *If $C(y)$ is strictly subadditive along a ray and y^* is any particular output vector on that ray, with $C(y^*) = C^*$, then the graph of $C(y^* - \Delta y)$ in the interval $y^*/2 \leq y^* - \Delta y \leq y^*$ must everywhere lie above the inverted*[8] *mirror image of $C(\Delta y)$ in the interval $0 \leq \Delta y \leq y^*/2$. That is, since by subadditivity $C(y^* - \Delta y) + C(\Delta y) > C(y^*)$, then*

$$(6) \quad C(y^* - \Delta y) > C(y^*) - C(\Delta y)$$

As (6) shows, Proposition 8 follows directly from the definition of subadditivity. Condition (6) also tells us, incidentally, that with subadditivity the increment in total cost resulting from an addition Δy to an output, must be less than the cost $C(\Delta y)$ of producing that addition all by itself (its "stand-alone cost").

Figure 3b indicates more explicitly the graphic implications of Proposition 8. Let the total cost curve in the interval between $y = 0$ and $y = y^*/2$ be *OABDE*. Now starting from C^*, the cost corresponding to y^*, draw (backwards) the curve $E'D'B'A'C^*$ which is the "upside-down" mirror image of *OABDE*. For example, with concave arc *OA* curving upward and to the right from *O*, arc C^*A' will be convex and curve downward and to the left from C^*. Now, Proposition 8 requires that the actual cost curve over the interval between $y^*/2$ and y^* (dotted curve EC^*) must everywhere lie above $E'D'B'A'C^*$.

This requirement is designed to assure us that the "incremental cost" IC^* of adding output Δy to output $y^* - \Delta y$ is less than the stand-alone cost *OS* of producing output Δy by itself, since, by construction, $OS = S'C^* > IC^*$.

VI. Some Implications for Evidence on Natural Monopoly

Propositions 6, 7, and 8 show that to test whether subadditivity is satisfied *just at a particular output level*, y^*, we can *not* examine only the cost curve in the vicinity of y^*. Because a claim of natural monopoly asserts that production by a single firm is cheaper than it would be in the hands of

[8] The center of inversion is the point $(y^*/2, C^*/2)$.

any and every possible combination of smaller firms, we must know the behavior of the cost curve *throughout its length in the interval between the origin and* y^*. This is a rather difficult prospect for those who bear the burden of proof of the presence or absence of natural monopoly!

On the other hand, Propositions 4 and 5 imply that the tests sometimes suggested to evaluate the cost advantages or disadvantages of monopoly have in another respect been excessively demanding. In a number of regulatory hearings, much stress has been placed on the allegation that the regulated firm in question had reached a size where "economies of scale have been exhausted," implying that since output is now being produced under constant ray average and perhaps marginal costs, several firms can provide it as cheaply as one. But this is simply not true in general (on this see, for example, Seneca). Indeed, it is easy to see that single firm production will always be cheaper so long as average costs decline strictly monotonically up to any output $(y^*/2) + \Delta$ for any $\Delta > 0$ and are level thereafter, where y^* is total industry production. For if two more firms were to provide the commodity instead, at least one such firm must produce no more than half of industry output and must therefore incur average costs greater than the minimum average cost attainable. That is,

PROPOSITION 9: *A condition sufficient for strict and output-specific subadditivity along a ray is that, with* y^* *the given output vector of the industry, ray average cost declines strictly throughout the interval between zero and* $y^*/2 + \Delta$ *for some* $\Delta > 0$, *and that it declines or remains constant in the interval to the right of* $y^*/2 + \Delta$ *and through* y^*.

VII. Transray Behavior and Multiproduct Subadditivity

From the single product case, we turn finally to the conditions under which a single firm is the most efficient supplier of *all* the products provided by some industry or at least of some specified subset of those outputs.

Since scale economies refer only to the technical gains from increases in volume of output rather than those accruing from production of several goods together, it is obvious that by themselves they cannot tell us whether it is cheaper to produce two different output bundles separately or together. The issue is one relating to the behavior of the cost function from one output ray to another, rather than along any one ray. It is therefore naturally to be suspected that evidence of the presence of scale economies will be insufficient to guarantee what we may refer to as transray subadditivity.

If that were all there is to the matter, the insufficiency of scale economies for natural monopoly might seem a trivial and uninteresting observation. But there is more to the issue.

The obvious extension of the concept of scale economies to the entire cost function is concavity. Concavity is, after all, a rather strong assumption. But it is easy to show that even strict concavity is neither sufficient nor necessary for subadditivity in an n-product cost function. First we show:

PROPOSITION 10: *Strict concavity of a cost function is not sufficient to guarantee subadditivity.*

PROOF by counterexample:[9]

Consider the cost function in two outputs

$$C = y_1^a + y_1^k y_2^k + y_2^a \qquad 0 < a < 1$$
$$0 < k < 1/2$$

Since the sum of several concave functions is itself concave, it is clear that the cost function is strictly concave because of the values of k and a. However, we have for

[9] I am indebted for this counterexample to Dietrich Fischer. It may seem at first that a case of superadditivity such as that in the example cannot occur in reality since the firm which finds it more expensive to produce two items together will turn them out separately (in different plants). But administrative and communication costs can still make it more expensive to produce this way than in two totally independent firms. That is why, in reality, some industries are characterized by many small firms, each with their different specializations. The cost functions are such that the giant multiproduct firm just cannot compete.

example, for $y_1^* = y_2^* = 1$:

$$C(y_1^*, 0) = 1 \qquad C(0, y_2^*) = 1$$
$$C(y_1^*, y_2^*) = 3 > C(y_1^*, 0) + C(0, y_2^*) = 2$$

Hence the function is not subadditive.

We also have immediately the basic result

PROPOSITION 11: *Scale economies are neither necessary nor sufficient for subadditivity.*

Nonnecessity was already proved in Proposition 5. To show insufficiency we need merely take the production function implicit in the preceding example to involve a single input (whose quantity is x) and whose price p is fixed. Then substituting $C = px$ into the cost function we see that it obviously exhibits scale economies throughout even though it is not subadditive.

It must be emphasized that this example does not represent some sort of pathological exception. Rather, as we will see next, strict concavity of a cost function involves an attribute which works in the direction opposite to that called for to yield transray subadditivity.

The main issue is what sorts of departure from concavity favor subadditivity? The answer is suggested by Figures 4a and 4b. Figure 4a depicts a cost function represented by surface OCC' which is strictly concave and exhibits scale economies throughout. Three cross sections along rays Ra, Rb, and Rc show the characteristic concave shape and, hence, the declining average costs which we have seen to suffice for subadditivity along a ray.

However, despite the concavity *and the presence of scale economies*, the cross section $CABDC'$ taken across these rays tells quite a different story. Because its lowest points are reached at the y_1 and y_2 axes, this concave transray cross section favors production of commodities in isolation. That is, it makes for increased cost of production using common facilities. This is precisely the opposite of what is wanted for transray subadditivity (or for an *interior* cost minimum along a fixed iso-revenue curve, as is indicated by Figure 4c, the iso-cost map corresponding to Figure 4a). Rather, subadditivity is favored by a cost function which, because of complementarity in production, is shaped like that in Figure 4b whose transray cross section $C^*A^*B^*D^*C^{*\prime}$ reaches its lowest points in the interior of the diagram where both commodities are produced together. The corresponding iso-cost map (Figure 4d) is obviously also conducive to an interior cost minimum along an iso-revenue locus.

We come now to our key result:

PROPOSITION 12: *Ray average costs that are strictly declining and (nonstrict) transray convexity along any one hyperplane* $\Sigma w_i y_i = w$, $w_i > 0$ *through an output vector* y *are sufficient to guarantee strict output-specific subadditivity for output* y.

PROOF:

The result has already been proved in Proposition 3 for the division of y into any y^a, y^b which lie in the same ray. It therefore only remains to prove for any $y^a + y^b = y$

$$C(y^a + y^b) < C(y^a) + C(y^b) \text{ if } y^a \neq wy^b$$

By the definition of ray average costs that are strictly declining we have for any $v > 1$

$$(7) \qquad vC(y) > C(vy)$$

Let $w_1, \ldots, w_n$ be any vector of positive constants defining the cross section along which y satisfies Definition 5 of transray convexity. Now define[10] v_a, v_b by $v_a \Sigma w_i y_{ia} = \Sigma w_i y_{ia} + \Sigma w_i y_{ib} = v_b \Sigma w_i y_{ib}$ and set

$$(8) \qquad k = 1/v_a$$

so that

$$1/v_b = 1 - 1/v_a = (1 - k)$$

[10]As is illustrated in Figure 5, the purpose of multiplying all the elements of y^a and y^b by v_a and v_b, respectively, is to expand each of these outputs along its own ray until it is on the same hyperplane of transray convexity $\Sigma w_i y_i = w$, which contains point $y^a + y^b$. That then permits us to apply Definition 5 of strict transray convexity to the three points $v_a y^a$, $v_b y^b$, and $y^a + y^b$, to show that the cost of the latter does not exceed a weighted average of the costs of the former.

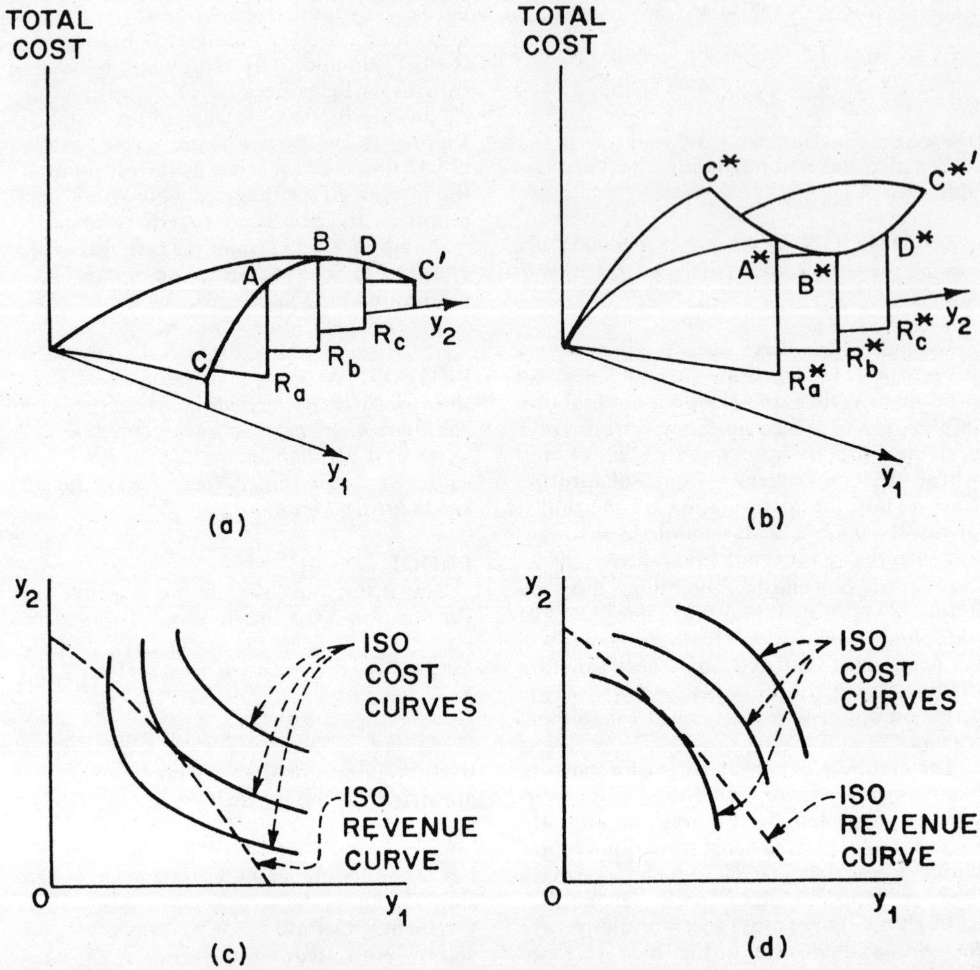

FIGURE 4

then by (7) and (3) in Definition 5

$$kv_aC(y^a) + (1 - k)v_bC(y^b) > kC(v_ay^a) + (1 - k)C(v_by^b) \geq C[kv_ay^a + (1 - k)v_by^b]$$

or since $kv_a = (1 - k)v_b = 1$ by (8) we have our subadditivity result

$$C(y^a) + C(y^b) > C(y^a + y^b)$$

Note that the proof does not require *strict* transray convexity, but it does have to assume that ray average costs are *strictly* declining over *part* of the region since the proof of Proposition 3, which is subsumed here, does require the latter. If, along the ray containing the industry output vector, average costs were not strictly declining, for example, if they increased proportionately with output, then several smaller firms might be able to produce the industry output vector at the same total cost as a monopolist. But, as Proposition 9 shows, the region in which ray average costs are *strictly* decreasing must only extend by any

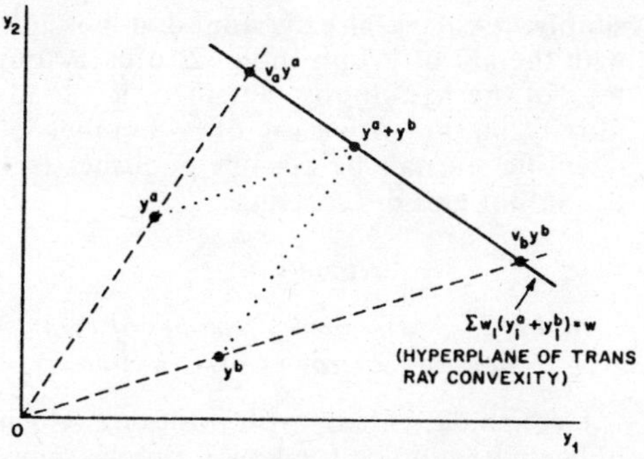

FIGURE 5

small amount beyond the *midpoint* of the ray between the origin and the outermost portion of the ray that is being tested for subadditivity.

The reason we do not need *strict* transray convexity also indicates why the conditions of Proposition 12 are not *necessary* for subadditivity. Let y be the vector sum of two output vectors y^a and y^b. Then y will be further from the origin than either y^a and y^b, and it will lie on a ray between the two. That is, it involves a larger scale than either of the component vectors *as well as* simultaneous production of the different commodities they include. Thus, even if there is no complementarity in the sense of strict transray convexity, if economies of scale are sufficiently strong, production of y by a single firm may still be the least expensive way to carry out the task.[11]

The fact that the conditions of Proposition 12 are not necessary implies that other and, perhaps, more familiar sufficient cost conditions for subadditivity may yet be found. It should be noted, however, that this may not be an important issue for empirical work in which data are likely to be analyzed with the aid of relatively simple mathematical forms for the cost function, whose subadditivity (or its absence) can be judged more directly.

VIII. Concluding Comment

The implications of the results of the preceding section should not be underestimated. It may seem as though ray subadditivity by itself is enough to constitute evidence for the presence of significant elements of natural monopoly in an industry and that transray subadditivity is little more than a bit of supplementary information. More specifically, it may seem that while transray subadditivity is required for natural monopoly in the production of several commodities together, ray subadditivity by itself gives us the essence of the natural monopoly, for then *each* good is still produced most cheaply by a single firm.

But that conclusion is quite misleading. To illustrate the point, suppose that the industry in question produces two commodities y_1 and y_2, and that, as in the case of Figure 6, a transray cross section has a number of minima. Then, despite strictly declining ray average costs, it can be cheapest for production to be carried out simultaneously by two or more firms. Though each firm will have a "monopoly" of production of the output *proportions* corresponding to its own ray, each will be producing the same commodities as the others. What sorts of monopolies would these really be if one were to "specialize" the production of y_1 and y_2 in a 50–50 ratio and another in a 45–55 ratio? Each firm would be producing the same two goods, only in (slightly?) different proportions, and that is surely no monopoly at all. In other words, *evidence of strict ray subadditivity is, by itself, evidence of virtually nothing of substance so far as natural monopoly is concerned.* It is consistent with the presence of a large number of firms in a cost-minimizing arrangement for the industry, and only requires slight dissimilarities in their product mix. It should

[11] Indeed, it can be shown that mild transray *concavity* can be compatible with subadditivity—the more rapid the rate of decline of ray average costs, the greater the permissible degree of concavity. The proof is a straightforward extension of the proof of Proposition 12. It can also be shown that if some outputs (or every output) in the industry product mix have their own fixed cost levels (a violation of transray convexity at the axes), then the cost function will still be subadditive if the conditions of Proposition 12 hold for the variable cost. The reason is that such fixed costs are always subadditive, and summation of two functions, one subadditive and the other strictly subadditive, always yields a strictly subadditive function.

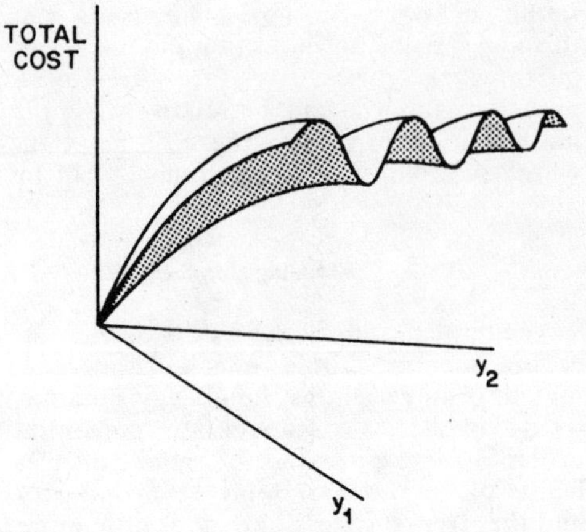

FIGURE 6

be noted that this is no extraordinary or pathological state of affairs. On the contrary, it is frequently found in multiproduct oligopoly industries in reality.[12]

We may note, finally, that though our natural monopoly criteria do not make for easy empirical testing, it is by no means unmanageable. Thus, as part of our research project on the cost of information supply, we have already found it possible with the aid of Proposition 12 to carry out tests of the hypothesis that there is subadditivity in the provision of a number of scientific journals by a single publisher (see the author and Braunstein).

[12]It can be proved that if the cost function is ray concave everywhere but not subadditive, then the number of firms that minimize the cost of producing the industry output vector will never exceed n, the number of different products supplied by the industry. This by itself means that in most multiproduct industries even where costs satisfy the ray concavity requirement (which is stronger than the conventional concept of scale economies) it is perfectly possible to have dozens of firms corresponding to the dozens of products supplied by the industry. Nor need these firms specialize in the production of single products. Rather, it may be optimal for them to operate along rays in the interior of product space, depending on the transray behavior of the cost surface, as is indicated in Figure 6 where it may obviously be more economical for two firms to operate at the low points of the scalloped cross sections than above the axes. Moreover, if, on the usual (but not quite accurate) criterion of scale economies, the cost function has declining ray average costs but is not concave everywhere, then the cost-minimizing number of firms can even exceed the number of products of the industry. Examples showing this, and other proofs underlying this discussion, were provided by Thijs ten Raa and Dietrich Fischer. These materials are presented in the Appendix (Propositions 13 and 14).

APPENDIX

On the Cost-Minimizing Number of Firms When Ray Average Costs Decline

I conclude with two propositions which indicate how much (or how little) we know about the natural number of firms in an industry, given information only about cost behavior along each ray (economies of scale) but no information on transray cost behavior (economies of scope) (see also the author and Fischer).

PROPOSITION 13 (Thijs ten Raa): *If the cost function is strictly output-ray concave, then the optimal number of firms cannot exceed n, the number of commodities produced by the industry.*[13]

PROOF:

It is sufficient to prove that for every $(n + 1)$-tuple of output vectors $y^1, \ldots, y^{n+1}$ there exists a cheaper n-tuple of output vectors with the same total output. Because in n-dimensional space any $n + 1$ vectors are linearly dependent, $y^1, \ldots, y^{n+1}$ must be linearly dependent. Hence, one of them, say, without loss generality y^{n+1} is a linear combination of the others:

$$y^{n+1} = \sum_{i=1}^{n} C_i y^i, \quad C_i \geq 0, \quad \text{not all zero}$$

Let $$\lambda \epsilon \left[0, \min_{i=1,\ldots,n} \left(1 + \frac{1}{C_i}\right)\right]$$

then

$$\forall i \epsilon \{1, \ldots, n\}: (1 + C_i - \lambda C_i) y^i, \quad \lambda y^{n+1} \epsilon \overline{\mathcal{R}^+_n}$$

[13]The proposition holds even if the concavity is *not* strict, provided there is no degeneracy in the sense used in linear programming.

and the sum of these $n+1$ vectors equals

$$\sum_{i=1}^{n} y^i + \sum_{i=1}^{n}(C_i - \lambda C_i)y^i + \lambda\sum_{i=1}^{n} C_i y^i = \sum_{i=1}^{n} y^i + \sum_{i=1}^{n} C_i y^i = \sum_{i=1}^{n+1} y^i$$

C is output ray concave, hence

$$\forall i \epsilon \{1,\ldots,n\}\colon\ C\{(1 + C_i - \lambda C_i)y^i\}$$

is a concave function of λ and so is $C(\lambda y^{n+1})$. Hence

$$\sum_{i=1}^{n} C\{(1 + C_i - \lambda C_i)y^i\} + C(\lambda y^{n+1})$$

is a concave function of λ. Hence its minimum occurs at one of the end points of λ's range, that is, at

$$\lambda = 0 \quad \text{or } \lambda = \min_{i=1,\ldots,n}\left(1 + \frac{1}{C_i}\right) = 1 + \frac{1}{C_j} \quad \text{for some } j\epsilon\{1,\ldots,n\}$$

When $\lambda = 0$, then the $(n+1)$th firm does not produce anything. When $\lambda = 1 + 1/C_j$, then the jth firm does not produce anything. In either case only n firms are left, producing the industry output more cheaply than when $\lambda = 1$ under which we have the original outputs $y^1,\ldots,y^{n+1}$. However,

PROPOSITION 14 (Raa and Fischer): *Declining ray average costs alone do not preclude the optimality of a number of firms larger than the number of products supplied by the industry.*

PROOF:

The following is an example in which it is optimal to have three firms producing two commodities when ray average costs are (not strictly) declining and there are no fixed costs.[14] Let

$$y^I = \left(1 + \frac{\sqrt{3}}{3}, 2\right)$$

[14]Note that the addition of any positive fixed cost will make the ray average costs decline *strictly*, without affecting the example.

and, to simplify the argument (letting us deal with only three rays in output space) let C be such that production is relatively cheap along rays involving three particular output bundles

$$(y_2 \equiv 0, y_1 \equiv 0 \quad \text{and} \quad y_2 = \sqrt{3}y_1)$$

but prohibitively expensive along all other rays. In addition, let the cost function satisfy

$$C\left(\frac{y_2\sqrt{3}}{3}, y_2\right) = 2y_2 \quad \text{for} \quad y_2 \geq 0$$

$$C(0, y_2) = \sqrt{3}\,y_2 \quad \text{for} \quad y_3 \geq 0$$

$$C(y_1, 0) = y_1 \quad \text{for} \quad y_1 \geq 1;\ \sqrt{3} - 1 < C\left(1 - \frac{\sqrt{3}}{3}, 0\right) < 1$$

$$C(y_1, 0) \quad \text{is linear for} \quad y_1 \epsilon \left[0, 1 - \frac{\sqrt{3}}{3}\right]$$

$$\text{and for} \quad y_1 \epsilon \left[1 - \frac{\sqrt{3}}{3}, 1\right]$$

Then y^I is produced more cheaply by

$$y^1 = (1,0),\ y^2 = \left(\frac{\sqrt{3}}{3}, 1\right) \quad \text{and} \quad y^3 = (0,1)$$

To show this, because of the linearity of C, it is sufficient to show that (y^1, y^2, y^3) is cheaper than

$$\left(\left(1 - \frac{\sqrt{3}}{3}, 0\right), \left(\frac{2\sqrt{3}}{3}, 2\right)\right)$$

and

$$\left(\left(1 + \frac{\sqrt{3}}{3}, 0\right), (0,2)\right)$$

the two pairs of output vectors capable of producing y^I. Thus:

$$C(y^1) + C(y^2) + C(y^3) = 1 + 2 + \sqrt{3} = 3 + \sqrt{3}$$

$$C\left(1 - \frac{\sqrt{3}}{3}, 0\right) + C\left(\frac{2\sqrt{3}}{3}, 2\right) > \sqrt{3} - 1 + 4 = 3 + \sqrt{3}$$

$$C\left(1 + \frac{\sqrt{3}}{3}, 0\right) + C(0,2) = 1 + \frac{\sqrt{3}}{3} + 2\sqrt{3} = 1 + \left(2\,\frac{1}{3}\right)\sqrt{3} > 3 + \sqrt{3}$$

REFERENCES

W. J. Baumol, "Scale Economies, Average Cost and the Profitability of Marginal-Cost Pricing," in Ronald E. Grieson, ed., *Essays in Urban Economics and Public Finance in Honor of William S. Vickrey*, Lexington 1976.

——, **E. E. Bailey, and R. D. Willig,** "Weak Invisible Hand Theorems on Pricing and Entry in a Multiproduct Natural Monopoly," *Amer. Econ. Rev.*, June 1977, *67*, 350–65.

—— **and D. Fischer,** "On the Optimal Number of Firms in an Industry," *Quart. J. Econ.*, 1977, forthcoming.

—— **and Y. M. Braunstein,** "Empirical Study of Scale Economies and Production Complementarity: The Case of Journal Publication," *J. Polit. Econ.*, 1977, forthcoming.

G. R. Faulhaber, (1975a) "Cross-Subsidization: Pricing in Public Enterprise," *Amer. Econ. Rev.*, Dec. 1975, *65*, 966–77.

——, (1975b) "Pricing Rules in Cooperative Markets," unpublished doctoral dissertation, Princeton Univ. 1975.

—— **and E. E. Zajac,** "Some Thoughts on Cross-Subsidization in Regulated Industries," paper presented at the International Conference in Telecommunications, England 1974.

G. Hanoch, "Homotheticity in Joint Production," *J. Econ. Theory*, Dec. 1970, *2*, 423–26.

——, "The Elasticity of Scale and the Shape of Average Costs," *Amer. Econ. Rev.*, June 1975, *65*, 492–97.

E. D. Lowry, "Justification for Regulation: The Case for Natural Monopoly," *Publ. Util. Fortnightly*, Nov. 8, 1973, *28*, 1–7.

P. Newman, "Some Properties of Concave Functions," *J. Econ. Theory*, Oct. 1969, *1*, 291–314.

J. C. Panzar and R. D. Willig, (1975a) "Economies of Scale and Economies of Scope in Multi-Output Production," unpublished paper, Bell Laboratories 1975.

—— **and** ——, (1975b) "Free Entry and the Sustainability of Natural Monopoly," unpublished paper, Bell Laboratories 1975.

R. A. Posner, "Natural Monopoly and its Regulation," *Stanford Law Rev.*, Feb. 1969, *21*, 548–643.

R. S. Seneca, "Inherent Advantage, Costs and Resource Allocation in the Transportation Industry," *Amer. Econ. Rev.*, Dec. 1973, *63*, 945–56.

W. W. Sharkey and L. G. Telser, "Supportable Cost Functions for the Multiproduct Firm," unpublished paper, Bell Laboratories 1977.

[26]

Pricing a new product: Eurotunnel

John Kay, Alan Manning and Stefan Szymanski

Eurotunnel, due to open in 1993, will link Great Britain with mainland Europe. Massive cost overruns have cast some doubts on its future profitability, but this article shows how its cost structure gives it critical advantages in pricing against its competitors. The prospectus assumption is that Eurotunnel and the ferries will charge broadly similar fares. In this article, we show that substantially undercutting ferry charges is a far more profitable strategy. Moreover, this result holds even if consumers regard the tunnel as a superior service and is robust to any response by the ferries themselves. Their best strategy is to seek niche markets and avoid direct competition with the tunnel. The article draws parallels for other firms introducing new products by applying new technology in established markets.

"The richest, the most civilised, and the freest countries in the world are now discussing, in fear and trepidation, the "difficult" question of whether a tunnel can be built under the English Channel.... On all sides, at every step one comes across problems which man is quite capable of solving *immediately*, but capitalism is in the way."

V I Lenin, Pravda Truda, No 6, September 17, 1913.

Introduction

New product launches are of several kinds. Most frequently a new product is introduced into an established market served by an established range. The new commodity may offer existing product characteristics in a new way. We might think of the launch of a new car, or mortgage, or washing machine. The range within which such a product might be priced will be set, within a relatively narrow band, by the price of existing products, and will be defined by the features of the new product. The task of pricing it involves assessing the "going rate" for that combination of features, and deciding whether to price a little below or a little above.

Sometimes a product is truly new. It meets a consumer need which was previously unfulfilled, and which may or may not be real. Twenty years ago neither video cassette recorders or video discs were available to consumers. VCRs succeeded, video discs did not. Wholly new products often fail: no market research, however, sophisticated, can definitively measure wants which consumers have had no opportunity to express in the market place. The pricing strategy required for these commodities must aim to maximise the probability that the product will succeed. But it must also be concerned to maximise the innovator's revenue from product development, which usually means that early sales must be at high prices. Pricing strategy for truly innovative products must aim to strike a balance between these two factors.

"Sometimes the superiority of the new product is so clear-cut that it wipes out existing products. More often, however, that process takes time."

This article considers a third type of product launch. A customer need is well established and met by existing products, but a new technology becomes available which meets these needs more fully or more cheaply. Sometimes the superiority of the new product is so clearcut that it immediately takes over the market. More often, however, that process takes time. This may be because many of the costs of established suppliers are sunk or fixed, and their variable costs are low, so that they can compete effectively in the short run (although not necessarily the long). Consumers may be wedded to existing products with which they are familiar. Or it may not pay an innovator to price so aggressively as to eliminate the competition, at least immediately. Commonly, although not necessarily, new products which fall into this category will reflect process rather than product innovation. The pattern we describe is common in pharmaceuticals, for example, but is more usual in industrial than in consumer markets.

"Many of the costs of established suppliers are sunk so that they can compete effectively in the short run."

The object of the article is to illustrate an analytic framework for dealing with these issues: the pricing strategy required of a new technology aimed at an established customer need. The case we use is one of the largest and most striking product launches of the 1990s: a competitive battle ahead which can be anticipated with a degree of certainty unusual in any market. The product in question is the Channel Tunnel between Britain and France, at present under construction and due to open for traffic in 1993.

The Eurotunnel prospectus suggests that the tunnel will aim to match the prices set by the ferries, which will in turn be somewhat lower than the current level of tariffs. The ferries have declared an intention to base their response on low cost competition on the short sea crossings. Neither of these strategies makes sense. The tunnel must price aggressively to secure volume, and by doing so it can secure profits considerably in excess of those shown in the prospectus, regardless of how the ferries respond. The ferries cannot compete effectively in direct opposition to the tunnel, and should concentrate their energies on other routes.

The competitive background: the existing market

The Tunnel will provide services in a well established market for transport between the UK and continental Europe. The crossing can at present be made by air or by sea.

Around 28 million people travel by air to and from the continent each year. Most of these are travelling to southern European holiday resorts and cannot realistically be considered part of the target market. Passengers from the UK to either France, Belgium or the Netherlands are more likely to consider direct rail links as an alternative to air travel: a market of around 6m passengers per annum. Air fares in this market have historically been heavily regulated and appear to have been well above competitive levels. Much liberalisation has already occurred, especially between the UK and the Netherlands. Increasing competitive pressures have emerged on all routes in recent years.

"The tunnel will provide services in a well established market."

The ferry market caters for accompanied vehicles (around 2.8m cars per annum), for freight (a similar number of vehicles), and for foot passengers (approximately 16m). Most of this traffic is concentrated on three corridors: Dover-Calais, Dover-Zeebrugge/Ostend, Felixstowe-Zeebrugge/Ostend. The first of these is the shortest sea route between the UK and France and is also the route taken by the Channel tunnel. The other two routes are primarily commercial freight routes connecting South-Eastern England with the Netherlands, Belgium and (indirectly) West Germany.

All three market segments have grown rapidly in the last decade – freight at 8% p.a., foot passengers at 6.5% p.a. and cars at 4.5% p.a. Indeed it is this growth which has made the tunnel commercially viable. The expansion of the market has been precipitated by a number of factors. The entry of the UK into the European Community is particularly significant. Community countries accounted for only 30% of UK trade in 1970; by 1987 this figure was over 50%. Market growth also reflects growing affluence within the UK (most of the passenger traffic originates from the UK) as more and more people can afford motoring holidays on the continent. Other specific factors include the development of continental coach services and the peculiarly British obsession with Duty Free Sales. The "excursionist" holiday, primarily undertaken to make purchases of duty free alcohol and cigarettes, currently accounts for around 3.4 million passenger trips.

"All market segments have grown rapidly. It is this rapid growth which has made the tunnel commercially viable."

The market is more or less evenly divided between 2 principal operators, P&O and Sealink, with around 80-90% of the market. The remainder is fought over by a competitive fringe (e.g. Sally Line, Brittany Ferries, Olau Line etc). P&O acquired its present position through the takeover of European Ferries in 1987 and also runs a substantial road freight business. Sealink is a consortium of National Ferry Companies of the Netherlands and France together with Sealink UK which was privatised in 1984 and taken over by Sea Containers, a container leasing company with some other passenger transport interests.

Although there is a high degree of concentration the existence of a competitive fringe ensures there is downward pressure on prices. Entry into the market is relatively cheap and failure need not be too costly (there is a well developed second hand market for ferries). This implies that it is difficult for the two majors to raise prices for extended periods since this will simply provoke entry. Indeed, there have been occasional price wars – the most recent between 1979 and 1981 saw prices fall by 18% in real terms.

That price war was in fact provoked by the intervention of the Office of Fair Trading which has regularly investigated the activities of the two major operators and which forced the abandonment of an earlier agreement which "harmonised" prices. An indication that price competition may be limited is the huge levels of excess capacity. Whilst average load factors are around 50% for most cross channel routes, the ferry companies have consistently invested in larger ships so that the average car ferry is now around four times the size of 20 years ago. Whilst this can partially be attributed to the efficiency of newer kinds of ships it is hard to believe this is the whole story. For example, larger ships mean larger crews which must be carried regardless of load factor, while smaller ships would increase flexibility.

The competitive background: Eurotunnel

The Channel Tunnel will be a 31 mile twin bore tunnel between Dover and Calais. It is scheduled to be opened in May 1993. The Tunnel will offer two main services. Foot passengers and rail freight will be able to travel through the tunnel on scheduled services offered by BR and SNCF (the UK and French national rail companies). Through rail services will connect London to Paris, Brussels and beyond. Eurotunnel will not charge travellers directly for this service and has negotiated a usage contract with BR and SNCF.

ET will also offer a shuttle service with specially designed trains carrying cars (with passengers), lorries and coaches between Dover and Calais. The journey time through the tunnel is expected to be 33 minutes. The crossing time of the fastest ferry is around 70 minutes.

The capacity of the system will be very large. A rough calculation based on Eurotunnel figures suggests that maximum capacity in 1994 will be double the size of *total* 1994 cross channel traffic demand (268% of current demand). Even on Eurotunnel's own forecasts, the market size in 2010 will still be only 95% of ET capacity. In principle at least, ET has the potential to satisfy the entire market for the foreseeable future. It also has first option on the construction of a further tunnel, which may, in the end, be an asset of considerable value.

"ET has the potential to satisfy the entire market for the foreseeable future."

The cost of constructing the Tunnel was estimated at around £5bn at the time of flotation in 1987. Since that time anticipated costs have risen substantially for reasons which are the subject of continuing, and unresolved, dispute between the company (ET plc) and the contractors. At the time of writing total cost estimates have risen to between £7bn and £8bn, but since around £2bn has already been spent, it is clear that suggestions of abandonment are far fetched. Aside from the loss of face to all parties, it is apparent that if it was deemed profitable to construct a tunnel two years ago for £5bn, then it is still worth spending £5bn today to achieve the same result. This illustrates an important characteristic of ET's competitive position. The huge amount of capital which must be committed to its construction, once 'sunk', plays no further role in deciding how the Tunnel should be operated although of course it affects the financial position of ET plc. The capital costs of the ferries are recoverable. Since they have a second hand value, they can be sold up and used in some other activity if the Dover and Calais trip becomes unprofitable.

The costs which matter when deciding how to operate the Tunnel and the ferries are marginal costs—which we discuss further below. According to our estimates, the Tunnel has a marginal cost (the extra cost of carrying one more passenger, car or lorry) around *one tenth* of the ferries. This reflects the fact that the Tunnel itself is a fixed hole in the ground with dedicated equipment and so the cost of running through another trainload of passengers or goods is very small. By contrast, running another ferry incurs substantial additional costs in the form of crew costs, fuel, port dues and so on, and in the long run the full capital costs of operation must be remunerated or the ferries will be used elsewhere or not replaced.

"The Tunnel has a marginal cost around one tenth of the ferries."

In our analysis we have assumed that the Tunnel is completed roughly on time and roughly within budget. This now seems increasingly unlikely. However, it does little to alter the nature of our results. Whilst higher construction costs or delayed opening will reduce the profits available for Eurotunnel's shareholders, this fact in itself should have no bearing on the way in which Eurotunnel attempts to generate the maximum level of profit possible, once it is opened.

Tactical competition

"There are three factors which are central to the outcome of tactical competition: relative product quality, substitutability and relative costs."

By tactical competition we mean price setting behaviour which takes no account of the possible impact that current profitability may have on future profitability. Tactical competition means that day to day price setting decisions are taken with a view to maximising current profits. Thus it does not allow for price strategies designed to build market share at the expense of current income or to persuade competitors to leave the market or refrain from entering it. There are three factors which are central to the outcome of this tactical competition – relative product quality, substitutability and relative costs.

(a) Relative product quality

It is by no means clear whether a tunnel or a ferry crossing is a superior product. The tunnel will certainly be faster but a sea trip will often be more pleasant. For example, consumers will typically view the prospect of a sea crossing differently from a trip through a tunnel. Experience may change these perceptions but in the extreme, a claustrophobe will never like travelling through a Tunnel whilst an agoraphobe will never happily choose to saunter on the open deck of a ferry. Product quality also depends on how well the product is adapted to its purposes. The tunnel will offer faster movement of freight between Dover and Calais but very little traffic originates at Dover or terminates at Calais. A crossing between Felixstowe and Zeebrugge is often a more appropriate routing.

We define an objective overall measure of service quality in each market segment by asking what relative prices would give each mode of operation an equal market share. If the tunnel would take 50% of the market for accompanied cars at a price premium of 20%, we judge that the tunnel's service is 20% superior. If it needs to undercut ferry charges by 30% to win 50% of the market, then it is inferior by that amount.

"It may be that the tunnel should charge a lower price even if its product is superior - it is often better to take profits in volume rather than in price."

Other things equal, the producer of a superior product can charge a higher price. But other things may not be equal. As we see below, it may be that the tunnel should charge a lower price even if its product is superior. It is often better to take profits in volume than in price.

(b) Substitutability

Tactical competition will also be influenced by the degree to which one product can be substituted for another. Substitutability and superiority/inferiority are quite distinct properties, although both are the characteristics of the underlying product. One good may be highly substitutable for another even though it is inferior—as with ordinary and long life light bulbs, or alkaline and zinc-carbon batteries. And related products may be poor substitutes even if they are of equal quality in the sense defined above. Two washing powders may have similar sized bands of loyal adherents, each of whom view their favourite product as clearly preferable. The powders are of equal quality but, in terms of customer perception, they are not easily substitutable.

"Substitutability and superiority are quite distinct properties. Related products may be poor substitutes even if they are of equal quality."

Our measure of substitutability is the elasticity of substitution—the rate at which changes in relative prices bring about changes in market share. If the elasticity of substitution is high then even if ferry and tunnel prices diverge by a small amount, a very large share of the market will go to the firm charging the lower price. If, on the other hand, the elasticity of substitution is low, then only very large differences in prices will cause customers to shift to the cheaper alternative. In the extreme, an infinite elasticity of substitution means that firms must charge identical prices if both are to stay in the market. A zero elasticity means that even if a competitor charged nothing, no customers would defect.

(c) Relative costs

It is by no means clear whether a tunnel will increase or reduce the average cost of crossing the channel. This depends not only on the size of final construction bills: it is also influenced by the ultimate level of demand for its services. This evaluation is relevant to an assessment of whether the tunnel should have been built, but not to tariff strategy now that the tunnel is certain to be built. But when setting prices it is marginal costs which are crucial, rather than fixed or average costs. Any price charged above marginal cost adds to profitability; but it never pays (in the short run at least) to charge below marginal cost. Of course, revenue over marginal cost is not pure profit; first it must cover fixed costs (such as the cost of construction of the ferries or the tunnel). However, the goal of the competitive firm must be to choose prices so as to maximise the surplus over marginal cost. If this surplus is insufficient to cover fixed costs then the firm faces bankruptcy, but this does not alter the argument since, by definition, any other price would actually reduce the surplus and therefore the likelihood of covering fixed costs.

"Relative marginal costs will be crucial in determining profitabiliy. The marginal costs of the tunnel are much lower than those of the ferries."

Relative marginal costs will therefore be crucial in determining profitability. As noted above, the marginal costs of the tunnel are much lower than those of the ferries. This is crucial to the competitive outcome.

The dynamics of market entry

Here we concentrate on the tunnel as entrant into the freight market. The prospectus envisages that the likely outcome of increased competition is that tariffs would fall by about 20%. This implies that both tunnel and ferry would charge about £150 for an average truck.

"The freight market is decidedly price sensitive."

We take this case as our starting point. The model used by the promoters suggests that the Tunnel is an inferior product in the freight market, taking about 18% of the overall market at equal prices. This reflects the unsuitability of the Dover-Calais route for most freight users. We need also to consider the extent of possible substitution. Our base assumption here is that this is relatively high. The freight market is decidedly a price sensitive one. Note here again the importance of the distinction between substitutability and inferiority. Even if the Tunnel is inferior for many users in this market, it is highly substitutable. They will always be ready to take advantage of it if the price is right.

On this basis, we show in Figure 1 the net revenues the Tunnel could anticipate from the freight market assuming that the ferry price is indeed £150. If the Tunnel also charges £150, these net revenues are around £125m per year. Figure 1 also shows, however, the profits which the Tunnel would make at alternative price levels.

As is general with such curves, the shape is an inverse v, rising to a maximum and then tailing off. Too low prices are insufficiently remunerative: too high prices damage volume. The position of the curve depends principally on the superiority or inferiority of the

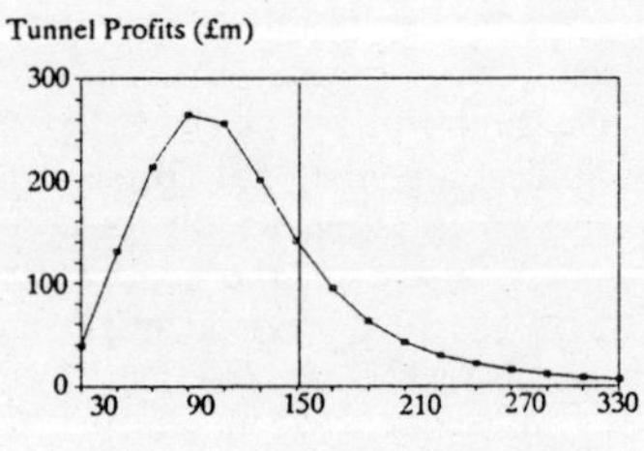

Figure 1
Tunnel profits for a range of tunnel prices given a ferry tariff of £150

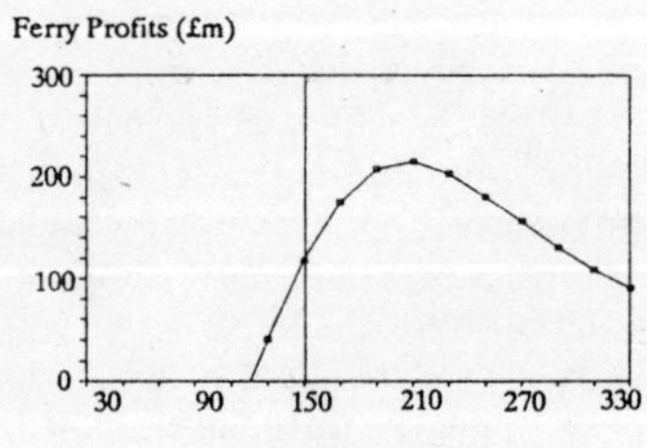

Figure 2
Ferry profits for a range of ferry prices given a tunnel tariff of £150

product. If the Tunnel was a poorer substitute for the ferry (road access was worse than anticipated, for example), then the whole curve would shift to the right. The slope of the curve depends primarily on the substitutability of the product. If the two products are very good substitutes, then profits will be very sensitive to the price charged and the curve will slope steeply away from the maximum.

"If the ferries did indeed charge £150, it would pay the tunnel to undercut it substantially."

Figure 1 shows that if the ferries did indeed charge £150, it would pay the Tunnel to undercut it substantially. The profit maximising price for the Tunnel is about £87, little more than half the ferry level, and at this price it would take the lion's share of the traffic (around three quarters of it, in fact). Profits would be approximately double the level implied in the prospectus projections. The additional volume is very attractive to the Tunnel because its marginal costs of operation are so low. The Tunnel could not expect, however, to price on this basis without some response from the ferries.

So in Figure 2 we consider precisely the same question from the perspective of the ferries. We assume a single decision maker for the ferries. (Agreement or merger between the two leading operators by 1993 is highly probable). What options are available to them if the Tunnel price is £150 as in the prospectus scenario? The net revenue curve for the ferries has the same inverse v shape as that of the Tunnel, but its position and slope are very different. This is because of the much higher variable cost base of the ferries. If the ferries match a tunnel price of £150 (as in the prospectus) they take most of the traffic and earn slightly more profits than the Tunnel (around £150m). Ferry revenues are much less sensitive to volumes than those of the tunnel, because of their higher costs. But for this reason it does not make sense for them to match the tunnel's price. It appears that if the Tunnel did indeed charge £150, the best strategy for the ferries would be to concede volume to the Tunnel and push their own price up to around £200. But, of course, this cannot be the final outcome. We know that it is not attractive to the Tunnel to charge £150: we suggested £87 was a better price. On the other hand, if the ferries did succeed in pushing up their prices to these levels it would make sense for the Tunnel to follow, at least partially.

"Ferry revenues are much less sensitive to volume: if the Tunnel charged £150, the best strategy would be to push their own price up."

Thus we need to consider the pricing strategies of the two parties simultaneously. But we can already see the key qualitative features of the solution. Given the massive variable cost advantage of the Tunnel, it must pursue a volume strategy. The best outcome for the ferries is to retreat into a niche market and take relatively high prices for those sectors of the market to which they can provide a premium product.

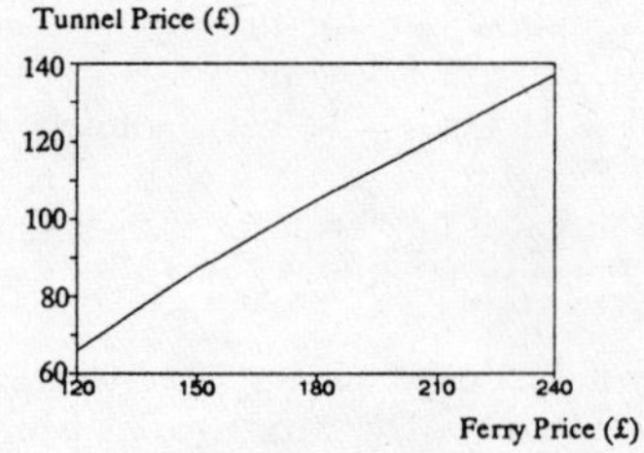

Figure 3
Tunnel reaction curve

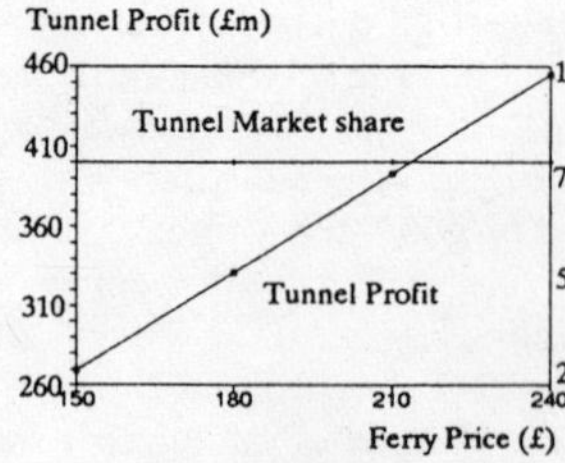

Figure 4
Tunnel profitability and market share on its reaction curve

Figures 3 and 4 summarise the strategies available to the two participants. Figure 3 describes the "reaction curve" of the Tunnel – the most remunerative price for the Tunnel – at each price which the ferries might set. Clearly, the higher the ferry price the higher the Tunnel price should be. But whatever the ferry price is, it always pays the Tunnel to undercut it. Since the Tunnel is assumed to be both an inferior product and a lower cost competitor this follows inescapably.

"Whatever the ferry tariff may be, the best strategy for the Tunnel is to price aggressively to win volume."

Figure 4 shows the implications of this reaction curve for Tunnel profits. The higher the price the ferries set, the higher is the level of Tunnel profitability. Figure 4 shows, however, that if the Tunnel prices correctly its profits are very sensitive to the level of ferry pricing but its market share is not. Whatever the ferry tariff may be, the best strategy for the Tunnel is to price aggressively to win volume.

In Figures 5 and 6 we present the analogous options for the ferries. Figure 5 shows the best price for the ferries to charge at different levels of Tunnel tariff. The ferry price rises with the Tunnel price, but generally less rapidly. Figure 6 shows how this determines the profit opportunities of the ferries. If the Tunnel prices very aggressively – say at £75 or below – the competitive position of the

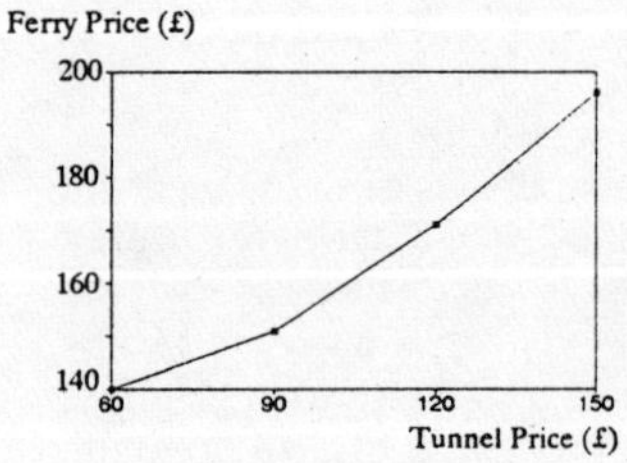

Figure 5
Ferry reaction curve

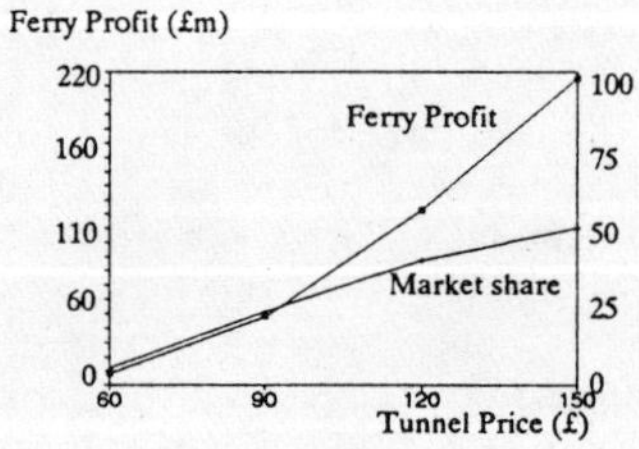

Figure 6
Ferry profitability and market share on its reaction curve

ferries is hopeless. The ferries cannot match these prices: even at much higher prices, more in line with ferry costs, market share is very low. A viable market for the ferries remains only if the Tunnel price is higher. As the Tunnel price rises, the ferry price rises also, but not as rapidly, so the ferry benefits both from higher margins and from higher market share.

It always pays the Tunnel to undercut – with its low marginal costs and inferior product; it always pays the ferries – with their much higher variable costs and variety of routes – to look for premium prices. Thus the two competitors' best strategies are potentially compatible. Figure 7 shows this by bringing together the reaction curves of the two competitors.

"While it always pays the Tunnel to undercut it always pays the ferries to look for premium prices."

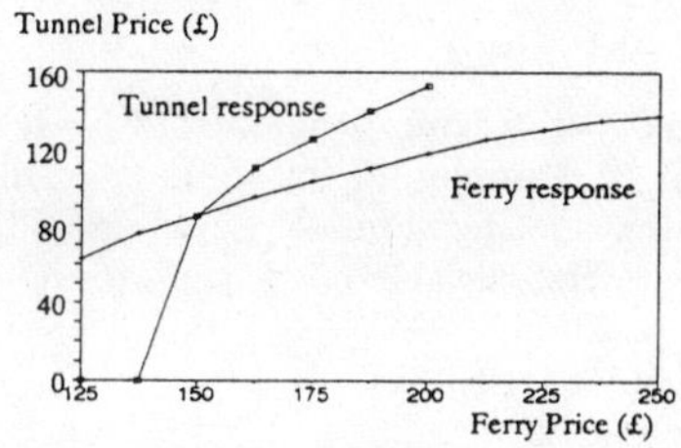

Figure 7
Finding the equilibrium price responses

There is a point at which the two reaction curves intersect. If the ferries set a price of £150, the best response for the Tunnel is to charge £87. If the Tunnel sets a price of £87, the best strategy for the ferries is to charge £150. It is easy to see from the diagram that this is the only pair of prices for which this property of mutual consistency of responses holds. If, for example, the Tunnel charged £100, the ferries should charge £170: but if the ferries did charge £170, then the Tunnel should set a tariff of £130. If the Tunnel did charge £130, the ferries should alter their price, and so on. In technical terms, the Tunnel price of £87 combined with a ferry price of £150 is a *Nash equilibrium* in strategies. It is the only Nash equilibrium for this particular competitive (non-cooperative) game.

Is such an outcome inevitable? Certainly it is profoundly unsatisfactory for the ferries. Their profits are less than half those they would earn in the prospectus scenario. Tunnel profits, by contrast, are twice as large. *But so long as the Tunnel makes appropriate strategic responses, this is the best they can do.* If they were to try to cut prices further to meet the Tunnel's competition, then the Tunnel should reduce prices still further, and the ferries face the

"Although the outcome is profoundly unsatisfactory for the ferries, it is the best they can do so long as the Tunnel makes appropriate strategic responses."

prospect of very low margins and low volumes. If the ferries raise prices, the Tunnel will not follow them up fully, and the loss of ferry traffic will more than offset its higher profitability. The ferries can earn more profits only if the Tunnel makes a strategic mistake. The prospectus scenario (of equal Tunnel and ferry prices) is an example of such a strategic mistake. In it, Tunnel profits are much less than they should be, and the ferries benefit accordingly. But barring such an error by the Tunnel there is no way in which the ferries can compete more effectively. Their only hope of making more profit is to cooperate with the Tunnel, tacitly or explicitly. We explore these possibilities in a later section.

Sensitivity analysis

Once a solution to a pricing problem has been derived, as in the previous section, it is important to see how sensitive that solution is to the underlying specification. We have identified the three key groups of parameters: variable costs, superiority/inferiority, and the elasticity of substitution.

"If ferry costs fell by the 40% envisaged by the anti-Tunnel campaigners, there is little joy in this scenario for anyone."

We first consider cost levels. It is sometimes suggested that the ferries may be able to respond to competition from the Tunnel by cutting costs substantially. Some steps have already been taken to achieve this – by reducing manning levels – but it has been claimed that a new generation of super-jumbo ferries would allow very low cost competition.

In Table 1 we show what might happen to our solution if ferry costs fell by the 40% envisaged by the anti-Tunnel campaigners. It can be seen that there is little joy in this scenario for anyone. The ferry operation is actually less profitable, and Tunnel revenues are

Table 1
Competitive outcomes if Ferry marginal costs fall by 40%

	Base Case		*Low Costs*	
	Tunnel	Ferries	Tunnel	Ferries
Price£	87	150	54	91
Profit £m	269	42	147	29
Market Share %	77	23	75	25

Notes:
(a) By profit we mean surplus over variable costs. This must cover all fixed costs including financing and dividend payments.
(b) All figures relate to a standard freight lorry one-way price.

much smaller. Lower prices do not increase the total market much – our base assumption for the freight market is that prices affect only the distribution of traffic. The problem for both parties is that the best strategy for the Tunnel is always to go for volume, whatever its opponent tries. If they are in a position to cut prices, that simply has the effect of depressing revenues for the whole industry. A cost reduction strategy might be successful if it could deter the Tunnel from entering – but it has not – or if it could persuade the Tunnel to abandon the market – but it cannot.

"If the Tunnel service is poorly regarded price cutting has to be more severe."

We have assumed, following the prospectus, that the tunnel is an inferior product in the freight market. Originally we accepted that at equal prices the Tunnel only took 18% of the market. Now suppose the Tunnel could take 50% at equal prices. The results are shown in Table 2. In this case the Tunnel need only undercut the ferry price by a small amount to obtain the traffic volumes it requires. If the Tunnel service is poorly regarded by prospective freight users, then price cutting has to be more severe, and profits are correspondingly reduced.

The outcome is most sensitive to the elasticity of substitution. If

Table 2
Competitive outcomes if Tunnel services and Ferry services are of equal quality

	Base Case		*Equal quality*	
	Tunnel	Ferries	Tunnel	Ferries
Price£	87	150	116	150
Profit £m	269	42	376	40
Market Share %	77	23	78	22

Notes:
(a) By profit we mean surplus over variable costs. This must cover all fixed costs including financing and dividend payments.
(b) All figures relate to a standard freight lorry one-way price.

the elasticity of substitution were much lower, then the consequences would be as in Table 3A (overleaf): everyone can charge much higher prices, and reap much higher profits. In fact this is not a realistic outcome. At this level of prices, ferry operation is so profitable that competition between ferry operators would push tariffs down to much lower levels. In Table 3B (overleaf) we also consider the implications for prices and profits if we assume that the maximum level of ferry tariff is £170.

"The Tunnel does better if its facilities are less directly substitutable for those of the ferries and so do the ferries themselves."

At first sight, it may seem surprising that the Tunnel does better if its facilities are less directly substitutable for those of the ferries. An elasticity of substitution of three (rather than five) raises profits by

Table 3A
Competitive outcomes if Ferry and Tunnel services are less substitutable

	Base Case		*Low elasticity of substitution*	
	Tunnel	Ferries	Tunnel	Ferries
Price£	87	150	118	234
Profit £m	269	42	311	210
Market Share %	77	23	63	37

Table 3B
Competitive outcomes if ferry and tunnel services are less substitutable and there is a price cap of £170 on the price of ferry services

	Base Case		*Low elasticity with price cap*	
	Tunnel	Ferries	Tunnel	Ferries
Price£	87	150	88	170
Profit £m	269	42	217	107
Market Share %	77	23	61	39

Notes:
(a) By profit we mean surplus over variable costs. This must cover all fixed costs including financing and dividend payments.
(b) All figures relate to a standard freight lorry one-way price.

"If the Tunnel and the ferries are poor substitutes, pressure on the general level of prices is correspondingly less."

over 30%. This is another aspect of the important distinction between superiority and substitutability. Two products are poor substitutes for each other if each has their own distinct clientele, for which one or other product is the more suitable. The inferior product is then the one which fewer people like. If everyone sees the relative merits of the products in much the same light, then they are highly substitutable (even if one or other is inferior). The Tunnel and the ferries are poor substitutes if they cater for largely distinct user groups—some have a strong preference for the Tunnel, others for the ferries. If that is the case, then the pressure on the general level of prices is correspondingly less, and all operations are more profitable. The greater the extent to which the two products focus on the same market, the stronger will be competitive pressures and the lower will be revenues all round. Here, as often, market segmentation is central to profitability.

Cooperative Solutions

So far our analysis has concentrated on decision making where both parties choose their best response independently of each other. In extreme cases as when the elasticity of substitution is very high this means that both sides push prices down in attempts to gain market share, with the result that both sides make lower profits. Both tunnel and ferries can do better by cooperating. The classic form of cooperation (collusion) is for both sides to agree to maintain high prices. Cooperative arrangements can be of two kinds, formal merger or informal collusion.

"Both tunnel and ferries can do better by cooperating."

The most extensive form of cooperation between the two parties would involve the tunnel buying out the ferries or concluding some written contract which specified exactly the choices (in particular, prices) to be made by each party. One way this might be achieved is through merger, as is common in other markets. Another method of cooperating used in other markets is licensing, although this is hardly possible in the case of Eurotunnel.

In the case of the cross-Channel market it should be obvious that a combined tunnel/ferry operation would earn the highest profit by running only tunnel services and ending ferry activities altogether. Given the substantial variable costs associated with ferry operations, the withdrawal of ferry services would reduce costs and enable the Tunnel to charge higher prices. The limit to prices in such a world would be the price at which new ferry operators would be tempted to enter the market.

"A combined operation would earn the highest profit by ending ferry services altogether."

Cooperation through merger is quite common when new products are introduced, or as results of a competitive battle, but they are not relevant in the present case. We can envisage no likely circumstances in which the competition authorities would permit the tunnel company to acquire major ferry operators. And although the Office of Fair Trading has considered the possibility of allowing horizontal agreements between ferry operators themselves, it seems inconceivable that they would allow the Tunnel to be party to such an arrangement.

Cooperative arrangements in this industry could therefore only be the product of informal arrangements. This may be achievable in a number of otherwise competitive situations, through price leadership or other forms of tacit collusion. But there are considerable obstacles to informal cooperation in the cross-Channel market. The Tunnel need not accept any solution which offers it less than the (substantial) revenues it would earn in a competitive outcome. Thus a prerequisite for cooperation is that the ferries accept that the tunnel will undercut their prices substantially and take a dominant share of profits and traffic. If they do accept that, then both parties

"These are considerable obstacles to informal cooperation in the cross-channel market. The ferries have very little to offer the Tunnel through a collusive arrangement."

could do better by allowing prices to edge up from competitive levels while still maintaining a substantial differential between ferry and tunnel prices.

We see no prospect of such an outcome in the freight market. Prices are set by individual negotiation between operators and large customers, and given the radically different cost structures of the two kinds of operator uncertainty about each other's actions would be an overwhelming obstacle to cooperative action. There are better prospects for keeping prices high in the consumer market, where fares are announced in public brochures, but here too the differences in costs make concerted action difficult to achieve.

The ferries have very little to offer the Tunnel through a collusive arrangement. Their prices are already high relative to the costs of the Tunnel and higher ferry profits are only likely to increase the already excessive capacity in the market. Indeed, our analysis suggests that the future of the ferry companies is bleak. We consider some alternative ferry strategies further below.

Influencing market structure

Until now we have assumed that the goal of both parties is short term profit maximisation. We now consider price strategies which might sacrifice immediate profits for longer term gains. We are not concerned here with very short term marketing activities. It might, for example, pay the Tunnel to make introductory offers to gain publicity and familiarise potential customers with its product. Such product launches are common in many markets although probably unnecessary in this: few manufacturers can anticipate having their product introduction celebrated jointly by the Queen of England and the President of France.

Firms can derive long term gains from short term behaviour in two ways. They may force rivals to leave the market. Or they can establish a reputation which will deter potential competitors from entering the market or induce actual competitors to modify their behaviour. The strength of both these strategies depends on the extent of commitment to the market and the degree of irrevocability of decisions to enter or to leave the industry.

"The construction of the Tunnel is irreversible. This is a source of financial weakness for the Tunnel company but of competitive strength for the Tunnel."

The construction of the Tunnel is irreversible: never have costs been so literally sunk. Once completed, it is there to compete forever with alternative forms of transport, while a ferry can be used on many different routes. This is a source of financial weakness for the Tunnel company but of competitive strength for the Tunnel itself. In particular, it rules out the possibility of predatory action *against* the

Tunnel since such actions can never lead to the withdrawal of the Tunnel (as distinct from Eurotunnel plc) from the market. It is possible, and by no means improbable, that Eurotunnel plc will face liquidation or financial reconstruction but the Tunnel will continue to transport passengers.

This is an extreme example of a common phenomenon. Where the costs of market entry are large, incumbents must distinguish between the financial strength of the entrant and the competitive strength of the product. If entry occurs, a lower cost product is unlikely to go away even if the company producing it fails to recover the costs of entry and loses money. The primary objective must be to deter entry, as indeed the ferries did for many years – a tunnel has been technically feasible for decades. But once entry has occurred (even if mistakenly) the nature of the market is forever changed.

Indeed Eurotunnel's financial weakness is in some respects a source of competitive strength. Because it has a huge burden of debt to carry it has to acquire a dominant market position or face acute refinancing problems. If the ferries themselves fear that ET may act as predator, they may rationally decide to quit the market rather than face future losses. Once ET achieves market dominance it will be able to deter potential competitors from entering the market, since it has already endured the substantial sunk costs of entry. A potential entrant, by contrast, will face at least some sunk costs in entering the market. When calculating the cost of competition therefore, the entrant will always find it more expensive than ET and so long as ET does not set its prices too high this means that entry will never be profitable (even if ET is making substantial profits). This will be true for a ferry operation and also, at some distant date, for a prospective second tunnel.

"The ferries have no long term strategic threats against the Tunnel but the Tunnel does against the ferries."

It follows that the ferries have no long term strategic threat which need disturb the Tunnel but that the Tunnel does against the ferries. The Tunnel cannot force the ferries to quit the market altogether, but it can force the ferries off the short sea crossings from Britain to France and this is what it should seek to do.

Most "strategic moves" involve costs as well as benefits if they cause the firm's profit levels to deviate from the short run maximum. A reputation for being a "tough character" or an aggressive competitor can act as a substitute for such strategic moves, but the problem with developing reputations is that they require the firm to take tough or aggressive actions, which in themselves may not be rational. Building a business on the basis of irrational decisions would seem to be a poor strategy. The only circumstance where strategic play can be both credible and make sense is where it involves sunk costs – irreversible investments which demonstrate the commitment of the firm to its market and deters competition from potential entrants. The cross channel market is a striking example. The ferries have negligible sunk costs, and for all their aggressive talk their commitment to the market in the long term is by no means assured. ET, however, by sinking £7bn into a hole in the ground which can only be recovered by charging tolls to cross the channel, have demonstrated their commitment to their market in dramatic form.

Market segmentation

"The ferries may be able to diversify away from direct competition. It will pay them to move into services which are less substitutable for the Tunnel."

So far we have concentrated largely on tunnel strategies and treated the ferry companies as followers rather than leaders. This is mainly because the relative marginal cost advantage of the tunnel gives it the ability to dictate market share. However, in strategic terms the ferries are not entirely powerless. It is clear that in the short term they can do very little to compete head on with the Tunnel in their principal markets. But they may be able to diversify away from direct competition with the Tunnel. This means segmenting the existing market and demonstrating some form of competitive advantage over the Tunnel in particular segments. This is equivalent to altering the values of the relevant parameters, relative service quality and the elasticity of substitution.

Since the Tunnel must pursue a volume strategy, it will pay the ferries to move into those services which are less substitutable for the tunnel. As we have already pointed out, the ferries may have a future in selling non-Dover services rather than competing on the Dover routes. In trying to move away from direct tunnel substitutes, however, the ferries are limited by the fact that demand is probably greatest on the Dover routes and less strong elsewhere. Services from Newcastle to Hamburg would not be close substitutes for the tunnel, but neither is there great demand for them!

Providing a different kind of service (rather than a different quality) is another way of altering the elasticity of substitution. One method is to become part of a wider service within which the basic service is an integral part. One example of this would be "Orient-Express" tours in which the sea crossing is an integral part of the "experience". Other examples include the way in which the ferry companies have developed the concept of the one day excursion to France as a particular product of which a sea crossing is an indispensable part (it will be interesting to see how successful Eurotunnel will be at marketing these kinds of services).

Improving service quality is a standard means of market segmentation and is consistent with the high price/low market share "niche" strategy which the ferries must pursue. However, it is worth pointing out in the light of our analysis that this kind of strategy may be less effective, given the cost structure of the market, than a strategy to change the elasticity of substitution. Comparing our base results (where the tunnel is inferior) to those in Table 2 (where the Tunnel is of equal quality) it is clear that improved service quality for the ferries mainly impacts on the pricing of the tunnel (pushing tunnel prices down) and has little impact on the prices or profitability of the ferries.Product differentiation is not identical to better service quality and it is differentiation which the ferries must pursue.

"Improving service quality is a standard means of market segmentation but may be much less effective than a strategy to change the elasticity of substitution."

Here again we see the critical nature of the distinction between superiority and substitutability. The ferries will not achieve profitable operations in the long term either by reducing costs or by improving the quality of their services. By doing these things they can certainly impose losses on the Tunnel, but they do not significantly enhance their own profits, since the basic economics of the market – the Tunnel is always a lower cost competitor – remain unchanged. They can only find a continuing role for themselves by developing services for which the Tunnel is not a direct competitor.

Conclusions

Our conclusions fall into two categories. There are those that arise from the techniques we have used for approaching this problem. There are also some general conclusions about likely strategy choices and outcomes in product launches.

The Channel Tunnel is unusually well documented in terms of the availability of public information, but the data available to us is probably no better than would normally be available to a firm introducing a new product. We have defined how the optimal reactions of competitors can be analysed, so that the response and counter response which might otherwise take place in real time can be analysed and anticipated in advance. We have shown how the sensitivity of this solution to the key parameters – the perceived superiority/inferiority of the new product and the elasticity of substitution between it and its competitors – can be measured. We have stressed the key difference between superiority and substitutability.

This non-cooperative solution sets lower limits to profits and prices. We have considered the profitability of accommodations, and also the attractiveness of strategies designed to alter the structure of

"Price similar products similarly is clearly inappropriate for a process innovator."

"Accommodation between competitors with very different cost structures is particularly difficult to achieve."

"Firms may be financially weak but strong competitors."

the market in the long term, by driving out the entrant or the incumbent. We have also noted the possibility of market segmentation which, in this case, is more readily available to the established firms than to the newcomer and may be an attractive response for them.

The naive approach in what we describe as the prospectus scenario – price similar products similarly – is clearly inappropriate for a process innovator. A firm which owns a lower cost technology must seek a dominant market share, and the superiority or inferiority of its product, and the degree of substitutability between it and established products, determines the level of prices at which it achieves this, but not the optimal outcome. Incumbents cannot compete effectively in the long run either by improving their product quality or by reducing their own variable costs (unless they can reduce them to levels below those of the entrant which is impossible in this case, and in most cases implausible). Their only viable strategy is product differentiation.

If accommodation is possible, it may be more profitable for all parties but, as we have seen, accommodation between competitors with very different cost structures is particularly difficult to achieve. And, paradoxically, firms with substantial sunk costs may be financially weak, but strong competitors nonetheless.

John Kay is Director of the Centre for Business Strategy, London Business School; Stefan Szymanski is a Research Fellow at the Centre for Business Strategy, London Business School; Alan Manning is Lecturer in Economics at the London School of Economics.

REFERENCES

Kay J, A Manning and S Szymanski (1989) The Economic Benefits of the Channel Tunnel, *Economic Policy*, No 8.

Journal of Economic Perspectives—Volume 8, Number 3—Summer 1994—Pages 145–162

Selling Spectrum Rights

John McMillan

"It has shades of the '49 California gold rush," remarked one industry observer. "It's the 21st century equivalent of the Oklahoma land rush," said another.[1] The sought-after item is the radio spectrum, which the U.S. government has put on the auction block. The wavelengths on offer, formerly reserved for the military, are to be used for newly invented personal communications services (PCS): pocket telephones, portable fax machines, and wireless computer networks.

The auction is one of the biggest and most complicated in history. The spectrum on offer is estimated by the Office of Management and Budget (1993, p. 21) to be worth $10.6 billion. Thousands of spectrum licenses are for sale.

The bidders include most U.S. telecommunications firms: long-distance, local, and cellular telephone companies and cable-television companies. After spending billions for the spectrum licenses, the firms will invest still bigger sums installing transmitters and developing a customer case. The return is highly uncertain. The new PCS operators will compete not only with each other but also with entrenched cellular-telephone companies. The PCS technology is still being developed. The potential size of the market is unknown. (Will cordless telephones eventually replace many of the telephones now tethered by wires? Will the new wireless multimedia systems—carrying video and data as well as the spoken word—be in wide demand?) Successful bidders face daunting risks, but could make huge profits.

[1] *Business Week*, November 29, 1993, p. 128; and Tom Wheeler, president of the Cellular Telecommunications Industry Association, in the *Financial Times*, October 18, 1993, p. VIII.

■ *John McMillan is Professor of Economics, Graduate School of International Relations and Pacific Studies, University of California, San Diego.*

The story of how the spectrum auction was designed is a case study in the policy application of economic theory. The major telephone companies and the government relied on the advice of theorists. Paul Milgrom, Robert Wilson, and Charles Plott were hired by Pacific Bell, Jeremy Bulow and Barry Nalebuff by Bell Atlantic, Preston McAfee by Airtouch Communications, Robert Weber by Telephone and Data Systems, Mark Isaac by the Cellular Telecommunications Industry Association, Robert Harris and Michael Katz by Nynex, Daniel Vincent by American Personal Communications, Peter Cramton by MCI, John Ledyard and David Porter by the National Telecommunications and Information Administration, and the author of this article by the Federal Communications Commission (FCC). This was perhaps the biggest use of economic theorists as consultants since that other telephone-industry revolution, the break-up of AT&T ten years earlier.

The analysis of how auctions work is one of the successes of modern mathematical economics. Developed to try out new ideas in game theory, auction theory has turned out to have considerable practical content. The theory looks at the strategy of competition: how bidders choose their bids, not knowing the value of the item for sale and not knowing what their rivals know; and what the seller can do to stimulate the bidding competition, not knowing how much any of the bidders is willing to pay.[2] When the theorists met the policy-makers, concepts like Bayes-Nash equilibrium, incentive-compatibility constraints, and order-statistic theorems came to be discussed in the corridors of power.

The Decision to Auction

Spectrum licenses used to be assigned by administrative decision. Prospective license-holders filed applications and the Federal Communications Commission held comparative hearings to decide which applicant was the most worthy. This method broke down under its cumbersomeness: there was a big backlog of unassigned licenses. Congress replaced it with lotteries, assigning each license randomly among the applicants. The lotteries succeeded in assigning licenses quickly, but the prospect of a windfall gain attracted large numbers of applicants: there were nearly 400,000 applications for cellular licenses. In one not atypical case, an obscure group called the RACDG partnership was chosen by lottery in 1989 to run cellular telephones on Cape Cod; the partners then sold their license to Southwestern Bell for $41 million. The total value of cellular licenses the government gave away during the 1980s, according to a

[2]Wilson (1969, 1977) started the theory of auctions. Milgrom and Weber (1982a) developed many of the ideas used in designing the spectrum auction. For surveys of the theory, see McAfee and McMillan (1987), Milgrom (1987, 1989), and Wilson (1992); and on its practical content, see McMillan (1992, chs. 11–13).

Commerce Department estimate, was $46 billion.[3] Congress could not shrug off such figures.

Auctioning spectrum rights is not a new idea. The U.S. Congress held hearings on it as early as 1958, and R. H. Coase advocated it in a 1959 article. A 1985 FCC discussion paper showed that auctions would be workable (Kwerel and Felker, 1985). New Zealand legislated spectrum auctions in 1989, as did the United Kingdom in 1990. It was not until August 1993, however, that Congress passed legislation giving the FCC the authority to auction licenses. The FCC was to "design and test multiple alternative methodologies" for competitive bidding, and auctioning was to begin in May 1994. Auctioning did not change property rights: the restrictions on what the spectrum can be used for remain as before. A license lasts for a fixed term of up to ten years, but renewal is almost automatic provided it is being used appropriately. The Act specifies a range of aims for the auction: achieving an "efficient and intensive use of the electromagnetic spectrum;" promoting rapid deployment of new technologies; preventing excessive concentration of licenses; and ensuring some licenses go to minority-owned and women-owned companies, small businesses, and rural telephone companies (U.S. Congress, 1993, pp. 80–83).

The Act downplays revenue as an objective, and by its actions also the government showed that revenue was not its overriding objective (as, indeed, it should not be). If revenue had been paramount, the government could have offered a single monopoly license in each region—at the cost, obviously, of creating future inefficiencies. The government allocated a large swath of spectrum for PCS (120 megahertz, as compared with 50 megahertz for cellular telephones), even though maximizing revenue would have meant allocating less spectrum. Nevertheless, the wide publicity given to the forecasts of over $10 billion to be raised in the auction put pressure on the FCC to generate revenue.

The FCC canvassed a variety of auction-design possibilities and made some preliminary recommendations in its October 1993 Notice of Proposed Rule Making, and then called for comments from the industry. Over 220 firms and lobby groups filed submissions (some written by academics). The auction structure chosen by the Commissioners in March 1994 followed the recommendations of the FCC officials. Although pork-barrel politics had shaped the debate on whether to use auctions, the auction-design process was driven not by politics, but by economics.

Theory helped to answer key questions of auction design. Which of the basic auction forms should the government use? An open auction, in which bidders raise their bids until only one remains, who wins and pays the final bid? A first-price sealed-bid auction, in which each bidder submits a single sealed bid

[3]For more on the methods the U.S. government has used for allocating the spectrum, see Kwerel and Felker (1985), Kwerel and Williams (1993), U.S. Department of Commerce (1991), and Congressional Budget Office (1992). The estimate of cellular-license values, based on the stock-market value of cellular firms, is from U.S. Department of Commerce (1991, p. D6). The Cape Cod story is from the *New York Times*, May 30, 1991, p. A1.

and the high bidder wins, paying that bid? Or a second-price sealed-bid auction, in which each bidder submits a single sealed bid and the high bidder wins, but the price is the second-highest bid? Should the licenses be auctioned in sequence, or should they all be bid for at once in a large simultaneous auction? Should the government help the bidders to aggregate licenses by accepting bids for combinations of licenses, or should it allow only bids for individual licenses? How should the auction be structured to promote the interests of minority-owned and other designated firms? Should the government demand royalty payments? Should reserve (or minimum) prices be imposed? How much should the bidders be informed about their competition? Faulty choices over issues such as these could mean the auction produces a mismatch of licenses to firms, or the government misses out on revenue it could have earned, or the auction in some way breaks down.

Cautionary Tales from the Antipodes

That auction design matters is illustrated by the experience of the innovator in the field of spectrum auctions, New Zealand, which began auctioning the spectrum for radio, television, and cellular-telephone use in 1990. Following the advice of a U.S.-U.K. consulting firm, National Economic Research Associates (NERA), the government adopted second-price auctions (NERA, 1988). Politically embarrassing newspaper headlines resulted, as winners paid prices far below their bids (Mueller, 1991). In one extreme case, a firm that bid NZ$100,000 paid the second-highest bid of NZ$6. In another the high bid was NZ$7 million and the second bid NZ$5,000. (NZ$1 equaled US$0.55.) An Otago University student bid NZ$1 for a television license for a small city; no one else bid so he won and paid nothing. The revenue fell far short of the advance estimate: the cellular licenses fetched NZ$36 million, one-seventh the NZ$240 million that NERA had predicted.

The auction form had a political defect. By revealing the high bidder's willingness to pay, the second-price auction exposed the government to criticism, because after the auction everyone knew that the firm valued the license at more than it paid for it. This scope for criticism would exist even if it was unjustified, in that the auction had generated the best possible price. But theory says the auction form had another defect. No reserve (or minimum) prices were imposed. More revenue would have been earned if there had been reserve prices because, when there are few bidders (as in New Zealand), a reserve price substitutes for the missing bidding competition. The government abandoned the second-price auctions following the complaints in the media, and now uses first-price sealed-bid auctions instead. The auctions worked better than the alternative, bureaucratic decisions. They assigned the spectrum to its highest-value users, and did so quickly and with low administrative costs. But less revenue was raised than could have been.

An Australian government auction illustrates that it pays to think through the details of auction design. Two licenses for satellite-television services were offered in April 1993 by first-price sealed-bid auction. What followed was high comedy—though it did not seem funny to the communications minister, Senator Bob Collins, who almost lost his job. An opposition politician called it "one of the world's great media license fiascoes." The licenses were won by dark-horse bidders called Hi Vision Ltd. and Ucom Pty. Ltd., who beat the favorites—including a consortium of the big players, Rupert Murdoch, Kerry Packer, and Telecom Australia—by offering startlingly high bids of A$212 million and A$177 million. (A$1 equaled US$0.68.) The government hailed the auction results as opening up "a whole new era," bringing new firms into the closed shop of the Australian television industry. The press quoted one of Hi Vision's directors expressing confidence in his firm's ability to raise the bid amount, despite having issued capital of just A$100.

It soon became apparent that the two parvenu bidders had, in the Australian argot, pulled the wool over the eyes of the government. They had no intention of paying their bids; they had bid high merely to guarantee they won. They had also put in a series of lower bids—reportedly up to 20 such bids at A$5 million intervals. The two proceeded to default on their highest bids, which meant that the licenses had to be re-awarded at the next-highest bids, also theirs. The government had neglected to require a deposit, so default cost the bidders nothing. The prices cascaded down as Ucom and Hi Vision failed to produce the cash for their bids. Four months later, after several defaults by the same two bidders, Ucom paid A$117 million for its license, A$95 million less than its initial bid. Shortly afterwards Ucom sold it to a firm called Australis Media Ltd., earning an agreeable A$21 million profit. The cascading continued on the other license for another five months, with Hi Vision dropping out but then other firms successively defaulting on their bids. The final price was A$77 million, A$100 million less than the original bid. The successful bidder for the second license was none other than Ucom—which then sold it to a joint venture called Continental Century.[4]

This botched auction delayed by almost a year the introduction of pay television into Australia, already one of the few countries in the world still without it. The flaw in the auction rules, the source of the cascading bids, was the absence of a penalty for default, which meant bids were not meaningful.

[4]The saga did not end with the award of the licenses. Outsmarted by the upstarts, the Murdoch-Packer-Telecom consortium belatedly tried some gaming of its own, seeking to undermine the auction. It investigated using alternative technologies for delivering pay television, to squeeze the two new entrants out of the market. It tried to make a side-deal to gain control of another satellite license that the government had reserved for the state-run Australian Broadcasting Corporation. When that failed it sued to overturn the auction outcome, alleging the government had not complied with the bid guidelines; it withdrew its suit five minutes into the court hearing. (This story has been pieced together from reports in the *Age*, the *Australian*, the *Australian Financial Review*, the *Financial Times*, and the *Sydney Morning Herald* between April 1993 and March 1994.)

The lesson is that the fine print matters. Any oversight in auction design can have harmful repercussions, as bidders can be counted on to seek ways to outfox the mechanism.

What Is the Role of Theory in Auction Design?

Any kind of auction will result in better matches of licenses to firms than allocating the licenses at random, as was done before. But some kinds of auctions work better than others: this was why so much effort went into designing the spectrum auction.

What makes the spectrum auction distinctive are the potential efficiencies from license aggregation. The FCC divided the United States geographically and the spectrum by wavelength, making over 2,500 licenses. There are 51 major trading areas (MTAs), each of which has two large blocks of spectrum (of 30 megahertz). There are also 492 basic trading areas (BTAs), subdivisions of the MTAs, each of which has four spectrum blocks (one of 30 megahertz and four of 10 megahertz). Efficiencies will be realized if bidders succeed in aggregating some of the licenses.

The aggregation efficiencies rest on both engineering and economics. First, firms that have several licenses can spread their fixed costs of technology acquisition and customer-base development. Second, problems of interference at the boundaries of license areas mean there are production-cost economies from operating adjacent licenses. Third, several different, incompatible technologies are vying to become the industry standard. Consumers will value roaming capability—the ability to use the same telephone when they travel around the country—and this is more likely to be achieved if some firms own enough licenses to cover reasonably large areas. As well as these complementarities, there is also the opposite kind of interdependency: substitution among licenses. Each region contains several slices of the spectrum, so a firm that fails to win one license may bid for another in its place, and the auction design must be flexible enough to allow bidders to switch. It is impossible to foresee what will comprise efficient aggregations of licenses. Different firms want different license combinations. The ideal auction procedure should therefore be flexible enough to enable the bidders to construct their own aggregations.[5]

The government's multiple aims complicated the task of auction design: achieving an efficient outcome, promoting minority-owned and other designed firms, preventing monopolization. An extra goal, not written in the legislation

[5]The secondary market in licenses will help to correct any mismatches of licenses to firms that result from defects in auction design (as it did when the licenses went by lottery). This does not, however, render auction design unimportant. The secondary market is likely to be thin; transactions costs will limit its ability to fix inefficiencies.

but critical, was that the auction not misfire and cause political damage. Revenue was low on the list. These objectives are not necessarily in conflict with each other. Pursuing efficiency, for example, is usually consistent with pursuing revenue (because efficiency usually means awarding the license to the bidder willing to pay the most). The auction designers took the view that, after the other aims had been met, the auction form should be chosen to maximize revenue.

Theory has limits. Any nontheorist will readily assent to this proposition; but it is useful to be specific about where those limits lie. First, while theory can identify the relevant variables, it cannot tell us much about their size. Theory sometimes shows that there are effects that work in opposite directions from each other, and data are needed to establish which effect is likely to be dominant. Second, transactions costs arise in carrying out some of the policies that the theory recommends, and these costs may swamp the theoretical benefits of the policies. Third, implementing a recommendation of the theory may require knowledge that is unavailable. In particular, some of what auction theory identifies as optimal seller strategies depend on the distributions of bidders' valuations, which were not known. Fourth, the theory does not specify an unambiguously best form for the spectrum auction, which is so complex that no existing theorem covers it.[6]

Each of these limits of theory was met during the spectrum-auction design process. Judgment and guesswork were needed to merge the various partial theories, to weigh the government's various objectives, to estimate the relative sizes of the different effects, and to evaluate whether a proposed scheme was workable. Laboratory experiments also were used to test whether people bid as the theory predicts, and to look for hidden gaps in the rules that might leave the auction open to manipulation by the bidders.

Open Auction or Sealed Bids?

The FCC, following the theorists' recommendation, chose an open auction ahead of a sealed-bid auction. The advantage of an open auction is that it

[6]The main shortcoming of the existing theory is the lack of a model of aggregation of the items for sale. Engelbrecht-Wiggans and Weber (1979), Milgrom and Weber (1982b), Palfrey (1983), Hausch (1986), McAfee and McMillan (1988), Maskin and Riley (1990), and McAfee and Vincent (1993) model auctions of multiple items, but without interdependencies. Gale (1990) models an auction with aggregation efficiencies and shows that the seller optimally bundles all the licenses; but the assumption that full aggregation is ideal makes this inapplicable to the PCS auction. Lang and Rosenthal (1991) model the auctioning of items that are substitutes for each other. Bernheim and Whinston (1986) characterize equilibria in the bidding for combinations of items, assuming the bidders know each others' valuations. Much of what is known about multi-unit auctions with interdependencies comes from experiments: Grether, Isaac, and Plott (1981, 1989), Rassenti, Smith, and Bulfin (1982), Banks, Ledyard, and Porter (1989), Brewer and Plott (1993).

reduces the force of the "winner's curse."[7] The high bidder is the one who most overestimates the value of the item for sale, and thus may find, too late, that it has paid more than the license is worth. However, with billions of dollars at stake (and, for that matter, having been advised by economists) the bidders might anticipate the winner's curse when they decide their bids. A bidding firm that understands the winner's curse avoids falling victim to it by bidding cautiously, discounting its own estimate of the license's value. This discount is large—and rational bidders bid low—if the estimates can range widely around the true value. If bidders bid to avoid the winner's curse, then anything that improves the bidders' information is to the government's advantage, in that it induces the bidders to be less cautious.

Theory says, then, that the government can increase its revenue by publicizing any available information that affects the licenses' assessed value: providing assurances about future regulatory developments, or announcing how much new spectrum will be allocated to telecommunications in the future.

By the same logic of winner's curse avoidance, an open auction yields more revenue than a sealed-bid auction (Milgrom and Weber, 1982a). In a first-price sealed-bid auction, the price is based solely on the winner's own initial value estimate. In an open auction, by contrast, each bidder gets some indirect information about the other bidders' estimates from their bids, so the bidders are more confident and, on average, bid higher.

Two caveats apply to the choice of an open auction. First, the spectrum-auction bidders are likely to be risk averse, given the huge sums being bid. Bidder risk aversion tends to make bids higher in a sealed-bid auction than in an open auction (Riley and Samuelson, 1981). Whether the winner's curse effect exceeds the risk-aversion effect is an empirical issue. Second, if bidder collusion is anticipated, the government might prefer a sealed-bid auction, because it deters collusion more effectively than an open auction (Milgrom, 1987). The FCC and the economist-consultants judged these two effects to be outweighed by the bidders' ability to learn from others' bids in the open auction.

Instead of using a conventional open auction, in which the bidders call out their bids, the FCC chose to run multiple rounds of sealed bids, announcing the bids after each round, and with a minimum bid increment between rounds. This has the informational advantages of a literally open auction, but offers the

[7] The winner's curse was first identified by Wilson (1969). Auction theory has two basic models: the common-value model and the independent-private-values model. The spectrum auction has aspects of both of these polar cases (so the bidders' valuations are affiliated: Milgrom and Weber, 1982a). Values are private insofar as different bidders have different stocks of capital, labor, and knowledge, and so different prospects for earning profits from the licenses. Values are common, on the other hand, insofar as there is uncertainty about technological possibilities and about consumer demand for the new mobile communication services: the bidders have their own estimates of technology and demand, but are trying to estimate the same number, the common value. The secondary market also induces a common-value aspect, as the bids reflect guesses of the prices that will rule there. Winner's curse effects reflect common values.

government extra control. With oral bidding, the bidders automatically know against whom they are competing. With multiple-round sealed bidding, the government can choose what to tell the bidders about the competition. Although the winner's curse idea suggests full information release—all bid amounts and bidder identities—fears of anticompetitive behavior suggest concealing the bidders' identities during the bidding: revealing identities may help bidders to collude. The compromise was to announce the bids during the bidding, but not the bidders' identities.

Simultaneous or Sequential Auction?

The most contentious question during the auction-design process was whether the licenses should be sold in sequence or simultaneously. The debate pitted theoretical virtues against practical feasibility. A simultaneous mechanism promises efficient aggregation of licenses; but the skeptics questioned whether it can realistically deliver on this promise.

Sequential auctions are the usual practice when multiple related items (parcels of real estate, coins, stamps) are sold. The advantage of the sequential method, as some of the economists pointed out, is its administrative simplicity; also, bidders know which licenses they already own and which have gone to others.[8] A drawback of the sequential mechanism in the case of spectrum licenses is that it impedes aggregation by eliminating backup strategies. A bidding firm may rethink its evaluation of one of the early licenses in the light of the bidding activity it observes on the later licenses; but in a sequential setting the bidder cannot go back. Also, predatory bidding can occur (Pitchik and Schotter, 1988). A bidder may try to drive prices for the early licenses up to excessive levels so the winners will be unable to afford to compete for the later licenses.

A simultaneous auction with multiple rounds of bidding allows bidders to take advantage of any information revealed during the bidding. It gives bidders, bidding license by license, full flexibility in constructing license aggregations, and in being able to switch to their backup aggregations should their first-choice aggregations turn out to be too expensive. Its symmetry prevents predatory bidding. Thus a simultaneous mechanism, if it works, creates better

[8]If a sequential mechanism is used, should the licenses covering the largest populations go first or last? For efficiency, the best ordering is large to small, as the large regions are the key parts of any aggregations. This ordering may mean sacrificing some revenue. The bidders learn from the early bidding, so the winner's curse discounts are smaller—and bids higher—the more regions have already been sold. If the smaller regions go first, then by the time the big regions are sold the winner's curse effect is reduced. An opposite revenue effect also exists, however: as the large-to-small ordering generates more efficiency, it raises the potential revenue and may raise realized revenue. Since Congress said efficiency had precedence over revenue, large-to-small was the recommended ordering.

license aggregations than a sequential mechanism. The crucial question about any simultaneous mechanism is whether it is workable. It will fail unless an effective stopping rule can be devised.

The two simplest stopping rules are inadequate. One would be to close licenses one by one, as the bidding ceases on each. But this is not really a simultaneous auction: it is effectively sequential, with a random ordering of the licenses. Another simple stopping rule leaves all licenses open until bidding ceases on all. This gives bidders complete flexibility in constructing aggregations, but gives them little incentive to bid actively: they could hold back, waiting for others to show their hands. A bidder wanting to game the mechanism could repeatedly bid on one small license, causing it to take interminably long to close. An effective stopping rule, then, must (1) end the auction in a reasonable time; (2) close the licenses almost simultaneously, to aid license aggregation; and (3) be simple enough to be understandable by the bidders.

Three stopping rules were discussed. One, offered by Paul Milgrom and Robert Wilson, keeps all licenses open until all close, but reduces gaming by means of an activity rule. Bidders must specify in advance, and pay deposits on, the total number of licenses they intend to own. In each round, a bidder must be active on a minimal number of licenses (a specified fraction of the bidder's pre-announced total), which means either being the current high bidder or putting in a bid that exceeds the current high bid by at least the specified increment. The mechanism has three phases, each with an increasingly stringent activity rule. A second stopping rule, offered by Preston McAfee, closes each license separately as the bidding stops on it, but tries to ensure that all licenses close at roughly the same time by slowing down the bidding as final prices are approached. It does this by reducing the minimum bid increment for a given license as the number of active bidders falls, so that when only two bidders remain the price rises slowly. The third stopping rule, offered by the FCC staff and the author of this paper, uses the skewedness of the population distribution among licenses. A relatively small number of licenses (one-fifth) account for 50 percent of the U.S. population: define these licenses to be the core. The all-open-until-all-close rule applies to the licenses in the core. After the core licenses close, all at the same time, the bidding continues in the remaining, smaller licenses, with license-by-license stopping on them. This mechanism therefore permits full efficiency in the core licenses, and sacrifices efficiency to speed of closing in the smaller licenses.

For bids to be meaningful, there must be some penalty on bidders who withdraw their bids (an important consideration, as the Australian example shows). If bids can be freely withdrawn, then the bidders cannot infer any reliable information from each other's bids. How to ensure sincerity of bidding without unduly restricting the bidders' flexibility to shift to backup plans needed a judgment call. One proposal was that, when a bidder withdraws while having the highest bid, the government require the bidder to pay the difference between its bid and the price at which the license ultimately sells (thus having the bidder compensate the government for the loss it causes by reneging on its bid).

The rules of a simultaneous auction, then, are necessarily quite complicated. Critics pointed to a risk of system breakdown: either from an inadvertent gap in the rules that allows bidders to game the mechanism, or from a clerical flaw in the bid-transmission process. The bidders also must be capable of processing a lot of information. The proponents of the simultaneous mechanism (including the author of this article) replied that the potential gains from achieving good license aggregations justified a little complexity.[9]

The FCC, in announcing the auction rules in March 1994, left itself the option of choosing from a range of auction forms, depending on the degree of license interdependency and whether the license values are high or low. "Because the Commission expects most licenses to be of high value and interdependent, it found that simultaneous multiple round auctions... should be the Commission's preferred auction design. ... Because of the superior information and flexibility provided by simultaneous multiple round auctions, this method will facilitate efficient aggregations across spectrum bands" (FCC, 1994, p. 2). The FCC left itself the possibility of using sequential auctions in those cases where the licenses have little interdependence, or single-round sealed bidding where there are large numbers of low-value licenses. For the simultaneous auction, the FCC chose the stopping rule that keeps the bidding open on all licenses until bidding stops on all. An activity rule would be used to ensure the auction closes within a reasonable time. Bidders would be required to pay a substantial deposit, so as to limit the bidding to serious bidders. Bid-withdrawal penalties were imposed to ensure sincere bidding. A high bidder withdrawing its bid during the course of the auction would have to pay the difference between its bid and the price for which the license ultimately sold. For withdrawing a bid after close of the auction there would be an extra 3 percent penalty.

Should Combinational Bids Be Permitted?

Should bidders be permitted to bid on combinations of licenses—that is, bids for bundles of licenses together—or should bids be accepted only

[9]A precedent—a large-scale simultaneous auction that worked—is the 1992 sale by Czechoslovakia (as it was then) of shares in nearly 1,500 state-owned firms (Svejnar and Singer, 1992). The auction was Walrasian. In the first round, the privatization ministry set a price per share. A bid, by vouchers, consisted of a request for a stated number of shares at the set price. In subsequent rounds, the ministry set the price as a function of earlier-round excess demands or supplies. Only five rounds were held, so price adjustments between rounds had to be large and misjudgments occurred, with some big swings from excess demand to excess supply and back. The Czechoslovakian auction was successful, however, in that it established equilibrium relative prices for the firms' shares, and disposed of all but 7 percent of the 22 million shares.

license-by-license? Private-sector auctions sometimes use combinational bidding when the items are worth more together than separately. When a factory is being sold, for example, the buildings and machines are offered as a set as well as piece by piece (Cassady, 1967, pp. 156–61). In the spectrum auctions it is possible that the license complementarities are large enough that, for efficiency, one or more firms should cover the entire country. This means winning every one of a large number of licenses (51 in the case of MTAs, 492 in the case of BTAs). With so many licenses to be won, it is possible that idiosyncratic events in a few auctions might prevent the efficient aggregation from being achieved. Because of a worry that the FCC had doomed the industry to fragmentation by dividing the nation into so many pieces, some suggested aggregation be aided by allowing nationwide bids, with the nationwide bid winning if it exceeds the sum of the highest bids on the individual licenses.

Theory says, however, that with nationwide bidding, licenses may not end up with the firms that are willing to pay the most (Palfrey, 1983). Nationwide bids can reduce the bidding competition, as the nationwide bidders refrain from driving up the separate-license prices. There is a free-rider problem. Separate-license bidders may not raise their bids by enough to beat a nationwide bidder because only part of the gain from raising their bid accrues to them. As a result, a nationwide bidder may win even though the total value of licenses if awarded separately would exceed the nationwide bidder's value. The auction is biased toward the nationwide bidders.[10] A variant of the nationwide proposal sought to mitigate this implicit favoritism by handicapping nationwide bidders: putting a premium on any nationwide bid, so it wins only if it is at least, say, 5 percent more than the sum of the individual bids (as is sometimes

[10] Imagine there are three bidders, E, W, and N, and two licenses, East and West (this example is due to Preston McAfee). Firm E values owning East alone at $2 billion, West alone at $1 billion, and the nation at $3 billion. Firm W values East at $1 billion, West at $2 billion, and the nation at $3 billion. Firm N values East at $1.6 billion, West at $1.6 billion, and the nation at $3.3 billion. Suppose first that nationwide bidding is not allowed. In the two open auctions, W wins West at a price slightly above $1.6 billion (which is the price at which the second-last bidder, who happens to be N, drops out), and E wins East at slightly above $1.6 billion. This is the ideal outcome, in that the licenses go to their highest-value users. The total value of the licenses to their new owners is $4 billion, of which the government gets a little over $3.2 billion. Now suppose there is a national auction in addition to the separate auctions. Anticipating winning the nationwide auction, N has no incentive to bid for the separate licenses. Only E and W bid for them, so the price in each stops at slightly more than $1 billion. All three bidders compete in the national auction. Firm N wins the nationwide bidding at slightly above $3 billion, which is where both E and W drop out. The nationwide bid of $3 billion exceeds the sum of the two separate bids, so the nationwide bidder N wins. This is not the efficient outcome: the total use-value is $3.3 billion and government revenue slightly above $3 billion. The free-rider point is that E and W would have to raise their nationwide bids by a total of $1 billion to beat N; but neither alone will raise its bid this much, as that would mean bidding more than value. Now make one change to the example: increase N's value of the nation to $4 billion, so ideally N would win the nation. But N wins even without nationwide bidding, by bidding slightly more than $2 billion in each separate auction.

done in the private sector; see Cassady, 1967, p. 160). Most of the economists recommended against permitting nationwide bids, even with a premium.

The ideal level of aggregation may not be nationwide. Some subnational aggregations are likely to be efficient. A more ambitious mechanism allows bidders to express their preferences over aggregations (Banks, Ledyard, and Porter, 1989). Bidders may bid for groups of licenses, in any combinations they choose. A group bid wins if it exceeds the sum of the individual bids. Experiments have found that this mechanism works better than separate-license bidding when the bidders' preferences are idiosyncratic, in that bidders rank the various aggregations differently. (One source of aggregation idiosyncrasies is government regulation: firms that already own cellular licenses are limited in the amount of PCS spectrum they can own in the same region.) If the different bidders have reasonably similar rankings across alternative aggregations, on the other hand, they can construct their own aggregations from individual auctions, and there is no need for combinational bidding. The disadvantage of the full-combinational mechanism is its complexity: both for bidders in understanding how it works and for the government in running it. A huge number of possible combinations exists (for the 492 BTA licenses, more than 10^{148}). Computer or other administrative breakdowns may occur. In the judgment of most of the economists involved in the auction design, the complexity costs outweighed the potential efficiency gains: the full-combinational mechanism was ahead of its time.

The FCC decided that bids for combinations of licenses should not be permitted in a simultaneous auction (at least not before significant proven advances have been made in combinational bidding procedures). If a sequential auction is used, and if it is clear that some particular level of license aggregation is efficient (such as nationwide), then the FCC might adopt combinational bidding, possibly with a bid premium.

How to Aid Designated Bidders?

Congress required the FCC to "ensure that small businesses, rural telephone companies, and businesses owned by members of minority groups and women are given the opportunity to participate in the provision of spectrum-based services" (U.S. Congress, 1993, p. 81). Theory says that auctions usually produce efficient outcomes: in most cases the winner is the bidder with the highest use-value for the license. This argues for laissez-faire: letting level-playing-field auctions determine who gets the licenses. Favoring certain bidders is justified, on the other hand, if bidders' willingness to pay does not reflect social value, because of externalities or capital-market imperfections, or for distributional reasons.

The FCC initially proposed that one-fourth of the spectrum for sale be set aside for bidding by the designated firms only. A skeptic might question this policy for its arbitrariness. Why does one-fourth give the right amount of correction: why not one-third or one-fifth? Also, setting aside some of the licenses lowers revenue by reducing the bidding competition. Theory offers an alternative way of aiding the designated bidders (Myerson, 1981; McAfee and McMillan, 1987, pp. 714–16). The government could allow any firm to bid on any license, but give the designated firms a price preference. With a preference of, say, 10 percent, a designated firm would win if its bid was no more than 10 percent less than the highest nondesignated-firm bid. This is a free-lunch policy. It would not only address the public-policy goal of increasing the number of licenses won by the designated firms, but it would also actually increase the government's revenue. Most of the designated bidders, presumably, have a lower willingness to pay for the licenses than the nondesignated firms (otherwise there would be little need for preferences). With level-playing-field bidding, they would therefore impose little competitive pressure on the nondesignated firms, who could get away with bidding relatively low. A price preference for the designated firms stimulates the bidding competition, forcing the nondesignated firms to bid higher. If the government sets the price preference at the right level, its revenue-raising effect (from the higher bids from the nondesignated firms) outweighs its revenue-lowering effect (from the chance that a designated firm wins and pays a low price). The net effect of the price preference, therefore, is to increase the government's revenue.

A difficulty in applying price preferences is in knowing the appropriate level at which to set them: the only practical approach would be to experiment with different levels (between, say, 5 and 15 percent). As with other choices between price and quantity tools (for example, in the environmental arena), quantity controls can seem more predictable, while price-based instruments seem more uncertain. But, as a rule of thumb, a 10 percent preference would result in about 10 percent more of the licenses being won by designated firms than would have happened without the preference.

In the end, the FCC retained the ability to favor designated bidders in a variety of ways, by using set-asides, price preferences, or installment payments. The FCC also said it would monitor any resale of licenses by these firms. To prevent what it called "unjust enrichment" by auction winners, the rules on resale require any designated firm selling its license to return to the government that part of the profit earned from the sale that is attributable to the artificially low purchase price.

Another kind of special treatment is the award of pioneer preferences. In December 1993 the FCC gave licenses to Omnipoint Communications, Personal Communications, and Cox Enterprises, as a reward for their having developed new PCS technologies. This removed from the auction three of the most valuable licenses, covering New York, Los Angeles, and Washington D.C. Had they been auctioned, they might have fetched up to $1 billion—an implausibly generous reward to the inventors.

Should Royalties or Reserve Prices Be Used?

Should winning bidders make a single up-front payment, or should the government extract royalties based on value in use? Theory says royalties increase the revenue from the sale. A three-way tradeoff exists (McAfee and McMillan, 1986; Laffont and Tirole, 1987). Royalties have two revenue-raising effects. First, royalties shift to the government part of the risk otherwise borne by the firm and, if the firm is risk-averse, raise the firm's willingness to pay. Second, and more subtly, royalties stimulate the bidding competition, for they reduce the effect of differences in valuations among the bidders. The cost of using royalties, on the other hand, is that they act as a disincentive to post-auction investment, since the license-holder keeps only a fraction of any revenue generated. The theory shows that, on balance, royalties benefit the government. Royalties on spectrum licenses are probably unworkable, however, since the government would have to compute the profits attributable to the licenses. In a telecommunications firm with multiple lines of business, it would be difficult to isolate the profit from the license alone, and easy for the firm to use creative accounting to understate it. The FCC decided against royalties.

Should the government impose reserve (or minimum) prices? Theory says it should. A reserve price, if set at the right level, can raise the government's revenue by driving up the price in the event that all bidders except one place little value on the license (Myerson, 1981; Riley and Samuelson, 1981). But the reserve price has its effect only when bidding competition is weak. The U.S. spectrum auctions (unlike in New Zealand, with its small population) will probably attract enough bidders to make reserve prices unnecessary. The FCC decided reserve prices, if used at all, would only be on licenses for which only two or three firms had applied to bid.

Spectrum Auctions and Auction Theory

Auctioning spectrum licenses is an idea whose time has come. Nations with inadequate telephone systems—less-developed countries and the formerly Communist countries—are leapfrogging technologies and going straight to wireless rather than laying wires. Once telecommunications ceases to be a state monopoly, a method for allocating the spectrum must be chosen: administrative process, lottery, or auction. An auction offers two advantages over the alternatives: it not only raises revenue, but also identifies the firms with the highest use-values for the spectrum. Egypt, India, and Colombia have auctioned cellular licenses. Argentina's 1993 cellular-license auction illustrates the variety of public-policy purposes to which auctions can be put. The competition was not over price, but over which bidder could offer to set up cellular-telephone service in the fastest time. A consortium including GTE and AT&T won by promising to provide cellular service across a vast area of Argentina's countryside in only one month.[11]

The FCC's spectrum auction is unprecedented in its use of economic theory in the design of the auction. The theorists' contribution showed in the choice of an auction with multiple rounds of bids; in the preference for a simultaneous auction when licenses are interdependent and have high value; in the form of the stopping rule and the use of an activity rule for the simultaneous auction; and in the nature of the bid-withdrawal penalties. The FCC's adoption of a simultaneous multiple-round auction ahead of a sequential or a single-round-sealed-bid auction—which are more conventional but arguably less effective for selling spectrum licenses—was a triumph for game theory. The auction runs through the summer and fall of 1994. The intriguing next step will be to appraise its performance.

■ *I thank the FCC staff for educating me in these issues: Jonathan Cohen, Jonathan Levy, Kent Nakamura, Robert Pepper, David Reed, John Williams, and especially Evan Kwerel. I thank also Roger Bohn, Peter Cramton, Peter Gourevitch, John Ledyard, Preston McAfee, Paul Milgrom, David Moore, Barry Nalebuff, Charles Plott, Daniel Vincent, Robert Weber, Bryce Wilkinson, and Robert Wilson for their suggestions, as well as editors Alan Krueger, Carl Shapiro, and Timothy Taylor; and the Sloan Foundation for its support of the PCS auction conference.*

[11] *Financial Times*, January 25, 1994, p. 6; *Wall Street Journal*, January 28, 1994, p. A8; *New York Times*, November 9, 1993, p. C16.

References

Banks, Jeffrey S., John O. Ledyard, and David P. Porter, "Allocating Uncertain and Unresponsive Resources: An Experimental Approach," *Rand Journal of Economics*, Spring 1989, *20*, 1–22.

Bernheim, B. Douglas, and Michael D. Whinston, "Menu Auctions, Resource Allocation, and Economic Influence," *Quarterly Journal of Economics*, February 1986, *101*, 1–32.

Brewer, Paul, and Charles R. Plott, "Decentralized Allocation of the Use of a Transportation Network," mimeo, California Institute of Technology, Pasadena, November 1993.

Cassady, Ralph, *Auctions and Auctioneering*. Berkeley: University of California Press, 1967.

Coase, R. H., "The Federal Communications Commission," *Journal of Law and Economics*, October 1959, *2*, 1–40.

Congressional Budget Office, "Auctioning Radio Spectrum Licenses," Washington DC, March 1992.

Engelbrecht-Wiggins, Richard, and Robert J. Weber, "An Example of a Multi-Object Auction Game," *Management Science*, December 1979, *25*, 1272–77.

Federal Communications Commission (FCC), "Notice of Proposed Rule Making," Washington DC, October 1993.

Federal Communications Commission (FCC), "FCC Adopts Rules to Implement Competitive Bidding to Award Spectrum Licenses," press release, Washington DC, March 8, 1994.

Gale, Ian, "A Multiple-Object Auction with Superadditive Values," *Economics Letters*, December 1990, *34*, 323–28.

Grether, David M, R. Mark Isaac, and Charles R. Plott, "The Allocation of Landing Rights by Unanimity Among Competitors," *American Economic Review Papers and Proceedings*, May 1981, *71*, 166–71.

Grether, David M, R. Mark Isaac, and Charles R. Plott, *The Allocation of Scarce Resources: Experimental Economics and the Problem of Allocating Airport Slots*. Boulder: Westview Press, 1989.

Hausch, Donald B., "Multi-Object Auctions: Sequential vs. Simultaneous Sales," *Management Science*, December 1986, *32*, 1599–610.

Kwerel, Evan R., and Alex Felker, "Using Auctions to Select FCC Licenses," OPP Working Paper No. 16, Office of Plans and Policy, FCC, May 1985.

Kwerel, Evan R., and John R. Williams, "Moving Toward a Market for Spectrum," *Regulation*, 1993, No. 2, *16*, 53–62.

Laffont, Jean-Jacques, and Jean Tirole, "Auctioning Incentive Contracts," *Journal of Political Economy*, October 1987, *95*, 921–37.

Lang, Kevin, and Robert W. Rosenthal, "The Contractors' Game," *Rand Journal of Economics*, Autumn 1991, *22*, 329–38.

Maskin, Eric, and John Riley, "Optimal Multi-Unit Auctions." In Hahn, F., ed., *The Economics of Missing Markets and Information*. Oxford: Oxford University Press, 1990, 312–33.

McAfee, R. Preston, and John McMillan, "Bidding for Contracts: A Principal-Agent Analysis," *Rand Journal of Economics*, Autumn 1986, *17*, 326–38.

McAfee, R. Preston, and John McMillan, "Auctions and Bidding," *Journal of Economic Literature*, June 1987, *25*, 699–738.

McAfee, R. Preston, and John McMillan, "Multidimensional Incentive Compatibility and Mechanism Design," *Journal of Economic Theory*, December 1988, *46*, 335–54.

McAfee, R. Preston, and Daniel Vincent, Daniel, "The Declining Price Anomaly," *Journal of Economic Theory*, June 1993, *60*, 191–212.

McMillan, John, *Games, Strategies, and Managers*. New York: Oxford University Press, 1992.

Milgrom, Paul, "Auction Theory." In Bewley, Truman, ed., *Advances in Economic Theory*. Cambridge: Cambridge University Press, 1987, 1–32.

Milgrom, Paul, "Auctions and Bidding: A Primer," *Journal of Economic Perspectives*, Summer 1989, *3*, 3–22.

Milgrom, Paul, and Robert J. Weber, "A Theory of Auctions and Competitive Bidding," *Econometrica*, September 1982a, *50*, 1089–122.

Milgrom, Paul, and Robert J. Weber, "A Theory of Auctions and Competitive Bidding II," mimeo, Northwestern University, 1982b.

Mueller, Milton, "Reform of Spectrum Management: Lessons from New Zealand," Policy Insight No. 135, Reason Foundation, Los Angeles, November 1991.

Myerson, Roger, "Optimal Auction Design," *Mathematics of Operations Research*, February 1981, *6*, 58–73.

National Economic Research Associates (NERA), *Management of the Radio Frequency Spectrum in New Zealand: A Report for the New*

Zealand Government. London: NERA, November 1988.

Office of Management and Budget (OMB), *Mid-Session Review of the 1994 Budget*, Washington, DC, September 1993.

Palfrey, Thomas R., "Bundling Decisions by a Multiproduct Monopolist with Incomplete Information," *Econometrica*, March 1983, *51*, 463–85.

Pitchik, Carolyn, and Andrew Schotter, "Perfect Equilibria in Budget-Constrained Sequential Auctions: An Experimental Study," *Rand Journal of Economics*, Autumn 1988, *19*, 363–88.

Rassenti, S. J., V. L. Smith, and R. L. Bulfin, "A Combinational Auction Mechanism for Airport Time Slot Allocation," *Bell Journal of Economics*, Autumn 1982, *13*, 402–17.

Riley, John, and William Samuelson, "Optimal Auctions," *American Economic Review*, June 1981, *71*, 381–92.

Svejnar, Jan, and Miroslav Singer, "The Czechoslovak Voucher Privatization: An Assessment of Results," mimeo, University of Pittsburgh, December 1992.

U.S. Congress, Omnibus Budget Reconciliation Act of 1993, Conference Report [HR 2264], Title VI, "Communications Licensing and Spectrum Allocation Improvement," Report 103-213, August 4, 1993.

U.S. Department of Commerce, *U.S. Spectrum Management Policy: Agenda for the Future*. Washington, DC, NTIA Special Publication 91-23, February 1991.

Wilson, Robert B., "Competitive Bidding with Disparate Information," *Management Science*, March 1969, *15*, 446–48.

Wilson, Robert B., "A Bidding Model of Perfect Competition," *Review of Economic Studies*, October 1977, *44*, 511–18.

Wilson, Robert B., "Strategic Analysis of Auctions." In Aumann, R. J., and S. Hart, eds., *Handbook of Game Theory with Economic Applications*, Vol. 1. Amsterdam: North-Holland, 1992, 227–80.

Economies of Scale, Natural Monopoly, and Imperfect Competition in an Experimental Market*

CHARLES R. PLOTT
California Institute of Technology
Pasadena, California

ALEXANDRE BORGES SUGIYAMA
University of Arizona
Tucson, Arizona

GILAD ELBAZ
IBM Corporation
San Jose, California

I. Introduction

This paper reports on the behavior of markets in which all agents have identical costs with economies of scale over the entire range of demand. Each firm, by choosing a larger scale of plant and a larger volume, can experience lower average cost. Thus, the markets are characterized by the fundamental technological property that has motivated decades of theorizing about natural monopoly and imperfect competition. The primary question posed by the research is whether or not a natural monopoly emerges and sets prices at monopoly levels, or whether the data are more closely approximated by some alternative model of imperfect competition, such as monopolistic competition, Cournot oligopoly, or contestable market theory.

Some of the principle results of the experiments reported here can, in retrospect, be interpreted as having been anticipated by the pathbreaking work of Coursey, Isaac, Luke and Smith [1, 69–84], and by Coursey, Isaac, and Smith [2, 91–113]. While these previous experiments involved economic environments that were much less complicated than the one studied here, the tendencies previously observed are clearly present in the behaviors reported here. So, in a sense, the results reported here can be interpreted as a major extension of the previous results, as well as replication and robustness check.

The similarities of experimental design with previous experiments rest on the facts of falling average cost and no barriers to entry that existed in all experiments. However, the number and

*This paper began with a project in an experimental economics class at Caltech in which G. Elbaz and A. Sugiyama were undergraduate students. In addition to the authors, Peter Ying contributed to the project during the initial stages of research. The comments of William Novshek are also appreciated. The financial support of the National Science Foundation and the Caltech Laboratory for Experimental Economics and Political Science is gratefully acknowledged.

nature of departures from the previous research are substantial. The markets studied here were much larger, so parameters took values in a more continuous manner. The experiments studied here involved two markets, so entry into the falling average cost market was accompanied by the opportunity cost of profits foregone in the alternative market. The alternative market was a computerized double auction which agents generally enjoy, so entry into the falling average cost market did not result from an attempt to relieve boredom, which one might have suspected played a role in previous studies. Agents entering the falling average cost market were required to make a choice of scale of plant that affected costs. Thus, the theory of cost minimization played an active role in developing models. This dimension was completely absent from previous experiments. Previous experiments used linear average costs that fell with volume until a capacity constraint was reached (within the range of demand) and then costs became vertical. Average costs in the experiments reported here were nonlinear and fell throughout the range of demand. In addition, the nonlinearities, scale economies, and demand were configured to create Cournot equilibria in the appropriate Cournot model of the environment. The Cournot equilibria were separated from the competitive (price equals average cost plus opportunity cost) equilibrium. In previous experiments the Cournot equilibrium was also the competitive equilibrium. The number of potential entrants used in previous experiments was small, ranging from two to four. In the experiments reported here, there were seven potential competitors. Briefly put, the choice of parameters for the experiments reported here was such that the economic environment was similar to those commonly found in the figures in economics textbooks.

II. Experimental Environment, Design and Procedures

A total of three experiments were conducted. Subjects were students at the California Institute of Technology and summer interns at Caltech. Some of the subjects were experienced in the operation of electronic markets. As it turns out, the empirical tendencies that were observed in the experiments are so pronounced that only three experiments appear to be needed to answer the original question posed. Since the experiments are expensive in terms of time and money, a decision was made to limit the number of experiments to three. Given the behavior exhibited by the twenty-one people studied, the expectation that anything would be learned from additional replications seems too low to justify the cost.

Each experiment consisted of 7 buyers and 7 sellers. Subjects with experience were placed in the more complex role of sellers. Two markets were created. They will be called market A and market B. The buyers could participate in both. Sellers could participate in either but not in both. In market A sellers had identical cost functions designed such that they were guaranteed a rent from participating in the market. The parameters were chosen such that in market A the rents per seller and the market price were (theoretically) independent of the number of sellers that chose to sell in that market. Market A was organized by a (computerized) double auction that fully occupied the attention of the sellers that chose to function in that market so they would not be motivated by boredom to enter market B.

Market B was different. Sellers that chose to operate in market B made irrevocable decisions about scale of plant, the quantity that they would offer for sale and the price they would post. Thus, the market organization was the standard posted price environment in which commitments were private information until the market opened. The only difference was that a seller could choose to drop out of the market once the decisions of other sellers were public but before

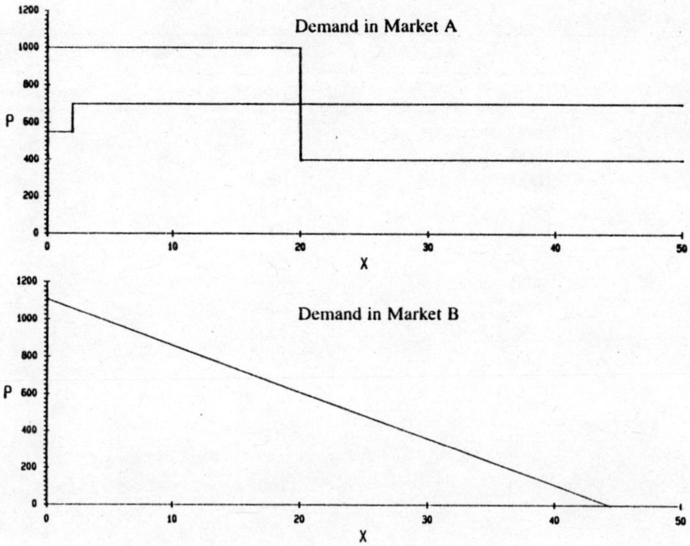

Figure 1.

the market opened. The decisions to drop out were also private (revealed simultaneously) and irrevocable. The dropout decision served to limit losses to the opportunity cost of market A profits foregone, and reduced the probability that subject bankruptcies would disrupt the experiment. In market B all sellers had the same cost function. The cost function was characterized by economies of scale.

In summary, the economic environment had the following properties:

1. Participation in market B involved an opportunity cost because reasonably predictable rents could be gained from participation in market A.
2. Participation in market A was "fun" in the sense that many people enjoy the speed and activity of the computerized double auction.
3. Participation in market B could be done without exposure to a major out-of-pocket loss. Sellers could "drop out" if they expected volume to be less than was anticipated at the time that scale of plant was chosen.
4. All transactions took place in a currency called francs. Each franc was converted to dollars at a rate of .0075 for buyers and .006 for sellers.

The Market Environment

A continuous approximation of market demands for markets A and B are contained in Figure 1. The equation for the continuous approximation of the market demand in market B is

$$P = 1110 - 25x. \tag{1}$$

Individual parameters for the demanders are in Table 1. Each of seven demanders made money by participating in market A and in market B. Each buyer had the same redemption values

Table I. Individual Incentives

	Market A		Market B
Unit	Demand*	Costs**	Market Demand***
1	1000	550	1085
2	1000	550	1060
3	1000	700	1035
4	400	700	1010
5	400	700	985
6	400	700	960
7	400	700	935
8	400	700	910
9	400	700	etc.
10	400	700	−25 each unit
11	400	700	—
12	400	700	—
13	400	700	—
14	400	700	—
15	400	700	—
16			—
17			—
18			—
19			

*All buyer agents (00 through 06) had the same demand as listed here.
**All seller agents (07 through 13) had the same costs as listed here.
***Individual agents demand rotated each period

in market A each period. That is, in market A both the market demand and the individual redemption values were constant over periods. In market B, the market demand was constant over periods but the redemption value of each individual changed from period to period. A fixed family of schedules was rotated among the individual demanders. The rotation schedule is contained in Plott, Sugiyama, and Elbaz [8]. The rotation convention was used because uncertainty about which model might be most accurate gave us little confidence in our ability to predict incomes of buyers. We wanted the income of all subject buyers to be sufficiently high to keep their interests. The rotation had a useful feature of removing dramatic asymmetries. Each of seven sellers had identical costs throughout the experiment. The fact that the costs were identical was not known by any agent in the markets. Each had the option of participating in either market A or in market B, but not in both. A seller that participated in market A used the cost schedule in Table I. For a single seller the graph of the (marginal) costs are included in Figure 1. As can be seen, the seller had two low cost units and then had constant cost afterwards for enough units to satisfy the entire demand.

Given these individual costs in market A, the market price (according to the competitive model) will be constant at 700 at all volumes near the demand (at 21 units) regardless of the number of suppliers in market A. As will be stated more clearly below, the equilibrium price will be near 700 and rents for all sellers in market A will be about 300 (2 units at 150 = 700 − 550 each) regardless of the number of other sellers in market A, as long as there are at least two.[1]

The costs of all seven suppliers were the same for market B. Each subject had separate tables

1. Typically, two or three sellers are enough for competitive equilibrium behavior in a double auction market.

(in different colors) for marginal cost, average cost, and total cost. The total cost table is shown as Table II. As can be seen, costs depended upon both scale of plant and volume of sales.

A continuous approximation to the underlying discrete parameter cost function has been useful in the development of behavioral predictions, as well as experimental design decisions. Figure 2 contains a graph of the long-run average cost curve in this continuous model, and also the short-run average costs for selected scales of plant. A continuous approximation of the market demand curve is imposed over the average cost for comparison.

The formula for the competitive model is as follows. The model is restricted to the values of parameters in the range of the tables of costs. The model begins with *short-run average cost* (*SRAC*) which depends upon output and the scale of plant (x, s). In the discrete values of costs in the table the scale of plant is indicated by letters of the alphabet, starting with the letter A. In the continuous model, if scale is A then $s = 11$; if scale is B then $s = 12$, etc., with a change of one in s as the letters change:

$$SRAC(x, s) = 3/4(x - s)^2 + 1/4(s - 40)^2 + 300. \tag{2}$$

The optimum scale of plant given a quantity x is indicated by $s^*(x)$. The formula is

$$s^*(x) = 10 + 3/4x. \tag{3}$$

Substituting (3) into (2), the *long-run average cost* function, *LRAC* (x) is obtained.

$$LRAC(x) = SRAC(x, s^*(x)) = 600 - 15x + 3/16x^2. \tag{4}$$

Of course this yields the *long-run total cost* (*LRTC*) and the *long-run marginal cost* (*LRMC*) as follows:

$$LRTC(x) = 600x - 15x^2 + 3/16x^3 \tag{5}$$

$$LRMC(x) = \partial LRTC(x)/\partial x = 600 - 30x + 9/16x^2. \tag{6}$$

The continuous model will be very useful to the interested reader. The complicated calculations for the equilibria of various models were first done in the context of the continuous model. The location of the equilibria in models based on discrete parameters was always nearby.

Market Organization

Market A was a computerized double auction. Market B was a posted price market. Both markets opened at the same time for trading. Sellers were informed about the market demand function in market B but they knew nothing about the market demand function in market A. Since market A followed standard procedures for MUDA markets,[2] only the timing and the details of market B need to be reviewed.

Before each period all seller agents were required to decide which market they would enter. After deciding they (privately) drew a large X through the record sheet of the market not chosen. Agents choosing market B would then fill in the blanks on their record for the period committing

2. See Plott and Gray [6, 245–58] for a detailed description of this market, or see Plott [5] for a description of the computerized version.

Table II. Cumulative or Total Costs

Total Units Sold	Production Schedule Choice ------------>																								
	A	B	C	D	E	F	G	H	I	J	K	L	M	N	O	P	Q	R	S	T	U	V	W	X	Y
1	585	587	590	596	603	613	624	638	653	671	690	712	735	761	788	818	849	883	918	956	995	1037	1080	1126	1173
2	1142	1142	1146	1154	1166	1182	1202	1226	1254	1286	1322	1362	1406	1454	1506	1562	1622	1686	1754	1826	1902	1982	2066	2154	2246
3	1675	1670	1672	1679	1693	1712	1738	1769	1807	1850	1900	1955	2017	2084	2158	2237	2323	2414	2512	2615	2725	2840	2962	3089	3223
4	2188	2176	2172	2176	2188	2208	2236	2272	2316	2368	2428	2496	2572	2656	2748	2848	2956	3072	3196	3328	3468	3616	3772	3936	4108
5	2686	2664	2651	2649	2656	2674	2701	2739	2786	2844	2911	2989	3076	3174	3281	3399	3526	3664	3811	3969	4136	4314	4501	4699	4906
6	3174	3138	3114	3102	3102	3114	3138	3174	3222	3282	3354	3438	3534	3642	3762	3894	4038	4194	4362	4542	4734	4938	5154	5382	5622
7	3656	3603	3565	3540	3530	3533	3551	3582	3628	3687	3761	3848	3950	4065	4195	4338	4496	4667	4853	5052	5266	5493	5735	5990	6260
8	4136	4064	4008	3968	3944	3936	3944	3968	4008	4064	4136	4224	4328	4448	4584	4736	4904	5088	5288	5504	5736	5984	6248	6528	6824
9	4619	4525	4448	4390	4349	4327	4322	4336	4367	4417	4484	4570	4673	4795	4934	5092	5267	5461	5672	5902	6149	6415	6698	7000	7319
10	5110	4990	4890	4810	4750	4710	4690	4690	4710	4750	4810	4890	4990	5110	5250	5410	5590	5790	6010	6250	6510	6790	7090	7410	7750
11	5613	5464	5338	5233	5151	5090	5052	5035	5041	5068	5118	5189	5283	5398	5536	5695	5877	6080	6306	6553	6823	7114	7428	7763	8121
12	6132	5952	5796	5664	5556	5472	5412	5376	5364	5376	5412	5472	5556	5664	5796	5952	6132	6336	6564	6816	7092	7392	7716	8064	8436
13	6672	6458	6269	6107	5970	5860	5775	5717	5684	5678	5697	5743	5814	5912	6035	6185	6360	6562	6789	7043	7322	7628	7959	8317	8700
14	7238	6986	6762	6566	6398	6258	6146	6062	6006	5978	5978	6006	6062	6146	6258	6398	6566	6762	6986	7238	7518	7826	8162	8526	8918
15	7834	7541	7279	7046	6844	6671	6529	6416	6334	6281	6259	6266	6304	6371	6469	6596	6754	6941	7159	7406	7684	7991	8329	8696	9094
16	8464	8128	7824	7552	7312	7104	6928	6784	6672	6592	6544	6528	6544	6592	6672	6784	6928	7104	7312	7552	7824	8128	8464	8832	9232
17	9133	8751	8402	8088	7807	7561	7348	7170	7025	6915	6838	6796	6787	6813	6872	6966	7093	7255	7450	7680	7943	8241	8572	8938	9337
18	9846	9414	9018	8658	8334	8046	7794	7576	7398	7254	7146	7074	7038	7038	7074	7146	7254	7398	7578	7794	8046	8334	8658	9018	9414
19	10607	10122	9676	9267	8897	8564	8270	8013	7795	7614	7472	7367	7301	7272	7282	7329	7415	7538	7700	7899	8137	8412	8726	9077	9467
20	11420	10880	10380	9920	9500	9120	8780	8480	8220	8000	7820	7680	7580	7520	7500	7520	7580	7680	7820	8000	8220	8480	8780	9120	9500
21	12290	11692	11135	10621	10148	9718	9329	8983	8678	8416	8195	8017	7880	7786	7733	7723	7754	7828	7943	8101	8300	8542	8825	9151	9518
22	13222	12562	11946	11374	10846	10362	9922	9526	9174	8866	8602	8382	8206	8074	7986	7942	7942	7986	8074	8206	8382	8602	8866	9174	9526
23	14220	13495	12817	12184	11598	11057	10563	10114	9712	9355	9045	8780	8562	8389	8263	8182	8148	8159	8217	8320	8470	8665	8907	9194	9528
24	15288	14496	13752	13056	12408	11808	11256	10752	10296	9888	9528	9216	8952	8736	8568	8448	8376	8352	8376	8448	8568	8736	8952	9216	9528
25	16431	15569	14756	13994	13281	12619	12006	11444	10931	10469	10056	9694	9381	9119	8906	8744	8631	8569	8556	8594	8681	8819	9006	9244	9531
26	17654	16718	15834	15002	14222	13494	12818	12194	11622	11102	10634	10218	9854	9542	9282	9074	8918	8814	8762	8762	8814	8918	9074	9282	9542
27	18961	17948	16990	16085	15235	14438	13696	13007	12373	11792	11266	10793	10375	10010	9700	9443	9241	9092	8998	8957	8971	9038	9160	9335	9565
28	20356	19264	18228	17248	16324	15456	14644	13888	13188	12544	11956	11424	10948	10528	10164	9856	9604	9408	9268	9184	9156	9184	9268	9408	9604
29	21844	20670	19553	18495	17494	16552	15667	14841	14072	13362	12709	12115	11578	11100	10679	10317	10012	9766	9577	9447	9374	9360	9403	9505	9664
30	23430	22170	20970	19830	18750	17730	16770	15870	15030	14250	13530	12870	12270	11730	11250	10830	10470	10170	9930	9750	9630	9570	9570	9630	9750
31	25118	23769	22463	21258	20096	18995	17957	16980	16066	15213	14423	13694	13028	12423	11881	11400	10982	10625	10331	10098	9928	9819	9773	9788	9866
32	26912	25472	24096	22784	21536	20352	19232	18176	17184	16256	15392	14592	13856	13184	12576	12032	11552	11136	10784	10496	10272	10112	10016	9984	10016
33	28817	27283	25814	24412	23075	21805	20600	19462	18389	17383	16442	15568	14759	14017	13340	12730	12185	11707	11294	10948	10667	10453	10304	10222	10205
34	30838	29206	27642	26146	24718	23358	22066	20842	19686	18598	17578	16626	15742	14926	14178	13498	12886	12342	11866	11458	11118	10846	10642	10506	10438
35	32979	31246	29584	27991	26469	25016	23634	22321	21079	19906	18804	17771	16809	15916	15094	14341	13659	13046	12504	12031	11629	11296	11034	10841	10719
36	35244	33408	31644	29952	28332	26784	25308	23904	22572	21312	20124	19008	17964	16992	16092	15264	14508	13824	13212	12672	12204	11808	11484	11232	11052
37	37638	35696	33827	32033	30312	28666	27093	25595	24170	22820	21543	20341	19212	18158	17177	16271	15438	14680	13995	13385	12848	12386	11997	11683	11442
38	40166	38114	36138	34238	32414	30666	28994	27398	25878	24434	23066	21774	20558	19418	18354	17366	16454	15618	14858	14174	13566	13034	12578	12198	11894
39	42832	40667	38581	36572	34642	32789	31015	29318	27700	26159	24697	23312	22006	20777	19627	18554	17560	16643	15805	15044	14362	13757	13231	12782	12412
40	45640	43360	41160	39040	37000	35040	33160	31360	29640	28000	26440	24960	23560	22240	21000	19840	18760	17760	16840	16000	15240	14560	13960	13440	13000

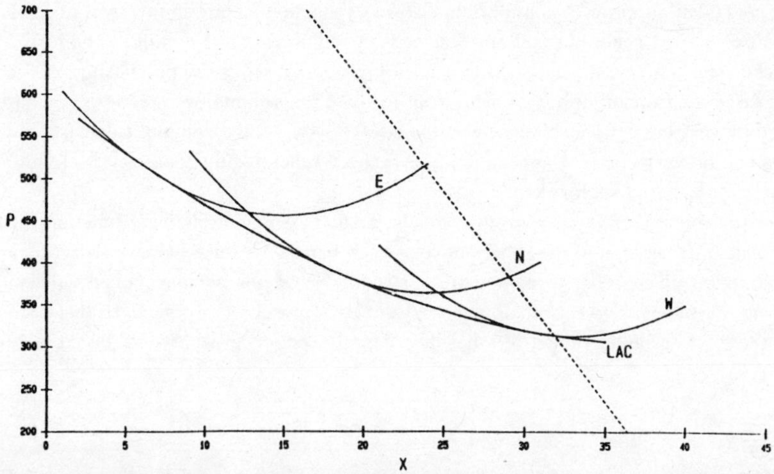

Figure 2. Long-Run Average Cost, Selected Short-Run Costs and Market Demand

themselves to a scale of plant, a quantity to be offered, and a price. The computerized MUDA program allows the simultaneous operation of multiple markets. Each of the seven sellers was assigned to a "personal market" in which no other seller could participate. The sellers would enter their (price, quantity) pairs in an order box fixed on their individual markets. At the appropriate (public) signal each seller would press the enter key, thereby making their private decisions public to all buyers and sellers as they were displayed by the computer as asks (to sell) in their individual markets. Once sellers had seen the asks of other sellers, they had the opportunity to cancel their own asks. This was done simultaneously on signal. Sellers canceling asks were not permitted to enter the A market. They did nothing for the remainder of the period. Thus, sellers who entered market B and canceled experienced the opportunity cost of A profits.

After sellers who had made the decision to enter market B had the opportunity to cancel, all markets opened for trading. Market A proceeded along the standard lines for the computerized MUDA. In market B, sellers who remained each had a price posted and a maximum quantity. At any time during a period buyers could toggle to any of these markets and purchase the number of units desired at the posted price, up to the amount for sale that the seller had left. Buyers could only accept the asks in these markets. That is, they could not tender bids in any market except market A.

A comment about the organization is in order. Market A was a double auction and it existed as a source of income and entertainment for those who chose not to enter market B. Market B was a posted price market because it is thought to provide the best circumstances for monopoly behavior [10, 83–106]. When the demand function is known, and prices are posted, the seller is most likely to successfully charge monopoly prices. Double auctions are known to have strong tendencies to converge to a competitive equilibrium even in the presence of monopoly. If market B had been a double auction, then any tendency to converge to a competitive equilibrium could have been attributed to the market microstructure alone, as opposed to the industrial organization. Thus, the posted price institution was thought to be a more favorable environment for the emergence of monopoly pricing than the double auction.

The cancellation property is important as a risk reduction feature in this type of market. If a seller chooses a large scale of plant and succeeds in selling only a few units, large losses can be experienced. Buyers have the capacity to punish high-priced sellers by purchasing only a unit or two. Similarly, well-meaning buyers who want to share the volume by spreading purchases over sellers can be very costly to a seller who does not otherwise get the volume. Likewise, accidental purchases can be very costly. Cancellation allows those sellers who choose relatively high prices the opportunity to avoid such risks.

The experiment contained one other special feature. A market demand function for market B was privately distributed to the sellers on a sheet of paper. All sellers knew what it meant. The demand function given sellers was actually 10 francs below the actual induced values. Buyers typically do not trade without a small profit margin for themselves. We believed that the function we gave them was a better model of what they would experience than would be the actual limit values.

Procedures

The experiments were conducted in the Laboratory for Experimental Economics and Political Science at Caltech. Subjects consisted of undergraduates, graduate students at the California Institute of Technology, plus high school students who were attending a special summer program. Most had previous experience in some type of computerized market. All had paged through a computerized instruction routine that familiarized them with key functions and the mechanics of making bids, offers, and acceptances.

In addition to the three experiments reported here, pilot experiments were conducted. The pilot experiments were discarded because they typically involved choices of parameters that were based on a miscalculation of the theoretical models. The parameters and procedures of one experiment were exactly like those reported in this paper but the data are not reported because one subject evidenced substantial confusion. The results of these unreported experiments appeared qualitatively similar to the experiments that are reported here. Space constraints effectively preclude their publication. Should anyone want to study them in detail, the data will be made available upon request.

Experimental sessions which lasted on the order of three hours began in the evening at about 7:00 P.M. The detailed instructions that were read to the subjects are contained in Plott, Sugiyama, and Elbaz [8]. In addition, the material presented on the chalkboard and the step-by-step procedures for conducting the experiment are also included.

The highlights of these experimental procedures are as follows. Subjects were paid a "show up" fee of $5.00 if they were extras and were turned away from participation. Subjects agreed to work off any losses incurred during the experiment at a rate of $10.00 per hour. Of course, buyers could make no losses unless they resulted from some sort of (foolish) speculation or from a typo. Contracts involving obvious typos that would result in large losses were always voided by the experimenter (a standard practice). However, sellers could make a loss. If a seller entered the B market at a substantial scale of plant and sold only a small number of units the losses could be considerable.

Sellers who wanted a sure return could participate in the A market. The design of this market was such that a rent of $1.80 per period was almost certain for participation in market A and the seller was exposed to no possibility of a loss. On average, each participant made approximately $30 from the experiments.

Each seller was provided cost schedules for market A sales.[3] For market B each seller had color-coded tables that gave marginal cost (pink), average cost (green), and total cost (yellow), of combinations of volume and scale of plant on 11 by 14 sheets of paper. Scale of plant could take 24 values, labeled *A* through *Y*.

Two practice periods were conducted. The parameters were the same as those that were used in the experiment. The mechanics of the experiment were very complex and many questions were prompted during these sessions. The answers to all questions were given publicly in a form that yielded no information about parameters that was not already public. After each period, for the first five periods (including the two practice periods), the accounting of each subject was checked and spot checks were made throughout the experiment.

III. Models

Ten different types of models can be applied to the economic environment. Of course these models share many basic principles but they also differ in many ways. Some give sharp predictions and the others remain vague. Where possible the models will be applied directly to the environment in a technical, mathematical fashion. Speculations and theorizing about which model might be expected to fit the data best are not considered to be part of the exercise at this stage of the experimental inquiry. Table III contains a summary of the predictions for those models for which predictions can be computed. The paragraphs below will briefly describe each model listed in the table.

A note on efficiency may be useful, especially for those who are not familiar with experimental economics. The measure invented by Plott and Smith [7, 133–53] is a direct adaptation of consumers' and producers' surpluses. The buyers receive franc redemption values from the experimenter that can be modeled as a (derived) demand function. The total value of francs redeemed by buyers is like the gross benefits to buyers from the units they acquired. Sellers pay francs to the experimenter for units sold. These payments are costs. The allocation that maximizes gross benefits minus costs is the most efficient. It is the one that maximizes franc earnings of subjects (exhausts all possible gains from exchange). Actual franc earnings divided by the maximum possible is the efficiency with which the system is operating.

Under ordinary modes of organization, 100 percent efficiency of operation is thought to be unattainable in the downward sloping average cost case. If a single price is charged, and if price is equated to marginal cost, then sellers would lose money. This degree of inefficiency is thought to be structural in the falling-average cost case.

Other practical sources of inefficiency exist. Tough bargaining sometimes results in failures to trade. Suppliers might choose the "wrong" scale of plant and thereby impose more costs on the system than necessary. Suppliers might choose to enter the B market and then cancel. The efficiency loss would be due to the opportunity cost of the low cost units that such suppliers could have delivered to the A market. Suppliers might choose an unnecessarily limiting quantity of x offer to the market B. In the section on models the efficiency of the equilibria allocation predicted

3. Rounding errors caused slight discrepancies between these schedules. For example, total cost at the contested market equilibria of scale *W* and volume 31 was 9765, if computed from the average cost table, and it was 9773 as listed on the total cost schedule, a difference of 4.8 cents.

Table III. Models and Predictions

Model	Market B						Market A			
	Number of Agents	Scale Choice	Market Price	Market Volume	Per Agent Volume	Per Agent Profit (Francs)	Number of Agents	Market Price	Market Volume	System Efficiency
1. Natural monopoly	1	M	684	17	17	4841	6	700	21	.80
2. Tacit collusion	—	—	—	—	—	—	—	—	—	—
3. Cournot (sym) duopoly	2	G,H	609	20	10	1400	5	700	21	.76
4. Cournot (asym) triopoly*	3		600	20			4	700	21	.70
	(1)	D,E			6	498				
	(2)	E			7	670				
Monopolistic Competition (Sym. Cournot)										
5. Quadopoly*	4	C,D	600	20	5	351	3	700	21	.67
6. Quintopoly*	5	C	600	20	4	228	2	700	21	.64
7. Perfectly contested (competitive)	1	W	325	31	31	302	6	700	21	1.00
8. Over-contested	5	W	325	31	(31,0)	(302,0)	2	700	21	.94
9. Unstable ("Bertrand")	—	—	—	—	—	—	—	—	—	—
10. Market collapse	0	—	—	0	0	—	7	700	21	.41

*For ease of computation a transaction cost was imposed as a parameter in price determination.

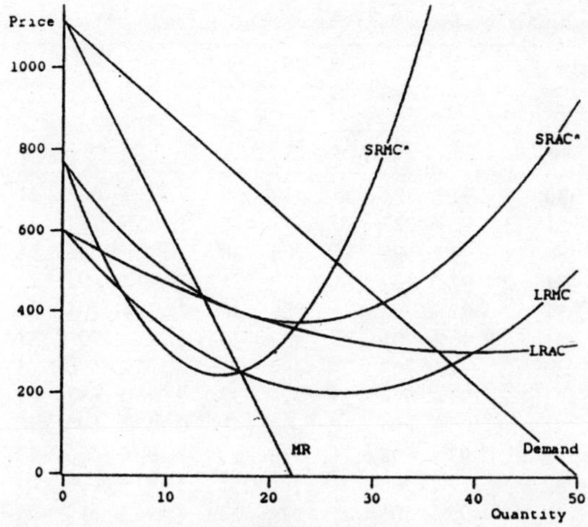

Figure 3. Monopolist in Market B: A Continuous Approximation

by each model is listed. The logic of each of these models justifies the nature and potential reasons for inefficiencies.

Natural Monopoly (Classical)

The classic model is natural monopoly. According to this model, because of the existence of economies of scale, competition will lead to the existence of a monopoly. All other sellers will participate in market A. This monopoly facing the market demand curve will choose the profit maximizing value of variables without regard to the effect that this action might have on the actions of other sellers, such as their proclivity to enter market B. That is, where $P = D(x)$ is the market demand function and long-run costs are $C(x, s(x))$ the monopolist sets the value of the variables to

$$\underset{x}{\text{maximize}}[D(x)x - C(x, s(x))].$$

For the parameters of the experiment the solution is a price of 684, a quantity equal to 17, a scale of plant of size M and a profit of 4841 in francs. These can be read from the table. Figure 3 demonstrates the model. For convenience the continuous model, which is only an approximation of the underlying parameters, is used in the figure. The accurate predictions based on the discrete environment are in Table IV.

Tacit Collusion

Collusion models are very numerous depending upon the complexity of the agreement that can be enforced. It is assumed here that collusion would lead to choices of variables that are good from the seller's point of view. We presume that the values would be something between Cournot and monopoly and that the volume would be similarly restricted.

Table IV. Experimental Results: Average Transaction Prices, Number of Entrants, Volumes, Efficiencies

	061191						062791						071891					
	A		B				A		B				A		B			
Period	$\overline{P}$	Vol.	$\overline{P}$	Vol.	*N*	Eff.	$\overline{P}$	Vol.	$\overline{P}$	Vol.	*N*	Eff.	$\overline{P}$	Vol.	$\overline{P}$	Vol.	*N*	Eff.
1	717	22	325	30	5	92%	584	25	412	26	3	83%	697	21	403	29	4	78%
2	691	21	312	31	3	92%	727	20	437	26	5	88%	704	21	351	30	5	85%
3	696	19	325	30	2	92%	696	21	402	30	2	89%	682	21	350	30	2	98%
4	685	21	324	31	2	97%	709	21	387	31	4	94%	693	21	340	28	3	93%
5	691	21	322	31	3	97%	702	21	355	30	2	96%	701	21	324	31	3	97%
6	703	21	315	31	4	95%	701	23	339	32	2	95%	703	21	319	31	2	98%
7	696	21	323	31	2	99%	702	21	330	31	4	95%	696	21	319	31	2	99%
8	700	21	320	31	2	99%	699	23	324	33	2	95%	697	21	318	31	3	97%
9	698	21	321	31	1	100%	696	22	—	0	0	40%	694	20	330	31	1	98%
10	701	19	400	28	2	93%	698	21	330	30	3	96%	696	23	325	31	2	96%
11	691	21	350	30	3	72%	700	21	326	31	3	97%	696	21	320	31	3	97%
12	698	21	345	28	3	90%	701	21	324	33	4	95%	696	21	321	31	1	100%
13	698	21	330	31	3	97%	700	21	335	30	2	98%	639	21	319	27	2	85%
14	700	21	335	31	2	99%	699	22	325	31	3	95%	696	21	330	31	1	98%
15	702	24	—	0	3	32%	700	22	330	31	3	95%	697	21	328	31	3	97%
16	700	21	328	32	2	92%	700	21	326	31	3	97%	695	21	324	33	3	97%
17	700	21	327	31	2	99%	700	21	327	31	2	99%	700	21	403	19	3	71%
18	700	22	326	31	2	97%	700	21	325	31	2	97%	697	23		0	3	34%
19	701	21	323	31	2	94%	691	19	437	26	1	93%	697	21	321	31	2	99%
AV.	698	21	331	29	2.5	91%	695	21	356	29	2.6	91%	694	21	336	28	2.4	90%

Cournot Models

Cournot models are all derived from the same general principles. Each competitor evaluates the market as if the quantity offered by the other sellers is a constant and the resulting market price is that determined by the sum of the quantities offered by sellers. For insights about the structure of these models, especially in the presence of non convexities as in the case with economies of scale, see Novshek [3, 61–70; 4].

Application of the class of models to any real market, especially the ones created for these experiments, might be met with three a priori criticisms/qualifications. First, the Cournot solutions to the technical problems are generally not unique. Typically, both symmetric solutions in which all firms act identically and asymmetric solutions, in which some firms are larger than others, exist. The symmetric solutions and those asymmetric solutions that have been identified and seem plausible have been included in Table III. The second qualification is that the principles that might govern entry into a market are not systematically integrated (unless lack of entry is treated as part of an asymmetric solution) into the analysis. For this reason, a special treatment of Cournot models, under a heading called monopolistic competition, is included. The third criticism is derived from the nature of the market structure itself. Agents in these markets post a price and a quantity. There is every reason to assume that the seller with the lowest price will sell all units that the seller offers, up to the demand function limits. The hypothesis that the quantity sold by other sellers remains constant, will almost certainly be violated. Thus, the structure of the decision problem might appear to resemble that of the Bertrand theory, more than Cournot, depending upon how the posted quantity is treated in the analysis.

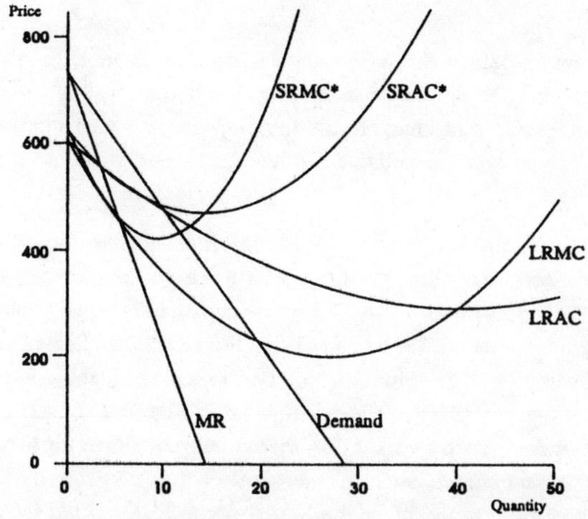

Figure 4. Quadopolist in Market B: A Continuous Approximation

All of the criticisms/qualifications are derived in part from the fact that the Cournot model is incomplete as a theory. It is silent about the nature of the price determination process. If sellers (or buyers) are supposed to be involved in price determination, then some sort of explicit coordination device must exist that guides sellers to settle on the same price, and guides buyers so that sellers share market volume in a Cournot fashion. Instead of dealing with all of this complexity, the Cournot model relies only on axioms typical of game theoretic representations of markets that assert that only one price exists, and further asserts that the one price is determined by the law of supply and demand once sellers' quantity choices are given. Nevertheless, Cournot models have broad experimental support and must be taken seriously in any environment until the data suggest otherwise.

The Cournot solutions for duopoly and for triopoly are also in Table III. Notice that the price predicted is 609 and then becomes 600, regardless of the number of firms. Of course, firm size must decrease as the number of firms increases. This means that the scale of plant chosen by firms must be smaller under triopoly than under duopoly.

Monopolistic Competition

The classical model of monopolistic competition is interpreted as a four firm Cournot market. Scale of plants are small in the equilibrium and the opportunity cost of 300 francs ($1.80) is barely covered by the 351 profit. Entry of another firm would force the profits to levels below the opportunity costs. In the table the Cournot equilibrium profits for quintopoly, a fifth firm, are less than the 300 francs opportunity cost for entering the B market. Again, notice from the table that the price predictions are the same, regardless of the number of firms.

In Figure 4 is shown a representative firm in the four firm equilibrium. The background shows the market demand function. The costs graphs are from the continuous approximation of costs given by equation (4).

Contested Markets

The contestable market literature has motivated researchers to look for two different types of phenomena in experimental data. The possible phenomenon are called "models" here, but they operate more like statements that characterize the extremes of what one might expect in data. Of course, those extremes and the relative tendencies toward them contain potentially useful information.

Perfectly Contested Market (Competitive) Equilibrium. This is the case in which only one seller exists in the market. The seller produces at a price and output that leaves price equal to average cost, including opportunity cost. The profits in market A and market B would be the same (thereby justifying the use of the term "competitive"). As indicated in the table, the price of the single entrant would be 325; volume would be 31; scale of plant would be W, and the other six sellers would be in market A. The relationships are in Figure 3.

Without side payments, such as a subsidy to compensate a firm for losses, and a completely different institutional arrangement, such as marginal cost pricing, or the incentive compatible equivalent, average cost pricing might be the best that can be expected from a consumer's point of view. It is used as a measure for 100 percent efficiency.

Over-Contested Market Equilibrium. This model postulates that the price and quantities sold would be the same as the perfectly contested outcome above. The only difference is the number of firms that have decided to enter. Previous experiments have defined this model to predict that all of the potential firms enter. Obviously, the plausibility of such phenomena would a priori seem low but this model is included as a benchmarker for completeness. The number, 5, is taken to be the maximum that could leave market A and still have it behave competitively.

Unstable ("Bertrand")

We do not know the equilibrium of the Bertrand model of these experimental markets. Presumably it involves some sort of mixed strategy. In the data this would appear as a type of variability in prices. At this point the model is included for completeness and to draw attention to the possibility that the data might not exhibit any type of monotone convergence property. It is also included to draw attention to the fact that the literature contains suggestions about how such variability phenomena might be modeled should it be observed.

Market Collapse (Type 1)

Entry into the contested market will involve a cost. The possibility of out-of-pocket losses also exists. Since there are no mechanisms for coordinating entry, sellers might all decide to operate only in the A market. Under such a circumstance the supply in B would be zero. The market would have collapsed. Type 1 collapse is the case when no firm enters the B market.

Market Collapse (Type 2)

The second type of collapse can occur when more than one firm decides to enter but all cancel leaving no one to supply the market. This is a type of coordination failure which can occur because the decisions to cancel market B offers are made simultaneously.

IV. Results

The central results are easy to state. The contestable markets model is the most accurate of those considered. After a brief review of the data, the discussion turns to making clear the strength of this central proposition. Following the main results, the remainder of this section is devoted to a discussion of a series of five observations about both individual and systems behavior.

A typical price time series for both markets are shown in Figures 5 and 6. Figure 5 contains the time series for market A, and Figure 6 contains the time series for market B. Vertical lines separate periods. The measure of time differs in the two figures. In market A the measure is seconds. In market B the measure is the number of events (e.g., asks, contracts) because the high speed with which events occur in clock time make them indistinguishable, given the units (seconds) in which clocktime is measured.

The horizontal lines in the figures show the price predictors for various models. The top line is the monopoly price. The second line is the price predicted by all Cournot and monopolistic competition models. The bottom line is the "competitive" price predicted by the contestable-market model. Contracts are indicated by circles in both the A market and the B market; and in market B the prices posted by sellers are displayed by small triangles. Cancellations in the B markets are not shown, but in most cases all sellers in the B market canceled, except the seller with the lowest posted price.

Figure 7 contains the price and volume data pooled across all experiments. Each dot represents a period in one of the three experiments. The market demand function and the predictions of selected models are also shown in the figure.

The visual impressions are that prices converged to the competitive equilibrium in market A and that prices converged to the one predicted by the contestable-market model in market B. These visual impressions are essentially correct. The first results reported in this section make the nature of the data that support these impressions precise.

The first result is a traditional statement intended to prevent any misconceptions about what is being reported. Sometimes experimental data are predicted by models in an accurate statistical sense. However, in most cases none of the models are statistically accurate. The first result makes clear that these models contain unanticipated and unexplained errors and, thereby, sets the stage for all subsequent analysis.

RESULT 1. *All models can be rejected as a statistically accurate representation of the data.*

Support. All models are static equilibrium models. However, the data for the B markets, such as the one contained in Figure 6, exhibits an obvious type of convergence pattern which is not captured by any of the models, even if a random error term is added. In the absence of additional theory appended to the models to take care of the dynamics, the models are rejected. ∎

The second result is perhaps the central result of the paper. It states that the contestable market theory is the one best supported by the data.

RESULT 2. *After the first six periods, all relevant economic variables (prices, volumes, profits, scale of plant choices, and efficiencies) are closer to the predictions of the two contestable market models than to the predictions of any other model.*

Support. Each of the variables will be discussed in order. All models predict competitive behavior in the A markets. The competitive price is 700 and the volume is 21. In 51 of the 57

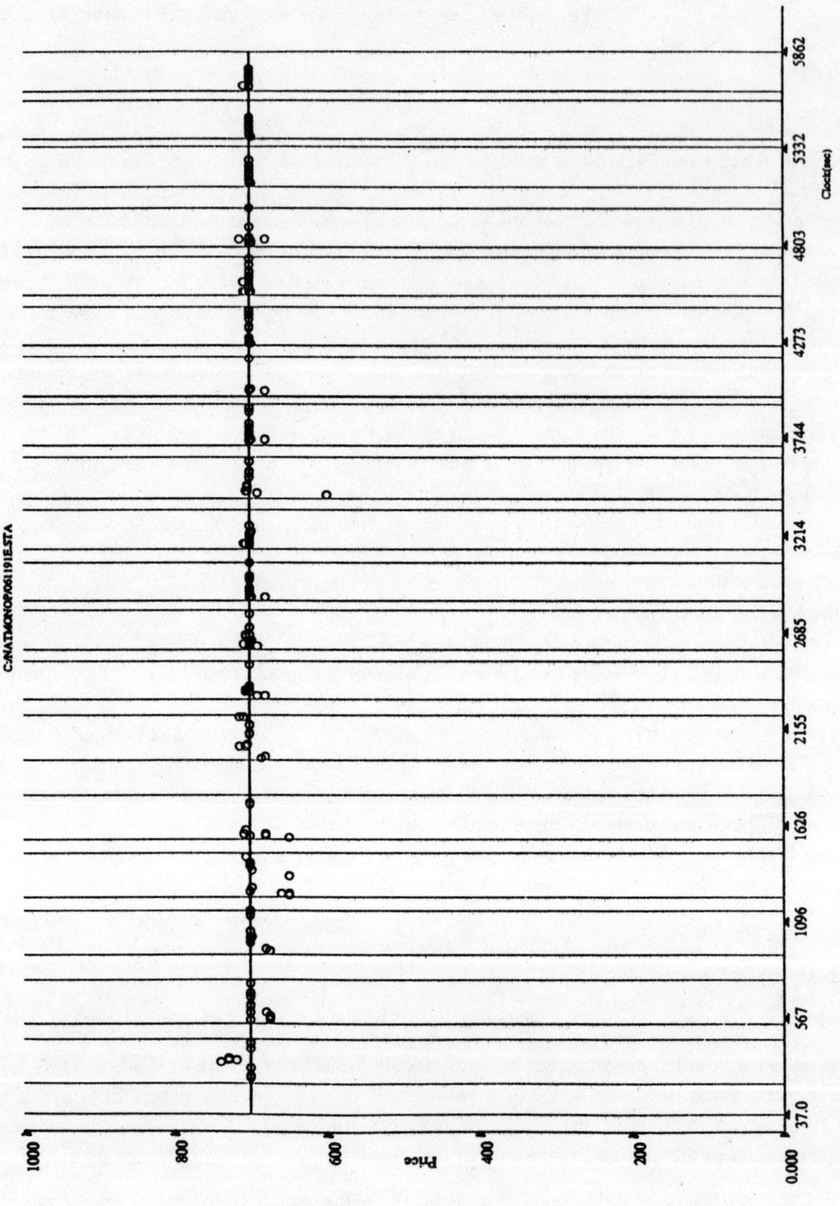

Figure 5. Market A, Price Time Series, Experiment 061191

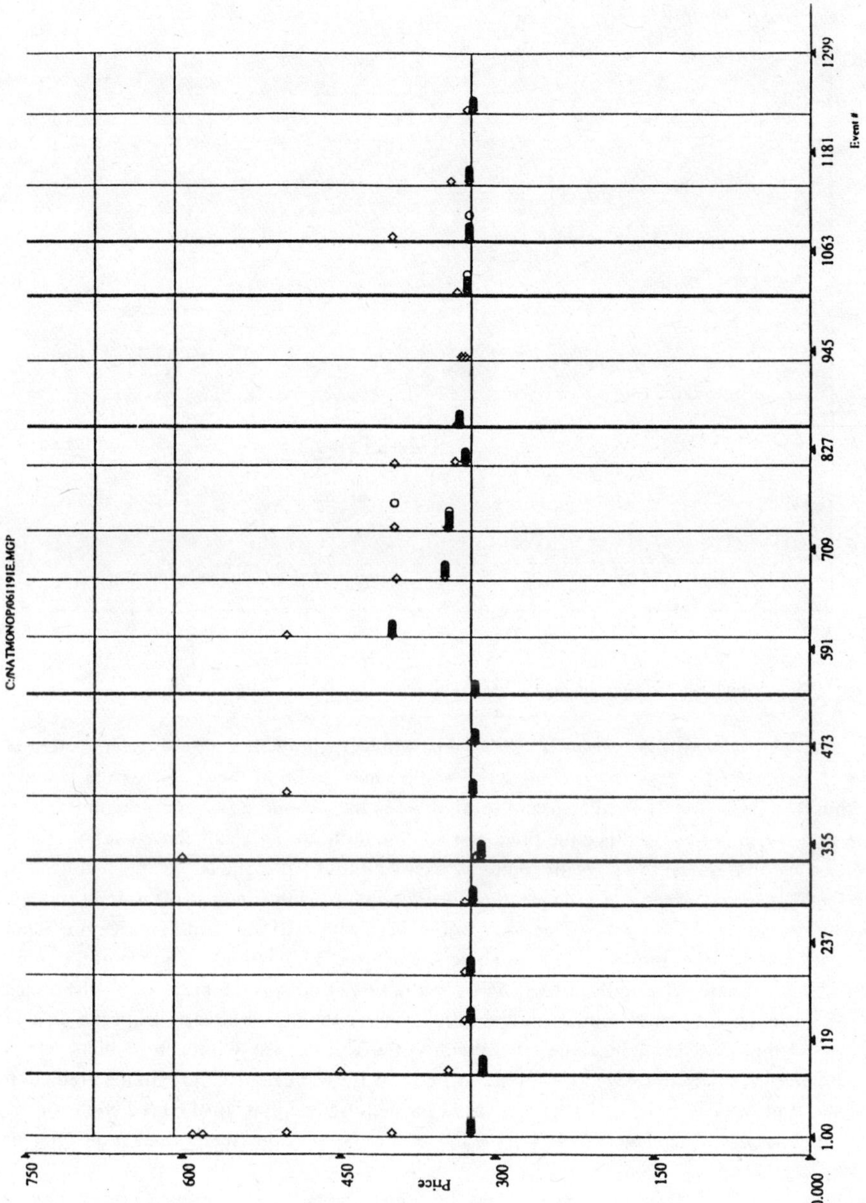

Figure 6. Market B, Price Time Series, Experiment 061191

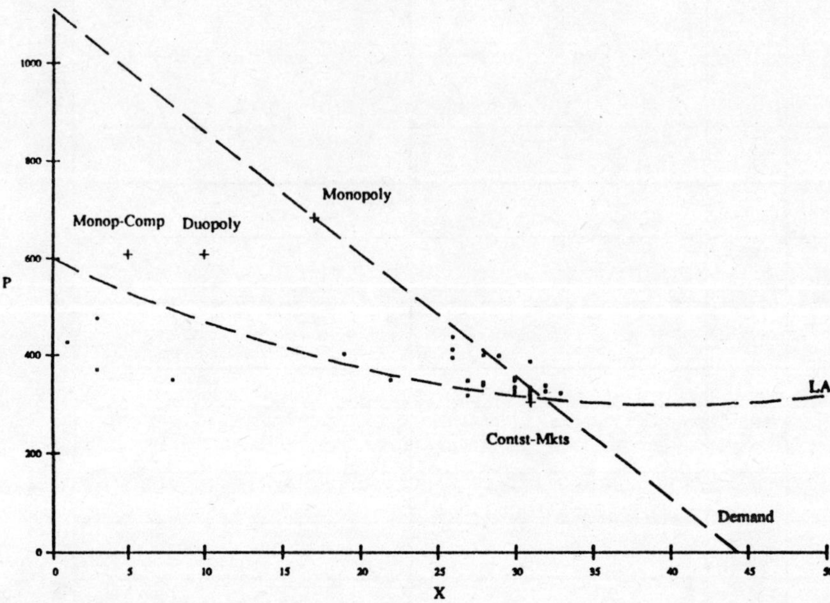

Figure 7. Period Prices and Quantities, All Periods, All Experiments

periods of all experiments the average price of the period was within 10 francs (6 cents for sellers and .75 of a cent for buyers) of the competitive equilibrium. In 56 of these periods the volume was within 3 units of the 21 predicted and in 41 periods the volume was exactly 21 units. The relevant data are in Table IV. Since the price and volume in the A markets behaved substantially as predicted by all models, the relevant comparisons are all in the B markets.

In the B markets prices and volumes tended to be closer to the contestable market models than any of the others. In 41 of the 57 periods, prices were within 10 francs of the price predicted by the contestable-market models (325). In no period was the price within 10 francs of the price predicted by the natural monopoly model (684), and in no period was the price within 10 francs of the price predicted by any Cournot model (609). The count comes directly from the data in Table IV and the predictions in Table III. Similarly, the volume was within three units of the contestable market prediction (31) in 49 of the 57 periods. It was never that close to the prediction of the natural monopoly model (17), and it was never within three units of the predictions of the Cournot models (20). Price and market volume figures support the contestable-market model over the others.

Volume of individual firms further support the contestability model over the Cournot models and the monopolistic competition models which, because of symmetry assumptions, predict that all B market entrants will have the same volume. In 53 of the 57 periods no more than one firm had positive sales in the B market. Thus, in 53 of 57 periods the data support contestability over monopolistic competition. In none of these three periods in which more than one firm made B market sales, was the distribution volumes near equality as predicted by the symmetric game models. As will be implicit in the discussions below, sellers that chose to enter the B market did not limit their quantities as required by the Cournot model and as they could have done under the procedures.

In market B profit levels predicted by competing models are in Table III. Profits should be at, or above 300, which is the (nearly) certain profit that can be obtained for participation in market A. Actual profits are in Table V,A. The listing of actual profits of sellers in market B are in Table V,B. The "active" firms referenced in the table are those that did not cancel their posted offer after they had seen the offers of other sellers. Shown also is the number of sellers that entered the B market at the beginning of the period.

Consider only the last four periods of the experiments after some level of equilibration has been achieved. The average profit of the firms that sell units over all three experiments is 451.6 francs per period. The average profit of all entrants is 184.0 francs per period. Thus, the average profit of sellers who entered market B is closer to the 302 predicted by the perfectly contested model than to the prediction of any other model, except quintopoly, which can be rejected since the number of sellers was always less than five. Consideration of more periods does not change this conclusion. In fact, the conclusion is only reinforced. The average profit earned per period by all entrants in market B, considering period 3 and later, for the three experiments was 29.4 francs, 279.0 francs, and 74.2 francs, respectively, far below that predicted by any model except quintopoly.

The frequency of scale of plant choices is contained in Table VI. Only three choices are at scale levels (D, E, G, and M) predicted by any of the alternative models to the contested market model. The contested market model predicts scale *W*, which is the mode of choices of sellers (41 choices out of 146 total). Over 40 percent of all choices are within one level of that predicted by the contestable-market model. The small mode at scale *K* is interesting because scale *K* was the example used in the instructions to illustrate the nature of costs.

Efficiency levels are reported in Table IV. The average efficiency level for the three experiments is .91, .91, and .90, which is much closer to the .94 predicted by the over-contested market model than it is the efficiency predicted by natural monopoly (80%), duopoly (76%), triopoly (70%), monopolistic competition (67%), or market collapse (41%). On average, the perfectly contested model is a better predictor of efficiency than any of the noncontested models.

In all dimensions the two contestable market theories are better predictors than the alternative models. If one is forced to choose between the perfectly-contested model and the over-contested model the choice will be the former. The average number of entrants per period is 2.56, which is closer to the one predicted by the perfectly contested model than the five predicted by the over-contested model. ∎

The next five observations focus on aspects of strategic behavior and on system behavior. The first four of the observations are related to individual behavior and the strategies that individuals employ. The fifth observation is a summary property of the system as a whole.

Observation 1 suggests that people bias their choices of prices in favor of those divisible by 5 and that individual strategies exhibit a degree of modification to take advantage of the underlying bias. For example, knowing about this bias, perhaps even in their own behavior, people sometimes reduce their own price by a unit. That is, rather than quote a price of 325 an individual might quote 324; or a 330 quotation would be modified downward to 329 rather than, say, increased to 331.

OBSERVATION 1. *Price choices are asymmetrically distributed downward around numbers that end in 0 or 5.*

Support. Actual prices ending in 0 or 5 accounted for a large percentage of choices (71 out of 146). Of the two, prices ending in 0 were the most common, occurring 50 times. Prices in a

Table V,A. Market A Profit by Experiment, Period, Individual

Individual	Experiment 061191							Experiment 062791							Experiment 071891						
Period	07	08	09	10	11	12	13	07	08	09	10	11	12	13	07	08	09	10	11	12	13
1	—	305	660	—	—	—	—	—	−2700	325	300	—	290	—	—	—	—	316	—	213	300
2	250	200	300	—	—	—	267	—	275	—	870	—	—	—	—	—	—	369	—	317	—
3	298	250	300	0	—	—	267	—	296	310	300	—	320	200	301	—	−86	300	290	314	—
4	249	210	299	198	—	—	220	—	344	—	400	—	—	350	—	300	147	300	—	308	—
5	—	215	300	196	—	—	290	—	311	0	300	—	336	300	—	450	156	310	—	300	—
6	—	335	350	270	—	—	—	—	301	—	300	310	309	293	444	300	212	298	—	303	—
7	—	290	300	258	304	—	265	—	309	—	—	—	330	300	300	300	272	298	—	253	—
8	—	320	300	298	300	—	290	—	300	290	300	—	299	290	298	300	—	302	231	—	—
9	300	300	300	298	304	—	260	293	265	297	275	297	300	280	298	301	298	302	286	200	—
10	299	300	310	—	305	—	300	—	280	—	300	—	300	280	300	300	298	298	—	210	—
11	—	310	—	—	325	100	283	—	301	—	300	—	304	302	—	300	298	301	—	224	—
12	—	300	—	—	302	260	300	—	—	—	300	—	303	325	300	300	298	300	296	306	—
13	—	300	—	—	290	260	300	—	300	300	301	—	307	300	297	902	—	300	300	219	—
14	—	300	300	—	300	300	300	—	300	—	301	—	304	281	300	298	296	298	300	220	—
15	—	302	—	—	308	298	350	—	300	—	300	—	300	303	—	305	298	305	—	221	—
16	—	302	300	258	—	303	345	—	305	—	300	—	302	302	301	298	—	302	—	186	—
17	—	301	300	—	303	301	300	—	300	—	300	300	302	303	299	300	—	300	300	—	—
18	—	300	305	—	302	298	300	—	0	—	300	300	295	300	288	303	—	303	—	226	—
19	—	301	300	—	301	306	320	—	201	294	260	290	300	281	298	300	—	298	300	232	—

Table V,B. Market B Volume and Profit, by Individual, by Period

Experiment 061191

Individual	07		08		09		10		11		12		13	
Period	Vol.	Profit	Vol.	Profit	Vol.	Profit	Vol.	Profit	Vol.	Profit	Vol.	Profit	Vol.	Profit
1	0	0					30	120	0	0	0	0	0	0
2							31	−194	0	0	0	0		
3									0	0	30	180		
4									31	271	0	0		
5	0	0							31	209	0	0		
6	31	−101							0	0	0	0	0	0
7	31	240									0	0		
8	0	0									31	147		
9											31	178		
10							28	2016			0	0		
11	22	−1166			8	−2936	0	0						
12	0	0			28	504	0	0						
13	31	457			0	0	0	0						
14	31	612					0	0						
15	0	0			0	0	0	0						
16	0	0							32	480				
17	31	364					0	0						
18	0	0					31	333						
19	0	0					31	−612						

Experiment 062791

Individual	07		08		09		10		11		12		13	
Period	Vol.	Profit	Vol.	Profit	Vol.	Profit	Vol.	Profit	Vol.	Profit	Vol.	Profit	Vol.	Profit
1	26	1950							0	0			0	0
2	26	2600			0	0			0	0	0	0	0	0
3	1	−456							29	2023				
4	31	2069			0	0			0	0	0	0		
5	0	0							30	900				
6	32	736			0	0								
7	0	0			0	0	0	0	31	364				
8	0	0							33	239				
9														
10	0	0			0	0			30	330				
11	0	0			0	0			31	240				
12	0	0	0	0	33	388			0	0				
13	0	0							30	480				
14	0	0			31	209			0	0				
15	0	0			31	364			0	0				
16	0	0			31	333			0	0				
17	0	0			31	364								
18	31	256			0	0								
19	26	2600												

Table V,B. Continued

Individual	Experiment 071891													
	07		08		09		10		11		12		13	
Period	Vol.	Profit	Vol.	Profit	Vol.	Profit	Vol.	Profit	Vol.	Profit	Vol.	Profit	Vol.	Profit
1	26	988	0	0	3	−1798			0	0				
2	3	−1048	0	0	0	0			0	0			27	263
3			0	0									30	870
4	28	112							0	0			0	0
5	0	0							31	178			0	0
6									31	23			0	0
7									31	116			0	0
8					0	0					0	0	31	85
9													31	302
10									31	302			0	0
11	0	0							31	132			0	0
12													31	178
13					27	−952							0	0
14													31	302
15	0	0							31	395			0	0
16					33	487			0	0			0	0
17					0	0					19	185	0	0
18					0	0			0	0			0	0
19					0	0							31	178

neighborhood, ±1, around 0 and 5, were also asymmetrically distributed, with the two numbers 9 and 4 being preferred to the two numbers 1 and 6 by a margin of 22 to 14. A hypothesis of equal probability can be rejected at .01 level of confidence. ∎

The second observation suggests that behavior does not reflect the belief that the behavior of others is independently random with probabilities represented by the relative frequencies of choices. Table VII shows the relative frequencies with which price choices were made, together with the expected profit that would result from various pricing decisions, given that the choices of others are drawn with probabilities equal to the frequencies in the table. If the system was at a Nash equilibrium, then the expected profit would be the same for all price choices.

OBSERVATION 2. *Pricing strategies are not Nash responses given the relative frequency of prices that was observed.*

Support. Consider the potential ask prices in Table VII. The high prices in the neighborhood of 360 and 385 would yield a profit of 150 percent or greater of the lower prices. ∎

The third observation is that scale choices of agents are optimal given actual volumes sold by sellers. This is particularly interesting because the scale choices are not optimal given the quantities offered for sale by sellers. Recall that sellers entering market B chose a scale, a price, and a quantity offered. The observation is that the scale choice suggests that sellers (correctly) expected to sell the market demand quantity but they offered a little more than that expectation in hope that the volume would be (possibly accidentally) higher.

OBSERVATION 3. *The scale chosen by agents tends to be optimum given the actual quantity sold. Actual quantity sold tends to equal induced market demand given the quote of price. Quantity*

Table VI. Frequency of Scale of Plant Choice in All Three Experiments, All Periods

Scale	Number of Choices	
A	3	
B	0	
C	3	
D	1	Cournot triopoly and more
E	0	
F	0	
G	1	Cournot duopoly
H	0	
I	1	
J	1	
K	9	
L	0	
M	1	Monopoly
N	0	
O	3	
P	1	
Q	0	
R	2	
S	8	
T	7	
U	25	
V	21	
W	41	Contested market
X	3	
Y	15	

Table VII. Relative Frequency of Price Choices in Periods beyond the Sixth and Expected Profits of Price Strategy

Price Range	Relative Frequency of Low Price Choices		Posted Price Strategy	Profit if Low Price	Prob.* of Low Price	Expected Profit
$318 \leq p \leq 324$	19/90	0.21				
$325 \leq p \leq 329$	22/90	0.24	325	302	0.79	238
$330 \leq p \leq 334$	10/90	0.11	330	457	0.54	256
$335 \leq p \leq 339$	5/90	0.07	335	612	0.43	257
$340 \leq p \leq 344$	4/90	0.04	340	630	0.39	220
$345 \leq p \leq 360$	6/90	0.07	345	780	0.33	250
$360 \leq p$	24/90	0.27	360	1230	0.27	307
			385	1980	0.27	528

*Computed neglecting ties.

offered for sale is greater than actual sales and the scale of plant chosen is too small given the quoted quantity.

Support. Figure 8 shows deviations of actual scale chosen from the theoretical optimum scale given the price quoted by the agent. If the seller has the lowest price then the demand function can be used to determine the quantity that will be sold. The quantity to be sold can be used to determine the optimal scale for that quantity. The figure shows deviations from this optimum where 0 indicates the optimum and ± 1 indicates one letter deviations from the optimum. As can be seen in the figure, the mode of choice is the optimum given the price.

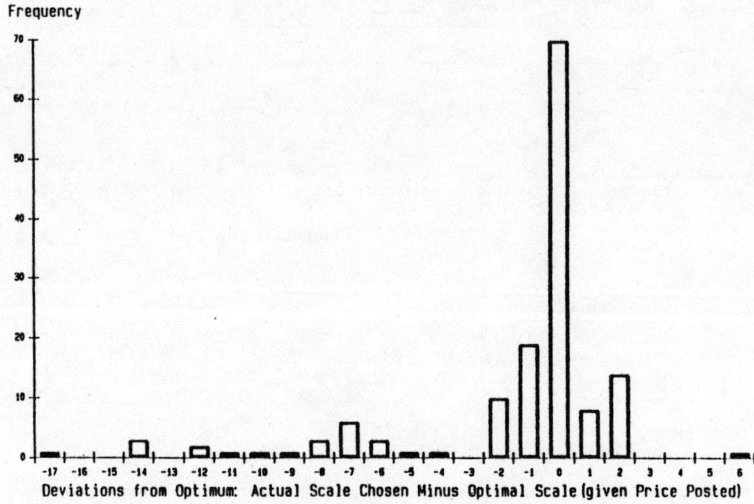

Figure 8. Deviations from Optimum: Actual Scale Chosen Minus Optimal Scale (Given Price Posted)

The same calculation can be made using the quantities offered for sale. Figure 9 shows deviation of scale choice from the optimum given the quantity offered. As can be seen, the scale choices tend to be smaller than this calculation of optimum. ▮

The next observation is that agents specialize in markets. Some agents are always in market A while others have a propensity to enter market B. Table VIII contains for each individual of each experiment, the total number of times during the nineteen periods of the experiment, the number of times the individual entered the B market. For example, the person with identification number 7 in experiment 061191 entered the B market 14 times out of the nineteen periods, while person 8 of that experiment never entered.

OBSERVATION 4. *The frequency with which market B is entered is not the same across sellers.*

Support. Test the hypothesis that the decisions made by the two individuals with the lowest propensity to enter, were independently drawn from the same distribution as the decisions of the two people with the highest propensity. The hypothesis is rejected at the .001 level of significance. ▮

The final Observation 5 concerns the behavior of the whole market system. As was noted in Result 2, efficiencies are not at 100% as they should be if both the competitive model and the perfectly contested market were working perfectly to predict behavior. On average, excluding the first periods, the system of both markets is operating at an efficiency level of about 91.3%. While this is much better than the 80% predicted by the natural monopoly model, or the 41% predicted by the market collapse model, these two models suggest sources of inefficiency that can be interpreted as the social cost of regulation. If more than one firm happens to enter the market there is an opportunity cost of profits foregone in market A. On the other hand, if there is under entry (no firm enters and sells) an efficiency loss will exist due to the loss of consumer surplus in market B. The observation is that the efficiency loss from these two sources amounts to about 67% of the 8.7% average loss in system efficiency (not including the first periods).

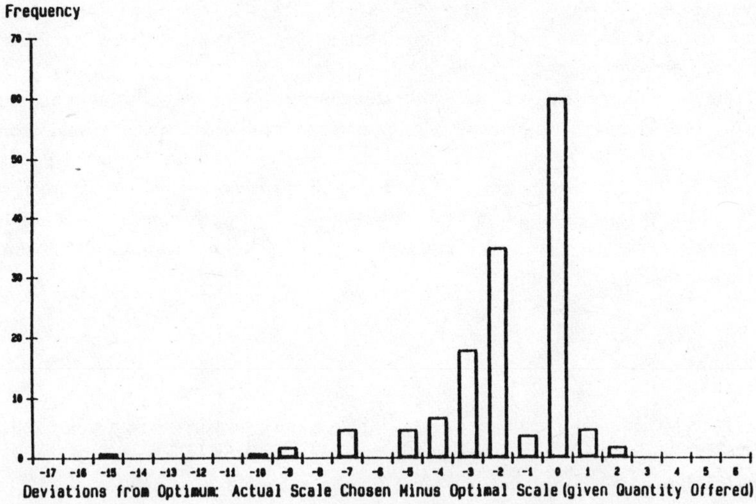

Figure 9. Deviations from Optimum: Actual Scale Chosen Minus Optimal Scale (Given Quantity Offered)

Table VIII. Number of Decisions to Enter the B Market in All Nineteen Periods: By Individual, by Experiment

	Individual Identification Number						
Experiment	7	8	9	10	11	12	13
061191	14	0	4	11	7	10	2
062791	18	1	12	1	14	2	2
071891	6	3	8	0	11	2	18

OBSERVATION 5. *Excluding first periods, efficiency loss due to over entry is about 2.19% and efficiency loss due to under entry is about 3.32%.*

Support. If exactly one firm leaves market A and enters market B the system can operate at 100% efficiency. This maximum possible efficiency expressed as a function of the number of entrants, n is: maximum possible efficiency $= 100 - (.01475)(n - 1)$ if $n > 0$. However, the maximum possible efficiency is .41 if $n = 0$. Thus, $(.01475)(n - 1)$ is the efficiency loss due to over entry and .59 is the efficiency loss due to no entry (or under entry). Of course, both over entry and under entry can occur at the same time if several firms enter and all cancel their asks and thus sell nothing.

The number of firms that left market A with an intent to enter market B each period of each experiment is contained in Table IV. Application of the formula to the numbers in the table produces for all experiments and for all periods (except the first periods), an average loss of .0219 due to over entry. The table also shows three periods, one in each experiment, in which no units were sold in market B due to no entry either by virtue of leaving market A and canceling (two periods) or by not leaving market A (one period). The efficiency loss averaged over all periods except the first periods, is 0.0332. ∎

If the efficiency losses identified in Observation 5 are interpreted as the cost of market regulation then the overall average efficiency loss of 8.7% can be decomposed into an implicit regulatory cost of 5.5% and "other inefficiencies" of 3.2%. Of course, whether or not this is the least expensive regulation possible is not addressed here. The major point is to identify the inefficiency and demonstrate that it can be measured.

Once the "regulatory cost" or "uncoordinated entry cost" is removed, the remaining 3.2% efficiency loss is of interest. This percentage represents the combined effects of typos, wrong scale choices, inefficiencies due to strategic maneuvering, inefficiencies due to posted prices above average cost, etc. The fact that the combined effect of all sources of inefficiency is small, strongly suggests that, with the exception of uncoordinated entry, the perfectly contested market theory is predicting almost perfectly. That is, the cost expended on this form of regulation has been almost perfect in achieving its desired effect.

V. Conclusions

This paper posed a series of questions. First, will increasing returns result in a single seller? Will the single seller charge a monopoly price? If a monopoly price is not charged, do models exist that accurately predict what the price will be?

The answer to the first question is "yes." For the most part, all sales tend to be made by a single agent. This is a particularly interesting result since neither monopolistically competitive or oligopolistic structures tended to evolve, even though they could have. In particular, the data provide no support at all for Cournot models of industrial structure and pricing.

The answer to the second question is "no." Even though sales were almost always by a single seller, monopolistic pricing did not emerge. Instead, the single seller sold at prices near those that would prevail if units were supplied at the lowest average cost that covered the opportunity cost of the supplying firm. The supplying firm chose to operate at a scale of plant and at prices such that consumers paid the lowest possible price subject to the constraint that the supplier did not make a loss. Briefly put, the system behavior was closer to that described by contestable market theory than any of the other models considered.

In some respects, the data here provide strong support for the conclusions drawn from other studies that experimentally examined the possibility of contestability theory. One could have been concerned that the results of other studies might have been due to subject boredom, the linearity of costs, the lack of latitude for monopolistically competitive organizations, etc. The results of this paper demonstrate that such concern about previous results are not well-founded. The fundamental tendencies reported by others were observed after all of the potential explanations were controlled.

To the extent that contestable market theory fell short of accurate predictions, the nature of the failure of contestability theory is interesting. The tendency to enter the "monopolized" market is too great and there is a chance that no one will enter. Firms tended to enter the industry in the hope that the incumbent would try to raise prices to near monopoly levels. Given the behavior of the incumbent, these firms would have been better off participating in alternative economic activity. In a sense, the policing activity was the cost of regulating the incumbent. Aside from this monitoring cost, the system worked substantially as predicted by contestability theory.

Obviously there exist many alternative ways to conduct experiments and check the robustness of the results reported here. Existing theory, especially game theory, is rich with suggestions for further experiments, Shapiro [9, 330–414]. Theoretically, the timing of decisions could switch market behavior between Bertrand and Cournot. Theories of signaling, repeated games, and other facets of dynamic rivalry, suggest variables and circumstances that might have dramatic effects on behavior. The message, at this point, seems to be that future research and experimental designs to explore these many possibilities should proceed on the presumption that contestability theory will have considerable exploratory power.

References

1. Coursey, Don, R. Mark Isaac, M. Luke, and Vernon L. Smith, "Market Contestability in the Presence of Sunk (Entry) Cost." *Rand Journal of Economics*, Spring 1984, 69–84.

2. Coursey, Don, R. Mark Isaac, and Vernon L. Smith, "Natural Monopoly and Contested Markets: Some Experimental Results." *Journal of Law and Economics*, April 1984, 91–113.

3. Novshek, William, "Finding All n-Firm Cournot Equilibria." *International Economic Review*, February 1984, 61–70.

4. ———. "On the Competitiveness of Large Cournot Markets." Unpublished manuscript, Purdue University.

5. Plott, Charles R. "A Computerized Laboratory Market System and Research Support Systems for the Multiple Unit Double Auction." Social Science Working Paper no. 783, Pasadena: California Institute of Technology, November 1991.

6. ——— and Peter Gray, "The Multiple Unit Double Auction." *Journal of Economic Behavior and Organization*, March 1990, 245–58.

7. ——— and Vernon L. Smith, "An Experimental Examination of Two Exchange Institutions." *Review of Economic Studies*, February 1978, 133–53.

8. ———, Alexandre B. Sugiyama, and Gilad Elbaz. "Economies of Scale, Natural Monopoly and Imperfect Competition in an Experimental Market." Social Science Working Paper no. 773, Pasadena: California Institute of Technology, revised February 1994.

9. Shapiro, Carl. "Theories of Oligopoly Behavior," in *Handbook of Industrial Organization*, vol. 1, edited by R. Schmalensee and R. D. Willig. Amsterdam: Elsevier Science Publishers B.V., 1989, pp. 330–414.

10. Smith, Vernon L. "An Empirical Study of Decentralized Institutions of Monopoly Restraint," in *Essays in Contemporary Fields of Economics in Honor of Emanuel T. Weiler (1914–1979)*, edited by George Horwich and James P. Quirk. West Lafayette, Indiana: Purdue University Press, 1981, pp. 83–106.

Part VI
Monopolistic Competition

[29]

THE JOURNAL OF
POLITICAL ECONOMY

Volume LXIX JUNE 1961 *Number 3*

THE ECONOMICS OF INFORMATION[1]

GEORGE J. STIGLER
University of Chicago

One should hardly have to tell academicians that information is a valuable resource: knowledge *is* power. And yet it occupies a slum dwelling in the town of economics. Mostly it is ignored: the best technology is assumed to be known; the relationship of commodities to consumer preferences is a datum. And one of the information-producing industries, advertising, is treated with a hostility that economists normally reserve for tariffs or monopolists.

There are a great many problems in economics for which this neglect of ignorance is no doubt permissible or even desirable. But there are some for which this is not true, and I hope to show that some important aspects of economic organization take on a new meaning when they are considered from the viewpoint of the search for information. In the present paper I shall attempt to analyze systematically one important problem of information—the ascertainment of market price.

[1] I have benefited from comments of Gary Becker, Milton Friedman, Zvi Griliches, Harry Johnson, Robert Solow, and Lester Telser.

I. THE NATURE OF SEARCH

Prices change with varying frequency in all markets, and, unless a market is completely centralized, no one will know all the prices which various sellers (or buyers) quote at any given time. A buyer (or seller) who wishes to ascertain the most favorable price must canvass various sellers (or buyers)—a phenomenon I shall term "search."

The amount of dispersion of asking prices of sellers is a problem to be discussed later, but it is important to emphasize immediately the fact that dispersion is ubiquitous even for homogeneous goods. Two examples of asking prices, of consumer and producer goods respectively, are displayed in Table 1. The automobile prices (for an identical model) were those quoted with an average amount of "higgling": their average was $2,436, their range from $2,350 to $2,515, and their standard deviation $42. The prices for anthracite coal were bids for federal government purchases and had a mean of $16.90 per ton, a range from $15.46 to $18.92, and a standard deviation of $1.15. In both cases the range of prices was significant on almost any criterion.

Price dispersion is a manifestation—and, indeed, it is the measure—of ignorance in the market. Dispersion is a biased measure of ignorance because there is never absolute homogeneity in the commodity if we include the terms of sale within the concept of the commodity. Thus, some automobile dealers might perform more service, or carry a larger range of varieties in stock, and a portion of the observed dispersion is presumably attributable to such differences. But it would be metaphysical, and fruitless, to assert that all dispersion is due to heterogeneity.

TABLE 1

ASKING PRICES FOR TWO COMMODITIES

A. CHEVROLETS, CHICAGO, FEBRUARY, 1959*

Price (Dollars)	No. of Dealers
2,350–2,400	4
2,400–2,450	11
2,450–2,500	8
2,500–2,550	4

B. ANTHRACITE COAL, DELIVERED (WASHINGTON, D.C.), APRIL, 1953†

Price per Ton (Dollars)	No. of Bids
15.00–15.50	2
15.50–16.00	2
16.00–16.50	2
16.50–17.00	3
17.00–18.00	1
18.00–19.00	4

* Allen F. Jung, "Price Variations Among Automobile Dealers in Metropolitan Chicago," *Journal of Business*, XXXIII (January, 1960), 31–42.

† Supplied by John Flueck

At any time, then, there will be a frequency distribution of the prices quoted by sellers. Any buyer seeking the commodity would pay whatever price is asked by the seller whom he happened to canvass, if he were content to buy from the first seller. But, if the dispersion of price quotations of sellers is at all large (relative to the cost of search), it will pay, on average, to canvass several sellers. Consider the following primitive example: let sellers be equally divided between asking prices of $2 and $3. Then the distribution of minimum prices, as search is lengthened, is shown in Table 2. The buyer who canvasses two sellers instead of one has an expected saving of 25 cents per unit, etc.

The frequency distributions of asking (and offering) prices have not been studied sufficiently to support any hypothesis as to their nature. Asking prices are probably skewed to the right, as a rule, because the seller of reproducible goods will have some minimum but no maximum limit on the price he can accept. If the distribution of asking prices is normal, the distributions of minimum prices encountered in searches of one, two, and three sellers will be those displayed in Figure 1. If the distribution is rectangular, the corresponding distributions would be those shown in Panel B. The latter assumption does not receive strong support from the evidence, but it will be used for a time because of its algebraic simplicity.

TABLE 2

DISTRIBUTION OF HYPOTHETICAL MINIMUM PRICES BY NUMBERS OF BIDS CANVASSED

No. of Prices Canvassed	Probability of Minimum Price of $2.00	Probability of Minimum Price of $3.00	Expected Minimum Price
1	.5	.5	$2.50
2	.75	.25	2.25
3	.875	.125	2.125
4	.9375	.0625	2.0625
∞	1.0	0	2.00

In fact, if sellers' asking prices (p) are uniformly distributed between zero and one, it can be shown that:[2] (1) The dis-

[2] If $F(p)$ is the cumulative-frequency function of p, the probability that the minimum of n observations will be greater than p is

$$[1-F(p)]^n = \left[\int_p^1 dx\right]^n .$$

tribution of minimum prices with n searches is

$$n(1-p)^{n-1}, \tag{1}$$

(2) the average minimum price is

$$\frac{1}{n+1},$$

and (3) the variance of the average minimum price is

$$\frac{n}{(n+1)^2(n+2)}.$$

Whatever the precise distribution of prices, it is certain that increased search will yield diminishing returns as measured by the expected reduction in the minimum asking price. This is obviously true of the rectangular distribution, with an expected minimum price of $1/(n+1)$ with n searches, and also of the normal distributions.[3] In fact, if a distribution of asking prices did not display this property, it would be an unstable distribution for reasons that will soon be apparent.[4]

For any buyer the expected savings from an additional unit of search will be approximately the quantity (q) he wishes to purchase times the expected reduction in price as a result of the search,[5] or

$$q\left|\frac{\partial P_{\min}}{\partial_n}\right|. \tag{2}$$

The expected saving from given search will be greater, the greater the dispersion of prices. The saving will also obviously be greater, the greater the expenditure on the commodity. Let us defer for a time the problem of the time period to which the expenditure refers, and hence the amount of expenditure, by considering the purchase of an indivisible, infrequently purchased good—say, a used automobile.

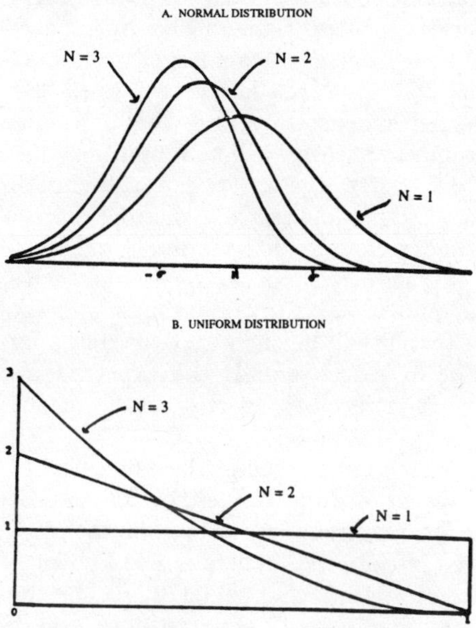

FIG. 1.—Distribution of minimum prices with varying amounts of search.

[3] The expected minimum prices with a normal distribution of mean M and standard deviation σ are

Search	Expected Minimum Price
1	M
2	$M - .564\sigma$
3	$M - .846\sigma$
4	$M - 1.029\sigma$
5	$M - 1.163\sigma$
6	$M - 1.267\sigma$
7	$M - 1.352\sigma$
8	$M - 1.423\sigma$
9	$M - 1.485\sigma$
10	$M - 1.539\sigma$

[4] Robert Solow has pointed out that the expected value of the minimum of a random sample of n observations,

$$E(n) = n\int_0^{\infty} p(1-F)^{n-1}F'dp,$$

is a decreasing function of n, and

$$[E(n+2) - E(n+1)] - [E(n+1) - E(n)]$$

is positive so the minimum decreases at a decreasing rate. The proofs involve the fact that the density function for the rth observation from the maximum in a sample of n is

$$n\binom{n-1}{r-1}F^{n-r}(1-F)^{r-1}F'dp.$$

[5] The precise savings will be (a) the reduction in price times the quantity which would be purchased at the higher price—the expression in the text—*plus* (b) the average saving on the additional purchases induced by the lower price. I neglect this quantity, which will generally be of a smaller order of magnitude.

The cost of search, for a consumer, may be taken as approximately proportional to the number of (identified) sellers approached, for the chief cost is time. This cost need not be equal for all consumers, of course: aside from differences in tastes, time will be more valuable to a person with a larger income. If the cost of search is equated to its expected marginal return, the optimum amount of search will be found.[6]

Of course, the sellers can also engage in search and, in the case of unique items, will occasionally do so in the literal fashion that buyers do. In this—empirically unimportant—case, the optimum amount of search will be such that the marginal cost of search equals the expected increase in receipts, strictly parallel to the analysis for buyers.

With unique goods the efficiency of personal search for either buyers or sellers is extremely low, because the identity of potential sellers is not known—the cost of search must be divided by the fraction of potential buyers (or sellers) in the population which is being searched. If I plan to sell a used car and engage in personal search, less than one family in a random selection of one hundred families is a potential buyer of even a popular model within the next month. As a result, the cost of search is increased more than one hundredfold per price quotation.

The costs of search are so great under these conditions that there is powerful inducement to localize transactions as a device for identifying potential buyers and sellers. The medieval markets commonly increased their efficiency in this respect by prohibiting the purchase or sale of the designated commodities within a given radius of the market or on nonmarket days. The market tolls that were frequently levied on sellers (even in the absence of effective restrictions on nonmarket transactions) were clear evidence of the value of access to the localized markets.

Advertising is, of course, the obvious modern method of identifying buyers and sellers: the *classified* advertisements in particular form a meeting place for potential buyers and sellers. The identification of buyers and sellers reduces drastically the cost of search. But advertising has its own limitations: advertising itself is an expense, and one essentially independent of the value of the item advertised. The advertising of goods which have few potential buyers relative to the circulation of the advertising medium is especially expensive. We shall temporarily put advertising aside and consider an alternative.

The alternative solution is the development of specialized traders whose chief service, indeed, is implicitly to provide a meeting place for potential buyers and sellers. A used-car dealer, turning over a thousand cars a year, and presumably encountering three or five thousand each of buying and selling bids, provides a substantial centralization of trading activity. Let us consider these dealer markets, which we shall assume to be competitive in the sense of there being many independent dealers.

Each dealer faces a distribution of (for example) buyers' bids and can vary his selling prices with a corresponding effect upon purchases. Even in the markets for divisible (and hence non-unique) goods there will be some scope for higgling (discrimination) in each individual transaction: the buyer has a maximum price given by the lowest price he encounters among the dealers he has searched (or

6 Buyers often pool their knowledge and thus reduce the effective cost of search; a few remarks are made on this method below.

plans to search), but no minimum price. But let us put this range of indeterminacy aside, perhaps by assuming that the dealer finds discrimination too expensive,[7] and inquire how the demand curve facing a dealer is determined.

Each dealer sets a selling price, p, and makes sales to all buyers for whom this is the minimum price. With a uniform distribution of asking prices by dealers, the number of buyers of a total of N_b possible buyers who will purchase from him is

$$N_i = K N_b n (1-p)^{n-1}, \qquad (3)$$

where K is a constant.[8] The number of buyers from a dealer increases as his price is reduced, and at an increasing rate.[9] Moreover, with the uniform distribution of asking prices, the number of buyers increases with increased search if the price is below the reciprocal of the amount of search.[10] We should generally expect the high-price sellers to be small-volume sellers.

The stability of any distribution of asking prices of dealers will depend upon the costs of dealers. If there are constant returns to scale, the condition of equal rates of return dictates that the difference between a dealer's buying and selling prices be a constant. This condition cannot in general be met: any dealer can buy low, and sell high, provided he is content with a small volume of transactions, and he will then be earning more than costs (including a competitive rate of return). No other dealer can eliminate this non-competitive rate of profit, although by making the same price bids he can share the volume of business, or by asking lower prices he can increase the rewards to search and hence increase the amount of search.

With economies of scale, the competition of dealers will eliminate the profitability of quoting very high selling and very low buying prices and will render impossible some of the extreme price bids. On this score, the greater the decrease in average cost with volume, the smaller will be the dispersion of prices.[11] Many distributions of prices will be inconsistent with any possible cost conditions of dealers,[12] and it is not evident that strict equalities of rates of return for dealers are generally possible.

If economies of scale in dealing lead to

[7] This is the typical state of affairs in retailing xcept for consumer durable goods.

[8] Since $n(1-p)^{n-1}$ is a density function, we must multiply it by a dp which represents the range of prices between adjacent price quotations. In addition, if two or more sellers quote an identical price, they will share the sales, so $K = dp/r$, where r is the number of firms quoting price p.

[9] For

$$\frac{\partial N_i}{\partial p} = -\frac{(n-1)N_i}{(1-p)} < 0,$$

and

$$\frac{\partial^2 N_i}{\partial p^2} = \frac{(n-1)(n-2)N_i}{(1-p)^2} > 0$$

if $n > 2$.

[10] Let

$$\log N_i = \log K + \log N_b + \log n + (n-1)\log(1-p).$$

Then

$$\frac{1}{N_i}\frac{\partial N_i}{\partial n} = \frac{1}{n} + \log(1-p) = \frac{1}{n} - p,$$

approximately.

[11] This argument assumes that dealers will discover unusually profitable bids, given the buyers' search, which is, of course, only partly true: there is also a problem of dealers' search with respect to prices.

[12] With the rectangular distribution of asking prices, if each buyer purchases the same number of units, the elasticity of demand falls continuously with price, so that, if average cost equaled price at every rate of sales (with one seller at each price), marginal costs would have to be negative at large outputs. But, of course, the number of sellers can be less at lower prices.

a smaller dispersion of asking prices than do constant costs of dealing, similarly greater amounts of search will lead to a smaller dispersion of observed selling prices by reducing the number of purchasers who will pay high prices. Let us consider more closely the determinants of search.

DETERMINANTS OF SEARCH

The equation defining optimum search is unambiguous only if a unique purchase is being made—a house, a particular used book, etc. If purchases are repetitive, the volume of purchases based upon the search must be considered.

If the correlation of asking prices of dealers in successive time periods is perfect (and positive!), the initial search is the only one that need be undertaken. In this case the expected savings of search will be the present value of the discounted savings on all future purchases, the future savings extending over the life of the buyer or seller (whichever is shorter).[13] On the other hand, if asking prices are uncorrelated in successive time periods, the savings from search will pertain only to that period,[14] and search in each period is independent of previous experience. If the correlation of successive prices is positive, customer search will be larger in the initial period than in subsequent periods.[15]

The correlation of successive asking prices of sellers is usually positive in the handful of cases I have examined. The rank correlation of anthracite price bids (Table 1) in 1953 with those in 1954 was .68 for eight bidders; that for Chevrolet dealers in Chicago February and August of 1959 was .33 for twenty-nine dealers—but, on the other hand, it was zero for Ford dealers for the same dates. Most observed correlations will, of course, be positive because of stable differences in the products or services, but our analysis is restricted to conditions of homogeneity.

As a rule, positive correlations should exist with homogeneous products. The amount of search will vary among individuals because of differences in their expenditures on a commodity or differences in cost of search. A seller who wishes to obtain the continued patronage of those buyers who value the gains of search more highly or have lower costs of search must see to it that he is quoting relatively low prices. In fact, goodwill may be defined as continued patronage by customers without continued search (that is, no more than occasional verification).

A positive correlation of successive asking prices justifies the widely held view that inexperienced buyers (tourists)

[13] Let the expected minimum price be $p_1 = f(n)_1$ in period 1 (with $f' < 0$) and let the expected minimum price in period 2, with r a measure of the correlation between sellers' successive prices, be

$$p_2 = \left(\frac{p_1}{f(n_2)}\right)^r f(n_2) .$$

If the cost of search is λ per unit, total expenditures for a fixed quantity of purchases (Q) per unit of time are, neglecting interest,

$$E = Q(p_1 + p_2) + \lambda(n_1 + n_2) .$$

Expenditures are a minimum when

$$\frac{\partial E}{\partial n_1} = Qf'(n_1) + Qr[f(n_1)]^{r-1} \times [f(n_2)]^{1-r} f'(n_1) + \lambda = 0$$

and

$$\frac{\partial E}{\partial n_2} = (1-r)Q[f(n_1)]^r \times [f(n_2)]^{-r} f'(n_2) + \lambda = 0 .$$

If $r = 1$, $n_2 = 0$, and n_1 is determined by $Qf'(n_1) = -\lambda/2$, the cost of search is effectively halved.

[14] See n. 13; if $r = 0$, $n_1 = n_2$.

[15] Let $f(n) = e^{-n}$. Then, in the notation of our previous footnotes,

$$n_1 - n_2 = \frac{2r}{1-r},$$

approximately.

pay higher prices in a market than do experienced buyers.[16] The former have no accumulated knowledge of asking prices, and even with an optimum amount of search they will pay higher prices on average. Since the variance of the expected minimum price decreases with additional search, the prices paid by inexperienced buyers will also have a larger variance.

If a buyer enters a wholly new market, he will have no idea of the dispersion of prices and hence no idea of the rational amount of search he should make. In such cases the dispersion will presumably be estimated by some sort of sequential process, and this approach would open up a set of problems I must leave for others to explore. But, in general, one approaches a market with some general knowledge of the amount of dispersion, for dispersion itself is a function of the average amount of search, and this in turn is a function of the nature of the commodity:

1. The larger the fraction of the buyer's expenditures on the commodity, the greater the savings from search and hence the greater the amount of search.
2. The larger the fraction of repetitive (experienced) buyers in the market, the greater the effective amount of search (with positive correlation of successive prices).
3. The larger the fraction of repetitive sellers, the higher the correlation between successive prices, and hence, by condition (2), the larger the amount of accumulated search.[17]
4. The cost of search will be larger, the larger the geographical size of the market.

An increase in the number of buyers has an uncertain effect upon the dispersion of asking prices. The sheer increase in numbers will lead to an increase in the number of dealers and, *ceteris paribus*, to a larger range of asking prices. But, quite aside from advertising, the phenomenon of pooling information will increase. Information is pooled when two buyers compare prices: if each buyer canvasses s sellers, by combining they effectively canvass $2s$ sellers, duplications aside.[18] Consumers compare prices of some commodities (for example, liquor) much more often than of others (for example, chewing gum)—in fact, pooling can be looked upon as a cheaper (and less reliable) form of search.

SOURCES OF DISPERSION

One source of dispersion is simply the cost to dealers of ascertaining rivals' asking prices, but even if this cost were zero the dispersion of prices would not vanish. The more important limitation is provided by buyers' search, and, if the conditions and participants in the market were fixed in perpetuity, prices would immediately approach uniformity. Only those differences could persist which did not remunerate additional search. The condition for optimum search would be (with perfect correlation of successive prices):

$$q\left|\frac{\partial p}{\partial n}\right| = i \times \text{marginal cost of search},$$

where i is the interest rate. If an additional search costs \$1, and the interest rate is 5 per cent, the expected reduction in price with one more search would at equilibrium be equal to $\$0.05/q$—a quantity which would often be smaller than the smallest unit of currency. But, indivisibilities aside, it would normally be

[16] For that matter, a negative correlation would have the same effects.

[17] If the number of sellers (s) and the asking-price distributions are the same in two periods, but k are new sellers, the average period-1 buyer will have lost proportion k/s of his period-1 search.

[18] Duplications will occur more often than random processes would suggest, because pooling is more likely between buyers of similar location, tastes, etc.

unprofitable for buyers or sellers to eliminate all dispersion.

The maintenance of appreciable dispersion of prices arises chiefly out of the fact that knowledge becomes obsolete. The conditions of supply and demand, and therefore the distribution of asking prices, change over time. There is no method by which buyers or sellers can ascertain the new average price in the market appropriate to the new conditions except by search. Sellers cannot maintain perfect correlation of successive prices, even if they wish to do so, because of the costs of search. Buyers accordingly cannot make the amount of investment in search that perfect correlation of prices would justify. The greater the instability of supply and/or demand conditions, therefore, the greater the dispersion of prices will be.

In addition, there is a component of ignorance duc to the changing identity of buyers and sellers. There is a flow of new buyers and sellers in every market, and they are at least initially uninformed on prices and by their presence make the information of experienced buyers and sellers somewhat obsolete.

The amount of dispersion will also vary with one other characteristic which is of special interest: the size (in terms of both dollars and number of traders) of the market. As the market grows in these dimensions, there will appear a set of firms which specialize in collecting and selling information. They may take the form of trade journals or specialized brokers. Since the cost of collection of information is (approximately) independent of its use (although the cost of dissemination is not), there is a strong tendency toward monopoly in the provision of information: in general, there will be a "standard" source for trade information.

II. ADVERTISING

Advertising is, among other things, a method of providing potential buyers with knowledge of the identity of sellers. It is clearly an immensely powerful instrument for the elimination of ignorance —comparable in force to the use of the book instead of the oral discourse to communicate knowledge. A small $5 advertisement in a metropolitan newspaper reaches (in the sense of being read) perhaps 25,000 readers, or fifty readers per penny, and, even if only a tiny fraction are potential buyers (or sellers), the economy they achieve in search, as compared with uninstructed solicitation, may be overwhelming.

Let us begin with advertisements designed only to identify sellers; the identification of buyers will not be treated explicitly, and the advertising of price will be discussed later. The identification of sellers is necessary because the identity of sellers changes over time, but much more because of the turnover of buyers. In every consumer market there will be a stream of new buyers (resulting from immigration or the attainment of financial maturity) requiring knowledge of sellers, and, in addition, it will be necessary to refresh the knowledge of infrequent buyers.

Suppose, what is no doubt too simple, that a given advertisement of size a will inform c per cent of the potential buyers in a given period, so $c = g(a)$.[19] This contact function will presumably show diminishing returns, at least beyond a certain size of advertisement. A certain fraction, b, of potential customers will be "born" (and "die") in a stable population, where "death" includes not only

[19] The effectiveness of the advertisement is also a function of the skill with which it is done and of the fraction of potential buyers who read the medium, but such elaborations are put aside.

departure from the market but forgetting the seller. The value of b will obviously vary with the nature of the commodity; for example, it will be large for commodities which are seldom purchased (like a house). In a first period of advertising (at a given rate) the number of potential customers reached will be cN, if N is the total number of potential customers. In the second period $cN(1-b)$ of these potential customers will still be informed, cbN new potential customers will be informed, and

$$c[(1-b)n - cN(1-b)]$$

old potential customers will be reached for the first time, or a total of

$$cN[1+(1-b)(1-c)].$$

This generalizes, for k periods, to

$$cN[1+(1-b)(1-c) + \ldots + (1-b)^{k-1}(1-c)^{k-1}],$$

and, if k is large, this approaches

$$\frac{cN}{1-(1-c)(1-b)} = \lambda N. \quad (4)$$

The proportion (λ) of potential buyers informed of the advertiser's identity thus depends upon c and b.

If each of r sellers advertises the same amount, λ is the probability that any one seller will inform any buyer. The distribution of N potential buyers by the number of contacts achieved by r sellers is given by the binomial distribution:

$$N(\lambda + [1-\lambda])^r,$$

with, for example,

$$\frac{Nr!}{m!(r-m)!}\lambda^m(1-\lambda)^{r-m}$$

buyers being informed of exactly m sellers' identities. The number of sellers known to a buyer ranges from zero to r, with an average of $r\lambda$ sellers and a variance of $r\lambda(1-\lambda)$.[20]

The amount of relevant information in the market, even in this simple model, is not easy to summarize in a single measure—a difficulty common to frequency distributions. If all buyers wished to search s sellers, all buyers knowing less than s sellers would have inadequate information, and all who knew more than s sellers would have redundant information, although the redundant information would not be worthless.[21] Since the value of information is the amount by which it reduces the expected cost to the buyer of his purchases, if these expected reductions are $\Delta C_1, \Delta C_2, \ldots,$ for searches of $1, 2, \ldots,$ the value of the information to buyers is approximately

$$\sum_{m=1}^{r} \frac{r!}{m!(r-m)!}\lambda^m(1-\lambda)^{r-m}\Delta C_m.$$

The information possessed by buyers, however, is not simply a matter of chance; those buyers who spend more on the commodity, or who search more for a given expenditure, will also search more for advertisements. The buyers with more information will, on average, make more extensive searches, so the value of information will be greater than this last formula indicates.

We may pause to discuss the fact that advertising in, say, a newspaper is normally "paid" for by the seller. On our analysis, the advertising is valuable to the buyer, and he would be willing to pay

[20] This approach has both similarities and contrasts to that published by S. A. Ozga, "Imperfect Markets through Lack of Knowledge," *Quarterly Journal of Economics*, LXXIV (February, 1960), 29–52.

[21] The larger the number of sellers known, the larger is the range of prices among the sellers and the lower the expected minimum price after s searches. But this effect will normally be small.

more for a paper with advertisements than for one without. The difficulty with having the sellers insert advertisements "free" and having the buyer pay for them directly is that it would be difficult to ration space on this basis: the seller would have an incentive to supply an amount of information (or information of a type) the buyer did not wish, and, since numerous advertisements are supplied jointly, the buyer could not register clearly his preferences regarding advertising. (Catalogues, however, are often sold to buyers.) Charging the seller for the advertisements creates an incentive for him to supply to the buyer only the information which is desired.

It is commonly complained that advertising is jointly supplied with the commodity in the sense that the buyer must pay for both even though he wishes only the latter. The alternative of selling the advertising separately from the commodity, however, would require that the advertising of various sellers (of various commodities) would be supplied jointly: the economies of disseminating information in a general-purpose periodical are so great that some form of jointness is inescapable. But the common complaint is much exaggerated: the buyer who wishes can search out the seller who advertises little (but, of course, enough to be discoverable), and the latter can sell at prices lower by the savings on advertising.

These remarks seem most appropriate to newspaper advertisements of the "classified" variety; what of the spectacular television show or the weekly comedian? We are not equipped to discuss advertising in general because the problem of quality has been (and will continue to be) evaded by the assumption of homogeneous goods. Even within our narrower framework, however, the use of entertainment to attract buyers to information is a comprehensible phenomenon. The assimilation of information is not an easy or pleasant task for most people, and they may well be willing to pay more for the information when supplied in an enjoyable form. In principle, this complementary demand for information and entertainment is exactly analogous to the complementary demand of consumers for commodities and delivery service or air-conditioned stores. One might find a paradox in the simultaneous complaints of some people that advertising is too elaborate and school *houses* too shoddy.

A monopolist will advertise (and price the product) so as to maximize his profits,

$$\pi = Npq\lambda - \phi(N\lambda q) - ap_a ,$$

where $p = f(q)$ is the demand curve of the individual buyer, $\phi(Nq\lambda)$ is production costs other than advertising, and ap_a is advertising expenditures. The maximum profit conditions are

$$\frac{\partial \pi}{\partial q} = N\lambda\left(p + q\frac{\partial p}{\partial q}\right) - \phi' N\lambda = 0 \quad (5)$$

and

$$\frac{\partial \pi}{\partial a} = Npq\frac{\partial \lambda}{\partial a} - \phi' Nq\frac{\partial \lambda}{\partial a} - p_a = 0 . \quad (6)$$

Equation (5) states the usual marginal cost–marginal revenue equality, and equation (6) states the equality of (price − marginal cost) with the marginal cost $[p_a/Nq(\partial\lambda/\partial a)]$ of advertising.[22]

22The marginal revenue from advertising expenditure,

$$\frac{Npq}{p_a}\frac{\partial \lambda}{\partial a},$$

equals the absolute value of the elasticity of demand by equations (5) and (6); see R. Dorfman and P.O. Steiner, 'Optimal Advertising and Optimal Quality," *American Economic Review*, XLIV (1954), 826.

With the Cournot spring (where production costs $\phi = 0$) the monopolist advertises up to the point where price equals the marginal cost of informing a buyer: the monopolist will not (cannot) exploit ignorance as he exploits desire. The monopolist will advertise more, the higher the "death" rate (b), unless it is very high relative to the "contact" rate (c).[23] The monopolistic situation does not invite comparison with competition because an essential feature—the value of search in the face of price dispersion—is absent.

A highly simplified analysis of advertising by the competitive firm is presented in the Appendix. On the assumption that all firms are identical and that all buyers have identical demand curves and search equal amounts, we obtain the maximum-profit equation:

$$\text{Production cost} = p\left(1 + \frac{1}{\eta_{qp} + \eta_{Kp}}\right), \quad (7)$$

where η_{qp} is the elasticity of a buyer's demand curve and η_{K_p} is the elasticity of the fraction of buyers purchasing from the seller with respect to his price. The latter elasticity will be of the order of magnitude of the number of searches made by a buyer. With a uniform distribution of asking prices, increased search will lead to increased advertising by low-price sellers and reduced advertising by high-price sellers. The amount of advertising by a firm decreases as the number of firms increases.

Price advertising has a decisive influence on the dispersion of prices. Search now becomes extremely economical, and the question arises why, in the absence of differences in quality of products, the dispersion does not vanish. And the answer is simply that, if prices are advertised by a large portion of the sellers, the price differences diminish sharply. That they do not wholly vanish (in a given market) is due simply to the fact that no combination of advertising media reaches all potential buyers within the available time.

Assuming, as we do, that all sellers are equally convenient in location, must we say that some buyers are perverse in not reading the advertisements? Obviously not, for the cost of keeping currently informed about all articles which an individual purchases would be prohibitive. A typical household probably buys several hundred different items a month, and, if, on average, their prices change (in some outlets) only once a month, the number of advertisements (by at least several sellers) which must be read is forbiddingly large.

The seller's problem is even greater: he may sell two thousand items (a modest number for a grocery or hardware store), and to advertise each on the occasion of a price change—and frequently enough thereafter to remind buyers of his price—would be impossibly expensive. To keep the buyers in a market informed on the current prices of all items of consumption would involve perhaps a thousandfold increase of newspaper advertising.

From the manufacturer's viewpoint, uncertainty concerning his price is clearly disadvantageous. The cost of search is a cost of purchase, and consumption will therefore be smaller, the greater the dispersion of prices and the greater the optimum amount of search. This is presumably one reason (but, I conjecture, a very minor one) why uniform prices are set by

[23] Differentiating equation (6) with respect to b, we find that $\partial a/\partial b$ is positive or negative according as

$$b \lessgtr \frac{c}{1-c}.$$

If $c \geq \frac{1}{2}$, the derivative must be positive.

sellers of nationally advertised brands: if they have eliminated price variation, they have reduced the cost of the commodity (including search) to the buyer, even if the dealers' margins average somewhat more than they otherwise would.

The effect of advertising prices, then, is equivalent to that of the introduction of a very large amount of search by a large portion of the potential buyers. It follows from our discussion in Section I that the dispersion of asking prices will be much reduced. Since advertising of prices will be devoted to products for which the marginal value of search is high, it will tend to reduce dispersion most in commodities with large aggregate expenditures.

III. CONCLUSIONS

The identification of sellers and the discovery of their prices are only one sample of the vast role of the search for information in economic life. Similar problems exist in the detection of profitable fields for investment and in the worker's choice of industry, location, and job. The search for knowledge on the quality of goods, which has been studiously avoided in this paper, is perhaps no more important but, certainly, analytically more difficult. Quality has not yet been successfully specified by economics, and this elusiveness extends to all problems in which it enters.

Some forms of economic organization may be explicable chiefly as devices for eliminating uncertainties in quality. The department store, as Milton Friedman has suggested to me, may be viewed as an institution which searches for the superior qualities of goods and guarantees that they are good quality. "Reputation" is a word which denotes the persistence of quality, and reputation commands a price (or exacts a penalty) because it economizes on search. When economists deplore the reliance of the consumer on reputation—although they choose the articles they read (and their colleagues) in good part on this basis—they implicitly assume that the consumer has a large laboratory, ready to deliver current information quickly and gratuitously.

Ignorance is like subzero weather: by a sufficient expenditure its effects upon people can be kept within tolerable or even comfortable bounds, but it would be wholly uneconomic entirely to eliminate all its effects. And, just as an analysis of man's shelter and apparel would be somewhat incomplete if cold weather is ignored, so also our understanding of economic life will be incomplete if we do not systematically take account of the cold winds of ignorance.

APPENDIX

Under competition, the amount of advertising by any one seller (i) can be determined as follows. Each buyer will engage in an amount s of search, which is determined by the factors discussed above (Sec. 1). He will on average know

$$(r-1)\lambda+\lambda_i$$

sellers, where λ_i is defined by equation (4) for seller i. Hence,

$$\frac{\lambda_i}{(r-1)\lambda+\lambda_i}$$

per cent of buyers who know seller i will canvass him on one search, and

$$\left(1-\frac{\lambda_i}{(r-1)\lambda+\lambda_i}\right)^s$$

per cent of the buyers who know i will not canvass him in s searches,

$$s \leq (r-1)\lambda+\lambda_i\,.$$

Therefore, of the buyers who know i, the proportion who will canvass him at least once is[24]

$$1-\left(1-\frac{\lambda_i}{(r-1)\lambda+\lambda_i}\right)^s.$$

If we approximate

$$\frac{\lambda_i}{(r-1)\lambda+\lambda_i}$$

by

$$\frac{\lambda_i}{r\lambda}$$

and take only the first two terms of the binomial expansion, this becomes

$$\frac{s\lambda_i}{r\lambda}.$$

The receipts of any seller then become the product of (1) The number of buyers canvassing him,

$$\frac{s\lambda_i}{r\lambda}\lambda_i N=T_i,$$

(2) the fraction K of those canvassing him who buy from him, where K depends upon his relative price (and the amount of search and the number of rivals), and (3) sales to each customer, pq. If $\phi(T_i Kq)$ is production costs and ap_a advertising costs, profits are

$$\pi=T_iKpq-\phi(T_iKq)-ap_a.$$

The conditions for maximum profits are

$$\frac{\partial\pi}{\partial p}=T_i\left(K\frac{\partial pq}{\partial p}+pq\frac{\partial K}{\partial p}\right)-T_i\phi'\left(K\frac{\partial q}{\partial p}+q\frac{\partial K}{\partial p}\right)=0 \qquad (8)$$

and

$$\frac{\partial\pi}{\partial a}=Kpq\frac{\partial T_i}{\partial a}-\phi'Kq\frac{\partial T_i}{\partial a}-p_a=0. \quad (9)$$

[24] The formula errs slightly in allowing the multiple canvass of one seller by a buyer.

The former equation can be rewritten in elasticities as

$$\phi'=p\left(1+\frac{1}{\eta_{qp}+\eta_{Kp}}\right) \qquad (8a)$$

Price exceeds marginal cost, not simply by $(-p/\eta_{qp})$ as with monopoly, but by the smaller amount

$$\frac{-p}{\eta_{qp}+\eta_{Kp}},$$

where η_{Kp} will generally be of the order of magnitude of the number of searches made by a buyer.[25] Equation (2) states the equality of the marginal revenue of advertising with its marginal cost. By differentiating equation (2) with respect to s and taking ϕ' as constant, it can be shown that increased search by buyers will lead to increased advertising by low-price sellers and reduced advertising by high-price sellers (with a uniform distribution of prices).[26]

By the same method it may be shown that the amount of advertising by the firm will decrease as the number of rivals increases.[27] The aggregate amount of advertising by the industry may either increase or decrease with an increase in the number of firms, s, depending on the relationship between λ and a.

[25] In the case of the uniform distribution, η_{Kp} is

$$\frac{-(s-1)p}{1-p}.$$

[26] The derivative $\partial a/\partial s$ has the sign of $(1+\eta_{Ks})$, and this elasticity equals

$$1+s\log[1-p]$$

with a uniform distribution of prices.

[27] By differentiation of equation (2) with respect to r one gets

$$r\frac{\partial a}{\partial r}\left\{\lambda_i\frac{\partial^2\lambda_i}{\partial a^2}+\left(\frac{\partial\lambda_i}{\partial a}\right)^2\right\}=\lambda_i\frac{\partial\lambda_i}{\partial a}\left(1-\frac{r}{K}\frac{\partial K}{\partial r}\right).$$

The term in brackets on the left side is negative by the stability condition; the right side is positive.

[30]

THE MARKET FOR "LEMONS": QUALITY UNCERTAINTY AND THE MARKET MECHANISM *

GEORGE A. AKERLOF

I. INTRODUCTION

This paper relates quality and uncertainty. The existence of goods of many grades poses interesting and important problems for the theory of markets. On the one hand, the interaction of quality differences and uncertainty may explain important institutions of the labor market. On the other hand, this paper presents a struggling attempt to give structure to the statement: "Business in underdeveloped countries is difficult"; in particular, a structure is given for determining the economic costs of dishonesty. Additional applications of the theory include comments on the structure of money markets, on the notion of "insurability," on the liquidity of durables, and on brand-name goods.

There are many markets in which buyers use some market statistic to judge the quality of prospective purchases. In this case there is incentive for sellers to market poor quality merchandise, since the returns for good quality accrue mainly to the entire group whose statistic is affected rather than to the individual seller. As a result there tends to be a reduction in the average quality of goods and also in the size of the market. It should also be perceived that in these markets social and private returns differ, and therefore, in some cases, governmental intervention may increase the welfare of all parties. Or private institutions may arise to take advantage of the potential increases in welfare which can accrue to all parties. By nature, however, these institutions are nonatomistic, and therefore concentrations of power — with ill consequences of their own — can develop.

* The author would especially like to thank Thomas Rothenberg for invaluable comments and inspiration. In addition he is indebted to Roy Radner, Albert Fishlow, Bernard Saffran, William D. Nordhaus, Giorgio La Malfa, Charles C. Holt, John Letiche, and the referee for help and suggestions. He would also like to thank the Indian Statistical Institute and the Ford Foundation for financial support.

The automobile market is used as a finger exercise to illustrate and develop these thoughts. It should be emphasized that this market is chosen for its concreteness and ease in understanding rather than for its importance or realism.

II. The Model with Automobiles as an Example

A. *The Automobiles Market*

The example of used cars captures the essence of the problem. From time to time one hears either mention of or surprise at the large price difference between new cars and those which have just left the showroom. The usual lunch table justification for this phenomenon is the pure joy of owning a "new" car. We offer a different explanation. Suppose (for the sake of clarity rather than reality) that there are just four kinds of cars. There are new cars and used cars. There are good cars and bad cars (which in America are known as "lemons"). A new car may be a good car or a lemon, and of course the same is true of used cars.

The individuals in this market buy a new automobile without knowing whether the car they buy will be good or a lemon. But they do know that with probability q it is a good car and with probability $(1-q)$ it is a lemon; by assumption, q is the proportion of good cars produced and $(1-q)$ is the proportion of lemons.

After owning a specific car, however, for a length of time, the car owner can form a good idea of the quality of this machine; i.e., the owner assigns a new probability to the event that his car is a lemon. This estimate is more accurate than the original estimate. An asymmetry in available information has developed: for the sellers now have more knowledge about the quality of a car than the buyers. But good cars and bad cars must still sell at the same price — since it is impossible for a buyer to tell the difference between a good car and a bad car. It is apparent that a used car cannot have the same valuation as a new car — if it did have the same valuation, it would clearly be advantageous to trade a lemon at the price of new car, and buy another new car, at a higher probability q of being good and a lower probability of being bad. Thus the owner of a good machine must be locked in. Not only is it true that he cannot receive the true value of his car, but he cannot even obtain the expected value of a new car.

Gresham's law has made a modified reappearance. For most cars traded will be the "lemons," and good cars may not be traded at all. The "bad" cars tend to drive out the good (in much the same way that bad money drives out the good). But the analogy with Gresham's law is not quite complete: bad cars drive out the good because they sell at the same price as good cars; similarly, bad money drives out good because the exchange rate is even. But the bad cars sell at the same price as good cars since it is impossible for a buyer to tell the difference between a good and a bad car; only the seller knows. In Gresham's law, however, presumably both buyer and seller can tell the difference between good and bad money. So the analogy is instructive, but not complete.

B. Asymmetrical Information

It has been seen that the good cars may be driven out of the market by the lemons. But in a more continuous case with different grades of goods, even worse pathologies can exist. For it is quite possible to have the bad driving out the not-so-bad driving out the medium driving out the not-so-good driving out the good in such a sequence of events that no market exists at all.

One can assume that the demand for used automobiles depends most strongly upon two variables — the price of the automobile p and the average quality of used cars traded, μ, or $Q^d = D(p, \mu)$. Both the supply of used cars and also the average quality μ will depend upon the price, or $\mu = \mu(p)$ and $S = S(p)$. And in equilibrium the supply must equal the demand for the given average quality, or $S(p) = D(p, \mu(p))$. As the price falls, normally the quality will also fall. And it is quite possible that no goods will be traded at any price level.

Such an example can be derived from utility theory. Assume that there are just two groups of traders: groups one and two. Give group one a utility function

$$U_1 = M + \sum_{i=1}^{n} x_i$$

where M is the consumption of goods other than automobiles, x_i is the quality of the ith automobile, and n is the number of automobiles.

Similarly, let

$$U_2 = M + \sum_{i=1}^{n} 3/2 x_i$$

where M, x_i, and n are defined as before.

Three comments should be made about these utility functions: (1) without linear utility (say with logarithmic utility) one gets needlessly mired in algebraic complication. (2) The use of linear utility allows a focus on the effects of asymmetry of information; with a concave utility function we would have to deal jointly with the usual risk-variance effects of uncertainty and the special effects we wish to discuss here. (3) U_1 and U_2 have the odd characteristic that the addition of a second car, or indeed a *k*th car, adds the same amount of utility as the first. Again realism is sacrificed to avoid a diversion from the proper focus.

To continue, it is assumed (1) that both type one traders and type two traders are von Neumann-Morgenstern maximizers of expected utility; (2) that group one has N cars with uniformly distributed quality x, $0 \leqq x \leqq 2$, and group two has no cars; (3) that the price of "other goods" M is unity.

Denote the income (including that derived from the sale of automobiles) of all type one traders as Y_1 and the income of all type two traders as Y_2. The demand for used cars will be the sum of the demands by both groups. When one ignores indivisibilities, the demand for automobiles by type one traders will be

$$D_1 = Y_1/p \qquad \mu/p > 1$$
$$D_1 = 0 \qquad \mu/p < 1.$$

And the supply of cars offered by type one traders is

$$(1) \qquad S_2 = pN/2 \qquad p \leqq 2$$

with average quality

$$(2) \qquad \mu = p/2.$$

(To derive (1) and (2), the uniform distribution of automobile quality is used.)

Similarly the demand of type two traders is

$$D_2 = Y_2/p \qquad 3\mu/2 > p$$
$$D_2 = 0 \qquad 3\mu/2 < p$$

and

$$S_2 = 0.$$

Thus total demand $D(p, \mu)$ is

$$D(p, \mu) = (Y_2 + Y_1)/p \qquad \text{if } p < \mu$$
$$D(p, \mu) = Y_2/p \qquad \text{if } \mu < p < 3\mu/2$$
$$D(p, \mu) = 0 \qquad \text{if } p > 3\mu/2.$$

However, with price p, average quality is $p/2$ and therefore at no price will any trade take place at all: in spite of the fact that *at any given price* between 0 and 3 there are traders of type one who are willing to sell their automobiles at a price which traders of type two are willing to pay.

C. Symmetric Information

The foregoing is contrasted with the case of symmetric information. Suppose that the quality of all cars is uniformly distributed, $0 \leqq x \leqq 2$. Then the demand curves and supply curves can be written as follows:

Supply

$$S(p) = N \qquad p > 1$$

$$S(p) = 0 \qquad p < 1.$$

And the demand curves are

$$D(p) = (Y_2 + Y_1)/p \qquad p < 1$$

$$D(p) = (Y_2/p) \qquad 1 < p < 3/2$$

$$D(p) = 0 \qquad p > 3/2.$$

In equilibrium

$$p = 1 \qquad \text{if } Y_2 < N \tag{3}$$

$$p = Y_2/N \qquad \text{if } 2Y_2/3 < N < Y_2 \tag{4}$$

$$p = 3/2 \qquad \text{if } N < 2Y_2/3. \tag{5}$$

If $N < Y_2$ there is a gain in utility over the case of asymmetrical information of $N/2$. (If $N > Y_2$, in which case the income of type two traders is insufficient to buy all N automobiles, there is a gain in utility of $Y_2/2$ units.)

Finally, it should be mentioned that in this example, if traders of groups one and two have the same probabilistic estimates about the quality of individual automobiles — though these estimates may vary from automobile to automobile — (3), (4), and (5) will still describe equilibrium with one slight change: p will then represent the expected price of one quality unit.

III. Examples and Applications

A. Insurance

It is a well-known fact that people over 65 have great difficulty in buying medical insurance. The natural question arises: why doesn't the price rise to match the risk?

Our answer is that as the price level rises the people who insure themselves will be those who are increasingly certain that they will need the insurance; for error in medical check-ups, doctors' sympathy with older patients, and so on make it much easier for the applicant to assess the risks involved than the insurance company. The result is that the average medical condition of insurance applicants deteriorates as the price level rises — with the result that no insurance sales may take place at any price.[1] This is strictly analogous to our automobiles case, where the average quality of used cars supplied fell with a corresponding fall in the price level. This agrees with the explanation in insurance textbooks:

> Generally speaking policies are not available at ages materially greater than sixty-five. . . . The term premiums are too high for any but the most pessimistic (which is to say the least healthy) insureds to find attractive. Thus there is a severe problem of adverse selection at these ages.[2]

The statistics do not contradict this conclusion. While demands for health insurance rise with age, a 1956 national sample survey of 2,809 families with 8,898 persons shows that hospital insurance coverage drops from 63 per cent of those aged 45 to 54, to 31 per cent for those over 65. And surprisingly, this survey also finds average medical expenses for males aged 55 to 64 of $88, while males over 65 pay an average of $77.[3] While noninsured expenditure rises from $66 to $80 in these age groups, insured expenditure declines from $105 to $70. The conclusion is tempting that insurance companies are particularly wary of giving medical insurance to older people.

The principle of "adverse selection" is potentially present in all lines of insurance. The following statement appears in an insurance textbook written at the Wharton School:

> There is potential adverse selection in the fact that healthy term insurance policy holders may decide to terminate their coverage when they become older and premiums mount. This action could leave an insurer with an undue proportion of below average risks and claims might be higher than anticipated. Adverse selection "appears (or at least is possible) whenever the individual or group insured has freedom to buy or not to buy, to choose the amount or plan of insurance, and to persist or to discontinue as a policy holder."[4]

Group insurance, which is the most common form of medical insurance in the United States, picks out the healthy, for generally

1. Arrow's fine article, "Uncertainty and Medical Care" (*American Economic Review*, Vol. 53, 1963), does not make this point explicitly. He emphasizes "moral hazard" rather than "adverse selection." In its strict sense, the presence of "moral hazard" is equally disadvantageous for both governmental and private programs; in its broader sense, which includes "adverse selection," "moral hazard" gives a decided advantage to government insurance programs.

2. O. D. Dickerson, *Health Insurance* (Homewood, Ill.: Irwin, 1959), p. 333.

3. O. W. Anderson (with J. J. Feldman), *Family Medical Costs and Insurance* (New York: McGraw-Hill, 1956).

4. H. S. Denenberg, R. D. Eilers, G. W. Hoffman, C. A. Kline, J. J. Melone, and H. W. Snider, *Risk and Insurance* (Englewood Cliffs, N. J.: Prentice Hall, 1964), p. 446.

adequate health is a precondition for employment. At the same time this means that medical insurance is least available to those who need it most, for the insurance companies do their own "adverse selection."

This adds one major argument in favor of medicare.[5] On a cost benefit basis medicare may pay off: for it is quite possible that every individual in the market would be willing to pay the expected cost of his medicare and buy insurance, yet no insurance company can afford to sell him a policy — for at any price it will attract too many "lemons." The welfare economics of medicare, in this view, is *exactly* analogous to the usual classroom argument for public expenditure on roads.

B. The Employment of Minorities

The Lemons Principle also casts light on the employment of minorities. Employers may refuse to hire members of minority groups for certain types of jobs. This decision may not reflect irrationality or prejudice — but profit maximization. For race may serve as a good *statistic* for the applicant's social background, quality of schooling, and general job capabilities.

Good quality schooling could serve as a substitute for this statistic; by grading students the schooling system can give a better indicator of quality than other more superficial characteristics. As T. W. Schultz writes, "The educational establishment *discovers* and cultivates potential talent. The capabilities of children and mature students can never be known until *found* and cultivated." [6] (Italics added.) An untrained worker may have valuable natural talents, but these talents must be certified by "the educational establishment" before a company can afford to use them. The certifying establishment, however, must be credible; the unreliability of slum schools decreases the economic possibilities of their students.

This lack may be particularly disadvantageous to members of

5. The following quote, again taken from an insurance textbook, shows how far the medical insurance market is from perfect competition:

> ". . . insurance companies must screen their applicants. Naturally it is true that many people will voluntarily seek adequate insurance on their own initiative. But in such lines as accident and health insurance, companies are likely to give a second look to persons who voluntarily seek insurance without being approached by an agent." (F. J. Angell, *Insurance, Principles and Practices*, New York: The Ronald Press, 1957, pp. 8–9.)

This shows that insurance is *not* a commodity for sale on the open market.

6. T. W. Schultz, *The Economic Value of Education* (New York: Columbia University Press, 1964), p. 42.

already disadvantaged minority groups. For an employer may make a rational decision not to hire any members of these groups in responsible positions — because it is difficult to distinguish those with good job qualifications from those with bad qualifications. This type of decision is clearly what George Stigler had in mind when he wrote, "in a regime of ignorance Enrico Fermi would have been a gardener, Von Neumann a checkout clerk at a drugstore." [7]

As a result, however, the rewards for work in slum schools tend to accrue to the group as a whole — in raising its average quality — rather than to the individual. Only insofar as information in addition to race is used is there any incentive for training.

An additional worry is that the Office of Economic Opportunity is going to use cost-benefit analysis to evaluate its programs. For many benefits may be external. The benefit from training minority groups may arise as much from raising the average quality of the group as from raising the quality of the individual trainee; and, likewise, the returns may be distributed over the whole group rather than to the individual.

C. The Costs of Dishonesty

The Lemons model can be used to make some comments on the costs of dishonesty. Consider a market in which goods are sold honestly or dishonestly; quality may be represented, or it may be misrepresented. The purchaser's problem, of course, is to identify quality. The presence of people in the market who are willing to offer inferior goods tends to drive the market out of existence — as in the case of our automobile "lemons." It is this possibility that represents the major costs of dishonesty — for dishonest dealings tend to drive honest dealings out of the market. There may be potential buyers of good quality products and there may be potential sellers of such products in the appropriate price range; however, the presence of people who wish to pawn bad wares as good wares tends to drive out the legitimate business. The cost of dishonesty, therefore, lies not only in the amount by which the purchaser is cheated; the cost also must include the loss incurred from driving legitimate business out of existence.

Dishonesty in business is a serious problem in underdeveloped countries. Our model gives a possible structure to this statement and delineates the nature of the "external" economies involved. In particular, in the model economy described, dishonesty, or the

7. G. J. Stigler, "Information and the Labor Market," *Journal of Political Economy*, Vol. 70 (Oct. 1962), Supplement, p. 104.

misrepresentation of the quality of automobiles, costs 1/2 unit of utility per automobile; furthermore, it reduces the size of the used car market from N to 0. We can, consequently, directly evaluate the costs of dishonesty — at least in theory.

There is considerable evidence that quality variation is greater in underdeveloped than in developed areas. For instance, the need for quality control of exports and State Trading Corporations can be taken as one indicator. In India, for example, under the Export Quality Control and Inspection Act of 1963, "about 85 per cent of Indian exports are covered under one or the other type of quality control."[8] Indian housewives must carefully glean the rice of the local bazaar to sort out stones of the same color and shape which have been intentionally added to the rice. Any comparison of the heterogeneity of quality in the street market and the canned qualities of the American supermarket suggests that quality variation is a greater problem in the East than in the West.

In one traditional pattern of development the merchants of the pre-industrial generation turn into the first entrepreneurs of the next. The best-documented case is Japan,[9] but this also may have been the pattern for Britain and America.[1] In *our* picture the important skill of the merchant is identifying the quality of merchandise; those who can identify used cars in our example and can guarantee the quality may profit by as much as the difference between type two traders' buying price and type one traders' selling price. These people are the merchants. In production these skills are equally necessary — both to be able to identify the quality of inputs and to certify the quality of outputs. And this is one (added) reason why the merchants may logically become the first entrepreneurs.

The problem, of course, is that entrepreneurship may be a scarce resource; no development text leaves entrepreneurship unemphasized. Some treat it as central.[2] Given, then, that entrepreneurship is scarce, there are two ways in which product variations impede development. First, the pay-off to trade is great for would-be entrepreneurs, and hence they are diverted from production; second, the amount of entrepreneurial time per unit output is greater, the greater are the quality variations.

8. *The Times of India*, Nov. 10, 1967, p. 1.

9. See M. J. Levy, Jr., "Contrasting Factors in the Modernization of China and Japan," in *Economic Growth: Brazil, India, Japan*, ed. S. Kuznets, *et. al.* (Durham, N. C.: Duke University Press, 1955).

1. C. P. Kindleberger, *Economic Development* (New York: McGraw-Hill, 1958), p. 86.

2. For example, see W. Arthur Lewis, *The Theory of Economic Growth* (Homewood, Ill.: Irwin, 1955), p. 196.

D. Credit Markets in Underdeveloped Countries

(1) Credit markets in underdeveloped countries often strongly reflect the operation of the Lemons Principle. In India a major fraction of industrial enterprise is controlled by managing agencies (according to a recent survey, these "managing agencies" controlled 65.7 per cent of the net worth of public limited companies and 66 per cent of total assets).[3] Here is a historian's account of the function and genesis of the "managing agency system":

> The management of the South Asian commercial scene remained the function of merchant houses, and a type of organization peculiar to South Asia known as the Managing Agency. When a new venture was promoted (such as a manufacturing plant, a plantation, or a trading venture), the promoters would approach an established managing agency. The promoters might be Indian or British, and they might have technical or financial resources or merely a concession. In any case they would turn to the agency because of its reputation, which would encourage confidence in the venture and stimulate investment.[4]

In turn, a second major feature of the Indian industrial scene has been the dominance of these managing agencies by caste (or, more accurately, communal) groups. Thus firms can usually be classified according to communal origin.[5] In this environment, in which outside investors are likely to be bilked of their holdings, either (1) firms establish a reputation for "honest" dealing, which confers upon them a monopoly rent insofar as their services are

3. *Report of the Committee on the Distribution of Income and Levels of Living*, Part I, Government of India, Planning Commission, Feb. 1964, p. 44.

4. H. Tinker, *South Asia: A Short History* (New York: Praeger, 1966), p. 134.

5. The existence of the following table (and also the small per cent of firms under mixed control) indicates the communalization of the control of firms. *Source*: M. M. Mehta, *Structure of Indian Industries* (Bombay: Popular Book Depot, 1955), p. 314.

DISTRIBUTION OF INDUSTRIAL CONTROL BY COMMUNITY

	1911	1931 (number of firms)	1951
British	281	416	382
Parsis	15	25	19
Gujratis	3	11	17
Jews	5	9	3
Muslims	—	10	3
Bengalis	8	5	20
Marwaris	—	6	96
Mixed control	28	28	79
Total	341	510	619

Also, for the cotton industry see H. Fukuzawa, "Cotton Mill Industry," in V. B. Singh, editor, *Economic History of India, 1857–1956* (Bombay: Allied Publishers, 1965).

limited in supply, or (2) the sources of finance are limited to local communal groups which can use communal — and possibly familial — ties to encourage honest dealing *within* the community. It is, in Indian economic history, extraordinarily difficult to discern whether the savings of rich landlords failed to be invested in the industrial sector (1) because of a fear to invest in ventures controlled by other communities, (2) because of inflated propensities to consume, or (3) because of low rates of return.[6] At the very least, however, it is clear that the British-owned managing agencies tended to have an equity holding whose communal origin was more heterogeneous than the Indian-controlled agency houses, and would usually include both Indian and British investors.

(2) A second example of the workings of the Lemons Principle concerns the extortionate rates which the local moneylender charges his clients. In India these high rates of interest have been the leading factor in landlessness; the so-called "Cooperative Movement" was meant to counteract this growing landlessness by setting up banks to compete with the local moneylenders.[7] While the large banks in the central cities have prime interest rates of 6, 8, and 10 per cent, the local moneylender charges 15, 25, and even 50 per cent. The answer to this seeming paradox is that credit is

6. For the mixed record of industrial profits, see D. H. Buchanan, *The Development of Capitalist Enterprise in India* (New York: Kelley, 1966, reprinted).

7. The leading authority on this is Sir Malcolm Darling. See his *Punjabi Peasant in Prosperity and Debt*. The following table may also prove instructive:

	Commonest rates for —		
	Secured loans (per cent)	Unsecured loans (per cent)	Grain loans (per cent)
Punjab	6 to 12	12 to 24 (18 ¾ commonest)	25
United Provinces	9 to 12	24 to 37 ½	25 (50 in Oudh)
Bihar		18 ¾	50
Orissa	12 to 18 ¾	25	25
Bengal	8 to 12	9 to 18 for "respectable clients" 18 ¾ to 37 ½ (the latter common to agriculturalists)	
Central Provinces	6 to 12	15 for proprietors 24 for occupancy tenants 37 ½ for ryots with no right of transfer	25
Bombay	9 to 12	12 to 25 (18 commonest)	
Sind		36	
Madras	12	15 to 18 (in insecure tracts 24 not uncommon)	20 to 50

Source: Punjabi Peasant in Prosperity and Debt, 3rd ed. (Oxford University Press, 1932), p. 190.

granted only where the granter has (1) easy means of enforcing his contract or (2) personal knowledge of the character of the borrower. The middleman who tries to arbitrage between the rates of the moneylender and the central bank is apt to attract all the "lemons" and thereby make a loss.

This interpretation can be seen in Sir Malcolm Darling's interpretation of the village moneylender's power:

> It is only fair to remember that in the Indian village the money-lender is often the one thrifty person amongst a generally thriftless people; and that his methods of business, though demoralizing under modern conditions, suit the happy-go-lucky ways of the peasant. He is always accessible, even at night; dispenses with troublesome formalities, asks no inconvenient questions, advances promptly, and if interest is paid, does not press for repayment of principal. He keeps in close personal touch with his clients, and in many villages shares their occasions of weal or woe. *With his intimate knowledge of those around him he is able, without serious risk, to finance those who would otherwise get no loan at all.* [Italics added.] [8]

Or look at Barbara Ward's account:

> A small shopkeeper in a Hong Kong fishing village told me: "I give credit to anyone who anchors regularly in our bay; but if it is someone I don't know well, then I think twice about it unless I can find out all about him." [9]

Or, a profitable sideline of cotton ginning in Iran is the loaning of money for the next season, since the ginning companies often have a line of credit from Teheran banks at the market rate of interest. But in the first years of operation large losses are expected from unpaid debts — due to poor knowledge of the local scene.[1]

IV. Counteracting Institutions

Numerous institutions arise to counteract the effects of quality uncertainty. One obvious institution is guarantees. Most consumer durables carry guarantees to ensure the buyer of some normal expected quality. One natural result of our model is that the risk is borne by the seller rather than by the buyer.

A second example of an institution which counteracts the effects of quality uncertainty is the brand-name good. Brand names

8. Darling, *op. cit.*, p. 204.
9. B. Ward, "Cash or Credit Crops," *Economic Development and Cultural Change*, Vol. 8 (Jan. 1960), reprinted in *Peasant Society: A Reader*, ed. G. Foster *et al.* (Boston: Little Brown and Company, 1967). Quote on p. 142. In the same volume, see also G. W. Skinner, "Marketing and Social Structure in Rural China," and S. W. Mintz, "Pratik: Haitian Personal Economic Relations."
1. Personal conversation with mill manager, April 1968.

not only indicate quality but also give the consumer a means of retaliation if the quality does not meet expectations. For the consumer will then curtail future purchases. Often too, new products are associated with old brand names. This ensures the prospective consumer of the quality of the product.

Chains — such as hotel chains or restaurant chains — are similar to brand names. One observation consistent with our approach is the chain restaurant. These restaurants, at least in the United States, most often appear on interurban highways. The customers are seldom local. The reason is that these well-known chains offer a better hamburger than the *average* local restaurant; at the same time, the local customer, who knows his area, can usually choose a place he prefers.

Licensing practices also reduce quality uncertainty. For instance, there is the licensing of doctors, lawyers, and barbers. Most skilled labor carries some certification indicating the attainment of certain levels of proficiency. The high school diploma, the baccalaureate degree, the Ph.D., even the Nobel Prize, to some degree, serve this function of certification. And education and labor markets themselves have their own "brand names."

V. Conclusion

We have been discussing economic models in which "trust" is important. Informal unwritten guarantees are preconditions for trade and production. Where these guarantees are indefinite, business will suffer — as indicated by our generalized Gresham's law. This aspect of uncertainty has been explored by game theorists, as in the Prisoner's Dilemma, but usually it has not been incorporated in the more traditional Arrow-Debreu approach to uncertainty.[2] But the difficulty of distinguishing good quality from bad is inherent in the business world; this may indeed explain many economic institutions and may in fact be one of the more important aspects of uncertainty.

University of California, Berkeley
Indian Statistical Institute — Planning Unit, New Delhi

2. R. Radner, "Équilibre de Marchés à Terme et au Comptant en Cas d'Incertitude," in *Cahiers d'Econometrie*, Vol. 12 (Nov. 1967), Centre National de la Recherche Scientifique, Paris.

[31]

Race and Gender Discrimination in Bargaining for a New Car

By IAN AYRES AND PETER SIEGELMAN*

More than 300 paired audits at new-car dealerships reveal that dealers quoted significantly lower prices to white males than to black or female test buyers using identical, scripted bargaining strategies. Ancillary evidence suggests that the dealerships' disparate treatment of women and blacks may be caused by dealers' statistical inferences about consumers' reservation prices, but the data do not strongly support any single theory of discrimination. (*JEL* J70, J15, J16)

The purchase of a new car typically involves negotiations between buyer and seller. Such negotiations may leave room for sellers to treat buyers differently on the basis of race or gender, especially because any individual buyer has little or no means of learning the prices paid by others. The tests we report in this paper confirm this possibility; we find large and statistically significant differences in prices quoted to test buyers of different races and genders. This is true even though the testers were selected to resemble each other as closely as possible, were trained to bargain uniformly, and followed a prespecified bargaining script.

Race or gender discrimination by sellers might be motivated by two broad kinds of forces. The first is noneconomic tastes for discrimination (including traditional forms of animus or bigotry) introduced into the market by a firm's owner, employees, or customers (Gary Becker, 1957). Even a market in which no participants are prejudiced might exhibit discrimination, however, if dealers use buyers' race or gender to make statistical inferences about the expected profitability of selling to them. Our study finds some evidence that is consistent with both broad theories of discrimination. Some discrimination may be attributable to seller animus. But our data also suggest that at least part of the observed disparate treatment of women and blacks is caused by dealers' inferences about consumer reservation prices.

Statistical inferences might disadvantage black or women consumers even though they are on average poorer than white males and should therefore have lower (opportunity) costs of search (George Stigler, 1968). Differences in information and (direct) search or negotiation costs might give white males lower reservation prices, despite their greater ability to pay and higher opportunity costs of search time. Moreover, profit-maximizing discrimination could well depend on more than a group's mean reservation price (Steven Salop and Joseph Stiglitz, 1977). It may be profitable for dealers to offer higher prices to a group of consumers who have a lower *average* reservation price, if the variance of reservation prices within the group is sufficiently large. Thus for example, suppose that a larger proportion of black (than white) consumers are willing to pay a high markup, even

*Ayres: Yale Law School, P.O. Box 208215, New Haven, CT 06520 (e-mail: AYRES@MAIL.LAW.YALE.EDU), Siegelman: American Bar Foundation, 750 N. Lake Shore Drive, Chicago, IL 60611 (e-mail: SIEGELMA@MERLE.ACNS.NWU.EDU). Kathie Heed, Akilah Kamaria, and Darrell Karolyi provided superb assistance with all phases of this project. Roz Caldwell prepared the manuscript with intelligence and good humor. We benefited from helpful comments by Jay Casper, Carolyn Craven, John Donohue, Richard Epstein, William Felstiner, Robert Gertner, James Heckman, and Carol Sanger, as well as substantial input from our colleagues at the American Bar Foundation. We especially want to acknowledge the invaluable advice of Peter Cramton and the sterling assistance provided by Michael Horvath.

though the mean (or median) black customer has a lower reservation price than her white counterpart. Knowing this, dealers might rationally offer higher prices to all black consumers.[1]

The rest of this paper proceeds in three sections. The first explains the audit method used to generate our data and discusses econometric specification. Section II then analyzes the empirical evidence for the existence of race and gender discrimination. Finally, Section III uses some ancillary data to explore the causes of the disparate treatment we found. There is some support for both statistical and animus-based theories of discrimination in the data.

I. Method

A. *Design of the Study*

This study used an audit technique in which pairs of testers (one of whom was always a white male) were trained to bargain uniformly and then were sent to negotiate for the purchase of a new automobile at randomly selected Chicago-area dealerships.[2] Thirty-eight testers bargained for 306 cars at 153 dealerships.[3] Both testers in a pair bargained for the same model of car, at the same dealership, usually within a few days of each other. Unlike most other audit studies, however, we allowed the composition of pairs to vary from audit to audit.[4] Dealerships were selected randomly; testers were randomly assigned to dealerships; and the choice of which tester in the pair would be the first to enter the dealership was also made randomly. The testers bargained at different dealerships for a total of nine car models,[5] following a uniform bargaining script that instructed them to focus quickly on one particular car and start negotiating over it. At the beginning of the bargaining, testers told dealers that they could provide their own financing for the car.

After deciding which car they were going to bargain over,[6] testers waited for an offer

[1]In other markets, competition often gives individual sellers an incentive to undermine price discrimination by offering posted prices with lower markups. The general failure of dealerships to opt for posted prices may be attributed to the high concentration of profits in a few car sales. Some dealerships may earn up to 50 percent of their profits from just 10 percent of their sales (Ayres, 1991 p. 854). Committing to posted prices would force dealerships to forgo these high-profit sales. If the extra profits from additional sales at a posted price are less than the forgone profits from selling a few cars at extremely high markups, individual dealers may not have a first-mover advantage in changing from bargained to posted prices. Nevertheless, recent evidence suggests that a move to posted prices for cars may be underway (Jim Mateja, 1992; Frank Swoboda, 1992).

[2]The technique is analogous to "fair housing" tests for discrimination in the real-estate market (John Yinger, 1986). Audit procedures were also used in tests of employment discrimination by Jerry Newman (1978), Shelby McIntyre et al. (1980), and in two recent Urban Institute studies (Harry Cross et al., 1990; Margery Turner et al. (1991). For an analysis of the strengths and weaknesses of this technique, see James Heckman and Siegelman (1992).

Because this study involves deception, it necessarily raises important questions of research ethics (Ayres, 1991; Michael Fix and Raymond Struyk, 1992). We minimized the effects of our tests on sellers by conducting tests at off-peak hours (mid-mornings and mid-afternoons during the week) and by instructing testers to abandon the test if all salespeople were busy with legitimate customers.

[3]We began with 404 tests, but because of discarded tests and scheduling difficulties, ended up deleting one of the observations for 98 audits, leaving us with 306 tests. While the techniques are somewhat more complicated, it is possible to analyze both the paired and unpaired observations together, using a variant of the approaches described here. We conducted extensive tests (see Ayres and Siegelman, 1992) to examine whether our results are in any way sensitive to the exclusion of the 98 "unpaired" observations. We concluded that they are not, and therefore we report only the results from the paired data set in the following analysis.

[4]In other words, rather than matching tester A with tester B for all tests, A was sometimes matched with B, sometimes with C, and so on.

[5]Testers in a pair bargained for the same car model, but the test allowed dealers to systematically steer testers to cars with different options. There is no evidence of this behavior: the average cost of the cars bargained for did not vary significantly by tester type. The nine models included a range from compacts to standard-size cars and included both imports and domestic makes. Human-subjects constraints prevent us from disclosing the identities of the car models.

[6]If they were shown more than one car of the type they were bargaining for, the testers were instructed to choose the car with the lowest sticker price.

from the dealer, or after 5 minutes elicited a dealer offer. Once the dealer made an initial offer, the tester waited 5 minutes and responded with a counteroffer equal to our estimate of the dealer's marginal cost for the car.[7] If the salesperson responded by lowering his or her offer, the test continued, with the tester's second counteroffer derived from the script in one of two ways.

At some dealerships, testers used a "split-the-difference" strategy. In these tests, the tester responded to subsequent dealer offers by making counteroffers that averaged the dealer's and the tester's previous offers. Thus, if a tester's first counteroffer was $10,000 and the salesperson responded with an offer of $12,000, the tester's next response would be $11,000. At other dealerships, the testers used a "fixed-concession" strategy in which their counteroffers (concessions) were independent of sellers' behavior. Testers began, as before, by making their first counteroffer at marginal cost. Regardless of how much the seller conceded, each subsequent counteroffer by the tester increased by 20 percent of the difference between the sticker price and the tester's previous offer.[8]

Under either bargaining strategy, the test ended when the dealer either (i) attempted to accept a tester's offer,[9] or (ii) refused to bargain further. During the course of negotiations, testers jotted down each offer and counteroffer, as well as options on the car and its sticker price. After leaving the dealership, each tester completed a survey describing ancillary details of the test (including the kinds of questions they were asked, the race and gender of the salesperson with whom they negotiated, etc.).

B. *Controls and Uniformity*

The paired audit technique is designed to eliminate as much intertester variation as possible, and thus to insure that differences in outcomes (such as prices quoted) reflect differences in *dealer* rather than tester behavior.[10] We began by choosing testers according to the following criteria:

(i) *Age:* All testers were between 28 and 32 years old.
(ii) *Education:* All testers had 3–4 years of postsecondary education.
(iii) *Attractiveness:* All testers were subjectively chosen to have average attractiveness.

The testers also displayed similar indicia of economic class. Besides volunteering that they did not need financing, all testers wore similar "yuppie" sportswear and drove to the dealership in similar rented cars.

The script governed both the verbal and nonverbal behavior of the testers, who volunteered very little information and were trained to feel comfortable with extended periods of silence. The testers had a long list of contingent responses to the questions they were likely to encounter. If asked, they gave uniform answers about their profession (e.g., a systems analyst at a large bank) and address (a prosperous Chicago neighborhood).

[7]Estimates of dealer cost were provided by *Consumer Reports* Auto Price Service and *Edmund's 1989 New Car Prices*. As we discuss below, making an initial offer at the dealer's cost reveals some sophistication on the buyer's part.

[8]That is, if the car had a sticker price of SP and the tester's last offer was LO, then the tester's next offer would be $LO + 0.2 \times (SP - LO)$. Since the gross margin $(SP - LO)$ decreases as the bargaining continues, the fixed-concession strategy produced smaller concessions in each subsequent round.

[9]The testers did not purchase cars. If a salesperson attempted to accept a tester offer, the tester would end the test, saying, "Thanks, but I need to think about this before I make up my mind."

[10]Heckman and Siegelman (1992 p. 188) point out that:

> Despite suggestive rhetoric to the contrary, audit pair studies are not experiments or matched pair studies. Race or ethnicity cannot be assigned by randomization or some other device as in... [a classical experiment]. Race is a personal characteristic and adjustments must be made instead on "relevant" observed characteristics to "align" audit pair members.

Because selling a car is a more discrete transaction than hiring an employee or renting out an apartment, the task of matching testers is substantially easier in this area.

Before visiting the dealerships, the testers had two days of training in which they memorized the bargaining script and participated in numerous mock negotiations that helped them negotiate and answer questions uniformly. Unlike many other audit studies, the testers did not know that another tester would visit each dealership, or even that the study tested for discrimination.[11]

Despite our efforts to insure uniformity, some differences between testers undoubtedly remained. Two important questions about such residual differences must then be asked: First, are they likely to be correlated with race or gender? If not, the remaining nonuniformity should not influence our conclusion that it is race and gender that generate different outcomes for the testers. Second, are the residual differences large enough to explain the *amount* of discrimination we report below? Although no experiment can eliminate all idiosyncratic differences in tester behavior, we feel confident that the amounts of discrimination we observed cannot plausibly be explained by divergence from the uniform bargaining behavior called for in our script.

C. *Econometric Specification*

In the analysis that follows, we consider four definitions of the dependent variable. The profit that the dealership would earn on its initial offer provides an especially well-controlled test for discrimination.[12] Because the initial offer was made by the dealer with relatively little intervention on the tester's part, it is unlikely that differences in first offers reflect differences in testers' abilities to follow our uniform bargaining script. On the other hand, the profit that the dealership would earn on its final offer more closely reflects the price a real consumer would pay. We use both percentage markup over marginal cost and actual dollar profits as dependent variables.

Table 1 presents some simple summary statistics that reveal the overall pattern of discrimination in dealer offers. White male testers were quoted initial offers that were roughly $1,000 over dealer cost. Offers to black males averaged about $935 higher than those to white males. Black female testers got initial offers about $320 higher than those white males received, while white females received initial offers that were $110 higher. These differences are statistically significant at the 0.05 level, except for white females.

Not surprisingly, the process of negotiation lowered dealers' average offers to all four tester types. However, dealer concessions further increased the disparities between white males and black testers, while only slightly narrowing the gap for white females. Thus, there is a stronger overall pattern of discrimination in final offers than in initial offers: black males were asked to pay $1,100 more than white males, black females $410 more, and white females $92 more. Although the differences in concessions by tester type were not statistically significant, it is striking that black male testers, despite receiving the highest initial offers, got the lowest average concessions ($290, or 15 percent) over the course of negotiations.

The results in Table 1 are suggestive but do not make full use of the information available from the audits. One improvement

[11] The testers were told only that we were studying how sellers negotiate car sales. For the importance of isolating participants from "experimenter effects" (behavior induced by an unconscious desire to produce the expected results), see Robert Rosenthal (1976).

[12] Profits on the initial offer were calculated as the difference between the dealer's first offer (before any bargaining took place) and our estimate of marginal cost for the car. Marginal cost was in turn derived as follows. We began with an estimate of the dealer's cost for the base model with no options, using data from *Consumer Reports* and *Edmund's*. We then subtracted the sticker price for the base car from the total sticker price (including options), giving the retail cost of the options. We applied an option-specific discount factor (dealer markup on each option, also derived from *Consumer Reports* and *Edmund's*) to each option price, to get the marginal cost of all the options. The marginal cost of the options was then added to the marginal cost of the base model to give the marginal cost of the car.

TABLE 1—SUMMARY STATISTICS ON PROFITS AND COSTS, BY TESTER TYPE

Tester type	Initial profit	Final profit	Concession[a]
White males (18 testers; 153 observations)			
Mean	1,018.7	564.1	454.6
Standard deviation	911.3	708.0	(44.6 percent)
Average markup (percentage)	9.20	5.18	
White females (7 testers; 53 observations)			
Mean	1,127.3	656.5	470.8
Difference from white male average	108.6	92.4	(41.8 percent)
Standard deviation	785.3	472.4	
Average markup (percentage)	10.32	6.04	
Black females (8 testers; 60 observations)			
Mean	1,336.7*	974.9*	361.8
Difference from white male average	318.0	246.1	(27.1 percent)
Standard deviation	887.8	827.8	
Average markup (percentage)	12.23	7.20	
Black males (5 testers; 40 observations)			
Mean	1,953.7*	1,664.8*	288.9
Difference from white male average	935.0	1,100.7	(14.8 percent)
Standard deviation	1,122.7	1,099.5	
Average markup (percentage)	17.32	14.61	
All nonwhite males (20 testers, 153 observations)			
Mean	1,425.5*	1,045.0*	380.5
Difference from white male average	406.8	481.0	(26.6 percent)
Standard deviation	973.6	989.9	
Average markup (percentage)	12.99	9.40	

[a]Average initial profit minus average final profit; average percentage concession is given in parentheses.

*Significantly different from the corresponding figure for white males at the 5-percent level.

would be simply to regress profits on a vector of variables thought to explain them, including dummy variables for tester race and gender. This ordinary least-squares (OLS) regression will produce unbiased estimates of the race and gender effects, as long as any variables that might be omitted from this equation are uncorrelated with the race or gender of the testers.

These estimates will be inefficient, however, because OLS fails to account for the correlation between errors for the two observations in a given audit (John Yinger, 1986). This correlation arises because there are unobservable variables whose effects are common to both testers in the same audit, including, for example, any factors that are unique to the specific dealership being tested. Since these variables are omitted from the OLS regression, their effect will be captured in the error term, imparting a correlation between errors at the same dealership.

We therefore exploit the panel structure of the data set, using the fact that we have two observations (one for a white male and one for one of the three other tester types) for each of the 153 audits. To capture the possibility of audit-specific errors we estimate the following fixed-effects model:

$$\Pi_{ai} = \mathbf{X}_{ai}\boldsymbol{\beta} + \mu_a + \varepsilon_{ai} \tag{1}$$

where Π_{ai} is dealer profit on the ith test ($i = 1, 2$) in the ath audit ($a = 1, \dots, 153$), $\mathbf{X}_{ai}$ is a matrix of dummy variables for tester race/gender, a constant, μ_a, is an unob-

TABLE 2—OLS AND FIXED-EFFECTS (ONE DUMMY PER AUDIT) REGRESSIONS OF INITIAL AND FINAL PROFITS AND MARKUPS ON RACE AND GENDER DUMMIES AND CONTROL VARIABLES

Variable	Initial dollar profit OLS	Initial dollar profit Fixed effects	Final dollar profit OLS	Final dollar profit Fixed effects	Initial percentage markup OLS	Initial percentage markup Fixed effects	Final percentage markup OLS	Final percentage markup Fixed effects
Race/gender dummies:								
Constant	1,014.95*		607.51*		0.114*		0.072*	
	(4.12)		(2.98)		(5.44)		(4.19)	
White female	192.38	55.10	174.68*	129.09	0.017	0.007	0.014	0.013
	(1.23)	(0.39)	(1.35)	(1.05)	(1.26)	(0.63)	(1.29)	(1.25)
Black female	404.28*	281.05*	504.64*	404.65*	0.039*	0.027*	0.045*	0.037*
	(2.75)	(2.13)	(4.15)	(3.49)	(3.09)	(2.42)	(4.45)	(3.87)
Black male	1,068.24*	1,061.17*	1,242.85*	1,061.27*	0.094*	0.091*	0.107*	0.090*
	(6.10)	(6.56)	(8.57)	(7.47)	(6.31)	(6.60)	(8.78)	(7.70)
Controls								
SPLIT[a]	20.30		−57.36		−0.02		−0.02	
	(0.15)		(−0.51)		(−1.52)		(−1.95)	
Time[b]	−1.73		−2.47		−0.0004*		−0.0004*	
	(−0.88)		(−1.52)		(−2.29)		(2.70)	
Experience[c]	−3.58		−0.50		0.00		0.00	
	(−0.43)		(0.07)		(0.10)		(0.56)	
First[d]	203.32		192.18		0.01		0.01	
	(1.69)		(1.93)		(1.30)		(1.48)	
$F_{[3, 298]}$:	12.91*		26.52*		14.04*		27.98*	
Adjusted R^2:	0.10	0.44	0.19	0.43	0.11	0.45	0.21	0.47
Standard error of the estimate:	914.35	723.2	757.1	635.6	0.078	0.06	0.064	0.05
Degrees of freedom:	298	150	298	150	298	150	298	150
N:	306	306	306	306	306	306	306	306

Note: The numbers in parentheses are t statistics.
[a]Dummy variable: 1 if tester used a split-the-difference bargaining strategy; 0 otherwise.
[b]Number of days between this test and the first day of testing.
[c]Number of prior tests by this tester.
[d]Dummy variable: 1 if tester was first in the pair; 0 otherwise.
*Statistically significant at the 5-percent level.

served, mean-zero, audit-specific error term,[13] and ε_{ai} is an independent, mean-zero error term.

Including an audit-specific fixed effect transforms each observation into a difference from its audit-specific mean. Thus, the fixed-effects regression (including only the race and gender dummies) is equivalent to a paired-difference estimate (Yinger, 1986).

[13]By definition, the factors that determine μ_a are shared by both members of an audit. Thus, μ_a must be uncorrelated with the race/gender dummies for audit a.

II. Results

A. *Tester Race and Gender Effects*

Table 2 reports the results of OLS and fixed-effects (one dummy per audit) regressions explaining raw profits and percentage markups associated with dealers' initial and final offers. Consistent with Table 1, the OLS regressions again suggest that a tester's gender and race strongly influence both the initial and final offers made by sellers. F tests for the joint significance of the three race/gender dummies (vs. a model with only control variables and a constant term) are significant in all four of the regressions. However, the size of the race and gender effects is generally somewhat smaller in the OLS estimates than is suggested by the raw comparison of means. As with the raw means, white females are quoted the smallest additional markups over white males, and black males the largest. The white female effect is not significant.

Allowing for audit-specific fixed effects does not change the basic story. There is strong evidence for the presence of heterogeneity among audits (the 153 audit dummies are jointly significant in all four specifications). But controlling for such effects does not have a dramatic influence on either the size or significance of the tester-type dummies. In the fixed-effects regressions, black males receive initial offers that generate dealer profits $1,100 (9 percentage points, or 81 percent) higher than those received by white males, with the disparity unchanged for final offers. While discrimination against black males does not increase in the final offers, this group still receives the smallest average concession (in both absolute and percentage terms). For black females, a gap of $280 in initial offers widens to just over $400 (3 percentage points higher markup) in final offers. Initial offers to white females are $55 higher than to white males, with final offers differing by $130. This amounts to about 1.7 percentage points of additional markup beyond the 11 percent quoted to white male testers. The estimated coefficients are significant for the black testers, although not for white females.

B. *Control Variables*

Our confidence in the methodology is supported by the finding that the variables testing whether the study was adequately controlled produced coefficients that were neither large nor statistically significant. We were concerned about possible secular trends in the car market because the tests were carried out over a period of $4\frac{1}{2}$ months. The regressions do indicate that there was a slight downward trend in car prices over the period covered by our tests; but given our testing procedures, this trend should not be correlated with race or gender and is therefore innocuous.[14] Another concern was that a tester's experience—the number of previous tests he or she had conducted—might influence the bargaining outcomes. The tables provide no evidence of any such experience effect.

We also examined whether the dealership's experience with the first tester affected its treatment of the second tester in the pair, as could happen, for example, if the seller learned that a test was taking place. (The two testers in a pair rarely negotiated with the same salesperson; and dealers never gave any indication that they suspected our testers were not bona fide buyers. Both of these facts suggest that the probability of discovery should have been low.) The order effect, captured by the FIRST dummy, was never statistically significant in any of the regressions in Table 2. Its magnitude, however, was surprisingly large, with the first tester asked to pay a $200, or 1 percentage point, higher markup than the second.[15]

The regressions in Table 2 also control for a bargaining-strategy effect. Buyers did slightly better with the split-the-difference strategy than with fixed concessions. However, this effect was quantitatively small and statistically insignificant.

[14]Since many car salespeople are paid on a commission basis, and since there are weekly and monthly quotas, we wanted to allow for possible day-of-week and week-of-month effects. In alternative specifications (not shown), we tested for these effects. They were uniformly small and insignificant, with the exception that dealerships' profits tended to be lower on Fridays. A referee suggested that this might be explained by dealers' inferences about consumers' propensity to engage in additional search. A consumer shopping on Friday may be more likely to visit other dealerships during the weekend, and dealers may therefore offer lower prices at the beginning of the weekend to forestall this additional search.

[15]One possible explanation is that sellers quoted lower prices to subsequent buyers because the failure to complete a sale to the first tester caused them to believe that demand conditions were worse than they had expected. While theoretically plausible, it seems unlikely that the "learning" effect from a single failed sale could explain so substantial a price decrease.

TABLE 3—OLS FIXED-EFFECTS (ONE DUMMY PER AUDIT) AND GLS (RANDOM-EFFECTS) REGRESSIONS OF FINAL PROFITS AND MARKUPS ON RACE AND GENDER DUMMIES, AUDIT-SPECIFIC EFFECTS

	Final dollar profit			Final percentage markup (actual coefficients × 100)		
Variable	OLS	Fixed effects	GLS	OLS	Fixed effects	GLS
Constant	564.09*	—	564.09*	5.18*	—	5.18*
	(9.16)		(9.11)	(9.94)		(9.89)
White female	92.40	129.10	103.83	0.86	1.26	1.00
	(0.76)	(1.04)	(0.96)	(0.84)	(1.25)	(1.12)
Black male	1,100.68*	1061.27*	1,088.40*	9.43*	8.96*	9.26*
	(8.13)	(7.47)	(8.87)	(8.24)	(7.70)	(9.12)
Black female	410.79*	404.65*	408.88*	3.71*	3.68*	3.70*
	(3.54)	(3.49)	(3.96)	(3.78)	(3.87)	(4.35)
Adjusted R^2:	0.18	0.43		0.18	0.47	
N:	306	306	306	306	306	306
Likelihood-ratio test (fixed effects vs. OLS):		325.12*			345.30*	
Breusch-Pagan test[a] (random effects vs. OLS, $\chi^2_{[1]}$):			14.52*			18.90*

Note: The numbers in parentheses are t statistics.
[a] Reject OLS in favor of random effects for large values of the test statistic.
* Significantly different from zero at the 5-percent level.

C. *Robustness*

The differences in prices quoted to the various tester types found in Table 2 are robust to a variety of alternative specifications and nonparametric tests.

1. *Fixed versus Random Effects.*—It is possible to compare the fixed-effects specification (one dummy variable for each of the 153 audits) described earlier with a random-effects (generalized least-squares [GLS]) specification in which each audit's error term is treated as a random draw from a common distribution. Table 3 presents such comparisons for the final profit and final markup equations, focusing on the tester-type variables (which vary within an audit).

Like the fixed-effects estimates, the GLS estimates indicate heterogeneity across audits: a Breusch-Pagan test indicates that the estimated variance of the audit-specific error term is significantly greater than zero in the random-effects specification. However, controlling for this heterogeneity (with either the random- or fixed-effects specifications) did not affect the size or significance of the tester-type coefficients.

2. *Individual-Tester Effects.*—Because we have multiple observations for each of the 38 testers (and testers were not paired with a single, fixed partner), we can also test for the presence of individual-tester effects. To do this, we simply reorganize the panel data by individual testers (for example, Π_{it} = dealer profit on the ith test for the tth tester) and compute a standard random-effects regression.[16]

[16] Note that the training and selection of the testers were designed to eliminate as much intertester variation as possible. Thus, we would expect to find little or no evidence of individual-tester effects in our data. For reasons described above, however, we cannot test for the presence of individual-tester effects that are correlated with testers' race or gender.

A fixed-effects specification with one dummy variable for each individual tester is equivalent to subtracting off the tester-specific mean for each variable. This means that any variables that do not vary over time for each individual tester (including the tester race and gender dummies) are indistinguishable from the

Rerunning the four specifications of Table 2, we found little evidence that significant individual-tester effects were present. For three of the four regressions, we found that the estimated variance of the individual-tester effects was less than zero, indicating that the individual effects were not statistically significant. (Positive variance estimates are not guaranteed in a finite sample, even though the variance is estimated consistently [William Greene, 1991 p. 493]). A Breusch-Pagan test statistic of 16.71 in the final dollar-profit regression indicates that there was some heterogeneity across testers (i.e., the variance of the individual-specific error was significantly greater than zero). The estimated coefficients in this regression, however, were virtually identical to the OLS and GLS estimates presented in Table 2, and all of the black-tester coefficients remained significant.

3. *Attempted Acceptances versus Refusals to Bargain Further*.—We also investigated whether our findings of race and gender discrimination might be linked to the fact that the dealerships' final offers were sometimes refusals to bargain further and sometimes acceptances of tester offers.[17] By adding an ACCEPT dummy (=1 if the seller attempted to accept a tester offer) to the regressions of Table 2, we found that sessions ending in attempted acceptances had a $400 lower final profit than those that ended in a refusal to bargain (t statistic of 4.20). The size of this acceptance effect, however, was the same for all testers: interacting the ACCEPT dummy with the tester type yielded small and insignificant coefficients.[18]

Dealers' willingness to offer lower prices to white males was reflected in a greater willingness to continue bargaining until an acceptable offer was made. When the tester was a white male, 25.6 percent of the tests ended in attempted seller acceptances; this figure was only 14.9 percent for the other tester types. The fact that sellers are more likely to accept offers from white males actually biases our estimates *against* finding discrimination, however, because acceptances only provide an upper bound for sellers' reservation prices. That is, in those cases where dealers attempted to accept an offer from a white male tester, the dealers might have been willing to make an even lower offer, which would have increased our measure of discrimination. Overall, our findings of discrimination do not seem to be sensitive to the fact that most negotiations did not end in an attempted acceptance.

4. *Nonparametric Tests for Race and Gender Effects*.—If race or gender were unrelated to the prices quoted to testers, we would expect that the benchmark white male testers would get lower offers than their audit partners half the time, while doing worse than their counterparts in the remaining half of the tests. As Table 4 indicates, however, this was not the case. Overall, white males did better than others in roughly two-thirds of the paired tests (for both initial and final offers). A likelihood-ratio test reveals that the differences from 50 percent were all statistically significant at the 5-percent level.

The disparities are even larger in dollar terms: in tests in which white male testers received the lower final offer, they did $897 better than their counterparts on average. Where the nonwhite males did better, they

individual-tester fixed effect and cannot be used, thus making the individual-tester, fixed-effect model inappropriate for examining race and gender effects (Jerry Hausman and William Taylor, 1981).

[17]In a parallel effort, we examined whether our results were affected by the fact that sellers sometimes made unsolicited initial offers and sometimes needed to have offers elicited by the testers. Logit regressions indicated that dealers were less likely to make an unsolicited initial offer to white males than to other tester types, but that this difference was not statistically significant. Solicited initial offers were significantly larger than unsolicited initial offers, but there was no statistical difference in final offers between tests that began with elicited initial offers and those that began with unsolicited offers by the seller.

[18]The ACCEPT variable may not be exogenous in these regressions, because higher profitability may cause the dealer to accept a tester's offer.

TABLE 4—PROPORTION OF TESTS IN WHICH WHITE MALE OBTAINED THE BETTER RESULT

Test	Percentages	
	Initial profits	Final profits
White males vs. all others (153 pairs)	68.0	66.7
White males vs. white females (53 pairs)	58.4	56.6
White males vs. black males (40 pairs)	87.5	85.0
White males vs. black females (60 pairs)	63.3	61.7

Notes: All values are significantly different from 50 percent at the 1-percent level using a likelihood-ratio test ($\chi^2_{[1]}$); in 43.5 percent of the tests, white males received an *initial* offer that was lower than the *final* offer made to the nonwhite male tester.

beat the white male by only $167. Perhaps even more startling, in 43.5 percent of the tests, white males received an initial offer that was lower than the *final* offer made to their audit-mate. That is, without any negotiating at all, 43 percent of white males obtained a better price than their counterparts achieved after an average of 45 minutes of bargaining. Wilcoxon signed-ranks tests (Morris DeGroot, 1986 pp. 573–76) similarly reveal that the median final and initial profits with white males were significantly lower than those with the other tester types. This suggests that white males did better on average not simply because a few of them received very low offers, but because the entire distribution of offers to white males was lower than for the other tester types.

Two conclusions emerge from this analysis. First, both final and initial offers display large and significant differences in outcomes by race and gender. For black males, the final markup was 8–9 percentage points higher (24 percent vs. 15 percent) than for white males; the equivalent figures are 3.5–4 percentage points for black females and about 2 percentage points for white females. Second, the results are robust. The magnitude and significance of the race and gender effects under various alternative specifications, combined with the insignificance of the individual-tester effects, reinforce our confidence in these conclusions.

III. The Sources of Discrimination

In this section we try to explain the race and gender discrimination uncovered in our testing. It is particularly difficult to distinguish between competing hypotheses without an explicit model of how bigotry or asymmetric information might influence sellers' bargaining behavior. Either animus or statistical inference might cause sellers to make higher take-it-or-leave-it offers to some groups. But when sellers can make alternating offers over time, as occurs during the purchase of a new car, the consequences of animus or asymmetric information become much murkier.[19]

Thus, our results should not be read as explicit tests of the two theories of discrimination. Instead, we simply explore the effects of some plausible covariates on the level of discrimination, as well as considering some ancillary evidence from other research. We conclude that the dealerships' disparate treatment of women and blacks may be caused by dealers' statistical inferences about consumers' reservation prices, but the results do not strongly support any single theory of discrimination.

A. *Animus-Based Discrimination*

Discrimination might be caused by the bigotry of a dealership's owners, employees, or customers. In this view, the higher prices paid by minorities and women serve to compensate the bigoted market participants for having to associate with the victims of discrimination (Gary Becker, 1957).

In Table 5, we report regressions (analogous to Table 2) testing whether the race

[19]For a bargaining-theoretic analysis of discrimination in the sale of new cars that shows how different animus-based and statistical theories disparately affect a seller's equilibrium negotiation strategy, see Narasimhan Srinivasan and Kuang-Wei Wen (1991) or Ayres (1994).

TABLE 5—OLS AND GLS (RANDOM EFFECTS, AUDIT-SPECIFIC ERRORS) REGRESSIONS OF INITIAL AND FINAL PROFITS/MARKUPS ON RACE/GENDER DUMMIES AND OTHER VARIABLES

	Initial dollar profit		Final dollar profit		Initial percentage markup		Final percentage markup	
Variable	OLS	Random effects	OLS	Random effects	OLS	Random effects	OLS	Random effects
Race/gender dummies:								
Constant	1,704.46*	1,713.50*	1,343.17*	1,338.14*	0.19*	0.19*	0.148*	0.147*
	(6.52)	(5.88)	(6.18)	(5.71)	(8.49)	(7.61)	(8.40)	(7.78)
White female	130.12	106.77	102.97	108.13	0.014	0.012	0.009	0.01
	(0.98)	(0.90)	(0.93)	(1.05)	(1.20)	(1.16)	(1.11)	(1.24)
Black male	985.19*	1,007.99*	1,156.55*	1,135.94*	0.084*	0.086*	0.098*	0.096*
	(6.59)	(7.49)	(9.32)	(9.75)	(6.61)	(7.60)	(9.74)	(10.15)
Black female	267.14*	272.16*	366.52*	375.65*	0.026*	0.027*	0.033*	0.034*
	(2.08)	(2.40)	(3.44)	(3.81)	(2.41)	(2.79)	(3.91)	(4.29)
Neighborhood variables:								
Income $\times 10^{-3}$	3.66	2.98	−0.21	−0.26	0.0002	0.0002	−0.0001	−0.0001
	(0.58)	(0.42)	(−0.04)	(−0.05)	(0.43)	(0.30)	(−0.20)	(−0.16)
Suburb[a]	−188.08	−165.09	162.76	−156.73	−0.014	−0.012	−0.01	−0.009
	(1.20)	(−0.97)	(−1.25)	(−1.14)	(−1.04)	(−0.84)	(−0.91)	(−0.83)
Black tester × suburb	166.29	107.64	170.35	165.42	0.022	0.018	0.021	0.021
	(0.60)	(0.43)	(0.74)	(0.76)	(0.94)	(0.85)	(1.13)	(1.18)
Minority-owned dealer[b]	102.25	77.53	138.70	135.49	0.004	0.0006	0.009	0.008
	(0.34)	(0.25)	(0.55)	(0.53)	(0.16)	(0.02)	(0.44)	(0.40)
Black tester × minority-owned dealer	62.80	224.86	−54.59	−2.80	0.025	0.04	0.008	0.013
	(0.13)	(0.52)	(−0.13)	(−0.01)	(0.60)	(1.12)	(0.26)	(0.43)
Percentage black in neighborhood	−50.62	−83.20	152.60	151.43	−0.002	−0.006	0.015	0.015
	(−0.18)	(−0.27)	(0.63)	(0.60)	(−0.09)	(−0.21)	(0.77)	(0.74)
Black tester × percentage black in neighborhood	−675.91	−641.54	−600.92	−607.22	−0.058	−0.054	−0.051	−0.053
	(−1.20)	(−1.26)	(−1.28)	(−1.37)	(−1.22)	(−1.25)	(−1.35)	(−1.47)
Seller interactions:								
Tester black male, seller white female	380.74	378.81	175.65	130.66	0.035	0.036	0.019	0.016
	(0.93)	(0.98)	(0.52)	(0.39)	(0.10)	(1.08)	(0.69)	(0.60)
Tester black male, seller black male	322.08	236.48	126.65	116.65	0.023	0.017	0.009	0.01
	(0.79)	(0.61)	(0.37)	(0.35)	(0.67)	(0.52)	(0.34)	(0.39)
Tester black female, seller white female	115.15	182.18	−73.29	−85.86	0.025	0.029	0.006	0.004
	(0.31)	(0.52)	(−0.24)	(−0.29)	(0.79)	(0.10)	(0.25)	(0.18)
Tester black female, seller black male	271.72	329.59	227.13	229.96	0.022	0.027	0.023	0.022
	(0.77)	(0.98)	(0.78)	(0.80)	(0.74)	(0.10)	(0.95)	(0.96)
Tester white female, seller white female	−389.30	−76.35	69.65	162.79	−0.026	−0.005	0.007	0.011
	(−0.87)	(−0.18)	(0.19)	(0.45)	(−0.69)	(−0.14)	(0.23)	(0.38)
Tester white female, seller black male	106.31	263.29	168.43	−126.48	0.005	0.019	−0.015	−0.013
	(0.35)	(0.93)	(−0.66)	(−0.52)	(0.19)	(0.79)	(−0.78)	(−0.67)
Adjusted R^2:	0.26		0.33		0.27		0.39	
Standard error of the estimate:	827.8		687.2		0.071		0.056	
Degrees of freedom:	281		281		281		281	
N:	306		306		306		306	

Notes: Numbers in parentheses are t statistics. See the text for explanation of the interpretation of the interaction effects. Note that all the regressions also include dummy variables for eight of the nine car models we tested, omitting the least expensive car.

[a] Dummy variable = 1 if dealership in suburb; 0 otherwise.

[b] Dummy variable = 1 if minority-owned dealer; 0 otherwise.

* Significantly different from zero at the 5-percent level.

and gender of the dealership's owner, employees, or customers influenced the amount of discrimination.[20] One conclusion emerges from Table 5: the neighborhood effects have virtually no power in explaining discrimination. Moreover, the tester-type dummies still have roughly the same size and significance level when the neighborhood effects are included.[21] This finding, along with some ancillary information, argues against standard animus-based theories as the primary explanation for the discrimination we observed.

1. *Owner Animus*.—If owners are the source of animus, black-owned dealerships should presumably exhibit less discrimination against blacks than dealerships owned by whites.[22] The regressions in Table 5 contain a dummy variable MINOWN fo minority-owned dealerships, as well as ar interaction dummy (equaling 1 when both the tester and the owner were black). None of these coefficients was significant in any o the regressions, indicating that the seller's race did not influence the bargaining outcome and that black testers did not fare better at black-owned dealerships.

Bigoted owners should also be more likely to discriminate against their own employees (with whom they presumably have to associate closely over an extended period of time than against their customers. Given tha owners are willing to hire nonwhite and nonmale *salespeople* (who comprised nearly one-fourth of those encountered in ou tests),[23] it seems implausible that they would need a $500 higher markup to compensate for selling to *customers* who are not white males.

2. *Employee Animus*.—Employees—in this case, salespeople—rather than dealership owners are another possible source o animus. Again, however, the magnitudes o the discrimination observed do not seem consonant with this source. For example, i is difficult to imagine that the $1,000 additional markup to black males represent compensation to white salespeople for the disutility of having to spend 45 minutes negotiating with them. The interaction effect in the regressions of Table 5 test whethe the gender and race of the salesperson affected the amount of discrimination. Th coefficients were uniformly insignifican

[20]To simplify interpretation of the interaction terms, we follow the procedure suggested by John Yinger (1986 p. 888). Consider, for example, the interaction of a white female tester with a black male seller. Let SBM be a dummy variable which is 1 if the seller is a black male, and let TWF be a dummy that is 1 if the tester is a white female. Then the normal interaction specification would be TWF×SBM. Instead, we use

$$\mathrm{TWF}\times\left(\mathrm{SBM}-\sum_{i=\mathrm{TWF}}\mathrm{SBM}_i/N_{\mathrm{TWF}}\right).$$

That is, we subtract the average value of SBM for all white female testers (simply the percentage of all white female tests in which the seller was a black male). This subtraction allows us to interpret the TWF coefficient as the average level of discrimination facing white female testers, while the interaction term represents the marginal effect of facing a black male seller.

[21]These regressions also contain dummy variables for eight of the nine car models (omitting the least expensive car). In other regressions, we investigated whether tester groups encountered different dealer behavior when bargaining for foreign or luxury cars. We included variables interacting the tester dummies with dummies indicating whether the car model was domestically produced and whether the car was an economy or standard/luxury model. These interaction coefficients were uniformly small and insignificant, indicating that the pattern of discrimination does not depend on the model class or whether the car is manufactured domestically.

[22]Because there are so few black-owned dealerships (we were able to identify only nine in our sample), they might be able to "free-ride" on the market discrimination by charging their black customers a price that reflects the discriminatory premium at white-owne dealerships. It is also theoretically possible that blac owners dislike dealing with blacks, but at a minimu this would implicate a nontraditional form of discrim nation. We used the "Black Pages," (an analogue the Yellow Pages which lists firms that are more tha 50-percent black-owned), supplemented by a City Chicago listing of minority-owned businesses as source Listing in either source is voluntary, so we may hav excluded some black-owned dealerships. We were u able to find any female-owned dealerships in analogo sources for women.

[23]Of the 306 tests, 23.2 percent involved salespeop who were not white males.

casting doubt on employee animus as a source of discrimination. Black testers did no worse when buying from white salespeople, nor did women get worse deals when the salesperson was male,[24] as one would expect if salesperson animus were the motive for discrimination. In addition, we would expect that bigoted salespeople would want to spend less time with non-white-male testers than with white males. In fact, however, salespeople spent nearly 13-percent longer negotiating with the "minority" testers than with the white males, which casts doubt on salesperson animus as the source of price differences.[25] We do not want to exclude this hypothesis completely, however, because our testers did report some instances of explicitly hostile racist or sexist language from the sellers.[26]

3. *Customer Animus.*—Fellow-customers should also be considered as a source of animus against black or women shoppers. For example, a dealership might charge more to black or female consumers if their presence in the showroom made it less likely that others (whites, men) would shop there. The evidence for this kind of discrimination is mixed. First, concerns about the reactions of other customers should lead dealers to shepherd blacks and women out of the showroom as rapidly as possible (to avoid their being seen by other potential customers). Yet it was white male testers, rather than blacks or white women, who had the shortest average negotiating sessions. In addition, the customer-based theory implies that the extent of customer prejudice should vary by neighborhood: black testers buying in a white neighborhood (where most other customers are likely to be white) should do worse than in a black neighborhood.[27] Table 5 does indicate that black testers shopping in black neighborhoods may receive lower offers. The coefficients on these interaction variables were large (roughly −\$500), but were poorly measured (t statistics between −0.9 and −1.3).[28]

In sum, animus-based theories of discrimination do not find support in our analysis of dealership characteristics. Consistent with Becker's analysis of the effects of competition on discrimination, the evidence for owner and employee animus is the weakest. The large but insignificant coefficients for

[24] In fact, an earlier pilot study (Ayres, 1991) found that women and blacks did *worse* when negotiating against a salesperson of the same race/gender and got their best deals, on average, from white males. The earlier study also found that testers were more likely to "draw" a salesperson of the same race and gender as themselves (who then tended to charge higher prices). We detected no evidence of steering in these data, however. The race and gender of testers and sellers appeared to be independent of each other, as the following table demonstrates:

	Seller			
Tester	White male	White female	Black male	Black female
White male	123	11	17	2
White female	37	4	11	1
Black male	46	6	7	1
Black female	29	5	6	0

$\left(N = 306 \text{ observations}; X^2_{[9]} = 5.64, p = 0.78\right).$

[25] The average test by a white male lasted 36.2 minutes. The average for the other testers was 40.8 minutes. Although the 4.6-minute difference is small, a t test reveals that the two means are significantly different at the 0.001 level. The shorter negotiations with white males could be explained by a dealer preference for wasting the time of minority buyers.

[26] Dealers made hostile race- or gender-based statements in about 4 percent of the tests.

[27] Neighborhoods are defined by what the City of Chicago (1992 p. 1) calls "Community Areas." Each has 30,000–60,000 people. "Community areas are defined by the city of Chicago as groups of census tracts. They were first identified in the 1930's by the Social Science Research Council of the University of Chicago. They correspond roughly to informally recognized neighborhoods such as Lakeview and Hyde Park. The boundaries have changed very little since their inception...."

[28] John Yinger (1986) concludes that, in the housing market, discrimination against blacks is motivated by realtors' perceptions that other renters or house buyers would disapprove of having a black neighbor. Interestingly, Yinger finds, as we do, that black females encounter substantially less discrimination than black males (p. 891). Because of the discrete nature of automobile purchases, animus by fellow consumers strikes us as inherently more plausible in the housing context than in the automobile showroom.

black testers in black neighborhoods might raise some concern, however, that customer animus may play a role in the higher prices charged to blacks.

B. *Statistical Theories*

"Statistical discrimination" is based not on a psychological distaste for associating with blacks or women, but rather on sellers' use of observable variables (such as race or gender) to make inferences about a relevant but unobservable variable (Edmund Phelps, 1972). In the labor market, productivity is the relevant unobservable variable. In car negotiations, dealers might use a customer's race or gender to make inferences about a buyer's knowledge, search and bargaining costs, or, more generally, her reservation price at the specific dealership. If sellers believe, for example, that women are on average more averse to bargaining than men, it may be profitable to quote higher prices to women customers.[29]

Dealers might also make racial or gender inferences about the expected costs of contracting—including, for example, the expected costs of default on car loans. The script attempted to eliminate cost-based statistical discrimination by having all testers volunteer early in the negotiations that they were providing their own financing. This disclosure indicated that the dealer should not have to bear a risk of buyer default.[30]

The plausibility of revenue-based statistical discrimination as an explanation for our results is heightened by the fact that salespeople have their own term for a kind of statistical discrimination, which they call "qualifying the buyer." "Qualifying" is the process of estimating how much the buyer is willing/able to pay on the basis of direct observation (how the buyer is dressed, what kind of car she is currently driving) and answers to questions the seller asks ("How did you get to the dealership?" "Have you visited other dealerships?"). This section looks at possible causes of statistical discrimination and examines whether they are consistent with the evidence.

1. *Search Costs*.—Sellers might perceive that race and gender are related to buyers' search costs for several reasons. For example, black consumers might have higher search costs because they are less likely than whites to own a car at the time they are shopping for a new one (and therefore might have more difficulty traveling to multiple dealerships) (Fred Mannering and Clifford Winston, 1991 p. 98).[31]

[29]As one car salesman turned consumer advocate (Darrell Parrish, 1985 p. 3) wrote:

> ...Salesmen... categorize people into "typical" buyer categories. During my time as a salesman I termed the most common of these the "typically uninformed buyer".... [In addition to their lack of information, these] buyers tended to display other common weaknesses. As a rule they were indecisive, wary, impulsive and, as a result, were easily misled. Now take a guess as to which gender of the species placed at the top of this "typically easy to mislead" category? You guessed it—women.

[30]Even though all testers volunteered that they did not need financing, dealers might disparately assess the credibility of this information depending on the gender and race of the tester. If statistically valid, this inference could form the basis for cost-based statistical discrimination.

Profit-maximizing dealers might also make inferences about the profits from ancillary sales, so statistical discrimination could also be caused by dealers' inferences about the likelihood of repeat purchases, referrals, or repair service. To dampen the importance of such inferences, testers initially volunteered to salespeople that they were moving out of the state within a month. However, having more than one tester make this representation at a single dealership increased the likelihood that dealers would suspect a test, and so this was discontinued.

[31]There is a large, uneven, and largely dated marketing literature which does seem to support the notion that "[v]ariation in prepurchase search behavior is related to racial differences" (Carl Block, 1972 p. 9). Laurence Feldman and Alvin Starr (1968 pp. 216–26) also conclude that there are differences in search behavior by race, although they find that these diminish after controlling for income. For a survey of studies examining differences in car ownership rates by race, see Raymond Bauer and Scott Cunningham (1970 pp. 157–60), who conclude that blacks are less likely to own a car than whites (even when controlling for income). For a theoretical examination of some possible effects of differences in search costs on the ability of sellers to discriminate, see Robert Masson (1973).

Our data provide some evidence that sellers considered search costs to be (differentially) important for different groups of testers. Non-white-male testers were more than 2.5 times as likely as white males to be asked how they got to the dealership, suggesting that dealers show particular interest in determining whether non-white-males have substantial opportunities to search. In addition, testers who revealed that they did not own a car were asked to pay $127 more while those who indicated that they had visited other dealerships saved $122 (although these results were only significant at a 20-percent level).[32]

The evidence does not uniformly support a search-cost explanation, however. If sellers are sensitive to buyers' search costs in setting prices, we would expect black testers to receive better deals (relative to whites) in the suburbs than at urban dealerships. By traveling the substantial distance from the center city to the Chicago suburbs (where very few blacks live), blacks are in effect signaling to suburban dealers that they are willing and able to undertake an extensive search for a car. Contrary to this theory, however, the coefficient for blacks negotiating in suburbs was a positive $64 for initial offers and $264 for final offers ($t$ statistics of 0.25 and 1.22, respectively). Moreover, initial and final offers for black testers in all-white neighborhoods were $675 and $600 higher than in all-black neighborhoods (t statistics of 1.20 and 1.28). The presence of black customers in white neighborhoods did not signal a willingness to search that translated into lower dealer offers.[33]

2. *Consumer Information.*—Race or gender may also be correlated with buyers' information about the car market. For example, a recent study by the Consumer Federation of America (1991) found that 37 percent of respondents did not believe that the sticker price on a car was negotiable. More important for our purposes, there were wide differences in consumer knowledge by race and gender. Sixty-one percent of blacks surveyed believed the price was not negotiable, while only 31 percent of whites believed this. Women were more likely than men to be misinformed about the willingness of dealers to bargain, although the disparities were not as great as between blacks and whites.[34]

Sellers in our study may have been motivated in part by such informational disparities in quoting higher prices to blacks and women. Dealers were somewhat more likely to volunteer information about the cost of the car to white males than to the other testers, possibly because they believed that white males already had such information.[35] More significantly, dealers made their first offer at the sticker price to 29 percent of nonwhite males, but initially offered the sticker price to only 9 percent of white male testers ($X^2_{[1]} = 25.9$). This suggests that sellers believed white males were more knowledgeable than other testers about the possibility of bargaining over sticker prices.

3. *Bargaining Costs.*—Another type of statistical discrimination might focus on

[32]These figures were derived by constructing dummy variables for the tests in which this information was revealed and by then rerunning the final-profit regression in Table 1. Testers revealed this information, however, only when dealers asked, and the decision to ask might not be exogenous to the dealer's final offer.

[33]Customer animus and search-cost theories of discrimination may not be independent. Neighborhoods with few black residents may also have stronger animus against black customers. This animus might swamp (or at least confound) the signaling effect and cause blacks bargaining in such neighborhoods to be quoted higher prices.

[34]Because the survey respondents were not limited to people who were actually interested in buying a car, the survey may overstate racial differences in information among the car-buying public (if nonbuying blacks are relatively less informed than nonbuying whites). George Moschis and Roy Moore (1981 p. 261), however, find "differences in consumer knowledge, skills and attitudes between blacks and whites" controlling for actual purchase behavior.

[35]White males were given unsolicited cost information in 55 percent of their tests, while all other testers were given such information in 48 percent of tests. The difference was not statistically significant at the 5-percent level, however.

buyers' aversion to conducting negotiations. Some buyers experience the process of bargaining as costly, while others apparently derive pleasure from the give-and-take of negotiations. The key question in the present context is whether these bargaining costs are correlated with race or gender. We have no direct evidence on this point,[36] but several findings suggest that dealers made it procedurally more difficult to purchase a car for "minority" testers. First, non-white-male testers were more often asked to sign purchase orders (40.2 percent vs. 27.6 percent for white males; $X^2_{[1]} = 7.14$) and to put down a deposit (37.7 percent vs. 25.6 percent for white males; $X^2_{[1]} = 6.78$). "Minority" testers were also much more likely than white males to be "bumped," that is, to have the dealership manager raise a salesperson's offer (7.0 percent vs. 1.5 percent; $X^2_{[1]} = 7.66$). Forcing non-white-male testers to overcome these additional procedural hurdles might have been one way dealers tried to take advantage of what they perceived as the higher aversion to bargaining of "minority" testers relative to white males.

IV. Conclusion

In negotiations for more than 300 new cars, Chicago car dealers offered black and female testers significantly higher prices than the white males with whom they were paired, even though all testers used identical bargaining strategies.[37] This race and gender discrimination is a robust result, and the magnitude of discrimination is large enough that it cannot credibly be attributed to residual nonuniformities between types of testers.

It is much more difficult to explain discrimination than to document its existence. The evidence that dealers occasionally used racist or sexist language, combined with the large (but statistically insignificant) savings that black testers encountered in black neighborhoods, justify lingering concerns about the possibility of animus or stereotypic discrimination. However, dealership conduct may be better explained as a form of statistical discrimination in which dealers use race and gender as a proxy for the customer's reservation price.

It may be that simple theories of discrimination fail to capture the mutually reinforcing nature of multiple causes. In the end, it may prove impossible to parse out the various elements of animus and rational inferences from irrational stereotypes. No single theory may be adequate to explain the observed discrimination against black men, black women, and white women. Whatever its causes, however, the discrimination uncovered in this study stands squarely in the face of earlier analyses that reject the possibility that discrimination can persist in a competitive market.

[36]The social-psychology literature does not seem to have reached a firm conclusion on whether women bargain differently from men or blacks from whites (Jeffrey Rubin and Bert Brown, 1975). A recent newspaper article (Warren Brown, 1990) interviewed dealers who suggested that middle-class black males associated needing to bargain with poverty and were thus reluctant to bargain.

[37]We should stress that these results may not be generalizable to a random sample of car buyers. Our testers employed a uniform bargaining strategy. If this strategy is atypical of the population at large, or if black and white consumers bargain differently, then the equilibrium amount of discrimination could be higher or lower than we observed.

REFERENCES

Ayres, Ian. "Fair Driving: Gender and Race Discrimination in Retail Car Negotiations." *Harvard Law Review*, February 1991, *104*(4), pp. 817–72.

______. "Further Evidence of Discrimination in New Car Negotiations and Estimates of Its Cause." Mimeo, Yale Law School, 1994.

Ayres, Ian and Siegelman, Peter. "Race and Gender Discrimination in Bargaining for a New Car." Working paper, American Bar Foundation, Chicago, 1992.

Bauer, Raymond and Cunningham, Scott. *Studies in the Negro market*. Cambridge, MA: Marketing Science Institute, 1970.

Becker, Gary. *The economics of discrimination*. Chicago: University of Chicago Press,

1957; 2nd. Ed., 1975.

Block, Carl. "Prepurchase Search Behavior of Low-Income Households." *Journal of Retailing*, Spring 1972, *48*(1), pp. 3–15.

Brown, Warren. "Who Gets the Best Deals on Wheels? Chicago Study Finds It's White Males." *Washington Post*, 14 December 1991, p. F1.

City of Chicago. "Chicago Statistical Abstract." Mimeo, 1992.

Consumer Federation of America. "U.S. Consumer Knowledge: The Results of a Nationwide Test." Washington, DC: Consumer Federation of America, 1990.

Cross, Harry; Kenney, Genevieve; Mell, Jane and Zimmerman, Wendy. *Employer hiring practices: Differential treatment of Hispanic and Anglo job seekers*. Urban Institute Report 90-4, Washington, DC, 1990.

DeGroot, Morris H. *Probability and statistics*, 2nd Ed. Reading, MA: Addison-Wesley, 1986.

Feldman, Laurence and Starr, Alvin. "Racial Factors in Shopping Behavior," in K. Cox and B. Enis, eds., *A new measure of responsibility for marketing*. Chicago: American Marketing Association, 1968, pp. 205–24.

Fix, Michael and Struyk, Raymond. "An Overview of Auditing for Discrimination," in Michael Fix and Raymond Struyk, eds., *Clear and convincing evidence*. Washington, DC: Urban Institute Press, 1992, pp. 1–67.

Greene, William. *Econometric analysis*. New York: Macmillan, 1990.

Hausman, Jerry and Taylor, William. "Panel Data and Unobservable Individual Effects." *Econometrica*, November 1981, *49*(6), pp. 1377–98.

Heckman, James and Siegelman, Peter. "The Urban Institute Studies: Their Methods and Findings," in Michael Fix and Raymond Struyk, eds., *Clear and convincing evidence*. Washington, DC: Urban Institute Press, 1992, pp. 187–258.

Mannering, Fred and Winston, Clifford. "Brand Loyalty and the Decline of American Automobile Firms." *Brookings Papers on Economic Activity*, Microeconomics 1991, pp. 67–103.

Masson, Robert. "Costs of Search and Racial Price Discrimination." *Western Economic Journal*, June 1973, *11*(2), pp. 167–86.

Mateja, Jim. "Escort Sticker Shock: One Price Sells 'em All." *Chicago Tribune*, 13 March 1992, p. C1.

McIntyre, Shelby; Moberg, Dennis, J. and Posner, Barry Z. "Preferential Treatment in Preselection Decisions According to Race and Sex." *Academy of Management Journal*, December 1980, *23*(4), pp. 738–49.

Moschis, George and Moore, Roy. "Racial and Socioeconomic Influences on Adolescent Consumer Behavior," in *Proceedings of the American Marketing Association*, Chicago: American Marketing Association, 1981, pp. 261–65.

Newman, Jerry. "Discrimination in Recruitment: An Empirical Analysis." *Industrial and Labor Relations Review*, October 1978, *32*(1), pp. 15–23.

Parrish, Darrell. *The car buyer's art*. Bellflower, CA: Book Express, 1985.

Phelps, Edmund. "The Statistical Theory of Racism and Sexism." *American Economic Review*, September 1972, *62*(4), pp. 659–61.

Rosenthal, Robert. *Experimenter effects in behavioral research*, 2nd Ed. New York: Irvington, 1976.

Rubin, Jeffrey and Brown, Bert. *The social psychology of bargaining and negotiation*. New York: Academic Press, 1975.

Salop, Steven and Stiglitz, Joseph. "Bargains and Ripoffs: A Model of Monopolistically Competitive Price Dispersion." *Review of Economic Studies*, October 1977, *44*(3), pp. 493–507.

Srinivasan, Narasimhan and Wen, Kuang-Wei. "Price Negotiations in New Car Purchases: A Game Theoretic Experimental Approach." Mimeo, School of Business Administration, University of Connecticut, 1991.

Stigler, George. "The Economics of Information," in *The organization of industry*. Chicago: University of Chicago Press, 1968, pp. 171–90.

Swoboda, Frank. "The Sacking of a Sales Force: Fla. Dealer Sells Twice as Many

Cars After Firing Showroom Staff." *Washington Post*, 27 February 1992, p. B9.

Turner, Margery; Fix, Michael and Struyk, Raymond. *Opportunities denied, opportunities diminished: Discrimination in hiring*. Washington, DC: Urban Institute Press, 1991.

Yinger, John. "Measuring Racial Discrimination with Fair Housing Audits: Caught in the Act." *American Economic Review*, December 1986, *76*(5), pp. 881–98.

[32]

Product Differentiation Advantages of Pioneering Brands

By RICHARD SCHMALENSEE*

This essay presents and explores a relatively simple market model in which rational buyer behavior in the face of imperfect information about product quality can give long-lived advantages to pioneering brands. The analysis has some implications for the variation in the strength of such advantages across markets with different basic conditions. Two sorts of evidence provide the motivation for this research.

First, Joe Bain's seminal empirical study of conditions of entry led him to conclude that "the advantage to established sellers accruing from buyer preferences for their products as opposed to potential entrant products is on average larger and more frequent in occurrence at large values than any other barrier to entry" (p. 216). Treating advertising as a proxy for product differentiation, a large literature has attempted to test this assertion by relating advertising to profitability in cross section.[1] It is interesting to note, however, that Bain concluded that advertising was *not* the main force at work:

> All of these things might seem to suggest the existence of fundamental technical considerations, institutional developments, and more or less fundamental consumer traits which make possible or even very probable the development of strong and stable product-preference patterns. They may also suggest that advertising *per se* is not necessarily the main or even the most important key to the product differentiation problem.... [p. 143]

Bain did not explicitly describe any mechanism by which product differentiation advantages might be created, but a number of his remarks pointed toward buyer uncertainty about product quality as centrally involved.[2]

Second, conventional wisdom in marketing and scattered recent empirical research support the notion that there are important advantages to being the first entrant in some sorts of markets. Marketers usually predict little success for "me too" brands, those claiming to be identical to established brands but selling at a lower price.[3] The success of generic and private-label brands of some consumer products makes it clear that the strength of any handicap under which such brands operate must vary considerably across markets of different sorts. Ronald Bond and David Lean (1977, 1979) find that important and long-lived advantages are enjoyed by pioneering brands of prescription drugs, advantages that can be overcome by later entrants only if they offer distinct therapeutic benefits, not just lower prices. Ira Whittin's study of cigarette market segments points in this same direction, as do the cross-section analysis of marketing costs by Robert Buzzell and Paul Farris, and the study of order-of-entry effects reported by Glen Urban and his associates.

The next section describes the assumptions and notation employed and outlines the analysis of Sections II–V. Buyer learning about quality takes place over time, so that buyers and sellers generally face dynamic decision problems when quality information

*Professor of applied economics, Sloan School of Management, Massachusetts Institute of Technology. I am grateful to the U.S. Federal Trade Commission for its support of this research. I am also grateful for helpful comments to Steven Salop, a referee, the managing editor, and seminar audiences at MIT, Chicago, Harvard, Princeton, Rochester, the Department of Justice, the Federal Trade Commission, and the Santa Barbara and San Diego campuses of the University of California. Naturally, only I can be held accountable for this essay's shortcomings and the opinions it expresses.

[1]William S. Comanor and Thomas A. Wilson and Harold Demsetz provide interesting overviews of this literature; see also my forthcoming essay, especially Section 3.

[2]See pp. 116, 140, and 142, as well as other discussions in ch. 4.

[3]For typical statements, see Kenneth Runyon, p. 214, or J. O. Peckham.

is incomplete. In order to render those problems more or less tractable, a number of rather drastic simplifying assumptions are made. Like most exercises in economic theory, this analysis should thus be thought of as a parable illustrating a general principle, not as a literal description of any particular piece of reality.[4] The findings and some of their implications for research and for public policy are summarized in Section VI.

I. Assumptions and Notation

Consider a narrowly defined product class, like freeze-dried instant coffee or stainless steel razor blades, such that individual consumers can be sensibly modeled as using at most one brand in the class at any instant. It is assumed for simplicity that brands in this class either "work" or "don't work"; they either perform as a brand in this class should, or they fail to perform acceptably. This makes it possible to describe uncertainty about the quality of a new brand by a single parameter, the subjective probability that it won't work. It is assumed that these products are what Phillip Nelson (1970) christened "experience goods," so that the only way a consumer can resolve uncertainty about quality is to purchase a brand and try it. One trial is both necessary and sufficient to determine whether or not any single brand works.

Consumers differ in their valuation of products in this class. Let the function $Q(v)$, $0 \leq v \leq V$, give the number of consumers willing to pay at least v for a brand in this class that is certain to work. Each consumer values a unit that doesn't work at $-\phi v$, with ϕ a nonnegative constant. (One might have $\phi > 0$ for a bleach that could ruin clothes, for instance.) Consumers are perfectly informed except about product quality, so that neither informative nor persuasive advertising occurs.

The time between purchases is assumed constant and equal to one period, so that trial of a new brand consumes the entire normal interpurchase time. This assumption can be altered without changing the basic results, as long as the cost of learning about a new brand's quality is not made negligible relative to current and expected future unit price. Let the one-period discount rate, assumed the same for all consumers, be r. All else equal, more frequent purchase implies a smaller value of r. Consumers are assumed to be risk neutral, to have infinite horizons, and to behave rationally in a sense to be made precise shortly.

The analysis below considers a two-stage scenario. In the first stage, a pioneering brand enters the market and attains steady-state equilibrium. I have in mind here the first appearance of a distinctly new product, like stainless steel razor blades. It is assumed that the first brand actually works for all buyers. If buyers knew enough about the costs of producing working and nonworking brands, and if they were very sophisticated, they might attempt to infer the pioneering brand's quality from its price or simply from its existence. It avoids serious game-theoretic problems and does little violence to reality, especially in the case of new products, to assume that buyers do not have enough information to behave in this fashion.[5] Instead, it is simply assumed that prior to the introduction of the first brand, all consumers have subjective probability π that it will not work, and all act to maximize the discounted value of expected utility. Trial of a new brand of unknown quality yields both an immediate utility payoff and information, the value of which depends on future prices of the brand. Section II analyzes the first

[4]A number of related works deserve mention here. Christian von Weizsächer, ch. 5, considers a basically competitive model of this sort of situation. The Bond and Lean (1979) model of first-entrant advantages relies heavily on assumptions about buyers' response to advertising. Cecelia Conrad presents a dynamic model resembling mine in some aspects, but she neglects the first brand's problems of getting buyers to learn about it. The development here traces its ancestry to the simple model in the Appendix of my 1979 article. Carl Shapiro's recent work has a number of formal similarities to mine.

[5]My 1978 article defends neglect of such signalling considerations in this general context. This assumption and the assumption that information sources such as word-of-mouth do not exist seem most plausible when quality is subjective, so that consumers can disagree about whether a brand actually works. In the interests of simplicity, I have not attempted to incorporate this sort of preference heterogeneity explicitly.

brand's pricing problem under the extreme assumption that buyers have static expectations about prices. Section IV examines the implications of the polar opposite extreme assumption of perfect foresight. Neither assumption is especially attractive, but together they should at least bound actual buyer expectations.

In the second stage of the scenario considered here, a second, objectively identical brand appears on the market. Innovation is ruled out in order to focus on the effects of order of entry and on related barriers to imitation. The second brand is also assumed to have exactly the same cost structure as the first. Two additional simplifying assumptions are made. First, it is initially assumed that the second brand is subjectively identical to the first at the introductory stage, so that the same value of π applies. It is straightforward to relax this assumption, and this is done in Section V. Second, it is assumed that the first brand does not change prices in response to entry and that the second brand knows this in advance. This is a much more passive response to new competition than is usually considered plausible.[6] In an undifferentiated world, this behavior would permit the second brand to undercut the first by an arbitrarily small amount, steal all the first brand's customers, and duplicate its profit performance. Regardless of cost conditions, it would thus make it impossible for the first brand to earn positive profits without attracting new entry. Despite this assumption, it is shown below that the addition of uncertainty about quality can make a profitable pioneering brand immune to subsequent entry. This assumption permits us to avoid (at least in this essay) modeling the complicated dynamic game between the first and second brands that would be played after the latter's entry.[7]

Section III analyzes the second brand's pricing problem for the case of static expectations and demonstrates that brand's order-of-entry disadvantage. Section IV shows that our basic conclusions are equally valid in the polar opposite extreme case of perfect buyer foresight. The consequences of relaxing the assumptions that buyers assign the same initial probability of inadequacy to both first and second brands, that they know for certain the value to them of a working brand, and that purchase is necessary to get information about quality are explored in Section V.

In my forthcoming essay, this basic setup is analyzed under the assumption that buyers correctly expect sellers never to change price. This very *ad hoc* pricing restriction drastically simplifies the model and turns out not to alter the basic nature of its conclusions. Since both brands actually work, each sells forever to those consumers who try it when it is introduced and to no others. Both brands then have well-defined demand curves, with the second brand's curve depending on the first brand's price. It is shown that the second brand's demand curve has the first brand's price as its intercept. It coincides with the first brand's demand curve only for prices distinctly below the first brand's price. This means that with economies of scale, the (common) long-run average cost schedule can lie everywhere above the second brand's demand schedule even though the first brand is earning positive profits. The analysis below obtains essentially the same results without restricting price changes. Since the second brand's demand curve turns out not to be easily defined in general, however, there does not seem to be a simple graphical description of the second brand's disadvantage.

II. Pricing the Pioneering Brand

In this section and the next, buyers have *static expectations*; they expect the most recently observed price to hold forever, even if price has changed in the past. Suppose that in order to try a new brand, a consumer ceases for the trial period to use a substitute that yields a nonnegative surplus, s. Assuming away income effects and indivisibilities, one can take $s=0$ for the first brand.

If a consumer would be willing to pay v for a working brand in this class, immediate

[6]See, for instance, Avinash Dixit and the references he cites.

[7]Conrad's paper illustrates the seriousness of these implications. It may be necessary to make basic changes in the model presented here in order to obtain a tractable post-entry game.

trial of a new brand selling at price p is rational if and only if the following inequality is satisfied:[8]

$$(1)\quad \pi[(-\phi v - p)+(s/r)]+(1-\pi)\times[(v-p)(1+r)/r] \geqslant s(1+r)/r.$$

The first bracketed term on the left gives discounted surplus if the new brand is tried, doesn't work, and the consumer switches back to the substitute. The second term on the left capitalizes the stream of surplus associated with buying a brand that works at price p forever, and the term on the right gives the capitalized benefit of continuing to purchase the substitute.

Inequality (1) can be rewritten simply as

$$(2)\qquad p \leqslant v(1-\tau)-s,$$

where the important quantity τ is defined by

$$(3)\qquad \tau = \pi r(1+\phi)/(1+r-\pi).$$

If $\tau = 0$, condition (2) indicates that the new brand will be purchased if and only if its net surplus, $v-p$, exceeds s. Larger values of τ always discourage trial of a new brand. As one would expect, τ is increasing in both π and ϕ, as these contribute to the expected cost of trial. Larger values of r, which correspond to lower purchase frequency, also increase τ. The lower is purchase frequency, the more important is any single purchase relative to the entire future stream of purchases. This makes the risk associated with trying a new brand loom larger relative to the alternative of sticking forever with the substitute. If $\tau \geqslant 1$, condition (2) shows that trial is so subjectively risky that it never occurs at positive p. To rule this out, let us assume $0<\tau<1$ in all that follows.

If the first brand on the market charges price p, and all buyers with $v>p$ are sure that it works, its sales equal $Q(p)$. Let $\Pi(p)$ be the per period profit function corresponding to this demand curve. When the first brand initially appears on the market, nobody is sure that it works, and condition (2), with $s=0$, implies that a price p will produce sales of $Q[p/(1-\tau)]$. Let the profit function corresponding to this less-attractive introductory-period demand curve be $\Pi^0(p)$, and assume both profit functions are globally strictly concave.

In period 1, let $\underline{P}=V(1-\tau)$, and in later periods let $\underline{P}$ equal the lowest price previously charged. The demand curve for the pioneering brand then has the general shape of the solid kinked curve in Figure 1. If $p<\underline{P}$, some new buyers are reached, and profits equal $\Pi^0(p)$. If $p \geqslant \underline{P}/(1-\tau)$, the only buyers are those who have purchased the brand at least once before, and profits are given by $\Pi(p)$. If $\underline{P} \leqslant p < \underline{P}/(1-\tau)$, current profits could obviously be increased, and no new customers are being informed, so that prices in this range can never be optimal.

If the pioneering brand adopts a *monopoly Q-constant* strategy, it maximizes profit subject to the constraint that it sell to the same buyers in all periods. This constraint implies that it charges a first-period price p^0 and a price p in all later periods such that $p^0 = p(1-\tau)$. (See Figure 1.) The optimal values of p and p^0 can then be obtained by maximizing $\{\Pi^0[p(1-\tau)]+(1/r)\Pi[p]\}$. This sort of low/high pricing sequence corresponds roughly to what is called "penetration pricing" in the marketing and managerial economics literature.[9] One can show that if marginal production cost is positive, a monopoly Q-constant policy yields an output level below that which would be chosen by an ordinary monopolist with profit function $\Pi(p)$ because of the extra marginal cost that the pioneering firm must incur in order to persuade buyers (by means of a low price) to try its *ex ante* risky product.

In Appendix A, it is shown that the monopoly Q-constant strategy just described is the best dynamic pricing policy for the first brand, as long as no thought is given to possible subsequent entry. In order to highlight those aspects of later entrants' prob-

[8] One can derive condition (1) with $s=0$ more rigorously by letting buyer utility be the sum of utility from this product class (either zero, v, or $-\phi v$) and income left over to spend on other goods. It is then straightforward to show that trial of the pioneering brand is optimal if and only if (1) holds with $s=0$.

[9] See Joel Dean for a brief discussion and a comparison with the alternative high/low strategy usually called "cream-skimming" and more commonly associated with durable goods.

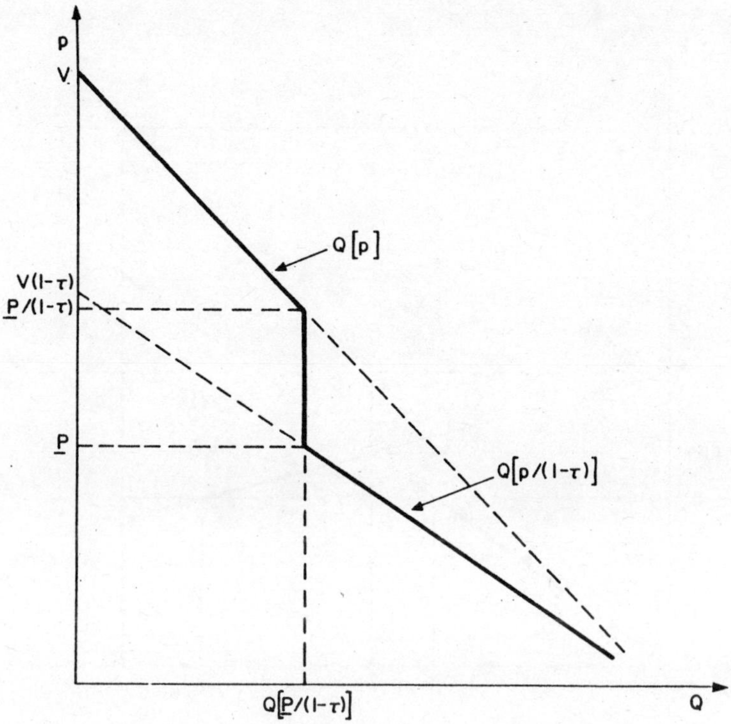

FIGURE 1. SINGLE PERIOD DEMAND FOR THE PIONEERING BRAND

lems that arise naturally, I assume away any such thoughts on the part of the first brand. Allowing the pioneering brand to price strategically could only strengthen the results obtained below at a high cost in added complexity. On the other hand, little is gained by confining the first brand to the monopoly Q-constant strategy defined above. It is thus assumed below only that the first entrant follows *some* Q-constant policy, charging price $P_1(1-\tau)$ in the first period and P_1 in all periods thereafter, and selling $Q(P_1)$ in all periods. Under any such policy, the levelized per period equivalent to the first brand's average revenue stream is simply

$$(4) \quad \bar{P}_1 = \left[\frac{r}{1+r}\right]\left[P_1(1-\tau) + P_1/r\right] = P_1\left[1 - \frac{r\tau}{1+r}\right].$$

III. Demand Conditions Facing a Later Entrant

Because the first brand has followed a Q-constant policy, the second brand faces two and only two distinct types of consumers. If the first brand's price is P_1, those consumers with $v \leq P_1$ have never tried the first brand. If the second brand then charges introductory price p, the condition for trial is again given by (2) with $s = 0$, as for the first brand:

$$(5a) \qquad v \leq P_1 \text{ and } p \leq v(1-\tau).$$

Consumers with high v's are a second type of buyer, as they have already tried brand one and found it to work. Because purchase of brand one yields a surplus of $(v - P_1)$, the

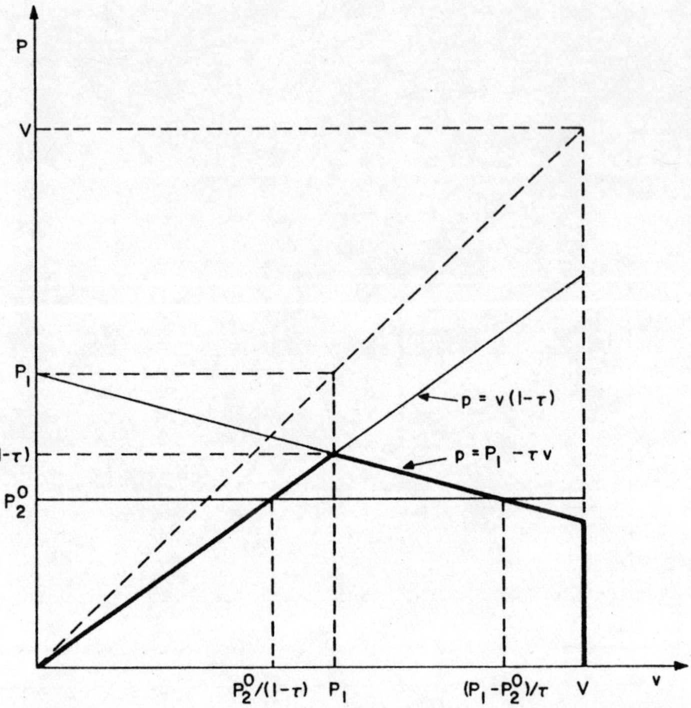

FIGURE 2. FIRST-PERIOD DEMAND PRICES FACING A LATER ENTRANT

condition for trial is given by (2) with $s = v - P_1$:[10]

$$v \geqslant P_1 \text{ and } p \leqslant P_1 - \tau v. \tag{5b}$$

Condition (5b) shows that consumers with large values of v are least likely to try brand two, even though they were most likely to try brand one. Their high valuation of brand one, after they have made the investment of trying it, gives them a high opportunity cost of trying brand two.

The demand conditions facing brand two in its first period are depicted in Figure 2. Prior to the second brand's appearance, the first brand (assumed to have completed the introductory phase of a Q-constant policy) charges P_1 and sells $Q(P_1)$. If the second brand charges an introductory price of P_2^0, its first-period customers are those with v's between the two intersection points of the $p = P_2^0$ line with the heavy kinked curve. As Figure 2 is drawn, the second brand sells

$$Q[P_2^0/(1-\tau)] - Q[(P_1 - P_2^0)/\tau]$$

in its first period. This is less than the first brand would have sold had it charged P_2^0 during *its* introductory period. Only if P_2^0 is less than $(P_1 - \tau V)$ are the second brand's introductory sales equal to those the first brand would have achieved at the same price

If the second brand undercuts the first brand's price sequence, $P_1(1-\tau)$ for one period and P_1 thereafter, by an arbitrarily small amount, it will sell only to those buyers with v's arbitrarily close to P_1. Such a policy would give the second brand a levelized aver-

[10]One can derive condition (5b) more formally using the framework sketched in fn. 8, above. The difference is that the alternative to trying the second brand yields utility of v from this product class for certain at a price of P_1.

age revenue equal to that of the first brand, $\bar{P}_1$, but it would make essentially zero sales. Under constant returns, entry will occur in spite of this disadvantage (though at arbitrarily small scale) if $\bar{P}_1$ exceeds unit cost.[11] With fixed costs or other economies of scale, however, it should be clear that $\bar{P}_1$ can be above the first firm's average cost (at output $Q(P_1)$) without provoking entry.

If the second brand charges *any* first-period price between $P_1(1-\tau)$ and $P_1-\tau V$, it makes fewer sales than the first brand would have made at the same introductory price. Since first-period sales translate into informed buyers willing to pay more because they know the brand works, this difference is the heart of the second brand's disadvantage. If the first seller of fluoride toothpaste can persuade those who care a lot about cavities to try one tube, and if the taste is acceptable to most consumers, the second brand of fluoride toothpaste will find it much harder to get a trial. It will be compared to a known, acceptable fluoride toothpaste, while the first brand was compared only to "ordinary" toothpaste.

If the second brand charges an introductory price less than $P_1-\tau V$, which is distinctly less than the first brand's introductory price, it thereby persuades all those who would have tried the first brand at that same price to try it. (That is, as Figure 2 should make clear, its first-period demand is given by $Q[P_2^0/(1-\tau)]$, the same function that held for the first brand at *all* prices.) It then has essentially the same second-period options the first brand would have had. (The second brand cannot sell anything if it charges a price above P_1, but this is not likely to be a relevant alternative.) If the first brand could have earned positive profit with a Q-constant strategy beginning with a very low first-period price, the second brand will find entry of the same sort attractive. Even with constant costs, however, it is obviously possible for the first brand to be highly profitable but entry at drastically lower prices to be unprofitable.

The preceding discussion establishes the *existence* of a barrier to entry. Profitable entry deterrence can occur in this model even though potential entrants have the exceptionally optimistic expectation that the first brand's price will never change, even if they steal all its customers. In order to investigate the *importance* of this barrier in general, it would be necessary to calculate the second brand's optimal price policy and the consequences of following it. This turns out to be very difficult. The argument in Appendix A establishing that the first brand's optimal policy involves only one price change can be applied to the second brand also. The problem is that it is not always optimal for the second brand to follow a Q-constant policy.

The nature of the difficulty here can be understood by examining the second brand's demand curve for periods after the first, as shown by the heavy kinked curve in Figure 3. As above, $\underline{P}$ is the lowest price *this brand* has ever previously charged, and P_1 is the first brand's price. Figure 3 is drawn assuming $\underline{P} > P_1-\tau V$. The flat portion of the demand curve at price P_1 corresponds to those consumers who have tried both brands and know that both work. The segment AB reflects those who have tried only the second brand because they found the first too expensive. A reduction in $\underline{P}$ increases the length of the flat segment (moves point A to the right) as well as that of the declining segment. If the optimal introductory price is above $P_1-\tau V$, it may be optimal to follow a Q-constant policy and go to a point like B thereafter. On the other hand, since a low introductory price increases the number of brand one's customers who engage in trial, it may be optimal to set a low introductory price for this purpose and then move to a point like A in Figure 3.[12] Finally, since a

[11] Note that if entry occurs at small scale, the pioneering brand loses only a few of its customers, so that the present value of its excess profits may still be positive. Thus even without scale economies, entry may not drive the pioneering brand to a zero (discounted) profit position. I am indebted to Dennis Carlton for this observation.

[12] If the first brand has followed a monopoly Q-constant policy, P_1 exceeds the static, perfect information monopoly price, as Appendix A shows. Thus marginal revenue just to the right of point A in Figure 3 exceeds the first brand's equilibrium marginal cost. If the second brand's marginal cost at the relevant output is no larger,

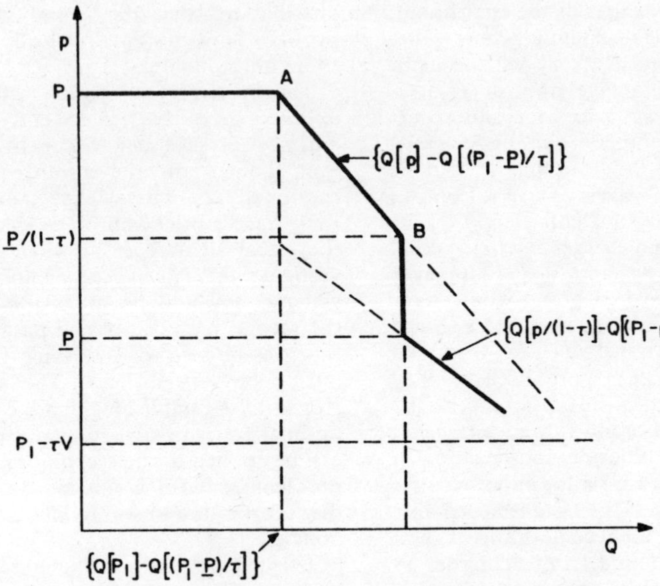

FIGURE 3. SINGLE PERIOD DEMAND FACING A LATER ENTRANT

reduction in the introductory price moves the whole segment AB to the right, it may be optimal to move to a point in the *interior* of that segment for periods after the first. If the optimal introductory price is below $P_1 - \tau V$, on the other hand, point A is unchanged by marginal variations in that price, and a Q-constant policy must be optimal. There are thus *four* distinct strategy types that may be optimal for the second brand in any particular situation, and it is apparently necessary in general to compare the profit streams they yield for given cost and demand functions and fixed P_1 in order to choose among them.

In lieu of any further general analysis, the remainder of this section examines the implications of a fairly tractable special case. Suppose that both brands have fixed, one-time setup costs F and zero variable costs. Let consumers' valuations be uniformly distributed over the unit interval, and let the scale of the market be normalized so that $Q(v)=1-v$. It is fairly straightforward to show that the present value of the first brand's profits (assuming no subsequent entry), W_1, is maximized by a Q-constant policy with $P_1 = 1/2$. Let W_2 be the maximum present value obtainable by the second brand, given that the first brand has followed the monopoly Q-constant policy. It is shown in Appendix B that if $r<1$, $\tau \leqslant 1/3$, and $\tau(1+4r)\leqslant 1$, the second brand optimally follows a Q-constant policy, and the net present values of the two brands are related by

$$W_2 = [W_1 + F]\left[1-\left(\frac{\tau}{1-\tau}\right)^2\right] - F. \tag{6}$$

If $\tau = 0$, $W_2 = W_1$; there is no quality uncertainty and there is obviously no barrier. If $F=0$, so that there are no scale economies, W_2 is positive if and only if W_1 is positive. The second brand is generally less profitable than the first, but its entry is not thereby deterred under our assumptions. In general, it is clearly possible for W_1 and F to be positive and yet for W_2 to be negative. The parameter τ completely describes the magni-

some equilibrium sales to new customers may thus be optimal.

tude of the second brand's demand disadvantage in this example. The larger is τ, the harder it is in general for *both* first and second brands to induce trial, and the worse is the *relative* position of the second brand.

IV. Implications of Perfect Foresight

The assumption of static expectations used above no doubt understates buyer sophistication in many situations. Experienced consumers have certainly observed low/high "penetration pricing" more than once. Moreover, new products are sometimes introduced at prices that are labeled "Introductory" and that sometimes are even described as being some definite amount below "Regular List Price." Though it undoubtedly *overstates* both buyer sophistication and seller predictability in many situations, the assumption of *perfect foresight* regarding price changes does illuminate the general implications of forward-looking behavior. It is an extreme assumption that is fairly tractable and should serve, along with the opposite extreme assumption of static expectations, to bound actual consumer behavior in this context.

Under perfect foresight, any consumer's purchasing behavior depends on the entire future time path of prices. But this picture becomes descriptively less plausible the more complex the time path considered. Moreover, one rarely observes "penetration pricing" strategies for new brands involving complex sequences of price changes. Thus nothing of empirical relevance is likely to be lost if we allow sellers only one price change, from an introductory price of p^0 to a "regular" price of p. Similarly, to facilitate comparison with the analysis above, all brands are restricted to strategies in which $p^0 \leqslant p$.[13]

If for some buyer $s \leqslant (v-p)$, a new brand will be tried in its introductory period, if at all, with the intention of buying it thereafter if it works. The condition for this sort of trial, following the development of (1), is[14]

$$(7)\quad p \leqslant v-s$$

$$\text{and}\quad \pi[(-\phi v-p^0)+(s/r)] + (1-\pi)[(v-p^0) + (v-p)/r] \geqslant s(1+r)/r.$$

Condition (7) can be usefully rewritten as

$$(8)\quad p \leqslant v-s$$

$$\text{and}\quad \hat{p}=\frac{p^0 r+p(1-\pi)}{r+(1-\pi)} \leqslant v(1-\tau)-s.$$

It is possible for consumers with $s \geqslant (v-p)$ nonetheless to try a new brand in the first period, with no intention of repurchasing it, if p^0 is low enough. The condition for first-period-only purchase of this sort is simply that first-period expected net benefits be positive:

$$(9)\quad p \geqslant v-s$$

$$\text{and}\quad p^0 \leqslant v[1-\pi(1+\phi)]-s = v(1-\tau')-s,$$

where the last equality serves to define τ'. Referring to (3), it is clear that $\tau' > \tau$. Let us assume that risk is sufficiently moderate that $\tau' < 1$, so that first-period-only purchase is at least possible in principle.

To consider the first brand's pricing problem, set $s=0$ in conditions (7)–(9), as in Section II. Appendix C establishes that the first brand optimally follows a Q-constant strategy under the assumptions here. That is, it charges $P_1(1-\tau')$ in the first period and P_1 thereafter, selling $Q(P_1)$ in all periods. The introductory price is kept low even though buyers have perfect foresight because of the seller's better information about quality. Buyers assume that they will repurchase the

[13] I conjecture that a strategy of this form is in fact optimal here, but I have not proven this to be true. Note that if $p^0 > p$, some consumers may rationally wait until the second period to buy.

[14] These conditions, both as they apply to the first brand and to later brands, can be derived more rigorously as outlined in fnn. 8 and 10, above.

product only with probability $(1-\pi)$, so that the second-period price is multiplied by this probability in condition (8), while the seller knows that they will repurchase for certain. The seller thus makes the second-period price as high as possible (given the optimal sales path) relative to the first-period price to take advantage of buyers' underweighting of the second and subsequent periods.

The first-brand's levelized average revenue under a Q-constant policy is given by (4) with τ' in place of τ. Since τ' is greater than τ, levelized average revenue at any P_1 (i.e., at any sales volume) is less under perfect foresight than under static expectations. It is harder to persuade rational consumers to try a risky new product if they know that today's low introductory price is temporary than if they expect it to hold forever, all else equal.

Now suppose the first brand has followed a Q-constant strategy and becomes established, and consider the demand conditions facing a later entrant. Buyers with v's less than the first brand's price P_1 have not tried that brand, so that conditions (8) and (9) still apply to them with $s=0$. Their behavior with respect to any second brand would thus be given by exactly the same conditions that governed their response to the first brand. Buyers with valuations above P_1 are buying the first brand and enjoying a surplus of $(v-P_1)$ per period. Substituting this surplus for s in conditions (8) and (9) yields $(P_1-\tau v)$ in place of $v(1-\tau)$ and $(P_1-\tau' v)$ in place of $v(1-\tau')$, respectively. The difference here is exactly like the difference between (5a) and (5b) under static expectations. Experience with brand one has altered the perceived opportunities facing some consumers in a way that makes trial of brand two less attractive.

As in the case of static expectations, the easiest buyers for brand two to steal from brand one are those with v's arbitrarily close to P_1. If the second brand just slightly undercuts the first brand's prices, it will get just those buyers. Exactly as before, the second brand cannot exceed the levelized average revenue earned by the first brand, and it can come close only by driving its own sales correspondingly close to zero. This means that if scale economies are present, entry deterrence is again possible even under our assumption of extreme entrant optimism that rules out price cuts by the first brand.

If the second brand elects to enter at a very low price, it can experience the demand conditions the first brand would have faced, just as under static expectations. If the second brand sets p^0 and p so that $\hat{p} \leqslant P_1-\tau V$, it will induce all of brand one's customers to try its product. It will then have essentially the same options that the first brand would have had, had it elected to charge such low prices. If the second brand sets $\hat{p}$ between $P_1(1-\tau)$ and $P_1-\tau V$, some buyers regularly consuming the first brand will rationally elect not to try the second, so that the second brand will wind up with lower sales than the first would have had. As in the case of static expectations, it may not be optimal for the second brand to follow a Q-constant strategy in all cases, so that evaluation of the importance of its order-of-entry handicap generally requires comparison of the profit implications of several different strategy types.

Such a comparison is not undertaken here. The objective of this section was to establish that in the basic model of Section I, late entrants have a demand disadvantage, which can be used to deter entry if economies of scale are also present, even if consumers do not have static expectations. By showing that a disadvantage of just this sort is present under the polar opposite assumption of perfect foresight, that objective has been achieved. The present values of the profits of all brands in this sort of model are affected by the form of consumers' price expectations, but expectation formation has nothing fundamental to do with the *differences* between the position of the pioneering brand and those of later entrants.

V. Extensions of the Basic Model

Let us first analyze the implications of relaxing the assumption that consumers are certain about the value of a brand that works, a rather restrictive assumption for new product classes. Consider a consumer who treats the valuation of such a brand as a random variable $v'=v+u$, where v is a constant as before and u is a random variable with mean zero and distribution function $F(u)$. We retain the assumption of risk neutrality, trea the valuation of a nonworking brand as nonstochastic, and assume that $F(u)$ is the same for all consumers. For simplicity, this section considers explicitly only the case of static expectations.

In Appendix D, it is shown that if $F[-\tau p/(1-\tau)]$ is positive, there is some chance that a consumer with $v = p/(1-\tau)$, the lowest value of v that makes trial optimal under certainty, will not repurchase the pioneering brand even if it works. This condition on F is shown to imply that some consumers with expected valuations below $p/(1-\tau)$ are induced to try the first brand *because* of their uncertainty about its value to them.[15] The possibility of low values of u does not offset the possibility of high values for households near the borderline. They will not repurchase the product if u is below their cutoff; whether it is barely below or far below doesn't matter. The analogy to stock options is immediate: here as there only one tail of the relevant distribution matters, so that increases in variance, all else equal, tend to enhance value.[16] If realized values of u do not differ markedly from expectations, this increased propensity to experiment enhances the first brand's profitability. It will generally be possible for it to charge a price *above* $p/(1-\tau)$ after the first period without losing all its customers.

If trial of the first brand serves to resolve all uncertainty about the valuation of working brands in the product class considered, later entrants lose this value-of-information-based demand for trial. The gap between demands for the pioneering brand and for later entrants can thus be *widened* by uncertainty about the valuation of the *product class*.

On the other hand, if later entrants differentiate their products, one effect may be to cause the valuation of their *brands* to be uncertain for some consumers. Appendix D indicates that if they can create enough uncertainty about their value to potential users, without lowering expected valuations, they may be able to overcome their other handicaps. This is at least consistent with the apparently greater popularity of attempting to differentiate new products from old, to claim new features of which consumers can be expected to have uncertain valuations, than of following the "me too" strategy of introducing a product "just like brand X only cheaper."

Let us now focus on a second restrictive assumption maintained in the analysis of Sections II–IV, the assumption that the pioneering brand and later entrants are subjectively identical when they first appear. Favorable experience with the pioneering brand may serve to reduce consumers' subjective probabilities that later entrant brands in the same product class won't work. This effect of course enhances the prospects of such entrants. Referring to Figure 2, if experience with the first brand is necessary and sufficient for greater optimism about later entrants, the $p = P_1 - \tau v$ locus that describes the introductory-period behavior of the first brand's customers should be replaced by a line $p = P_1 - \tau'' v$, with $\tau'' < \tau$. (The relevant kinked schedule then has a vertical segment at $v = P_1$.) Unless $\tau'' < (P_1/V)\tau$, later entrants still find it harder to get the first brand's customers to try their product than the first brand found it to attract them initially. Note that small drops in τ'' help later brands only slightly; the relation is continuous.

Similarly, if nonusers of the first brand become more optimistic about the likelihood that brands in this class will work, the $p = (1-\tau)v$ line in Figure 2 is replaced by a steeper line with the same intercept, reflecting the lower relevant value of τ. Again, this sort of change in perceptions advantages later entrants in a continuous fashion. Presumably this sort of second-entrant advantage is most important for "me too" brands that do *not* differentiate themselves from the pioneering brand, so that this effect and valuation uncertainty are unlikely both to benefit any particular later entrant noticeably.

Finally, let us consider the implications of relaxing the assumption that consumers can learn about quality only through purchase.

[15] If consumers were risk averse, this might well be reversed; see the Appendix to my 1979 article.

[16] Mark Rubinstein and John Cox provide a clear and thorough discussion of stock option valuation. Uncertainty increases the propensity to purchase because of the value of information in the model of Sanford Grossman, Richard Kihlstrom, and Leonard Mirman.

As long as one follows Nelson (1974) and assumes that advertising for experience goods cannot credibly convey complete information about product quality, the addition of advertising to this model in an appropriate fashion should cause no fundamental changes. The demand handicaps facing late entrants here should simply render their advertising outlays less productive.

If information about new brands is valuable enough, one can expect consumers to use word-of-mouth and other similar channels (such as specialized publications) to seek it. If a new brand is sufficiently attractive that condition (1) is satisfied and trial would be optimal, the expected value of perfect quality information is easily shown to be $[\pi(s+p+\phi v)]$. This suggests that consumers are more likely to search out additional sources of information for items with high unit cost, all else equal. Since information transmission among consumers tends to eliminate the imperfect information on which this model's conclusions rest, this in turn suggests that the mechanism presented here is likely to be more important for products with low unit cost, all else equal.[17] Finally, Michael Porter has noted that for some products, which he and the marketing literature call "shopping goods," retailers are important sources of information about quality. Where retailers can reliably evaluate quality and offer their reputations as hostages for the accuracy of those evaluations, one would expect the mechanism presented here to be relatively unimportant.[18]

VI. Summary and Conclusions

In this model, brands enter sequentially, and consumers are initially skeptical about their quality. When consumers become convinced that the first brand in any product class performs satisfactorily, that brand becomes the standard against which subsequent entrants are rationally judged. It thus becomes harder for later entrants to persuade consumers to invest in learning about their qualities than it was for the first brand. Even if late entrants expect the pioneering brand not to lower its price if they enter, their entry may be deterred if economies of scale are present. Even without scale economies, late entrants are disadvantaged relative to pioneering brands. We have thus found a product differentiation advantage of early entry that has nothing to do with advertising or consumer irrationality. This finding suggests the value of looking at consumers' acquisition and use of information generally, paying less attention to advertising in particular than has been done in much of the industrial organization literature.

The basic mechanism presented here seems sufficiently general that it should be operative in most markets for experience goods. It is obviously not of central importance in many such markets, however. Even though the analysis here is based on the implausible assumption that established firms don't react to entrants, it does give rise to some hypotheses about differences in the strength of first-entrant advantages that may deserve some empirical attention. The example considered in Section III found the second brand's disadvantage to be increasing in τ. This suggests that high risk (relative to unit cost) and low purchase frequency increase the height of the entry barrier considered here. This is consistent with Bain's (p. 142) finding that infrequency of purchase contributes to strong product differentiation. Similarly, the barrier presented here depends on overall scale economies, which clearly vary in importance across markets.[19] Finally, the discussion of alternative information sources in Section V suggests that first-entrant advantages are greater for products with low unit cost and for "convenience goods," for which retailers do not provide much information.

[17] The mere existence of word-of-mouth information transfer will not generally serve to eliminate first entrant advantages. If information spreads via some sort of diffusion process from users to nonusers, later entrants' greater difficulty in getting initial trial of their products will still leave them at some disadvantage.

[18] I am indebted to Christian von Weizsächer for this point. It seems consistent, at least, with Porter's cross-section regression results.

[19] Michael Spence has recently provided a useful analysis of the interaction of scale economies in production and advertising.

If the mechanism presented here is especially important in some market, it follows that a "me too" strategy is especially unattractive to potential entrants. If the product involved is such that differentiation is feasible, it is especially likely to be attempted by new entrants. Thus, where the mechanism considered here is important, the quality-matching, price-cutting competition most commonly assumed in economic analysis is likely to be unimportant. Successful entrants will generally have differentiated themselves sufficiently from their predecessors as to appear "pioneering" to at least a sizeable segment of buyers. A traditional industrial organization economist might be inclined to treat the product differentiation and non-price rivalry in such a market as a cause of entry barriers, but this analysis suggests that these features may actually be caused by the same underlying basic conditions that give pioneering brands important demand advantages.

The analysis here does not seem to lead to any simple, general public policy prescriptions, Pioneering brands should generally be rewarded for innovating and bearing risk. After a new and *ex ante* risky brand has become established, its trademark performs the valuable function of transmitting information about quality to experienced buyers, information that is not easily transmitted in other ways. By granting pioneering brands exclusive use of their trademarks forever, society grants something like a patent with infinite life. As with patent policy, trademark policy can only be analyzed in second best terms. Like the patent grant, the potential monopoly position of pioneering brands trades off static efficiency against the incentive to innovate. It is no easier to analyze particular proposed changes in the length or terms of the trademark grant, in general or in any particular industry, than to perform the corresponding analysis of patent policy. As is often the case in second best situations, decisions may well turn on very difficult questions of fact.

Appendix A

In order to show that the monopoly Q-constant policy defined in Section II is optimal under static expectations, I first show that such a policy is optimal if only one price change is made, then it is shown that it is optimal to make only one price change. Because of strict concavity, the profit functions $\Pi^0(p)$ and $\Pi(p)$ defined in the text have unique maximizers, M^0 and M, respectively. If $C[Q]$ is the relevant cost function, we have $\Pi(p) = pQ(p) - C[Q(p)]$ and $\Pi^0(p) = pQ[p/(1-\tau)] - C[Q(p/(1-\tau)]$. It is immediate that $\Pi[p/(1-\tau)] > \Pi^0(p)$ for $p > 0$. Examination of the first-order conditions and use of concavity establishes that $M^0 \geqslant M(1-\tau)$, with equality only when marginal cost is zero.

If the monopolist's first-period price is p^0, its profit is simply $\Pi(p^0)$. It can't then be optimal to change to a price p *below* p^0 and hold that price forever, as the firm will then earn $\Pi^0(p)$ forever, and it could do better either by charging p in all periods or by charging p^0 in all periods. From the discussion of Figure 1, if the monopolist changes to a price above p^0, it will charge at least $p^0/(1-\tau)$. Since any such change increases per period profit, the monopoly will want to make it as soon as possible. Thus if only one price change is made, it will be a price increase from p^0 in the first period to $p \geqslant p^0/(1-\tau)$ in the second and later periods. The best policy of this sort must maximize $\{\Pi^0(p^0)+(1/r)\Pi(p)\}$ subject to $p(1-\tau) \geqslant p^0$. Since $M^0 \geqslant M(1-\tau)$, the constraint will be satisfied with equality, and the optimal one-change policy is thus the monopoly Q-constant policy defined in Section II of the text.

Now let us show that it is optimal to change price only once. The problem here is stationary, with the state of the system in any period completely described by $\underline{P}$, the lowest price previously charged. By stationarity, if it is ever optimal to price above $\underline{P}$ and to leave the state of the system unchanged, it must be optimal to charge the same price forever afterward.

We can also establish that any optimal sequence of price changes must be finite and must end with a change to a price at least equal to $\underline{P}/(1-\tau)$, with that price maintained thereafter. If price changes only a finite number of times, and the final change is to a price less than $\underline{P}/(1-\tau)$, profits can be increased by charging $\underline{P}/(1-\tau)$ instead of the final price. If it is optimal to change price an infinite number of times, stationarity implies that price is a monotone decreasing sequence decending toward some nonnegative limit. Call that limit $P^\infty(1-\tau)$. Then per period profit approaches $\Pi^0[P^\infty(1-\tau)] \leq \Pi[P^\infty]$, with equality if and only if $P^\infty = 0$. If $P^\infty \leq M$, such a sequence is dominated by one that involves increasing price to M as soon as a price below $M(1-\tau)$ is charged in the original sequence. If $P^\infty > M$, the uniqueness of M implies that one can find $P' > P^\infty$ such that $\Pi(P^\infty) > \Pi(P') > \Pi^0[P^\infty(1-\tau)]$, and profit can be increased by charging P' for all periods after the original sequence drops below $P'(1-\tau)$. Thus it cannot be optimal to change price infinitely often.

Combining the results of the preceding two paragraphs, if a one-change price policy is not optimal, any optimal sequence must have prices P_a, P_b, and P_c charged in successive periods, with $P_c \geq P_b/(1-\tau)$ charged thereafter, $P_b < P_a$, and P_a less than $\underline{P}$ at the start of the relevant period. If a sequence of this sort is optimal and a one-change policy is not, it must be that

$$\Pi^0(P_a)+\frac{1}{1+r}\left[\Pi^0(P_b)+\frac{1}{r}\Pi(P_c)\right] > \Pi^0(P_b)+\frac{1}{r}\Pi(P_c).$$

But rearrangement and use of $\Pi[P/(1-\tau)] \geq \Pi^0[P]$ yields directly

$$\Pi^0(P_b)+\frac{1}{r}\Pi(P_c) < \frac{1+r}{r}\Pi^0(P_a) \leq \Pi^0(P_a)+\frac{1}{r}\Pi[P_a/(1-\tau)].$$

This inequality implies that discounted profits would be increased if the monopolist moved to $P_a/(1-\tau)$ from P_a rather than going to P_b and P_c. This contradicts the initial assumption that a one-change policy was not optimal, and the proof is complete.

Appendix B

If the first brand in the example at the end of Section III follows a Q-constant strategy, the present value of its profit stream is

$$\text{(A1)}\quad W_1 = [P_1(1-\tau)][1-P_1] + (1/r)[P_1][1-P_1] - F, \\ = P_1(1-P_1)[(1-\tau)+(1/r)] - F.$$

This is maximized by setting $P_1 = 1/2$, as asserted in the text.

Suppose that the second brand charges p^0 in its introductory period, with $P_1 - \tau \leq p^0 \leq P_1(1-\tau)$. Then its first-period profit (and revenue) function is

$$\Pi^0(p^0; P_1) = \frac{p^0}{\tau}\left[P_1 - \frac{p^0}{1-\tau}\right].$$

In the second and later periods, if the second brand charges p its profits are given by

$$\Pi(p; p^0, P_1) = \frac{p}{\tau}[P_1 - p^0 - \tau p],$$

for $p^0/(1-\tau) \leq p \leq P_1$. The second brand's objective function is

$$\text{(A2)}\quad W_2(p^0, p; P_1) = \Pi^0(p^0; P_1) + (1/r)\Pi(p; p^0, P_1) - F.$$

If $p^0 < P_1 - \tau$, the relevant objective function is identical to that of the first brand, and a Q-constant strategy must be optimal by the arguments in Appendix A.

Let us evaluate optimal strategies of the types mentioned in the text. Considering point A in Figure 3, one can set $p = P_1$ in (A2) and maximize W_2 with respect to p^0. Under the assumption $r<1$, the maximum occurs at the lower corner where $p^0 = (P_1 - \tau)$ and all brand one's customers have been persuaded to try brand two. Let W_2^A be the value of W_2 corresponding to this strategy. Considering point B in Figure 3, one can set $p = p^0(1-\tau)$ in (A2) and again maximize with respect to p^0. If $P_1 \geq 2\tau/(1+\tau)$, W_2 is again maximized at the point $p^0 = P_1 - \tau$. To simplify matters, let us assume that P_1 takes on its monopoly value, 1/2, and that $\tau \leq 1/3$, so that this corner solution is the relevant one. Direct comparison then establishes that the corresponding value of W_2, call it W_2^B, strictly exceeds W_2^A.

The third strategy type involves $p^0/(1-\tau) < p < P_1$, corresponding to points strictly between A and B in Figure 3. If such a strategy is optimal, the value of p that yields an unconstrained maximum of $\Pi(p; p^0, P_1)$, call it $p^*(p^0; P_1)$ must lie in this interval. (If not, the optimal price in periods after the first must be a corner solution at one of the endpoints.) Substituting $p^*(p^0; P_1)$ into (A2) and differentiating, one finds that $W_2[p^0, p^*(p^0, P_1); P_1]$ is *decreasing* in p^0 over the entire relevant range as long as $\tau(1+4r) \leq 1$. Assuming this last condition satisfied, as it is when $r \leq 1/2$ under our assumption that $\tau \leq 1/3$, and using $P_1 = 1/2$, the relevant lower bound on p^0 turns out to be $P_1 - \tau = P_1(1-\tau)/(1+\tau)$. At this point, however, $p^*(p^0; P_1) = p^0/(1-\tau)$, and we are at a point like B once again. Under these assumptions, in short, there exists no optimal strategy of the third (interior) type. Finally, the optimal Q-constant strategy for $p^0 \leq P_1 - \tau$ must have this constraint holding with equality, since the objective function is the same strictly concave one that held for the first brand and that is maximized at $p^0 = (1-\tau)/2 > (1/2) - \tau$. We are again at a point like B in Figure 3; this fourth strategy type also yields a present value of profits equal to

$$\text{(A3)} \quad W_2^B = (1/4)[(1-2\tau)(1+r-r\tau)] / \left[r(1-\tau)^2\right] - F.$$

Setting $P_1 = 1/2$ in (A1) and substituting into (A3), we obtain equation (5) in the text.

APPENDIX C

To prove the optimality of a Q-constant policy under the perfect foresight assumptions of Section IV, let us first show that if it is optimal for the first brand to make any sales at all, it is optimal to make sales in all periods after the first. If this were not true, then (9) would imply the optimality of selling $Q(v^0)$, for some v^0, in the first period at v^0 per unit, then choking off demand with $p = V$ thereafter. Using (8), the pioneering brand can sell $Q(v^0)$ in all periods after the first (since the brand always works) by setting $p = v^0$ and $p^0 = v^0[1-\tau-\tau(1-\pi)/r] = (1-\tau')v^0$. It follows directly from condition (9) that this p^0 induces no first-period-only trial for $v < v^0$, so that $Q = Q(v^0)$ in all periods. But this pricing pattern yields equivalent levelized average revenue of

$$\text{(A4)} \quad \bar{p} = \frac{r}{1+r}\left[p^0 + \frac{1}{r}p\right] = \left(1 - \frac{r\tau'}{1+r}\right)v^0.$$

Since $\bar{p}$ exceeds $(1-\tau')v^0$ for all finite r, the optimality of sales after the first period is established.

We can now show that the pricing pattern just described maximizes the present value of revenues from any fixed set of customers to be served in all periods. That is, assuming $Q(v^0)$ sold in all periods after the first and neglecting the profit implications of any first-period-only trials, the pricing pattern just described is profit maximizing. A comparison of (8) and (A4) shows that p has a larger impact relative to p^0 on the seller's present value, a multiple of $\bar{p}$, than on the buyers' cutoff criterion, $\hat{p}$. Buyers treat the probability that they will ever pay p after trial as $(1-\pi)$; the seller knows that the product works and thus treats this probability as one. Accordingly, the seller can increase the present value of revenues without excluding customers by raising p as high as possible and lowering P^0 so as to keep $\hat{p}$ constant. Clearly p can be raised no higher than v^0 if all buyers with $v \geq v^0$ are induced to try the brand, and this yields exactly the pricing policy described in the preceding paragraph.

Let $Q(v^0) > 0$ be the first brand's optimal sales in all periods after the first. The preceding paragraph has established that $p^0 = (1-\tau')v^0$ and $p = v^0$ maximize the revenue derived from those sales. The second-period price, p, cannot be increased without reducing second-period sales. If p is decreased and p^0 increased so as to hold second-period sales constant, first-period sales are unaffected and discounted revenues fall. If the pricing pattern just described is not optimal, it therefore can only be the case that it is better to charge a lower value of p^0, say $(1-\tau')(v^0-X)$, leave p fixed, and increase first-period sales by $[Q(v^0-X)-Q(v^0)]$. If such a change increases discounted profit, however, it can be further increased by lowering p by the same percentage amount to (v^0-X) and enjoying exactly the same sales increase in all later periods. But this contradicts the initial assumption that $Q(v^0)$ was the optimal sales level in periods after the first. The optimal policy must thus be a Q-constant policy, as described at the start of this paragraph.

Appendix D

Under the assumptions given in the first paragraph of Section IV, the condition for trial corresponding to (2) can be shown to be

$$\text{(A5)} \quad p \leq v(1-\tau)-s+z(1-\pi),$$

where z is defined by

$$\text{(A6)} \quad z=\left\{\int_{u^*}^{\infty} u dF(u)-\tau v F(u^*)\right\} \Big/ \{1+r-[\pi+(1-\pi)F(u^*)]\},$$

and

$$\text{(A7)} \quad u^*=s-(v-p).$$

The quantity z is multiplied by $(1-\pi)$ in (A5) because it picks up uncertainty about the value of a brand conditional on its working. The quantity in brackets in the denominator in (A6) is the unconditional probability that it will not be worthwhile to purchase in periods after the first; purchase of a working brand is not rational if u turns out to fall below u^*. The denominator is always positive.

Consider the demand conditions facing a pioneering brand charging price p in its first period. Then (A5) applies with $s=0$ and $u^*=-(v-p)$. If the range of u is finite, there will exist a v large enough so that $f[-(v-p)]=0$ and thus $z=0$. The derivative of the numerator of (A6) with respect to v is $\{F'(p-v)[p-v(1-\tau)]-\tau F(p-v)\}$. This quantity is nonpositive for all $v \geq p/(1-\tau)$, and it is negative for some v in this interval if $F[-\tau p/(1-\tau)]$ is positive. This condition means that there is some chance that a working brand will not be repurchased: if $v=p/(1-\tau)$ and $u<-\tau p/(1-\tau)$, the consumer's actual valuation, $v'=v+u$, is less than p and purchase of the working brand is not optimal. If this condition is satisfied, it follows that z is positive in a neighborhood of the cutoff valuation under certainty, $v=p/(1-\tau)$. It thus follows that some consumers with expected valuations below this critical level elect to try the pioneering brand, as asserted in the text.

Now consider a later entrant. Valuation uncertainty acts as above on consumers who have not tried the first brand. For those currently buying the first brand, on the other hand, s must be set equal to $(v-P_1)$, as before, in conditions (A5)–(A7). Thus u^* equals $[-(P_1-p)]$ for all those buyers, independent of v. If $F(u^*)$ is positive, there is a positive probability that the new brand will be sufficiently worse than the old that it won't be worth purchasing even at its lower price. (By assumption, the expected valuation of the new brand equals the actual valuation of the old.) It is easy to show that if this is true, z is positive for $v=P_1$ and decreasing in v. All else equal, valuation uncertainty makes it easier for an entrant to attract at least the low-v customers of the pioneering brand; z may be negative for large enough v.

REFERENCES

Bain, Joe S., *Barriers to New Competition*, Cambridge: Harvard University Press, 1956.

Bond, R. S. and Lean, D. F., "Sales, Promotion, and Product Differentiation in Two Prescription Drug Markets," Staff Report to the U.S. Federal Trade Commission, Washington, 1977.

______ **and** ______, "Consumer Preference,

Advertising, and Sales: On the Advantage from Early Entry," Working Paper 14, Bureau of Economics, U.S. Federal Trade Commission, Washington, October 1979.

Buzzell, R. D. and Farris, P. W., "Marketing Costs in Consumer Goods Industries," Report 76-111, Marketing Science Institute, Cambridge, August 1976.

Comanor, William S. and Wilson, Thomas A., "Advertising and Competition: A Survey," *Journal of Economic Literature*, June 1979, *17*, 453–76.

Conrad, C. A., "The Pioneering Brand Hypothesis or Does Number Two Try Harder," Studies in Industry Economics No. 119, Department of Economics, Stanford University, 1980.

Dean, Joel, "Pricing Pioneering Products," *Journal of Industrial Economics*, July 1969, *17*, 165–79.

Demsetz, Harold, "Accounting for Advertising as a Barrier to Entry," *Journal of Business*, April 1979, *16*, 1–10.

Dixit, Avinash K., "The Role of Investment in Entry-Deterrence," *Economic Journal*, March 1980, *90*, 95–106.

Grossman, Sanford J., Kihlstrom, Richard E., and Mirman, Leonard J., "A Bayesian Approach to the Production of Information and Learning by Doing," *Review of Economic Studies*, October 1977, *40*, 537–47.

Nelson, Phillip, "Information and Consumer Behavior," *Journal of Political Economy*, March/April 1970, *78*, 311–29.

______, "Advertising as Information," *Journal of Political Economy*, July/August 1974, *82*, 729–54.

Peckham, Joseph O., "Can We Relate Advertising Dollars to Market Share Objectives?," in *Proceedings of 12th Annual Conference*, Advertising Research Foundation, New York 1966.

Porter, M. E., *Interbrand Choice, Strategy, and Bilateral Market Power*, Cambridge: Harvard University Press, 1976.

Rubinstein, Mark and Cox, John C., *Option Markets*, Englewood Cliffs: Prentice Hall, 1980.

Runyon, K. E., *Consumer Behavior and the Practice of Marketing*, Columbus: C. E. Merrill, 1977.

Schmalensee, Richard, "A Model of Advertising and Product Quality," *Journal of Political Economy*, June 1978, *87*, 485–504.

______, "On the Use of Economic Models in Antitrust: The ReaLemon Case," *University of Pennsylvania Law Review*, April 1979, *127*, 994–1050.

______, "The New Industrial Organization and the Economic Analysis of Modern Markets," in W. Hildenbrand, ed., *Advances in Economic Theory*, Cambridge: Cambridge University Press, forthcoming.

Shapiro, Carl, "Consumer Information, Product Quality and Seller Reputation," mimeo., U.S. Federal Trade Commission, July 1980.

Spence, A. Michael, "Notes on Advertising, Economies of Scale, and Entry Barriers," *Quarterly Journal of Economics*, November 1980, *95*, 493–508.

Urban, G. L., Johnson, P. L., and Brudnick, R. H., "Market Entry Strategy Formulation: A Hierarchial Modeling and Consumer Measurement Approach," Working Paper 1103-80, MIT Sloan School of Management, December 1979.

von Weizsäcker, C. C., *Barriers to Entry*, New York: Springer, 1980.

Whitten, Ira T., "Brand Performance in the Cigarette Industry and the Advantages of Early Entry," Staff Report to the U.S. Federal Trade Commission, Washington, 1979.

THE JOURNAL OF INDUSTRIAL ECONOMICS
Volume XXVIII December 1979 No. 2

THE WELFARE ECONOMICS OF PRODUCT VARIETY: AN APPLICATION TO THE READY-TO-EAT CEREALS INDUSTRY

F. M. Scherer*

I. INTRODUCTION

Ever since the publication of Chamberlin's *Theory of Monopolistic Competition* [6], economists have known that how well a market economy solves the three-way trade-off among product variety, economies of scale, and purity of competition critically affects the level of economic welfare. Following a long period of neglect, there has recently been an explosion of work on the theory of optimal product variety. Although unsettled questions remain, the theory reveals that whether monopolistic competition yields the welfare-maximizing amount of product variety, too little, or too much, depends upon the relationships among several potentially observable variables. Except for the rather special cases of television programming and service competition among publicly regulated airlines,[1] there has been little effort to apply the theory to real-world market situations. This paper attempts to extend the set of applications to a situation in which the visible hand of regulation was largely absent.

The focus is the US ready-to-eat (RTE) breakfast cereal industry, which is the subject of a major antitrust case brought by the Federal Trade Commission.[2] The FTC's complaint alleges that leading manufacturers Kellogg, General Mills, Post (i.e. General Foods), and Quaker,[3] accounting for approximately 90% of RTE cereal sales during the late 1960s, collectively monopolized the industry and engaged in diverse monopolistic practices. One charge is that the four respondents deterred new entry by proliferating product varieties, thereby leaving insufficient room for viable newcomers.[4] In other words, they pre-empted the entry of what otherwise would have been new monopolistic competitors and thereby prevented the emergence of a more atomistic market structure. The FTC did not address the question of whether product proliferation was carried beyond the point at which some plausible index of social welfare was maximized. To take

* The author is grateful to Ronald Braeutigam, Richard Schmalensee, John Beggs, William Burnett and an anonymous referee for helpful comments.

[1] See Steiner [32], Spence and Owen [31], Noll *et al.* [22] and Douglas and Miller [9].

[2] In the matter of Kellogg *et al.*, FTC docket no. 8883. The author appeared as an expert witness for the government on matters for the most part only indirectly related to the subject of this paper.

[3] In 1978, at the conclusion of the government's case in chief, Quaker was dismissed as a respondent.

[4] For the theory of this allegation, see Schmalensee [28].

that last difficult step is the aim of this paper. The paper begins by reformulating the received theory of optimal product variety in a more empirically tractable form, proceeding then to relate the available evidence to the theory.

Before we begin, an overview of the RTE cereal industry's structure and performance may be useful. The SIC industry of which it is the principal component, 'cereal preparations', is one of the 20 most concentrated four-digit US manufacturing industries. Among 412–451 four-digit industries, cereal preparations had in both 1967 and 1972 one of the ten lowest ratios of materials plus plant payroll costs to industry sales—52% in both years.[5] It also had less plant capital and inventory per dollar of sales than the average manufacturing industry. Thus, in-plant costs were unusually low. Obversely, advertising expenditures and profits were unusually high. Among 324–329 four-digit manufacturing industries for which comparable input–output statistics are available, cereal preparations had the second highest ratio of advertising outlays to sales—22% in 1963 and 18·5% in 1967.[6] Accounting profits after taxes plus interest averaged 19·8% of assets for the RTE operations of leading firms Kellogg, General Mills, General Foods, Quaker, and Ralston between 1958 and 1970. For all manufacturing corporations, the comparable figure was 8·7%. Or when advertising expenditures are capitalized and depreciated at an annual exponential decay rate of 35%, the adjusted 1958–70 after-tax return on assets for the five RTE firms was 17·8%, compared to 8·4% for all manufacturing corporations.[7]

From the perspective of this article, an especially important feature of the RTE industry's recent history has been the introduction of numerous new product variants. Key innovations are widely considered to have been pre-sweetened cereals, with Post's introduction of Sugar Crisp in 1950 marking the first major success; nutritional cereals (with Kellogg's Special K leading the way in 1956);[8] and natural cereals (long available from fringe sellers, but enjoying a demand surge in the early 1970s). We concentrate here on the principal firms' activities following the introduction of Special K and preceding the natural cereal boom. At the end of 1957, the six largest companies had a total of 38 RTE brands in national distribution. From then to the close of 1970, they carried 51 new brands beyond the regional test stage while withdrawing 22, leaving a total of 67 brands in

[5] Analysis of company data showed that the RTE subset of cereal preparations had an even lower ratio. See pp. 28,183–95 of the FTC hearing transcript, which will subsequently be cited as TR.

[6] TR 27,676–8, citing Ornstein [23, pp. 77–85].

[7] Testimony of Thomas R. Stauffer at TR 19,069 ff., summarized in FTC exhibit CX-701. (The prefix CX indicates that an exhibit was introduced by complaint counsel (i.e. the FTC). A second set of initials, if any, reveals the company from whose records the document came. A third letter, if any, identifies the exhibit page.)

[8] On these two, see p. Z72 of the General Foods 1967 task force study included as exhibit CX-GF-4039. The same document observes at p. Z74 that 'Good ideas for new cereals are scarce'.

national distribution in December 1970. Many of the new brands failed to achieve viable market shares, and of the 51 brands launched between 1958 and 1970, only five—Kellogg's Froot Loops, General Mills' Total, Post's Alpha Bits and Quaker's Life and Captain Crunch—succeeded in obtaining for a year or more a market share of at least 2%. Thus, the newer products characteristically filled only small niches in the spectrum of consumer demands. In contrast, older brands showed considerable staying power. Only two pre-1958 brands were withdrawn from national distribution during the 1960s, and the 29 leading brands of 1960, with 83% of total industry pound volume then, retained 74% of the market in 1970 despite the competition of numerous products. The key question is, was the cereal makers' proliferation of product variants carried beyond the point at which economic welfare was maximized?

II. THE THEORY

The problem of optimal product variety has been approached theoretically in several ways: using geographic spatial analogies following the lead of Hotelling,[9] in an orthodox consumer utility function framework,[10] with Lancasterian characteristics preference models,[11] and using demand function and consumers' surplus methods. The model employed here is a hybrid, adapting Spence's areas-under-the-demand-function focus [29], [30] to a Loesch–Hotelling [19], [12] spatial approach. As a hybrid, it sacrifices elegance to bring into clear focus relationships one can observe and attempt to measure.

Figure 1 provides the simplest possible view. The horizontal axis represents a one-dimensional space over which a product's real or perceived characteristics might vary—e.g. in the degree of nutrient fortification, or sweetness, or crunchiness, or (with discrete rather than continuous variation) shape. Consumers' preferences for a given characteristic are described by their location in product characteristics space. If, for example, the relevant dimension is sweetness, a consumer who likes a relatively sweet product will have his or her preference located farther to the right, e.g. at point B, than a consumer (e.g. at A) preferring a less sweet product. We assume provisionally a uniform distribution and intensity of preferences over the relevant spatial segment, ignore the problem of finite segment bounds and assume income effects to be insignificantly small.[12] Adapting Spence's perspective to the Loesch–Hotelling framework, the vertical ordinate of Figure 1 for any given point in (horizontal) product characteristics space measures the integral under the inverse demand function for all consumers

[9] See Hotelling [12], Lovell [18], Meade [20], Stern [33], and Hay [11].

[10] See Usher [35], Dixit and Stiglitz [8], and Leland [17].

[11] Lancaster [14], [15], [16], and Archibald and Rosenbluth [4].

[12] Since RTE cereal purchases represent only a very small proportion of the average household's expenditures, ignoring income effects causes no appreciable problems. See Willig [36].

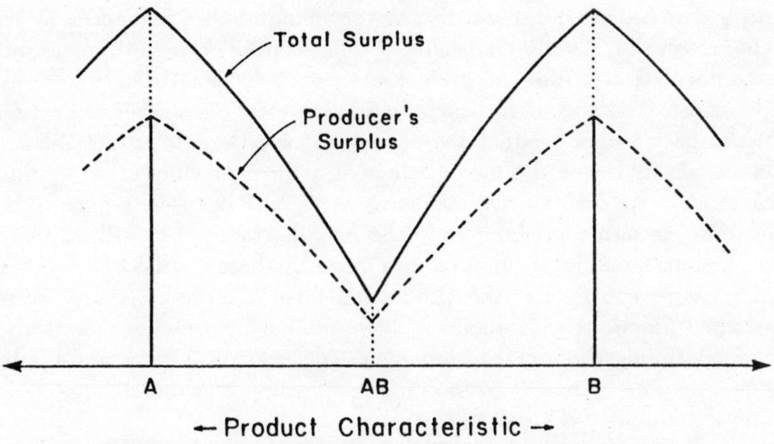

FIGURE 1. Surplus Functions in Product Characteristics Space

whose preferences (or the relevant part of whose preferences[13]) match that point, given the prices of the product(s) purchased by those consumers and also the prices of all substitute and complement products. It is convenient to net out from this value the variable costs of production and distribution. Thus, Figure 1 presents two sets of tent-like functions. The upper (solid) function shows at any abscissa point the total surplus (consumers' plus producer's) realized from sales to consumers with preferences at any given point in product characteristics space. These ordinate values, it must be emphasized, are uniquely defined only for a specific set of products and product prices. Our analysis must deal therefore only with incremental localized product availability changes.

Figure 1 assumes the supply of only two products *A* and *B*. These products have characteristics exactly matching the preferences of consumers located at points A and B in characteristics space. By assumption, however, consumer preferences are distributed uniformly over space. Those whose preferences are imperfectly satisfied by *A* or *B* must either buy *A* or *B* or spend more of their income on unrepresented (perhaps quite different) products. The loss of utility experienced by a consumer with preferences at, say, boundary point AB from having to make do with imperfect substitute *A* or *B* is analogous in a geographic spatial model to the transportation cost a consumer incurs securing output from a geographically distant plant under FOB pricing. Given downward sloping demand functions, a higher delivered price in the uniform density geographic model means that less will be consumed by distant customers than by customers located near the plant, all else equal. In the variable product characteristics case, the loss of utility from consuming less-than-ideal products leads analogously to a lower

[13] There is no reason why a single consumer cannot have multiple locations, reflecting a preference for variegated products.

quantity demanded, the more distant the demander's preferences lie from the characteristics of available products. This, combined with the assumption of a uniform distribution of preferences over characteristics space, gives rise to the tent shape of the surplus functions, whose maxima are at the points in space where product characteristics exactly match preferences.

Let us consider now the introduction of a third product *C* at a point in characteristics space intermediate between A and B, as in Figure 2. This means that consumer preferences in the neighborhood of C will be satisfied better, leading to an increase in consumption by those consumers, and hence to increases in consumers' and producer's surplus represented by the new tent-shaped functions with maxima above point C. Purchases will normally be divided among products at boundaries (i.e. AC and CB) where the total surplus functions intersect. Assuming uniformly distributed preferences, this implies an equal division of the market.

Whether or not product C will be offered depends critically upon the fixed costs of launching it—e.g. the required investment in research and

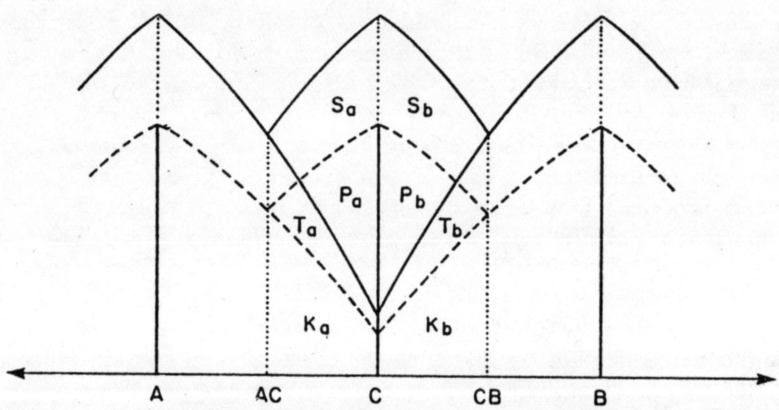

FIGURE 2. The Consequences of Product Launching

development, plant and introductory marketing—and upon market structure. To mesh these pieces of the problem, it is desirable to let the producers' and consumers' surplus functions measure discounted present values rather than single-period flows. Market structure matters then in the following sense. If the market is (at least locally) monopolized and entry at C by outsiders is blocked, the relevant surplus (or more accurately, discounted present value of quasi-rents) to the producer of *A* and *B* contemplating introducing *C* is the diamond-shaped area consisting of T_a, T_b, P_a and P_b—T_a and T_b being transfers from consumers' into producer's surplus and P_a and P_b pure producer's surplus increases. On the other hand, if entry is possible, a monopolistic competitor considering offering *C* in competition with other firms' products A and B and assuming, Cournot-like, that C is priced at the same level as the unchanged prices of A and B, perceives itself as gaining that diamond-shaped surplus *plus* K_a and K_b, which represent transfers of quasi-rents from the producers of A and B to the producer of C. Such transfers are often referred to as 'cannibalization' among business people, and we shall name them accordingly.[14] The monopolistic competitor unconcerned about whence K_a and K_b come views itself as gaining a larger surplus through new product introduction than does the monopolist. It is entirely possible that fixed launching costs exceed $T_a+T_b+P_a+P_b$ but are less than that sum plus K_a and K_b. If so, product C will be introduced by a monopolistic competitor but not by a monopolist. This is the principle underlying economists' conclusion that greater product variety will emerge under monopolistic competition than under pure monopoly.[15]

Consider now a modification in the structural assumptions. If a monopolist supplies A and B but entry into C is open, the monopolist may choose also to offer C and pre-empt entry that would otherwise cause it to lose surplus K_a and K_b. If so, as much product variety may emerge under such entry-deterring monopoly (or oligopoly) as under monopolistic competition, other things (such as price) being held equal.

It remains to be seen whether the variety of products supplied under monopolistic competition or entry-deterring monopoly is optimal. Assuming that a dollar of consumers' surplus is valued equally with a dollar of producers' surplus, a new product should be introduced if its addition to surplus net of transfers—that is, pure producers' surplus increase P_a+P_b plus consumers' surplus gains S_a+S_b—exceeds the fixed costs of introduction. That diamond-shaped area may be either larger or smaller than the wall-tent shaped surplus area guiding the decisions of monopolistic competitors or entry-deterring monopolists. As Figure 2 is drawn, the two areas are of similar magnitude, and so decisions motivated by profit maximization under actual or potential monopolistic competition will tend also to advance social welfare.

This is not necessarily so, however. Figure 3 provides a counter-example. The extent of cannibalization K_a plus K_b by product C is large relative to the net increase in social surplus S_a plus S_b. (Note that all producers' surplus gains now come as transfers from what was consumers' surplus when there were only two products.) If fixed costs are smaller than $K_a+K_b+T_a+T_b$ but larger than S_a+S_b, excessive product proliferation will occur.

Figure 3 differs from Figure 2 largely in the gentler slope of its surplus functions, which in turn, given uniform preference density over characteristics space, reflects greater substitutability of the products. When products are relatively good substitutes for one another, as in Figure 3, not much

[14] See also Scherer [25, pp. 392–4], where a distinction is drawn between new market and market-sharing innovations.

[15] See Lancaster [15], Archibald and Rosenbluth [4], and Spence [29], [30].

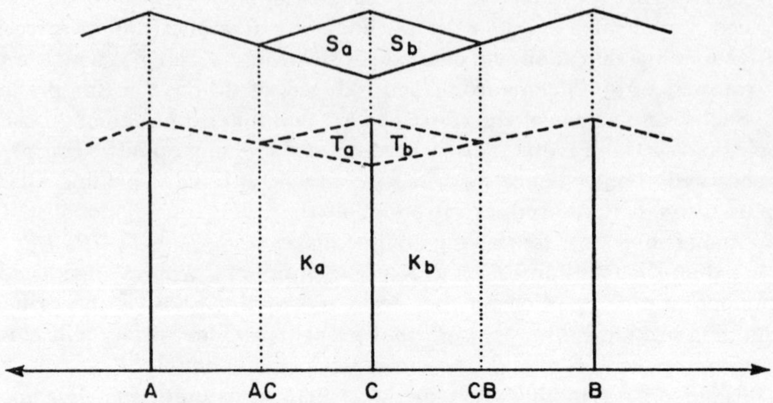

FIGURE 3. Launching of a Close-substitute Product

demand is choked off when consumers have to make do with a product that departs by some given amount from their 'ideal' characteristics. In the limiting case of perfect substitutes (reflected by horizontal surplus functions), adding a new product has no demand-expanding effect, and so there is nothing but cannibalization. Quite generally, the better substitutes existing and new products are for one another, the more likely it is that additional product launchings will add more to costs than to social benefits, all else equal.[16]

Cannibalization is also apt to be high relative to surplus gains net of transfers when the ratio of producers' to consumers' surplus is high. This in turn has two main determinants. First, as Spence has emphasized, when sellers maximize profits under the conventional assumptions of monopolistic competition, producer's surplus is higher relative to consumers' surplus with inverse demand functions that are concave downward (i.e. relatively flat-topped) than with convex functions.[17] Second, one would expect higher producers' surpluses, the more sellers respect their interdependence in pricing and co-operate toward joint profit-maximizing policies rather than viewing (as we have assumed thus far) the prices of spatially proximate products as insensitive to their own price and product launching choices.

Summing up, we have identified four potentially observable characteristics associated with a tendency toward excessive proliferation of product variants: high substitutability among the variants, modest increases in producers' surplus net of cannibalization or (assuming constant prices and unit costs) in sales volume, a high ratio of producers' to consumers' surplus, and (following from these three) extensive cannibalization. Also, fixed

[16] See also Spence [29], [30].

[17] See Spence [29],]30]. With linear demand functions and constant marginal costs, consumers' surplus is a constant one-half of producers' surplus regardless of the specific parameter values, assuming conventional monopoly profit maximization.

product launching costs must be substantial, but less than the gross producers' surplus (including cannibalization) realized by an added product variant.

Four further complications must be noted. Thus far, we have assumed that the prices of products *A* and *B* remain fixed when product *C* is introduced at the same price. A new entrant could, however, be greeted by a price war, or the new entry might be accommodated by the raising of existing product prices.[18] Assuming that pre-entry prices exceed marginal cost, uniform price increases reduce total surplus and hence shift the total surplus functions downward; uniform price decreases have the opposite effect (unless and until marginal cost is undercut). For non-uniform or discriminatory price changes, it is more difficult to state simple generalizations.

Second, our analysis has no way of determining what set of prices is globally optimal in either a first-best or second-best sense. It can only evaluate the desirability of marginal changes in the array of products. Given this limitation, the most that can be said is that if the prices of pre-existing products remain unchanged or increase in response to the introduction of a new product variant, the price effects of the introduction on non-local welfare will be either neutral or adverse incrementally. Thus, any surplus of launching costs over *local* net surplus gains will not be compensated by surplus gains attributable to second-order price effects in other regions of product characteristics space.

Third, consumer preferences may not be uniformly distributed and of uniform intensity over product characteristics space. This, we shall see, will cause empirical difficulties.

[18] For the analogous case of new plant entry into geographic space with linear point-in-space demand functions, it can readily be shown that the entry of a new plant at the boundary between two existing plants will induce an *increase* in prices if the operators of the old and new plants maximize joint profits. The proof here follows Hay [11].

Let the demand function for consumers located Z kilometers from a plant be linear, e.g.

$$q_z = a - b\,(P_0 + tZ), \tag{1}$$

where P_0 is the price FOB plant and t is the transport cost per kilometer for a unit of product. Assume that demand is uniformly dense over one-dimensional geographic space. Then for a plant shipping out to M kilometers in each direction from its location, the total quantity sold is:

$$\begin{aligned} Q &= 2\int_0^M [a - b\,(P_0 + tZ)]\,dZ \\ &= 2\,aM - 2b\,P_0M - bt\,M^2. \end{aligned} \tag{2}$$

With constant marginal cost c and fixed costs of F, the plant's profit is:

$$\pi = (P_0 - c)\,(2aM - 2b\,P_0M - bt\,M^2) - F. \tag{3}$$

If each plant has the same marginal production cost c and transportation cost t and if all co-operate to maximize joint profits, the optimal location of a new plant will be midway between existing plants, all sellers will charge the same price, and conjectural variations can be ignored. Under these assumptions, profits are maximized by setting $\partial\pi/\partial P_0 = 0$, from which one obtains the relationship:

$$P_0^* = a/2b + c/2 - tM/4. \tag{4}$$

Clearly, as entry reduces the spacing M between plant boundaries, the joint profit-maximizing price P_0^* rises.

Finally, we must relax the assumption of Figures 1–3 that product characteristics space is one-dimensional. In the more realistic multi-dimensional case, any additional product variant is apt to interact with several or many existing products, not two. This appears at first to add no important complications.[19] If the products are close substitutes, the total amount of cannibalization will be high and the net growth of producers' and consumers' surplus may be small. If they are distant substitutes and the new product fills an important unserved niche in product characteristics space, the obverse is more apt to be true. Extending this reasoning to the case of very many potential substitutes,[20] what is sacrificed when a new product's sales come in infinitesimally small increments from products scattered throughout a preponderantly competitive economy will for the most part be units of consumption at the margins where price equals marginal cost, and no appreciable surplus, consumer or producer, is foregone. If the new product yields a surplus over launching costs, welfare is undoubtedly increased. More perplexing is the situation in which product interactions occur weakly over a large number of dimensions within a world of monopolies, to use Mrs. Robinson's phrase [24, p. 307]. Then the market's invisible hand may lead new product suppliers into incurring costs to swap one surplus for another, but it will be difficult or even impossible in practice to detect that welfare has been reduced.

III. THE CEREAL INDUSTRY EVIDENCE

We turn now to the evidence, taking up in turn the costs of new RTE product launching, the extent to which sales gains were real as compared to cannibalistic, various aspects of pricing behavior, and an attempt to estimate the magnitude of added consumers' surpluses.

A. *The Costs of New Product Launching*

The earliest recognizable costs of launching a new cereal product into the market are those associated with research, development, market research, and test marketing. According to a survey of 21 new cereal products by Buzzell and Nourse [5, pp. 91–4], research and development costs in the 1959–64 period averaged $122,000, market research costs $60,000 and the excess of other marketing costs over product sale gross margins during the period of test marketing approximately $740,000. These costs, like most others, have undoubtedly risen over time with inflation. Therefore, we shall to the maximum degree possible emphasize cost and sales data centered on 1962 for purposes of comparison.

Investment outlays for the equipment needed to produce a new product

[19] We ignore here the possibility that the character of pricing interactions and the strength of entry deterrence may change with *N* neighboring products as compared to two. On this, see Schmalensee [28].

[20] For an extreme view, see Triffin [34].

vary with the degree to which existing capacity can be used with minimal rebuilding. At one extreme were products such as Total or Sugar Frosted Flakes, which merely required the addition of vitamin or sugar enrobing equipment to standard wheat or corn flakes lines.[21] At the other extreme would be a product such as Quaker's Life, whose complex shape necessitated a multi-million dollar investment in newly designed machinery. Appreciable start-up costs might also be incurred in debugging production equipment, but no evidence on their magnitude is available.

For many consumer goods, and perhaps especially for ready-to-eat cereals, expenditures on introductory advertising and other types of sales promotion (such as special displays, free samples and coupon campaigns) are a major element of new product launching costs. Although considerable variation can be observed between products, the need to attain a threshold level of awareness in national 'roll-out' campaigns imposes a rough lower bound on the level of introductory advertising outlays.[22] A study of 25 relatively successful RTE cereals introduced between 1957 and 1967 showed average advertising expenditures to have been $805,000 in the first two months of national distribution and $3·5 million over the first 14 months, after which the average rate of spending tended to stabilize temporarily at $115,000 per month.[23] Whether in calculating introductory advertising costs one should truncate at 14 months with the stabilization of monthly outlays is a difficult question. The same study showed that market shares stabilized at an average of 0·9% after two years.[24] At 1962 industry levels, this implies annual sales on the order of $4·5 million per brand and, with advertising outlays averaging $1·16 million per year in the third year, an advertising/sales ratio of 26%.[25] Since the comparable ratio for all products, old and new, was 17%, this suggests that launching costs may have continued into the third year of national sales. On this and related issues more will be said later.

We find then that average launching costs in the early 1960s were at

[21] Of course, if a new product increases company demand for the products made on such machines, as appears to have been true initially for both Total and Sugar Frosted Flakes, an investment in complete new lines may be necessary. This is not always so, however. During the late 1960s, both General Mills and Post emphasized the development of new products that could use existing excess capacity.

[22] On the threshold costs of launching new cigarette brands, see Scherer *et al.* [27, p. 249].

[23] From a 1970 Quaker Oats Co. study included in the cereal case record as CX-Q-177. For similar figures, see Buzzell and Nourse [5, p. 98].

[24] Had less successful brands been included, the average market share would have been much lower. The Quaker Oats study reports that between 1958 and 1970, 76 brands were introduced into either test market or national distribution and that only 54% of these remained on the market in 1970. Early market success had some impact on introductory advertising levels, but not a great deal. Of the 25 brands analyzed, the six most successful, with an average market share of 1·67% at the end of the third year, had initial 14 month advertising outlays of $4·4 million. The six least successful, with an average share of 0·34%, spent $3·2 million on average during their first 14 months.

[25] Applying the 0·9% market share, which is based upon poundage, directly to total 1962 industry sales, the product sales estimate is $3·7 million. An upward adjustment was made to reflect the fact that newer cereals were priced roughly 30% higher per pound than old cereals—i.e. those on the market by 1954.

least \$4·4 million per product (i.e. \$122,000 + 60,000 + 740,000 + 3·5 million) and perhaps, if new production facilities were needed and extensive promotional activity other than advertising was undertaken, a good deal more.

B. *Real Growth* vs. *Cannibalization*

The cereal antitrust case record yields mixed and even contradictory documentary and testimonial evidence on the degree to which new products contributed to genuine market growth, as distinguished from cannibalizing existing product sales and quasi-rents. In a 1966 speech to his field sales personnel, a Kellogg vice-president lamented the appearance of 'so many meaningless new products' and 'the futility and the wastefulness of having *too* much of a good thing'.[26] The same official observed three years later that 'for the past several years, our individual company growth has come out of the other fellow's hide'.[27] Analyzing the sources of anticipated patronage for its OKs product, introduced nationally in 1959, Kellogg marketing staff listed as last of five in importance 'people who are not eating any ready-to-eat cereals currently'. Brand-switching consumers of rival products Cheerios and Alpha-Bits were listed first.[28] A 1958 Post (i.e. General Foods) memorandum observed similarly that 'the pre-sweetened market is beginning to show signs of inexpansibility' and that expected rival product introductions would 'further fraction the category and make the marketing of established pre-sweets more difficult in FY 1960'.[29] A marketing analysis for a new pre-sweetened Post product introduced in the late 1960s estimated that half the product's sales came from cannibalization of an older Post brand, 30% from cannibalization of a rival Kellogg product and the rest from all other RTE cereals.[30] Similarly, a 1971 General Mills analysis found that in the highly fractionated, mature market for pre-sweetened cereals, 'much of the new product growth has come at the expense of established pre-sweets, which, as a category, have shown regular declines'.[31]

One can also find statements imputing to product innovation a favorable impact on overall market growth. There appears to be something approaching consensus that the appearance of the first nationally advertised pre-sweets and nutritional cereals during the 1950s had a genuine growth-stimulating effect. A 1954 statement of Post cereal marketing philosophy indicated that 'Both new products, specifically pre-sweetened cereals, and regular products have contributed to the industry growth'.[32] A 1965 General

[26] Speech text of C. H. Tornabene, CX-K-549Q and R (emphasis in original).

[27] CX-K-744B.

[28] CX-K-396A.

[29] CX-GF-16D.

[30] CX-GF-1425I

[31] CX-GMI-2178. Other references to extensive cannibalization include CX-GF-4B, CX-GF-18L, CX-GF-325F, CX-GF-602B, CX-GF-1302B, CX-GF-1445W, CX-GF-1410O, CX-GF-3000 Z 155, CX-K-409B, CX-K-7181J and CX-GMI-570 Z 13.

[32] CX-GF-4A. But compare p. B of the same document. See also CX-GF-3000 Z 51.

Mills memorandum said that 'In the early 1950s the advent of pre-sweetened cereals opened whole new avenues of volume and profit potential' and that 'the sales of pre-sweetened cereals have expanded the total cereals market and have not adversely affected sales of regular cereals'.[33] Discussing the forthcoming introduction of a pioneering high-nutrition cereal, a Kellogg executive predicted in 1956 that 'with Special K, the possibilities are almost unlimited for getting new users who seldom use any ready to eat cereal'.[34]

How does one reconcile these differing views, some of which are squarely inconsistent? One variable apparently influencing company perspectives was the overall state of demand. Over the two decades following World War II, the RTE industry experienced nearly continuous pound sales growth averaging 3.5% per annum. Decision-makers' attitudes were buoyant, and many attributed at least a part of their good fortune to the concurrent surge of new product introductions. However, from 1966 to 1970 the growth rate dropped virtually to zero and continuing new product activity came to be viewed more skeptically, with visibly more awareness of cannibalization. Also, a more sanguine view of new products' pure growth-inducing effect tended to be taken by the executives of General Mills, which gained market share during the 1960s, than by officials of Kellogg, which only maintained its share until the the late 1960s and General Foods, which lost ground. It seems clear too that industry analysts devoted inadequate attention to the simultaneous movement of demographic variables and as a result, their accounting of the sources of growth was often incomplete.

An attempt to take the fullest possible range of relevant variables into account was made by Richard Schmalensee in an unpublished statistical study of annual RTE cereal consumption per capita from 1953 to 1971.[35] Among the variables included in his time series were the following:

- *Q* Pound sales per capita.
- *Y* Real disposable income per capita.
- *Dem* Population weighted by an index of cereal consumption in various age groups, divided by total population.

Using the Cochrane–Orcutt transformation (with $\rho = 0{\cdot}575$) to minimize inefficiency owing to autocorrelation, he estimated the following regression, with *t*-ratios given in parentheses:

$$\text{Log } Q = -0{\cdot}02 + \underset{(4{\cdot}89)}{5{\cdot}90} \log Dem + \underset{(4{\cdot}74)}{0{\cdot}32} \log Y;\ R^2 = 0{\cdot}974,\ \text{D.W.} = 1{\cdot}64.$$

Both the income and weighted demographic variables were statistically significant. When a measure of the number of brands nationally distributed in each year was added to the regression, its *t*-ratio was only 0·42, suggesting that the increasing number of brands over time had no significant identifiable

[33] CX-GMI-111A. See also CX-GMI-262B and CX-GMI-263A.
[34] Speech text of Mard Leaver, CX-K-560C. See also CX-K-5651.
[35] I am indebted to Professor Schmalensee for providing these materials.

effect on consumption. Also insignificant was a variable measuring the proportion of working wives. Because the data were insufficient to estimate a properly identified simultaneous equation system and also because of multicollinearity, relative price indices had implausible positive signs and were therefore excluded.

The coefficients in Schmalensee's regression can be interpreted as elasticities, and the high value of the *Dem* coefficient is puzzling. Schmalensee's *a priori* hypothesis was that its value should be near unity. One apparent reason for the unexpectedly high value was that the income and demographic variables were strongly collinear up to 1965, after which per capita income continued to grow while the growth of cereal consumption and the demographic variable slackened—the latter because children are particularly heavy RTE cereal eaters and the cohort of children 12 years old and under fell in size from 1965 to 1970. The demographic variable was therefore forced to bear the burden of explaining the post-1965 stagnation of consumption growth, taking on an implausibly large coefficient value as a consequence.

A simpler but in some ways more revealing picture of these developments by five-year intervals is provided by Table I. The first numerical column

TABLE I

GROWTH TRENDS IN US RTE CEREAL CONSUMPTION AND POPULATION, 1950–70[a]

Year	*RTE cereal consumption* (000 *lb*)	% *growth, five years*	*Population* (000)	% *growth, five years*	*Weighted population*	% *growth, five years*
1950	609,800	—	150,697	—	147,896	—
1955	783,067	28·4	165,248	9·7	165,269	11·8
1960	940,584	20·1	180,670	9·3	181,456	9·8
1965	1,177,546	25·2	194,593	7·7	197,343	8·8
1970	1,183,100	0·5	204,879	5·3	204,779	3·8

[a] *Sources*: Cereal consumption, CX-101E. Population, US Bureau of the Census, *Current Population Reports*, Series P-25, Nos. 470 and 519; and *Statistical Abstract of the United States*: 1957.

shows pounds of RTE cereal sold through grocery stores and the second column gives five-year growth rates. There follow two sets of demographic indices, one using a simple population count and the other a population index with age groups weighted by relative intensity of consumption.[36] The rapid growth of cereal consumption, the stagnation of the late 1960s and (in the weighted population index) the waning of the post-World War II baby boom are all evident. What stands out is that in every five-year period but the last, the rate of cereal consumption growth is more than double the growth rate of the weighted population variable. This would

[36] With 1·000 being the average for all consumers, the weights by age group are: 12 years and under, 1·417; 13–19, 1·023; 20–44, 0·699; and 45 and older, 0·973. The source is CX-GF-3000K.

appear to indicate that something more than mere demographic change—conceivably, the proliferation of pre-sweetened and nutritional cereal variants—stimulated consumption growth.

This is still not the full story, however. Consumers evidently choose RTE servings more on the basis of bulk—e.g. filling a standard 23 in^3 cereal bowl—than on the basis of weight.[37] Pre-sweetening raises product weight without necessarily affecting bulk. Census data show that sugar use by the cereal industry increased from 67·8 million pounds in 1954 to 420 million pounds in 1972. RTE cereal output meanwhile grew by 613 million pounds. Thus, roughly 57·5% of the cereal output increase consisted of sugar. Assuming that consumers would otherwise have dipped commensurately into their sugar bowls in the absence of pre-sweetening,[38] this part of the industry's recorded output growth is merely a transfer akin to vertical integration and not real growth. Applying the 57·5% transfer factor to the Table I data for 1955–70 (the period corresponding most closely to that for which Census data are available), one finds that total non-sugar growth of RTE consumption was 21·7%. This compares closely with the 23·9% growth of weighted population, suggesting that most if not all of the industry's non-sugar growth corresponded to demographic changes. Although other variables such as increasing real incomes, a rise in the proportion of working wives, a general trend toward consumption of convenience foods, the appearance of other new convenience breakfast foods, and relatively rapidly rising RTE cereal prices were at work, this plus Schmalensee's regressions suggest rather strongly that one cannot attribute much real growth of RTE cereal consumption to the proliferation of new product varieties. It follows that new products must have cannibalized the actual and potential sales and surpluses of older products extensively.

C. *Profits and Prices*

If new products cannibalized producers' surpluses from existing products while adding to fixed costs, all else equal, one might expect to observe a decline in industry profitability. No such decline is evident. If anything, the trend was toward rising accounting returns on assets during the 1960s.[39] The cereal makers avoided a decline in returns by effecting general price increases and by seeking on new products relatively high gross margins. As a 1962 General Foods marketing plan observed, the newer products

[37] See CX-GMI-279D and testimony at TR 14,454 and 17,445.

[38] The assumption is debatable. Many pre-sweetened cereals consist of 40% or more by weight of sucrose—the equivalent of adding two and a half heaping teaspoons of sugar to an average 1·4 oz serving of unsweetened puffs or flakes. To the extent that consumers would not consciously have added as much sugar, the problem of unknowing overdose raises doubts about the premise accepted here that consumers know what they are getting. On this, see CX-GF-4039 Z 7.

[39] CX-701 C-P.

carried higher profit margins to make their introduction affordable.[40] Between 1952 and 1970, the average wholesale price per pound of RTE cereals sold through grocery stores rose by 81% while the general wholesale price index for finished consumer food products rose by 20·4%.[41]

An example of the premium pricing strategy adopted for new products can be seen in Kellogg's Sugar Frosted Flakes, the best-selling pre-sweet in 1970. The product is obtained by applying a sugar frosting to the venerable corn flake. Following an increase in the price of corn flakes effective July 25th, 1970, the wholesale list price of Kellogg's Corn Flakes in an 18 oz package was 34·44 cents/lb while the price of Sugar Frosted Flakes in a 20 oz package was 44·67 cents/lb. The main physical difference between the two is that the sucrose content of the Corn Flakes is approximately 7·8%, while it is 29·0% for Sugar Frosted Flakes.[42] To make a pound of Sugar Frosted Flakes, one in effect adds 0·23 lb of sugar to 0·77 lb of Corn Flakes. In mid-1970, 0·23 lb of refined cane sugar could be purchased on the spot market for 2·55 cents. Thus, using 2·55 cents worth of sugar to convert Corn Flakes into Sugar Frosted Flakes yielded additional revenue of 18.15 cents.[43] The variation of product characteristics accompanied by heavy advertising (in this case, emphasizing brand 'spokesman' Tony the Tiger) made it possible to segregate markets and practice price discrimination.[44]

It is also possible, though less clearly supported, that prices on older products were raised more rapidly than corresponding increases in their cost. This is the reaction one would expect from joint profit-maximizing sellers in geographic space when new plant entrants pack the relevant space more densely.[45] Although it is uncertain whether the analogy can be extended to the case of more dense product characteristics space packing, it is clear that the cereal companies exhibited considerable concern about achieving a structure of old and new product prices that maximized collective profits.[46]

Pricing in the cereal industry was definitely more complex than our initial theoretical exposition supposed. Nevertheless, three inferences appear warranted. The average level of prices rose in real terms as a consequence of new product introductions. With uniform demand, this should have

[40] CX-GF-17E. See also page L of the same document, noting that General Foods set a gross margin target of 16 cents per lb for older *exclusive* products and 21 cents/lb on new products. The average wholesale price per pound of all General RTE cereals at the time was 32 cents/lb.

[41] Cereal sales and quantity data are from CX-101 E and F; wholesale price index data are from the *Economic Report of the President*.

[42] From measurements by Dr. Ira L. Shannon, Veterans Administration Hospital, Houston, reported in 'Sugars in Breakfast Cereals', *Chicago Tribune*, October 30th, 1977, Sec. 1, p. 4.

[43] i.e. $44{\cdot}67 - 0{\cdot}77 \times 34{\cdot}44 = 18{\cdot}15$. According to the 1972 *Census of Manufactures*, Vol. II, p. 20D-8, materials costs averaged 38% of sales for the cereals industry as a whole in 1970.

[44] See also Adams and Yellen [2], [3].

[45] See note 18 *supra*.

[46] On this facet of the cereal makers' conduct, see the author's testimony at TR 27,819–20, 27,828–29, 27,915–18 and 28,495–504.

shifted total surplus functions downward on average, all else equal. But there was also a probable increase in the dispersion of prices. Since some products (such as corn flakes, which experienced competitive pressure from private labellers) remained available at relatively low prices, it is conceivable, although by no means certain, that demands of low reservation price consumers continued to be satisfied.[47] If dead-weight welfare losses were attenuated as a result, the downward shift of total surplus functions could have been mitigated. Finally, for reasons considered in section II and also as a consequence of price discrimination, it seems likely that for any given set of total surplus functions, the ratio of producers' to consumers' surplus rose relative to what it would have been under a regime of constant and uniform prices. Substantial redistributions from consumers' to producers' surplus must have occurred. And the relatively high gross margins secured by the cereal oligopolists must have stimulated product proliferation beyond what it would have been had there been more competitive pressure on prices.[48]

D. *Consumers' Surplus Increments*

To advance farther, we must accept assumptions that cannot be conclusively supported by the available evidence. Opting to err on the side of overstating benefits, let us assume that total surplus curves were not shifted downward at all on the average as a result of the price increases attending product proliferation. Consistent with the evidence that cannibalization was extensive (and hence that spatially proximate differentiated products were fairly close substitutes) and with the related demographic evidence that product proliferation did not significantly increase physical consumption, we assume that producers' surplus gains were transfers from what otherwise would have been consumers' surplus. In other words, the situation is better described by Figure 3, with non-cannibalized producers' surplus gains T_a and T_b reflecting transfers from pre-existing consumers' surplus, than by Figure 2, in which producers' surplus gains P_a and P_b come from the growth of consumption without offsetting *old* consumers' surplus reductions. To the extent that these assumptions are valid, the increases in welfare net of transfers before launching costs are deducted must be associated solely with the consumers' surplus increments S_a and S_b.

These are not measurable in terms of the analysis presented thus far. However, they have an exact counterpart in the consumers' surplus areas under what might be called the *ceteris paribus* demand function—that is, an inverse demand curve drawn under the assumption that all other products but the one in question continue to be available, so that what is measured is the consumers' surplus gain from having the additional

[47] Cf. Scherer [26, pp. 254, 258, 340] and Adams and Yellen [2], [3].
[48] Compare Schmalensee [28].

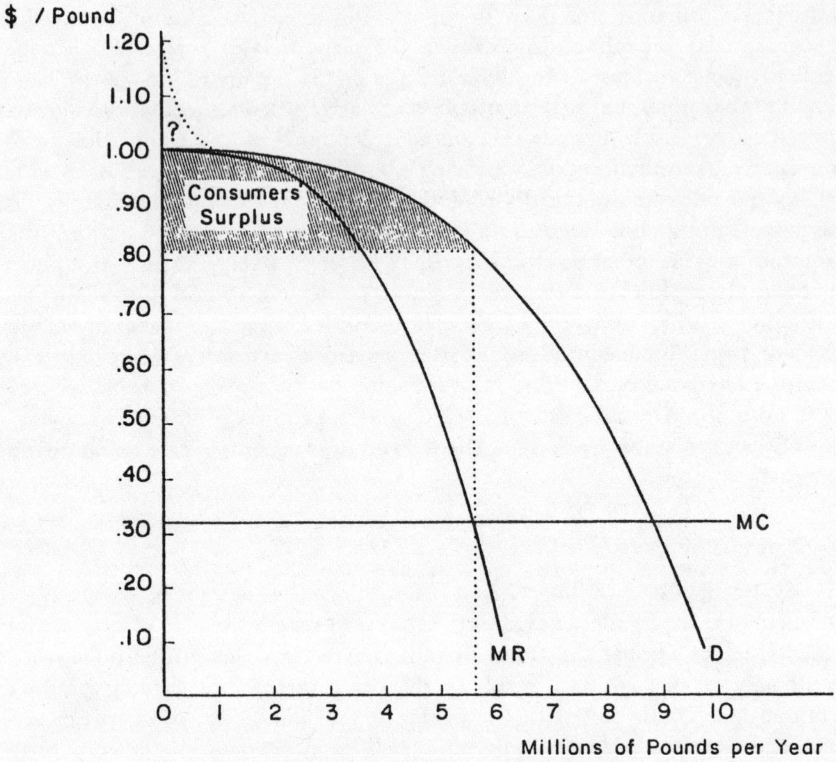

FIGURE 4. Demand Function for an Additional Product

product.[49] There is reason to believe that these demand functions, at least for most of the newer cereal products, tend to be concave downward, as illustrated in Figure 4.[50] The absence of a steep slope at low quantities is suggested *inter alia* by evidence that consumers do not exhibit much brand loyalty. Thus, a Kellogg memorandum addressed to the Federal Trade Commission observed that 'the fickleness of consumers toward RTE cereals means that manufacturers must continually remind consumers of their products or run the risk of being forgotten when the buying decision is

[49] Compare Spence [29, p. 219]. This approach accepts *inter alia* the assumption of well-defined independent consumer preferences. At least for children's cereals, the assumption is arguable. Thus, a General Foods task force concluded that children's advertising should among other things stress 'helping join the crowd' (CX-GF-4039Z97). This implies contrived interdependence of preferences, violating a basic assumption of traditional consumer choice theory.

[50] The demand function in Figure 4 satisfies the equation $P = 1 - 0{\cdot}001\ Q^3$, where Q is denoted in millions of pounds per year. With the assumed marginal cost of 32 cents/lb, the profit-maximizing price–cost relationships appear representative of 1970 experience for relatively new RTE products.

made'.[51] Similarly, an internal General Foods planning memorandum characterized the cereal business in 1966 as exhibiting a 'multiplicity of brands and categories with little, if any, brand loyalty'.[52] On the other hand, there may be a few consumers with intense loyalty to particular new products. Their existence would give rise to the convex-downward demand curve extension above the question mark in Figure 4.[53]

Insight into the function's curvature in the vicinity of prevailing prices is provided by the testimony of cereal company executives and internal decision making memoranda. For products that are similar to one another, but less close substitutes than, say, Kellogg's Corn Flakes and Post Toasties, retail shelf prices can apparently diverge by 'a few cents a pack' without having much impact on volume.[54] But wider differentials were said in 1967 to become a potentially 'significant factor in people switching', or move products into 'the trouble area', or even, in the case of low-volume products, 'greatly weaken our efforts' to keep them in business.[55] Cereal makers generally chose not to maintain differentials wider than 4 cents per pack on similar products, which means that they must have considered their demand functions to become quite elastic at prices exceeding those of the nearest substitutes by more than that magnitude.

In view of this, we estimate that the *average* consumer surplus on a typical 11 oz package was 7 cents in 1970. This overstates the surplus for marginal consumers and understates it for especially loyal and/or price insensitive infra-marginal consumers. The implied consumers' surplus per pound is 10·2 cents, or 20% of average 1970 wholesale sales revenue per pound.[56]

We seek to compare such consumers' surpluses on new brands, representing the social gain net of transfers, with the average launching cost of a brand, estimated conservatively at $4·4 million for 1962. We assume that the ratio of incremental consumers' surplus to wholesale sales is 0·2. If manufacturer sales volume associated with a percentage point of market share in year t is $V(t)$, the market share achieved in year t is $M(t)$, and the discount rate is r, we want to know whether the estimated discounted pre-

[51] CX-K-1090Z21.

[52] CX-GF-48576.

[53] The 13-year-old son of a referee for this paper is apparently one such exception. Ignoring such exceptions leads to mismeasurement, but the error is probably offset by the neglect of surplus-decreasing price effects and the fixed investment necessitated by new product launchings.

[54] Testimony of Kellogg executive R. F. Nicholls at TR 12,547 and 12,613.

[55] See the testimony of General Mills executive Robert Bodeau at TR 16,609 along with CX-GM-278 and CX-GM-280. See also General Foods new product pricing analyses CX-GF-137M and CX-GF-1412J.

[56] Note that this surplus rate is fairly high in comparison to the four leading cereal producers' before-tax profit return on sales, which was approximately 15% in 1964. See National Commission on Food Marketing [21, p. 206]. The rate is low compared to gross margins (averaging about 50%) and the price minus variable manufacturing cost margin (averaging about 62%).

sent value of consumers' surplus increments:[57]

$$(1) \qquad S \equiv \sum_{t=0}^{H} \frac{(0{\cdot}2)\ M(t)\ V(t)}{(1+r)^t} \geqslant \$4{\cdot}4 \text{ million.}$$

Market share data for products introduced between 1958 and 1970 were available through 1975 at best, and there are gaps in many of the series.[58] Internal gaps were filled by linear interpolation. When the available data covered fewer than 20 years of product life, market shares were estimated through year 20 by linear extrapolation and a remainder term for years 21 to infinity was computed, assuming conservatively a continuation of year 20's observed or estimated share.[59] A discount rate of 0·09 was used, reflecting the average of values employed by Kellogg and Quaker in investment decisions.[60] This may well exceed the economy-wide return on investment, but it is below the marginal rate confronting a typical consumer buying on installment credit. Because the launching cost estimate is centered on 1962, the product sales data must be benchmarked accordingly, even though new products were introduced more or less continuously between 1958 and 1970, with inflation of both launching costs and sales figures occurring as time passed. This was taken into account by making two alternative sales per market share point assumptions: a $1·0 million value associated with 1962 sales levels and a $1·46 million value associated with 1967 sales.[61]

Inequality (1) was estimated for all new RTE cereals introduced between 1958 and 1970 experiencing any appreciable success on the market. Taking 1962 sales as the benchmark, 17 brands satisfy the inequality—that is, they yielded estimated net consumers' surplus in excess of estimated average launching costs.[62] With 1967 sales as the benchmark, the list is expanded to 22 brands.[63] The other 29 brands known to have been launched nationally clearly fail the test, having cost more to launch than they added to consu-

[57] Note that launching costs are not incurred precisely at time $t=0$. Of the estimated $4·4 million, $922,000 is incurred over several years prior to $t=0$ and the remainder in the 14 months following $t=0$. Any error introduced by centering the cost estimate on $t=0$ is undoubtedly small. First year sales were discounted at midyear, i.e. with $t=0{\cdot}5$, with annual incrementing from that value for subsequent years.

[58] CX-434.

[59] Many products were withdrawn from the market before year 20, in which case market shares subsequent to withdrawal were uniformly zero.

[60] See CX-Q-188B and CX-K-9020B.

[61] Since the market share data are denominated in pounds, the sales figures have been inflated by 23% relative to total industry values to reflect the higher average price per pound of newer cereals. Taking sales benchmarks for years later than 1967 would not materially change the results because all the brands at the margin of satisfying inequality (1) had rapidly declining market shares over time, and all but one were introduced by 1963.

[62] They are Cocoa Crispies, Product 19, Bran Buds, Froot Loops, Apple Jacks, Cocoa Puffs, Frosty Os, Lucky Charms, Total, Post Oat Flakes (including Fortified Oat Flakes), Crispy Critters, Honeycombs, Alpha Bits, Life, Quisp/Quake (launched jointly), regular Captain Crunch and Corn Chex.

[63] The five are OKs, All Stars, Twinkles, Country Corn Flakes and Team. Although the data for brands achieving relatively small market shares are less complete, increasing the value of a market share point by as much as 50% would appear to add at most only a very few brands to the list of new products satisfying the inequality.

mers' surplus. And although launching costs were presumably much lower, a similarly adverse verdict must be rendered for at least 25 new products whose introduction was terminated after test marketing but before nationwide distribution commenced. Thus, the analysis of consumers' surplus increments suggests that product proliferation was carried well beyond the point at which marginal social benefits equalled launching costs.

Among the numerous doubts one might raise concerning these calculations, only one will be added here. The 'fixed' launching cost estimate is quite conservative in excluding plant investment and start-up costs and in terminating the accumulation of introductory advertising outlays at 14 months. Sustaining advertising costs—i.e. those incurred indefinitely after the product is launched—pose peculiarly difficult welfare accounting problems. If a potential new product were not introduced, sustaining advertising costs would not be incurred. Neither would the product's production and physical distribution costs. But given the apparently high degree of cannibalization, production costs avoided if a new product is not introduced will be offset by additional costs of turning out more of the old products. That the same offsetting will occur with respect to advertising costs is much less certain. There are threshold effects in sustaining as well as introductory advertising,[64] and it seems reasonable to assume that with fewer products, lower total advertising outlays would be required to have each product reach its threshold level of effectiveness. Also, many of the advertising messages concerning spatially adjacent products are mutually cancelling, conferring a net benefit on neither producers nor consumers. In view of the generally high advertising/sales ratios prevailing in the cereal industry, incremental increases in sustaining advertising and/or mutual cancellation of claims owing to brand proliferation entail costs whose present value could be large relative to the value of initial product launching costs. To the extent that this is true, substantially larger values of S in inequality (1) may have been needed to offset the total social costs of product proliferation.

E. *Conclusion*

In drawing conclusions at the end of such an analysis, one recognizes it is not only the cereal industry's products that can be flaky. It seems undeniable that some ready-to-eat product innovations have yielded net consumers' plus producers' surpluses well in excess of launching costs. But equally clearly, conditions in the industry exhibit several hallmarks of the scenario in which the supply of product variety is overstimulated: high substitutability, extensive cannibalization, concave-downward inverse demand functions, ample producers' surplus margins (plus the monopoly power to sustain them), and substantial product launching costs. In view of these

[64] See Comanor and Wilson [7, pp. 49–53], Lambin [13, pp. 94–8, 127–9], Ackoff and Emshoff [1] and Scherer *et al.* [27, pp. 249–50].

qualitative features and the crude quantitative findings, it appears probable that product proliferation has, at least at the margin, cost more than it was worth.

NORTHWESTERN UNIVERSITY ACCEPTED NOVEMBER 1978

REFERENCES

[1] Ackoff, Russell L. and Emshoff, James R., 'Advertising Research at Anheuser-Busch, Inc. (1963–68)', *Sloan Management Review* (Winter 1975), pp. 1–15.

[2] Adams, W. J. and Yellen, Janet L., 'Commodity Bundling and the Burden of Monopoly', *Quarterly Journal of Economics* (August 1976), pp. 475–98.

[3] —— 'What Makes Advertising Profitable?', *Economic Journal* (September 1977), pp. 427–49.

[4] Archibald, G. C. and Rosenbluth, Gideon, 'The "New" Theory of Consumer Demand and Monopolistic Competition', *Quarterly Journal of Economics* (November 1975), pp. 569–90.

[5] Buzzell, Robert D. and Nourse, R. E., *Product Innovation, the Product Life Cycle and Competitive Behavior in Selected Food Processing Industries, 1947–64* (Arthur D. Little, Inc., Cambridge, 1966).

[6] Chamberlin, Edward H., *The Theory of Monopolistic Competition* (Harvard University Press, Cambridge, 1933).

[7] Comanor, William S. and Wilson, Thomas A., *Advertising and Market Power* (Harvard University Press, Cambridge, 1974).

[8] Dixit, Avinash K. and Stiglitz, Joseph E., 'Monopolistic Competition and Optimum Product Diversity', *American Economic Review* (June 1977), pp. 297–308.

[9] Douglas, George W. and Miller, James C., III, *Economic Regulation of Domestic Air Transport* (Brookings, Washington, 1974).

[10] Greenhut, Melvin L., *A Theory of the Firm in Economic Space* (Appleton-Century-Crofts, New York, 1970).

[11] Hay, D. A., 'Sequential Entry and Entry-deterring Strategies in Spatial Competition', *Oxford Economic Papers* (July 1976), pp. 240–57.

[12] Hotelling, Harold, 'Stability in Competition', *Economic Journal* (March 1929), pp. 41–57.

[13] Lambin, Jean-Jacques, *Advertising, Competition and Market Conduct in Oligopoly over Time* (North-Holland, Amsterdam, 1976).

[14] Lancaster, Kelvin, 'A New Approach to Consumer Theory', *Journal of Political Economy* (April 1966), pp. 132–57.

[15] —— 'Socially Optimal Product Differentiation', *American Economic Review* (September 1975), pp. 567–85.

[16] —— 'Monopolistic Competition as a Perfect Market Structure', processed (October 1977).

[17] Leland, Hayne E., 'Quality Choice and Competition', *American Economic Review* (March 1977), pp. 127–37.

[18] Lovell, Michael C., 'Product Differentiation and Market Structure', *Western Economic Journal* (June 1970), pp. 120–43.

[19] Loesch, August, *The Economics of Location*, 2nd edn, trans. W. H. Woglom (Yale University Press, New Haven, 1956).

[20] Meade, J. E., 'The Optimal Balance between Economies of Scale and Variety of Products', *Economica* (November 1974), pp. 359–67.

[21] National Commission on Food Marketing, *Studies of Organization and Competition in Grocery Manufacturing*, Technical Study No. 6 (Washington, June 1966).

[22] NOLL, ROGER G., PECK, M. J. and McGOWAN, J. J., *Economic Aspects of Television Regulation* (Brookings, Washington, 1973).

[23] ORNSTEIN, STANLEY I., *Industrial Concentration and Advertising Intensity* (American Enterprise Institute, Washington, 1977).

[24] ROBINSON, JOAN, *The Economics of Imperfect Competition* (Macmillan, London, 1934).

[25] SCHERER, F. M., 'Research and Development Resource Allocation under Rivalry', *Quarterly Journal of Economics* (August 1967), pp. 359–94.

[26] —— *Industrial Market Structure and Economic Performance* (Rand McNally, Chicago, 1970).

[27] SCHERER, F. M., BECKENSTEIN, ALAN, KAUFER, ERICH and MURPHY, R. D., *The Economics of Multi-plant Operation: An International Comparisons Study* (Harvard University Press, Cambridge, 1975).

[28] SCHMALENSEE, RICHARD, 'Entry Deterrence in the Ready-to-Eat Breakfast Cereal Industry', *Bell Journal of Economics* (Autumn 1978), pp. 305–327.

[29] SPENCE, MICHAEL, 'Product Selection, Fixed Costs and Monopolistic Competition', *Review of Economic Studies* (June 1976), pp. 217–35.

]30] —— 'Product Differentiation and Welfare', *American Economic Review* (May 1976), pp. 407–14.

[31] SPENCE, MICHAEL and OWEN, BRUCE, 'Television Programming, Monopolistic Competition and Welfare', *Quarterly Journal of Economics* (February 1977), pp. 103–26.

[32] STEINER, PETER O., 'Program Patterns and Preferences and the Workability of Competition in Radio Broadcasting', *Quarterly Journal of Economics* (May 1952), pp. 194–223.

[33] STERN, NICHOLAS, 'The Optimal Size of Market Areas', *Journal of Economic Theory* (April 1972), pp. 154–73.

[34] TRIFFIN, ROBERT, *Monopolistic Competition and General Equilibrium Theory* (Harvard University Press, Cambridge, 1960).

[35] USHER, DAN, 'The Welfare Economics of Invention', *Economica* (August 1964), pp. 279–87.

[36] WILLIG, ROBERT D., 'Consumer's Surplus without Apology', *American Economic Review* (September 1976), pp. 589–97.

Part VII
Humour

[34]

Richard Zeckhauser (1988), 'Puzzle 2: Cheaper by the Half-Dozen', *Journal of Economic Perspectives*, 2 (4), Fall, 182 and 185.

Puzzle 2: Cheaper by the Half-Dozen

Richard Zeckhauser (Harvard-JFK School) tells of a puzzle from dining in *The Ocean Club* restaurant (located in the Charles Hotel, Cambridge, MA). This restaurant offers half-portions of the main course entrees for less than half the price of the full portion. When Richard and his companions used this option, they discovered that the half-portions were at least half the size of the full portions and more than that, they came with full portions of the accompanying vegetables. As economists, they debated possible explanations. Could it be that the restaurant wanted to encourage people to try more than one dish? If diners most clearly remembered their favorite dish, then this incentive to sample would increase the chance that someone would find a "winner" and this would lead to great word of mouth advertising. Or did this half portion ordering reduce the variance in the distribution of orders so that there would be less spoilage and hence lower costs? To settle the dispute, the maître d' was called over. What was his explanation? Hint: No one at the table guessed correctly.

Answer to Puzzle 2

The maître d' listened patiently to all the alternatives and rejected each one. The true reason, he explained was that this was an *irrational* thing to do. People noticed this discrepancy quite regularly and told their friends about this inconsistency on the menu. As a result, this generated tremendous word of mouth publicity for the restaurant at very little cost. This puzzle is simply one more feather in their cap. In the spirit of Sherlock Holmes, when all explanations appear to fail, the explanation must be that there is no explanation.

Joseph Quinn (1989), 'Comment on Puzzles from Fall 1988', *Journal of Economic Perspectives*, 3 (3), Summer, 173–4.

Comment on Puzzles from Fall 1988

Puzzle 2: Cheaper By the Half Dozen. Finally, we have our latest entry in the "markets are efficient after all" column. This puzzle reported on the Ocean Club restaurant that offered half-portions for less than half price. The proffered explanation was that this seeming irrationality made for good word of mouth (and *JEP*) publicity. Perhaps there was too much of a good thing. Joseph Quinn (Boston College) writes: "You will not be surprised, and perhaps even pleased, to know that the Ocean Club went belly up during the summer, and they closed both of their locations. We all know that coincidence does not imply causation, but there may be a story here nonetheless. The Ocean Club may have been one of those establishments that lost money on every transaction, but made up for it on volume."

Name Index

The International Library of Critical Writings in Economics

1. Multinational Corporations
   Mark Casson
2. The Economics of Innovation
   Christopher Freeman
3. Entrepreneurship
   Mark Casson
4. International Investment
   Peter J. Buckley
5. Game Theory in Economics
   Ariel Rubinstein
6. The History of Economic Thought
   Mark Blaug
7. Monetary Theory
   Thomas Mayer
8. Joint Production of Commodities
   Neri Salvadori and Ian Steedman
9. Industrial Organization
   Oliver E. Williamson
10. Growth Theory (Volumes I, II and III)
   R. Becker and E. Burmeister
11. Microeconomics: Theoretical and Applied (Volumes I, II and III)
   Robert E. Kuenne
12. The Economics of Health (Volumes I and II)
   A.J. Culyer
13. Recent Developments in Macroeconomics (Volumes I, II and III)
   Edmund S. Phelps
14. Urban and Regional Economics
   Paul C. Cheshire and Alan W. Evans
15. Modern Public Finance (Volumes I and II)
   A.B. Atkinson
16. Exchange Rate Economics (Volumes I and II)
   Ronald MacDonald and Mark P. Taylor

17. The Economic Value of Education: Studies in the Economics of Education
Mark Blaug

18. Development Economics (Volumes I, II, III and IV)
Deepak Lal

19. The New Classical Macroeconomics (Volumes I, II and III)
Kevin D. Hoover

20. The Economics of the Environment
Wallace E. Oates

21. Post Keynesian Theory of Growth and Distribution
Carlo Panico and Neri Salvadori

22. Dynamic Labor Demand and Adjustment Costs
Giorgio Galeazzi and Daniel S. Hamermesh

23. The Philosophy and Methodology of Economics (Volumes I, II and III)
Bruce J. Caldwell

24. Public Choice Theory (Volumes I, II and III)
Charles K. Rowley

25. Evolutionary Economics
Ulrich Witt

26. Economics and Psychology
Shlomo Maital and Sharone L. Maital

27. Social Choice Theory (Volumes I, II and III)
Charles K. Rowley

28. Non-Linear Dynamics in Economic Theory
Marc Jarsulic

29. Recent Developments in Experimental Economics (Volumes I and II)
John D. Hey and Graham Loomes

30. Monopoly and Competition Policy (Volumes I and II)
F.M. Scherer

31. The Economics of Technical Change
Edwin Mansfield and Elizabeth Mansfield

32. The Economics of Exhaustible Resources
Geoffrey Heal

33. The Economics of Institutions
Geoffrey M. Hodgson

34. The Economics of Transport (Volumes I and II)
Herbert Mohring

35. Implicit Contract Theory
Sherwin Rosen

36. Foundations of Analytical Marxism (Volumes I and II)
John E. Roemer

37. The Economics of Product Differentiation (Volumes I and II)
Jacques-François Thisse and George Norman

38. Economic Growth in Theory and Practice: A Kaldorian Perspective
John E. King

39. Markets and Socialism
Alec Nove and Ian D. Thatcher

40. Recent Developments in the Economics of Education
Elchanan Cohn and Geraint Johnes

41. The Theory of Inflation
Michael Parkin

42. The Economics of Location (Volumes I, II and III)
Melvin L. Greenhut and George Norman

43. Financial Intermediaries
Mervyn K. Lewis

44. The Political Economy of Privatization and Deregulation
Elizabeth E. Bailey and Janet Rothenberg Pack

45. Gender and Economics
Jane Humphries

46. Macroeconomics and Imperfect Competition
Jean-Pascal Bénassy

47. Labor Economics (Volumes I, II, III and IV)
Orley C. Ashenfelter and Kevin F. Hallock

48. The Economics of Altruism
Stefano Zamagni

49. The Economic Analysis of Rent Seeking
Robert D. Tollison and Roger D. Congleton

50. Economics and Biology
Geoffrey M. Hodgson

51. The Economics of Ageing
John Creedy

52. Fiscal and Monetary Policy (Volumes I and II)
Thomas Mayer and Steven M. Sheffrin

53. The Economics of Information (Volumes I and II)
David K. Levine and Steven A. Lippman

54. Transaction Cost Economics (Volumes I and II)
Oliver E. Williamson and Scott E. Masten

55. Agricultural Economics
George H. Peters

56. International Debt (Volumes I and II)
Graham Bird and P. Nicholas Snowden

57. Economics and Discrimination (Volumes I and II)
William A. Darity, Jr

58. Business Cycle Theory
Finn E. Kydland

59. International Trade (Volumes I and II)
J. Peter Neary

60. The Money Supply in the Economic Process
Marco Musella and Carlo Panico

61. Small Firms and Economic Growth (Volumes I and II)
Zoltan J. Acs

62. Producer Cooperatives and Labor-Managed Systems (Volumes I and II)
David L. Prychitko and Jaroslav Vanek

63. Ethics and Economics (Volumes I and II)
Alan P. Hamlin

64. The Economics of the Family
Nancy Folbre

65. The Economics of Training (Volumes I and II)
Orley C. Ashenfelter and Robert J. LaLonde

66. Chaos Theory in Economics: Methods, Models and Evidence
W. Davis Dechert

67. General Equilibrium Theory (Volumes I, II and III)
Gérard Debreu

68. Economic Growth: Theory and Evidence (Volumes I and II)
Gene M. Grossman

69. Long Wave Theory
Christopher Freeman

70. The Economics of Communication and Information
Donald M. Lamberton

71. The Foundations of Public Finance (Volumes I and II)
Peter Jackson

72. The Theory of the Firm
Mark Casson

73. The Economics of Uncertainty (Volumes I and II)
John D. Hey

74. The Economics of Global Warming
Tom Tietenberg

75. The Development of Ecological Economics
Robert Costanza, Charles Perrings and Cutler Cleveland

76. Economic Growth in the Long Run: A History of Empirical Evidence (Volumes I, II and III)
Bart van Ark

77. The Economics of Productivity (Volumes I and II)
Edward N. Wolff

78. The Economics of Population: Key Modern Writings (Volumes I and II)
Julian L. Simon

79. Political Business Cycles
Bruno S. Frey

80. Cultural Economics: The Arts, the Heritage and the Media Industries (Volumes I and II)
Ruth Towse

81. Law and Economics (Volumes I, II and III)
Richard A. Posner and Francesco Parisi

82. Independent Central Banks and Economic Performance
Sylvester Eijffinger

83. Culture, Social Norms and Economics (Volumes I and II)
Mark Casson

84. Industrial Policy and Competitive Advantage (Volumes I, II and III)
David B. Audretsch

85. The Economics of Housing (Volumes I and II)
John M. Quigley

86. Economic Demography (Volumes I and II)
T. Paul Schultz

87. Trade and the Environment: Economic, Legal and Policy Perspectives
Alan M. Rugman and John J. Kirton with Julie A. Soloway

88. The Economics of Fiscal Federalism and Local Finance
Wallace E. Oates

89. Price Theory and its Applications
Bernard Saffran and F.M. Scherer

90. Women in the Labor Market (Volumes I and II)
Marianne A. Ferber

91. Market Process Theories (Volumes I and II)
Peter Boettke and David Prychitko

Future titles will include:

Mathematical Economics
Graciela Chichilnisky

Input-Output Analysis
Heinz Kurz, Erik Dietzenbacher and Christian Lager

The Economics of Unemployment
P.N. Junankar

The Economics of Energy
Paul Stevens

The Economics of Science and Innovation
Paula E. Stephan and David B. Audretsch

International Finance
Robert Z. Aliber

Welfare Economics
William J. Baumol and Janusz A. Ordover

The Economics of Inequality and Poverty
A.B. Atkinson

The Economics of Crime
Isaac Ehrlich

The Economics of Integration
Willem Molle

The Rhetoric of Economics
Deirdre McCloskey

The Economics of Defence
Keith Hartley and Nicholas Hooper

Consumer Theory
Kelvin Lancaster

The Economics of Business Policy
John Kay

Microeconomic Theories of Imperfect Competition
Jacques Thisse and Jean Gabszewicz

The Economics of Increasing Returns
Geoffrey Heal

The Balance of Payments
Michael J. Artis

Cost-Benefit Analysis
Arnold Harberger and Glenn P. Jenkins

Gender in Economic and Social History
K.J. Humphries and J. Lewis

Privatization in Developing and Transitional Economies
Colin Kirkpatrick and Paul Cook

The Economics of Intellectual Property
Ruth Towse

The Economics of Tourism
Clem Tisdell

The Economics of Organization and Bureaucracy
Peter Jackson

The Economics of Commodity Markets
David Greenaway and Wyn Morgan

Realism and Economics: Studies in Ontology
Tony Lawson

New Developments in Game Theory
Eric S. Maskin

The International Economic Institutions of the Twentieth Century
David Greenaway

The Economics of Structural Change
Harald Hagemann, Michael Landesmann and Roberto Scazzieri

Economic Justice
Harold Hochman and Georgio Brosio

The Economics of Famine
Jean Drèze

The Foundations of Regulatory Economics
Robert B. Ekelund

The Economics of the Welfare State
Nicholas Barr

Path Dependence and Economic Dynamics
John Cantwell

Alternative Theories of the Firm
Richard Langlois, Paul Robertson and Tony F. Yu

Economic Anthropology
Stephen Gudeman

The Economics of Executive Compensation
Kevin F. Hallock and Kevin J. Murphy

The Economics of Marketing
Martin Carter, Mark Casson and Vivek Suneja

Foreign Exchange Intervention: Theory and Evidence
Sylvester C.W. Eijffinger

The Economics of the Mass Media
Glenn Withers

The Foundations of Long Wave Theory
Francisco Louçã and Jan Reijnders

The Economics of Budget Deficits
Charles Rowley

Economic Forecasting
Terence C. Mills

The Economic Theory of Auctions
Kenneth G. Binmore and Paul Klemperer

Corporate Governance
Kevin Keasey, Steve Thompson and Mike Wright